The Cultural Politics of

An innovative history of the politics and practice of the Caribbean spiritual healing techniques known as obeah, and their place in everyday life in the region. Spanning two centuries, the book results from extensive research on the development and implementation of anti-obeah legislation. It includes analysis of hundreds of prosecutions for obeah, and an account of the complex and multiple political meanings of obeah in Caribbean societies. Diana Paton moves beyond attempts to define and describe what obeah was, instead showing the political imperatives that often drove interpretations and discussions of it. She shows that representations of obeah were entangled with key moments in Caribbean history, from eighteenth-century slave rebellions to the formation of new nations after independence. Obeah was at the same time a crucial symbol of the Caribbean's alleged lack of modernity, a site of fear and anxiety, and a thoroughly modern and transnational practice of healing itself.

DIANA PATON is Reader in Caribbean History at Newcastle University. She is the author of *No Bond but the Law: Punishment, Race and Gender in Jamaican State Formation, 1780–1870* and co-editor of *Gender and Slave Emancipation in the Atlantic World* and *Obeah and Other Powers: The Politics of Caribbean Religion and Healing*.

*Critical Perspectives on Empire*

*Editors*

Professor Catherine Hall
*University College London*

Professor Mrinalini Sinha
*University of Michigan*

Professor Kathleen Wilson
*State University of New York, Stony Brook*

*Critical Perspectives on Empire* is a major series of ambitious, cross-disciplinary works in the emerging field of critical imperial studies. Books in the series explore the connections, exchanges and mediations at the heart of national and global histories, the contributions of local as well as metropolitan knowledge, and the flows of people, ideas and identities facilitated by colonial contact. To that end, the series not only offers a space for outstanding scholars working at the intersection of several disciplines to bring to wider attention the impact of their work; it also takes a leading role in reconfiguring contemporary historical and critical knowledge, of the past and of ourselves.

A full list of titles published in the series can be found at:
www.cambridge.org/cpempire

# The Cultural Politics of Obeah
*Religion, Colonialism and Modernity in the Caribbean World*

Diana Paton
*Newcastle University*

# CAMBRIDGE
UNIVERSITY PRESS

University Printing House, Cambridge CB2 8BS, United Kingdom

One Liberty Plaza, 20th Floor, New York, NY 10006, USA

477 Williamstown Road, Port Melbourne, VIC 3207, Australia

4843/24, 2nd Floor, Ansari Road, Daryaganj, Delhi - 110002, India

79 Anson Road, #06-04/06, Singapore 079906

Cambridge University Press is part of the University of Cambridge.

It furthers the University's mission by disseminating knowledge in the pursuit of education, learning and research at the highest international levels of excellence.

www.cambridge.org
Information on this title: www.cambridge.org/9781107615991

© Diana Paton 2015

This publication is in copyright. Subject to statutory exception and to the provisions of relevant collective licensing agreements, no reproduction of any part may take place without the written permission of Cambridge University Press.

First published 2015
First paperback edition 2017

*A catalogue record for this publication is available from the British Library*

*Library of Congress Cataloging in Publication data*
Paton, Diana, 1969 –
The cultural politics of Obeah : religion, colonialism and modernity in the Caribbean world / Diana Paton, Newcastle University.
   pages   cm. – (Critical perspectives on empire)
Includes bibliographical references and index.
ISBN 978-1-107-02565-3 (hardback) – ISBN 978-1-107-61599-1 (paperback)
1. Obeah (Cult) – Political aspects – Caribbean Area.   2. Religion and politics – Caribbean Area.   3. Caribbean Area – Social conditions.   I. Title.
BL2532.O23P38   2015
299.6'7 – dc23      2015012661

ISBN   978-1-107-02565-3   Hardback
ISBN   978-1-107-61599-1   Paperback

Cambridge University Press has no responsibility for the persistence or accuracy of URLs for external or third-party internet websites referred to in this publication, and does not guarantee that any content on such websites is, or will remain, accurate or appropriate.

For Kate

# Contents

| | |
|---|---|
| *List of figures* | *page* viii |
| *List of tables* | ix |
| *Acknowledgements* | x |
| *List of abbreviations* | xiii |
| Introduction | 1 |
| 1  The emergence of Caribbean spiritual politics | 17 |
| 2  Obeah and the slave-trade debates | 43 |
| 3  Creole slave society, obeah, and the law | 76 |
| 4  Obeah and its meanings in the post-emancipation era | 119 |
| 5  Obeah in the courts, 1890–1939 | 158 |
| 6  Obeah prosecutions from the inside | 208 |
| 7  Protest, development, and the politics of obeah | 241 |
| 8  The post-colonial politics of obeah | 274 |
| Conclusion | 314 |
| *Bibliography* | 317 |
| *Index* | 347 |

# Figures

| | | |
|---|---|---|
| 1.1 | Graman Quacy | *page* 33 |
| 2.1 | Three-Fingered Jack | 73 |
| 3.1 | 'Negro Superstition' | 107 |
| 5.1 | Arrests or prosecutions for obeah and related offences in Jamaica and Trinidad, 1890–1939 | 166 |
| 5.2 | Charles Dolly in the Antigua gaol | 178 |
| 5.3 | 'Obeah' in Jamaica, *The Graphic*, 2 July 1898 | 181 |
| 6.1 | 'Mammy Forbes, the Healer' | 231 |
| 6.2 | Advertisement for the DeLaurence company | 236 |
| 8.1 | Arrests or prosecutions for obeah and related offences in Jamaica, 1940–1989 | 278 |

# Tables

| | | |
|---|---|---|
| 5.1 | Arrests and prosecutions for obeah and related offences | *page* 163 |
| 5.2 | Gender of defendants in obeah and related cases | 167 |
| 5.3 | Numbers of defendants in obeah and related cases | 170 |
| 5.4 | Outcomes of obeah cases | 171 |
| 5.5 | Punishments of those found guilty in obeah and related cases | 173 |
| 5.6 | Extent of prison sentences in obeah-related cases | 175 |
| 5.7 | Appeals against obeah and related convictions | 176 |
| 8.1 | Outcomes of Jamaican obeah and related cases, 1940–1989 | 279 |
| 8.2 | Punishments of those found guilty in Jamaican obeah and related cases, 1940–1989 | 280 |

# Acknowledgements

This book has benefited from the support of innumerable individuals and institutions over many years; I could not have completed it without their help. Research and writing was supported by Newcastle University and by much-appreciated grants from the British Academy, the Arts and Humanities Research Council, and the Leverhulme Foundation. Maarit Forde, now of the University of the West Indies, St Augustine, served as the Research Associate on the Leverhulme Research Project that supported the research. It is a pleasure to formally thank her for her work in that role and her support thereafter. Helen McKee, Jen Kain, and Suzie Thomas all also provided valuable research assistance, for which I am very grateful. I also appreciate the work of the staff of the many libraries and archives where I worked on this book. In the UK: the Robinson Library, Newcastle University; the National Library of Scotland; the National Archives; the British Library; Cambridge University Library; Liverpool University Library; the Bodleian Library and Rhodes House Library, Oxford University; and the SOAS and Senate House Libraries, University of London. In the United States: the Schomburg Center for Research in Black Culture, the New York Public Library, and Northwestern University Archives. In the Caribbean: the University of the West Indies libraries at Mona, Cave Hill (especially the law library), and St Augustine; the library of the University of Guyana; the National Library of Jamaica; the African Caribbean Institute of Jamaica; the Jamaica Archives; the National Archives of Trinidad and Tobago; the Barbados Museum and Historical Society; and the National Archives of Guyana. Research trips have been both more comfortable and more fun as a result of the hospitality of Mónica Moreno Figueroa and Hettie Malcolmson; Miranda Mindlin, Tim Nicholls, Jessie Nicholls-Mindlin and Ben Nicholls-Mindlin; Patrick and Mary Quinn; Greg Grandin and Manu Goswami; Tracy Robertson, Melanie Newton, Velma Newton, Suzanne Trill, Bridget Brereton, Peggy Soltau, Zoe Laidlaw, Lloyd D'Aguilar, and Annie Paul. Thanks to them all.

# Acknowledgements

In writing a book as wide-ranging as this, I have inevitably relied on the knowledge of others. Friends and colleagues far and wide have generously shared notes, references, and unpublished work; pointed me to sources, both primary and secondary; given me tips about conducting research in multiple locations; invited me to present papers and listened to the results; and commented on papers and drafts of chapters that eventually became the book. For all this and more I am grateful to a remarkable group of scholars whose work on the Caribbean and beyond has influenced mine: Rosanne Adderley, Henrice Altink, Mandy Banton, Jean Besson, Ken Bilby, Nigel Bolland, Bridget Brereton, Vince Brown, Randy Browne, Trevor Burnard, John Cowley, Owen Davies, Juanita de Barros, Richard Drayton, Jerry Handler, Gad Heuman, Bobby Hill, Natasha Lightfoot, Melanie Newton, Stephan Palmié, Christer Petley, Steven Pierce, Lara Putnam, Kate Quinn, Kate Ramsey, James Robertson, Gemma Robinson, Gemma Romain, Leah Rosenburg, Gunvor Simonsen, David Trotman, Leon Wainwright, and Tim Watson. Mary Turner supported this project (sometimes critically) from the start, but sadly did not live to see the result. She is much missed. I am grateful also for the encouragement, support, and sharing of knowledge of Newcastle comrades and colleagues (current and former): Joan Allen, Claudia Baldoli, Helen Berry, Jeremy Boulton, Sarah Campbell, Nicola Clarke, Barbara Cochrane, David Creese, Janice Cummin, Martin Farr, Susan-Mary Grant, Xavier Guégan, Rachel Hammersley, Pat Harrison, Jens Hentschke, Ben Houston, Tim Kirk, Nina Laurie, Mónica Moreno Figueroa, Carolyn Pedwell, Matt Perry, Susanna Phillippo, James Procter, Felix Schulz, Neelam Srivastava, Naomi Standen, Sam Turner, and Jaap Wisse.

Initial versions of much of the material in this book were presented at the conferences of the Society for Caribbean Studies, the Association of Caribbean Historians, the Caribbean Studies Association, the Caribbean Research Seminar in the North, the Society of Early Americanists, the Society for the Social History of Medicine, the North American Conference on British Studies, the Omohundro Institute of Early American History and Culture, and *Interventions*. I have also presented this work at conferences and seminars at Oxford University, the Institute for Historical Research (London), New York University, Pittsburgh University, Tulane University, and the Universities of Bristol, Cambridge, Edinburgh, Glasgow, Manchester, Newcastle, Nottingham, Oxford, Sheffield, Toronto, and York. I thank the audiences for their feedback, which significantly improved the book. An earlier and significantly different version of part of Chapter 1 was published in the *William Mary Quarterly*, and of part of Chapter 5 was published in *Obeah and Other Powers: The Politics* of *Caribbean Religion and Healing*, published by Duke University Press. At Cambridge University Press and the Critical Perspectives on Empire series I thank Michael Watson, who has supported and encouraged me along the way, Kathleen Wilson for initially suggesting that the book might work in the series, and Catherine Hall for her continued enthusiasm, support, and advice over many years. Thanks also to all those who have helped in the production of the book, especially Rosalyn Scott, Jo Breeze, Jane Read, and Mary Starkey.

Though I was not able to answer all their queries or satisfy all their criticisms, this book is undoubtedly better than it would have been because of the advice of those who have read and responded to parts of it along the way, including the readers of the proposal for Cambridge University Press. Many are named above, but I must single out for thanks a few who were there at the end: Randy Browne, Kate Ramsey, and Tim Watson all took time from their own work to provide thoughtful suggestions on parts of the manuscript. Lara Putnam advised and supported me from the early stages of writing, shared many conference panels, was enormously generous with her own knowledge of Caribbean history, and commented insightfully on the whole manuscript.

For moral and practical support I am grateful to my family, born and made: to Alistair Chisholm, Geof Ellingham, Judith Green, Jon Green, David Epstein, Rona Epstein, and Debbie Epstein. Miriam and Polly Chedgzoy didn't exactly help with the research or writing, but made my life much richer and more fun than it otherwise would have been during the process. I thank them for encouraging me to make this book a finished one. Finally, I offer gratitude and love to Kate Chedgzoy, for teaching me so much, and for the life we have made together.

# Abbreviations

| | |
|---|---|
| Add Ms | Additional Manuscripts, British Library, London |
| BT | Board of Trade, Public Records Office, National Archives, Kew, England |
| CO | Colonial Office, Public Records Office, National Archives, Kew, England |
| CUL | Cambridge University Library |
| FCO | Foreign and Commonwealth Office, Public Records Office, National Archives, Kew, England |
| *FP* | *Falmouth Post* |
| JA | Jamaica Archives, Spanish Town |
| NLS | National Library of Scotland, Edinburgh |
| *POSG* | *Port of Spain Gazette* |

# Introduction

Obeah's persistent presence haunts Anglo-Creole Caribbean history. For a long time obeah was the ultimate signifier of the Caribbean's difference from Europe, a symbol of the region's supposed inability to be part of the modern world. It has been, that is, a foundational category in the positioning of the Caribbean within what Michel-Rolph Trouillot termed the 'Savage Slot' in Western thought; a crucial part of the way in which 'the West' produces 'the Caribbean' as its other.[1] In the post-independence era the negative construction of obeah was inverted by some, so that obeah came to be seen as the spiritual centre of enslaved people's resistance, something that might be celebrated – so long as it was safely in the past. In published accounts of Caribbean history and culture stretching from the eighteenth to the twenty-first centuries obeah is frequently glossed as, and thus reduced to, the European concepts of 'witchcraft or sorcery'.[2] More sympathetic texts explore its origins in Akan, Sierra Leonean, and Central African concepts of healing, harm, and the divine.[3] Yet despite their differences, paradigms that understand obeah as backwardness and those that position it as resistance share a great deal. For both, obeah is the most vivid and enduring symbol of and inheritance from Africa within the Anglo-Creole Caribbean; for both, it is particularly strongly associated with slavery; for both, it marks out the Caribbean's difference from Europe and thus helps – despite all the evidence – to position Europe as rational and anti-superstitious. For both, it is a singular phenomenon whose meaning provides a focal point for interpreting Caribbean culture.

Yet the meaning of obeah has never been so straightforward. As a term, 'obeah' has always referred to multiple phenomena. At the most obvious

---

[1] Trouillot, *Global Transformations*, chapter 1. My focus in this book is the Anglo-Creole Caribbean, made up of the territories that were at one time British colonies. To avoid repetition I sometimes use 'Caribbean' as shorthand.
[2] For examples see Bilby and Handler, 'Obeah'.
[3] For instance Fernández Olmos and Paravisini-Gebert, *Creole Religions of the Caribbean*, 131–42.

level, it describes practices involving ritual attempts to manipulate a world of spiritual power. But the practices included and excluded by that term, and the ethical directions connoted by it, have varied greatly depending on the speaker's point of view. Obeah is also, importantly, a term that has for more than two centuries been animated by the use of law, because of its status as a crime. With few exceptions, obeah is not and has not been a term that people use to describe their own practices, and therefore it has rarely been reclaimed as positive from within. Those people who, now and in the past, undertake practices that others describe as obeah generally consider themselves to be doing something else. They often make use of designations that invoke the modernity rather than the primitivism of their knowledge, such as 'science-man', 'scientist', 'doctor-man', or 'professor'. Efforts to rewrite obeah in more positive terms have tended to come from the safe distance of the academy, of cultural nationalist politics, or of both.

This book was not written to pin down, once and for all, this elusive creole cultural phenomenon. Rather, it unpicks the multiple meanings of the term obeah, and considers the cultural, political, and social effects of the consolidation of that term as a means of describing and defining a very wide range of practices that, broadly speaking, involve the ritual manipulation of spiritual power. *The Cultural Politics of Obeah* argues that, precisely because of its indeterminacy and multiple meanings, obeah has been a telling category over a long period, one that has frequently marked out critical debates about the status of the Caribbean and its people; about power, race, nation, and citizenship. This book thus investigates the construction of obeah by multiple parties and in multiple ways. Like a musical recording, it utilizes several tracks that have been produced separately but are best heard (or read) together. One track provides a (selective) history of representations. How has the term 'obeah' been applied to changing and often locally specific sets of practices? How have colonial, nationalist, and popular definitions and representations of obeah contrasted, and overlapped? What cultural work have they done in the construction of the Caribbean? To what has the Caribbean been constructed as an 'other' through representations of obeah?

A second track traces the history of state policy towards a legal category, 'obeah', that was itself repeatedly produced by state power – including the power of low-level actors within what we might call the everyday state. How did obeah feature in Caribbean law, in different times and places? How were these laws enforced, at whose instigation, and with what effects? The third track within the book provides a history of popular interactions with and contributions to both the first and second tracks. How did participants in popular religious movements, parts of whose practice were sometimes referred to as 'obeah', understand and relate to that term? How did their vulnerability to prosecution for the crime of obeah affect their collective worship and spiritual practice? How did their understanding of obeah, which often included the use of the term to describe dangerous and hostile power used by others, contribute to popular political discourse?

Since the eighteenth century obeah has had a privileged place in understandings of what is both illicit and powerful about subaltern Caribbean religion. This book argues that concern about obeah was repeatedly linked to debates about the political status of the region and its people. Obeah was a significant presence in many contested political issues. It was mobilized in conflicts about the slave trade and the abolition of slavery; it was present in debates about the contraction of representative government in the late nineteenth century; it helped people to understand the meaning of the uprisings of the 1930s; and questions about it were raised when independent states were established in the 1960s, 1970s, and 1980s. At the same time, the illegality of obeah, and the means by which this illegality was enforced, had a profound effect on the practice of religion and its place in everyday life. The book therefore moves among its three tracks of representation, state activity, and everyday behaviour in order to break down conventional boundaries between social history and the history of politics and representation. I hope that in doing so I am better able to explain not just the complex formation of obeah, but more generally the relationship of everyday politics – particularly the politics of religion – to the world of formal politics. This book also stresses interconnections across the Caribbean region, comparisons between different territories within the region both within and beyond the British Empire, relationships across British imperial space, and the persistence of both representations and legal practices concerning obeah over long periods of time. The history of the cultural politics of obeah demonstrates the ongoing reverberations and connections among places divided by language, distance, or political experience but linked by movement of people and/or colonial status.

This book has been written at a time when official representations and interpretations of obeah are undergoing change. Until recently obeah was interpreted by those with cultural power in the Caribbean either as profoundly negative or as an embarrassing relic and sign of ignorance. At this stage just one example will suffice. Frank Cundall, the British founder of the Institute of Jamaica (IoJ), in 1908 completed a book-length manuscript, 'The British West Indies Today', intended to inform potential tourists, settlers, and investors about opportunities in Britain's Caribbean colonies. Cundall was committed to developing cultural institutions within the region, and was far from the most hostile of observers of what he understood as the region's African-derived cultural practices. His description typifies one form of insider's representation of obeah. It combines genuine interest, evidenced through details available to Cundall largely as a result of obeah's illegality, with clear condescension:

> Obeah, or as it is called in some of the islands Wanga, may be described as the art of imposing upon the credulity of ignorant persons by means of feathers, bones, teeth, hairs, cat's claws, rusty nails, pieces of cloth, dirt, and other rubbish, usually contained in a wallet. The obeah man is usually dirty and unkempt, with a slouching gait and averted face. The cult sometimes develops into poisoning, by means of ground glass, arsenic, or prepared vegetable extracts.
>
> The obeah man provides charms to make a woman's lover true, to bring success to a business, to obtain a verdict in a police or law-court, to cure the sick – often by removing substances from the wound, to harm a rival, to keep thieves off a provision ground by means of little black wooden coffins, and bottles filled with some dirty mixture, and, in fact, to do anything that his clients may be fools enough to believe. In Trinidad recently one Obeahman purveyed means to facilitate burglary in the shape of a mixture intended when smoked in a pipe by a burglar to induce sleep on the inmates of the house – consisting of crushed bones, tobacco & scraps of paper! He used also to catch a supposed lost shadow (or soul) but that is rarely heard of now-a-days.
>
> His symbol is a stick carved with twisted serpents, from which, by some the word obeah has been derived – *ob* being Egyptian for serpent; but it is more probably connected with the Efik *ubio*, a charm to cause sickness or death.[4]

Cundall's successors at the Institute of Jamaica take a different approach, revealing a transformation in official perceptions. In the last ten years two exhibitions produced under the Institute's auspices have normalized obeah by depicting it as part of the landscape of Jamaican religion. In 2006, nearly a century after Cundall wrote, the Institute's exhibition 'Of Things Sacred', curated by Wayne Modest, included obeah as one of a series of Jamaican 'sacred traditions' displayed to the public through material culture, text, and image. Obeah was the first 'tradition' presented to the visitor, and thus played a role as a precursor or predecessor of other Jamaican religions.[5] In 2011 the African Caribbean Institute of Jamaica – a sub-unit of the IoJ – staged a smaller exhibition, 'Guzzum Power: Obeah in Jamaica', that, as the title suggests, focused entirely on obeah. This exhibition presented obeah as a living component of the Jamaican present, 'one of the most powerful West African influences

---

[4] Frank Cundall, 'The British West Indies Today', unpublished manuscript, National Library of Jamaica, MS 934, 96.
[5] 'Of Things Sacred', unpublished catalogue, Institute of Jamaica archives.

Introduction

in Jamaica' and 'part of the social fabric' of the island.[6] Its choice of language was a far cry from that of Cundall, and, indeed, from that of exhibitions of the late 1960s, when an exhibition commemorating the centenary of the founding of the Jamaica Constabulary Force included a 'gruesome corner' which displayed 'many implements of obeah'.[7] Today, even official government bodies recognize obeah as part of everyday life. In its 2003 Standard Occupational Classification, designed to develop the categories provided by the International Labour Organization and to be used with the census, the Statistical Institute of Jamaica (STATIN) introduced a new occupational category 'obeah man/woman' as a sub-category to the larger ILO-sponsored subgroup of 'astrologers'.[8]

There has thus been substantial change in the public status of obeah in the Caribbean in the recent past. This change is marked by the recent decriminalization of obeah in Anguilla (1980), Barbados (1998), Trinidad and Tobago (2000), and St Lucia (2004).[9] It is a shift that echoes the changing status of religions associated with Africa in other parts of the Americas. In Brazil, Candomblé was from the 1930s promoted as a 'national "folk" institution' and eventually became a national symbol, even while, as J. Lorand Matory explains, it provided 'convenient journalistic canvases for escapist white fantasies and political allegories'.[10] In Cuba, santería has, as Stephan Palmié points out, moved from being 'the object of state-sponsored denunciation' to being officially pronounced part of the Cuban revolution's struggle against global capitalism.[11] In Haiti, religious freedom was guaranteed by Article 297 of the 1987 Constitution, adopted after the overthrow of Jean-Claude Duvalier. Article 297 specifically overturned earlier anti-Vodou laws that prohibited 'superstitious practices'.[12]

Yet despite partial decriminalization, the status of obeah has changed much less than has that of these other African Atlantic religions. Obeah differs from Candomblé, Vodou, and Afro-Cuban religion in its lack of self-confident promoters and interpreters. In Brazil, Haiti, and Cuba intellectuals who identified with Candomblé, Vodou, and santería, respectively, pressed for change in the status of those religions from the

---

[6] Weise, *Guzzum Power*.
[7] 'Constabulary Force Exhibition Nov. 28–29', *Gleaner*, 13 November 1967.
[8] Statistical Agency of Jamaica, *Jamaica Standard Occupational Classification 2003*, Annex II, minor group 515. Copy in author's possession, from STATIN. The occupation had the alternate title of 'Mother', 'Reader-man', or 'Shepherd', and the occupational summary was one who 'gives spiritual guidance, administers and mixes potions'.
[9] Handler and Bilby, *Enacting Power*, xiii.
[10] Matory, *Black Atlantic Religion*, 164, 166. [11] Palmié, *The Cooking of History*, 20.
[12] Ramsey, 'Vodouyizan Protest'. As Ramsey explains, Article 297 was abrogated in 2012, although the effects of this are as yet unclear.

late nineteenth and early twentieth centuries. They often acted as informants for anthropologists, who used their words to produce new narratives. J. Lorand Matory, David Brown, and Stephan Palmié have shown that for Brazil and Cuba respectively, important figures such as Seu Martiano de Bomfim and Fernando Guerra played critical roles in the early twentieth century, both in providing the information and more importantly in coaxing a particular interpretation out of critical intellectuals such as Raymundo Nina Rodrigues and Fernando Ortiz.[13] In Haiti, similar processes led to the re-evaluation of Vodou by Anténor Firmin and later Jean Price-Mars.[14] In the Anglophone Caribbean a tiny number of spiritual practitioners who considered themselves to be practising obeah contributed to the twentieth-century anthropological record. Particularly significant were the Jamaican spiritual workers who acted as informants for Joseph Moore and Donald Hogg.[15] But the work of these anthropologists was much less influential than that of their peers who studied Cuba, Brazil, and Haiti. This was partly because the British Caribbean colonies were for a long time considered the least anthropologically interesting part of a region that was itself a backwater for the discipline of anthropology, because its religious and cultural forms appeared insufficiently exotic.[16] While an important body of anthropological work on religion in the region was produced, it for good reasons focused on discrete religious formations such as Revival, Orisha Worship/Shango, and the Spiritual Baptist tradition, rather than the difficult-to-define 'obeah', a term often used by critics of all these religious groups to condemn aspects of their practice. Today, while the status of Revival, Orisha, and Spiritual Baptism has been transformed to the point where in Trinidad and Tobago a national holiday, Spiritual Baptist Liberation Day, celebrates the repeal of the Shouters' Prohibition Ordinance, 'obeah' continues to raise considerable concern and anxiety.[17]

Obeah remains illegal in much of the Caribbean, and not simply due to omission. When, in 2013, the Jamaican government removed flogging as a judicial punishment from the Jamaican judicial system so as to be able to sign the United Nations Convention against Torture, it amended

---

[13] Matory, *Black Atlantic Religion*; Brown, *Santería Enthroned*; Palmié, *Wizards and Scientists*.
[14] Fluehr-Lobban, 'Anténor Firmin'; Ramsey, *The Spirits and the Law*.
[15] Moore, 'Religion of Jamaican Negroes'; Hogg, 'Jamaican Religions'.
[16] On the Caribbean as an overlooked region in early anthropology because it troubled the foundations of the discipline see Trouillot, 'The Caribbean Region', 20–1.
[17] On the changed status of the Spiritual Baptist faith in Trinidad and Tobago see Glazier, *Marching the Pilgrims Home*; Henry, *Reclaiming African Religions in Trinidad*, 39, 50–74. The Shouters' Prohibition Ordinance made practice of the Spiritual Baptist faith illegal. It was in force from 1917 to 1951.

the Obeah Act of 1898. The amendment removed the punishment of flogging, but left the criminal status of obeah untouched.[18] A public debate followed in which some called for decriminalization, but were opposed by as many others who argued that to decriminalize obeah would be anti-Christian.[19] The catalogue to 'Guzzum Power' demonstrated similar anxiety. It included a 'General Disclaimer' on its opening page that warned, or perhaps reassured, readers that 'None of the material contained in this document should be construed as instructions or guides to the practice of obeah, which is illegal in Jamaica. The information is for general information purposes only.'[20] Similar concerns perhaps underlay STATIN's decision to locate its new occupational category of 'obeah man/woman' within the subgroup 'astrologers' rather than in other possible locations such as 'traditional and complementary medicine associate professionals', examples of which include 'Herbalist, Witch doctor, Village healer, Scraping and cupping therapist', or 'Religious Associate Professionals' (group 3414), a group which included 'faith healer, monk, nun, lay preacher'.[21] STATIN's choice of the 'astrologer' category tellingly located the position of obeah in Jamaica today apart from the religious or healing roles that those who practise the activities of giving 'spiritual guidance' or 'administer[ing] and mix[ing] potions' usually consider themselves to undertake. Thus, despite the very real changes in the official response to obeah since Cundall's time, the shift to an interpretation of obeah as an everyday part of Caribbean life with parallels in every society rather than a concern or an embarrassment has been decidedly partial.

In writing about obeah I have tried to steer a course between two risks. On the one hand is the risk of reiterating the exoticization of Caribbean life that forms the heart of many depictions of obeah. Mervyn Alleyne critiques the 'obsession with obeah in White studies of Jamaican society', suggesting that this is 'symptomatic of the inability and unwillingness of Europeans to understand the culture of Africans'.[22] That obsession is also implicitly critiqued by Michel-Rolph Trouillot, who reveals the pre-occupation of anthropology and other Western scholarship with aspects

---

[18] The Obeah (Amendment) Act 2013, www.japarliament.gov.jm/attachments/341_The%20Obeah%20%28Amendment%29%20Act,%202013.pdf, last visited 9 May 2014.
[19] Balford Henry, 'Senators to Push for Decriminalisation of Obeah', *Jamaica Observer*, 29 February 2013.
[20] Weise, *Guzzum Power*.
[21] International Labour Organisation, International Standard Classification of Occupations 08 and International Standard Classification of Occupations 88, both available at www.ilo.org/public/english/bureau/stat/isco/isco08/index.htm, last viewed 30 October 2012.
[22] Alleyne, *Roots of Jamaican Culture*, 83.

of cultures subjected to anthropological study that 'prove' their difference and otherness.[23] In this book I hope to avoid reproducing these problems, through my efforts not to uncover the 'real' obeah, but rather to show how the variety of practices and beliefs that have been deemed to be obeah have been regulated, suppressed, discussed, represented – and how all of these activities have been part of the process by which obeah has been produced and stabilized as an object. The repeated reiteration of the lexical item 'obeah' eventually led to the existence of a set of practices which observers and participants all, more or less, know to be obeah. But that 'more or less' matters, because a lot remains unknown. By taking apart the production of the sense that 'obeah' is a coherent phenomenon, and by investigating the ways in which the belief in its existence played out in the very concrete fields of legislating, policing, prosecuting, and punishing, we see that its existence and reproduction, as an object of comment and suppression, has been part of the dynamics of colonial and post-colonial power over more than two centuries.

Running counter to the risk of exoticism is the risk that in turning away from trying to study the history of obeah as object, we end up with a story that is only about the top-down imposition of power. It would be ironic if, at the point at which 'obeah' became a sign of resistance rather than of evil, works of scholarship such as this one argued that it was not created by enslaved and colonized people at all, but rather was a construction of the colonizer. This is not my argument. Rather, I want to draw attention to the way in which obeah was a *mutual* construction, made in the spaces between the powerful's imposition and the colonized's resistance; but also, and more importantly, moving beyond assumptions about the permanent division between the always-imposing colonizer and the always-resisting colonized.

I hope that this work will have implications for understanding the political dynamics of culture beyond the Anglophone Caribbean. In particular, I hope it will allow us to move beyond some debates in African Atlantic and colonial history in which positions have become entrenched. Perhaps most entrenched of all is the debate between constructivists and realists. On one side are scholars who emphasize the constructed nature of the categories through which we apprehend the world – categories such as caste or tribe – and in particular the way in which new discursive categories were frequently produced in colonial contexts.[24] The work of constructivist scholars has, however, been criticized by those who emphasize the long-standing existence of phenomena that came to be

---

[23] Trouillot, *Global Transformations*, 18–20.
[24] See for instance Ranger, 'The Invention of Tradition'; Dirks, *Castes of Mind*.

Introduction

categorized in new ways by colonial discourse.²⁵ This debate has parallels, in African Atlantic studies, in the long-standing conflicts between those who, following Sidney Mintz and Richard Price, emphasize creolization and the importance of cultural construction in colonial slave societies, and others, following Melville Herskovits, who argue for the continued resonance of specific African ethnic identifications in diaspora.²⁶ There has recently been an enormous expansion of work in the latter vein, stimulated in particular by new research on the slave trade that has significantly improved our understanding of the origins of Africans in the Americas.²⁷ Yet this work at times reaches an impasse. After tracing a particular cultural form to Yoruba, Igbo, Akan, or Kongo predecessors, what is the next analytic step? (The same problem – though with a different political charge – arises in studies of cultural practices in the Americas deriving from Europe.) Vincent Brown has tried to shift the terms of the debate on Africans in the Americas. He suggests that rather than ask 'How African was it?' we should instead ask 'What was it used for? What were its consequences?'²⁸ These are the kinds of questions that guide this study of obeah. I ask not just what obeah was used for and what its consequences were, but also, what was the concept of obeah in its representation by colonial authorities and writers used for? What was the creation of a crime of obeah used for?

Repeatedly, debates about obeah – at least, those debates about obeah that have left archival and printed records – have been organized through binary oppositions structured by arguments about the appropriate legal and political response that states should take to it. As I show in more detail later in this book, until about the 1830s the repressive view was that obeah practitioners were genuinely powerful ritual specialists, who controlled other people, either stimulating them to rebellion or damaging their health. Prosecution and harsh punishments were required to restrain the power of obeah. The growing dominance of an Enlightenment approach to the supernatural meant that the acceptance of the reality of obeah's spiritual power was no longer an intellectually respectable viewpoint by the late nineteenth century, but the argument for severe

---

25 For one example see Pennington, *Was Hinduism Invented?*
26 Mintz and Price, *The Birth of African-American Culture*; Herskovits, *Myth*.
27 The Transatlantic Slave Trade Database developed by David Eltis, David Richardson, and colleagues has been very influential here. See www.slavevoyages.org. Significant work influenced by this paradigm includes Falola and Childs, eds., 'The Yoruba Diaspora'; Konadu, *The Akan Diaspora*; Sweet, *Recreating Africa*; Gomez, *Exchanging our Country Marks*.
28 Brown, *The Reaper's Garden*, 8. Also see J. Lorand Matory's important critique of the debate between 'retention'-focused scholars and constructivists: Matory, 'The "Cult of Nations"'.

measures continued to be made. Advocates of this view changed their explanation for why obeah was damaging, but maintained the claim that it *was* destructive and therefore must be met with harsh repression. The problem was now diagnosed as one of fraud and charlatanism which allegedly kept the Caribbean population uncivilized, and interfered with proper judicial processes and medical procedures. Adherents of the repressive view saw obeah practitioners as people who exercised illegitimate power over the mass of the population and thus stood in the way of what they understood to be the proper hierarchies of an orderly society. Advocates of this view drew on theories of punishment rooted in retributionist arguments to make the case for the criminalization of obeah and the maintenance of its illegal status, for treating it as a specific crime rather than an aspect of other crimes, and for severe punishments: torture and the death penalty during slavery; flogging and long prison sentences in the period since 1838. They tended to make claims for absolute racial difference and hierarchy. The descendants of Africans, they argued, were inherently irrational, prone to superstitious beliefs and thus likely to believe in obeah. Harsh punishments were necessary due to this inherent racial inferiority. If obeah practitioners were not prosecuted and subjected to strong repression, the punitive faction argued, their power was reinforced because people believed that they were more powerful than the state.

Opposing these racial determinists were the advocates of a more liberal position, who argued for more than a hundred years that belief in obeah was inevitably dying away through the logical movement of Caribbean culture towards modern, rational belief systems and/or Christianity. Supporters of this viewpoint, from William Wilberforce in the 1820s, through Charles Frederick Lumb, a judge in Jamaica in the 1890s and 1900s, to writers in the Jamaica *Gleaner* in the 1960s, argued against the passage and maintenance of specific laws against obeah and against the infliction of particularly harsh punishments for it.[29] Such punishments, they claimed, drew attention to the significance of obeah and thus reinforced the power of its practitioners. To the extent that they believed that obeah should be criminalized – and most liberals did believe that some of its practitioners should be prosecuted – they thought that it should be combined with other offences such as vagrancy or small-scale theft, and should receive the relatively 'minor' punishments accorded these crimes. This view was often deeply enmeshed with a liberal approach to colonial

---

[29] Wilberforce, *An Appeal*, 29; Judgment in the case of Rex v. Chambers, 29 May 1901, enclosed in CO 137/620, Hemming to Chamberlain No. 406, 5 July 1901; 'Jottings', *Gleaner*, 6 February 1960.

power and penal policy that understood the growth of imprisonment as a modern replacement for 'backward' corporal punishments, and also envisaged colonial rule as a process of educating a backward population. In this paradigm, harsh punishments such as torture or flogging were not appropriate in a British colony or a modern society for any crime, and drew shame on those who implemented them. Moreover, the criminalizing of magical acts was problematic because it tended to reinforce popular belief in the power of those prosecuted. It was better to practise a liberal policy that used missionary work, education, and the improvement of health services to gradually change people's views. As the practice of obeah was already dying away of its own accord, this should not be a difficult task.

As this book documents, these opposed views about obeah policy were repeated, with relatively little change in their substance, over several hundred years, from the point when obeah shifted, in colonial authorities' views, from being considered primarily as a weapon of autonomous opponents – Maroons and enslaved rebels – to being understood as a crime of dominated people – slaves and later colonial subjects. They remain a prominent part of discourse about obeah in the Caribbean. While the adherents of these two positions frequently became highly antagonistic to each other, their views nevertheless had a great deal in common. They shared a sense of obeah as a singular object, and a view that the existence of this object indicated the Caribbean region's lack of modernity. The opposition between these two views left little space for alternative understandings of obeah, either as a real form of dangerous power that might be made use of by ritual specialists, or as a healing and protective resource.

On the fringes of this binary debate there often lurked an anxiety that not all participants in fact subscribed fully to the shared view of obeah as impossible and fraudulent. Scandals and hints that wealthy – or at least 'respectable' – members of Caribbean society might be making use of the services of ritual specialists repeatedly undermined the agreement expressed within the structure of the two-sided debate that its participants were united in their modernity and superiority to the everyday 'folk' of the region. Such scandals tended to push both sides in the debates back towards assertions of their shared disbelief and rationalism.

This book examines the development of these two opposed but interlocked viewpoints, the oscillation between the two, and their connections to different political positions. In doing so, it also raises additional questions that are harder to address. How did the oscillating, yet in many ways similar, top-down debates about obeah affect the beliefs and practices of ordinary people in the Caribbean, including ritual specialists, those who routinely sought their help, and those who did not? And, perhaps even more importantly, how did the beliefs and practices of ordinary Caribbean folk contribute to the debate among the elite and to the outcomes of their debates? It is much more difficult to answer these questions, especially the latter, than it is to document the range of views among the elite. I have tried to address them by careful investigation of the processes of obeah trials and in particular of popular response to them. This analysis reveals a widespread popular ambivalence towards obeah, in which the term is understood to mean supernatural danger used against the speaker, while the practices associated with the term are understood to be legitimate, if risky, methods of spiritual protection.

*The Cultural Politics of Obeah* uses the methods of criminal justice history and cultural history, drawing on each to shed light on what it finds through the other. I began the research using cultural history approaches, in an effort to understand what had gone into the production of the relatively narrow range of sources that had previously been used to establish scholarly knowledge about obeah. I investigated the conditions of production of the archival and printed materials that have formed the backbone of scholarship on obeah to date. This led to my initial question: how did the myriad phenonema described by the term come to be considered part of the singular category 'obeah'? In order to address this, in Chapter 1 I examine how the crime of obeah came to cohere into a singular phenomenon, something that is naturalized as one object in retrospect but which could have been interpreted in other ways, as indeed did happen in some other European colonies. Chapter 2 then examines the political context of the production of a formative set of sources about obeah, the 1789 Parliamentary Report into the Slave Trade. It demonstrates that sources that have often been understood as straightforward descriptions of obeah practice were in fact produced within a vociferous debate about the slave trade, largely by the pro-slave-trade side.

While these discussions enable me to trace the changing significance of obeah within systems of representation, they might on their own be rather free-floating, telling us about colonial discourse at the expense of colonial society. I wanted to know more about obeah as it was interpreted in everyday life. For this reason I adopted also the methods of criminal justice history, a form of social history that usually begins with quantitative analysis of data gathered from sources produced within the criminal justice system and then uses that material to shed light on questions related to power, culture, and social relationships within the society that generated the records.[30] Because the category at the heart of this

---

[30] For a paradigmatic example of work within this field see Beattie, *Crime and the Courts*.

book was in part a product of criminal justice systems, it became central to discover how it was legally defined, how the law against obeah was applied, who was prosecuted under it and why, what those prosecuted were doing, and how they understood their practice. Chapter 3 applies these questions to the later period of slavery, after obeah had become a crime in Jamaica. It shows how the category of obeah became consolidated in the early nineteenth century as part of a policy of 'ameliorating' slavery. The chapter then analyses trial records to ascertain what types of behaviours led to prosecution and punishment at this time. In order to produce this analysis I collected as many cases as I could from as many places as possible during slavery. Most of these were found in Colonial Office files, but they are not the product of a comprehensive search, because the records of the slavery-era courts have not been systematically preserved. I was, however, able to conduct some quantitative analysis of a few bounded datasets from the period between 1806 and 1825, and to combine these with close readings of a selection of the court cases where detailed records do survive. On the basis of these methods I show that, during slavery, obeah was usually prosecuted only when it involved some kind of perceived harm to the system of slavery: either because it involved rebellion, or because it involved the harming of one enslaved person by another (and thus damage to property).

With Chapter 4 we move to the post-slavery period, examining the reformulation of obeah law in the late nineteenth century. Metropolitan policy towards obeah shifted in this period. Mid-century, British policy was that colonies should incorporate prohibitions against obeah into vagrancy laws, with much less significant punishments. By the beginning of the twentieth century the Colonial Office advocated a policy of singling out obeah in specific legislation, with punishments that included flogging. This shift took place in the context of broader debates about the alleged success or failure of emancipation, as independent popular religion became increasingly powerful and increasingly political, and in the context of imperial expansion in Africa.

Chapters 5 and 6 return to the criminal justice history approach, to find out how obeah was prosecuted in the wake of the new legislative framework for obeah discussed in Chapter 4. In the absence of official court records, I turned to newspaper reports as my primary means of finding obeah cases. For reasons explained in more detail in Chapter 5, I searched systematically for prosecutions for obeah and related offences in two jurisdictions, Trinidad and Jamaica, beginning in 1890. The material collected is analysed in Chapter 5 for what it tells us about the process of prosecution, and in Chapter 6 for what it reveals about everyday practices of spiritual healing in the early twentieth-century Caribbean.

Criminal justice history approaches have the advantage of bringing us reasonably close to the people we are trying to study. Even though they reveal people under pressure, and only those unlucky individuals who were prosecuted, they do enable us to encounter ordinary people rather than the abstractions that tend to appear in the kinds of sources that have traditionally been used to study obeah. But in their very abundance the records located through these methods have the limitation of requiring some kind of quantification in order to make sense of them. We can end up examining what is countable rather than what is important. I did perform some basic quantitative analysis of the material collected from newspapers, the results of which appear in Chapters 5 and 8. But I have made more qualitative use of the material, examining in more detail some individual cases of particular interest, such as those of Polydore of Jamaica and Pierre of Grenada (discussed in Chapter 3), and, in the twentieth century, to give just a few examples, Charles Dolly, who moved around the eastern Caribbean, Henry Padmore of Grenada and Trinidad, and Rose Anne and George Forbes of Jamaica (discussed in Chapters 6 and 7). The nature of the English criminal justice system and its colonial offshoots means that in none of these cases do we have the kind of extended record of interrogation produced by the Inquisition in the colonies of Spain and Portugal. I have not been able to trace the extended life history of any single healer in the way that James Sweet has recently traced the life of the African-born healer Domingo Álvares.[31] Nevertheless, the fragmentary stories of the people who found themselves subject to prosecution for obeah over the roughly two centuries examined in this book tell us much about life, power, and daily politics in the Caribbean.

Chapter 7 moves to the politics of obeah in the first half of the twentieth century. It shows how the development or expansion of multiple religious movements in this period was seen as increasingly threatening by colonial authorities, and faced significant repression in ways connected to, though not identical with, the repression of obeah. After the region exploded in the labour rebellions of the 1930s the Moyne Commission, which investigated the rebellions, briefly considered obeah and other aspects of African-oriented religion in its report. The Moyne Commission's analysis signalled the dominance of a new approach to understanding the Caribbean's relationship to Africa. New modes of anthropological thinking had raised the status of African religion, such that obeah now came to represent the Caribbean's degeneration from a purer African past, rather than a sign of continuity.

[31] Sweet, *Domingo Álvares*.

Chapter 8 combines the criminal justice history and cultural history approaches to analyse debates about obeah in the independence period. It shows that, for Jamaica at least, obeah prosecutions declined after the Second World War and almost completely ended after independence. Yet independent states in the Caribbean did not decriminalize obeah. Instead, the status of obeah became enmeshed in political conflicts over the limits of transformation wrought by independence, in particular as Black Power advocates challenged the first generation of nationalist leaders. The book ends by analysing representations of obeah on the Caribbean stage in the independence era, considering both popular comic drama and serious theatre.

Inevitably, I have had to be selective in what I analyse. This book is already long; if I had discussed all the topics that might legitimately have been included, it would have been prohibitively so. There are some important representations of and debates about obeah that I have not been able to attend to. For instance, I pay little attention to Benjamin Moseley's *A Treatise on Sugar*, which introduced the story of Three-Fingered Jack to the British public. Nor do I discuss in any detail either the important novel *Hamel, The Obeah Man*, or Matthew Lewis's *Journal*. For the twentieth century I was not able to include, for instance, discussion of the role of obeah in popular music, such the Mighty Sparrow's 'Melda' (Obeah Wedding) or the recordings of the Bahamian musician who styled himself Exuma, the Obeah Man; nor do I discuss the works of the Catholic missionary and amateur ethnographer Joseph J. Williams. Similarly, I have not attempted to examine either obeah prosecutions or religious movements for all times and places. Luckily, there is a rich and rapidly expanding literature in Caribbean studies that has considered many of these topics and themes, and to which this book seeks to contribute.[32]

David Scott has argued that studies of the Caribbean have too often been framed within the narrative form of Romance, telling stories of 'salvation and redemption' and imagining a 'utopian horizon toward which the[ir] emancipationist history' moves.[33] My work on *The Cultural Politics of Obeah* is located within a similar critique, and similarly aims to move beyond stories of overcoming. But rather than reframing Caribbean studies as Tragedy, as Scott proposes, I hope to reveal the reverberations

---

[32] Much of this work is cited elsewhere in this book, but on the specific topics mentioned in this paragraph see Wisecup, 'Knowing Obeah'; Ward and Watson, 'Introduction'; Nordius, 'Racism and Radicalism'; Ward, '"What Time has Proved"'; Brathwaite, 'The African Presence'; Sandiford, *Theorizing a Colonial Caribbean-Atlantic Imaginary*, 123–44; Bilby, 'An (Un)natural Mystic'; Dillon, 'Obi'; Palmié, 'Other Powers', 321–5.

[33] Scott, *Conscripts of Modernity*, 7–8.

between the colonial past and the post-colonial present. This book thus examines the complex history of the construction and reconstruction of obeah as discursive category, legal artefact, and everyday practice. It develops a non-teleological narrative about the formation of a particularly symbolically charged means of understanding the Caribbean's culture, one that has also for centuries been central to representing relationships between Africa, Europe, and the Caribbean.

# 1 The emergence of Caribbean spiritual politics

In 1760, in the wake of the events that we know as Tacky's Rebellion, the Assembly of Jamaica passed a comprehensive Act intended to ensure the security of slavery against rebellion. Tacky's Rebellion was the most substantial uprising by enslaved people of the eighteenth-century British-colonized Caribbean. The full title of the Act passed in its aftermath was 'An Act to remedy the evils arising from irregular assemblies of slaves, and to prevent their possessing arms and ammunition and going from place to place without tickets, and for preventing the practice of obeah, and to restrain overseers from leaving the estates under their care on certain days, and to oblige all free negroes, mulattoes or Indians, to register their names in the vestry books of the respective parishes of this Island, and to carry about them the certificate, and wear the badge of their freedom; and to prevent any captain, master or supercargo of any vessel bringing back slaves transported off this Island'.[1] The Act's emphasis on tickets, registration, and certification suggests a concern with monitoring space and people in order to be able to track and thus prevent insurrectionary activity. Such provisions were widespread in slave societies, and became increasingly so in the second half of the eighteenth century. Alongside these standard security provisions, though, was a relatively brief clause designed to 'prevent the practice of obeah'. By passing this clause, the Jamaica Assembly took a word that had hitherto been relatively rarely used, and gave it legal status and definition. It created a new crime that would eventually be prosecuted across the British colonies in the Caribbean, not just during the era of slavery but into the late twentieth and even twenty-first centuries. The Assembly's influential choice to make obeah into a crime departed from earlier responses to slave rebellions or Maroon anti-slavery activity in the Anglophone Caribbean, even where 'obeah' had been implicated in their organization. It also differed from the decisions of state authorities in other slave societies.

---

[1] The original Act is in CO 139/21.

What underlay the Assembly's decision, and what were its implications? The significance of the passage of the 'Act to remedy the evils arising from irregular assemblies of slaves' in 1760 has rarely been discussed, while the question of why, for most of the eighteenth century, no explicit legislaion restricted the practices that came to be known as obeah, has not been raised. However, if we extend our view over time and across space, both the contingency and the significance of that decision in 1760 become clearer. This chapter attempts to understand the Jamaican decision to criminalize obeah by considering it in relation to earlier British colonial responses to the use of spiritual power by enslaved Africans, which did not make use of criminal law. It both charts and explains the narrowing, over the course of the eighteenth century, of the terms through which African spiritual power was interpreted. It argues that Jamaican legislators' decision to imbue an African-derived word with meaning in British imperial law must be understood in the context of several important factors, in particular the shift towards a state-organized legal framework for responding to enslaved insurgency and resistance, and the decriminalization of witchcraft in English law earlier in the eighteenth century.

The African captives trafficked in huge numbers to the Caribbean and elsewhere in the Americas from the sixteenth to the nineteenth centuries brought with them a complex range of understandings of the powers that animated the spiritual world, their manifestations in the world of the living, and the relationship between these worlds. Spiritual powers, and the individuals who had specialist skill and knowledge to manipulate them, were specific, and named with many different words. While we can be sure that many of these terms, and the ideas they encoded, crossed the Atlantic, what is accessible to us now must surely be only a small selection of the words that circulated among Africans in the seventeenth- and eighteenth-century Americas. African religious ideas were undergoing considerable development in this period, partly in response to the devastation caused by the Atlantic slave trade. We do know, though, that terms like *calundú (quilondo), ganga (nganga), wanga/ ouanga, Vaudoux/Vodun/Vodou,* and *gris-gris* found their way from Central Africa, Dahomey, and Senegambia, respectively, to the Americas.[2]

Europeans who moved to the Americas also brought with them ideas and practices about the power of witches; about the healing powers of

---

[2] Sweet, *Recreating Africa*, 144–59; Sweet, *Domingo Álvares*, 17–19; Pettinger, 'From Vaudoux to Voodoo'; Hall, *Africans in Colonial Louisiana*, 163–5; Pluchon, *Vaudou, sorciers, empoisonneurs*, 16.

wise men and cunning folk; about God, saints, and the devil. Like African ideas, those of Europe were in flux in this period. Under the pressure of the extensive changes in European society in the wake of the reformation and as the process of 'Enlightenment' developed, the idea that humans might directly communicate with the devil, or might be able to access spiritual power to make changes for good in the world, became less respectable. Disbelief in witches and magic became a mark of intellectual credibility among the elite and the middle class. Nevertheless, for the majority of the population in much of Europe, magical explanations of misfortune and the ongoing presence of the dead in the world of the living remained important.

If, in the early eighteenth-century British-colonized Caribbean, the powers of the spiritual world and the practices designed to influence them were known by many names, both European and African in derivation, by the end of that century one term had become dominant: obeah. The term obeah had been defined in law in Jamaica and was spreading across the Caribbean; evidence about enslaved people's day-to-day religious practice also suggests its increasing importance as an everyday term. This rise to prominence of 'obeah' as a conceptual framework for making sense of Africans' and African Caribbeans' relationship to the spiritual world is the foundation of the rest of the story that this book seeks to tell, for the long-standing illegality of obeah both depended on and perpetuated it.

This chapter focuses more on how Europeans in the Caribbean interpreted African spiritual power than on African interpretations. This is partly a consequence of the available evidence: it is much easier to know how colonists interpreted African spiritual power than how enslaved people themselves understood that power. Precisely because they were not explicitly illegal until 1760, it is only occasionally that the healing and solidarity-building practices that came to be known as obeah are revealed in the sources that remain. The construction of obeah as a crime in 1760, and the subsequent laws that built on that illegality, brought African efforts to manipulate the spiritual world into view more systematically, and thus provide us with greater insight into how spiritual workers and those they sought to help understood their practice. However, this chapter does analyse moments of crisis such as the war between the Maroons and the British in early eighteenth-century Jamaica, and the planned rebellion in Antigua in 1736, as well as the reaction to them by colonial authorities. These events provide hints into the significance, for enslaved Africans, of obeah during its formative period.

Much of the historiography of obeah has prioritized the identification of the specific African origins of that term – a problem to which I will return later in the chapter.³ In so doing, it has overlooked a point that is more surprising: that an African, rather than a European, term became dominant at all. This was not inevitable; indeed, it was not even frequent within the Americas. In many other locations European colonists described what Africans did to manipulate the spiritual world with words deriving from European languages, usually terms for witchcraft. Direct equivalents of the crime of obeah did not exist elsewhere. In Brazil, people accused of using African religious magic were usually taken before the Inquisition as *feiticeiros/as*. These, and the related *feitiço*, are terms with their own interesting history, deriving from Portuguese interaction with Africans on the Atlantic coast, as William Pietz documents.⁴ In addition the term *calundú*, probably deriving from the Kimbundu word *quilundo*, came to be used for divination ceremonies involving the possession of human beings by spirits, but did not acquire legal status.⁵ In the Spanish colonies the Inquisition investigated people for *brujería* and *hechicería*.⁶ The actions that led to prosecutions for obeah in Britain's Caribbean colonies would most likely have been construed as poisoning in the French Caribbean and the British North American colonies.⁷

Some scholars state that 'obeah' was made illegal in the Danish West Indies before it was criminalized in the British colonies. Neville Hall writes that a clause of the Danish West Indian slave code promulgated by Govenor Philip Gardelin in 1733 authorized flogging or death as a punishment for 'obeah'. Hall's claim is followed by Kwasi Konadu, who states that in the Danish colonies obeah was legally prohibited and punishable by death.⁸ Others state that the Gardelin slave code authorized flogging for witchcraft.⁹ In fact, the Gardelin code, which was published

---

³ See for example the works cited in notes 36–47 in this chapter.
⁴ Pietz, 'The Problem of the Fetish II'. Pietz shows that the term 'fetish' derived from the Portuguese *feitiço* (charm/spell), which was linked to *feitiçaria* (witchcraft). In the coastal African context *feitiço* became *fetisso*, and then moved into Dutch as *Fetiche* and English as *fetish*. The Dutch and English terms lacked the sense of malevolence associated with the Portuguese.
⁵ Sweet, *Recreating Africa*, 144–5; Sansi, 'Sorcery and Fetishism'; de Mello e Souza, *The Devil and the Land of the Holy Cross*.
⁶ Bristol, *Christians, Blasphemers, and Witches*, 150; Maya Restrepo, '"Brujeria"'; Ortiz, *Brujas e inquisidores*.
⁷ On poison in the French colonies see Pluchon, *Vaudou, sorciers, empoisonneurs*; Weaver, *Medical Revolutionaries*; Debbasch, 'Le crime d'empoisonnement'; Leti, 'L'empoisonnement'. For British North America see Morgan, *Slave Counterpoint*, 612–20; Schwarz, *Twice Condemned*, 92–113; Parish, *American Curiosity*, 274–9. For an important discussion of both witchcraft and poison across early North America see Games, *Witchcraft in Early North America*.
⁸ Hall, *Slave Society in the Danish West Indies*, 58; Konadu, *The Akan Diaspora*, 103.
⁹ Caron and Highfield, *The French Intervention*, 15; Sensbach, *Rebecca's Revival*, 22; Westergaard, *The Danish West Indies*, 167.

in Dutch and Danish, uses neither the term obeah nor an equivalent of witchcraft, but rather the word *towernarye*, probably a misspelling of the Dutch *tovernerij*, meaning magic, which was spelled *tovernery* in eighteenth-century Dutch. It was *tovernery* by slaves, which the code describes as involving cloth bundles containing carved images, feathers, and nails which could do harm, that was made punishable by whipping. It also specifically prescribed poisoning of masters by slaves, punishable by 'pinching' with red-hot pincers and breaking on the wheel.[10]

Thus Britain's Caribbean colonies, and specifically in the first instance Jamaica, were unique in their decision to give legal status to an African-derived term, rather than in interpreting African spiritual activity under the rubrics of poisoning, witchcraft, or magic. The 'obeah' that emerged in this environment shaped Jamaican culture and the culture of the Anglo-Creole Caribbean in the eighteenth and nineteenth centuries. In adopting and generalizing the term 'obeah' and translating it as 'witchcraft', British colonists in Jamaica made a consequential choice. This legal language assimilated a range of African practices to the early modern European crime of witchcraft, but also produced a conceptual space between them. Where colonists in most parts of the Americas assimilated African practices to European witchcraft, Jamaican authorities distanced the two. The new crime of obeah drew on the legal definition of witchcraft, but named it as something else.

The decision to criminalize obeah in Jamaica, and the fact that the crime then appeared in legal practice and cultural discourse in much of the Anglo-Creole Caribbean, had significant consequences both for the politics of slavery and for the understanding, interpretation, and framing of African-oriented religious practice after slavery. As later chapters will demonstrate, the fact that obeah had been constructed as a crime during slavery, rather than simply as an aspect of Caribbean religion or culture, meant that after slavery it formed a central means of stigmatizing, and often of continuing to criminalize, much of the religious practice of Caribbean working people. It is therefore important to ask how people in Jamaica and elsewhere in the British-colonized Caribbean came to live in a world where obeah was a crime, while people in other slave societies did not. Why were the roughly equivalent categories of *conjure* or *root work*

---

[10] The Gardelin Slave code, 5 September 1733, English translation available online at http://www.eurescl.eu/images/files_wp3/danishregulations/17330905.pdf. This translation cites Rigsarkivet 390 Generaltoldkammeret, Vestindiske og guineiske sager, Visdomsbog, 1733–83 [Danish National Archives. 390. The Chamber of Customs, West Indian and Guinean Cases, Book of Wisdom, 1733–83], 359–63 for a Danish version, 285–91 for a Dutch version Thanks to Gunvor Simonsen for alerting me to this source and for sharing with me images of the Danish and Dutch originals.

in the United States and *quimbois* in Martinique and Guadeloupe, which were regarded by slave-holding elites in those places with suspicion and disapproval, not also made into central foci of criminal law?[11] Why, by the late period of slavery, were French colonials who encountered enslaved peoples' ritual practices so afraid of poison, while in Britain's Caribbean colonies slave-holders discussed poison with considerably less anxiety, but considered obeah a very serious social problem? Addressing these questions helps us to see obeah as a category with a history, something that came into being at a particular moment and under particular conditions. The rest of this chapter looks first at African and then European concepts of witchcraft, the spiritual world, and spiritual power, before examining how they came together in the Caribbean and were ultimately made into the crime of obeah.

Africans who arrived in the American colonies in the seventeenth and eighteenth centuries originated in societies in which the use of spiritual power played a significant role. They came from a range of cultural regions, which can broadly and schematically be divided into West-Central Africa (Kongo-Angola), the Bight of Biafra (predominantly Igbo), the Bight of Benin (Fon–Ewe–Yoruba), the Gold Coast (mainly Akan), Sierra Leone (Mende and Temne, among others), and Senegambia (Mande, Bambara, and Wolof, with a strong Muslim influence).[12] These societies differed in their religious practices and their understanding of the significance and working of spiritual power. For instance, people in the Gold Coast region and in Senegambia understood the soul to be divisible into two or more parts, which in Jamaica became the 'duppy' and the 'shadow'.[13] In Sierra Leone, specialist knowledge was developed within organizations such as the Poro and Sande societies.[14] In some regions, especially in Muslim West Africa and in Kongo-Angola, objects imbued with spiritual power, known as *minkisi* (sing. *nkisi*) in Kongo, played a significant role in mediating between the living and the dead. *Minkisi* were 'ritual object[s] invested with otherworldly power,

---

[11] On *conjure* see Fett, *Working Cures*, 84–108; Chireau, *Black Magic*; Young, *Rituals of Resistance*, 120–45. On *quimbois* see Ebroin, *Quimbois, magie noire et sorcellerie aux Antilles*, 150–3.

[12] For broad descriptions of Atlantic African cultural regions in the era of the slave trade see Hall, *Slavery and African Ethnicities*; Morgan, 'Africa and the Atlantic', 229–31. On the difficulty, but also usefulness, of specifying regions within Atlantic Africa see MacGaffey, Cultural Tradition'.

[13] On the Gold Coast see McCaskie, *State and Society*, 167–8. On Senegambia see Baum, *Shrines of the Slave Trade*, 48-49. On both see Gomez, *Exchanging our Country Marks*, 49 and 111–12.

[14] Day, *Gender and Power in Sierra Leone*.

allowing [them] to affect special spiritual and material functions in the world'.[15] The names of the spirits or deities in different cultures also differed in different places, and these varieties of names also travelled across the Atlantic, so that today we have, for instance, *lwa* in Haiti and *orisha/orisa* in Brazil, Cuba, and Trinidad, all terms that probably have Yoruba origins.[16]

Nevertheless, despite these specificities, many of which also became important in the Americas, there were significant commonalities that united early modern Atlantic African understandings of the relationship between the living and the dead. Africans universally understood the dead, in the form of ancestors and spirits, to have influence over the lives of living humans, and believed that the spiritual world could act on the physical world.[17] Ancestors and spirits thus needed to be cared for and respected. There were also more distant gods alongside those that operated more intimately and locally, and were thus more easily contacted by human beings.

In all early modern African cultures people consulted ritual specialists whose knowledge of the spiritual world enabled them to help with problems affecting both bodily health and the health of a person's relationship to the world. Ritual specialists also advised political leaders, including through divination that revealed when times were auspicious for activities such as war, and administered oaths that created community and solidarity. Specialists could, with the appropriate knowledge, use spiritual means to protect, to heal, and to attack others. They often used 'medicines' – spiritually powerful substances that could, with appropriate treatment, act on the bodies and minds of humans. Protection against spiritual attack was a necessary aspect of daily life. Physical substances could have powerful effects, and these often depended on the ritual context in which they were consumed, touched, or simply placed in proximity to a person.[18] African terms for such powerful substances were often translated into European languages as 'poison'. This was in

---

[15] Young, *Rituals of Resistance*, 110–12. See also the definition given by Wyatt MacGaffey: 'ritual complexes intended to bring about improvements in the well-being of individuals and groups, curing disease, identifying and punishing wrongdoers, averting misfortune, and favoring fertility and prosperity'. MacGaffey, *Kongo Political Culture*, 12.
[16] Ramsey, *The Spirits and the Law*, 19.
[17] Gomez, *Exchanging our Country Marks*; Thornton, *Africa and Africans*, 236–53. Thornton emphasizes the compatibility of African and European approaches to the 'other world' inhabited in part by the dead.
[18] Vansina, *Paths in the Rainforest*, 95–7; Sweet, *Recreating Africa*, 104–6; Sweet, *Domingo Álvares*, 17–24; Peel, *Religious Encounter*, 48–9; McNaughton, *The Mande Blacksmiths*, 44.

some ways an appropriate early modern translation, for early modern Europeans strongly associated poisoning with magic. It is one that can, however, cause confusion if it is assumed to refer to substances that provoke purely pharmacological reactions. It is also misleading in that African spiritual medicines were not only used to cause harm.[19]

Early modern African approaches to the spirit world tended to be holistic rather than focused on the ethical direction of spiritual work. They did not emphasize a fundamental division between 'good' and 'evil' in the use of spiritual power, nor did they frame the importance of the dead in the lives of the living as the specifically negative 'witchcraft' of European societies. Rather, concern with the spirit world formed part of a pervasive cosmology that related to the whole of life. Spiritually powerful individuals such as *nganga*s or *okomfo*s could be dangerous, precisely because of their power, but they were not inherently evil. Even the Akan *obayifo*, translated by early twentieth-century ethnographers as 'witch', was really, it has recently been argued, a more neutral term for one who makes use of spiritual power.[20] Indeed, it seems likely that concern specifically about witchcraft is in West Africa a phenomenon that dates from the era of the slave trade, and may well have been caused by it. According to Rosalind Shaw the earliest detailed written account of Sierra Leone, from the early sixteenth century, 'makes no mention of witchcraft or techniques of witch-finding', but does describe 'divination for sickness, remedial sacrifice, and burial practice'.[21] Similarly, one of the most detailed and closely observed accounts of West Africa in the era of the slave trade, Willem Bosman's *New and Accurate Description of the Coast of Guinea*, contains extensive discussion of religion and of spiritually induced harm and protection in the Gold Coast, but makes only one reference to an individual being a sorceress or witch (the Dutch word is *toverhoer*, literally whore who works magic).[22] While the concept of witchcraft may have existed in these societies without leaving behind written documentation, the absence of such documentation suggests that witchcraft was of lesser concern than in early modern Europe and in later

---

[19] Paton, 'Witchcraft, Poison', 246–8.
[20] Konadu, *The Akan Diaspora*, 140; Blay, 'Obeah'.
[21] Shaw, *Memories of the Slave Trade*, 211–12. Shaw is discussing Valentim Fernandes's 1506–10 *Description de la Côte Occidentale d'Afrique (Sénégal au Cap de Monte, Archipels)* (originally in Portuguese). See also Austen, 'The Moral Economy of Witchcraft'; Sweet, *Recreating Africa*, 162–3.
[22] Bosman, *New and Accurate Description*, 385. Bosman, a Dutch slave trader, lived at Elmina in the late seventeenth and early eighteenth centuries. For the Dutch see *Nauwkeurige beschryving van de Guinese Goud, Tand- en Slave-Kust* (Utrecht, 1704). Thanks to Jaap Wisse and Henrice Altink for help with Dutch. On Bosman see Pietz, 'The Problem of the Fetish, IIIa'.

periods in African history.[23] Even so, there was clearly a strong sense in many West African societies that the world was a spiritually dangerous place, in which people could be harmed by the spiritual work of other people, and directly by spirits themselves. Thus while many West Africans who ended up enslaved in the Americas would have been familiar with the idea of the witch, the more important idea for them was that certain individuals could manipulate spiritual power for a range of purposes that were not directed in a single moral or ethical direction.[24]

A concern with the problem of witchcraft seems to have been more widespread, at an earlier date, in West–Central Africa than in West Africa. Jan Vansina argues that the idea of witchcraft and the witch is a very long-standing part of Central African culture. The idea of witchcraft as human evil promoted an ethos of apparent equality, as the powerful were often suspected of using supernatural power, including witchcraft.[25] According to John Thornton, witches were an established presence in seventeenth- and eighteenth-century Kongo, where they were understood to do their evil work by eating their victims, symbolically and sometimes literally.[26] Witches were just one element in a wider landscape of spiritually powerful humans, ancestors, and spirits.[27]

Thus, Africans who were brought to the Americas as slaves shared a sense that harm could be done to people through spiritual or occult means, that physical substances (poisons) could be involved in such attacks, and that spiritual power could also protect and heal. For at least some Africans the slave trade was contributing to the formation of an increasingly threatening sense of the power of witchcraft and witches in the world around them. Nevertheless, they were embedded in a wider sense that the physical world was in constant relationship with a spiritual world, in which the power of the dead to intervene in the lives of the living, and the need to ensure that they did so in positive ways, was ever present.

Europeans also understood the visible, human world to exist in relation to an unseen world. For them the unseen world was more sharply divided in ethical orientation than it was for Africans. This was most obviously the case in the distinctions between God and the devil, heaven and hell. For some – Catholics – there were spiritual intermediaries, the saints. The focus on good and evil led to an emphasis on the possibility of an alliance between human beings and evil powers, and thus to the idea of the witch,

---

[23] Shaw, *Memories of the Slave Trade*, 212.
[24] For similar points see Bilby and Handler, 'Obeah'.
[25] Vansina, *Paths in the Rainforest*, 96–8.
[26] Thornton, *The Kongolese Saint Anthony*, 42–4.    [27] MacGaffey, *Religion and Society*.

who was characteristically female. From the fifteenth to the seventeenth centuries anxiety about witchcraft in Europe led to the execution of thousands of individuals who were convicted of the crime, most of whom were female. As Lyndal Roper notes, the witch was imagined as the inverse of the young, fertile woman. Rather than providing nourishment to others, her body had become a source of danger: she produced poison in her breasts instead of milk.[28] This idea of the spiritually evil person was to be significant in framing European understandings of African spiritual work and ritual specialists in the Caribbean.

Prosecutions for witchcraft took place, albeit with greater or lesser intensity, throughout early modern Europe, including in all the countries that would become colonial powers in the Americas.[29] The establishment of the American colonies roughly coincided with the most intense period of witch hunting, from the late sixteenth to the mid-seventeenth centuries. By the time the plantation system and the Atlantic slave trade boomed in the late seventeenth and eighteenth centuries, however, large-scale European witch panics had ended. The belief that the physical, visible world was only one part of a wider cosmos remained, but the possibility of human action in relation to that other world was in retreat. Witchcraft trials declined in France, England, Spain, Portugal, and the Netherlands during the seventeenth century, and witchcraft was decriminalized across Europe between the late seventeenth and late eighteenth centuries, beginning with France in 1682. Brian Levack argues that the primary cause of decriminalization was the imposition by centralized state legal systems of limits on the prosecutorial activities of local judicial institutions; that is, that it was connected to the development of the absolutist state.[30] Central state authorities' concern about witchcraft trials was also stimulated by the increasing prominence of ways of thinking about science, religion, history, and politics that were less congruent with demonology.[31] Despite this, for most Europeans witchcraft and magic remained real phenomena long after they were no longer crimes subject to prosecution. Cunning men and women, folk healers, spirits, and ghosts continued to be important parts of popular culture well into the nineteenth century, when they were reinvigorated by new mystical ideas such as spiritualism and theosophy.[32]

---

[28] Roper, *Oedipus and the Devil*, 209. See also Purkiss, *The Witch in History*, 134.
[29] For an overview of the chronological and geographical distribution of European witch trials see Levack, *The Witch-Hunt*, 185–232.
[30] Levack, 'Decline and End'.
[31] For important explorations of the complex issues at stake here see Clark, *Thinking with Demons*, 683–6; Porter, 'Witchcraft and Magic', 193–218.
[32] Vincent, *Literacy and Popular Culture*, 171–4; Davies, *Witchcraft, Magic and Culture*; Davies, *Popular Magic*; Oppenheim, *The Other World*; Dixon, *Divine Feminine*.

The Europeans who became slave-holding colonists in the seventeenth- and eighteenth-century Caribbean thus drew on a shared Christian history in which witchcraft existed as part of a wider religious landscape. Coming from a range of social backgrounds, it is likely that their understanding of witchcraft varied widely. For some, including most of the elite, belief in witchcraft indicated the believer's failure to adapt to changing intellectual developments. For others it was a continuing live reality. The French Dominican priest Jean-Baptiste Labat is a good example of such an individual. Born in the 1660s, Labat lived through the period in which witchcraft was decriminalized, but maintained belief in the power of the supernatural. As Doris Garraway notes, his application of 'the discourse of colonial demonology to African practices of magic' indicates 'the persistence of colonial beliefs in the occult supernatural at the beginning of the eighteenth century, when the European witch craze was undeniably in decline'.[33]

There were, then, considerable similarities but also quite profound differences between European and African approaches to spiritual power, witchcraft, and the role of ritual specialists – the elements that would eventually fuse into the colonial creole idea of obeah. And yet it was not until well after Caribbean colonies became plantation societies that obeah became the dominant, and the legal, term for African spiritual power. The next section of the chapter investigates several occasions when practices and concepts referred to as obeah (or obey, obia, obi) were clearly significant for enslaved people, and were known to be so by slave-holders, but when these practices and concepts did not cohere or congeal into an object of knowledge thought to be characteristic of Africans. The chapter ends by exploring the events of Tacky's Rebellion and their aftermath. What had changed by 1760?[34]

First, though, we should recognize that in order for the consolidation of obeah as an object of knowledge, produced through law and state power, to take place, it was necessary for the lexical item obeah to be available to people in the colonies. Where, then, did it come from, and why was it selected as the lexical term under which to criminalize African spiritual practice?

This is far from a new question. Indeed, it has been a matter of considerable interest to both popular and academic audiences since the

---

[33] Garraway, *The Libertine Colony*, 165.
[34] Elsewhere I have considered Tacky's Rebellion and its aftermath in the light of a comparison with contemporaneous events in Saint-Domingue, where Makandal's conspiracy, which made use of broadly similar spiritual medicines to those indicated by the term 'obeah', came to be understood by planters as 'poisoning' and also fed into the construction of Vodou as a religion. See Paton, 'Witchcraft, Poison'. This chapter includes some material that is reworked from that article.

eighteenth century. As the next chapter will explore in more detail, a prominent eighteenth-century speculative etymology argued that the term derived from the ancient Egyptian word *ob*, serpent. This explanation dominated in the nineteenth century and continued to have influence in the twentieth before eventually losing out to approaches that identified West African languages as sources of the word's etymological root.[35] Current scholarship is divided between proponents of two arguments. The first, a revision of the long-standing claim first made by the American Jesuit missionary and ethnologist Joseph J. Williams, who lived in Jamaica for several years in the 1920s and 1930s, is that obeah – as a term at least, and probably as practice too – derives from the Akan (Twi) word *obayifo*, traditionally translated as witch. The argument for an Akan etymology for the term obeah was promoted by Orlando Patterson, and has been recently updated by Kwasi Konadu.[36] Like his predecessors, Konadu argues that obeah is related to the Twi *obayifo*, but he claims that rather than directly deriving from that term, it actually comes from *bayi*, a term that he suggests has neutral rather than negative connotations, and means the neutral force used by the *obayifo*.[37] Other recent scholarship emphasizes the potential for the Akan *obayifo* to use *bayi* to

---

[35] The Egyptian etymology derived from Jacob Bryant's *A New System of Ancient Mythology* (1774). It was reproduced, sometimes with an additional connection to Hebrew, in abolitionist memoirs such as Madden, *A Twelvemonth's Residence*, II, 71; generalist periodicals such as *Chamber's Edinburgh Journal* ('Sketches of Superstitions: Fetishes – Obeah', *Chamber's Edinburgh Journal*, 14 December 1839, 374–5) and *Notes and Queries* (Henry H. Breen, letter to *Notes and Queries* 80, 10 May 1851, 376); the popular writings of colonial officials such as Hesketh J. Bell (Bell, *Obeah*); accounts by people from the Caribbean such as the black Jamaican Anglican minister Thomas R. Banbury (Banbury, *Jamaica Superstitions*, 6); and the anonymous author of an article published in the Guyanese journal *Timehri* in 1919. From some of these sources it was reproduced in reviews and other popular newspaper articles. For instance reviews of Hesketh Bell's *Obeah* in the *Manchester Examiner*, 27 November 1889 and the *Daily Chronicle*, 28 December 1889 both reproduce it. (Both in CUL, Sir Henry Hesketh Bell Collection, Royal Commonwealth Society Library, GBR/0115/RCMS 36 (henceforth Bell Papers), 36/1, Scrapbooks 1889–99). See also 'The Cult of Obeah – A Curse to Jamaica', *Gleaner*, 9 April 1932. The etymological claim even found its way into scholarship in the United States, in the form of W. E. B. DuBois's *The Negro Church* (1903). None of these citations discussed the claim that Caribbean obeah derived from an Egyptian term in any detail; its use served primarily to demonstrate the authors' scholarly approach to the subject. Although this etymology was no longer taken seriously by most scholars by the early twentieth century, versions of it, clearly drawing on the account by Stephen Fuller, Edward Long and James Chisholme discussed in the next chapter (see pp. 55–6), still appear on esoteric and New Age websites such as http://www.angelfire.com/electronic/awakening101/obeah2.html and http://www.witch-lovespells.com/what_is_obeah.html, both accessed 14 February 2011.)
[36] Patterson, *Sociology of Slavery*, 185–6.
[37] Konadu, *The Akan Diaspora*, 140. For further elaboration of this argument see Konadu, *Indigenous Medicine*, 50–1.

bring good fortune as well as to harm.³⁸ Still others, however, define *bayi* as 'witchcraft'.³⁹ Konadu bases his argument not just on phonological similarity, but also on the presence of the lexical item *obeah* in places where significant numbers of enslaved people came from the Gold Coast – most of the British colonies, as well as Suriname and the Danish Virgin Islands – and its absence from most of North America, where there were fewer enslaved people of Akan origin.⁴⁰

The attribution of Akan origin to the term obeah has long been contested, and is no longer the most widely accepted etymology. In the early twentieth century Harry Johnston argued that 'obeah' was 'a corruption of an Efik or Ibo word from the north-east or east of the Niger delta, which simply means "Doctor"', a derivation endorsed by Melville Herskovits in 1934.⁴¹ More recently, the case for an Igbo origin of the term has been strongly put forward by Douglas B. Chambers and taken up by Handler and Bilby. Handler and Bilby argue that the Akan *obayifo* was not likely to be the root of obeah because in its early usage *obeah* (or *obia*) did not have negative connotations, unlike *obayifo*. Instead, they claim, citing the Nigerian scholar John Anenechukwu Umeh along with Johnston and others, that the compound Igbo term *dibia*, meaning 'master of knowledge and wisdom', is a likely etymological source for Caribbean *obeah*.⁴² Captives from the Bight of Biafra, Chambers notes, were present in significant numbers – indeed, in larger numbers than were people of Akan origin – in all the places where the term obeah (or its cognates) is found in early sources.⁴³ Citing Handler and Bilby's work, the 2004 *Oxford English Dictionary* amended its entry for obeah. The 1989 entry cited Efik and Twi origins for the term but the current edition, while stating that the term's etymology is 'uncertain', gives the Igbo and Ibibio etymologies first.⁴⁴

Meanwhile, other etymologies also circulate. Alongside Igbo and Ibibio origins, the *OED* also proposes Edo *obi* (which it translates as 'poison')

---

38 Blay, 'Obeah'.
39 Allsopp, *Dictionary of Caribbean English Usage*, 412.
40 Konadu, *The Akan Diaspora*, 140. Handler and Bilby dispute Konadu's etymological claims on the basis of personal communication from the Ghanaian musicologist J. H. Nketia, whom they cite as stating that both *bayi* and *obayifoo* have strong negative connotations. Handler and Bilby, *Enacting Power*, 111n115.
41 Johnston, *The Negro*, 253n. Melville Herskovits to Joseph John Williams, 18 January 1934, Herskovits Papers, Northwestern University Archives, Evanston Ill., Series 35/6, Box 26, Folder 9.
42 Handler and Bilby, 'Early Use and Origin', 91–2; Umeh, *After God is Dibia*.
43 Chambers, 'Ethnicity in the Diaspora', 38; Chambers, 'My Own Nation', 88–90.
44 'obeah, adj. and n.', OED Online, June 2013, Oxford University Press. Available at www.oed.com/view/Entry/129542?isAdvanced=false&result=1&rskey=JSyRzW& (accessed 20 June 2013).

and Efik *ubio* ('fetish').[45] Donald Hill states that the term is of Fon origin.[46] Others have suggested that the word may derive from Yoruba obi divination, in which coconut or cowrie shells are interpreted to determine responses to questions posed by the diviner.[47] As the multiplicity of possible original terms suggests, this controversy is unlikely to be definitively resolved. Perhaps it is most likely that in encounters between Akan speakers' discussions of *bayi* and *obayifos* on the one hand, and Igbo and Ibibio speakers' references to individuals as *dibia* on the other, both recognized similarities in meaning and sound of the others' words, leading to its emergence in Jamaican and in other creole languages as a single term. Nevertheless, Konadu's argument does fit with the clear identification of early prominent 'obey men' and 'obia men' with Akan names, origins, or associations. Examples include Quawcoo, the spiritual adviser to Court, the leader of the 1736 Antiguan conspiracy; Graman Quacy (or Kwasi), the spiritual healer of eighteenth-century Suriname; and the unnamed 'obiah man' who advised the Gold Coast-born Tacky in Jamaica in 1760.[48] Yet although many of the early individuals identified as obeah men were Akan, there are also eighteenth-century examples of people practising obeah who are identified as being of other African ethnicities. Among them are the 'woman of the Popo country', who will be discussed in the next chapter, and the less well-known 'Rock alias Venture', an 'elderly Negro man of the Papaw country' advertised in Jamaica in 1791 as a runaway who 'passes amongst the negroes for a great obeah man'.[49] At an early point, then, activity identified as 'obeah' was attributed to individuals with a range of African origins.

Moreover, discussions of origins do not tell the whole story. In particular, they omit the spread of the term 'obeah' across the colonies acquired by the British in the late eighteenth and nineteenth centuries. In places such as Trinidad, Grenada, and Dominica, where enslaved people came later, and fewer of them from the Gold Coast, legislation was also passed against obeah, and the term also came to be widespread in popular usage by the nineteenth century – although sometimes it competed more openly with other terms.[50]

---

[45] Ibid. An online etymological dictionary also cites the Efik and Twi derivations. Douglas Harper, 'Obeah', Online Etymology Dictionary, available at www.etymonline.com/index.php?term=obeah, last consulted 20 June 2013.
[46] Hill, *Caribbean Folklore*, 21.
[47] Edmonds and Gonzalez, *Caribbean Religious History*, 233n231.
[48] Kwaku and Kwasi are both Akan day-names. Tacky's Rebellion was led by Akan-origin Africans.
[49] *Royal Gazette*, 22 January 1791.
[50] Direct arrivals from Africa to Dominica, Grenada, and Trinidad are revealed by this search of the Slave Voyages database: http://slavevoyages.org/tast/database/search.faces?

Thus the term obeah and the many variants found in the seventeenth and eighteenth centuries – obi, obey, oby, obia, obea – reflect the mutual comprehensibility, for African captives from the Gold Coast, the Bight of Biafra, and elsewhere, of a cultural perspective in which the dead could intervene in the lives of the living, and spiritual power was an important force for everyone. These terms existed alongside others for spiritual power, including *wanga*, *gris-gris*, *nganga* (ganga), *confou*, and *axe*, that were more prominent in other locations but which did not become part of a legal vocabulary. It was the prominence of obeah, both the term and the practice it connoted, in the Akan-led rebellion of 1760 that drew the attention of the Jamaican colonial authorities. For reasons that are hard to reconstruct, they used the spelling 'obeah' in their law of 1760. This law then came to stand for all kinds of uses of spiritual power in English eyes as well as those of enslaved Africans. The term was diffused around the other English and British colonies, and to Britain itself, as the British Empire in the Caribbean expanded in the late eighteenth and early nineteenth centuries.

In addition to its widespread use in British colonies, the term *obeah* was also widely used in Suriname, where it remains current among today's Maroons, although without the negative connotations it has in the Anglophone Caribbean.[51] Accounts of the healer Graman Quacy in eighteenth-century Suriname show that at that time the term was used without negative implications, not only by Maroons but also in colonial society. John Gabriel Stedman described Quacy as a *locoman*, diviner, and sorcerer (rather than an obeah man) who made and sold 'obias or amulets' that made their wearers 'invulnerable'.[52] Quacy, who is depicted in Figure 1.1 in European fine clothing, acquired his freedom, and even became well off through his work. His powers were respected and used by both black and white people in Surinamese society. Bilby and Handler argue that the neutral meaning of obeah in Suriname, which was a British colony until 1677, suggests that the original meaning in Britain's Caribbean colonies was also largely positive. They explain that the negative implications of the term obeah developed in the British world after Suriname was taken over by the Dutch, and thus did not affect that colony. In Suriname neither 'obeah' nor 'obia' became a term with a specific meaning in law;

yearFrom=1514&yearTo=1866&mjslptimp=33800.34400.34500. Although it omits the significant importation of enslaved people from other colonies, this search gives some indication of origins.

[51] Bilby and Handler, 'Obeah', 155.
[52] Stedman, *Narrative*, 582. For discussion of Quacy see Price, 'Kwasimukamba's Gambit'; Davis, 'Judges, Masters, Diviners'; Parish, 'Diasporic African Sources', 290–3; Watson, *Caribbean Culture*, 20–3.

instead, the religion winti, which was for a long time forbidden by law, was a closer equivalent.[53]

The Surinamese experience may explain why obeah was not criminalized anywhere in the British colonies prior to 1760. In seventeenth- and eighteenth-century Suriname obeah was considered a useful force, even by planters and the colonial state, who used Graman Quacy's powers to counter the resistance and rebellion of enslaved people and Maroons. An analogous situation may have prevailed in the early English Caribbean, alongside a policy of, in Tim Watson's terms, 'accommodating, tolerating, and understanding...Jamaican culture and religion'.[54] Over the course of the eighteenth century, however, the perception that African spiritual power and knowledge could be controlled through such alliances shifted, especially as it was increasingly associated with anti-slavery solidarity. Increasing planter concern about obeah's potential for rebellion eventually culminated in the law of 1760.

Events that drew slave-holders' attention to obeah's potential as a force for resistance and for building solidarity took place in the 1730s, in Antigua and Jamaica. In Jamaica the planter class tried, and failed, to gain a military victory over what they termed the 'rebellious Negroes', that is, the well-established Maroon communities, the Leeward Maroons led by Cudjoe in central Jamaica and the Windward Maroons led by Nanny and Quao in the east of the island.[55] These communities traced their origins to the English conquest of Jamaica from Spain in 1655. Since then they had become well established, and formed a significant barrier to the continued expansion of the plantation system. In the 1730s, with the slave trade expanding and planter desire to bring new land into cultivation by enslaved people, the war between the British and the Maroons intensified. To their surprise, British troops were unable to gain a decisive victory over the Maroons, and instead the colonial government eventually came to terms with them, signing treaties in 1739 with first Cudjoe and then Quao.[56]

As Barbara Kopytoff described in her classic article 'The Early Political Development of Jamaican Maroon Societies', obeah men and women played significant roles among both the Leeward and Windward Maroons. Kopytoff argues that their political role was more significant among the more politically fragmented Windward Maroons.[57] The powerful spiritual work of the 'First Time' Maroons – those who fought the

---

[53] Van Wetering, 'Polyvocality and Constructions of Syncretism'; Handler and Bilby, 'Early Use and Origin', 98–9n26.
[54] Watson, *Caribbean Culture*, 18.   [55] Metcalf, *Royal Government*, chapter 2.
[56] Bilby, *True-Born Maroons*, 168–80, 260–88.
[57] Kopytoff, 'Early Political Development', 298–301.

The emergence of Caribbean spiritual politics

Figure 1.1 Graman Quacy, as depicted by William Blake.
*Source*: John Gabriel Stedman, *Narrative of a Five Years' Expedition, against the Revolted Negroes of Suriname, from the year 1772 to 1777* (London, 1796). Courtesy of the National Library of Scotland

war against the British and won the treaties – remains an essential part of Maroon mythology and identity. Nanny's spiritual power is at the root of one of the foundational stories of Jamaican nationalism, especially since her elevation to the status of National Hero in 1977.[58] Contemporary written sources corroborate the presence of spiritual leaders known as Obia or Obea men or women during the 1730s. A Leeward Maroon woman captured by British troops after a skirmish in 1730 during which her husband was killed told her captors that her husband was 'one of the rebellious leaders and Chief Obia Man'.[59] After the treaties were signed, a retrospective account described the Maroons as 'very superstitious' and noted the significance to them of 'a person whom they called Obia Man whom they greatly revered'. The Maroons' Obia Man practised divination: 'his words carried the Force of an Oracle with them, being consulted on every occasion'. This observer also suggested that the 'Obia man' had lost prestige due to his failure to protect them during the final stages of the war: 'at present this Obia man is disregarded for having assured them this last town was inassailable by the Whites who in a few days after this report, convinced them of the Falseness of it, by burning their houses & bringing them to a submission'.[60] Philip Thicknesse, a British soldier who captained troops in the 1730s war against the Maroons, referred to the existence of both an 'Obea woman' and of 'Obea women' among the Windward Maroons, also on occasion using the spelling 'Obeah woman'. Thicknesse claimed that this woman (or women), who historians have usually assumed was Nanny, was a vigorous advocate of ongoing war against the British, who opposed the treaty of 1739, and supported dealing harshly with captured enemies. The Windward 'Obea women', Thicknesse claimed, wore the teeth of dead British soldiers as trophies, 'drilled thro' and worn as ankle and wrist bracelets'.[61]

The Maroons were also reported, according to the testimony of another captive, Sarra, to use sacred oaths to ensure loyalty among those who

---

[58] Bilby, *True-Born Maroons*, 38–40, 202–13; Sharpe, *Ghosts of Slavery*, 17–29. For popular attention to Nanny as obeah woman see Cousins, *Queen of the Mountain*; Gottlieb, 'The Mother of us All'.
[59] 'An Extract of Col. Campbell's letter concerning the examination of some rebellious negros lately taken', CO 137/47, f. 91. A similar but not identical extract of Campbell's letter is found in Hunter to Newcastle, 23 January 1730/1, CO 137/53, f. 303, where Hunter's covering letter identifies the woman as a 'negro woman prisoner' brought in by 'a small party sent out from the leeward'. See also Calendar of State Papers Colonial, America and West Indies, Volume 38: 1731 (1938), no. 25, pp. 14–31, which renders the word 'obia' as 'obra'. The original MS clearly reads 'obia'.
[60] I. Lewis to James Knight, 20 Dececember 1743, British Library Add Ms 12431, f. 99.
[61] Thicknesse, *Memoirs and Anecdotes*, 120–1, 126.

joined them: 'They give encouragement for all sorts of Negroes to joyn them, and oblige the men to be true to them by an oath which is held very sacred among the Negroes, and those who refuse to take that oath, whether they go to them of their own accord or are made Prisoners, are instantly put to Death.'[62] Although Sarra did not use the term obeah or obia to refer to such oaths, his description anticipates accounts of oaths in other times and places that also constructed spiritual solidarity, and were often termed obeah oaths.[63]

Spiritual protection, termed obeah (or Obia or Obea) thus emerges as a centrally important part of the Maroons' fighting strategy. Sarra's evidence also suggests that the Maroons' sense of collectivity was produced at least in part through religion. Despite this, the British who were fighting them paid relatively little attention to these elements. Obeah does not appear in any sustained way in colonial discussions of strategy, nor was there any effort at the time to restrict the use of obeah or spiritual power more generally among enslaved people. The colonial government's primary concern was with the difficulty of combating the Maroons in Jamaica's mountainous terrain, and with the possibility that their internal enemies might successfully ally with the Spanish. In this context, it is unsurprising that the Jamaican government did not legislate against obeah in the 1730s. Obeah was associated with the 'wild negroes', not those who remained on plantations. Such 'wild negroes' could only be fought by war or diplomacy, not through the courts or the law.

In the same period as the British–Maroon war in Jamaica, enslaved people on plantations in Antigua also seem to have been using spiritual power that they termed 'obeah', again without any legislative response. In late 1736 planters in Antigua came to suspect that a large-scale conspiracy was planned against them, led by a mixture of 'Cormantees' and Creoles. The uprising was planned to begin during a ball to celebrate the coronation of George II, which would be attended by the island's main planters, but plans for it were discovered before the ball began. The suspected ringleaders were quickly arrested and interrogated. A four-strong commission of planters was appointed to investigate; over the next nine weeks its members took evidence, heard confessions, ordered punishments and wrote a 'Report... upon the Weighty Affair of the late Conspiracy of our slaves'.[64] In the end forty-seven people were executed and forty-three banished from Antigua. Because the uprising was halted

---

[62] 'The further examination of Sarra alias Ned taken by order of his Excellency', 1 October 1733, CO 137/54, f. 354. Another copy is at CO 137/21, f. 42.
[63] Mullin, *Africa in America*, 41, 67–68; Stewart, *Three Eyes*, 43.
[64] 'Report of our Proceedings upon the Weighty Affair of the late Conspiracy of our slaves', 30 December 1736, CO 9/10, ff. 97–114.

before it took place, it has never been clear how extensive the planning was. The major historians of the event, however, are convinced that it represented a genuine plan. The conspiracy – even if its extent was exaggerated in its repression – revealed a complex network of relationships between Akan-speaking enslaved people and those born in Antigua, many of whom are likely to have been of Akan parentage.[65]

The conspiracy was organized through religious ceremonies and loyalty built through religious oaths, which were described in detail in the planters' report:

> The manner of administering the oath was, by drinking a health in liquor, either rum or some other, with grave dirt, and sometime cocks blood, infused; and sometimes the person swearing, laid his hand on a live cock. The words were various, but the general tenor was, to stand by and to be true to each other, and to kill the whites, man, woman & child to assist in the execution of this, when called upon by the Chief, and to suffer death rather than discover; with damnation and confusion to those who should refuse, or having drank and sworn, should afterwards discover, sometimes too, the person swearing chew'd malageta pepper.[66]

Here the report's authors drew on evidence taken at multiple trials to produce a composite picture of an oath which conspirators were said to have taken on multiple occasions and in 'no less than seven places'. Their main interest was in the content of the oath itself, rather than on who administered it. Nevertheless, the report went on to state that on one occasion where the oath was taken the leader and host Secundi 'had called to his assistance, a Negro Obiaman or Wizard who acted his part before a great number of slaves, assembled at Secundi's to take the oath, and assured them of success'.[67] The 'Obiaman' in question was Quawcoo, who was tried on 11 December 1736, when he was described as 'an Old Oby Man and Physition and Cormantee'. Quawcoo was one of three men to be described in the trials as an obeah man; the other two were Caesar, who belonged to the governor, and John Obiah.[68] Quamina, the main witness against Quawcoo, said that he had known Quawcoo in 'Cormantee Country' and declared himself to be 'afraid of this Obey Man' who was 'a Bloody fellow'. Quamina also described Quawcoo's administration of the blood oath:

> Quawcooo put Obey made of Sheeps Skin upon the ground, upon and about the bottle of Rum, and the Chequeen upon the bottle. Then took the Cock cut open his Mouth and one of his Toes and so poured the Cocks blood Over

---

[65] Gaspar, *Bondmen and Rebels*, 227–54 and *passim*; Craton, *Testing the Chains*, 120–4; Konadu, *The Akan Diaspora*, 133–40.
[66] 'Report' CO 9/10, f. 106.   [67] Ibid.   [68] Gaspar, *Bondmen and Rebels*, 246.

all the Obey, and then Rub'd Secundi's forehead with the Cocks bloody Toe, then took the Bottle and poured some Rum upon the Obey, Drank a Dram and gave it to Secundi and made Secundi Swear not to Discover his name. Secundi pledged him and swore not to Discover his name to any body. Secundi then asked him when he must begin to Rise. Quawcoo took a string ty'd knots in it and told him not to be in a hurry for that he would give him notice when to Rise and all should go well and that as he tyed those knots so the Baccarararas should become arrant fools and have their mouths stopped and their hands tyed that they should not Discover the Negro's Designs. He made believe that he would make the Bacarrarraras fools and that they would find nothing of it out.[69]

This detailed account of oathing reveals a more complex role for the obeah man than the report's condensed version allows. Quawcoo conducted the oath as the report's composite description presents it, but was also involved in divination, using a knotted string in order to identify an auspicious time for the rising to take place, and also to exert spiritual control over the whites (the 'Baccarararas' or 'Bacarrarraras'). Quamina's evidence suggests that Quawcoo was a significant person, although he does not appear in many other accounts of the events of the conspiracy. 'Obey' here describes a spiritually powerful object, made of sheep's skin, which the 'Obey man' (or 'Obia man') placed on the ground and sacrificed a cock and made a libation of rum over.

Quawcoo also participated at an earlier stage in the conspiracy, giving advice to the Akan leader Court and showing him the ceremonial material for the ritual dance. Quawcoo showed Court how they 'played with the Ikem, in his Country'. He also demonstrated how to fight with a wooden cutlass, and blew 'with an Oben ie an Elephant's tooth', and had a 'sheep skin on his thigh'. Konadu argues that these materials and the rituals revealed in the evidence demonstrate that what was taking place was an Antiguan version of the Akan *odwira* festival, which celebrated the New Year and recognized the power of the *ahene* (ruler).[70] Quawcoo's involvement clearly demonstrates that in his role as an 'obey man' he acted as both spiritual adviser and diviner.

Despite this detailed description of the use of an 'Obey' and the specialist who knows how to use it as an 'Obey man'/'Obiaman', white people in Antigua did not focus primarily on obeah in their response to the conspiracy. In its aftermath a number of security measures were taken, particularly focusing on limiting the ability of enslaved people to

---

[69] 'Tryal of Quawcoo an Old Oby Man and Physition and Cormantee belong to Mr Wm Hunt', 11 December 1736, in Minutes of Chief Governor and Council, St Johns, Antigua, 12 January 1737, CO 9/10. See also Gaspar, *Bondmen and Rebels*, 237.
[70] Konadu, *The Akan Diaspora*, 135–7.

congregate in towns.[71] But control over enslaved people's religious practice or spiritual work was not seen as an essential part of the response to the conspiracy.

These events in both Antigua and Jamaica suggest a world in which rituals, objects, and specialists linked to immanent power had broad purposes but strong political resonances, and the term 'obia' was part of the lingua franca used by Africans and their descendants to designate many of these purposes and resonances. Compared to later constructions of obeah, whether as healing or as witchcraft, the early eighteenth-century meaning of obeah was much more expansive. It was far from the private, individualized encounter between specialist and client described by, among others, Orlando Patterson.[72] Rather, the obeah practitioner was a person at the heart of the community whose knowledge contributed to critical political decisions such as when to rise against slavery.

Twenty-three years after the Antigua events there was another conspiracy, again led by enslaved Coromantees. This time the location was Jamaica, and the plan became an actual rebellion, the most threatening to the planter class in a British colony in the eighteenth century. Enslaved people successfully took power, albeit briefly, over significant parts of Jamaica. It took months for the plantocracy to fully regain control of the island. At Easter, 150 slaves under the leadership of a 'Coromantee' named Tacky attacked the fort at the town of Port Maria. They seized gunpowder and muskets, then marched southwards, gathering recruits as they went. Tacky's forces had connections with an island-wide network of rebels. Over the next few weeks uprisings took place in the parishes of Clarendon, St Elizabeth, St James, and Westmoreland, while a conspiracy was detected in the Kingston–Spanish Town area. Although British forces fairly quickly inflicted sufficient military damage on the rebels to prevent them overthrowing the island's rulers, they were unable to crush the rebellion completely. Rebel camps continued to exist for months, especially in Western Jamaica.[73]

The Saint Mary rebels' solidarity derived at least in part from the leadership of a man later described by planters Stephen Fuller, James Chisholme, and Edward Long as 'the chief Instigator and Oracle of the Insurgents'. This man was said to have 'administered the Fetish or solemn

---

[71] Lanaghan, *Antigua and the Antiguans*, I, 108.
[72] Patterson, *Sociology of Slavery*, 188.
[73] Brown, *The Reaper's Garden*, 148–9; Craton, *Testing the Chains*, 125–39; Metcalf, *Royal Government*, 150–1. For a new approach to Tacky's Rebellion see Brown, 'Slave Revolt in Jamaica'. Maria Alessandra Bollettino argues that these events should be understood as a 'series of insurrections', rather than a unified Akan-led revolt. Bollettino, 'Slavery, War, and Britain's Atlantic Empire', chapter 5, quotation on 191.

Oath to the Conspirators, and furnished them with a magical Preparation which was to render them invulnerable'.[74] Edward Long in his *History of Jamaica* used similar language. He described the man as 'a famous obeiah man or priest, much respected among his countrymen', and noted that the 'obeiah man' and 'others of his profession' had 'administered a powder' to the rebels which when 'rubbed on their bodies, was to make them invulnerable'. These priests also persuaded the rebels that Tacky was ritually protected and 'could not possibly be hurt by the white men'. Long argued that the arrest and execution of this man relatively soon after the start of the rebellion deterred some possible followers from joining the rebels. Nevertheless, he said, others continued to be persuaded of Tacky's invulnerability.[75]

Tacky and his 'obeiah man' thus behaved similarly to Court and Quawcoo in Antigua, although with more success. In both contexts the leaders hoped to use spiritual power to promote solidarity and thus to mobilize a collective military campaign. Although the accounts of the specific ritual activities undertaken by Tacky's obeah man are less detailed than the evidence of Quawcoo's actions, it seems likely that in Jamaica too the rituals drew on Akan ideas and practices.

Despite the similarities between the role of obeah in Antigua in 1736 and Jamaica in 1760, the response of the Jamaican authorities in 1760 was significantly different to that of their predecessors. The Antiguan authorities had focused on restricting enslaved people from congregating. In the 1730s the Jamaicans had had to be satisfied with making treaties with the Maroons. In recognizing them as a sovereign polity, albeit one with obligations to the British Crown, the Jamaican government made no attempt to intervene in Maroon religious life. The planter class in 1760 was in a different situation. Like the planters of Antigua, Jamaican planters were concerned with questions about absenteeism, the ability of slaves to move around, and the need for a strong militia. For the first time, however, they also focused on obeah itself as a problem. As Fuller, Chisholme, and Long reported, 'the Examinations which were taken' after the rebellion 'opened the Eyes of the Public to the very dangerous Tendency of the Obeah Practices, and gave birth to the Law which was then enacted for their Suppression and Punishment'.[76] In the wake of Tacky's Rebellion, the Jamaican House of Assembly passed a law that attempted to prevent future rebellions.[77] Like the Antiguan

---

[74] 'Copies of certain of the evidence submitted to the committee of Council for Trade and Plantations in the course of their enquiry into the state of the African slave trade', 1788, BT 6/10.
[75] Long, *The History of Jamaica*, II, 451–2.  [76] 'Copies of certain of the evidence.'
[77] 'An Act to remedy the evils arising from irregular assemblies of slaves....', CO 139/21.

response to the 1736 conspiracy, this Act sought to secure slave society by restricting assemblies of slaves, 'free negroes, mulattoes or Indians', and the possession of arms by slaves. But in addition, it prohibited obeah.

The 1760 Act's anti-obeah clause drew on the concept of witchcraft in English law and Christian religion. It prohibited the practice of what it termed 'Obeah or Witchcraft', making conviction punishable by death or transportation off the island. This phrasing is ambivalent about whether 'witchcraft' is intended as an explanatory term, a kind of translation or gloss – 'obeah, that is, witchcraft' – or as an alternative to obeah, an additional thing that was prohibited. In the long term the former meaning predominated, and obeah came to be defined increasingly as a form of witchcraft. The Act described obeah as 'the wicked Art of Negroes going under the appellation of Obeah Men and Women, pretending to have Communication with the Devil and other evil spirits'. It thus drew on elite European ideas of the witch, in which communication with, and more specifically the making of pacts with, the devil was a constituent part of the phenomenon of witchcraft. At the same time, it creolized this concept by suggesting the possibility of communicating with 'other evil spirits'. The act also included a long list of materials – 'Blood, Feathers, Parrots Beaks, Dogs Teeth, Alligators Teeth, Broken Bottles, Grave Dirt, Rum, Egg-shells' – that might be used in the practice of 'Obeah or Witchcraft'. This suggests that the legislators were also engaging with the material details of Jamaican ritual practice.[78]

The choice to name obeah as a crime in 1760, rather than to subsume it within a larger concept of witchcraft, was partly determined by the fact that witchcraft in England had been decriminalized by the time of Tacky's Rebellion. In 1736 the English parliament passed a new Witchcraft Act, which repealed the sixteenth- and seventeenth-century Witchcraft Acts that had previously governed the legal approach to the crime. The new Witchcraft Act represented a transformation in elite understandings of witchcraft. As well as decriminalizing witchcraft, it created a new crime: to '*pretend* to exercise or use any kind of Witchcraft, Sorcery, Inchantment, or Conjuration'.[79] Under the Witchcraft Act it also became an offence to accuse someone of practising witchcraft.[80] This new Act represented an attempt to generalize the idea that witchcraft was not possible – a view that had become widespread among the elite – to the wider population. Its main purpose was to suppress popular belief in witchcraft.

---

[78] For further discussion of this Act see Handler and Bilby, *Enacting Power*, 46; Anderson, 'Gnostic Obia', 114–16.
[79] Davies, *Witchcraft, Magic and Culture*, 2.
[80] Bostridge, 'Witchcraft Repealed'; Bostridge, *Witchcraft*; Davies, *Witchcraft, Magic and Culture*.

Jamaican legislators thus could not resurrect older legislation against witchcraft. They probably would not have wanted to even if they could have done so, since many of them regarded themselves as men of the Enlightenment and were engaged with Atlantic debates about science and reason. And yet the 1736 Witchcraft Act, which set out the relatively minimal penalty of a year's imprisonment for 'pretending to exercise or use any kind of Witchcraft, Sorcery, Inchantment, or Conjuration', would not have helped authorities to combat the kind of use of spiritual power seen in Tacky's Rebellion.[81] The obeah law bore traces of scepticism and anti-supernaturalism: it prohibited 'pretending' to communicate with the devil and 'pretending' to have supernatural power, rather than actually doing those things. It also emphasized the problems caused by 'deluding' others into believing in their power. But Jamaican legislators did not consider creating a crime of accusing someone of practising obeah. Whereas the main purpose of the English Act was to suppress belief in witchcraft, the makers of Jamaican anti-obeah legislation were far more concerned with suppressing obeah itself – even while they purported not to believe in its power. Their concern may indicate that at least some of the legislators – and perhaps even more of their constituents – were actually less secure in their conviction that obeah did not really work than they acknowledged. But whether or not they were convinced that Africans were able to muster supernatural power against them, they had just seen the very real consequences of the solidarity that obeah practice could promote, in the form of the rebellion. As Vincent Brown suggests, the new legislation was a response to the fact that 'Jamaican masters could not abide sources of authority they did not wholly control'.[82] In making a law against obeah, the Jamaican legislators gave slave-holders the ability to prosecute – and thus rid themselves of – enslaved people whose use of spiritual power was *not* in itself directly related to rebellion, as well as those whose use of obeah was specifically directed at mobilizing resistance. In practice, as Chapter 3 shows, the new power to prosecute would be used primarily in response to rebellion and to the use of obeah in conflict between slaves; but the law had wider potential. The ability to prosecute enslaved people for obeah allowed for the possibility of combating the power and authority of African spiritual leaders that was not at present being used for rebellious purposes, but might eventually come to be used for rebellion. By bringing obeah under the purview of criminal law, Jamaican legislators attempted to individualize and domesticate what was in the context of Tacky's Rebellion a collective practice. In the challenging circumstances faced by slave-holders in the aftermath

---

[81] Levack, *The Witchcraft Sourcebook*, 171–2.    [82] Brown, *The Reaper's Garden*, 149.

of Tacky's Rebellion, even apparently non-confrontational uses of obeah seemed to present a threat.

We return then, to the question: what had changed since the 1730s? Although it is hard to definitively answer that question, the difference may ultimately come down to the greater legislative response in general of the second half of the eighteenth century, which in turn was a sign of a commitment to manage slavery through everyday state measures, as well as extraordinary violence. In Antigua, despite the recommendations of the report, no law was made in response to it. By the 1760s new slave codes were becoming a standard part of the management of slavery in the Caribbean. And therefore, in response to a major rebellion in which spiritual power, named in this case as obeah, played a prominent role, legislators outlawed obeah. In doing so they created a crime that would spread across the Anglophone Caribbean, and that would outlast both slavery and colonial rule.

## 2 Obeah and the slave-trade debates

In the years between the passage of Jamaica's 1760 'Act to remedy the evils arising from irregular assemblies of slaves' and the end of slavery, obeah increasingly preoccupied observers of and commentators on Caribbean societies, whether located within the Caribbean or in Britain. Laws against obeah proliferated across the colonies, and were frequently enforced. Discussions of obeah became pervasive in analyses of and commentaries on slavery. This chapter and the next investigate the process by which obeah moved from a marginal to a central position in discussions of slavery and slave society. Chapter 2 examines discussions of obeah that were primarily located outside the Caribbean, and were connected in particular to the increasingly contentious debates about the legality and morality of the slave trade that dominated the last years of the eighteenth century and the first decade of the nineteenth. Chapter 3 investigates the spread and implementation of laws against obeah in the Caribbean, using evidence that also gives us some insight into enslaved people's use of spiritual power. Notable is the contradiction between the increasing emphasis on obeah as a sign of African-ness in the Caribbean at a time when the number of African-born people in the region was declining. The widespread urge on the part of Britons and Anglo-Caribbean people to tell stories about obeah, both in the Caribbean and in the metropolis, suggests that such stories did more than simply describe the realities of Caribbean life. In their emphasis on the occult power of enslaved people they expressed and displaced an anxiety on the part of observers of the Caribbean about their own illegitimate power, enforced by violence, transforming such anxiety into an argument about racial hierarchy.[1] And yet these stories were always ambivalent, operating, as Simon Gikandi argues, 'in a fascinating dialectic of attraction and revulsion', and allowing scope for vicarious identification with a version of the slave rebel, alongside fear of rebellion.[2]

---

[1] For a similar argument, focused primarily on representations of Haitian Vodou as 'black magic', see Murphy, 'Black Religion'.
[2] Gikandi, *Slavery and the Culture of Taste*, 259; see also Jaudon, 'Obeah's Sensations'.

Let us begin with one of the most frequently retold obeah stories, which was said to have taken place on a plantation in Jamaica. An English planter, unnamed but described as a 'Gentleman of the strictest veracity' who had been away from his Jamaican estates, returned in 1775 to find them in disarray. Many of his 'Negroes' had died during his absence; many of those still alive were in very poor health. Despite his effort to provide appropriate medicine and nursing care, people continued to sicken and die. Indeed, so bad was the sickness that 'two or three were frequently buried in one day'. For an entire year he struggled against sickness and death on his estate, suspecting, but unable to prove, that it was caused by obeah. Around a hundred slaves had died over a period of fifteen years.[3]

The estate was eventually saved by a seriously ill woman. This woman told the planter that her octogenarian stepmother, a woman 'of the Popo country' (that is, from Dahomey in what is now Benin) 'had put *Obi upon her* as she had also done upon those who had lately died; and that the old Woman had practised *Obi* for as many Years past as she could remember'. The woman's story was confirmed by other enslaved people on the plantation. In response, the planter ordered six white servants to force open the accused woman's house. Inside, they found the roof and walls 'stuck with the Implements of her Trade, consisting of Rags, Feathers, Bones of Cats, and a thousand other Articles'. Under the bed was an earthen jar, which contained:

a prodigious Quantity of round Balls of Earth or Clay of various dimensions, large and small, whitened on the Outside, and variously compounded, some with Hair and Rags or Feathers of all Sorts, and strongly bound with Twine, others blended with the upper section of the Skulls of Cats, or stuck round with Cats Teeth and Claws, or with Human or Dogs Teeth, and some Glass gummy Substance... and many little Bags stuffed with a variety of Articles.[4]

For the planter, these materials confirmed the accusation of obeah. He ordered that the woman's house be pulled down and its contents burnt. Rather than prosecute her, he sold the woman to 'a party of Spaniards' who took her to Cuba. From then on, the plantation thrived: 'his Negroes

---

[3] 'Report of the Lords of the Committee of Council appointed to the Consideration of all Matters relating to Trade and Foreign Plantations: submitting to his Majesty's consideration the evidence and information they have collected in consequence of his Majesty's Order in Council, dated the 11th of February 1788, concerning the present State of the Trade to Africa, and particularly the Trade in Slaves; and concerning the Effects and Consequences of this Trade, as well in Africa and the West Indies, as to the general Commerce of this Kingdom' (henceforth 'Report'), *PP* 1789, vol. 69, 217–18.
[4] Ibid., 218.

seemed all to be animated with new Spirits, and the Malady spread no farther among them'.[5]

This narrative followed many of the conventions of fiction, but was presented as truth. It first appeared in print as part of a seven-page section about obeah in Jamaica included in the Committee on Trade and Plantations (the Board of Trade) of the British Privy Council's 'Report... concerning the Present State of the Trade to Africa, and particularly the Trade in Slaves'. The report was the outcome of the first parliamentary enquiry into the slave trade, which took place over several months in 1788 and 1789. Kenneth Bilby and Jerome Handler describe this section of the report as 'one of the earliest Jamaican sources on obeah, and one of the most detailed of the eighteenth century'.[6] It may well be the most influential description of obeah that has ever been produced.[7] It was quoted (with acknowledgement) in Bryan Edwards's *History, Civil and Commercial, of the British West Indies* (1793).[8] From there, as I show in the last section of this chapter, it was rapidly integrated into fictional and dramatic works.

The dynamic of secrecy and revelation in the telling of the story drew on melodrama and Gothic fiction, and appealed to writers and readers of that genre. It worked by emphasizing the threat posed by enslaved people's esoteric knowledge but also by domesticating that threat, and thus conveyed a taste of danger while reaffirming the power of white knowledge. In addition, the story tapped into conventional British understandings of witchcraft. By describing the obeah practitioner as an old, isolated, marginal woman, and a stepmother, who brings ill-health and misfortune to the community as a whole, the story of the Popo woman solidified the association between the obeah practitioner and the European witch that had been made in the 1760 Jamaican anti-obeah law's designation of the crime it defined as 'obeah or witchcraft'. The witch-like obeah woman and her literary descendants were convincing to British audiences, who were unaware that, as we will see in later chapters, most of those prosecuted for obeah were male, that their practice was most frequently related to healing rather than doing harm, and that they were as likely to be in the prime of life as they were to be elderly and isolated.

The story of the Popo woman has also been significant for twentieth- and twenty-first-century historical scholarship. Probably its most influential citation has been in Orlando Patterson's account of obeah in *The*

---

[5] Ibid.  [6] Bilby and Handler, 'Obeah', 158.
[7] For recent reproductions of this passage see Bewell, *Medicine*, 193–8; Earle, *Obi* (2005), 168–81.
[8] Edwards, *History*, II, 95–7.

*Sociology of Slavery*, which used it to develop a structural-functionalist account of slave society. The accusation against the old woman, Patterson argued, was 'a case of post hoc witchcraft accusation along the well known African pattern, which is known to be particularly evident during periods of epidemics'.[9] Other scholars have used the story to show that colonial whites blamed obeah for inexplicable deaths, or alternatively, that the obeah woman was a revered figure in Caribbean slave society.[10] Londa Schiebinger argues that it shows that Europeans' response to obeah was to attempt to destroy it rather than to harness its power, while Sylvia Frey and Betty Wood argue that it demonstrates that 'sacred specialists' could use knowledge of 'drugs and magic... to manipulate and control relationships with owners or to intimidate fellow bondpeople'.[11] These scholars have asked what the story tells us about slave society, but not what its publication reveals about late eighteenth-century debates about slavery and the slave trade. Meanwhile, literary critics have undertaken important analyses of representations of obeah in British culture at the turn of the eighteenth century. They have frequently focused on texts that draw on the story of the Popo woman, but have rarely examined the original text itself.[12]

This chapter bridges the gap between historical and literary analyses of obeah by reconstructing the route through which obeah came to form a substantial part of British representations of African Caribbean culture. It puts the larger text from which the story of the Popo woman is taken into context by analysing the Jamaican material alongside other accounts of obeah submitted to the same committee. Defenders of the slave trade from Antigua, Barbados, Grenada, and St Kitts also answered questions about obeah, but there were significant differences between their descriptions and analysis of obeah and those of the Jamaican planters. The report contains two pro-slave-trade tactics for discussing obeah, one Jamaican, the other Eastern Caribbean. They shared some assumptions but were not easily compatible. These two tactics presented in their earliest forms the two discourses on obeah that would dominate discussions of the subject until the mid-twentieth century. While the Jamaican contribution

---

[9] Patterson, *Sociology of Slavery*, 193. Patterson quotes from the manuscript source that was printed in the report, held in the UK National Archives, BT 6/10, rather than from the published report.
[10] Bush, 'Defiance or Submission?', 161. See also Bush, *Slave Women*, 76; Mair, *Historical Study*, 265, 409n219. In 1926 Frank Pitman used the story of the Popo woman as one among several cases demonstrating the prevalence of the 'nefarious art' of obeah in early Caribbean societies. See Pitman, 'Slavery', 652–3.
[11] Schiebinger, 'Scientific Exchange', 316–17; Frey and Wood, *Come Shouting to Zion*, 58.
[12] To my knowledge the only work to explore the original Popo woman story from a literary point of view is Jaudon, 'Obeah's Sensations'.

presented obeah as threatening and dangerous, the Eastern Caribbean witnesses presented it a problem of the past that was on the verge of disappearing, and at times suggested that obeah should be understood not as an indication of racial difference but as a sign of the universality of 'superstition'. Neither tactic became an important part of the debate about the slave trade itself. The Eastern Caribbean accounts were for a long time forgotten, but the Jamaican representation of obeah had an extensive afterlife, beyond rather than within discussion of the slave trade. It strongly influenced less explicitly political writing about the Caribbean, especially in fictional and dramatic works, which were significant for the formation of race in this period.

The depiction of obeah in the Jamaican submission to the committee also introduced an important trope that would remain significant in representations of obeah for many years. It emphasized the enormous power of obeah practitioners over slaves, depicting them as knowing charlatans whose ability to trick other enslaved people demonstrates the majority's credulity and foolishness. This was particularly significant in late eighteenth-century Britain, where the power of those who claimed to control mysterious forces and knowledge, in particular in relation to healing and the body, was a significant area of debate, and where ghost stories and other elements of the supernatural were becoming a form of entertainment for metropolitan sophisticates while remaining part of everyday life for much of the population. Ghosts and other forms of magic were prominent on stage and in fiction, and the ability to enjoy the thrill of the ghost story as pleasurable entertainment was becoming a marker of the modernity of a metropolitan audience.[13] In this context, the depiction of people in the Caribbean as not only believers in the power of obeah but also as able to derive political force through this belief was a powerful sign of Caribbean difference to British audiences. As Hugh Hodges points out, obeah 'became an enormous resource for colonial writers looking for evidence of the depravity of Jamaican [and, I would add, Caribbean] culture'.[14]

The Board of Trade's more-than-400-page report was a product of the intense controversy about the slave trade that raged across the British Atlantic world from the 1780s to 1807, and was particularly fierce from 1788 to 1792, when parliamentary votes on several occasions seemed likely to bring an end to the trade. In the voluminous scholarly discussion of the debates about abolition, the content of the parliamentary investigations has attracted relatively little attention.[15] Historians have

[13] Clery, *Supernatural Fiction*.  [14] Hodges, *Soon Come*, 22.
[15] For an exception see Davis, *The Problem of Slavery*, 420–34.

focused primarily on the propaganda directly controlled by anti-slavery campaigners and on abolitionist campaigning, while literary scholars have, not surprisingly, focused on novels, dramatic works, and poetry.[16] Nevertheless, the parliamentary inquiries and the reports that they produced played an important role in shaping wider ideas about slavery and race; as Seymour Drescher notes, parliamentary reports 'provided the basis of most arguments used in both polemical and analytical discussions of the British slave system'.[17] Contemporaries were aware of the significance of parliamentary inquiries: both sides of the debate about the slave trade, and later slavery, worked hard to ensure that their views were effectively represented in the final products.[18]

In 1788, when the inquiry that produced the 'Report... concerning the Present State of the Trade to Africa' was commissioned, such investigations were a new and rapidly expanding form of knowledge production about the colonies. Previous inquiries had taken place in relation to North America and India.[19] Through inquiries, the government emphasized that its decisions were based on evidence rather than interest. Inquiries could also provide a means by which a political lobby could draw attention to its point of view on a contentious issue. Witnesses to parliamentary inquiries phrased their testimony as empirical observation based on experience, rather than partisan argument. Getting arguments that supported one's point of view into a published parliamentary report was thus an important means of carrying forward a political debate. The circulation of descriptions and analyses of obeah in the context of a parliamentary report gave them a more authoritative status than that of similar material published in other locations.

William Pitt's government commissioned the inquiry into the 'African Trade' in February 1788, in response to the anti-slavery campaign that began in the mid-1780s. The Society for the Abolition of the Slave Trade had been established in 1787 and in its first year published anti-slave trade pamphlets in editions of thousands; it also began a substantial

---

[16] The literature is very extensive. Among the most important historical works on the debate about the abolition of the slave trade are Anstey, *The Atlantic Slave Trade*; Blackburn, *Overthrow*; Davis, *The Problem of Slavery*; Jennings, *Abolishing the British Slave Trade*; Oldfield, *Popular Politics and British Anti-Slavery*; Drescher, *Capitalism and Antislavery*. Significant work by literary scholars includes Boulukos, *The Grateful Slave*; Lee, *Slavery and the Romantic Imagination*; Waters, *Racism*; Richardson, 'Romantic Voodoo'; Watson, *Caribbean Culture*; Carey, *British Abolitionism and the Rhetoric of Sensibility*; Ellis, *The Politics of Sensibility*; Swaminathan, *Debating the Slave Trade*.

[17] Drescher, *Econocide*, 10.

[18] Jennings, *Abolishing the British Slave Trade*, 45–6, 52–5; Anstey, *The Atlantic Slave Trade*, 289–96.

[19] Marshall, 'The British State', 180.

petitioning campaign.[20] In response, an Order in Council instructed the Board of Trade to investigate 'the African Trade' and in particular to examine 'the Practice and Manner of purchasing or obtaining Slaves on the Coast of Africa, and the Importation and Sale thereof... and also... the Effects and Consequences of this Trade, both in Africa and in the said Colonies and Settlements, and to the general Commerce of this Kingdom'.[21]

The commissioning of this investigation put pro-slavery forces on the defensive. Prior to 1788 they had produced pamphlets and tracts but had not believed slavery to be seriously under threat.[22] In 1788, however, with the prime minister aligned with anti-slave-trade campaigners and the movement against the slave trade gathering strength, they felt the pressure to seriously organize for the first time. The Society of West India Merchants and Planters established a special subcommittee to coordinate their response, prepared many pamphlets for publication, and gathered and coached witnesses who could supply written and oral testimony to the inquiry. They focused on presenting the slave trade as essential to British prosperity, conditions in the plantation colonies as benign, and Africa as degraded.[23]

The Board of Trade, which undertook the inquiry, was split between abolitionists and defenders of slavery. It included powerful critics of slavery in Prime Minister William Pitt, William Wyndham Grenville, and the evangelical Bishop of London, Beilby Porteus, but also significant opponents of abolition such as Lord Sydney, the minister with responsibility for the colonies, and Henry Dundas, who would in 1792 propose the amendment that inserted the word 'gradual' into Wilberforce's motion for the abolition of the slave trade, thus gutting it of content.[24] The Board's chair, Lord Hawkesbury, was a defender of slavery; its secretary was George Chalmers, a pro-slavery figure who had spent his young adulthood in Maryland, where slavery played a significant economic role, and would go on to become Agent for the Bahamas.[25] Thus, although pro-slavery forces perceived the Board of

---

[20] Jennings, *Abolishing the British Slave Trade*, 44; Ragatz, *The Fall of the Planter Class*, 250–1.
[21] BT 6/12, f. 1, African Trade: Order in Council directing the Committee for Trade forthwith to take into Consideration the present State of the Said Trade, 11 February 1788.
[22] Swaminathan, *Debating the Slave Trade*, 191–203.
[23] Anstey, *The Atlantic Slave Trade*, 287–91.
[24] The attendance at the Board of Trade meetings can be followed in its minutes in BT 6/12.
[25] On Hawkesbury see Anstey, *The Atlantic Slave Trade*, 289. On Chalmers see Porter, *Abolition*, 24–5.

Trade inquiry as an attack, its agents included many of their allies. It gave them a platform from which they could address the critiques of slavery that had been gaining momentum since the 1770s, as well as an opportunity to put their own case. Indeed, according to Thomas Clarkson, abolitionists initially feared that only pro-slavery witnesses would be heard.[26] In the end the inquiry solicited written and verbal evidence from tens of witnesses, mainly slave traders, planters, and colonial agents, but also some anti-slave-trade activists, including Clarkson, John Newton, Alexander Falconbridge, and James Ramsay. Although many former slaves lived in London at the time, the Board of Trade did not invite them to give evidence. Even Olaudah Equiano, who wrote to the committee with ideas about the colonization of Africa, was not invited to testify.[27] As a result, those who were deemed to have the necessary experience to be valid witnesses to slavery and the slave trade were primarily those who benefited from them and stood to gain from their preservation.

The committee organized its report into three sections: on Africa; on the middle passage; and on 'treatment of slaves in the West Indies'. This structure allowed for at least two contested overall interpretations, depending on the reader's stance on the slave trade. A pro-slave-trade reading moved from an emphasis on the degradation and barbarity of Africa, to an account of the care taken by captains and surgeons aboard the slave ships, and finally to an interpretation of life in the West Indies dominated by descriptions of the 'good treatment' of enslaved people. The anti-slave-trade witnesses tried to inject an alternative reading, in which Africa was a continent whose problems were exacerbated by the slave trade but which might move towards civilization through 'legitimate' trade, the middle passage was dominated by terror and abjection, and West Indian slave societies were lawless places dominated by the unconstrained despotic power of slave-owners.

The accounts of obeah appear in the final section, on the West Indies. This, the longest part of the report, was organized by colony. The evidence about each colony was presented as responses to a series of fifty-three numbered questions, in many cases with the words of several witnesses divided up as answers to each question. The questions themselves, including a series of questions about obeah, were published as an appendix to another volume of *Parliamentary Papers*.[28]

---

[26] Clarkson, *History*, I, 476.
[27] Caretta, *Equiano*, 4. For Equiano's letter see 'Report', 98–9. On former slaves resident in London in this period see Gerzina, *Black London*.
[28] 'Appendix Paper A: Heads of Inquiry transmitted to the Agents of the West India Islands', in A Statement of the Laws at Large, Respecting Negroes in the West India Islands, *PP* 1789 lxx, 391–5.

This presentation made the report's discussion of obeah appear natural and inevitable. Nevertheless, closer inspection reveals some peculiarities. Although representatives of many of the colonies responded to the questions about obeah, more did not. The answers from Montserrat, for instance, jump straight from question 21 to question 28, with a note inserted that 'no answers have been returned' to the 'Head[s] of Inquiry respect[ing] the Practice of Obeah'. Likewise, the witnesses from Nevis, Dominica, St Vincent, Bermuda, and the Bahamas did not answer the questions about obeah.[29]

The manuscript records of the Board of Trade reveal why the witnesses from these colonies failed to respond. They demonstrate that it was by no means inevitable or even anticipated that accounts of obeah would appear in the report. The committee began its work by writing to the agents for the West India Islands, the secretary of the Committee of Merchants Trading to Africa, and colonial governors, inviting them in general terms to supply information on the topics listed in the Order in Council (that is, 'the Practice and Manner of purchasing or obtaining Slaves on the Coast of Africa, and the Importation and Sale thereof... the Effects and Consequences of this Trade both in Africa and in the said Colonies and Settlements, and to the general Commerce of this Kingdom').[30] The West India agents' reply stated that they needed time to consult those they represented, and asked for 'heads of enquiry' to tell them what to investigate.[31] The committee agreed a set of initial questions to put to the agents, about law, subsistence, work, disease and health, population increase and decrease, and the availability of Christianity via Baptism, missionaries, and 'religious Institutions'.[32] Obeah was not mentioned at all, and nor was anything else about African religion or culture in the Caribbean. The focus of the questions was on 'treatment': what was done by slave-holders to enslaved people, not enslaved people's activity or beliefs.

How, then, did material about obeah come to feature so prominently in the final report? It was introduced through an apparently throwaway mention in the initial evidence submitted by the Jamaican witnesses. Information about Jamaica was coordinated by Stephen Fuller, the Agent for Jamaica, a Member of Parliament and very active member of the

---

[29] 'Report', 352, 359, 414, 429, 440, 448.
[30] BT 6/12, Minutes of the Board of Trade, 12 February 1788, ff. 2–3.
[31] Ibid., minutes of meeting of 15 February 1788.
[32] Ibid., minutes of meeting of 18 February 1788, ff. 19–24. Compare these questions with Hawkesbury's broader proposals for 'Heads of Examination', dated 12 February 1788, BL Add Ms 38416, ff. 13–19. For another discussion of the questions posed by the Board of Trade see Lee, *Slavery and the Romantic Imagination*, 130–1 and 245 n126. Lee misunderstands the inquiry, suggesting that the questions were posed in Jamaica by the Jamaican Privy Council.

Society of West India Planters and Merchants.[33] Fuller produced his responses in collaboration with Edward Long and James Chisholme; all three attended the Board of Trade meeting on 1 April to present their account.[34] Long, who had lived for twelve years in Jamaica before returning to London in 1769, was already well known for his *History of Jamaica*, published in 1774.[35] James Chisholme was a prominent Scottish planter.

Fuller, Long, and Chisholme introduced the subject of obeah to the inquiry in two sentences in their written statement to the Board of Trade. These sentences formed part of their response to the question: 'Are they [Negro slaves] subject to any peculiar Diseases to which White Inhabitants or Free Negroes are not subject; and if they are so subject, assign the causes?'[36] The question was designed to probe one of the key abolitionist charges against slavery in the West Indies: that it was unhealthy – indeed, deadly. The question thus formed part of a contemporary expanding debate about slavery and demography that was of critical importance for both sides of the slave-trade controversy.[37] Fuller, Long, and Chisholme's answer was, like most of their evidence, extensive and detailed. It portrayed the planters as people who provided for the needs of enslaved people out of self-interest and because it was the right thing to do, while attributing problems in West Indian society to the behaviour of enslaved people. The answer first listed yaws, coco-bays, leprosy (Greek and Arabian), and elephantiasis as diseases that affected slaves more than whites, then argued that poorer health among enslaved people was largely due to differences in '*Manners*', by which, the authors explain, they meant participation in '*Negro Plays* or nocturnal Assemblies,' early sexual activity by women, 'intemperance', and the prevalence of venereal disease. It is at this point that they bring in a brief discussion of obeah:

We may add the effects of Witchcraft or *Obeah*, which whether they arise from a distempered imagination, and credulity, or from poison, secretly administered, are very fatal to many of the Slaves. The Legislature of Jamaica, in order to check, as much as lies in its Power, this destructive practice, inflict Death upon conviction of *Obeah-men* or pretended wizards.[38]

Fuller, Long, and Chisholme gave no detailed explanation of obeah in this initial document; rather, they presented it as a synonym for witchcraft,

---

[33] On Fuller's activity see Anstey, *The Atlantic Slave Trade*, 288.
[34] BT 6/12, Minutes of the Board of Trade, 1 April 1788, ff. 82–3.
[35] On Long see Lewis, *Main Currents*, 109–16. For biographical information see Morgan, *Materials*, 2.
[36] 'Report', 211.  [37] On this debate see Paugh, 'The Politics of Childbearing'.
[38] 'Report', 211–12.

thus defining it as something whose primary use is hostile and which is used by one individual against another. They did not at this point mention the reason that obeah had been made a criminal offence: its use to build solidarity and thus to promote armed rebellion. Instead, they subtly emphasized their own and their readers' cultural distance from enslaved people. By listing only imagination, credulity, or poison as possible causal mechanisms through which obeah might work, by making this one among many examples of the choices or practices of 'Negroes' by which they brought poor health on themselves, and by describing obeah men as 'pretended Wizards', they assumed that readers shared with them the understanding that obeah could not work through spiritual power; that its effectiveness must be explained or explained away. Their brief account of the purpose of the Jamaican law against obeah omitted its origin as a counterinsurgency measure adopted in response to a slave rebellion.

From here, Fuller, Long, and Chisholme moved away from the topic of obeah, going on to explore the prevalence of tetanus in newborns. They argued that there was less discrepancy in infant mortality between enslaved and free children in Jamaica than between the children of the 'labouring poor' and those of 'parents in more opulent circumstances' in Britain. This, they claimed, was because 'the Preservation of the Infant Brood in Jamaica is so very important an Object with the Planters'.[39]

Obeah thus made its initial appearance in official imperial knowledge as part of an explanation for the poor health and high mortality rates of enslaved people, an explanation that emphasized the virtue of slaveholders and the vices of slaves, and thus deflected systematic criticism of slavery. The practice of obeah became one among many misguided and damaging 'manners' of enslaved people. Collectively these dangerous 'manners' referred to the areas of life that allowed enslaved people the greatest autonomy: night-time gatherings, sexuality, and religion. In making these associations, the Jamaicans made some critical moves in establishing obeah's place in British understandings of the Caribbean and of slave society.

These two sentences might have been the beginning and end of the Board of Trade's consideration of obeah. However, they sparked significant interest among members of the committee. At the end of the meeting at which the Jamaicans' material was read, the committee decided to pose an additional set of detailed questions about the topic to all the West Indian agents, including the Jamaicans:

---

[39] Ibid., 212.

Whether Negroes called Obeah-men, or under any other Denomination practicing Witchcraft, exist in the Island of ___?

By what Arts or by what Means do these Obeah-men cause the Death, or otherwise injure those who are supposed to be influenced thereby, and what are the Symptoms and Effects that have been observed to be produced in People who have been supposed to be under the Influence of their Practices?

Are the Instances of Death or Diseases produced by these Arts or Means frequent?

Are these Arts or Means brought by the Obeah-men from Africa, or are they Inventions which have originated in the Island?[40]

These questions were unusual within the framework of the inquiry; no other piece of testimony prompted the committee to pose supplementary questions. The Jamaicans' initial framing of obeah as a problem for planters because it led to the deaths of slaves clearly influenced these questions. The new questions sought to investigate the link between obeah and high mortality rates. They assumed, without asking, that obeah was a form of witchcraft; that its primary purpose was to cause harm; and that obeah men, where they exist, cause death and injury. In adding the final question, about whether the obeah men's 'arts or means' were brought from Africa or originated in the West Indian colonies, they foregrounded a discussion of origins that has animated much analysis of obeah since. The Board of Trade's supplementary questions suggest a fascination with colonial witchcraft beyond other elements of slave society. Through these questions, attention to the 'treatment' of slaves became refocused on the exotic.

Fuller, Long, and Chisholme apparently jumped at the chance to expand on their opening lines about obeah. They responded twelve days later with answers that filled nineteen pages of the manuscript evidence, and supplemented these a couple of days after that, in response to a further supplementary question from the Board of Trade, with another fifteen pages of material compiled from information provided by other 'Jamaican Gentlemen'. Their document did not respond directly to the questions asked. Instead, it was a hybrid essay that combined the anecdotal with the apparently scholarly and was produced by many individuals who themselves relied on knowledge gained from talking to others, including, they attest, some enslaved people in Jamaica. The document is, not surprisingly, contradictory, amplifying some of the assumptions of Fuller, Long, and Chisholme's original brief discussion of obeah but also revealing breaks and slippages within those assumptions, especially

---

[40] The questions are recorded in the minutes of the meeting of 12 April, BT 6/12, ff. 98–100, which make it clear that they were posed on 1 April.

in relation to the question of the means by which obeah works and the purposes of its use.[41]

The Jamaicans' essay begins with speculation on the etymology of the word obeah, based on 'the learned Mr Bryant's commentary upon the word *Oph*'. Arguing that 'the Term *Obeah, Obiah*, or *Obia* [is] the Adjective, and *Obe* or *Obi* the Noun Substantive; and that by the Words *Obiah* Men or Women, are meant those who practice *Obi*' they link these terms to the ancient Egyptian word for serpent, Ob or Aub, to Moses's prohibition of enquiry of the 'Daemon Ob' and to the biblical woman (or witch) at Endor, known in the Hebrew Bible as Oub or Ob.[42] The 'learned Mr Bryant' was Jacob Bryant, whose *A New System, or an Analysis of Ancient Mythology* was a work of speculative mythological history that attempted to find correspondences between ancient mythologies and the biblical account of Noah's flood. Bryant's biographer describes his *New System* as a 'fantastic hodgepodge of spurious etymology... and riotous imagination', but at the time of its publication in 1774 it was a well-received contribution to a prominent intellectual tradition.[43] Fuller, Chisholme, and Long use Bryant's commentary to argue that obeah is essentially a form of serpent worship that the Bible designates as evil. 'Mr Fuller', they note (perhaps distancing Long and Chisholme from Fuller on this), believes that 'Obeah' or 'Oby' 'is a manifest Trace of the *Manichean* Heresy, which prevailed for many Years in Arabia, Egypt and Africa, and might possibly take its rise from the Temptation of Eve in Paradise'.[44] They support this claim with the information, derived from William Snelgrave's *New Account of Guinea*, that snake worship was prevalent in Whydah (Ouidah).[45] As noted in the previous chapter, this etymological discussion was very influential, and has been reproduced almost as frequently as the story of the Popo woman. It is a complex opening to an account that as a whole is committed to the idea of obeah as a sign of difference and otherness. By inserting obeah within a world history of Christianity and ancient civilizations Fuller, Long, and Chisholme suggest that Africans share in a unified world history of humanity, even if their role in this world history is as heretics or worshippers of evil. Meanwhile their speculation on the etymology of 'myal' connected the term to Classical civilization, through the claim that it derives from the Greek words μύω (close or secret) or μυέω (to initiate into religious

---

[41] BT 6/10, ff. 171–90, 513–28. This material appears in 'Report', 215–21.
[42] 'Report', 215–16.
[43] Dennis R. Dean, 'Bryant, Jacob (*bap.* 1717, *d.* 1804)', *Oxford Dictionary of National Biography*, Oxford University Press, 2004 (www.oxforddnb.com/view/article/3795 (accessed 24 January 2011)).
[44] 'Report', 218.   [45] Snelgrave, *New Account*, 10–12.

mysteries).⁴⁶ These terms would, for educated eighteenth-century readers, have connected myal to the Eleusinian mystery cults of ancient Greece, a surprisingly respectable, though non-Christian, lineage.⁴⁷ These relatively positive associations were only fleetingly made in the Jamaicans' submission, but suggest an intriguing thread of ambivalence and a degree of respect towards African Jamaican religion within the overall hostility of the Jamaicans' submission.

The Jamaicans' contribution went on to generalize about what 'negroes' do and believe, recounted elements of Jamaican history, most notably Tacky's Rebellion of 1760 and the law against obeah that followed it, and then told several stories about the use of obeah, including the story of the Popo woman. At its heart remains the question of population. Fuller, Chisholme, and Long stressed that obeah men were widely distributed on Jamaican estates, and vividly described the fear produced in those who found that 'Obi' had been set for them. Such individuals, they stated, would 'fall into a Decline, under incessant Horrour of impending Calamities'. They imagine that any minor pain confirms that they are victims of obeah: 'immediate Despair takes place, which no Medicine can remove, and Death is the certain Consequence'. Thus, the authors 'cannot but attribute a very considerable Portion of the annual Mortality among the Negroes of Jamaica to this fascinating Mischief'.⁴⁸ Obeah was thus a serious current threat to the working of the plantation system and contributed significantly to one of the problems of slavery that was most frequently commented on by abolitionists: its high mortality. In attributing a substantial proportion of deaths to obeah, the Jamaicans were careful to maintain their own standpoint of Enlightenment rationality, stating that this mortality was caused not by actual magical practice but by the 'terrified' and 'disturbed Imagination' of those who believed themselves to be subject to obeah.

Long, Chisholme, and Fuller's analysis of high mortality as the result of obeah emphasized the power of the obeah practitioner. They drew a contrast between the majority of the enslaved population who experienced obeah primarily as its victims, and the skill, knowledge, and power of the obeah practitioners. The former are 'deluded', 'weak', and 'credulous', while obeah men, and in particular a sub-category of that group 'called Myal-Men', are skilled enough to use a 'narcotic potion' to induce a 'trance or profound sleep of a certain Duration', thus

---

[46] 'Report', 218.
[47] Parker, *On Greek Religion*, 250–5. Thanks to David Creese for help in translating and understanding the Greek reference.
[48] 'Report', 216.

convincing spectators that they are able to 'reanimate dead Bodies'. This skill and knowledge was used exploitatively, for instance in providing an 'extremely lucrative' trade for the 'Wretches' who 'manufacturer and sell their *Obies* adapted to different Cases and different Prices'.[49] This depiction of people who have the extraordinary power of bringing the dead back to life essentially described what would become known in the Haitian context as the zombie, although the Jamaicans are clear that what they are discussing is not a real magical power but a knowing manipulation.

The Jamaicans' pairing of the obeah practitioner and the deluded victim of obeah relied on an implied third figure: the planter, whom they implicitly contrast to the obeah practitioner. Obeah in the Jamaicans' description became both a mirror to and an alibi for slavery and the slave trade. The lucrative and unjust trade under discussion becomes the one in 'Obies' rather than in human beings. Rather than slave-owners using their power and knowledge for exploitative purposes, it is obeah men who do so. And rather than the system of slavery leading to the high mortality of the plantations, it is the slaves' belief in obeah that is responsible. As Srinivas Aravamudan argues, such stories 'arose from a denial of the material and pathogenic circumstances within which obeah could operate along with a heightened belief in the slave's psychosomatic susceptibility to suggestion'.[50]

Even while they sought to contrast the legitimacy and benevolent power of the slave-owners, who elsewhere they described as providing food, clothing, and housing for slaves, with the illegitimate and cruel power of the obeah men, Fuller, Chisholme, and Long's description suggests that the difference is less absolute than they would like. The 'Negroes', they wrote, 'revere' and 'consult' as well as 'abhor' the obeah practitioners, gaining from them 'the Cure of Disorders, the obtaining Revenge for Injuries or Insults, the conciliating of Favour, the Discovery and Punishment of the Thief or the Adulterer, and the Prediction of future Events'. That is, enslaved people rely on obeah practitioners for many of the things that one might expect a benevolent authority figure to provide.[51] Indeed, it was the obeah man's disruption of the supposedly natural lines of authority and dependence between planter and slave that the Jamaicans found most disturbing about obeah. The passage suggests that the depiction of obeah is being used to allay a hidden concern that the planters'

---

[49] Ibid. This section and some other elements of the report are reproduced in Williamson, *Contrary Voices*, 319–23, where they are mistakenly attributed to Richard rather than Stephen Fuller. Extensive passages are also quoted in Payne-Jackson and Alleyne, *Jamaican Folk Medicine*, 67–8.
[50] Aravamudan, 'Introduction', 31.   [51] 'Report', 216.

power might not really be as benevolent as the pro-slavery party liked to suggest.

Chisholme, Fuller, and Long also submitted several additional original papers to accompany their report, producing a composite, multi-layered document. The additional material they sent included some more mundane and everyday examples of obeah practice, which passed almost unnoticed in later discussion and reproduction of the material published in the report.[52] The most significant of this additional material was a paper submitted separately by a Mr Rheder which reiterated crucial elements of what Fuller, Long, and Chisholme had already said, including the obeah man's ability to bring the apparently dead back to life. Rheder added some details of the colonial response to Tacky's Rebellion, including the information that 'On the other Obeah-men, various Experiments were made with Electrical Machines and Magic Lanthorns, which produced very little Effect; except on one who, after receiving many severe Shocks, acknowledged his Master's Obeah exceeded his own.'[53] As Vincent Brown observes, this probably constitutes the first recorded use of electric shock as a form of torture.[54]

There are contradictions within the Jamaican evidence, in part produced by the fact that it compiles material from a number of other sources. The emphasis on the white observers' distance from the 'superstitious' beliefs of enslaved people is subtly disrupted by the most memorable and vividly depicted account of obeah in the report, the story of the woman of the Popo country, which Fuller submitted as an additional 'Paper' described as the evidence of 'a Planter in Jamaica, a Gentleman of the strictest Veracity, who is now in London'.[55] The story is designed to illustrate a point that has been made earlier: that obeah was responsible for many deaths in the colonies. However, while the passage written

---

[52] These included an account of a Wainman who responded to the loss of a steer by going to a 'noted Obiah-man'; a narrative about a journey from Spanish Town to Kingston during which a boy refused to proceed beyond a 'Glass Bottle hung by the Neck upon a Stick which was fixed in the Ground'; and two accounts of obeah trials, one arising from the use of obeah by an enslaved man against a planter family, and the other from a case in which a man was said to have put obeah on his wife because he suspected her of being unfaithful: ibid., 218–20. For discussion of the story of the boy's fear of the bottle see Jaudon, 'Obeah's Sensations'.

[53] 'Report', 219. Essentially the same account also appears on a subsequent page, under the heading 'Obiah Trials', where it is described as coming from 'another Jamaica Gentleman': ibid., 221. It seems that Mr Rheder both gave his account to Fuller and supplied it directly to the Board of Trade.

[54] Brown, 'Spiritual Terror and Sacred Authority', 38, 52n86; see also Aravamudan, 'Introduction', 27; Schiebinger, 'Scientific Exchange', 321–2; Delbourgo, *A Most Amazing Scene*, 126–7; Jaudon, 'Obeah's Sensations'.

[55] 'Report', 217.

by Fuller, Chisholme, and Long repeatedly emphasizes that obeah works through fantasy and imagination, the unnamed gentleman's paper shows no trace of this scepticism. The tale is told matter-of-factly: the planter comes to suspect that 'Obiah Practice' is the cause of the deaths among his slaves, the discovery of the 'balls of Earth or Clay' and other materials in the woman's house are proof of her practice of obeah, and the reader is left to infer from the fact that deaths on the plantation end when she is sent to Cuba that her obeah practice was indeed responsible for the high mortality rates. Nothing in the 'Gentleman's paper' suggests that the deaths were caused by suggestion, poison, or anything other than the spiritual power of obeah. Thus the Jamaicans' emphasis on their own scepticism in the first section of their evidence is undone by this additional testimony, especially because it was such a powerful narrative, which attracted repetition and elaboration.

The story of the Popo woman subtly queries the Jamaican legislative strategy of combating obeah through criminalization. In the report it follows information about the passage of the 1760 law against obeah, which itself notes the law's lack of success. Despite 'the many Examples of those who from Time to Time have been hanged or transported', obeah continues to be practised. In the case of the Popo woman, the planter in question 'declined' to prosecute the woman. The report presents this as a decision taken 'from a Principle of Humanity' on the grounds that prosecution would have led to her death, despite the fact that the law allowed for transportation as an alternative punishment, and there is evidence that this – which is effectively what happened to the Popo woman – was regularly used.[56] As much as being a humanitarian decision, the planter's action derived from a desire to maintain himself as the sovereign actor on the plantation in a situation where his authority had been called into question.

The story of the Popo woman had wider implications, affirming that planter domination was normal and appropriate. The planter's behaviour and position in this story fits within the wider narrative that the defenders of slavery were trying to sustain: that planters' relation to their slaves is essentially one of protection and direction, analogous to the English landowner's relation to his tenants.[57] While the planter is unaware of the true

---

[56] Ibid., 217–18. For examples see the cases of Sarah (1772), Solomon (1776), and Neptune (1782), all from 'Copy of the Record Book of the slave trials of St. Andrew Jamaica from 17 March 1746 to 16 Dec. 1782', enclosed in Metcalfe to Russell No. 51, 5 April 1840, CO 137/248. This source is discussed in Paton, 'Punishment, Crime, and the Bodies of Slaves'.

[57] For a similar argument in relation to Long's *History of Jamaica* see Bohls, 'The Gentleman Planter'.

nature of what is happening, in part because of his absence, the estate is disordered and people die. As soon as he knows the identity of the suspect, he is able to act against her in a way that was apparently impossible for the enslaved residents, who have known her identity all along but cannot defend themselves against her. He moves decisively, revealing the materials used in her obeah practice and then ridding the estate of her. In this, he is able to elicit the support of the other enslaved people, who provide 'general Acclamations' as the woman's house is burned. The anecdote ends with satisfying resolution: as the correct order of power is re-established on the estate, so health returns to its residents. Obeah, readers are encouraged to conclude, is a threat, but one that can be controlled as long as proper plantocratic hierarchies are maintained. This, combined with the emphasis on obeah as an explanation for mortality, was the dominant message of the Jamaican evidence. It formed the first of two pro-slave-trade obeah narratives in the report.

Agents for the other West Indian colonies responded to the supplementary questions more slowly and with less enthusiasm, but produced an alternative pro-slave-trade account of the meaning of obeah, in which its absence rather than its presence revealed the legitimacy of slave society. In this account obeah was said to be a thing of the past, and its absence from the present revealed the value of slavery in civilizing Africans. The Agents for Barbados (John Brathwaite), Antigua (William Hutchinson), and Grenada and St. Kitts (Charles Spooner) took over a month to send in much shorter answers than those of Fuller, Chisholme and Long. Accompanying Hutchinson's answers was the statement of the physician James Adair, who also gave evidence on behalf of Antiguan planters, and submitted what he described as his 'answers to the additional queries, chiefly respecting the Obeah men' in June 1788.[58] Adair had lived in Antigua for twenty years and would later include part of his evidence to the inquiry in a pro-slavery pamphlet entitled *Unanswerable Arguments against the Abolition of the Slave Trade*.[59] The Barbadian Council and Antiguan Council and Assembly also submitted brief answers.[60]

---

[58] BT 6/10, 'Answers returned by Mr Hutchinson, Mr Brathwaite, Mr Spooner and Mr (John) Rheder to the following questions respecting the practice of obeah in the West India Islands', ff. 529–52 and 'Answers delivered in by Dr Adair respecting the obeah men in Antigua, 24 June 1788', ff. 679–86; BT 6/12, Minutes of Board of Trade meeting of 16 May 1788, ff. 113–16 and 24 June 1788, ff. 136–7. This material is printed in the report at 301–2 (Barbados), 336–8 (Antigua), and 375–6 (Grenada and St Kitts).

[59] Adair, *Unanswerable Arguments*. For more on Adair see Whyte, *Scotland and the Abolition of Black Slavery*, 156–7.

[60] The other colonies represented in the report – Montserrat, Nevis, Dominica, and St Vincent – did not have agents; their evidence came from their legislatures, governors, or from private individuals in the colonies, who did not respond to the supplementary questions.

The witnesses from the Eastern Caribbean produced accounts that were different in both tone and substance to those from Jamaica. While sharing some core points with the Jamaicans' contributions, they stuck more closely to the questions asked, portrayed obeah as less threatening, and provided much less detail about particular cases. Most accepted that obeah practitioners were exclusively African born. Brathwaite, the Jamaicans, Hutchinson, and Adair shared the view that their 'Arts... are most probably brought from Africa', while Spooner agreed that obeah was originally African and that Creoles did not practise it. The Antiguan Council and Assembly dissented from this unanimity, but not to argue for a different origin. Instead, they stated that they did not know whether obeah originated in African or locally: 'no Persons have ever thought it worth their while to inquire'. Only the Council of Barbados disagreed, stating that the 'Professors [of obeah] are as often Natives as African'.[61]

The Eastern Caribbean witnesses also agreed that an important part of the obeah practitioners' skill was based on knowledge of the medicinal properties of plants. Fuller, Long, and Chisholme had noted that obeah practitioners exhibited 'skill in plants of the medicinal and poisonous Species'.[62] Brathwaite similarly suggested that 'Some of them have knowledge in Simples [herbal or 'bush' medicine], and can apply them with Success in the Cure of Wounds.'[63] Spooner likewise emphasized obeah practitioners' knowledge of bush medicine: 'from their Skill in Simples, and the Virtues of Plants, they sometimes operate extraordinary Cures in Diseases which have baffled the Skill of regular Practitioners, and more especially in foul Sores and Ulcers'. Spooner openly acknowledged his own consultation with obeah practitioners, stating that he had himself 'made use of their Skill' in treating ulcers 'with great Success'.[64]

But there were also significant differences between the Jamaican and Eastern Caribbean accounts of obeah. The Antiguan Council attacked the very line of questioning that referred to obeah men 'practicing Witchcraft' and asked about the 'instances of Death or Diseases' that they caused. While it was true, argued the Council, that 'some few Negroes called Obeah-men exist... in this island' they could not possibly practise witchcraft, because witchcraft did not exist: 'the Idea of a Possibility of that Art has been long ago exploded in Great Britain, and consequently in every part of the Dominions inhabited by Persons educated there, and entertaining the same sentiments'.[65] For similar reasons, there were

---

[61] 'Report', 337, 338, 376, 302.   [62] Ibid., 216.   [63] Ibid., 301.
[64] Ibid., 376. Spooner's evidence is quoted in Goveia, *Slave Society*, 248. Other extracts from the Eastern Caribbean witnesses' testimony on obeah is reproduced in Craton, Walvin, and Wright, *Slavery, Abolition and Emancipation*, 95–7.
[65] 'Report', 337.

not and could not be any instances of obeah causing death, because any symptoms that arose were the result of 'fear and superstition', not obeah. The Antiguans emphasized the modernity of the colonial elite, stressing that their understanding of the need to reject belief in witchcraft was superior even to that of the members of the Board of Trade. Implicitly, they also positioned themselves as more rational and enlightened than their Jamaican colleagues.

Some of the other Eastern Caribbean witnesses acknowledged that obeah could damage health and even lead to death, attributing this to either poison or suggestion. They also shared with the Jamaicans the view that obeah was powerful because of the fear of 'superstitious Negroes'.[66] Governor Parry of Barbados discussed the 'superstitions' that he said were 'almost insurmountable' among enslaved people in Barbados, and stated that 'Even the better sort amongst them almost universally believe in Witchcraft.'[67] None of the Eastern Caribbean witnesses, however, produced vivid accounts of obeah as a current danger. Instead, in the most striking difference between the Jamaican and Eastern Caribbean evidence, they all presented obeah as something that was in decline, and that they expected would continue to decline. Brathwaite and Hutchinson believed that the deaths produced by obeah were, in Brathwaite's words, 'less frequent now than formerly', while Adair said that there were fewer obeah practitioners in Antigua than there used to be, and stated that he had never seen an instance of death caused by obeah.[68] For all these witnesses, obeah was fading away as a result of the declining proportions of Africans among the enslaved population. According to Brathwaite, the Barbadian-born enslaved people were now 'more civilized, and from being better informed ... not so easily deluded'.[69] Hutchinson presented the most substantial account that situated obeah as a historical rather than a current problem: 'In the Infancy of planting,' he wrote, 'when the West India Islands were stocked by imported Negroes only, the Obeah-men ... were almost unrestrained from doing what Mischief they pleased.' Now, although 'A few Negroes called Obeah-men do *yet* exist in the Island of Antigua', they have 'lost their Influence and terrifying Power ... there being few or none, except imported Negroes, who continue to view them as in any degree supernaturally endowed'.[70] Adair went so far as to claim that enslaved people pretended to be afraid of obeah as a form of malingering, in the 'Hope of temporary Exemption from Labour, or as an Excuse of Delinquency'.[71] The Eastern Caribbean witnesses' testimony thus solidified a sense of cultural difference between creole and African-born enslaved people. In this their evidence again contrasted with that of the Jamaicans, who stated

[66] Ibid., 301.  [67] Ibid., 300.  [68] Ibid., 301, 336.  [69] Ibid., 301.
[70] Ibid., 337.  [71] Ibid., 337.

clearly that obeah practitioners were respected and feared by 'the Negroes in general, whether Africans or Creoles,' although they also noted that practitioners were 'Natives of Africa, and none other'.[72]

Like the Jamaicans, the Eastern Caribbean witnesses noted obeah practitioners' manipulation of power. But where the Jamaicans emphasized that the pairing of powerful obeah man and deluded slave marked the difference of both to European society, the Eastern Caribbean witnesses made comparisons that tended to assimilate obeah to European practices. Brathwaite described the arts of the obeah men as 'like those adopted in Europe, by the more cunning and designing'.[73] Spooner likewise emphasized the similarity to supernatural practices in Britain: Obeah 'must be considered in the same Light as Witchcraft, Second-sight, and other pretended supernatural Gifts and Communications among White Men'.[74] In making such comparisons, these witnesses brought the Caribbean and Britain into a single frame of reference. The 'superstition' of enslaved people in the Caribbean was analogous to that of those British people – implicitly the poor – who similarly believed in supernatural practices. Some witnesses went further, comparing the power of the obeah practitioners to animal magnetism, the new, fashionable but controversial medical technique invented by Franz Mesmer. Brathwaite said that obeah was not quite like 'animal magnetism, but as ridiculous, and perhaps as difficult to be described'.[75]

Practitioners of animal magnetism claimed to be able to heal by using the magnetic power that they said resided in all living things, including human beings. Their practice typically involved inducing a deep, trance-like sleep in a usually female patient, passing their hands close to her body, and then waking her up. Animal magnetism was most influential in Continental Europe in the eighteenth century, but attracted widespread interest in Britain in the 1780s. Critics of the practice, including James Adair, attacked it for its quackery and improper manipulation of the practitioner's power, also suggesting that it was sexually improper. In invoking 'animal magnetism', Spooner and Brathwaite were emphasizing the manageability of obeah: a sign of difference, but not of danger. It is notable that the Jamaicans, who could have compared the 'trance or profound sleep' they described obeah practitioners producing to the trance induced by animal magnetizers, did not make this comparison; they preferred to emphasize the difference, rather than the similarity, between obeah and European practices.[76]

---

[72] Ibid., 216.   [73] Ibid., 301.   [74] Ibid., 376.   [75] Ibid., 301
[76] On animal magnetism in Britain see Fara, 'An Attractive Therapy'; Cooter, 'The History of Mesmerism'. Fara mentions that James Adair was a critic of animal magnetism. Mesmerism was also influential in Saint-Domingue; see McClellan, *Colonialism and Science*, 175–9; Regourd, 'Mesmerism in Saint Domingue'.

Whereas the Jamaicans knew the law that made obeah illegal in Jamaica, several of the Eastern Caribbean witnesses were unsure of obeah's legal status. In fact, with the exception of Dominica, which passed an anti-obeah law in 1788, obeah was not illegal elsewhere in the Caribbean at this time.[77] Brathwaite stated that he 'should think that some Law has been enacted to punish them', but could not locate it. The Barbadian Council was similarly relaxed. It stated confidently that there was no law against obeah, and candidly admitted that 'Of their Arts we know nothing'.[78] Like Brathwaite, Hutchinson, of Antigua, was uncertain of the legal status of obeah but did not see it as a problem: he 'believe[d] that there is no Law... which specifies the Crime of practicing these Arts... it was never thought... to be an Offence so frequently committed there as to require their particular Notice'.[79] Fifty years after the 1736 conspiracy discussed in the previous chapter, the significance of the obeah men in those events had been forgotten. Adair disagreed with Hutchinson on the question of law, stating that he 'believes, but cannot positively assert, that Obeah-men are restrained by Law from the Exercise of their Arts'. The Antiguan Council was more confident than Hutchinson or Adair, stating positively that 'No Laws whatever exist for the particular Punishment of these few Imposters', but that they were sometimes punished 'as Cheats and Rogues'.[80] Spooner likewise stated that there were no laws against obeah in any of the Leeward or Ceded Islands.[81]

The 1789 Board of Trade report thus enabled careful readers to discern an emerging contrast between Jamaica and the Eastern Caribbean colonies. The theme of rebellion that was so prominent in the Jamaican account was absent from the others, and the Jamaicans presented obeah as a live problem, while for the rest of the region it was a thing of the past. Moreover, for the Jamaicans obeah was a crucial sign of race, which profoundly revealed the otherness of the enslaved population. For the Eastern Caribbean witnesses, in contrast, obeah could be explained by analogy to British and European 'superstitions' such as rural folk medicine and even semi-respectable heterodox forms of healing such as animal magnetism.

What accounts for the differences between these two narratives? The most obvious explanation would be that that it derives from substantial differences in the actual situation in Jamaica compared to that in the Eastern Caribbean colonies of Antigua, Barbados, Grenada, and St Kitts. African-derived forms of spiritual healing and mobilization of

[77] Handler and Bilby, *Enacting Power*. [78] 'Report', 302, 301. [79] Ibid., 337.
[80] Ibid., 337, 338. [81] Ibid., 376.

spiritual power may genuinely have been more widespread in Jamaica than elsewhere. If we take at face value the witnesses' claim that obeah was practised exclusively by Africans, this makes sense. Barbados was already a substantially creole society by the late eighteenth century.[82] The other long-established British colonies such as Antigua and St Kitts had similar population dynamics, if not so thoroughly creole. The slave trade to Antigua, Barbados, and St Kitts had peaked in the 1760s. In contrast, the slave trade to Jamaica would not peak until the 1790s.[83] The population of Jamaica remained significantly African born. In 1817, ten years after the abolition of the slave trade, 37 per cent of enslaved people were African; the late eighteenth-century figure would have been much higher.[84] Jamaican planters therefore depended more on the continuing import of Africans than did those in the Eastern Caribbean. It seems likely that their awareness of this dependence drove their greater anxiety about the power of Africans, expressed through their concern about obeah.

But the higher concentration of Africans in Jamaica compared to the Eastern Caribbean cannot account for the whole difference between their representatives' accounts of obeah. Later Caribbean history shows clearly that Caribbean-born people could and did sustain the practices of ritual spiritual healing, divination, and protection that came to be known as obeah. It would be surprising if locally born enslaved people in Antigua, Barbados, and St Kitts were not already making use of these practices. As the next chapter will discuss in more detail, the governing classes of the colonies whose representatives in 1788 claimed that obeah was becoming obsolete would, with the exception of St Kitts, all pass laws to prohibit its practice before the end of slavery, suggesting that as time passed they became less, not more, convinced that obeah was dying away. A straightforward correlation between Africans in the population and slave-holder concern about obeah does not in itself explain the different contributions to the report.

More important was the fact that the Jamaican witnesses had recent and concrete experience of the way that Africans' use of spiritual power and protection could directly endanger their power. The memory of Tacky's Rebellion, even thirty years on, gave obeah a greater significance for Jamaican planters than for those from other colonies which had not experienced a recent rebellion in which African spiritual power

---

[82] Beckles, *A History of Barbados*, 64.
[83] For comparative figures of imports of enslaved people to these colonies over time see the Trans-Atlantic Slave Trade Database, www.slavevoyages.org.
[84] Higman, *Slave Populations of the British Caribbean*, 116.

played a significant role. While some of the extended commentary of the Jamaicans must come from the personal enthusiasms and, perhaps, obsessions of the authors, particularly Edward Long, the experience of rebellion made obeah a compelling concern for all Jamaican planters, in a way that it was not for those from other parts of the region. It is this experience of rebellion that most effectively explains the difference between Jamaican and Eastern Caribbean accounts of obeah in 1789.

Despite the significant space it occupied in the Board of Trade report, there was little initial public response in Britain to its discussion of obeah. Participants in the pamphlet war that developed between 1789 and 1792, although they frequently reprinted extracts from the report, rarely reproduced or discussed the sections that dealt with obeah. Nor did the evidence taken by the House of Commons in 1790 include material about obeah. For all its length and detail, and for all the Board of Trade's apparent conviction that it would be valuable in informing the discussion, the report's information about obeah had an oblique relationship to the debate on the slave trade. Although intended by Chisholme, Fuller, and Long as a contribution to the argument in defence of the slave trade, the wider West Indian interest did not, apparently, find it useful.

At first sight, the relevance of the discussion of obeah to the slave-trade debate seems to be similar to that of the discussion of religion in Africa, which was explored at length by the Board of Trade and played a more substantial role in the response to the Board's report. Hawkesbury was clear that one of the things the committee needed to establish was 'the state of the countries from whence the slaves are brought', of which 'their religious principles' formed one element.[85] Knowledge of the 'state' of African societies allowed judgements to be made about the slave trade. Witnesses were asked to classify and describe African religion. They usually labelled it as pagan and emphasized the worship of 'idols' or 'fetiches' and the practice of 'superstitions'.[86] Negative depictions of African societies contributed to the argument that the slave trade was justified because the people enslaved were uncivilized – and in particular were not Christian. Thus enslaving them was not a moral problem. Anti-abolitionist witnesses were particularly keen to describe scenes of human sacrifice in Africa.[87] In doing so, they drew on a discourse dating back to the early eighteenth century; an influential example was William Snelgrave's *New Account of Some Parts of Guinea and the Slave Trade* (1734),

---

[85] 'Copy of the Heads of Examination proposed by L. Hawkesbury to the Committee for Trade & Plantations on the 12th Feby 1788.' BL Add Ms 38416, Liverpool Papers Vol. 127: Papers relating to the slave trade.
[86] 'Report', 9–21.   [87] Ibid., 14–19.

which used accounts of human sacrifice in Dahomean religion to justify the slave trade.[88] Even those who had nothing to say about human sacrifice were asked if they had witnessed it. Abolitionists, meanwhile, argued that the slave trade encouraged the negative characteristics of African societies. Its abolition, they claimed, could lead to the Christianisation and civilization of Africa.

Descriptions of obeah seemed to extend the knowledge of religion produced by the witnesses to African societies. The people who were largely 'pagan' in Africa were 'superstitious' in the Caribbean; their susceptibility to the power of obeah men sprang from their lack of knowledge of Christianity and their failure to share in Enlightenment scepticism of the kind outlined by the Antiguan Council. Yet while the accounts of African religion served clearly to justify the slave trade, descriptions of obeah had a more ambivalent effect. Although initially intended to explain away high mortality rates, the detail presented about obeah suggests an excessive preoccupation with it. Overall, the Eastern Caribbean witnesses' argument that obeah was an unthreatening phenomenon that was already in the past was a more effective means of defending the slave trade than was the Jamaican witnesses' evidence. One of the pro-slave-trade witnesses' principal claims was that African societies were so barbaric that removing people from them, even into plantation slavery, was a positive step. The Jamaicans' revelation that obeah was widespread and dangerous worked against this argument, because it implied that any such benefit was slight. If obeah men in the Caribbean endangered other enslaved people and threatened rebellion, and obeah men were overwhelmingly African born – both points made by the Jamaican witnesses – readers might conclude that the opponents of the slave trade were justified in suggesting that no more Africans should be brought to the colonies. This was particularly likely in light of claims elsewhere in the pro-slavery evidence that significant numbers of those who underwent the middle passage did so as punishment for witchcraft.[89] The argument that superstitious belief in obeah was responsible for a high proportion of excess mortality in the plantation colonies could at best be only a partial justification for these deaths. For when accompanied by emphasis on the paternal authority of planters, high death rates surely implied that planters were failing in their responsibilities by not transmitting Enlightenment anti-superstitious principles to their slaves. Indeed, elsewhere in their defence of slavery, Jamaican planters argued that they took great 'anxiety, trouble,

---

[88] Snelgrave, *New Account*. For a discussion of the significance of this work see Boulukos, *The Grateful Slave*, 57–9.
[89] 'Report', 13, 22, 29, 33, 34, 37, 41, 42, 43, 46, 57.

and expence... in civilizing these slaves', as part of which process they 'remov[ed] their cruel and superstitious notions'.[90] The introduction of lengthy and vivid descriptions of obeah into the slave-trade debates implied, in contrast, that black people's 'superstitious notions' had by no means been removed. It could therefore be seen as a tactical error on the part of the Jamaican pro-slavery advocates. The Jamaicans' fascination with and anxiety about African difference and power overwhelmed their tactical nous. The other respondents' emphasis on obeah as a thing of the past suggests their sense that such arguments would be more valuable for defending the slave trade. There is an irony here, given that of all the planters whose representatives gave evidence about obeah, the Jamaicans needed the slave trade the most.

However, if the emphasis on obeah was a slip on the part of the Jamaican planters, it was not one on which abolitionists could easily capitalize. Very little abolitionist propaganda took up the question of obeah. One rare statement that did was made by the Society for the Abolition of the Slave Trade on 20 July 1790. In a response to a wide range of pro-slavery propaganda points, the society rebutted the Jamaicans' claim that obeah was responsible for the deaths of many slaves. It noted the planters' argument that high mortality in the colonies required the continuation of the slave trade, and that this mortality was due in part to 'the supposed Effect of a certain Species of Magic or Witchcraft called Obeah, which some few of the Negroes are said to practice on others'. In response, the society suggested other causes for the health problems of slaves, which, it said, 'may naturally be expected to arise from Dejection of Heart, from the Insufficiency or bad Quality of Food, from Excess of Labour, and Severity of Punishment'. Regarding the contribution of obeah to the death rate, the society argued that 'the Negroes are not less superstitious in their own Country, yet there they increase by Births'. Moreover, 'they are ignorant, but capable of Instruction, and the Terrors of Superstition will soon vanish before the Beams of Knowledge, if they are placed in the Way of receiving them'.[91] Thus, obeah could not explain the mortality rates of the colonies, and the difference between Europeans and Africans was not immutable.

This response notwithstanding, abolitionists in general paid little attention to obeah. They were keen to point out the failings of West Indian society, but they did not want to produce a portrait of Africans (in Africa

---

[90] *Proceedings of the Hon. House of Assembly of Jamaica, on the Sugar and Slave Trade, in a session which began the 23rd of October, 1792* (St Jago de la Vega: Alexander Aikman, by order of the House, 1792) 19. Copy in BL Add Ms 12432.
[91] *The General Evening Post* (London), 3–5 August 1790, Burney Collection online.

or in the Americas) as too 'other'. In particular, they did not want to risk portraying Africans as dangerous or threatening. Obeah, it seemed, was not 'good to think' about the slave trade with, and it disappeared quickly from the explicit slave trade debates.

Yet the Jamaicans' focus on obeah, while a tactical error in the immediate and narrowly defined context of the debate about the slave trade, was in the longer term a valuable intervention on the side of the plantocracy. If discussion of obeah was unhelpful in convincing the British public of either side's position on the slave trade, it was more significant in forming perceptions of race in wider discussions of Africans and African Americans. From the point of view of the defence of slavery, rather than the slave trade, and of the development of racism, it was an extremely significant contribution. Its focus on the persistence of African 'superstition' in the Caribbean helped to sustain a powerful image of black inferiority.

Representations of obeah proliferated in the 1790s, but not in explicitly polemical work relating to the slave trade. Rather, as Alan Richardson has shown, obeah featured in works of fiction and in descriptive writing that purported to stand above or to one side of that heated debate.[92] Such works had implications for the debate about slavery without directly intervening in it, and made important contributions to their readers' perceptions of race. Passages on obeah appeared in several 'descriptive accounts' published around the time of the 1789 report, including Peter Marsden's *Account of the Island of Jamaica* (1788) and Thomas Atwood's *History of the Island of Dominica* (1791).[93] Benjamin Moseley's *A Treatise on Sugar* included an extremely influential discussion of obeah as part of an explanation of the story of Three-Fingered Jack, which Moseley introduced to a British audience.[94] But even more influential than Moseley was Bryan Edwards's *History, Civil and Commercial, of the British Colonies in the West Indies*, first published in 1793. This work was also responsible for ensuring the wide circulation of the account of obeah in the 1789 report.

Edwards's *History of the British Colonies* was a formative pro-slavery and white creole work which sought to demonstrate the value of the colonies and the legitimacy of slavery, against increasingly influential abolitionism.[95] Indeed, as Lowell Ragatz noted, without the abolitionist controversy 'it would probably never have been written', and the interest in the West Indies aroused by the campaign against the slave trade

---

[92] Richardson, 'Romantic Voodoo'.
[93] Marsden, *An Account of the Island of Jamaica*, 40; Atwood, *History of Dominica*, 268–72.
[94] Moseley, *A Treatise on Sugar*, 173–80.  [95] Edwards, *History*, II.

accounted in part for its success.[96] It was not, however, an explicitly political work: Edwards presented his project as a neutral history rather than an intervention into the slave trade debate. It was, in Tim Watson's terms, a work of creole realism.[97] Obeah was relevant to Edwards's project in a way that it was not to more explicitly political interventions. While the political debate now focused narrowly on the slave trade, the wider need of pro-slavery forces was to establish race as a secure category of difference; that is, to make the case for the inferiority of Africa and Africans. Edwards's book begins with a long if selective account of the geography, topography, history, and natural history of the British Caribbean colonies, but devotes most of its space to discussing contemporary society and economy in the Caribbean, including comments on the practice of the slave trade, the characteristics of each group of Africans, methods of agriculture, and governmental institutions. Although Edwards claimed to discuss the British colonies in the West Indies as a whole, and presented some material on the Eastern Caribbean, he had lived in Jamaica and not elsewhere in the region, and the bulk of the material he included was based on Jamaica.[98]

Edwards's *History* includes detailed accounts of many aspects of cultural life among the enslaved population. His discussion of obeah immediately follows a discussion of funerals, at the end of a section that describes the cultural practices of slaves in relation to issues such as sexuality, music, and respect for elders. Edwards wrote that:

when, at any time, sudden or untimely death overtakes any of their companions, instead of rejoicing at such an event, they never fail to impute it to the malicious contrivances and diabolical arts of some practitioners in *Obeah*, a term of African origin, signifying sorcery or witchcraft, the prevalence of which, among many of their countrymen, all the Negroes most firmly and implicitly believe.[99]

Thus for Edwards, as for Long, Fuller, and Chisholme, the stimulus for discussion of obeah is the death of enslaved people. Edwards, however, subtly moves away from the earlier account in that he does not attribute these deaths directly to belief in obeah, but rather states that enslaved people make such an attribution. At this point Edwards introduces a long quotation from the 1789 report, speculating that 'the public are chiefly indebted for it to the diligent researches, and accurate pen, of Mr. Long'.[100] The material he presents includes all of the obeah-related material transmitted by Fuller, but not the answers given by the non-Jamaican

[96] Ragatz, *The Fall of the Planter Class*, 259.  [97] Watson, *Caribbean Culture*, 17–20.
[98] On Edwards see Lewis, *Main Currents*, 113–15, and Blouet, 'Bryan Edwards'.
[99] Edwards, *History*, II, 88.  [100] Ibid., 88–99, quotation at 88.

respondents to the Board of Trade's inquiries. Thus in Edwards's rendition the Jamaican material came to stand for obeah across the whole of the West Indies.

Edwards did not comment on the material he quoted. His choices were, however, significant, because his *History* was much more widely read than the Board of Trade's report. It went through five editions between 1793 and 1819, and influenced many prominent accounts of obeah, in both fiction and non-fiction, from that period. Not only did writers read Edwards and form their understandings of obeah on the basis of his text, many of them also reproduced his material on obeah in whole or in part, giving the Jamaicans' 1789 testimony a wider readership.[101] They often did this by using footnotes, so that words attributed to Edwards (though usually in fact from the report) explain or support the narrative within which they are embedded. Thomas Winterbottom's *Account of the Native Africans in the Neighbourhood of Sierra Leone* compared the use of 'greegrees and fetiches' to guard against danger in Sierra Leone with the fear of 'obia' in the West Indies, including a long quotation from Edwards's *History* in a footnote to support the comparison.[102]

A similar use of Edwards's work appears in many of the plays, novels, and short stories of the period that turned to obeah to represent Caribbean life. Reference to Edwards's *History* often buttressed these works' claims to realism and to be grounded in knowledge of the reality of life in the colonies. In Maria Edgeworth's short story 'The Grateful Negro' (written in 1802 and published in 1804) Esther, an 'old Koromantyn negress' who has convinced her 'countrymen' that she is 'possessed of supernatural powers', instigates rebellion by 'stimulat[ing] the revengeful temper' of another slave, Hector. Caesar, Hector's friend and the 'Grateful Negro' of the story's title, tries to persuade Hector not to rebel, and when persuasion fails, threatens to reveal the plot to the whites. In order to prevent Caesar's betrayal, Esther poisons Caesar's wife Clara with deadly nightshade and claims that only her own magic power can bring Clara back to life. By attacking Clara, Esther hopes to control Caesar and thus prevent him from betraying the planned rebellion.[103] Esther is described by the narrator as a 'sorceress' and 'hag', never as

---

[101] As Handler and Bilby point out, Edwards's account was to 'serve as the authority for many nineteenth and twentieth-century writers', who, they argue, used it selectively, shifting increasingly towards a view of 'obeah as entirely malignant in nature'. Bilby and Handler, 'Obeah', 177n. For a recent reproduction of Edwards's material on obeah see Sernett (ed.), *African American Religious History*, 19–23.

[102] Winterbottom, *An Account of the Native Africans* (1969), 251, 262–4.

[103] Edgeworth, 'The Grateful Negro'. For analysis of the story see Boulukos, 'Maria Edgeworth's "Grateful Negro"'; Botkin, 'Questioning the "Necessary Order of Things"'; Richardson, 'Romantic Voodoo'.

an obeah woman. She is modelled on a European witch, even using a cauldron. However, Edgeworth links her to obeah when she is first introduced by quoting from Edwards's *History* in a footnote, inserted at a point where Hector, the rebel leader, resolves 'to have recourse to one of these persons* who, amongst the negroes, are considered as sorceresses'. The footnote after 'persons' introduces the account of the 1760 rebellion and the story of the Popo woman with the explanation that 'The enlightened inhabitants of Europe' may find it hard to believe that Caribbean 'negroes... respect and dread' obeah practitioners, but that Edwards's 'unquestionable authority' makes these reports of Caribbean 'superstitious credulity' convincing.[104]

Perhaps the most widely known fictions of obeah at the turn of the nineteenth century were the multiple renditions of the story of Three-Fingered Jack, which appeared on the stage, in novels, and in chap books (see Figure 2.1).[105] The story derives from real events that were introduced to the British public in Benjamin Moseley's 1799 *Treatise on Sugar*, but took on a life of its own.[106] It was connected to obeah both through the name of the central character, which was also used as the title of many of the novels and plays – Obi, or Three-Finger'd Jack – and because Jack uses obeah to consolidate his power, often with the help of an obeah woman. Although he is depicted differently in different renditions of the story, Jack is almost always a classic outlaw, reminiscent of older English outlaw heroes such as Robin Hood and, in particular, Dick Turpin. As such, he was an ambivalent figure: both a disturber of the plantation hierarchy and a hero. His story always ends with his defeat and death and the re-establishment of the traditional hierarchy of slave society.[107]

The two most important prose fiction accounts of the story of Three-Fingered Jack, William Burdett's sixty-page novella *Life and Exploits of*

---

[104] Edgeworth, 'The Grateful Negro', 56–7. Obeah also appears briefly, and without explicit reference to Edwards, in Edgeworth's 1801 novel *Belinda*, where it is used to demonstrate racial difference and the credulity of black people, through the character of a black servant, Juba. Edgeworth, *Belinda*, esp. 172–4. For analysis of obeah's role in *Belinda* see Watson, *Caribbean Culture*, 37–49; Harvey, 'West Indian Obeah'; McCann, *Cultural Politics in the 1790s*, 192–9.

[105] The most important of these were Burdett, *Life and exploits of Mansong*; Earle, *Obi*; Fawcett, 'Obi, or, Three-Finger'd Jack!'; Murray, 'Obi; or, Three-Finger'd Jack'. For a bibliography of additional versions see Paton, 'Histories of Three-Fingered Jack'. For a more extended analysis of the significance of Three-Fingered Jack see Paton, 'The Afterlives of Three-Fingered Jack'.

[106] Moseley, *A Treatise on Sugar*, 173–80.

[107] For critical analysis of the various versions of the Three-Fingered Jack story see Aravamudan, 'Introduction'; Bohls, *Romantic Literature*; Waters, *Racism*, 26, 66–9; O'Rourke, 'The Revision of Obi'; Botkin, 'Revising the Colonial Caribbean'; Charles Rzepka, 'Obi Now'; Cox, 'Theatrical Forms'; Wisecup, 'Knowing Obeah'; Sandiford, *Theorizing a Colonial Caribbean-Atlantic Imaginary*, 132–9.

Obeah and the slave-trade debates 73

Figure 2.1 Three-Fingered Jack, as depicted in an 1835 chapbook, part of 'The Young Gentleman's Library'.
*Source*: *Three-Fingered Jack* (London: Orlando Hodgson, 1835). Courtesy of the National Library of Scotland

*Mansong, commonly called Three-finger'd Jack, the Terror of Jamaica*, and William Earle's *Obi, or Three Fingered Jack* both drew on Edwards's quotation of the Board of Trade report. Although the source for these novels in terms of plot was Moseley's *A Treatise on Sugar* and the stage pantomime *Obi, or Three Finger'd Jack*, they both include a near-identical verbatim quote taken from Bryan Edwards's discussion of obeah which they insert in footnotes immediately after the introduction of the first obeah practitioners in their novels.[108] The anonymously published plantation novel *The Koromantyn Slaves* also included an incident closely modelled on the story of the Popo woman, which it acknowledged in a footnote was 'extracted from Edwards's History of the West Indies'.[109]

British representations of obeah and of the Caribbean incorporated Edwards's presentation of obeah as a sign of racial difference. Burdett's obeah man, Amalkir, is a clearly negative character, who 'dwelt in a loathsome cave, far removed from the inquiring eye of the suspicious whites, in the Blue Mountains'. Amalkir was elderly and diseased: 'old and shrivelled; a disorder had contracted all his nerves, and he could hardly crawl'.[110] Bashra, one of two obeah men in William Earle's *Obi*, is 'wrinkled and deformed', with snail trials on his 'shrivelled feet', living in a 'sequestered' hut or cell that is filled with 'foul uncleanliness'.[111] This characteristic isolated and grotesque obeah man formed a powerful and highly persistent stereotype. Yet it was not quite as simple as that. The stories and arguments reproduced by Edwards contained many possibilities for slippage out of their original framework. Some writers depicted complex obeah men whose use of magical power against their enemies was fully justified. The most significant to do so was William Earle who, despite relying heavily on material from the 1789 report (via Bryan Edwards) and Edward Long's *History of Jamaica*, as well as on Benjamin Moseley's account of Three-Fingered Jack, and despite making use of the figure of the grotesque and isolated obeah man, presents obeah as a legitimate response to oppression. Jack, the hero, is 'noble' and 'a man'; he uses obeah in an attempt to gain revenge on Captain Harrop, the evil slave-trader who has kidnapped his mother. Bashra, despite his deformities, works obeah in the context of supporting Jack's struggle. There is also another obeah man, Feruare, who turns out to be the long-lost father of Jack's mother Amri. Like Jack's, Feruare's use of obeah is depicted as prompted by legitimate desire for revenge, since he was tricked into

---

[108] Earle, *Obi* (1800), 72–82; Burdett, *Life and exploits of Mansong*.
[109] *The Koromantyn Slaves*, 180–1. [110] Burdett, *Life and exploits of Mansong*.
[111] Earle, *Obi* (2005), 104.

slavery while trying to rescue his daughter from enslavement.[112] Even so, Earle's representation was unusual. There was little complexity in the more popular theatrical versions of Three-Fingered Jack in which the obeah woman is described as a 'hag' or 'an old decrepid Negress, dressed very grotesequely'.[113]

Edwards's *History* thus amplified the influence of the Jamaican material in the report, giving it a new and wider audience. Indeed, had Edwards not reproduced it, it seems likely that the obeah elements of the report would have been lost until revisited by late twentieth-century scholars, as was the case with the material about obeah in Barbados, Antigua, Grenada, and St Kitts. Edwards's choices contributed to making the Jamaican testimony, with its contradictions, vivid stories, etymological speculations, and emphasis on mortality and rebellion, the foundational text for reflections on obeah in British writing over the next two centuries. The Board of Trade report contained two contradictory accounts of obeah, one of which presented it as a powerful sign of Caribbean difference, while the other presented it as something that hardly mattered. It was the former story of obeah as a powerful force in Caribbean society and a powerful marker of racial otherness that emerged as dominant by 1800 in British accounts. In the Caribbean, too, this narrative became increasingly dominant, even in places such as Barbados and Antigua where Agents and legislative bodies had declared obeah not to be a problem in 1788. By the end of slavery, most of these colonies had followed Jamaica in criminalizing obeah. The next chapter investigates this dramatic shift.

---

[112] Ibid.
[113] 'Hag' is from the cast list to the melodrama version; 'decrepid Negress' from the pantomime's stage directions. *Obi or, Three Fingered Jack*, 1; Fawcett, 'Obi, or, Three-Finger'd Jack!', I.iii.

# 3  Creole slave society, obeah, and the law

Between the publication of the Board of Trade's report into the slave trade in 1789 and the abolition of slavery in 1834 the meaning of obeah shifted. What had been a preoccupation of Jamaican planters became a crime across the Caribbean. What had primarily worried planters for its connection to rebellion became a matter that was equally of domestic concern, something that alarmed whites both because it indexed damaging conflict among enslaved people and because it might lead to insurrection. Meanwhile, what was meant by 'obeah' became both more diverse and more unified across the region; practices that had been conceived under a range of different terms became increasingly linked by the increasingly wide-ranging catch-all heading of 'obeah'. As the British Empire expanded, terms used for spiritual healing and the use of spiritual power in colonies of other European powers became absorbed into the idea of obeah.

This was the period of the 'amelioration' of slavery, when the plantocracies tried, unsuccessfully, to adjust and stabilize the system of slavery, hoping to fend off both insurrectionary change from below and the threat of metropolitan abolitionism from without. After the abolition of the slave trade from the beginning of 1808, the populations of even the most African of the colonies began to shift decisively towards the creole. This was also the period during which missionaries made extensive efforts to make converts among the enslaved population. In this period the practices that were becoming more clearly known as 'obeah' also became more clearly creole and at the same time more clearly a permanent part of Caribbean culture, even while many in authority continued to profess the belief that they were things of the past, liable to disappear over time.

This later period of slave society is also the one for which historians have most thoroughly investigated obeah, beginning with the classic studies by Orlando Patterson and Kamau Brathwaite in the 1960s and 1970s. Patterson and Brathwaite's work posed alternative interpretations that have continued to influence scholarship. For Patterson, obeah's functions included the detection of crime and the healing of sickness, but it was most importantly a form of witchcraft accusation through which frustrations among enslaved people were expressed and projected onto the weaker members of society.[1] For Brathwaite, on the other hand, obeah was part of the creole culture created by enslaved people, functioning primarily as a means of resistance to slavery, both in providing a site for rebellion and through creating an alternative space for structures of authority.[2]

Although Patterson discussed obeah at greater length than did Brathwaite, and his work on the subject was initially very influential, Brathwaite's interpretation has had greater impact in the long term. It has recently been extended by Vincent Brown, who argues that obeah and myal in Jamaica were 'spiritual arts [that] held a supernatural political authority among the enslaved'. They were, he claims, 'used both to mediate conflict and to instigate it; they were both a threat to communal equilibrium and a powerful social discipline. Sometimes, too, they provided an axis for insurrectionary action.'[3] This analysis importantly emphasizes the multiple roles of the manipulation of spiritual power in establishing and sustaining relationships among enslaved people, and between the enslaved and the free. As Brown also notes, the illegality of obeah outlawed 'alternative authority and social power'.[4]

This chapter extends Brown's analysis by investigating in more depth the workings of that ban on alternative authority and social power in a broader space than Jamaica and with greater attention to change over time. It argues that the last fifty years or so of slavery were particularly important for the consolidation of the idea of obeah across the British-colonized Caribbean. Rather than see this period as one in which obeah began to disappear, as, for instance, does Michael Mullin, I show that this was the time when it became a firmly entrenched part of Caribbean law.[5] In doing so, it swept up a range of other ideas about the supernatural and about spiritual power that had been significant in eighteenth-century Caribbean society, creating out of them a fully creole phenomenon which paradoxically emphasized its Africanness.

This chapter investigates the remaking of obeah in this context of a changing slave society. It begins by examining the consolidation of the idea of obeah – both the term itself and that particular spelling of it. It shows how events in the colonies of Trinidad and Berbice that were

---

[1] Patterson, *Sociology of Slavery*, 190–5.
[2] Brathwaite, *The Development of Creole Society*, 162–3, 298.
[3] Brown, *The Reaper's Garden*, 145.   [4] Ibid., 150.   [5] Mullin, *Africa in America*, 184.

initially conceived of as something other than obeah were later remembered as moments of obeah. The stability of obeah as a phenomenon thus became projected into the past. It then investigates the spread of the obeah laws across the Caribbean, and the implementation of those laws in the last years of slavery. The crime of obeah was in this period one that carried extremely severe penalties, and prosecutions for it took place only in specific circumstances. Any investigation of the social and cultural function of obeah within slave communities, a theme that has preoccupied historians, has to be undertaken while recognizing that the evidence we have about obeah largely results from its illegality. It is therefore crucial to understand how laws against obeah worked and how they were used.

The consolidation of obeah and its laws took place in a Caribbean that was a major theatre of war, first in the Seven Years War of 1756–63 and then in the Revolutionary and Napoleonic Wars between 1789 and 1815. As a result of these conflicts, British territory in the region expanded dramatically. Dominica, Grenada, and Tobago were added through the Treaty of Paris of 1763, and St Vincent in 1783. Trinidad was occupied in 1797; St Lucia in 1803. Demerara, Essequibo, and Berbice were taken from the Dutch in the 1790s, becoming the new colony of British Guiana in 1831. In each of these locations the transfer of power from one colonial ruler to another meant reformulation of law and government. The Crown Colony system of direct rather than elected rule was developed to integrate these new colonies in which the free population was not British, and was often heavily dominated by people of colour. Metropolitan British governments did not trust these free but conquered populations with the electoral powers that existed in the older British colonies.[6]

The acquisition of new colonies also meant that new elites with their own traditions of how to respond to enslaved peoples' use of spiritual power were brought into the British Empire. This included both the prior legal frameworks of Spanish, French, and Dutch colonies and the cultural orientations of their ruling groups – including whether or not they considered such matters a problem. The process resulted in a kind of intra-European creolization, as different forms of European rule interacted with one another. As a consequence, in many places British colonial authorities responded to African spiritual work in complex ways that did not draw solely on British experience and discourse but took place in relation to the longer history of the particular colony concerned. The most important example of this process took place in Trinidad.

[6] Duffy, 'World-Wide War'; Cox, 'The British Caribbean'.

Trinidad was before 1797 in formal terms a Spanish colony, with a Spanish governmental and judicial system. After the opening up of Spanish Trinidad to increased settlement through the 'cédula of population' of 1783, part of the Bourbon reforms, a large influx of French Caribbean colonists, particularly from Martinique, migrated to the colony. Many brought with them enslaved people who had previously lived in Martinique and elsewhere in the Caribbean. The population rose from around 3,000 in 1782 to around 19,000 in 1789, and then increased again in the 1790s with a new influx of royalist refugees from Saint Domingue.[7] As a result, after British forces under Sir Ralph Abercromby took Trinidad from Spain in 1797, the planter class in the island was largely French speaking. Abercromby quickly left Trinidad, appointing as military governor of the island one of his officers, Colonel Thomas Picton. Picton retained this position until 1801. The new governor rapidly became embroiled in what James Epstein has described as a 'Scandal of Colonial Rule'.[8] By 1804 Picton had been recalled to London to be prosecuted for the torture of a young woman (or possibly child) of colour, Luisa (also known as Louisa) Calderón, who was accused of theft. Calderón had been subjected to a form of torture known as 'picqueting', in which she was tied up by the wrists with her foot resting on a sharp stake or 'picquet'. Legally, the case turned on whether or not torture was permitted under Spanish law, which still applied in the colony despite the British occupation. It produced a significant debate about the nature of colonial rule, and also led to the elaboration of a new set of justifications for 'modern' colonialism, in contrast to Picton's model of government.[9]

Although Picton became infamous for the torture of Luisa Calderón, this was far from his only use of torture. In fact, at the heart of the conflicts in Trinidad during Picton's governorship was the issue of African-derived spiritual power. Torture of Africans accused of sorcery drew much less attention than did the treatment of Calderón, but is at least as important for understanding Picton's rule. The relevant events began in 1801 with a large number of sudden and unexplained deaths on Coblenz estate, owned by the Baron de Montalembert, a royalist in exile from republican and anti-slavery Saint-Domingue. In response, and on the advice of both Montalembert and Hilaire de Begorrat, a planter from Martinique, Picton established a commission to investigate the deaths. Large numbers of people were arrested and held in the Port of Spain

[7] Epstein, *Scandal of Colonial Rule*, 97.   [8] Ibid.
[9] As well as Epstein's *Scandal of Colonial Rule*, the following works include important accounts of the Picton controversy: Millette, *The Genesis of Crown Colony Government*; Havard, *Wellington's Welsh General*; Candlin, *The Last Caribbean Frontier*; Naipaul, *The Loss of El Dorado*.

gaol, charged with crimes described in different sources as 'witchcraft, sorcery, divination, and poisoning', 'poisoning by means of sorcery or witchcraft', 'sorcery and poisoning', 'the false art of divination', 'sorcery and poison by means of charms', or 'sorcery, divination, and poisoning by charms'.[10] La Fortune, to take one example, was prosecuted for 'having by his knowledge in the black art discovered the use of herbs, of having by poison caused sickness among many slaves, and been the author of the loss of many slaves on different estates, of having distributed and sold pretended Charms & of having dangerous connections'.[11] For nine months the commission interrogated substantial numbers of slaves, sentencing sixteen to drawn-out public executions involving mutilation of the body of the executed. At least six more remained in the local gaol for an extended period. Many of those eventually executed were kept in prison for months before their deaths, and interrogated repeatedly. A second commission that began in late 1802 arrested and tortured more enslaved people. We know the names of some of the commission's victims, and the manner of their deaths. We also know that while a few of them were women, most were men, suggesting that this colonial response to 'witchcraft' did not simply import a European stereotype of the witch as archetypally female. We know very little else about the suspects, except that some of them protested their innocence, and one of them invoked God just prior to her execution.[12]

The white population was divided on the causes of the unexplained deaths on Coblenz and elsewhere. William Fullarton, who arrived in Trinidad in 1803 to govern alongside Picton and quickly became his harshest critic, wrote that many attributed the deaths to 'change of climate, bad food, unhealthy situations and other cause of sickness and despondency'. The French planters, however, attributed 'all of these calamities... to sorcerers and poisoners by means of charms'.[13] They worked within a Franco-Caribbean paradigm, in which 'obeah' was not a powerful term, but poisoning – sometimes explicitly thought of as

[10] Individual accounts of the cases can be found in CO 295/13 and CO 295/5, which also includes a 'List of Persons put to death and of those who have suffered different kinds of punishment'. See also CO 295/15, Fullarton to Windham 22 July 1806; Fullarton, *Substance of the Evidence*; Gloster, *Letter to the Earl of Buckinghamshire*; de Verteuil, *A History of Diego Martin*; Wise, *Historical Sketches*, II.
[11] 'Extracts from the Sentences pronounced on Negroes &c by the Judicial Commission of which Mr Sargent was President and by the Judicial Commission of which Mr Begorrat was President', CO 295/5, f. 76v.
[12] Manuel, Pierre François, and La Fortune are all recorded as having protested their innocence. Thisbe said to the spectators at her execution, in French, that 'she hoped she was going to be happy with God'. Fullarton, *Substance of the Evidence*, 65; McCallum, *Travels in Trinidad*, 192–4.
[13] Fullarton to Windham, 22 July 1806, CO 295/15.

magical, at other times as purely material – was the source of enormous anxiety.[14] The Baron de Montalembert, for instance, described how enslaved people on his estate were 'suddenly attacked by a cruel distemper' which led to 'Negroes of my Plantation [being] imprisoned for Poison', eschewing any attention to magic.[15] The interpretation of poisoning was also accepted by Picton and his British allies, who believed that Trinidad required strong, authoritarian rule. One British traveller, for instance, described matter-of-factly the hanging, decapitation, and mutilation of a 'Gang of Negroes discovered who poisoned a great number of persons, their fellow slaves'.[16] Yet it is clear that for many in Trinidad, both enslaved and free, this 'poisoning' was not purely material and pharmacological. Another British resident of Port of Spain wrote that the city's inhabitants were 'accustomed' to 'frequent accounts of the supposed effects of sorcery'.[17] A Martinican planter, Louis Pelete, described a 'poisoning affair' that took place on his plantation in 1803 (after Picton's poisoning commissions), noting that when eight enslaved people suddenly died of the 'bloody flux' the 'loss seemed to me to be produced by supernatural causes'. Pelete described a little leather bag containing 'nails, hair and other trash' which 'these poisoners call their Guard' and which they thought made them invulnerable.[18]

The term 'obeah' was not used to describe the events investigated by the commission or the later incidents of poisoning. This was not because the language of obeah was unavaible. In 1800 Picton had issued a slave code which provided for the punishment of 'any Negro who shall assume the reputation of being a spell-doctor or obeah-man'.[19] Fullarton, in his attacks on Picton, thought it relevant to refer to the evidence provided to the Board of Trade in 1789, in which Agent Spooner had noted that there were no laws against obeah in any of the Leeward or Ceded Islands.[20] Yet no one seems to have proposed the use of the 1800 slave code's provision against obeah when confronted with the

---

[14] The most in-depth discussion of the poisoning allegations is in Candlin, *The Last Caribbean Frontier*, 96–117, although I do not think the evidence bears out his claim that 'on Trinidad... it [the occult-infused poisoning outbreak] was called Obeah' (103).
[15] CO 295/5, Baron de Montalembert to General Picton and Commodore Hood, 11 April 1803.
[16] Letter from unidentified correspondent to George Cumberland, 23 May 1802, British Library Add Ms 36499, f. 104.
[17] CO 295/14, f. 62, Thomas Higham to Earl Camden, 5 October 1804, enclosed in Hislop to Windham, No. 22, 29 April 1806.
[18] CO 295/14, f. 40, Statement of Louis Pelete, 18 November 1805, enclosed in Hislop to Windham, No. 18, 1 April 1806. My translation.
[19] Ordinance of the Governor, Lt.-Colonel Thomas Picton, reprinted in Carmichael, *History of Trinidad and Tobago*, 379–83.
[20] CO 295/15, Fullarton to Windham, 22 July 1806.

alleged crimes of Thisbe, Manuel, Pierre François, and the other enslaved people brought before the poisoning commissions. At this point obeah in Trinidad apparently connoted something different – though what, exactly, it did refer to is unclear.

As the events of Picton's governorship receded into the past, however, retrospective descriptions of what happened on Coblenz and other plantations began to present them as instances of obeah. An 1812 pamphlet reveals the beginning of this process. Its author, John Sanderson, had been one of the leaders of the opposition to Picton's rule. He argued that the combination of Spanish and English law that governed Trinidad led to errors of judgement and the misapplication of law. To drive home his point, he discussed the commissions of 1801 and 1802, describing their practice as 'torture to extort confessions of sorcery, witchcraft, and obeism'.[21] Sanderson retains some of the key terms of earlier accounts, which referred to the commissions dealing with 'witchcraft, sorcery, divination, and poisoning' or 'sorcerers and poisoners by means of charms'. However, he omits 'poison', instead referring to 'obeism'; the shift to construing these events as examples of obeah had begun. By 1838 the Anglo-Trinidadian novelist and writer E. L. Joseph made obeah more central. In his *History of Trinidad* Joseph presented Picton's 'sanguinary tribunal' as an unfortunate lapse on the part of a popular and effective governor who 'preserved the island' from its population of African 'savages' and disreputable mixed-race Spanish 'peons'.[22] Joseph described the tribunal as being for the 'suppression of sorcery, or, as it is called, obi ... or obiah'.[23] Joseph was a liberal who disapproved of such prosecutions because they strengthened belief in obeah and the power of the obi man, encouraging what he termed 'obi seekers' – those who attributed all kinds of health problems or misfortunes to 'obi'. His concern about such 'obi seekers' suggests that by the time he was writing 'obi' had become widespread as a way of understanding and explaining harm and danger – a category that applied to the use of power by others. 'Obi', Joseph concluded, 'was the scape goat of the West Indies.' His account mentioned poison, but only as a subsidiary crime; for Joseph and his readers, the lessons to draw from the Picton story were about obeah.[24]

---

[21] Sanderson, *An Appeal to the Imperial Parliament*, 27. On Sanderson see Epstein, 'The Radical Underworld Goes Colonial', 154–7; Epstein, *Scandal of Colonial Rule*, 124–7.

[22] Joseph, *History of Trinidad*, 206. Joseph was born in London and lived in Trinidad from 1817 until his death in 1838. For this and further biographical information, see Brereton et al., 'Introduction', xix–xxi.

[23] Joseph, *History of Trinidad*, 212.

[24] There are similarities here to the process described by James Sweet for Brazil, where magical practices that drew on Portuguese predecessors came to be seen as African. See Sweet, *Recreating Africa*, 187–9.

When Picton's commissions were remembered after slavery, they were even more systematically assimilated to a narrative about obeah. In 1854 Mary Fanny Wilkins, an American-born resident of Trinidad, published a novel, *The Slave Son*. It featured a character, St Hilaire Cardon, based on St Hilaire Begorrat, the Martinican–Trinidadian planter who led the poisoning commissions under Picton.[25] While the novel is explicitly set in the 1820s, part of the plot describes events very similar to those of Picton's poisoning commissions. Like Joseph's historical account, this fictional retelling repeatedly locates the plantation deaths within the context of obeah. During a discussion with Dorset, an English character who represents the ameliorationist view of slavery, Cardon describes how the 'murdering work, or Obiah, as they call it, has been going on for the last two years', and states that 'if I could only find out the sorcerer, or Obiah man, as they call him, I would hang him up on the very first tree'.[26] While he also argues that the mysterious plantation deaths are caused by poison and refers to what is taking place as 'the poisoning work', the use of poison has become part of the armoury of the obeah practitioner, rather than the prime cause of anxiety. The novel even extends the term 'obiah' to a description of Martinique, which Cardon had visited in 1822 during a poisoning scare.[27] Cardon's account in the novel again states that the deaths were due to poison, but locates this within the context of obeah: 'The Obiah had spread its ravages to such a fearful extent, that a Court was instituted', he tells Dorset.[28] For Wilkins, obeah had come to be a dominant category, subsuming poisoning, sorcery, and other terms that had been used in Trinidad in the early years of British colonization. Wilkins's book speaks to the process whereby 'obeah' increased its linguistic range, as Anglo-Creole ways of thinking displaced the earlier Franco-Creole alternatives.

Twenty years after Picton's poisoning commissions, evidence about a similar case in Berbice allows us to capture a moment when 'obeah' was coming into play as the dominant term for African spiritual power, but had not yet gained hegemony. It also, more than the sources from Trinidad, provides evidence about the terms and interpretations used by enslaved people in discussing and describing the nature and use of spiritual power. As on Coblenz in Trinidad, the events in Berbice took place in the context of unexplained sickness and death among enslaved people. Whereas in Trinidad the sources reveal the planters' response

---

[25] Wilkins, *The Slave Son*.   [26] Ibid., 182.
[27] The Martinican poisoning scare described in the novel refers to real events of 1822. Despite the novel's usage of 'obiah', in Martinique this was understood as an outbreak of poisoning, not obeah. Savage, 'Between Colonial Fact and French Law'.
[28] Wilkins, *The Slave Son*, 299.

to unexplained death, in Berbice the sources, deriving from the trial of a Berbice-born enslaved man named Willem, focus initially on enslaved peoples' actions.

While the people from whom testimony was taken disagreed on many aspects of the case, it seems that, in response to sickness and death on plantation Op Hoop van Beter, particularly among children, the estate's drivers, Primo and Mey, summoned Willem from a neighbouring plantation to investigate.[29] Willem is variously described in the sources as 'Attetta Sara', 'Monkesi Sara', 'Abdie Toboko', a 'Confou man' (a term used both on its own and as a translation for 'Obiah Man') and as the Minje Mama.[30] On arrival he organized the performance of a divinatory ritual known as the Mousckie dance, Mackize dance, Mousiki dance, Water Mama dance, and, most frequently, as the Minje Mama dance. This ritual dance was regularly undertaken on the estate, and was connected to water spirits.[31] The dance was designed to locate the 'bad person' responsible for recent deaths. In the course of the dance a woman, Madalon, was identified as the 'bad person', and Willem instructed others to flog her. In a presumably coincidental echo of the 'piqueting' torture inflicted on Luisa Calderón in Trinidad, she was then tied by her hands to a mango tree so that her 'toes could just touch the ground', and beaten further.[32] Although her body was never found, several people testified that Madalon died on the mango tree, and that she was then cut down, her body weighted, and sunk in the Berbice river.

This episode had been widely discussed by historians, where it has been used to emphasize the significance of African religious concepts and practice in creolizing Berbice, the importance of African-derived water spirits, the role of African religious leaders as healers, and, most recently, the violence that obeah rituals could entail.[33] Interpretations among historians about its meaning have differed significantly, but most refer to the incident as one involving obeah. This is not surprising, since the Parliamentary Paper that published the details of Willem's trial is entitled 'Trial of a Slave in Berbice, for the Crime of Obeah and Murder'. Yet if we look carefully at the trial record itself, it is clear that Willem was not tried for obeah. The subsidiary title of the document is 'Proceedings of the Court of Criminal Justice of the Colony Berbice, on the trial of the Negro Willem ... for murder of the Negress Madalon', with no mention of obeah or indeed of any crime other than murder. The initial complaint

[29] 'Trial of a Slave in Berbice', *PP* 1823 (348) xviii.
[30] Ibid., 22, 23, 25, 27, 29, 32.    [31] Ibid., 23–4, 14.    [32] Ibid., 20.
[33] De Barros, '"Setting Things Right"'; Gill, 'Doing the Minje Mama'; Thompson, *Unprofitable Servants*, 181–2; Mullin, *Africa in America*; Viotti da Costa, *Crowns of Glory*; Browne, 'The "Bad Business" of Obeah'.

against Willem, in September 1821, stated that he had 'been engaged with other negroes . . . in dancing the so called Minje Mama dance, which is strictly forbidden by the existing laws of the colony' and that he was suspected of being responsible for the death of Madalon.[34] The primary focus throughout the trial documents is on the Minje Mama dance.

The term 'obeah' and its cognates appear in the records of Willem's trial more than in the Trinidadian poisoning commissions, but were clearly not the most significant categories for any of the participants. Their usage suggest that a process was taking place in Berbice in which obeah was beginning to emerge as a significant term for the use of spiritual power, but had not yet become dominant. 'Obeah' appears first in the questioning of W. Sterk, a planter from a neighbouring plantation and officer in the militia, who had initially arrested Willem. Sterk reported that an enslaved man, David, had 'confessed' to him that Willem had 'blamed him as being one of the Obii people on the estate', had attempted to 'flog the Obeah work out of his head', and had later struck him again for sending insufficient payment for this beating. Sterk also reported that David said that Willem had told him 'that Obeah people were not allowed to wear any thing of value'. David himself denied this 'confession'.[35] Even if we assume that David did communicate to Sterk what Sterk said he did, we still need to deal with the problem of translation. Although the records of Willem's trial are in English, the everyday vernacular of Berbice was the creole language known as Berbice Dutch.[36] The terms 'Obii' and 'Obeah' in Sterk's account may have been David's Berbice Dutch terms, but it is at least as likely that they were translations of another Berbice Dutch term.

The issue of translation is even more apparent in the second appearance of the term 'obeah', which occurs in the examination of 'the negro Isaac', from Op Hoop van Beter. Isaac was one of the enslaved people who testified about Willem's orchestration of the Minje Mama dance and Madalon's death. He is quoted as describing Willem both as 'Minje Mama' and as 'a real Obiah man (Confou man)'.[37] Like David, Isaac probably spoke in Berbice Dutch, so the phrase 'Obiah man (Confou man)' seems to be an interpreter's idiom. Possibly Isaac used a Berbice Dutch cognate term for obeah, which the interpreter believed needed to be explained to the reader. If this is so, it suggests that 'Confou man' was a more familiar term for a spiritual worker than 'obeah man' – a suggestion supported by the fact that 'Confou man' appears much more

---

[34] 'Trial of a Slave in Berbice', 5.   [35] Ibid., 21–2.
[36] Browne, 'The "Bad Business" of Obeah', 457–8; Gill, 'Doing the Minje Mama'.
[37] 'Trial of a Slave in Berbice', 25.

frequently in the trial records than does 'obeah man'. Alternatively, Isaac may have used the term 'Confou man', which the interpreter rendered 'Obiah man', but then felt the need to gloss with Isaac's term. Or Isaac himself may have used both terms. At several other points in the multiple trials, Willem is described as a 'Confou man' without the gloss.[38] Either way, the fact that obeah needed qualification – whether by Isaac or an interpreter – is suggestive.

The third use of the term obeah in the trial records took place in Willem's 'confrontation' at the courthouse in New Amsterdam on 3 November 1821. On this occasion, Willem was charged with 'causing the Minje Mama dance to be performed on plantation Op Hoop van Beter, professing himself to be an Obeah man; and for directing and causing, as an Obeah man, several of the slaves of said latter estate to be flogged', such that Madalon 'was found dead the morning succeeding the evening she had been severely maltreated'.[39] 'Obeah' had crept into the legal definition of what was at stake, although it was still subordinate to the Minje Mama dance, and was soon pushed aside. At the conclusion to Willem's trial, in January 1822, 'obeah' was no longer mentioned. This document stated that he was accused of 'treasonable practices, by deluding the minds of the negroes... from their obedience to the laws of the land, and their proprietors, by instituting and causing to be danced... the Minje Mama dance, and... occasioning the death of the negress Madalan'.[40] The two constants in the charges against Willem were the death of Madalon and the Minje Mama dance.

One final use of the term obeah is found in the concluding proceedings in the trial of a driver on Op Hoop van Beter, Kees Logie, for 'aiding, abetting, and assisting' Willem in inflicting violence on Madalon. The Fiscal's account of the charges against Logie summarized his plea in mitigation: the 'dread and fear' he felt of Willem's power, because Willem 'was esteemed a great Obeah man, and the Minje Mama'.[41] Logie's initial interrogation does describe his fear of Willem, but refers to him not as an Obeah man but as a 'Confou man'.[42] The term obeah appears to have been introduced by the Fiscal.

Obeah as a term and a category thus played a relatively minor role in the trial, while 'Minje Mama' and 'Confou' were far more significant. Given this, the labelling of the trial when printed in the Parliamentary Papers as 'for the crime of obeah and murder' is of considerable interest. How did the shift come to happen? It seems that the label was assigned because the first report of Willem's trial to reach Britain was not the trial record itself

---

[38] For instance, ibid., 27.  [39] Ibid., 33.
[40] Ibid., 39.  [41] Ibid., 44.  [42] Ibid., 29.

but a letter from John Wray, a missionary with the London Missionary Society. In a long letter written in February 1822 to William Hankey, the society's treasurer, Wray framed the events in relation to obeah. 'I have frequently related to you the awful effects of Obeah among the Negroes of this Colony,' he opened his letter, 'but one has lately occurred which surpasses any thing I have known before.' Wray went on to describe in detail the events revealed at Willem's trial, as well as his own frequent visits to Willem while he was awaiting execution. According to Wray, 'The superstitious Negroes on the Estate fancied that somebody was practising Obeah among them, in consequence of which, many of their Children and others died.' Wray explained that the 'Minggie or Water Mamma' had led people on the estate to accuse Madalon of 'Obeah'.[43]

It seems likely that it was Wray's letter, arriving in London in late spring 1822, that led to the request in the House of Commons in July for the printing of 'any information which may have been received concerning the trial of a slave, for the crime of obeah, in the colony of Berbice'. We can assume that an anti-slavery Member of Parliament – perhaps William Wilberforce, who had earlier been the recipient of another letter from Wray about the trial for obeah of an enslaved man named Hans – made that request, because of the case's propaganda value for the anti-slavery cause.[44] Whoever made the request in Parliament understood Willem's trial to be about obeah, and although we cannot be sure that he had read John Wray's account, it seems likely that this was the reason.

Wray presented the situation as one in which Willem and others on Op Hoop van Beter were responding to Madalon's obeah. But none of the uses of 'obeah' in the trial records relate to Madalon. The other documents suggest that Willem and those who followed him understood the problem with Madalon to be that she had a 'bad story' or 'bad thing' in her head, or that she was a 'bad woman' who was the 'cause of the healthy people on the estate becoming sick'.[45] As recent studies of the case have suggested, this 'badness' was effectively a synonym for witchcraft.[46] According to Willem, beating would remove the 'bad thing' and thus cure the estate of sickness. Willem and others were clearly working with an understanding of hostile spiritual power. But they did not describe this as obeah; rather, to the extent they used that term at all, they did so to describe Willem's power, the power to counter the

---

[43] John Wray to William Hankey, 6 February 1822, SOAS, Council of World Missions Archives, British Guiana–Berbice Incoming Correspondence, Box 1a, 1813–1822, Folder 6.
[44] John Wray to William Wilberforce, 29 October 1819, ibid., Folder 5.
[45] 'Trial of a Slave in Berbice', 32.
[46] Browne, 'The "Bad Business" of Obeah'; Gill, 'Doing the Minje Mama'.

'bad thing'. Obeah, for the residents of Op Hoop van Beter, was at most one among many terms that might be used for a powerful spiritual worker, whose practices could include violence against those understood to be bringing spiritual and physical harm to the community. In framing these events, along with the others that he had 'frequently related' to Hankey, as 'obeah', John Wray was most likely drawing on his British understanding of Caribbean spiritual power, acquired through exposure to material such as the popular version of the Three-Fingered Jack story, and Bryan Edwards's account of the obeah law in Jamaica, to which he referred in an earlier letter.[47] He may also have been translating terms from Berbice with which he was familiar into terms that he thought would be easier for his English audience to understand. In doing so, he set in motion an interpretation of the events as an 'obeah case' in which both Willem and Madalon are understood as obeah practitioners, an interpretation that has dominated the historiography. The complex events in which Willem, Madalon, and others were enmeshed reveal a great deal about perceptions in early nineteenth-century Berbice of spiritual danger, techniques designed to overcome it, and the power relations among those involved. The reduction of these events to an example of obeah removes the specificity of what went on in Berbice at this time, imposing an apparent clarity on the messiness of a situation in which obeah was indeed illegal, but where that term was only one of several through which African spiritual power was understood.

In Trinidad and British Guiana, and most likely also in other new colonies, the category 'obeah' was undergoing expansion in the early nineteenth century. During the same period there were shifts in the legal meaning of obeah across the Caribbean. Even in Jamaica, where obeah was most established as the appropriate category for dealing with African spiritual power, there were significant changes. Although the original anti-obeah law was made in response to the use of ritual oaths in Tacky's Rebellion, over time colonial authorities came to see the use of oaths as a separate problem to obeah, and prosecuted it under different laws. Jamaican slave codes included provisions against 'unlawful oaths', as separate clauses to those that prohibited 'obeah'. Individuals whom we might think of as making use of obeah were sometimes prosecuted under the oathing laws, rather than the obeah laws. For instance, two men, Quashie and Cudjoe, lived as armed Maroons in Jamaica for at least six months before their capture in 1821. They were tried by the St Catherine slave

---

[47] John Wray to William Wilberforce, 29 October 1819, SOAS, Council of World Missions Archives, British Guiana–Berbice Incoming Correspondence, Box 1a, 1813–1822, Folder 5.

court for rebellious acts, illegally bearing arms, and being incorrigible runaways, as well as for administering unlawful oaths and being present when unlawful oaths were administered. They were not however prosecuted for obeah, despite facing charges at a point when obeah was a commonly prosecuted offence in Jamaica.[48] Nor were George and Pompey, of Westmoreland, Jamaica, charged with obeah. Instead, both were sentenced to transportation for 'attending meetings for administering of unlawful oaths, drinking human blood mixed with rum, and other unlawful purposes'.[49] Certainly oath-taking, obeah, and rebellion continued to be associated with one another, for instance in the 1823 Jamaican conspiracy discussed later in this chapter, but it had also become possible to legally separate obeah from the sacred oath involving blood and grave dirt that had at the time of Tacky's Rebellion been seen as an essential part of it.

Even where the term 'obeah' was used, there was no consensus at the turn of the eighteenth century on how it should be spelled. The 1789 Board of Trade report, Edward Long, Bryan Edwards, and the 1760 Jamaican law all predominantly or exclusively used the spelling 'obeah', which became the most widely used spelling across the Caribbean. However, alternative usages including obea, obiah, obia, obi, obeism and even obye were also common.[50] These variant spellings, found in the writings of court scribes, governors, planters, and the keepers of parish records, suggest that knowledge of obeah among literate and relatively powerful people was transmitted primarily orally rather than through written texts, and that it travelled along multiple paths rather than being diffused from a small set of sources. The spoken word 'obeah' must have been in widespread use across the Caribbean. By the end of slavery, however, there was more uniformity. Other spellings remained possible, especially 'obiah' and 'obi', but 'obeah' had become the norm.

Thus at the turn of the eighteenth century there was no unitary understanding of or term for African spiritual power among Caribbean elites, but there was a trend towards understanding such power within the

---

[48] CO 140/112, *Votes of the Assembly of Jamaica in a session begun November 1 and ended December 19, 1825*, Appendix 61, p. 396.
[49] Ibid., Appendix 59, p. 374.
[50] For an example of 'obea' see St Thomas in the Vale, Vestry Minutes, 11 July 1795, Jamaica Archives, Local Government 2/1, 1. Both 'obiah' and 'obia' were used in the Jamaicans' submission to the Board of Trade as alternatives to obeah. For another use of 'obiah' see John Wray to William Hankey, 6 February 1822, SOAS, Council of World Missions Archive, British Guiana–Berbice Incoming Correspondence, Box 1a, 1813–1822, Folder 6. 'Obi' was widespread in accounts of Three-Fingered Jack. 'Obeism' was used by Joseph Sanderson, as quoted above. 'Obye' is used in a letter from Grenada in CO 101/44, Maitland to Windham No. 67, 7 December 1806.

overarching framework established by the criminalization of 'obeah'. An important part of this process towards consolidation took place through the passage and application of legislation. While Jamaica's 1760 law remained the only anti-obeah statute for nearly thirty years, in the fifty years between 1788 and 1838 at least ten other colonies passed laws against obeah.[51] (The exceptions, colonies that did not pass obeah laws before the end of slavery, were the Bahamas, Bermuda, St Kitts, St Lucia, the Virgin Islands, and the Turks and Caicos Islands.) Everywhere in the Anglo-Creole Caribbean except Jamaica, obeah as an object of legislation was a product of the late slavery period. In this period slave-holders aimed to stabilize and justify the system of slavery, in a policy that came to be known as 'amelioration'. The extension of laws against obeah was an important part of the amelioration process.

The connection between anti-obeah law and amelioration was most striking in Dominica, where legislative prohibition of obeah was initially included in the colony's first 'ameliorative' slave code, an 'Act for the Encouragement, Protection, and better Government of Slaves', passed in 1788.[52] The colony's governor explained that the new Act, which replaced a previous 'Act for Suppressing of Runaway Slaves', was 'framed upon more liberal, just, and humane principles' than its predecessor.[53] The adoption of provisions against obeah across most of the Caribbean was part of this wider shift towards an allegedly liberal and humane slavery, although in most colonies it took place in stand-alone pieces of legislation rather than in comprehensive slave codes. Obeah became illegal as part of the process whereby the system of slavery was 'modernized' and reordered under pressure from abolitionism and its own contradictions and tensions.[54]

The original Jamaican anti-obeah provision clearly influenced several other colonies. Phrases that derived from it appeared in later laws of British Honduras, Antigua, and Barbados.[55] Still, the expansion of obeah

---

[51] Antigua, Barbados, Berbice, British Honduras, Dominica, Grenada, Montserrat, Nevis, St Vincent, and Trinidad. For a full account of these laws, with the exception of that in Montserrat, see Handler and Bilby, *Enacting Power*. For ease of reference, further references to Caribbean legislation in this chapter cite Handler and Bilby's work rather than the original primary sources wherever possible. For the Montserrat 1819 'Act for the Punishment of Obeah' see Third report of the commissioner of inquiry into the administration of civil and criminal justice in the West Indies. Antigua, Montserrat, Nevis, St Christopher, and the Virgin Islands, *PP* 1826–7 (36), 33.
[52] Handler and Bilby, *Enacting Power*, 81–2.
[53] CO 71/14, Orde to Sydney, 4 October 1788, ff. 169–84.
[54] For parallel arguments in different contexts see Dayan, *The Law is a White Dog*; Khalili, *Time in the Shadows*.
[55] Handler and Bilby, *Enacting Power*, 54, 72, 96, quoting laws passed in Barbados in 1806, Antigua in 1809, and British Honduras in 1791.

legislation was more complex than simple adoption by one colony of legislation from another. The wording of the relevant acts differed substantially across colonies, suggesting that these provisions were adopted independently. Nevertheless, anti-obeah statutes agreed on some fundamentals. While descriptions of what was meant by 'obeah' varied quite widely, almost all the slavery-era laws referred in some form to 'pretending to supernatural power', a phrase that became the lowest-common-denominator legal definition of obeah.[56] In all the colonies obeah was a serious crime, punishable by death. Most also provided for an alternative punishment of transportation, while Dominica and St Vincent made it possible for courts to order flogging rather than the death penalty.[57] Several also implicitly or explicitly referred to obeah as a form of witchcraft, either by using that term, as did the Jamaican and Dominican laws, or by reference to communication with the devil, as did Jamaica, Barbados, and Belize.[58]

In defining obeah as a problem, the colonial legislation referred to two concerns: rebellion, and damage to health. The Jamaican 1760 'Act to remedy the evils arising from irregular assemblies of slaves' was entirely framed around the need to prevent rebellion. Its obeah clause, although not directly mentioning rebellion, referred to it obliquely in its explanation that obeah needed to be illegal because obeah practitioners gave enslaved people 'Belief of their having full Power to exempt them whilst under their Protection from any Evils that might otherwise happen'. Slave codes in Jamaica and Dominica in 1788 were the first to explicitly mention rebellion in connection with obeah. The Dominican law stated that obeah 'frequently stimulate[s] them [slaves] to acts of mutiny or rebellion against their masters, renters, managers and overseers', while the Jamaican code referred to 'slave[s] who shall pretend to any supernatural power to affect the health or lives of others or promote the purposes of Rebellion'.[59] The Barbadian House of Assembly also included explicit reference to rebellion when it renewed its anti-obeah legislation in 1818,

---

[56] Legislation that included some version of this phrase includes Acts passed in Jamaica (in 1760, 1761, 1781, 1788, and 1801) British Honduras (1791), Barbados (1806, 1816, 1818), Dominica (1788, 1799, 1818, and 1821) Berbice (in 1810 – a proclamation rather than legislation), and St Vincent (1824). The only Acts that I am aware of that prohibited obeah without any mention of pretending to use any supernatural power were passed in Trinidad in 1800, St Vincent in 1803, and Jamaica in 1833. For sources for all these acts see ibid.
[57] Ibid., 81, 92, referring to laws passed in Dominica in 1788 and St Vincent in 1803.
[58] Ibid., 46–9, 54, 81–2, 96, referring to laws passed in Jamaica in 1760 and subsequently, Dominica in 1788, Barbados in 1806 and Belize in 1791.
[59] Ibid., 47, 82.

two years after the major uprising on that island.⁶⁰ The concern about the health of enslaved people was expressed in the Jamaican 1788 law, which added the phrase 'to affect the health or lives of others' after 'who shall pretend to any supernatural power'.⁶¹ It appeared also in, for instance, the preamble to the Barbados Act of 1806, which stated that 'valuable slaves have lost their lives or have otherwise been materially injured in their health' due to obeah, and the Berbice Ordinance of 1810 which referred to damage done by obeah to the 'life, health, or happiness of any other slave or individual'.⁶² The exception to this rule was St Vincent, which passed legislation punishing obeah with death in 1803 and renewed it in 1824 and 1833, but described obeah in terms that made it seem much less threatening: it was used, the laws stated, for curing disease, protection or injury of persons or things, discovery of hidden matter or things, recovery of stolen or lost goods, or the administration of love potions or philtres.⁶³

Overwhelmingly, the obeah laws made obeah into a racial crime. Most defined those subject to anti-obeah legislation as slaves, who by definition were people of African descent.⁶⁴ But some held out the possibility that obeah practitioners might be free. The Belize law of 1791 referred to 'any free person of colour or slave', while the Nevis law applied to 'all negroes and coloured persons whatsoever', thus racializing the crime while not associating it only with enslaved status.⁶⁵ St Vincent, again, was distinctive, its 1803 law applying to 'any person, either white, coloured, or a slave'.⁶⁶ This and Barbados's 1826 Consolidated Slave Act were the only slavery-era obeah laws that allowed the possibility that obeah practitioners might be white.⁶⁷ Thus with very few exceptions

⁶⁰ Ibid., 54.   ⁶¹ Ibid., 47.
⁶² Ibid., 54. Proclamation of the Governor and Court of Policy, Berbice, 2 April 1810, T 1/3482. Thanks to Randy Browne for sharing this document with me. The proclamation is extracted in Thompson, *Documentary History*, 149, but is not mentioned in Handler and Bilby's *Enacting Power*.
⁶³ Handler and Bilby, *Enacting Power*, 92–3.
⁶⁴ This is true of all the Jamaican and Dominican slavery-era laws, as well as those of Barbados in 1806 and Trinidad of 1800. Ibid.
⁶⁵ Ibid., 96 (Belize). 'An Act for punishing, with death, all negroes and coloured persons whatsoever, who shall practise what is called confu, or obeah doctor, or who shall take away, or attempt to take away, the life, or injure the health, of any person or persons whatsoever' (Nevis), referred to in Third report of the commissioner of inquiry into the administration of civil and criminal justice in the West Indies. Antigua, Montserrat, Nevis, St. Christopher, and the Virgin Islands, *PP* 1826 (36). I have not been able to locate the original text or date of this Act, which is not mentioned in Handler and Bilby's *Enacting Power*.
⁶⁶ Amended in 1821 to 'whether free or slave'. Handler and Bilby, *Enacting Power*, 92–3.
⁶⁷ Ibid., 55. In addition, Barbados's 1818 anti-obeah law theoretically applied to all 'persons' rather than just enslaved people. This change from the 1806 law was apparently a matter for debate: the amendment was made between the initial passage of the Bill

slavery-era anti-obeah laws assumed that obeah was something done by people of African descent, defined as slaves, Negroes, or persons of colour. Indeed, in all colonies except St Vincent and Barbados, a white person could theoretically practise the arts defined as obeah without breaking any law.

The development of colonial law also suggests the instability of official concepts of obeah, and the multiplicity of terms in play for what would later stabilize around that single term. As mentioned above, Nevis passed a law prescribing death for 'all negroes and coloured persons whatsoever, who shall practise what is called confu, or obeah doctor'. Dominica similarly provided for the punishment of slaves who 'are what is commonly called Obeah or doctor Men.'[68] These laws' use of equivalent or alternative terms to obeah ('confu', 'spell-doctor', 'doctor Men') and their use of the term 'doctor' demonstrate the range of expressions for spiritual power in those colonies. Obeah was the term that circulated most widely across the colonies, appearing in multiple laws around the Caribbean. Many colonies, however, had their own local alternatives.

When considered in the light of the accounts of obeah given in 1789 to the Board of Trade and discussed in the previous chapter, which understood it as strongly correlated to the proportion of Africans in the population, the expansion of obeah law during the late period of slavery seems contradictory. If obeah was associated with Africans, why should laws against it proliferate at the moment when Africans were a diminishing fraction of the population? The colonial archives provide little help in explaining this contradiction. Official correspondence contains practically no discussion about why Caribbean legislatures gradually decided to legislate against obeah. Governor Orde of Dominica, for instance, in a letter outlining the conflicts leading up to the passage of the 1788 slave code, and the new provisions that it contained, did not even mention the substantial innovation involved in making obeah illegal.[69] Other colonial governors likewise submitted legislation containing new anti-obeah provisions without commentary or justification.[70] Legislative provisions against obeah had come to seem obviously necessary, despite their novelty.

In the absence of direct testimony from their proponents, we must infer the reasons for the passage of obeah laws. It seems likely that, perhaps counterintuitively, obeah was made illegal at the point at which

by the Assembly and its approval by the council. CO 31/47, Meeting of the General Assembly, 30 June 1818, f. 195v.
[68] Handler and Bilby, *Enacting Power*, 81. The use of the term 'confu' in Nevis echoes the description of Willem as a 'confou man' in Berbice at around the same time.
[69] CO 71/15, Orde to Sydney, 4 October 1788.
[70] For instance, from Barbados, CO 28/98, Warde to Bathurst No. 9, 24 October 1826.

slave-holders were becoming more in control; that is, its illegality was a sign of the successful institutionalisation of slavery. In earlier periods obeah was involved in warfare between slave-holders and their opponents – Maroons or rebellious slaves. In such circumstances a legislative response was beside the point; colonial forces used military means in an effort to suppress obeah and the military tactics associated with it. By the nineteenth century, notwithstanding the external threat from abolitionism and the fact that this period saw the largest rebellions in Anglo-Creole Caribbean history, in Barbados (1816), Demerara (1823) and Jamaica (1831), state authorities were more firmly in control on a day-to-day basis. In this context, anti-obeah law was part of a wider amelioration policy that sought to extend the remit of law into new areas of life, including religion, while fending off abolitionist claims that slavery was an unsustainable and immoral system.

Also significant was the expansion of missionary work in the Caribbean. Missionaries did not actively seek the passage of anti-obeah legislation. Indeed, sometimes they argued against it. John Wray of Berbice, for instance, critiqued the use of law to combat obeah, arguing that 'light and knowledge alone can root out this evil'.[71] Missionaries hoped to win over the people's hearts and minds to a non-Africanized Christianity, rather than use the law against African religion. Nevertheless, the expanded missionary presence in the nineteenth century made African religion a site of everyday contestation on estates and an increased part of the discourse on slavery in Britain. As Dianne Stewart notes, missionaries 'arrived with the agenda of demolishing African culture and religion'.[72] Missionaries reported their attempts to persuade enslaved people to 'throw aside their Obeah', and celebrated the displacement of 'obeism and sorcery' with 'the promises of Scripture', while accounts of Caribbean society regularly depicted scenes revealing the conflict between missionary religion and enslaved people's allegiance to obeah.[73] Anti-obeah legislation responded to the missionary agenda by reasserting the planters', as opposed to the missionaries', authority over the religious practice of enslaved people.

---

[71] John Wray to William Wilberforce, 29 October 1819, SOAS, Council of World Missions Archives, British Guiana–Berbice Incoming Correspondence Box 1a, 1813–1822, Folder 5.
[72] Stewart, *Three Eyes*, 80.
[73] Lang, 'Extract of the Diary', 365; Religious Tract Society, Missionary Records: West Indies, quoted in Stewart, *Three Eyes*, 85. See also John Wray to Charles Bird, 25 August 1829, enclosed in Beard to Murray, 25 September 2819, in Copy of any Reports which may have been received from the Protectors of Slaves... Part II: Berbice, *PP* 1830–1 (262) xv, 48–9. For depictions of missionary attempts to persuade enslaved people to repudiate obeah, see Williams, *Hamel*; Williams, *A Tour through the Island of Jamaica*, 194.

Scholars have rightly argued that, prior to the passage of anti-obeah laws, slave-owners usually expressed interest, rather than fear, in enslaved people's ritual work to invoke the power of the spirits. Vincent Brown, for instance, cites Thomas Thistlewood's description of an enslaved man, Guy, who in 1753 'acted his Obia &c. with singing, dancing, &c. odd enough', and his observation the following year of Jinney Quashe, who 'pretend[ed] to pull bones, &c. out of several of our Negroes for which they was to give him money'.[74] Such activity would, after 1760 in Jamaica, have been potentially punishable with death. Even then, however, the existence of laws against obeah did not mean that all ritual work that might have been prosecuted under such laws reached the courts. Sometimes those with the power and desire to prosecute enslaved people were not aware of what was happening in slaves' spiritual lives, or could not muster the evidence required to make an obeah charge stick. Duncan, an enslaved man in Jamaica, was prosecuted for horse-stealing and running away, rather than for obeah, despite his reputation as a well-known obeah practitioner. According to the chief magistrate in the case this was because enslaved people were so afraid of 'his supernatural power' that they 'would not give evidence against him, fearful their lives would be endangered thereby'.[75] Their reluctance to give evidence may have been rooted in solidarity or dependence as much as fear, but whatever the reason, it meant that prosecution for obeah was not an option available to Duncan's owner. Even if it had been, the prosecution of an enslaved person for obeah, as for any other transgression, was a serious step. Although planters received compensation when their slaves were sentenced to death or transportation, it was still likely to cause them financial loss and other forms of disruption.[76] Planters' everyday power, without recourse to the law, was sufficient that they often chose not to prosecute. Prosecution, after all, would make public their inability to deal privately with the problem of obeah, and was thus a last resort. As a result, even after the passage of the obeah laws plantation managers frequently responded to ritual practice that they considered dangerous with the private weapons that slavery placed in their hands: sale, flogging and other forms of violence.

Thus for example when Thomas Thistlewood recorded in 1780 that he had caught 'Mr Wilson's Will (who is an Obiah, or Bush Man) . . . in

---

[74] Journal of Thomas Thistlewood, quoted in Brown, 'Spiritual Terror and Sacred Authority', 35. See also Watson, *Caribbean Culture*, 18; Handler and Bilby, 'Early Use and Origin'.

[75] Robert Vassall to the Right Hon. Lord Holland, 14 May 1822, BL Add Ms 51819, ff. 13–14.

[76] On the compensation system see Gaspar, '"To Bring their Offending Slaves to Justice"' and Paton, 'An "Injurious" Population'.

Abba's house, at work with his Obiah', he understood Will's actions to be more troubling than he had the actions of Guy and Jinney Quashe more than two decades earlier. He did not, however, attempt to have Will prosecuted. Instead, he returned him to his owner, Mr Wilson, who 'flogged [Will] well'.[77] Another case from around the same time that probably involved spiritual work involved an enslaved man known as 'Doctor Caesar' on Rozelle plantation. Initially accepted as a medical practitioner within the plantation, Doctor Caesar became known to the estate managers as a troublemaker and was severely flogged. Just before he was about to be 'sold off the island' he successfully escaped on a ship for London. While the plantation manager's reports about Caesar's activities focus on his use of arson and of 'stirring up' the other plantation slaves rather than on his medical and healing knowledge, it seems likely that he was a man whose knowledge of ritual healing was part of what gave him authority within the plantation, enabling him to 'stir up' the rest of the community.[78] Nevertheless, the management's preferred response was not prosecution but sale. The story of the Popo woman in the 1789 Board of Trade report, discussed in the previous chapter, is another example of this kind of response to obeah. The planter who related that case did not prosecute the accused woman, but instead sold her to slave-trading Spaniards, who probably took her to Cuba.

Similar informal measures of control continued into the 1820s. When the authorities at plantation Dentichem in Berbice believed that an enslaved man named Tobias was 'practicing obeah on the estate' they confined him in the stocks rather than prosecute him, and later sold him.[79] In another incident in Berbice the same year, a planter offered in defence against his slave's complaint of mistreatment that the complainant was a bad character and a 'dealer in obeah'. This did not provoke any discussion of why the complainant had not been prosecuted for obeah, suggesting that it was common and accepted not to prosecute known obeah practitioners.[80] In a Jamaican case from the same period, an overseer witnessed an enslaved man 'depositing something which he knew to be an Obiah-Spell' in a hole he had dug. The next day the overseer told the man that he 'could *Hang* him for what he had done', but in fact chose not to prosecute, instead 'charging him to escape to America or some other place'.[81] The Jamaican novel *Marly* presented a fictionalized account of a similar incident, in which Hampden, an estate driver, was accused of using obeah to make two other

---

[77] Hall, *In Miserable Slavery*, 279. See also Burnard, *Mastery, Tyranny, and Desire*, 224.
[78] Graham, *Burns and the Sugar Plantocracy*, 55–6; citing National Register of Archives of Scotland 3572/3/6–7.
[79] Further Papers Relating to Slaves in the West Indies, *PP* 1825 (476) xxv, 76–7.
[80] Ibid., 63 and 66.   [81] Brown, *The Reaper's Garden*, 151.

enslaved people sick. Although everyone was convinced of Hampden's guilt, the overseer 'conceived it would be a pity to trust his case in the hands of public justice', and instead ordered that Hampden be flogged and removed from his position of driver. 'He expressed himself even sorry to go this far, but if something was not done to satisfy the negroes, they might lodge a complaint, where Hampden would not be so leniently dealt with.'[82]

When plantation authorities did prosecute, they often did so after a long period during which they had been aware that the person prosecuted had a reputation as a spiritually powerful individual. Matthew Lewis eventually prosecuted his slave Adam after recording instances of obeah in his diary for months.[83] George Kerr of Jamaica, prosecuted in 1822 for obeah, had been flogged for 'myal dancing' at some point previously, probably years earlier.[84] The existence of the crime of obeah provided planters with a weapon against enslaved people's use of spiritual power, but prosecution was not something they undertook lightly. The prosecutions for obeah that did take place, then, reveal only a small section of the overall landscape of ritual spiritual activity in the Caribbean of the late slavery period. Activity that led to prosecution was a particular subset of all the spiritual work that would come to be known as obeah.

How, then, was anti-obeah legislation used? It is, unfortunately, not possible to give a comprehensive account of all obeah prosecutions. The records of slave courts are not held in any central location, and were often not retained at all, so the evidence we have about obeah trials is dispersed among many other types of document, making it extremely time consuming to locate.[85] In what follows, I reconstruct some of what went on in obeah trials during the slavery period, using them primarily as a way of understanding what types of actions provoked prosecution, while also trying to see what we can learn about the context and meaning of such actions for the individuals engaged in them. I rely extensively

---

[82] *Marly*, 129. The logs of punishments on managers' orders in Berbice also attest to the use of flogging as a privately inflicted punishment for obeah. See the 'Abstracts of Offences committed by Male and Female Plantation Slaves in the Colony Berbice' for 1828 and 1829 in Copy of any Reports which may have been received from the Protectors of Slaves... Part II: Berbice, *PP* 1830–1 (262) xv, 19–20, 103–5. Thanks to Randy Browne for reminding me of this source.

[83] Lewis, *Journal of a West Indian Proprietor*, 87–93, 221–3.

[84] Unsigned letter, dated Content, October 1822, JA 1A/2/1/1 Hanover Slave Court, Hanover Courts Office, Lucea.

[85] The process has been helped by recent improvements, led by Mandy Banton, in cataloguing the Caribbean records held at the UK National Archives. Enhanced cataloguing descriptions enabled me to locate many more records referring to obeah than would otherwise have been possible, but the cataloguing has been a partial process, not covering every colony.

on Jamaican materials, supplemented with evidence documenting obeah prosecutions from elsewhere in the Caribbean, where I have been able to locate it.

The earliest prosecutions for obeah come, unsurprisingly, from the period shortly after the passage of Jamaica's 1760 'Act to remedy the evils arising from irregular assemblies of slaves'. It is possible that the first trial under the Act took place in November 1765, in the wake of another, smaller, rebellion, also in St Mary's. In its aftermath, among the tens of individuals hanged or transported was one, Quaon, who was said to be 'an obeaman' who 'could give them obeah which would protect them from musket Balls or any other Weapon'. Quaon was burnt alive. However, it seems more likely that he was tried for rebellion than specifically under the 1760 Act against obeah. The fact that Quaon was burnt alive, a punishment usually reserved for traitors, and not one specified in the 1760 Act, also suggests that this was not a trial for obeah.[86] The next year provides more definite uses of anti-obeah legislation. The St Thomas in the East slave court at Morant Bay sentenced an enslaved man named Philander to death for practising obeah; he was hanged. That court saw the prosecution of at least two more enslaved men for obeah in the next sixteen years.[87] A set of slave-court records from the parish of St Andrew, near Kingston, includes the prosecution in 1767 of Mary for 'having material in her possession relative to the practice of obeah or witchcraft'; of Sarah in 1772 for 'for having in her possession, cats teeth, cats claws, cats jaws, hair, beads, knotted cloths, and other materials relative to the practice of obeah to delude and impose on the minds of the negroes'; of Solomon in 1776 for possession of obeah materials; of Tony in 1777 for 'practising obeah or witchcraft on a slave named Fortune by means of which the said slave became dangerously ill', and of Neptune in 1782 for 'making use of rum, hair, chalk, stones and other materials relative to the practice of obeah or witchcraft'.[88] The St Ann vestry paid £40 in compensation to the owner of Guy, who had been executed for the

---

[86] On Quaon see Information of Cuffee, 8 December 1765, Examination of slaves in connection with premature slave revolt in St Mary's Parish, 1765, English Miscellaneous Manuscripts Collection, Ms. 753, box 5, folder 1762–1765, Manuscripts and Archives, Yale University Library (quote), and Clements Library Michigan, Lyttelton Papers Oversize, Bayley to Lyttleton, December 1765, both cited in Robertson, 'The Experience and Imagination of a Slave Revolt', 19. I thank James Robertson for his generosity in sharing this paper and details of his notes from these sources with me.

[87] Hill, *Light and Shadows*, Appendix, p. 147–8, quoting from trial book of slaves, kept at the Vestry Office at Morant Bay, Jamaica. I have not located Hill's original source.

[88] 'Copy of the Record Book of the slave trials of St Andrew Jamaica from 17 March 1746 to 16 Dec. 1782', enclosed in CO 137/248, Metcalfe to Russell No. 51, 5 April 1840, ff. 216–26. For more extensive discussion of these records see Paton, 'Punishment, Crime, and the Bodies of Slaves'.

practice of obeah in 1772.[89] Little detail or context is included about any of these cases. Most frustratingly, in all except the case of Tony, the records of these prosecutions tell us nothing about the use to which the defendants put the material that they were prosecuted for owning. Did they use their assemblages in order to protect, to heal, to stimulate rebellion, for divination? Some or all of these, or for purposes we cannot intuit? We cannot answer these questions, but these cases nevertheless suggest an on-the-ground sense among slave-holders that obeah was both a form of witchcraft, and was genuinely powerful.

The most detailed early obeah case I have found is that of George, prosecuted at the Morant Bay slave court in 1787, whose trial was reported in the London newspapers because a colonist wrote home about it. George was charged with 'laying obeah, and procuring a phial of strong poison to destroy the white people on Stanton estate'. The estate's enslaved population had asked George for assistance in killing their overseer 'and others to whom they had taken a dislike', because of his 'reputation among the slaves as an adept in the occult sciences'. George was sentenced to an aggravated form of the death penalty, designed to display the power of the plantocratic state. After being hanged his head was severed and displayed on a pole at the Stanton estate.[90] The display of the heads of executed slaves was standard practice for enslaved people who challenged slavery in the Caribbean, making use of a traditional European punishment for traitors and rebels.[91] George's skills and knowledge appear to have been used as part of collective political action by slaves – and it was this kind of use of spiritual power that attracted prosecution. The combination of obeah with poisoning and with collective consultation of the specialist by enslaved people was particularly unsettling for Jamaican whites.

Some comprehensive reports of prosecutions from Jamaican slave courts survive from the first three decades of the nineteenth century. These provide little detail of the nature of the events that led up to prosecution, but do reveal roughly how frequently obeah was prosecuted, the conviction rates and punishments meted out. I located three sets of such cases, involving a total of 140 prosecutions. The first covers the years 1806 to 1811, and includes 18 cases of obeah out of a total of 241 cases from 4 Jamaican parishes (along with several others of poisoning

---

[89] St Ann Vestry Orders JA Local Government 2/9/1, 1767–90.
[90] 'Extract of a letter from Kingston, Jamaica, October 6', London *General Evening Post*, Issue 8447, 8 January 1788–10 January 1788, Burney Collection online. The same story was also published in the *Morning Chronicle and London Advertiser*, 8 January 1788; in the London *Gazetteer and New Daily Advertiser*, 9 January 1788, and in *Gentleman's Magazine*, February 1788, p. 106.
[91] Gatrell, *The Hanging Tree*, 281, 298–9.

or possessing poison).[92] Another set includes 79 obeah cases of a total of 1,151 cases from the years 1814–18.[93] The third covers 1820–5, with 43 cases of obeah out of a total of 484 cases, along with a few for 'unlawful oaths'.[94] Obeah, then, was regularly, if not frequently, prosecuted in Jamaica in the early nineteenth century: around eleven cases per year were recorded in the two data sets that include the whole of Jamaica. Obeah cases accounted for between 7 and 9 per cent of all trials reported in these records. Jamaican residents in the first three decades of the nineteenth century would have been familiar with obeah prosecutions, although not everyone would have directly known someone who was so prosecuted.

Prosecution for obeah did not necessarily mean conviction: only 55 per cent of those prosecuted were convicted.[95] This relatively low conviction rate may suggest an additional reason why planters in many instances preferred to deal privately with those whose spiritual work they found threatening. The death sentence was in the 1800s and 1810s routinely used to punish those convicted of obeah, but even then conviction did not mean an automatic death sentence. Rather, transportation – that is, publicly administered sale into the overseas slave trade – was the most frequently inflicted punishment, meted out to 78 per cent of all those convicted across all three sets of records.[96] The dominance of the use of transportation as a punishment increased over time. Six of the fourteen people convicted between 1806 and 1811 were executed, but only one person convicted in 1820–5 received the death penalty, and his sentence was commuted to transportation for life.

Obeah – like most offences – was largely a crime for which men faced prosecution. The three data sets are consistent in this regard: between

---

[92] *PP* 1814–15 vii (478), Morrison to Bathurst, 28 January 1813, enclosing: 'A list of slaves tried, and sentenced to death, or transportation for life, in the said parish of Vere under the Consolidated Slave Laws, from 31 December 1802 to 31 December 1811' (106–8); 'A List of Convictions and Punishments of Slaves, in at Slave courts in the Parish of Westmoreland, commencing 1810' (114); 'A List of all Negro or other Slaves tried . . . in the parish of St Elizabeth . . . from the year 1808 to the present period' (118–21); and 'St Mary Parish: Extracts of Convictions 1806–1812' (123–8).

[93] CO 137/147. An analysis of the obeah cases from this source is presented in Brown, 'Spiritual Terror and Sacred Authority'. Brown discusses eighty-five cases, because the source includes a duplicate page for the parish of Hanover, which he counted twice.

[94] CO 140/112, Appendices 59 and 61.

[95] This excludes the records from Vere and St Mary, which did not record those found not guilty. It counts those tried for multiple crimes and found guilty of one of them, for instance cases in which someone was tried for both obeah and possession of obeah materials, and was found guilty only of the latter. For comparison, the conviction rate for all St Andrews prosecutions was 76 per cent, for all 1814–18 prosecutions was 72 per cent, and for all 1821–5 prosecutions was 65 per cent.

[96] On transportation as a punishment in the Caribbean see Paton, 'An "Injurious" Population'.

88 and 90 per cent of those prosecuted were male, a figure that roughly matches rates of prosecution of enslaved women for all crimes in this period.[97] As well as being more likely to be prosecuted, men were slightly more likely to be convicted than were women: 56 per cent of men prosecuted were convicted, but only 40 per cent of women. The dominance of men among those prosecuted belies the cultural prominence of female obeah practitioners in the British imagination, and to some extent among Caribbean commenters too.

Prosecutions followed legislation in singling out ritual practice in two main settings: either it was undertaken in the context of broader anti-slavery activity or it led, or was thought to lead, to harm to the health of other enslaved individuals. Obeah was sometimes suspected in cases that appear to involve individual opposition to slavery. James, of St Elizabeth, Jamaica, for instance, was prosecuted in 1814 for 'arson in burning down his master's house, obeah and running away'.[98] Similarly Stewart, also of St Elizabeth, was charged with obeah and running away, and found guilty only of the former, for which he was nevertheless transported for life.[99] Others were found guilty of obeah alongside 'being armed and for making use of rebellious and threatening language' towards the overseer of his estate, or with 'violently assaulting' an overseer.[100]

Many of the extant cases suggest that those prosecuted for obeah were individuals who acted not just as individual rebels but as combined spiritual and political leaders. Brutus, enslaved in Trelawney, Jamaica, was sentenced to imprisonment in the workhouse for life for obeah in 1788 – an unusual punishment at a point when workhouses held few life prisoners. The archival records do not reveal the events that led to his prosecution. However, he later escaped from the workhouse and by 1792 was reported to be the leader of a small group of Maroons, among whom he was known as 'Captain Brutus'. Brutus's knowledge of obeah apparently earned him respect and authority amongst his peers. The group maintained solidarity through the use of an oath that bound those taking it not to leave the group or to 'reveal any of their secrets' if caught, and involved 'mix[ing] part of the blood of each in a calabash with water and money'. The group was also said to have a 'fortune teller, who can discover any of the party who will prove false to his oath'.[101] Similar cases took place

---

[97] For all prosecutions, men were 87 per cent of the defendants in the 1814–18 records and 91 per cent of defendants in the 1821–5 records. One exceptional crime, where women predominated as defendants, was poisoning.
[98] CO 137/147, f. 52.     [99] CO 137/147, f. 53.
[100] CO 137/147, f. 55 (case of Limerick) and f. 57 (case of Frank).
[101] For Brutus's obeah conviction and eventual execution see *Diary or Woodfall's Register* (London, England), 28 March 1792, issue 941 (Burney Collection online), reprinting

in 1807, when Captain, described by a witness against him as a 'skilful Obeah man' who was to 'swear the Negroes' in a planned rebellion, was transported off the island, and in 1823, when Fortune was transported for life for using 'supernatural power... and... certain charms and spells' to persuade seventeen enslaved people from Caenwood Estate 'to abscond with him for the purpose of living in the wood'.[102]

In Grenada, too, knowledge of obeah was reported as a source of authority over other enslaved people that might lead to marronage or rebellion. In 1806 a man who 'practiced what is termed obye' and was 'connected with a great many others' was executed. The group with which he was 'connected' had reportedly 'acquired ascendency over the other Negroes, very dangerous to the safety of the colony'. Like Brutus, this expert in obeah was a leader who was thought to be likely to inspire active opposition to the colonial regime.[103]

The most substantial nineteenth-century case in which obeah was used to organize rebellion comes from the plans of a group of enslaved people in Jamaica in 1823. Late that year Jamaican whites feared conspiracy in the parishes of St Mary, St James, and St George. Some of these fears seem to have been based on little more than rumours among enslaved people that freedom was coming soon, rather than any planned uprising. The evidence for a 'conspiracy' in St James was based solely on talk at a dance. Yet the plans in the parish of St George appear to have been real enough. Several individuals from Balcarres estate testified that enslaved people had been acquiring weapons, practising mustering, and planning to unite with slaves on other estates at Christmas time. Among those executed for 'rebellious conspiracy' as a result of the plot was Jack, who was also charged with obeah.[104] Jack was apparently the ritual leader of the event, supporting Henry Oliver, the conspiracy's central organizer. One witness, a runaway who reported the plot, described how Oliver and Jack prepared a blood oath. Oliver cut his finger and put the blood into 'a large basin standing in the middle' of the room. Jack 'then threw a quart

---

item from Jamaica *Royal Gazette*, 21 January 1792. For the oath and fortune teller see CO 137/90, Williamson to Dundas, 12 February 1792, enclosing 'Minutes of Examination of a Negro Slave named Lucky the property of Mr James Cotton', 31 December 1791. For more general discussions of the significance of the 'blood oath' see Mullin, *Africa in America*, 67–8; Stewart, *Three Eyes*, 43.

[102] Examination of Frank, in Minutes of Council, 9 March 1807, enclosed in CO 137/118, Eyre Coote to Windham, 10 March 1807, f. 116; JA Local Govt St George 2/18/6 General Slave Court 1822–1831, case of 1 January 1823.

[103] CO 101/44, Maitland to Windham No. 67, 7 December 1806.

[104] Papers relating to the manumission, government and population of slaves in the West Indies, 1822–1824, *PP* 1825 xxv (66), 82–109; JA Local Govt St George 2/18/6 General Slave Court 1822–31. Jack's trial is also discussed in Mullin, *Africa in America*, 182–3; Hart, *Slaves Who Abolished Slavery*.

of rum into it, and something else, [either] grave dirt or gunpowder'.[105] All the conspirators drank the ritually powerful mixture, swearing an oath of secrecy and solidarity as they did so. After drinking, Oliver reportedly said, 'So help me God you must stand to the battle.'[106]

In addition to the blood oath, witnesses described Jack's preparation of 'a quantity of pounded bush with which he anointed the bodies of the conspirators' in order to give them strength and make them invulnerable. He reportedly told each individual to whom he gave some of the bush: 'Well, you see this bush here; this is to give you strength when you go up to your busha's house, and if any buckras come to help, you are to stand boldly to the battle, and do not fear any hurt, as this bush will save you.'[107] Another witness, a participant in the plan who gave evidence to save himself, described Jack as 'the obeah man' and emphasized how he organized 'the swear' and 'rubbed bush' on the conspirators' naked bodies in order to give them strength.[108] Jack himself admitted to being present at 'the swear', although he denied organizing it. He said at his trial that 'he knew that his doctoring was what Buckra called obeah. Buckra had their own fashion; in Guinea, negro could doctor.' For Jack, it seems, 'obeah' was an outsiders' term; what he was doing was 'doctoring'.[109] Witnesses also referred to him as 'the doctor' as well as 'the obeah man'.

These events in Jamaica in 1823 are part of a lineage that also includes the events in Antigua of 1736 and Jamaica of 1760. In all three cases enslaved people used spiritual power to build solidarity and in an attempt to render themselves invulnerable. The meaning of obeah in this context primarily related to the activities of an individual who played the role of spiritual adviser to a political leader. This appears to have been the dominant meaning of the term for enslaved people, of greater significance than the more personal and individualized role of the healer and spiritual consultant that would come to dominate accounts of obeah in later decades, and was already becoming prominent in representations.

Cases like this were the kind of events that planters and slavery's defenders discussed most frequently when they described obeah as a problem. But obeah law was also used in other circumstances, when there was no threat of armed uprising or even marronage. In these cases,

---

[105] *PP* 1825 xxv (66), 88, evidence of Charles Mack in trial of Henry Oliver, 19 January 1824.
[106] Ibid., 84–5, examination of Charles Mack, 7 January 1824, and 88, evidence of Jean Baptiste Corberand.
[107] Ibid., 85 examination of Charles Mack, 7 January 1824 and 88, evidence of Charles Mack in trial of Henry Oliver, 19 January 1824.
[108] Ibid., 93, evidence of Jean Baptiste Corberand, 5 February 1824.
[109] Ibid., 108–9, confession of Jack, 8 April 1824.

prosecutors believed that obeah had been used to harm other slaves. Most frequently, this harm was understood to have directly involved the hostile use of obeah. For example Marcia, Richard Baker, and John Thomas were convicted in Jamaica in 1815 for 'the practice of obeah and for giving deleterious matter to a negro girl named Sally Bradford by means of which she died'; Marcia was hanged and the two men transported.[110] In a similar case the following year, Maurice and London were found guilty in Portland of obeah activity which allegedly nearly led to the death of a woman named Eliza.[111] Likewise 'Joseph alias Bellyful' was convicted of obeah for having harmed 'the minds and healths' of two enslaved women from the same estate, and for having damaged the health of another slave, Cupid, through a preparation of 'poisonous and deleterious matter' in rum.[112] In Grenada, Elly and Frances were convicted in 1812 of 'practising Obi and threatening the lifes [sic] of several slaves' on the estate where they lived.[113] Such cases were explicitly framed as being about the damage to the property of the planters who claimed ownership of the enslaved individuals concerned, rather than as a matter of concern for the slaves hurt. Indictments in this type of obeah case typically described the damage caused by the crime of obeah with phrases such as 'to the material injury of the proprietor' or 'owner'.[114]

A prosecution arising from events on Lloyds estate, Jamaica, in 1829 left more detailed evidence. The case developed out of conflict between two enslaved people, Industry and Bella, who was a 'Guinea Negro' (that is, an African). According to evidence presented in court, a boy, Richard Chambers, acting on Industry's instructions, put a 'black something' described as 'like a small potatoe or Indian arrowroot' under the 'door mouth' of Bella's house, and another in the thatch of her roof. Another enslaved woman, Ann Williams, saw Chambers putting the things in Bella's house, and told her what she had seen. Although Bella stated in court that she had 'never had any quarrel' with Industry, she interpreted these 'somethings' as spiritually powerful items that had been 'put there for bad'. When Bella found the objects she told the driver, and with him reported her finding to the overseer, Edmund Sharpe, leading to

---

[110] CO 137/147, f. 53. [111] CO 137/147, f. 72.
[112] JA Local Govt St George 2/18/6 General Slave Court 1822–31, case of 2 October 1822. For similar cases see, from CO 140/112, case of Harry, Appendix 59, p. 375, and of Thomas Liddle, Appendix 61, p. 397; from the St George Slave Court, case of Bob Burrows, 5 April 1827; and from JA 1A/2/1/1 Hanover Slave Court, case of Isaac Lowe, 9 April 22. (This case is also recorded in CO 140/112, Appendix 59, p. 383.)
[113] CO 101/58, f. 80, enclosed in Riall to Bathurst, 17 September 1818, No. 15.
[114] All the indictments for obeah from the St George General Slave Court, 1822–31, include phrases of this kind. See JA Local Govt St George 2/18/6.

Industry's prosecution. In court, Bella was asked if she had ever cursed Industry, and denied having ever done so.[115]

Industry's prosecution demonstrates one method by which an accused obeah practitioner might hurt another person: the use of a spiritually powerful object hidden in the house of the intended victim. This was a familiar part of the repertoire of obeah practice, and appears in many contemporary and later accounts of obeah.[116] It also demonstrates the unanimous belief of the people involved, including Sharpe, that the 'somethings' were harmful, or at least intended to harm. It seems likely that this incident was the culmination of other events that led the Lloyds estate managers to prosecute Industry – a process that led to his removal from the estate and the payment of some compensation to his owners.

In cases of obeah arising from interpersonal relations among enslaved people, one often senses additional layers of complexity that are only hinted at in the documents. The more detail we have about such cases the more complicated they become. An example where more information is preserved than in the case of Industry is the prosecution of Andrew Marble in St Catherine, Jamaica, in 1824, which was summarized in the court records as 'for practising of obeah and for having articles notoriously used in such practice in his possession'.[117] A newspaper report of the trial provides additional detail, revealing that the prosecution took place in the aftermath of the death of an old woman, Pamila, who had been ill for two years. Edmund Whittaker, the property's overseer, testified that Pamila had reported to him that Marble, a field slave on the property, had 'obeahed' her and that 'that no other but prisoner [i.e. Marble] could cure her'. This is an important, and rare, example of the use of obeah (in this case the verb 'to obeah') in the reported speech of an enslaved person. Whittaker responded by directing Marble to try to cure Pamila, which he did, conducting divination and healing rituals.[118] Using items from a bag containing 'soap, berries, chalk, and shell', Marble threw six of them in water, examining which floated and which sank. He diagnosed that there was 'an iron bar across [Pamila's] back bone, under her skin' and that 'she had too many things in her skin, besides the iron bar, for there was toots, and glass, and nough sunte that was

---

[115] CO 137/209, Sligo to Glenelg No. 315, 9 February 1836. Industry was sentenced to transportation, but was never transported. He spent years in prison before being released.
[116] For instance Moseley, *A Treatise on Sugar*, 172–3.
[117] CO 140/112, *Votes of the Assembly*, Appendix 61, p. 399.
[118] 'Trial for Practicing Obeah', *Liverpool Mercury*, 25 August 1825, in Album of Anti-Slavery News Cuttings, 1824–1826, Merseyside Maritime Museum D/CR/13, in *Slavery, Abolition and Social Justice* (online collection) (Marlborough: Adam Matthews Digital, 2007). For another discussion of this case see Murray, 'Three Worships'.

causing her illness'.[119] Then, according to another enslaved man who was present at the time, Marble 'put his mouth to [her] skin, held it hard, and shook it like a dog biting, and spit out some glass and teeth'. This is the earliest specific example I have found of a curative method that appears in a number of later obeah cases, in which a spiritual worker extracts objects from the body of a person in an effort to heal him or her. It echoes Benjamin Moseley's description from 1799: 'When the patient is nearly exhausted... OBI brings out an old rusty nail, or a piece of bone, or an ass's tooth, or the jaw-bone of a rat, or a fragment of a quart bottle, from the [affected body] part; and the patient is well the next day.'[120] Marble's attempt to heal Pamila was unsuccessful, as was that of the white doctor who attended her, and whose medicine she refused to take except when administered by Marble. Marble was prosecuted only after Pamila died, and was convicted of possessing obeah materials rather than of obeah itself. His case suggests the ambivalent role of ritual specialists on Caribbean plantations. He appears to have attempted to heal Pamila in good faith, and in his defence he stated that 'he was not an Obeah man to kill, but an Obeah man to cure', Nevertheless Pamila was convinced, according to several witnesses, that Marble's ritual practice was the original cause of her illness, and for that reason also believed that he was the only one who could make her well again.

Another Jamaican trial a few years later reveals a similar ambivalence in the practice of a ritual specialist. The most substantial evidence in the trial of Polydore came from an enslaved woman, Jane Henry, whose brother, Reid Bayley, was very sick: 'All what the Doctor could do was no use he was getting worse.' According to her testimony, she heard of the reputation of an elderly man, Polydore, who could 'give advice' and 'give bath', and went to him to ask him to help. Polydore told Jane that baths would not help her brother because 'he had [her] brother in a cotton tree' – that is, he had trapped Bayley's shadow (soul) in a tree, causing him to fall sick. A few months earlier, Polydore told her, a man named John Reeves had come to him asking him to attack Reid Bayley. He had done so through a ritual involving a cock and a pint of rum, with which he had successfully trapped her brother's shadow in the cotton tree behind her house. Now that Jane was there, Polydore was prepared to work to release her brother's shadow. At his request, she and two friends returned at midnight with a cock, two dollars, and a pint of rum. Polydore 'threw

---

[119] 'Toots' appears to mean 'tooths' (teeth). I am not sure what 'nough sunte' means. Deryck Murray, who has written about this case in detail, also states that he does not know the phrase's meaning. Ibid.
[120] Moseley, *A Treatise on Sugar*, 172.

Figure 3.1 'Negro Superstition': A representation by the British artist Richard Bridgens of a divination ritual in Trinidad. Bridgens does not describe the event depicted as obeah.
© The British Library Board, 789.g.13, plate 21

part of the rum on the cotton tree and took the rest to his house, held the live cock in his hand by [its] two legs and beat his head on the cotton tree until he killed it. The blood gushed onto the tree.' Back at his house, Polydore put chalk on their hands which he mixed with rum 'until it came like soap suds and then rubbed it on the dead cock'. He then told Jane and her companions that 'he had pulled her bro[ther] out of the cotton tree . . . that nothing would hurt her Brother and he would get better'.[121] When she returned to her estate, Jane Henry reported what had happened to the estate overseer, who, we must assume, brought the prosecution.

Polydore was both assumed cause and attempted healer of Reid Bayley's illness. In both this case and that of Andrew Marble the evidence

---

[121] CO 137/209, Sligo to Glenelg No. 315, 9 February 1836, enclosing notes from trial in St Dorothy Special Slave Court, 28 July 1831. For a longer summary of the case and some of the documents see Diana Paton and Gemma Romain, 'Polydore, Jamaica, 1831', www.obeahhistories.org/polydore.

that the men practised obeah was derived not from any efforts to hurt, but rather from their attempts to heal. Such cases tended to be subsumed in white representations by a larger sense that obeah practice was used to harm other enslaved people, when it was not being used in rebellion. These cases suggest a more complex ritual economy, however; not one in which we can straightforwardly say that ritual practitioners were working to protect, but rather one in which those with specialist knowledge were involved in healing and harming, working for whoever was prepared to pay them to do so. The term 'obeah' when used by enslaved people often carried a sense of threat or danger, as in Pamila's statement that she had been 'obeahed', but could also imply protection, as in Marble's claim to be an 'an Obeah man to cure'.

Andrew Marble's prosecution reveals something else important about obeah in this period. Despite its reputation as something that took place in secret and its identification with esoteric African knowledge, this case suggests that the arts that were increasingly described as obeah were well integrated into the daily life of plantations. Deryck Murray has analysed this case as an example of the division between European and African modes of knowledge in the slavery-era Caribbean.[122] Yet important elements of the evidence suggest the integration rather than the division of knowledge between white and black on the estate. Pamila complained to the overseer that she had been 'obeahed' by Marble, expecting that he would recognize and understand the complaint. Whittaker's initial response was not to contest Pamila's analysis, nor to prosecute Marble for obeah, but rather to ask Marble how he did it, and whether he could cure her. That is, he not only recognized Pamila's claim as serious, but attempted to make use of Marble's skills: he instructed Marble to heal Pamila, and even had him locked in the plantation stocks when he initially refused. The case thus suggests that the overseer had some regard for Marble's power and skill, and also that Marble saw his own knowledge as in certain respects equivalent to that of the white doctors. He reportedly treated Pamila for a while, but then refused to continue unless he was paid 'as other doctors'.

Other evidence also suggests that obeah could be part of a shared knowledge that crossed boundaries between enslaved and free, and to some extent black and white. In a Jamaican trial from 1789 in which two slaves were prosecuted for stealing money from their master, John Fry, a newspaper reported that Fry 'had exercised the art of Obeah on the slaves to compel a discovery'.[123] Similarly, in 1821 in Berbice an

---

[122] Murray, 'Three Worships'.
[123] *Diary or Woodfall's Register*, 7 September 1789 (Burney Collection).

enslaved woman complained that her mistress, a free woman of colour, made her 'drink a parcel of clay taken from Griffith's grave, and mixed with rum' in order to ascertain whether she was guilty of theft.[124] The divination technique, involving rum and grave dirt, was not in this case labelled obeah, but nevertheless involved elements that frequently were described with that term. In these cases slave-holders used methods of mobilizing spiritual power conventionally associated with enslaved people in order to maintain their power over slaves. While we know that Jenney's mistress was a woman of colour, it is not clear if Fry was black or white. Either way, all these cases suggest that techniques involving the use of spiritual power were part of the everyday culture of slave society, not part of a secret world of black knowledge.

Prosecutions also reveal the connectedness of enslaved people and those who managed plantations. Jane Henry reported her experience with Polydore to the manager of the estate, who brought the prosecution. Similarly, the prosecution of Industry relied on the willingness of several enslaved men and women to give evidence against the accused man. The court heard not only Bella's evidence, but also that of Ann Williams, who warned Bella about what had happened; William Smith, Bella's friend and probably her partner, who was lying down in her house at the time when Williams came to warn them of the event; and even the boy Richard Chambers, who admitted to placing the object in Bella's house, but apparently was not blamed for doing so. Andrew Marble's conviction also relied on the testimony of his fellow slaves. Obeah then, even during slavery, cannot be explained entirely in relation to resistance, rebellion, or even healing; it was also entangled in complex interpersonal relationships that could cross boundaries between slave and free. Perhaps it was this that the planter Thomas Roughley was objecting to when he wrote that a good overseer 'above all things... must not encourage the spirit of Obea' in slaves.[125] There was a conflict between everyday management of plantations, which accepted the reality of obeah or at least acknowledged its importance to enslaved people, and the kind of management advocated by the new style of 'progressive' planter, such as Roughley, who refused to give credence to belief in it.

Many of the cases involving harm seem to have arisen in the context of sexual coercion of women by men. This was part of the context in the case of Andrew Marble, where the overseer reported that Pamila had

---

[124] Complaint of Jenney against her Mistress, the Coloured woman Elizabeth Ann Sanders, alias Elizabeth Atkinson, 1 August 1821, *PP* 1825 (476) xxv, 45–6, also in Thompson, *Documentary History*, 158.
[125] Roughley, *The Jamaica Planter's Guide*, 41.

told him that Marble had initially 'obeahed' her because 'she would not be intimate with him'. In an 1831 prosecution that arose from events on Lloyds estate (the same estate where Industry was prosecuted), several people testified that Thomas House, who had been head driver, had threatened them or their wives with harm – presumably through spiritual techniques, although this was not stated explicitly in the evidence – if the women did not 'sleep with him'. One of the women, Sally Doman, said that House told her that 'if she would not consent to have him she would be rotten before she died'. As a result of these threats, Doman 'gave herself up to prisoner to save her life'. House also succeeded in getting another woman, Prue, to have 'connection' with him, although at least one other managed to resist his threats. His activities seem to have been directed towards dominating other men through domination of 'their' wives, as well as at dominating women. Prue's husband, William Morrison, testified that House said to him: 'go on boy I'll make you leave that woman and lay by the fire side', adding that 'if he don't do it he did not come out of Eboe woman's belly'.[126] The last statement suggests a sense of power associated with his mother's Igbo background, and provides an example of continuity of African ethnic identifications among Caribbean-born enslaved people.[127]

An incident that took place on Trouthall estate in Clarendon, Jamaica, brings together many of these themes, including sexual power, plantation conflict, and the integration and communication of knowledge tactics between plantation managers and enslaved people. It is worth exploring in some detail, not only because of what it reveals about planter policy towards obeah, but also because it is a rare example that gives us considerable insight into the interpretation of obeah within plantation communities. Over the summer of 1809 three children of one enslaved woman, Johannah, died. The deaths of George, Joe, and their unnamed sibling drew the attention of Trouthall's attorney, William Anderson. Anderson wrote about them in some detail in a letter to the estate's owner, James Chisholme, explaining that 'nothing will convince [their mother Johannah] or her family but that they were killed by Obeah'.[128]

---

[126] CO 137/209, Sligo to Glenelg No. 315.
[127] On the formation of Igbo as an identity in the context of the Atlantic slave trade see Byrd, *Captives and Voyagers*, esp. 17–31; Chambers, 'Tracing Igbo'.
[128] William Anderson to James Chisholme, 6 September 1809, NLS, Nisbet Papers, MS 5466. Except where otherwise noted all details about these events are from this source. For another discussion see Brown, 'Spiritual Terror and Sacred Authority'. James Chisholme was probably the same planter who collaborated with Edward Long and Stephen Fuller to present evidence to the parliamentary inquiry discussed in Chapter 2.

From Johannah's point of view – at least as reported by Anderson – the events revolved around her intimate relationships with men. Her husband, and the father of her three children, was a carpenter at Frankfield, a neighbouring estate. He had built Johanna a 'fine house'. About a year earlier, however, Johannah had been the recipient of the 'addresses' of Napier, the estate's second driver and boatswain, who tried to persuade her to leave the carpenter for him. Johannah refused him, but shortly afterwards her relationship with her husband came to an end. Apparently this was because of his jealousy when he heard about Napier's attentions to Johannah. Napier then assumed that he would now be able to establish a relationship with Johannah, but she was having none of it: indeed, 'she was more averse from the injury of losing her husband'.

After Johannah's second refusal of Napier, things turned nasty. We learn of this via Anderson's reports of what he was later told by Johannah, her mother, and brother. According to Anderson's letters, Napier began to threaten Johannah, telling her that he would 'do her bad', and in particular threatened her not to take 'any others but him' – that is, not to form any new relationship. Johannah had up to this point dealt with Napier on her own, but now went to the estate's head driver and complained. The head driver 'reprimanded [Napier] in her presence' and said that he would bring Napier to Anderson if the threats continued, but did not at this point inform Anderson of the conflict. This provides a small window into something that must have taken place very frequently on Caribbean plantations – enslaved people's use of informal structures of authority to deal with conflict, structures of authority that referred only indirectly to the white power structure.

At some point shortly after the encounter between Johannah, Napier, and the head driver, two of Johannah's children died. Anderson attributed the deaths to putrid sore throat, a common term for a range of infectious throat inflammations which often led to death. There were epidemics of putrid sore throat around the Atlantic world in the 1730s, and then intermittent outbreaks for the rest of the eighteenth century and into the nineteenth.[129] Anderson's letters suggest that one of these outbreaks took place in Jamaica in 1808–9. Johannah's two children were the 'first that had the disease in this vicinity', indicating that others later went on to experience it. Nevertheless, hers were the only children who died, making the explanation of putrid sore throat alone unsatisfying to her. Johannah, her brother Harry Brown, her mother, and apparently others on the estate attributed the children's deaths to the malevolent use of spiritual power, which they termed obeah. (As Anderson put it, 'nothing

---

[129] Landers, *Death and the Metropolis*, 240.

will convince her or her family but that they were killed by Obeah as none died but hers'.) It was this sorcery, which they believed Napier had initiated, that had caused the children to be the first ones hit by the epidemic, and to die as a result.

We have no record of how Johannah and her family initially responded to George and Joe's illness and death. She may well have consulted someone else who could manipulate the power of obeah in the hope of saving her children's lives, as did one of her Jamaican predecessors, Abba, who was enslaved to the infamous diarist Thomas Thistlewood. As noted above, Thistlewood recorded in 1780 that he had caught Will 'in Abba's house, at work with his Obiah'. Thistlewood claimed that Will had 'made [Abba] believe' –though Abba was probably not difficult to persuade – that another woman, Damsel, 'was the occasion of her children being sick & her miscarriage, etc.'. The implication was that Damsel had used obeah to cause this damage.[130] However, if Johannah, like Abba, attempted to use the power of obeah to combat spiritual assault, it was not fully effective. A few months later her third child became very ill.

Johannah now decided to act by going to the source of the problem. Echoing Pamila's actions in relation to Andrew Marble, she and her mother 'went to Napier to beg him for the child's life'. They did not, it seems, believe that Napier himself was an obeah practitioner, but rather that he had consulted someone who was, in order to harm Johannah and her children. It later emerged that Napier was rumoured to have made (in Anderson's words) 'visits in the night to a professor of that dread trade; an old hag', who had also reportedly come to Trouthall to do her work. Getting 'no satisfaction', Johannah's brother Harry Brown physically seized Napier and said he would bring him to Anderson. To prevent this happening, Napier promised to 'clear the yard of what was doing the mischief', and Brown released him in order to allow him to do so. This is a second occasion in which conflict was dealt with amongst enslaved people, using the threat of white authority but not actually involving the white plantation hierarchy. Anderson later interpreted Napier's statement as a confession that he had previously acted to spiritually assault Johannah and her family. Anderson interpreted 'clearing the yard' to mean physically removing the spiritually powerful assemblage of materials that had been previously placed there in order to cause harm: assemblages described in other sources, such as the case of Industry, as buried in the ground over which people would walk, or inserted into the fabric of their houses, and including grave dirt, feathers, egg shells, and so on.[131]

---

[130] Hall, *In Miserable Slavery*, 279; see also Burnard, *Mastery, Tyranny, and Desire*, 224.
[131] For cases involving the use of egg shells, see case of Winter, 1776, in Hill, *Light and Shadows*, 148, quoting Extracts from the Trial Book of Slaves, kept at the Vestry Office

This may well have been what Napier meant, but he may also have been using the term 'clearing' as it was later used by myalists in the 1840s and followers of Revival Zion in the twentieth century, where it referred to a ritual practice for the eradication of evil.[132]

Whatever his specific meaning, Napier did not fulfil his promise immediately, but instead left the estate the next morning, prompting Johannah, Harry Brown, and their mother to seek out Anderson. It is only at this point that they informed Anderson what had taken place. Napier was caught the next day when he returned to visit 'a girl that had some of his clothes', and was locked up on the estate. Anderson kept him confined for three months and also 'punished' him in ways that he did not explain, probably implying physical violence. After this, Napier was sent back to work, although probably not as a driver.[133] Anderson's letter provides no further information about any later interactions between Napier and Johannah, but Johannah's third child seems to have died after Napier was locked up. This suggests that, from Johannah's point of view, Napier's incarceration did little to help her: the obeah he had mobilized against her continued to work. In the longer term, many questions remain. Did Johannah find a more powerful spiritual worker who helped her to repel Napier's attacks? Did the two come to some kind of grudging accommodation? Did Napier continue to use (or be suspected of using) obeah as a means of sexual predation and violence?

The answers to those questions are almost certainly unknowable, but it is worth noting that Napier's hostility towards Johannah was not the first time that he had used threats of spiritual assault against those with whom he was in conflict. Anderson reported that the previous year Napier had successfully broken up another couple, London and his wife, and 'got hold of' the (unnamed) woman. According to London's complaint to Anderson, Napier had 'threatened him [London] almost the same words he did Johanna' when he saw London watching the newly formed couple.

Our ability to see only what the enslaved people on the estate allowed Anderson to know, or in the case of Thomas House, the testimony given in court, limits our understanding of the many aspects of these encounters that were surely kept hidden from Anderson and from the court. Nevertheless, both Napier and House could be understood as examples of a substantial group in hyper-masculine plantation slave societies such as Jamaica: men with some authority who used threats of harm – spiritual or otherwise – to maintain sexual dominance over women and to displace

---

at Morant Bay, Jamaica; case of George Kerr, 1822, JA 1A/2/1/1 Hanover Slave Court, Hanover Courts Office, Lucea.

[132] Stewart, *Three Eyes*, 182, 284n130; Besson, *Martha Brae's Two Histories*, 243.
[133] Anderson to Chisholme, 8 February 1810, NLS, Nisbet Papers, MS 5466.

the power of other men. This is a category that includes slave-holders and also some enslaved men. As Trevor Burnard notes, the relationship between slave-owners and male slaves could be one of 'two men within the same patriarchal social order, albeit in different positions within that order'.[134] Napier's actions, however, went too far, disrupting his subordinate position within this patriarchal framework. It was this disruption to the expected sex–race hierarchy of everyday life that Anderson and, back in the metropolis, Chisholme, found distressing.

Chisholme, Anderson, and white Jamaican men like them did not object to men intruding into stable relationships between enslaved men and women, so long as those other men were white. Frequent letters from the late 1790s and early 1800s record Chisholme's encouragement of relationships between white men and black women. He agreed to manumit several 'mulatto' and 'quadroon' children and buy 'New Negro' replacements for them. He even congratulated the previous attorney, James Craggs, on his sexual prowess. 'I will send you a manumission for the mulatto child Fanny, the daughter of Feany's Sarah', he wrote in 1796, adding that he 'rejoice[d] my old friend to find, you have still so much young blood about you'.[135] While we lack detailed information about the relationships that led to the births of these children, it is likely that at least some of them involved the breaking up of other relationships very much in the way that Napier attempted. The difference was that the white personnel on the estate would not have needed to invoke spiritual threats in order to establish their dominance, as they had more access to mundane means of achieving their goals.

Anderson did not prosecute Napier through the formal courts, explaining that although he would have liked to 'ma[k]e an example (much wanted)' of Napier, he could not do so because of the temporary lack of appropriate law due to the disallowance of the 1808 Consolidated Slave Law.[136] If he had brought Napier to trial, the records produced by the case would probably have been similar to those produced by the prosecutions of Industry and Thomas House, individuals who used their

---

[134] Burnard, *Mastery, Tyranny, and Desire*, 204. For another analysis of sexual and domestic violence committed by enslaved men against enslaved women see Browne, 'Slavery and the Politics of Marriage'.

[135] Chisholme to James Craggs, 31 December 1796, NLS, Nisbet Papers, Letterbook of James Chisholme, MS 5476.

[136] The 1801 Consolidated Slave Law expired at the end of 1807, and had been replaced by a similar law, passed in 1808. However, the king disallowed this Act in April 1809 because of its anti-missionary provisions. A new law, without the offending clause, was passed in December 1809 and approved, but still in February 1810 Anderson was complaining that 'still there is no law to try slaves by, till those at last sessions are published'. Anderson to Chisholme, 8 February 1810, NLS, Nisbet Papers, MS 5466.

own or others' esoteric knowledge to harm others, although sometimes in complex situations in which they might also undo the damage they had done.

The evidence about obeah prosecutions during slavery as a whole, then, suggests that they took place in one of two types of situations. The first was in reaction to rebellion or other forms of oppositional activity such as running away. The second involved events like those in the cases of Thomas House, Industry, or Polydore, in which the person prosecuted was alleged to have harmed another enslaved person. Planters also felt themselves to have been damaged in these circumstances by the loss of production entailed in the death or illness of enslaved people, and the disruption to the smooth running of the estate produced by anxiety about obeah. But the details of these cases, which frequently arose out of reports by one enslaved person to overseers and other plantation managers of the alleged destructive activity of other slaves, suggests that they were often driven by conflict among enslaved people rather than by the agendas of plantation managers. That is, overseers were willingly drawn into conflicts, taking sides with one group or individual in order to maintain as much stability as they could.

Descriptive rather than legal sources, the later history of the use of spiritual power in the Caribbean, and our knowledge of analogous practices in other societies all suggest that these two types of circumstances – involving rebellion on the one hand, harm on the other – cannot have been the only ways in which enslaved people made use of spiritual power in the early nineteenth-century Caribbean. In Berbice in 1824 the role of Mamadoe as a 'sort of doctor' who prescribed herbal cures in a ritual only came to light when Mamadoe was killed and his suspected murderer was thought to be the husband of a woman who he had failed to cure.[137] John Stewart, while foregrounding the 'evil' and 'wicked' nature of obeah, admitted that it could also be used as a 'guard or watch' in provision grounds, 'scaring away the predatory runaway and midnight plunderer'.[138] The novel *The Koromantyn Slaves* (1823) gave a similarly

---

[137] Investigation into the probable circumstances of the death of the Negro Mamadoe, 8 November 1824, in CO 116/140, 'Berbice: Complaints of Slaves made to the Fiscal commencing 26 October 1824 to 7 January 1825'. For discussion of Mamadoe's murder see Browne, 'The "Bad Business" of Obeah', 476. Browne writes that Rhina, Mamadoe's suspected killer, said that in his country 'the way they treat Obiah man is to kill them', implying that Rhina considered Mamadoe to be an obeah practitioner. In fact this phrase appears in the testimony of the attorney, Duncan Fraser. No direct testimony from Rhina is included in the evidence, but another enslaved man reported that he threatened to treat Mamadoe as 'dirty people' were dealt with in his 'own country' (Kongo). 'Obeah men' appears to be Fraser's explanation of 'dirty people'.

[138] Stewart, *A View of the Past and Present State of the Island of Jamaica*, 276–9.

extensive list of reasons for which obeah practitioners might be consulted: 'for the cure of disorders, the obtaining of revenge for real or supposed injuries, the conciliating of favour, the discovery and punishment of misdemeanours or crimes, or the prediction of future events'.[139] Writing of Dominica, Thomas Atwood described how enslaved people there consulted 'Obeah men and women' for 'for spells and charms against sickness, to prevent their being robbed, or to find out the thief, and to punish those who do them any injury'.[140] Neither planters nor the slavery-era state was interested in prosecuting such uses of obeah, which in some circumstances could facilitate the maintenance of order within slavery. Obeah was not a problem worthy of risking the removal of slaves via transportation or the death penalty, except when it disrupted the productivity of the plantation system.[141]

Over the course of the nineteenth century, as more and more colonies passed laws against obeah, and consolidated them through prosecutions, obeah law became a significant area for the expression of colonial difference. The Caribbean colonies had laws prohibiting actions that in England were not illegal, just as they had laws that enshrined a system of social and labour relations – slavery – that was not protected under English law. In English law, putting 'something' in the fabric of someone's house with malicious intent, as Richard Chambers was reported to have done in the trial of Industry, might have been construed as trespass, but it could not be a serious crime, punishable with the death penalty. However much slave-holders emphasized that African slaves believed in obeah while they themselves did not, colonial law worked on the assumption that obeah did exist and could cause harm. Indeed, as the existence of slavery itself became increasingly controversial, this difference between English and colonial law became an angle from which anti-slavery activists, and to some extent representatives of the imperial state, attacked the planter class. This argument was employed in the first years of the nineteenth century by William Fullarton in Trinidad, who argued that Picton was wrong to establish the poisoning commissions. 'Pretended sorcerers', he argued, should not be harshly punished, but instead should be subjected 'to those punishments which may render them objects of ridicule and contempt among their companions'.[142] William Wilberforce criticized Caribbean legal approaches to obeah from a similar perspective in an 1823 pamphlet. 'The idea of rooting out any form of pagan superstition

---

[139] *The Koromantyn Slaves*, 177.   [140] Atwood, *History of Dominica*, 270.
[141] For the argument that obeah was 'used primarily to regulate relationships among the slaves' and was therefore met by whites with 'uneasy tolerance' see Turner, *Slaves and Missionaries*, 57.
[142] CO 295/15, Fullarton to Windham, 22 July 1806.

by severity of punishment', he wrote, 'has long been exploded among the well-informed.' He even claimed that such laws were counterproductive, asserting confidently that 'it has been established that the devilish engine of persecution recoils back on its employers, and disseminates the very principles it would suppress'.[143] By the early 1830s, as the abolition of slavery became increasingly likely, colonial policy turned against prosecutions for obeah. Anti-obeah provisions in slave law did not lead the Colonial Office to refuse assent to those laws – in contrast to, for instance, provisions that limited the possibility of missionary work among enslaved people.[144] But when asked to affirm severe punishments for obeah, such as transportation, the Colonial Office began to refuse. Thus, when details of the Jamaican cases of Thomas House, Industry, and Polydore were sent to England for confirmation of the punishment of transportation, the colonial secretary responded that the three men should be released. The reasons given were specific to each case, but included a general argument against such punishments. Advocating 'religious instruction' rather than prosecution as a solution to obeah, the response argued against transportation as a penalty for obeah on the grounds that 'To vulgar apprehension it will probably appear that the Rules of the country participate in the feelings of the multitude respecting an offence to the commission of which so grave a penalty as transportation for life is attached'.[145] This analysis positioned the colonial elite as backward by its association with obeah, just as it was backward because of its complicity in slavery.

The colonists attempted to rebut such claims as part of their wider intervention into the slavery debates. One of the most forceful was Alexander Barclay, a Jamaican planter and Assembly member. Barclay justified the laws against obeah on the grounds that it was 'calculated to put an end to the most fatal and destructive of [enslaved people's] superstitions' and argued that obeah was dying out anyway, under the pressure of the 'influence of Christianity' and creolization.[146] Such arguments were weakened as defences of the planter class by the fact that planters had opposed both the introduction of Christianity via missionaries and the end of the slave trade, and by the evidence of continuing prosecutions for obeah in the colonies.

And yet, at the same time as planters defended the obeah laws, the application of such laws was beginning to change. As this chapter has shown, prosecutions for obeah had been directed at enslaved people

---

[143] Wilberforce, *An Appeal*, 29.
[144] For disallowance of anti-missionary laws see Turner, *Slaves and Missionaries*, 120–2.
[145] CO 138/59, Glenelg to Sligo No. 249, 12 April 1836.
[146] Barclay, *A Practical View*, 190–1.

whose practice either involved rebellion or harm of another individual. The range of activities described as obeah by other sources, such as interventions to protect health, cure illness, ward off theft and other forms of harm, were not targeted by the law. In 1833, however, between the passage of the Abolition Act and the actual abolition of slavery, a new kind of obeah case took place in Grenada. This was a case that would find many echoes in the post-emancipation world. Directed not against a slave but against an elderly free African man, the evidence against Pierre consisted purely of accounts of his spiritual healing practice. Although a plantation attorney claimed that the 'negroes' on his estates were acutely frightened of the 'supernatural powers' that Pierre 'had long pretended to and practiced', the witnesses who testified in court reported visiting Pierre for treatment for their own illnesses and those of their children. Pierre's medical practice is described in detail in the witnesses' accounts. Like Andrew Marble he removed objects from the bodies of patients, including frogs, fish bones, and scorpions. He also prescribed and dispensed mixtures including spiritually powerful material such as scrapings from alligator's teeth and stag's horns along with rum, honey, and water to others to drink. In court, Pierre denied that he was an obeah practitioner, and instead stated that he could not have 'done what he has done without assistance of good spirits ... that God gives him the sense to do what he has done'.[147]

The prosecution of Pierre, despite the fact that no evidence was presented that claimed that his spiritual practice involved harm or rebellion, was a novel form of regulation. As subsequent chapters will show, it was one that would take hold with force in the years after slavery. These new prosecutions attempted to use law to stigmatize African-oriented ritual healing practices and to brand them criminal, whatever purpose they were directed towards. A new means of racializing the population was taking hold. During slavery, such measures were not considered necessary, but now, with the threatening erasure of racial distinctions, Caribbean elites reached for clearer boundaries of respectability and legitimacy.

[147] CO 101/78, Smith to Stanley No. 5, 6 March 1834.

# 4 Obeah and its meanings in the post-emancipation era

The English historian James Anthony Froude's account of his visit to the Caribbean left a lasting impression on the British public. In *The English in the West Indies*, published in 1888, half a century after the abolition of slavery, Froude presented repeated anecdotes illustrating the 'superstition' of Caribbean people. Describing the large cotton tree in Port of Spain, Froude informed his reader that 'the ceiba is the sacred tree of the Negro, the temple of Jumbi the proper home of Obeah', inviting English readers to marvel at the foolishness which meant that Caribbean people were reluctant to cut down such trees.[1] The larger purpose of Froude's book was to make the case for continuing British authoritarian rule of the Caribbean colonies. The region's people were insufficiently civilized to govern themselves, Froude claimed: 'left entirely to themselves, they would in a generation or two relapse into savages'.[2] Froude's words suggest the political significance of obeah in the late nineteenth century. It had become entwined with a complex debate about Caribbean modernity, civilization, political rights, and the region's connection to Africa.

The most amplified voices in this debate were those of people like Froude, who described the region in racialized terms as backward, uncivilized, and primitive. Froude claimed that Caribbean people were drawn to obeah, and presented this as a sign of their primitiveness and lack of political capacity. But he was contested by a series of writers and activists who sought to speak back to such claims. Most prominent among them was the black Trinidadian intellectual and political reformer John Jacob Thomas of Trinidad, who published a scathing critique of Froude, *Froudacity*, in 1889.[3] Like contemporaries in Haiti, Thomas aimed to demonstrate that the region and its people were in fact modern, and did indeed deserve political rights. As I will show later in this chapter, in order to make this case, Thomas denied the significance of obeah in Caribbean life. Since obeah had come to symbolize Africa in the Caribbean, denying

[1] Froude, *The English in the West Indies*, 61.
[2] Ibid., 50.   [3] Thomas, *Froudacity*.

its significance also meant distancing the region from its African connections. The ironic effect was to reinforce European cultural hegemony even while contesting white political rule.

This late nineteenth-century debate stands at considerable distance, both chronological and conceptual, from the debates and judicial practices of the late slavery period discussed in the previous chapter. Politically, it set the scene for a substantial expansion and harshening of obeah law in the 1890s and the first decade of the twentieth century across most of the Caribbean region, and for the acceptance rather than questioning of those legal changes by the British government. This was a significant shift from the role of obeah in law and discourse in the late slavery and early post-emancipation period, when the Colonial Office had criticized obeah prosecutions.

This chapter investigates legal and political changes in relation to obeah from the end of slavery to the adoption of the Leeward Islands Obeah Act of 1904. It first explains obeah's legal status in the immediate aftermath of slavery, and the shifts that began to take place in the 1850s, when colonial administrators across the region and in Britain debated the correct response to obeah. In this period colonial authorities and missionaries hoped and expected that Caribbean populations would choose to adopt British cultural mores. Emancipation was understood by many in both Britain and the Caribbean as a politically freighted test or, in Seymour Drescher's terms, a 'Mighty Experiment'.[4] The outcome of that experiment – not just economic, but also cultural and political – became a litmus test regarding race, in which obeah played a significant role. Would obeah, as missionaries and abolitionists had predicted during slavery, wither away once former slaves were free to choose to adopt British culture and Christianity? In this context colonies such as Jamaica and British Guiana that adopted specific laws targeting obeah were on the margins of the debate, and had to justify their practice to a Colonial Office whose personnel often disapproved of such laws.

The second half of the nineteenth century saw a significant shift in such evaluations of the Caribbean's possibilities. The Morant Bay Rebellion in Jamaica in 1865 symbolized for many the failure of the post-emancipation settlement, but it in fact took place in an already established atmosphere of racial hostility and a sense that Caribbean populations would not, after all, become just like Britons.[5] This conclusion led many in Britain to believe that the Mighty Experiment of emancipation had failed. The shift can already be seen in works like Charles Kingsley's *At Last* of

---

[4] Drescher, *The Mighty Experiment*.
[5] Heuman, *'The Killing Time'*; Kostal, *A Jurisprudence of Power*.

1871, but was encapsulated most prominently in Froude's *The English in the West Indies* and the debate in response to it.[6] The second part of the chapter thus attends in detail to Froude and his respondents, examining how obeah functioned in these texts. It focuses in particular on how the debate used claims about obeah to position Britain's Caribbean colonies in relation to Haiti. For people writing and thinking about the Anglo-Creole Caribbean, Haiti became a repeated and immediate point of comparison. The 'black republic' became a powerful symbol of racial atavism, with its religious practices, labelled 'voodoo', singled out for attack. Many, including Froude, presented the British colonies as similar to Haiti or in danger of becoming so, sometimes with the proviso that all that prevented the one becoming the other was the strict enforcement of laws against obeah. On the other hand, defenders of the British colonies could and did argue that the comparison was slanderous, emphasizing the difference between their own societies and Haiti. This position accepted the premise that obeah was like 'voodoo', and was equally hostile to both, but denied the significance of obeah or, more generally, of African-oriented religion in the Caribbean.

The debate sparked by Froude's book set the stage for a new round of legislation in the 1890s and early 1900s, in which singling out obeah for legislative action became the preferred response of colonial governments, approved by the British Colonial Office. The chapter also examines this legislation and the arguments that surrounded it, arguing that as well as the post-Morant Bay debate about race, the concurrent expansion of British colonial rule in Africa and the encounter with 'witchcraft' there provided another important context in which the Caribbean's ruling groups made sense of and responded to obeah.

For the majority of the population these debates about legal responses to obeah were distant, if not irrelevant. The chapter also examines, as far as is possible, popular views and experiences of spiritual power, authority, and danger in the second half of the nineteenth century. It addresses this through a reconsideration of the many African-oriented religious movements of the period, which sought to use spiritual weapons to combat spiritual threats. For some of those involved, what they were doing was combating obeah, but in a very different way to that envisaged by the law and by those involved in the debate set off by Froude. Ironically, popular attempts to defeat obeah were themselves incorporated into official definitions of obeah, and became vulnerable to prosecution.

In most colonies the end of slavery meant that laws against obeah, along with a host of other statutes, lapsed. Anti-obeah provisions had been

[6] Kingsley, *At Last*.

largely incorporated into slave codes or in laws that referred specifically to slaves. Once this category of persons no longer existed, the laws made to govern them no longer had meaning. The early post-emancipation period was thus a time of intensive law making, as colonial legislatures sought to find new ways to control the people who had once been slaves.[7]

As Jerome Handler and Kenneth Bilby have explained, anti-obeah provisions were in many colonies incorporated into new Vagrancy Acts, intended to replace controls that had been enacted through the private power of the planter with the judicial authority of the state.[8] The earliest of these were passed in Jamaica in 1833 and Antigua in 1834, in anticipation of the abolition of slavery. Establishing a trend that other colonies would follow, these laws were modelled on the 1824 English Vagrancy Act. They inserted the term 'obeah' into a clause from the English Act that defined 'rogues and vagabonds' to include 'persons pretending or professing to tell fortunes, or using any subtle craft, means, or device, by palmistry or otherwise, to deceive and impose'.[9] Where obeah during slavery had usually been a capital offence, as part of vagrancy it was a low-level crime tried in magistrates' courts. Jamaica's 1833 law, which was disallowed by the Colonial Office in 1836 for being too vague and too harsh, made being a 'rogue and vagabond' – including obeah – punishable with up to six months' imprisonment, or two years and flogging for a second offence under the act.[10] Antigua imposed a punishment of three months' imprisonment.[11] In 1838 a Colonial Office circular to all colonies proposed that they adopt vagrancy laws modelled on England's 1824 Act, but with the addition of providing a punishment of twenty-eight days' imprisonment for obeah.[12] Such laws were adopted in the decade after 1838 in Trinidad, the Bahamas, Barbados, Dominica, Jamaica, and St Kitts and Nevis (which also included Anguilla).[13] They demonstrate

[7] This was true for many areas of legislation, not just the laws respecting obeah. See Paton, *No Bond But the Law*.
[8] Handler and Bilby, *Enacting Power*, 42–4.
[9] For discussion of the anti-fortune-telling provisions of the 1824 English Vagrancy Act (5 Geo. IV, c 83) see Perkins, *The Reform of Time*, 41–3; Davies, *Witchcraft, Magic and Culture*, 54.
[10] An Act to Restrain and Punish Vagrancy, *PP* 1836 (166-I) xlviii, 244–7, clauses 3, 4, 6, and 9. For its disallowal see CO 138/59, Glenelg to Sligo No. 250, 13 April 1836. See also Handler and Bilby, *Enacting Power*, 48. Handler and Bilby report the penalty under this Act as 'one to three months in jail with hard labor', overlooking clause 9 which allows for longer sentences and flogging.
[11] Handler and Bilby, *Enacting Power*, 72.
[12] Order in Council on Vagrancy (enclosure 2), 7 September 1838, enclosed in Lord Glenelg to the Governors of British Guiana, Trinidad, and St Lucia, and Mauritius, 15 September 1838, Papers Relative to the West Indies. Part I. Circular Instructions, Jamaica and British Guiana, *PP* 1839 (107-I) xxv, 4–13 (page images 10–19).
[13] Handler and Bilby, *Enacting Power*, 50, 56, 58, 66–7, 76, 83.

that imperial officials in London and elites in the Caribbean continued to think of obeah as a problem, but a relatively minor one, which did not require legislation on its own terms or severe punishments. Incorporating 'obeah' into a list of other activities was a relatively low-key and liberal approach, characteristic of an early post-emancipation policy that focused primarily on missionaries and education, rather than law, as the means to transform popular religious belief and practice. As an Antiguan stipendiary magistrate explained, the death penalty was not an appropriate punishment for obeah because it 'only confirmed [the majority of the population] in their belief that supernatural powers were really possessed by [those convicted], of which they could be only deprived by death'. The present law, though, was difficult to obtain convictions under, because potential witnesses feared supernatural retribution. He concluded that 'education alone therefore would seem to be the means peculiarly fitted for the improvement of the Negroes in this as in many other respects'.[14]

In a few colonies this policy was already being questioned by the 1850s. First to change the law was Antigua, which amended its Vagrancy Act in 1851, extending the punishment for obeah to a maximum of one year's imprisonment, and also added the punishments of flogging for men and solitary confinement for women. The preamble to the Act complained that the three-month punishment for obeah in effect since 1834 had been 'quite inadequate to repress the Commission of the said Offences', and stated that 'notwithstanding the general advance of civilization and the spread of religious knowledge and education [these crimes] are unhappily greatly on the increase, to the demoralization of the lower classes'.[15] Within the next five years the legislatures of Jamaica and British Guiana passed laws dealing specifically with obeah.[16] These laws singled out obeah (and, in Jamaica, myalism) as the subject of legislation, extended the maximum period of imprisonment for practising it to a year, and introduced flogging as a punishment. The Guyanese act also made consulting an obeah practitioner a criminal offence. This was an important extension of the scope of the law, which had previously only penalized those who themselves undertook ritual activity.

Those advocating distinctive laws and flogging made the apparently common-sense argument that, since obeah was a problem, the solution was criminalization and corporal punishment. In St Vincent the attorney

[14] William Walker to Major John MacPhail, 24 July 1841, enclosed in CO 7/68, MacPhail to Russell, 26 August 1841.
[15] CO 8/28 ff. 110–12, 'An Act... having reference to the punishment of persons pretending to be dealers in Obeah', Antigua 1851. See also Handler and Bilby, *Enacting Power*, 72–3.
[16] Handler and Bilby, *Enacting Power*, 50–1, 62.

general noted that the change in the law resulting in the criminalization of 'occult practices' in 1854 had 'been loudly called for by the most injurious results of late years in this colony resulting from Obeah and other like practices'. He assumed without needing to explain that increased punishment would lead to the diminution of these 'injurious results'.[17]

Calls for stricter and specific obeah laws were not limited to a plantocratic elite. In British Guiana the governor stated that the new law was desired by 'persons of all classes, clergy, magistrates and planters, without distinction'.[18] While the governor's understanding of 'all classes' was undoubtedly not inclusive of all Guyanese, his claim does suggest that there was a relatively broad consensus among the middle class as well as planters in support of it. In Jamaica the Obeah Act was proposed by John Castello, a brown newspaper proprietor and member of the Town Party, which represented the interests of urban merchants and coloured people rather than whites and planters.[19] Castello's law was passed after several years during which his newspaper, the *Falmouth Post*, had joined with other papers to argue for flogging as a punishment for obeah as well as for certain other crimes.[20] Some Jamaican judges and juries had also argued for a change in the law for some time, and it was passed unopposed by the Jamaican House of Assembly and Council.[21] In both colonies, then, the call for harsher punishments encompassed or was even led by middle-class groups that considered themselves liberal or progressive in the context of Caribbean society.

Arguments for the reinvigoration of the obeah laws frequently linked obeah to other allegedly negative characteristics of the Caribbean population, which, through repeated discussion, became discursively associated with one another. These shortcomings frequently included the absence of patriarchal family life, especially the prevalence of non-marital unions

[17] CO 260/81, Report of Attorney General of St Vincent, enclosed in Colebrook to Grey No. 66, 28 September 1854. The governor of Antigua made similar assumptions. See CO 7/98, Mackintosh to Grey, 5 April 1851.
[18] CO 111/304, Wodehouse to Grey No. 15, 24 January 1855. For further discussion of the 1855 Guyanese law see Moore, *Cultural Power*, 145–7.
[19] CO 137/331, Barkly to Labouchere No. 52, 9 April 1856. On the Town Party see Heuman, *Between Black and White*, esp. 136–52; Holt, *The Problem of Freedom*, 218–23.
[20] For instance, 'Middlesex Assizes', *Colonial Standard*, 25 February 1850; 'Dealers in Obeah', *Falmouth Post* (henceforth *FP*), 7 June 1850; 'Obeahism, and the depravity of our peasantry', *FP*, 13 September 1850; 'Subjects for the Consideration of the Legislature', *FP*, 18 February 1851.
[21] For instance, comments of Judge Roberts at Hanover Quarter Sessions, as reported in *FP*, 14 May 1850; statement of Grand Jury at Cornwall Assize Court as reported in *FP*, 16 July 1850; comments of Judge Farquharson at St Ann's Quarter Sessions, as reported in *FP*, 15 July 1851; statement of Grand Jury at Surrey Assizes, as reported in *FP*, 12 August 1853. CO 137/331, Barkly to Labouchere No. 52, 9 April 1856.

and 'illegitimate' children, and the population's 'idleness', that is, people's reluctance to engage in waged plantation work. As Castello's *Falmouth Post* put it, describing the Jamaican parish of Hanover:

> It appears that there is not a resident Clergyman... that the people live in great fear of 'Obea' – and that superstition prevails to such an extent, as to be truly alarming. The males work upon the ignorant minds of the females – adultery and concubinage are freely indulged in – wives are deserted, and characterless wretches supply their places – and vice of every description, is rampant.[22]

As would become increasingly common over the course of the nineteenth century, obeah was here connected to gender disorder, each 'problem' apparently reinforcing the other and, in the minds of middle-class observers such as Castello, moving the population away from the standards of 'civilization'.

Despite the forcefulness with which arguments for harsh obeah laws were expressed, and their dominance in Jamaica and British Guiana, in this period an alternative view was in the ascendant as official British colonial policy. Successive colonial secretaries supported what came to be understood as a Barbadian model: the tactic of restraining obeah only through vagrancy legislation, and enforcing this relatively lightly. Barbadian opposition to new obeah laws was most powerfully expressed by William Colebrooke, the governor of Barbados and the Windward Islands from 1848 to 1856. In Barbados the anti-obeah laws of the slavery era had been repealed in 1842 and the anti-obeah provisions of the vagrancy law of 1840 seem not to have been enforced. Colebrooke, who it seems did not realize that the 1840 law prohibited obeah, claimed in 1854 that in Barbados 'such offences' were punished under 'Laws which contain no express allusion to that superstition [i.e. obeah]', and went so far as to argue that this had led to the 'entire extinction of the practice of Obeah in this populous island'; indeed, that 'with the present generation all knowledge of its former existence has been lost'.[23] Colebrooke made these comments in the course of explaining his refusal of assent to a new Vincentian law in 1854 that singled out obeah as a crime. After several months during which it resisted Colebrooke's advice, the St Vincent legislature eventually agreed to remove the explicit reference to obeah, but retained the punishment of flogging and up to a year's imprisonment for the crime of 'palmistry... any subtle craft or occult science'.[24] Since by

---

[22] 'Practice of Obeah in the parish of Hanover', *FP*, 26 April 1850.
[23] CO 260/81, Colebrooke to McDonell, 28 February 1854, enclosed in Colebrook to Grey No. 66, 28 September 1854.
[24] CO 260/81, Colebrook to Grey No. 66, 28 September 1854; for the text of the Act see CO 262/16, ff. 504–21. See also Handler and Bilby, *Enacting Power*, 93.

then it was widely known that the law was intended for the purpose of prosecuting obeah practitioners, it seems unlikely that this change had much effect. Colebrooke also wrote directly to the governor of the Leeward Islands, advocating that that colony adopt the Barbadian policy.[25] The Colonial Office was persuaded of his view, and circulated his advice to other governors in the region. Colonial Office officials also criticized Jamaica's Obeah and Myalism Act on the grounds that 'practices having no foundation except in abject credulity are rather apt to gain strength than to lose it when they are severely treated as the objects of special and severe legislation'.[26]

As this comment suggests, the main argument against harsher punishments for obeah was that they led to its persistence rather than its eradication. Thomas Witter Jackson, a brown Jamaican stipendiary magistrate, submitted a lengthy critique of Jamaica's 1856 obeah law, arguing that it 'conjured up and revived the terrors of those idolatries so destructively felt in the days of slavery, but which were happily fast disappearing from among us'. Acknowledging that 'belief in obeah and the superstitious practices this gives rise to are evils', he described them as 'diseases of the mind' which should not be punished by either imprisonment or the whip. Instead, Jackson proposed moral instruction, combined with ridicule: 'The most appropriate and efficacious punishment would be to put a fools cap on his head and expose him, in the market place, to the ridicule of children.' The law, he suggested, led to false accusations and also reinforced the belief in obeah among those who witnessed the trials.[27] Jamaica's attorney general similarly, but unsuccessfully, opposed the increasing reach and severity of obeah legislation, arguing that it 'extended and elevated... the superstition... to higher ranks of society than it was wont to soar at when treated with comparative contempt'. He also emphasized that 'superstition' was not confined to the Caribbean, pointing to the recent British case of James Tunnicliff, a 'cunning man' whose trial for fraudulently obtaining money in the course of treating someone who believed himself to be bewitched had recently attracted extensive publicity.[28] William Colebrooke also referred to British

---

[25] CO 260/81, Colebroke to Grey No. 81, 8 December 1854, enclosing Colebrooke to the Governor of the Leeward Islands, 25 November 1854.

[26] Letters from Colonial Office to governors of Trinidad, British Guiana, Bahamas, and Jamaica, 15 January 1855, filed with CO 260/81, Colebrooke to Grey No. 81, 8 December 1854. Criticism of the Jamaican Act is in CO 138/71, Lytton to Darling No. 4, 15 June 1858.

[27] T. Witter Jackson, Report on St Thomas in the Vale, 6 August 1857, enclosed in CO 137/366, Darling to Labouchere No. 47, 19 March 1858.

[28] CO 137/336, Darling to Stanley No. 49, 26 March 1858. On the Tunnicliff case see Davies, *Murder, Magic, Madness*, 30–1.

practice, arguing that Caribbean law should, like British law, allow for prosecutions for fraud but should not single out obeah by name. These men thus advocated an approach to Caribbean ritual spiritual practice that was, at least explicitly, non-racial.

This debate ended without the adoption of a uniform legal response to obeah across the region. In Antigua the legislature at least partially accepted Colebrooke's advice, and in 1857 returned to the situation that had existed prior to the passage of its 1851 law, that is, with obeah, along with fortune telling and palmistry, punishable by three months' imprisonment.[29] On the other hand, the governments of British Guiana and Jamaica both resisted pressure to revise their laws. The difference in policy was justified by the fact that Jamaica and British Guiana were, they claimed, less civilized and more African than Barbados. Henry Barkly, governor of Jamaica, contrasted Barbados and Jamaica in order to justify his consent to the 1856 Obeah Act. Playing down obeah might be appropriate in the former, he claimed, because African influence was there dying out due to education and supervision of the population. Things were different in the 'mountain fastnesses' of Jamaica, however, 'where the face of a white man is often not seen from one year's end to another'. In addition to the influence of the Maroons, 'who retain the language and customs of their African ancestors', Barkly suggested that the arrival of indentured 'liberated Africans' had 'revive[d] and perpetuate[d] the belief in obeah, which . . . is as universal now as it was during slavery'.[30] A missionary in British Guiana also argued that the influx of new Africans after the end of slavery was increasing the prevalence of 'heathenish and wicked practices' or 'Congfou', which he translated as 'wizards or obeah'.[31] These discussions thus secured the connection between Africa, obeah, and 'backwardness'.

The participants in these debates understood themselves to have very different points of view, but shared more than they disagreed about. The entire discussion was framed within a discursive field in which all involved assumed that the goal of policy was to end belief in and practice of obeah, and all thought that the acts defined by obeah laws as criminal should be punishable. Participants presented alternative views on how to govern popular religion, which nevertheless aimed for the same endpoint. The Barbadian path was one of hegemony and governmentality, in circumstances where the population was tightly controlled through a

---

[29] Handler and Bilby, *Enacting Power*, 73.
[30] CO 137/331, Barkly to Labouchere No. 52, 9 August 1856.
[31] Rattray to Tidman, 21 March 1849, SOAS, Council on World Missions archives, British Guiana – Demerara Incoming Correspondence, Box 7, Folder 4, and 4 March 1850, Box 7, Folder 5.

still-vigorous plantation system and where the island's topography enabled easier control of the population, as Barkly's comments about Jamaica's 'mountain fastnesses' suggest. The Jamaican and Guyanese strategy used legal force in a context where elites felt they had less cultural control over the population. At this point the liberals, who opposed the singling out of obeah, were dominant; the Jamaicans and Guyanese had to justify why their laws differed from what the Colonial Office hoped would be a uniform policy across the Caribbean.

The Colonial Office's advocacy of a policy of cultural hegemony through education and religious mission did not last. By the 1890s the Colonial Office stood on the other side of the debate, defending separate and specific obeah laws. Before discussing those laws in detail, I here trace some of the discursive changes that enabled this shift. Much of the debate about obeah in the second half of the nineteenth century was directly connected to the wider question of political rights for Caribbean people, and was routed through discussion of Haiti.

Britons both in Britain and the Caribbean had discussed Haiti ever since the nation was formed in 1804.[32] But the independent nation became a much more frequent reference point after the publication of Spenser St John's book *Hayti, or the Black Republic* in 1884. St John had been the British government's representative in Haiti; his book gave an account of that country's history, government, and economy. The book was loaded with racist hostility to black political authority. It argued that the only hope for Haiti was control by the 'mulatto element' who were also the 'civilising element'; as mulatto power was in decline and white immigration was not encouraged, he argued, the country was tending to 'sink into the state of an African tribe'.[33]

St John's book was widely read both in Britain and the Caribbean. Its most sensational element was its claim that Haiti was dominated by cannibalism, performed as part of the Vodou religion. As Kate Ramsey emphasizes, the reputation Haiti acquired from St John's account was supremely ironic. It arose from a case of murder in 1863 that was allegedly undertaken as part of a Vodou ceremony, although the evidence for that was very limited. The convicts in what came to be known as the *affaire de Bizoton* were publicly executed. The murder case became widely known because of the vigour with which the Haitian government pursued not only those culpable of the murder but *voduisants* more generally. Fabre Geffrard, the president of Haiti, instructed authorities to vigorously enforce the provision of the Code Penal that prohibited 'spells'.

---

[32] Brereton, 'Haiti and the Haitian Revolution'; Hörmann, 'Thinking the Unthinkable'.
[33] St John, *Hayti* (1884), vii.

The point, from the Haitian elite's point of view, was to emphasize that Haitians condemned ritual murder and cannibalism; that it was aberrant in Haitian life.[34] The Haitian government could not control representations of the incident, however. St John's account presented the crime as characteristic of Haiti, rather than an aberration.

The image of Haiti that St John's work established for English-language readers stuck, despite the efforts of Haitian writers to contest it. After 1884, discussion of Britain's Caribbean colonies was routinely conducted with reference to this image of Haiti. The discussion took place in the context of the new political settlement created in the aftermath of the Morant Bay Rebellion, in which representative government was removed from the Caribbean (except in Barbados) in favour of Crown Colony rule. For many British observers the Morant Bay Rebellion and the shift to Crown Colony rule proved the failure of emancipation – something they had suspected for some time. Increasingly, this was an openly racialized view, in which political rights were seen as impossible to grant because of the racial inferiority of the region's inhabitants. Simply put, the Caribbean was too African for its people to govern themselves.

The pattern was established by the English historian and travel writer James Anthony Froude's notorious *The English in the West Indies* (1888), a book that in many ways was an extended consideration of the extent to which the Anglophone Caribbean colonies were like Haiti.[35] Froude assumed that his readers were familiar with and endorsed St John's depiction of Haiti. He then wrote as if obeah were identical with Vodou, and directly connected both with cannibalism and child sacrifice. *The English in the West Indies* indicates how St John's book was rapidly reduced to its claim that Haitian 'Vaudoux' involved ritual cannibalism and child murder. Froude summarized St John's account of Haiti as follows:

> The republic of Toussaint l'Ouverture... had, after ninety years of independence, become a land where cannibalism could be practiced with impunity. The African Obeah, the worship of serpents and trees and stones, after smouldering in all the West Indies in the form of witchcraft and poisoning, had broken out in Hayti in all its old hideousness. Children were sacrificed as in the old days of Moloch and were devoured with horrid ceremony.[36]

For Froude, alleged Haitian cannibalism was but an extreme example of the generic phenomenon of 'African Obeah', a practice which, like an inadequately suppressed fire, had been 'smouldering' across the West

---

[34] Ramsey, *The Spirits and the Law*, 83–6.
[35] Froude, *The English in the West Indies*. Discussions of Froude that note his attention to Haiti include Benn, *The Caribbean*, 67–8; Smith, *Creole Recitations*.
[36] Froude, *The English in the West Indies*, 111.

Indies until the right conditions of independence from white rule allowed the fire to blaze brightly in Haiti. Obeah, rather than 'Vaudoux', was the dominant term for him and his readers in considering the negative religious associations between Africa and the Caribbean. The original source of the West Indian fire was Africa, but there is an ambivalence in Froude's emphasis on obeah's African origin. By comparing Haiti's alleged cannibalism to 'the old days of Moloch' Froude invokes the god to whom the ancient Israelites sacrificed their children. He thus connects African and European traditions even while emphasizing the difference between them.

Froude's repeated use of Haiti as a negative example and his casual references to 'eat[ing] the babies' and 'babies... offered to Jumbi' imply that he fully accepted St John's claims regarding cannibalism.[37] There is, however, an important section of *The English in the West Indies* in which Froude presents himself as a sceptic, even comparing the accusations about Haitian cannibalism to the blood libel against the Jews and to the European witch trials, in both of which, he claims, 'the belief had created the fact, and accusation was itself evidence'.[38] Announcing that he will go and investigate St John's claims himself, Froude spends two hours in Jacmel, where despite seeing 'a large menacing-looking mulatto, like some ogress of the "Arabian Nights", capable of devouring, if she found them palatable, any number of salt babies', he discovers no evidence for cannibalism or ritual murder.[39] Nevertheless, he repeatedly reasserts allegations of cannibalism, to the point where St John, in the second edition of *Hayti*, noted that Froude had endorsed his claims.[40] His work thus suggests the power of the accusation of cannibalism even when its author has to acknowledge that it cannot be sustained as a reality.

For Froude, what was at stake in the discussion of Haiti was political. The republic provided both a reference point and a vision of the British colonies' negative potential future, should authoritarian imperial rule not be maintained. Froude frequently uses Haiti as an apparently throwaway comparator, with the assumption that readers will know immediately what is implied. For instance, in discussing the future of Grenada, Froude counterposes the strong colonial government of British India to independent Haiti, declaring that the alternative to 'an English administration pure and simple, like the East Indian' is 'a falling eventually into a state like that of Hayti, where they eat the babies, and no white man

---

[37] Froude, *The English in the West Indies*, 175.  [38] Ibid., 112–13.
[39] Ibid., 164. Froude's description of the Haitian woman in terms of the Arabian Nights follows a pattern of discourse identified by Mimi Sheller as 'Orienting the Caribbean'. See Sheller, *Consuming the Caribbean*, 107–42.
[40] St John, *Hayti* (1889), 255.

can own a yard of land'.[41] Haiti's negative example is compressed here into two characteristics: cannibalism – more specifically, cannibalism of children, an accusation made obsessively by Froude – and the refusal to allow white land ownership. At other points Froude feels no need even to specify the nature of Haiti's negative example. Arguing against representative government in Trinidad, he writes that if 'we force them to govern themselves' – denying the existence of legitimate Trinidadian demands for representative government – 'the state of Hayti stands as a ghastly example of the condition into which they will then inevitably fall'.[42] Similarly, with regard to Jamaica, Froude claims that 'nothing but a strong government could prevent the island from lapsing into the condition of Hayti'.[43]

Froude was not the only writer to make such arguments and to connect them to politics and colonial power. Many others who discussed obeah in this period were concerned with its similarities to and differences from Vodou, and with whether religious practices in the Anglophone colonies involved human sacrifice and/or cannibalism. A review of Hesketh Bell's book *Obeah* claimed that it showed that 'the character of the negro of the West Indies, in spite of the many years during which he has been in contact with civilisation, has improved but little', but at least 'he' had not 'reverted', like the population of Haiti, to cannibalism and a 'perfectly savage life in the woods'.[44] British writers in the 1890s and 1900s concluded that obeah was mild in comparison to 'voodoo', testimony, many of them thought, to the advantage of British colonial rule. 'They [Jamaicans] are all believers in "Obie"-worship, which is identical with Voudoux', claimed one, who thought that 'were it not for the strong arm of the law' 'the same ceremonies and orgies would be practised in Jamaica as in Haiti'.[45]

Froude's viewpoint summarized a widely held late nineteenth-century understanding of the Caribbean which drew on the arguments that had been presented in the 1850s in defence of the obeah laws of Jamaica and British Guiana. Many writers, both from outside the Caribbean and living there, described the region's history in terms of the failure of emancipation, a failure caused by the moral shortcomings of the people. Obeah was one sign of this moral failure, along with illegitimacy, irreligion, and idleness. Such ideas were everywhere in this period: in books, newspaper and magazine articles, letters to the editor, and, we

---

[41] Froude, *The English in the West Indies*, 50.  [42] Ibid., 71.  [43] Ibid., 178.
[44] Review of Hesketh Bell, *Obeah*, *Manchester Examiner*, 26 November 1889, clipping in Bell Papers, Scrapbooks 1889–1899.
[45] Kennedy, *Sport, Travel, and Adventure*, 335.

must assume, in popular discussions. One fairly typical letter to the editor of the Jamaica *Gleaner* in 1899 summed up this point of view with the claim that 'It is impossible for us to claim to rank among the civilised peoples of the globe with our 65% of illegitimate births, with the belief in obeah and other superstitions, and with the alarming prevalence of praedial larceny which characterize the people of this land.'[46] Similarly, an article in *Harpers* entitled 'What is the Matter with Jamaica?' attacked the alleged refusal of the population to work, the prevalence of 'illegitimacy', and the fact that 'the obeahman is a power in the land, and voodooism a religion'.[47]

Assumptions like Froude's underlay the shift towards harsher obeah laws at the turn of the nineteenth century, details of which I turn to in the next section. Proponents of stronger laws argued that new legislation was needed to prevent Anglophone Caribbean people's threatened 'reversion' to a lower position on the scale of civilization. Within the Caribbean, many members of the middle class were particularly concerned about this because they wanted to show that their colonies were rapidly becoming civilized. The new Jamaican and Leeward Islands obeah laws, passed in the 1890s and 1900s, were said to demonstrate to potential settlers and tourists that these British islands were not Haiti. Thomas Banbury, for instance, a black Jamaican clergyman, wrote approvingly in 1894 of a harsher law passed two years earlier, arguing for the need for 'strenuous efforts to put down and stamp out... obeahism'.[48]

Froude's claims about the Caribbean did not go uncontested. Even his own book contained counter-currents. He reported an extended discussion about Haiti and St John's representation of it with Sir Conrad Reeves, the black chief justice of Barbados. Froude does not name Reeves, but lists him, alongside Frederick Douglass, as an example of a black intellectual who despite his eminence does not prove anything about black intellectual capacity as a whole. Froude's report of his conversation with Reeves indicates the chief justice's understanding of the wider implications of St John's allegations, appreciating that they would be interpreted as applying to black people everywhere. Reeves, says Froude, 'took leave of me with an expression of passionate anxiety that it might be

---

[46] 'The Education Question', *Gleaner*, 10 March 1899.
[47] 'Phil Robinson on Jamaica', *Gleaner*, 19 December 1898, reprinting 'What is the Matter with Jamaica' from *Harpers*. For an analysis of similar discourses about African Caribbeans and the argument that they were represented as culturally naked, in contrast to the representation of Indo-Caribbeans as bearers of an inferior culture, see Munasinghe, 'Culture Creators and Culture Bearers'.
[48] Banbury, *Jamaica Superstitions*, iii.

found possible to remove so black a stain from his unfortunate race'.[49] That 'stain' was particularly focused around obeah which, through its connection with St John's allegations about Haiti, was now associated with the ritual murder of children.

As well as Reeves's rebuttal within the book itself, *The English in the West Indies* led to a series of responses by writers within and outside the Caribbean that defended Caribbean people from Froude's attack. Here I consider the work of John Jacob Thomas, Nicholas Darnell Davis, and C. S. Salmon. All understood the implicit and explicit references to obeah contained in Froude's claims that Britain's Caribbean colonies would become 'another Hayti' if granted representative government. The most lastingly influential response was by Thomas. His *Froudacity: West Indian Fables Explained*, published a year after *The English in the West Indies*, opens with a sarcastic précis of Froude's work that stresses Froude's 'perpetual reference to Hayti'. Thomas also explores the threat that if granted political reform the British colonies would degenerate from being 'ostensibly civilized' into 'revellers... in orgies of devil-worship, cannibalism, and obeah'.[50] Thomas repeatedly invoked this triad of negative traits, referring for instance to the 'relapse into obeahism, devil-worship, and children-eating' and to 'the obeah, the cannibalism, the devil-worship' that Froude predicted would take place should greater representative government be achieved.[51]

For Thomas, obeah was part of a tightly interconnected set of negative stereotypes of the Anglophone Caribbean that he wanted to counter. He never explained what he understood by 'obeah' or 'obeahism', but claimed that Froude exaggerated its significance. While importantly contesting Froude and exposing his ignorance of the region about which he wrote, this response nevertheless left in place the association of obeah with cannibalism and devil worship that Froude had established. In this, *Froudacity* differs from Thomas's earlier work, *The Theory and Practice of Creole Grammar* (1869), which includes phrases in its section on 'idioms' that Thomas translates as 'to injure him by means of witchcraft', 'to cast an obeah spell', and 'having no obeah charms'. Here, then, he presented obeah as ordinary rather than scandalous.[52] In *Froudacity*, in contrast,

---

[49] Froude, *The English in the West Indies*, 113.
[50] Thomas, *Froudacity*, 53. Thomas has been extensively discussed by many scholars, including Smith, *Creole Recitations*; de Barros, '"Race" and Culture'; Brereton, 'John Jacob Thomas'.
[51] Thomas, *Froudacity*, 72, 175.
[52] Thomas, *Theory and Practice*, 118–19. Smith, *Creole Recitations*, 17, also discusses this issue.

Thomas treated Froude's suggestion that obeah was a significant part of Anglophone Caribbean societies as if it were as clearly and as patently untrue a slur as were allegations of cannibalism.

*Froudacity* also accepted Froude and St John's portraits of Haiti, referring, for instance, to the 'hideous orgies of heathenism' there.[53] Where Thomas differs from Froude is in his assertion that the comparison of the British colonies to Haiti is unfair and inappropriate, being based only on 'origin and complexion'.[54] He thus argued against Froude's racial determinism in order to distance the black population of the British West Indies from that of Haiti. In contrast to Haitians, who acquired their independence as 'perfectly illiterate barbarians', Thomas argued, (Anglophone) West Indian blacks are 'free, educated, progressive, and at peace with all men'.[55] In order to make the case for political reform in the Anglophone Caribbean, Thomas was thus forced to distance Anglophone Caribbean culture from association with Haiti, which, in turn, stood for association with Africa. West Indian blacks, according to Thomas, are not African at all, but rather are Christian. This is particularly telling since elsewhere in *Froudacity* Thomas shows his awareness of specific African ethnic groups in Trinidad, listing 'the Madingoes, Foulahs, Houssas, Calvers, Gallahs, Karamenties, Yorubas, Aradas, Cangas, Kroos, Timnehs, Veis, Eboes, Mokoes, Bibis, and Congoes, as the most numerous and important of the tribal contribution of Africa to the population of these Colonies'.[56]

Thomas invoked obeah only in relation to comparisons of the Anglophone Caribbean to other places: Haiti and Africa. He used it to imply that Froude's references to obeah were unjust to Caribbean people, who were in fact modern, not African, the two categories being counterposed. For more extensive discussion of obeah in a response to Froude, we must turn to Nicholas Darnell Davis's bitterly satirical article 'Mr Froude's Negrophobia, or Don Quixote as Cook's Tourist', published in the Guianese Agricultural Society's journal *Timehri* in 1888.[57] Davis was born in Grenada to white parents and spent most of his adult life in British Guiana working for the colonial government.[58] He argued that Froude's claims that the British West Indies were becoming like Haiti was merely the suggestion of 'nameless slanderers'. Davis did not fully accept Froude and St John's depictions of Haiti. Froude, he said, 'seems to have accepted as evidence against the Haytians, yarns told him by sailors: tales they had heard from others, who had, in turn, been told by

---

[53] For a similar point see Benn, *The Caribbean*, 69.   [54] Thomas, *Froudacity*, 53.
[55] Ibid., 54.   [56] Ibid., 168.   [57] Davis, 'Mr Froude's Negrophobia'.
[58] On Davis's career see Higman, *Writing West Indian Histories*, 52–3.

someone else'.⁵⁹ Still, his main purpose was not to defend Haiti, and he rapidly backed away from doing so in order to focus his attack on Froude's depiction of the Anglo-Creole Caribbean. Like Thomas, he argued that the comparison was unfair. Haitians, he maintained, could not be said to have *relapsed* into barbarism because they were never civilized, having achieved their revolution as 'pure barbarians'.⁶⁰ In this they were very different to black people in the Anglophone Caribbean, who had attained civilization over the many years since the abolition of the slave trade and slavery. This argument was almost identical to Thomas's. For both it was the Anglophone Caribbean's distance from Africa (in terms of the birthplace of its population) that proved its civilization. Africa became the antonym for civilization and, in asserting the Caribbean's civilization, Davis denied its connection with Africa.

Davis clinches his case for the difference between Haiti and the Anglophone Caribbean through a discussion of obeah. He moves into this discussion immediately after attacking Froude's claims that the West Indies were 'tending towards Haytia' (*sic*), without pausing to explain why obeah is relevant.⁶¹ Haiti, it seems, self-evidently suggested obeah. As with Thomas's triad of 'Obeah, cannibalism and devil-worship', obeah and Haitian 'barbarities' were, for Davis, part of the same phenomenon, and obviously should be discussed together.

Davis's discussion of obeah was more extensive than Thomas's, but their arguments are very similar. Where Thomas implied that obeah is irrelevant because the Caribbean population is at heart Christian, Davis made the argument explicit. However, because Davis discussed obeah in more detail than did Thomas, he could not deny that it existed:

What is the fact? In a precarious sort of way the superstition of Obeah does still exist in some of the West Indian islands. How could it be otherwise? It is but eighty two years since Englishmen ceased to take part in the Slave Trade. Up to 1806 thousands of slaves were brought year by year to the Islands from Africa ... These people were all steeped in the superstitions of the Dark Continent. Again, it is but fifty years since Slavery was abolished in the Islands, and, whilst it existed, there was little done to Christianise the people. What has been done is the outcome mainly of but fifty years: a mere drop in the Stream of Time.⁶²

In contrast to Froude's view of obeah as a slow-burning smoulder that might break into open flame at any moment without the right precautions, for Davis it was a phenomenon in gradual but inevitable decline, with only a 'precarious' existence in 'some of the West Indian islands'. Davis's argument echoed the line taken by abolitionists during the debates over

---

⁵⁹ Davis, 'Mr Froude's Negrophobia', 121.
⁶⁰ Ibid., 122.   ⁶¹ Ibid., 117.   ⁶² Ibid., 117–18.

slavery, who asserted that it was simply a matter of time before the African origins of enslaved people ceased to matter. For Davis, obeah's decline demonstrated the impressive capacity of black people for self-improvement. 'All things considered,' he asked, 'is it not matter for wonderment that the cult of Obeah is not more in vogue than is actually the case?'[63]

Davis's point, like Thomas's, was political: he wanted to refute Froude's argument against representative government. Even while pronouncing 'Long may Britannia's Sceptre rule the Western Main!' he tentatively raised the possibility of West Indian independence, suggesting that 'in ages now far off, the connection between Great Britain and her West Indian Possessions may be dissolved'. More immediately, he proposed the moderate goal of 'a prolonged Apprenticeship to the business of Representative Government'.[64] Yet, like Thomas, Davis's deep disagreement with Froude on political matters concealed some important shared assumptions about Africa and African-derived religions, represented as 'obeah'. Froude, Thomas, and Davis all saw obeah as essentially African, essentially superstitious, and essentially negative. As a cultural legacy of slavery, it existed unchanged over time. All agreed that African religious practices were incompatible with self-government and civilization. Thus it was critical to Davis's argument that he could demonstrate that obeah was a relic of the past that was being swept away by modernity. Inverting the image of the powerful obeah man, Davis argued that education and Christianity were displacing obeah: 'A much more powerful Medicine Man now roams at large. This is the Schoolmaster. Working hand in hand with him are the Ministers of Religion.'[65] For Davis, these twin aspects of modern British civilization would render critiques like Froude's unnecessary and obsolete.

Joining Thomas and Davis in attacking Froude was C. S. Salmon, whose *The Caribbean Confederation*, published in 1888, argued for a locally self-governing confederation of the Caribbean colonies within the British Empire. Salmon had spent time in Sierra Leone working for a merchant house, was the colonial secretary and acting administrator in the Gold Coast from 1869 to 1872, and later president of Nevis. In Africa he was a critic of Crown Colony rule and a supporter of a British Empire that ruled through 'traditional' chiefs. Anticipating the idea of 'indirect rule' later spelled out by Frederick Lugard, he opposed explicit imperial intervention in the cultural affairs of the colonized.[66] He presented a more detailed account of African society than either Thomas or Davis, arguing that the continent is diverse, that many areas are governed by

[63] Ibid., 119.  [64] Ibid., 129.  [65] Ibid., 119.  [66] Omosini, 'C. S. Salmon'.

Africans in an orderly and respectably patriarchal way, and that British intervention has been the cause of much of Africa's problems. Africa may not have been civilized, but for Salmon this was not a problem so long as its traditional rulers were allowed to continue ruling, under the tutelage of the British Empire.

The Caribbean posed a problem for this kind of vision of empire, because it lacked hierarchies that could easily be deemed 'traditional'. Salmon resolved this contradiction by arguing that Caribbean black people were different to those in Africa. His purpose in *The Caribbean Confederation*, he explains, is to 'show the fitness of the black British subjects in the West Indies for admission into the communities of the British Empire, by allowing them, together with the white races in the colonies, to share in the privileges of British subjects everywhere – by having a full share in their local self-government'.[67] Salmon mentions obeah twice, once in summarizing Froude's discussion of Haiti, where he states dismissively that Froude 'talks of Obeah and children killed and salted', and once in a quotation from Froude, the paragraph quoted above that begins 'the republic of Toussaint L'Ouverture'.[68] For Salmon, then, obeah was significant as a symbolic attack that negatively connected the Anglophone Caribbean with Haiti. Like Thomas and Davis he recognizes the centrality of Haiti to Froude's attack on black people in the Anglophone Caribbean, emphasizing this by including the phrase 'with a true explanation of the Haytian mystery' in his book's subtitle. In contrast to Thomas and Davis, who accepted that Haiti was backward and cannibalistic, Salmon argued that Froude and St John's depictions of Haiti were exaggerated and based on insufficient evidence. In addition, he argued that even should the allegations of cannibalism be proved true, 'all that can be said about it is that the Haytian pagans have developed a new and abominable form of pagan rite for which there is no counterpart in Africa itself'.[69] Salmon associates obeah only with Haiti, not with Africa, and thus not with the Anglo-Creole Caribbean. He sees it as a New World corruption of an African 'paganism' that, while a 'bad faith', is nevertheless sincerely practised.[70] Haiti, Salmon argues, does not prove anything about the capacity for self-government of 'the British black man' – a phrase he adopts in pointed contrast to Froude's use of the terms 'the Negro' and 'the black'.

Froude's respondents all put the case for Caribbean self-government in some form, but all did so in a way that accepted rather than contested the view that obeah, as a symbol of the Caribbean's connection with

---

[67] Salmon, *The Caribbean Confederation*, 4.
[68] For the Froude quotation see above, p. 129. For Salmon's use of it see *The Caribbean Confederation*, p. 91. Ibid., 91.
[69] Ibid., 93.   [70] Ibid., 91.

Africa, was incompatible with it. All felt that they had to respond to his representation of obeah and to the way he linked it with Haiti. At least in the case of Thomas and Salmon, the fact that their references to obeah are brief but highly symbolically charged (linking it with cannibalism) suggests discomfort in having to address the issue. Thomas, Salmon, and Davis all presented Caribbean culture as worthy of self-government only to the extent that it met externally posed tests of rationalism and civilization.

Such assumptions were very widespread, not just the arguments of a handful of intellectuals. Plentiful examples can be found in the pages of prominent colonial newspapers such as Jamaica's *Daily Gleaner* and the *Port of Spain Gazette*. For instance, a *Gleaner* correspondent in 1898 countered the statement that the parish of Clarendon was served by 'dozens' of obeah men with the argument that such claims must be rebutted, not only because of their inaccuracy but also because they caused:

> an incalculable amount of harm not only to the district or parish in question but to the island at large. They are simply arguments in favour of the contention by some in our midst that the churches are failures, and that the money spent on education is worse than wasted and as far as outsiders (foreigners) are concerned, the island is thereby made to occupy a much lower place in their estimation than it would otherwise occupy.[71]

Promoting Jamaica required the island to cultivate an image as a modern place.

Taking the other side of the argument, a pamphlet published in 1871, some years before Froude's book, used obeah to show the necessity for European dominance over 'the Negro'. Without European influence, the author wrote, black people in the Caribbean would 'sink back into the good-humoured, lazy, sensual and intensely superstitious African'.[72] This propensity to obeah demonstrated, allegedly, 'how essentially different is the nature of the negro' to that of the English public.[73] Black people were 'children to be disciplined by the white clergy and laity among them'. They should not be given ideas about political rights, as this would 'stimulate [them] into assertions of independence sure to culminate in a rising'.[74] Discourse about the Caribbean had become locked in a dynamic in which commenters either condemned the region's population for its Africanness, which was equated with backwardness, or promoted and boosted the region by denying its connections with Africa.

---

[71] 'Obeah in Clarendon', *Gleaner*, 15 December 1898.
[72] A Fellow of the Royal Geographic Society, *Jamaica and its Governor*, 28.
[73] Ibid., 30.  [74] Ibid., 31.

It is, perhaps, unsurprising that moderate imperialists such as Salmon, white creoles in the colonial service such as Davis, or correspondents to colonial newspapers would take up such a position. Perhaps for this reason, their work has attracted less attention and debate than has Thomas's. Because Thomas is made to bear the weight of vindicationist hopes, and because his work, as Denis Benn puts it, 'mark[s] the tentative starting point of a systematic intellectual tradition of nationalist protest in the region', his writing has been vigorously scrutinized, with some seeing him as a forerunner of Black Power while others criticize him for his hierarchical and pro-imperial stance.[75] Placing his work alongside that of other writers who responded to Froude suggests the shared milieu within which they all wrote. The recurrence of similar ways of thinking about obeah within texts that in other respects are quite different strongly suggests the difficulty of approaching the issue differently when the challenge was to undercut powerful racist ideas such as Froude's. The significance of these writers, especially Thomas, as vindicationist promoters of the idea of black potential and actual achievement in a context of racist social evolutionist thought which denied it, is clear. Yet the framework shared by Thomas with writers such as Davis and Salmon makes it important to unpack the assumptions in their work, for such assumptions were carried into future Caribbean nationalisms. Although over the course of the twentieth century the moderate political reforms advocated by late nineteenth-century activists came to be perceived by nationalists as far too limited, most Caribbean nationalism continued to treat cultural practices perceived as African within the framework of the obeah debates described here.

I end this section by considering another work that responded to *The English in the West Indies*: Hesketh Bell's *Obeah: Witchcraft in the West Indies*. Like *Froudacity*, *Obeah* was published in 1889, and like the works of Thomas, Salmon, and Davies it attacks Froude for his insufficient knowledge of the region.[76] Bell was a white colonial administrator, who had, like Salmon, spent time in Africa. He wrote *Obeah* during his time as a junior official in the colonial service in Grenada.[77] Bell's work shares some of the approach of the vindicationist texts already discussed, most notably a final chapter that presents the Caribbean as an attractive prospect for white settlers. But it differs significantly from the other responses because although it does rebut Froude, it is not

---

[75] Benn, *The Caribbean*. I am using 'vindicationist' to describe a strategy of contesting racism by demonstrating the impressive achievements of black or Caribbean people, following Scott, *Conscripts of Modernity*, 79–83.
[76] Bell, *Obeah*.   [77] Hesketh Bell, introductory notes to synopsis of diaries, Bell Papers.

primarily intended as a serious intervention into a political debate, but rather as a popular and humorous work, aimed at entertaining what its author hoped would be a large audience.[78]

Unlike Thomas, Salmon, and Davis, Bell makes no effort to argue that obeah is not significant in the Caribbean. Instead, for him it is all around, but, rather than a sign of threat and danger, it is comic. The opening chapter of *Obeah* exemplifies this approach. It describes an encounter with an unnamed white planter in Grenada who complains about theft of plantains from his farm. Exasperated, the planter decides to have the garden 'dressed', paying an obeah man, Mokombo, to use his powers to prevent further theft. The planter presents a double face with regard to obeah: he allows the black population to think that he really believes in the power of obeah: 'Are you quite ready to work Obeah properly for me?' he asks Mokombo.[79] In contrast, to the narrator he mocks black belief in obeah, emphasizing his cleverness in being able to take advantage of black credulity and superstition.[80] After a scene in which Mokombo 'dresses' the crops and has left, the planter takes down one of the glass vials that Mokombo has tied to the tree and opens it, declaring that it contains 'nothing but sea-water, with a little laundry blue in it, and ... a dead cockroach floating on the top'.[81] Yet the planter's smugness, with which Bell as narrator aligns himself, reveals his own ignorance, for the fact that the obeah bottle's material contents can be identified as everyday objects undermines their spiritual power no more and no less than the knowledge of the physical make-up of communion wine undermines the meaning of communion for Catholics. As a review of *Obeah* recognized, the planter in employing the obeah man has acknowledged the power of obeah and been drawn into its worldview.[82] Emphasizing one's non-belief to an outside audience does not mitigate the fact that obeah's power is being invoked.

[78] Bell's ambitions for commercial success are clear from the synopses of his diaries for 1890 and 1891, held at Cambridge University Library. Bell destroyed the originals after making the synposes.
[79] Bell, *Obeah*, 2.
[80] A similar incident takes place later in the book, this time with Bell himself in the role of successful manipulator of black superstition: when a bottle of whisky is stolen from him, he goes along with a 'boy' servant's suggestion that all his staff be asked to drink eau-de-Cologne, in the expectation that the thief would 'swell up and bust' as a result of obeah if he or she did not confess. Like the planter's, Bell's pretended belief is successful: his cook confesses that she took the whisky, confirming the 'boy's' belief in the power of obeah. Ibid., 63–4.
[81] Ibid., 4.
[82] Review of Obeah in *Literary World*, 28 February 1890, Bell Papers, Scrapbooks 1889–1899. This review described the planter's use of obeah against theft as 'humiliating'.

Bell thus constructs obeah very differently to the other texts considered in this chapter. Where Thomas and his peers connected obeah to cannibalism and presented it as something that would be frightening were it not so insignificant and archaic, Bell presented it as omnipresent but not frightening or threatening; rather, it is relatively harmless, and thus comic. Yet, at the same time, the book recounts events that imply that supernatural powers are not merely the product of the superstitious imaginations of the gullible. In the second chapter the narrator reports an event he says was told to him by a Roman Catholic priest who had lived in Trinidad. The priest stayed overnight in a house from which 'an old coloured woman who... was looked on with a good deal of dread by the people', along with all her heavy furniture, disappeared overnight from a room without external doors, without disturbing the parson who was sleeping in the other, interconnecting room. Although the narrator mocks this story, the parson's statement that he has 'never been able to explain [the incident] satisfactorily' stands as the final comment. While the priest goes on to refer to local 'unreasoning belief in the powers of the Obeah or Wanga man', the story seems more calculated to suggest the reality of such powers.[83]

Bell's quasi-ethnographic approach leads him to undo, at least partially, the opposition in the more explicitly political works between African or Haitian culture, associated with superstition, on the one hand, and European culture, associated with rationalism, on the other. Although he invites the implied rationalist white British reader to join him in feeling superior to those whose beliefs he describes, he also insists that his readers should not judge 'the credulity of negroes' too harshly, and compares them to 'our lower classes' and the 'beliefs and ideas so rampant among the most civilized people of Europe during the middle ages'.[84] Thus, while for most of the book he places all supernatural belief under the sign 'obeah', he at a few important moments recognizes the universal appeal of the supernatural. He includes, for instance, an account of British and French girls with 'magnetic' powers that allow them to move objects without touching them, and a matter-of-fact description of 'English "Ghosts," German "Geiste," French "Revenants"... [and] West Indian "Jumbies" or "Duppies"'. He also connects Grenadian 'loupsgarou' (or 'Loogaroos') with European 'vampires'.[85] These moments to some extent participate in a discourse of class condescension which associated European working-class and poor rural people with racial 'others'. At the same time, they opened the way for an understanding of obeah that did not

[83] Bell, *Obeah*, 18–20.    [84] Ibid., 70.    [85] Ibid., 99–102, 121, 161–70.

align Europe with enlightenment, rationalism, and civilization on the one hand, and Africa with supernatural belief and barbarism on the other. Unwittingly, Bell's book created an ambivalent yet significant space in which the practices designated obeah might be understood as ordinary, as part of everyday life.

Yet if *Obeah* makes its subject matter ordinary, it does so precisely because it does not attempt to argue for political rights for Caribbean people. Bell criticized Froude's lack of research, but accepted his argument that most Caribbean people were not 'ready' for the vote.[86] Nowhere in this debate did anyone argue that people for whom the practices designated as obeah were part of everyday life could be legitimate participants in political debate and government. Indeed, in the late nineteenth-century obeah debates, a position corresponding to what was probably the view of the majority of Caribbean people – a view in which the supernatural healing, divining, and protective practices designated obeah were a powerful but normal and actually or potentially positive part of everyday life – was unenunciable, and apparently incompatible with political claim making.

This debate of the late 1880s and 1890s thus wove the question of obeah into discussions about the Caribbean's political representation and, more broadly, its relationship to the modern world. It was followed by renewed legislation about obeah, which drew on the discursive patterns established by Froude and his respondents. Discussion about changes to the obeah laws retrod some of the paths of the discussion of the 1850s, with Barbadian elites continuing to focus on obeah within the context of vagrancy while Jamaica led the way on specific obeah legislation, but the balance had shifted. Now the Colonial Office, rather than supporting the Barbadians, defended Jamaican policy against critics of corporal punishment, and supported the extension of Jamaican anti-obeah law to other colonies.

The legislation passed in this period varied in specifics, but the new laws tended, in comparison with early post-emancipation laws, to increase maximum penalties and extend the use of flogging, expand the definition of the crime 'obeah', create additional offences such as consulting an obeah practitioner and distributing obeah-related literature, and make prosecutions easier and more routine. In Jamaica five Obeah Acts were passed between 1892 and 1903.[87] The most significant was the 1898 Obeah Act, which in only slightly modified form remains in force

---

[86] Ibid., 197. Bell made an exception for Barbados.
[87] Handler and Bilby, *Enacting Power*, 51–3.

today.[88] The Leeward Islands legislated against obeah in 1892 and then again in 1904, when it copied Jamaica's 1898 Obeah Act.[89] British Guiana adopted a new and more substantial obeah law in 1918, building on its 1856 Act and also on some vagrancy legislation.[90] Flogging as a punishment for obeah had already been extended to Trinidad and Tobago in 1868 and to St Lucia in 1872.[91] This period of law making was particularly important because in many parts of the Caribbean the laws passed in this period governed obeah for the next several decades.

There were some exceptions to the pattern of expanding the scope of the obeah laws. Barbados reaffirmed its inclusion of obeah as part of vagrancy law, and its relatively minor punishment for the offence: its revision of the law in 1897 left the punishment for practising obeah at the twenty-eight days' imprisonment established in 1840.[92] Grenada's punishment for obeah, reaffirmed in 1897, was also relatively mild: three months, without the possibility of flogging.[93] But by 1904 these punishments for obeah had become the exception. In most parts of the region the crime was punishable for men with flogging, and with solitary confinement for women.

This new legislation was debated in newspapers, in legislative debates, and in official correspondence. Newspapers carried reports about legal developments and prominent cases in other colonies, so that legislation and practice in one colony could influence policy in others.[94] Supporters of the new legislation continued to assert that harsh punishment was a natural corollary of the existence of obeah and the harm that it did. The administrator of St Lucia, for instance, emphasized that the 1872 anti-obeah Ordinance was necessary due to the 'very grave consequences which have lately been proved to ensue from the practice of "obeah"'.[95] Others argued that flogging for obeah was essential because it exposed the obeah practitioners' lack of power. According to the attorney general of the Leeward Islands, whipping made 'an "obeah man" ... thereafter

---

[88] For contemporary commentary on this act see Thornton, '"Obeah" in Jamaica'. Thornton claimed that before the 1898 Act it was impossible to secure a conviction for obeah that was not vulnerable to appeal for technical reasons.

[89] Handler and Bilby, *Enacting Power*, 69–70. The Federal Colony of the Leeward Islands was created as a legislative unit in 1871 out of the colonies of Antigua, Barbuda, the British Virgin Islands, Montserrat, Saint Kitts, Nevis, Anguilla, and Dominica.

[90] Ibid., 63–4.  [91] Ibid., 59–60 (Trinidad), 89 (St Lucia).

[92] Ibid., 56.  [93] Ibid., 86–7.

[94] For instance, 'Obeahism in Jamaica', *Port of Spain Gazette* (henceforth *POSG*), 27 April 1892; 'Is it Obeah?', *POSG*, 25 January 1902; 'Obeah Fetish: Other Colonies Grappling with the the Evil', *Gleaner*, 9 November 1907.

[95] CO 321/12, Des Voeux to Hennessy, 13 June 1876, enclosed in Hennessey to Carnavon No. 24, 1 July 1876.

an object of ridicule instead of dread'.⁹⁶ He also justified the provision regarding instruments of obeah on the grounds that ordinary people were so afraid of obeah that they would never give evidence against obeah practitioners. It was difficult, he noted, 'to get black men (and even some white men) to give evidence against a popular "obeah man"'.⁹⁷ Missionaries also supported extension of the obeah law. Moravian and Wesleyan ministers in the Leeward Islands were said to be 'so impressed' by the new 1904 Leeward Islands Obeah Act 'that they read and explained [its provisions] from the pulpit'.⁹⁸

Arguments for the new laws frequently invoked a racial logic linked to ideas about progress and modernity to explain their necessity. Jamaica's chief justice, for instance, wrote in defence of the colony's 1898 Obeah Act that 'the belief in Obeah is not confined to the lowest and most ignorant class. It [impedes] the life of the negroes generally and retards their progress as a race.'⁹⁹ Such views drew on the kind of discourse put forward by Froude. But the argument for harsher obeah laws could also be given a patriotic twist. Defending the implementation of flogging in two recent cases, the *Antigua Standard* argued that the continued existence of obeah was 'a reproach which every lover of these beautiful islands, every philanthropic Christian man and woman, should endeavour to have removed'. Education and Christianity alone had not had the required effect, and so, the paper argued, flogging would help.¹⁰⁰

Whereas the Colonial Office had in the 1850s argued against flogging and supported the governor of Barbados's arguments against specific laws, by the early twentieth century London officials took a harsher line. In a 1909 investigation into flogging for obeah, officials argued in its favour. 'As regards flogging,' wrote one, 'surely the practice of obeah is rather more "demoralizing" and brutal than the penalty for it . . . it would be a mistake to begin the reform of the instrument in the case of this crime.'¹⁰¹ By 1918 a Colonial Office official stated that 'no measures can be too strong to put down these malpractices'.¹⁰² This was a major shift from earlier interpretations, and we can see in these views the influence of the debate in the wake of Froude's *The English in the West Indies*. The fact that not even vindicationist creole patriots such as Thomas had

---

[96] Remarks of the Attorney General, enclosed in CO 152/284, Cox to Lyttleton No. 207, 4 May 1904.
[97] Ibid. [98] CO 152/286, Knollys to Lyttelton No. 109, 21 March 1905.
[99] CO 137/625, Sir F. Clarke, Memorandum, 'As to the Obeah Law', 24 September 1901.
[100] 'Obeah', *Antigua Standard*, 17 September 1904.
[101] CO 137/676, Minute of 'G. G.' on J. Cowell Carver to Secretary of State for the Colonies, 27 January 1909.
[102] CO 111/617, Collet to Long No. 279, 31 July 1918.

contested an interpretation of obeah as essentially negative contributed to the dominance of such positions.

Nevertheless, the tightening of the law did not take place without controversy. Arguments against the new laws reiterated those made in the 1850s by William Colebrooke, the governor of Barbados. In Jamaica, although each change in the obeah law between 1892 and 1903 passed the legislature without difficulty, there was some political opposition to many of the Acts.[103] Opponents worked within a larger discourse that accepted the need to eradicate obeah, but argued against the extension of punishment for it. William Andrews, a 'coloured' member of the Jamaican Legislative Council, opposed the 1893 Obeah and Myalism Amendment Act and conducted a series of public meetings in his constituency where he declared his opposition to it, along with other political matters. First establishing that he understood obeah as 'simply and purely absolute nonsense' that would 'result in their [the Jamaican people] coming back to the old state of things', he nevertheless opposed specific legislation to counter it. If obeah practitioners killed through poison, they should be prosecuted for murder; otherwise, they should simply be ridiculed. Flogging was a 'brutal, wicked and demoralising practice'. Moreover, Andrews opposed specific legislation because it was a mark of colonial difference: in England, he pointed out, fortune tellers were patronized by the 'best men in the land', and were not subjected to flogging.[104] Andrews received support from members of the black middle class, including S. C. Morris, who identified himself in a letter to the *Gleaner* as a descendant of slaves. Morris described flogging for obeah as a relic of slavery, and argued that there was considerable use of obeah practitioners by respectable professionals: if 'the more intelligent and influential' were to refuse to associate with the 'professors of this superstition' then the latter would be bankrupted, and would no longer be a problem.[105] Regular letters to the editor of the *Gleaner* also opposed flogging for obeah, sometimes in the context of more general attacks on flogging.[106] The views of Andrews and Morris correspond, in everyday political terms, with the ideas put forward by people such as John Jacob Thomas and Nicholas Darnell Davis in the sphere of published books and pamphlets: Andrews and Morris, like Thomas and Davis, argued that the Caribbean was more advanced, more modern, and therefore more like Britain, than the proponents of anti-obeah legislation were prepared to recognize.

---

[103] See reports on debate on the 1892 and 1893 Acts, *Gleaner*, 6 April 1892, 14 April 1893, 15 April 1893, 20 May 1893.
[104] 'Mr Andrews Visits his Constituents', *Gleaner*, 26 May 1893.
[105] 'Obeahman and the Cat', *Gleaner*, 6 June 1893.
[106] For instance, 'The Empire of the Whip', *Gleaner*, 1 November 1899.

In 1909 the sentencing of Richard Aitken, a successful Jamaican ritual practitioner, to six months' imprisonment, eighteen lashes, and two years police supervision led to an extended controversy about flogging. Aitken had been arrested as a result of entrapment, and made a powerful speech in court attacking this mode of police practice: 'It is a great provocation and temptation,' he said. 'Is it right that when a man is gone to his bed at night another man should come to him with money to tempt him? To ask him to do such thing that he don't want to do?' Perhaps because of these words the *Gleaner* picked up on this case, publishing editorials that condemned flogging in general as ineffective, 'brutal', and 'barbarous'.[107] These editorials attracted supportive letters to the editor, amplifying its arguments against entrapment and flogging.[108] Some of these, like the *Gleaner* editorials, used the language of modernity, suggesting that it was the use of flogging, rather than obeah, that was 'barbarous'. In addition, a Kingston resident, J. Cowell Carver, sent newspaper reports of the case directly to the Colonial Office, leading it to ask the Jamaican governor to investigate, while the British Humanitarian League, a liberal organization that campaigned against all forms of corporal punishment, also queried the Colonial Office about the extent to which flogging was used as a response to obeah.[109]

These letters were met with opposing views from other correspondents who supported flogging, arguing that it was indeed effective. Several presented the debate as one that divided the 'sentimental' or 'educated' elite of Kingston from people living in 'the country'. Rural residents, they claimed, understood the reality of the harm caused by obeah, including regular murders.[110] Nevertheless, the opponents of flogging won a temporary victory. In April the Legislative Council passed a motion condemning judicial flogging, the debate about which focused largely on flogging for obeah. Although the motion did not become law, the governor, Sidney Olivier, wrote the following year to all magistrates advising them not to order the punishment of flogging for obeah convicts.[111] It appears that no floggings took place for the next few years, until in September

---

[107] 'Eighteen Lashes' and 'Drastic Legislation', *Gleaner*, 16 and 27 January 1909. A further editorial on the case appeared on 12 February.
[108] Letters to the editor in support of the editorial appeared on 28 and 29 January and 1 February 1909.
[109] CO 137/676, J. Cowell Carver to Secretary of State for the Colonies, 27 January 1909. For the concurrent debate on judicial flogging in England, with which the Humanitarian League was primarily concerned, see McLaren, *The Trials of Masculinity*, 15–26.
[110] Letter from 'Justice', *Gleaner*, 18 February 1909. For similar views see letters on 23 February and 9 March 1909.
[111] *Gleaner*, 5 and 15 January 1910.

1913 regular flogging was resumed, on the grounds that obeah practitioners believed that the punishment had been abolished, and it therefore needed to be used to refute this belief.[112]

In this discussion about flogging obeah became a site for elaboration of the larger questions that preoccupied people involved in Caribbean politics at the turn of the century. What kind of people lived in the Caribbean? How did they respond to violent and other kinds of punishment? Where did the region fall on the largely unquestioned scale that ranked countries and peoples according to their 'level' of civilization, and what was the role of the state in moving it 'up' that scale? How did the fact that the majority of the population was of African descent determine the answers to these questions? Debates circled around these problems, without ever questioning the scales of value that were being applied.

Thus far we have been examining the rise in the new obeah laws in relation to discourses of race and modernity in the Caribbean, and specifically to the debate about the region's political status that took place in the wake of the publication of Froude's *The English in the West Indies*. But other factors also contributed to the proliferation of laws and prosecutions at this time. During slavery, prosecutions for obeah almost always involved either an attempted rebellion or clear evidence of harm against another person. The next two chapters examine obeah prosecutions between 1890 and 1939, and will demonstrate that they often took place in circumstances where no party was obviously hurt and where no clear resistance to authority was involved. The late nineteenth- and early twentieth-century state in the Caribbean was much more active in intervening in people's cultural lives than was the slavery-era state, even if the penalties during slavery were more severe. Why did state authorities across the Caribbean feel it necessary to intervene in everyday worship, healing, and belief at the turn of the twentieth century, when they had not felt this to be necessary before?

Brian Moore and Michele Johnson argue that the Jamaican obeah laws were part of a wider attempt to impose 'Victorian' values on the population: an attempt to produce cultural hegemony, which they argue was unsuccessful.[113] It would also be possible to interpret these laws and prosecutions in Foucauldian terms, as a sign of an increasingly disciplinary state attempting to use productive power to mould a population in a particular direction.[114] Both of these arguments are persuasive, but neither addresses the chronological question. Why was the concern with

---

[112] 'Obeah Case at Chapelton', *Gleaner*, 10 September 1913.
[113] Moore and Johnson, *Neither Led nor Driven*, 14–15 and chapter 12 *passim*.
[114] Foucault, 'Governmentality'.

popular religious and healing practice so pronounced in the decades following the 1890s, rather than in the 1840s and 1850s, when specific obeah legislation was unusual and demands for prosecutions were much less pronounced? After all, the immediate post-slavery period was the high water mark of what, after Catherine Hall, we could call the era of 'civilizing subjects'.[115] In the mid-nineteenth-century period studied in Hall's book of that name, considerable effort was put into transforming the cultural orientation of former slaves, especially by missionaries. Yet in that period the use of the law to suppress popular religious and healing practices, while certainly not absent, was far less marked than in the late nineteenth and early twentieth centuries.

Hall's book implicitly suggests part of the reason for this: the late nineteenth-century concern with popular religion is a sign of the law stepping in where the missionaries were perceived to have failed. In the immediate post-slavery period colonial authorities thought that natural processes of social development of a free people would lead to the adoption of British middle-class values. This tended to lead to the assumption that beliefs and practices perceived as African would eventually die out of their own accord. As the British colonial secretary put it in 1836, echoing a view that had often been expressed during the debates over slavery, African 'superstitions... opinions and barbarous habits' would eventually 'yield to the influence of Christianity and civilization'.[116] Yet even in the immediate aftermath of emancipation there were indications that, rather than adopting British culture, Caribbean people were making their own cultures. This became particularly clear in Jamaica in the early 1840s when what became known as the 'myal outbreak' revealed a popular religiosity organized around a millenarian African Christianity. Myalists aimed to root out evil – usually referred to as obeah – through ecstatic rituals involving singing and dancing, attempts to 'dig up' obeah, and the use of physical violence against those thought to be harbouring evil within them.[117] The leader of one group of myalists said that he was 'sent by God to cleanse the earth'; obeah 'must be dug up, before the

---

[115] Hall, *Civilising Subjects*.
[116] CO 138/59, Glenelg to Sligo No. 249, 12 April 1836. For similar claims made during slavery see the note to an anonymously published set of poems: 'It [obeah] has for some time been losing ground, and will probably disappear entirely, as soon as Christianity shall have been generally established throughout our West-Indian Colonies; it being confidently believed by the negroes that Baptism is a certain preservative against the effects of Obeah' (*Poems Chiefly on the Superstition of Obeah*, 20). And in 1843 the missionary James Phillippo claimed that this was indeed taking place: 'the spell of Obeism and its kindred abominations is broken', he wrote. Phillippo, *Jamaica*, 263.
[117] Schuler, *'Alas, Alas, Kongo'*; Stewart, *Three Eyes*; Alleyne, *Roots of Jamaican Culture*; Austin-Broos, *Jamaica Genesis*, 51–5.

Lord Jesus would come again'.[118] The rapid rise of myal after emancipation reveals the extent to which, at least in Jamaica, the meaning of obeah as dangerous spiritual power, rather than as neutral or protective, had become dominant.

Those concerned with governing Jamaica expressed concern about the politics of the 'myal outbreak'. Governor Elgin complained that it led to 'the labourers in a body abandoning their work, and devoting themselves entirely to the celebration of the myalist rites'. Although there were no indications that myalism involved attacks on the power structure of Jamaican society, the *Falmouth Post* nevertheless feared that it would lead to overt rebellion: state action to suppress the movement was necessary, or 'the colony from one end to the other, may be lighted by rebellious torches'.[119]

Such fears seemed to become more significant during the last third of the nineteenth century and the first decades of the twentieth, when Revivalist religions that fused Christianity with African-derived ritual and experiential elements such as spirit possession and speaking in 'unknown tongues' were increasingly public and prominent. W. F. Elkins noted more than thirty years ago that this 'growth in revivalism... influenced the rising national consciousness of the Jamaican masses... and helped shaped popular resistance to colonialism.'[120] These religions were the primary location in which independent consciousness, contradicting the everyday ideology of the elite, developed. The Mothers, Shepherds, and Brothers who provided leadership within them were working-class sufferers themselves, and their positions of community authority provided a potent counterpoint to the colonial structures in which light skin, masculine gender, and mastery of British culture coalesced with wealth as the sources of status and power. They undermined colonial hierarchies, providing an alternative structure of authority and hierarchy. Spiritual and ritual healing were central elements of the practice and belief of these religions. As Diane Austin-Broos points out, in an argument that could be applied more widely across the region, 'healing became a central motif in Jamaican Christian practice'.[121]

Probably the most numerically significant religious movements were what the anthropologist George Simpson called the region's 'Revivalist cults', which consolidated themselves in many colonies in this period.[122] These religions developed in the context of revivals during the 1850s

---

[118] *FP*, 19 October 1842.   [119] Ibid.
[120] Elkins, *Street Preachers*, 6.   [121] Austin-Broos, *Jamaica Genesis*, 43.
[122] Simpson, *Black Religions in the New World*. Simpson's categories have been criticized, and to some extent revised, for instance in Houk, *Spirits, Blood and Drums*. They nevertheless remain useful as a heuristic device.

and 1860s which began within the missionary churches and were influenced by British and North American Revival movements.[123] Caribbean Revival quickly became independent, merging worship of the Holy Spirit with African-derived practices and theologies. The result was religions characterized by possession states and altered consciousness, 'trumping' (counter-clockwise movement) to induce these states, and an emphasis on the role of ancestral spirits in the human world. Although usually led by male 'teachers' and 'shepherds', Revival-inspired religions had a strong place for women as second-tier leaders.[124]

Associated with Revival, although sometimes operating independently, were balm yards: centres that offered protective and curative spiritual and herbal healing in the context of religious diagnosis.[125] Balm yards served large numbers of people. For instance, by the 1930s a balm yard in Trench Pen, Kingston, was said to provide healing and protective baths for at least twenty-five people each day, as well as having beds for several patients who lived within the centre. Although the balm yard was located in one of the poorest urban communities, those who attended it were not confined to poor Kingstonians. The *Gleaner* reported that it was visited by a 'vast amount of people of every class and colour drawn from the metropolis and all over the island'.[126]

In Jamaica Revival religion was known as Revival Zion or Pocomania (Pukumina).[127] Revival was both strengthened and politicized in the late nineteenth century by the leadership of the healer and preacher Alexander Bedward, who created a mass religious movement (Bedwardism), attracting thousands to his 'healing stream' at August Town, close to Kingston.[128] In Trinidad, too, religious revival created communities whose worship included trances, spirit possession (or manifestation of the Holy Spirit), and spiritual travelling.[129] By 1898 the term 'Shouter' seems to have been in common use: the *Port of Spain Gazette* reported on a house that was 'every Sunday night filled with a congregation of "Shouters"'.[130] The term 'Spiritual Baptists' was also in use at an early date; a group engaged in 'preaching and singing' in the streets of Port

---

[123] Austin-Broos, *Jamaica Genesis*, 55–9.
[124] Ibid., 83–7; Elkins, *Street Preachers*, 10–18.
[125] On recent Jamaican balm healing see Payne-Jackson and Alleyne, *Jamaican Folk Medicine*; Wedenoja, 'Mothering and the Practice of Balm'.
[126] 'With the Pocomaniacs – At the Balmyard', *Gleaner*, 1 August 1936.
[127] On the Jamaican 'Revival Complex' see Chevannes, *Rastafari*, 23–33; Hodges, *Soon Come*.
[128] Chevannes, *Rastafari*, 79–82; Burton, *Afro-Creole*, 116–19.
[129] Glazier, *Marching the Pilgrims Home*; Laitinen, *Marching to Zion*; Lum, *Praising His Name*.
[130] 'The "Shouters" at Tunapuna', *POSG*, 26 October 1898, 4.

of Spain was described with that term in 1908.[131] Spiritual Baptist practice included rituals of initiation via 'mourning', involving seclusion for several days, speaking in tongues, and the ringing of bells and drawing of seals. Like Jamaican Revivalists and Pocomania worshippers, Spiritual Baptists dressed distinctively, often entirely in white. The movement was allied to similar groups in St Vincent, Grenada, and British Guiana, due to connections established through the circuits of movement around the southern Caribbean. In Guyana Revivalists were organized as Jordanites or the White-Robed Army.[132]

Considerably smaller than the Revivalist movements were what Simpson called 'neo-African cults', in particular the Shango (or Orisha Worship) movements in Trinidad and Grenada. In Trinidad this movement was stimulated by the arrival of 'liberated Africans' from Yoruba-speaking areas in the 1840s and 1850s, who founded 'Yarraba' communities in Belmont.[133] Members of Orisha communities worshipped the Yoruba orishas, especially but not exclusively Shango (Xango). There was considerable overlap between participants in Spiritual Baptist and Orisha religious ceremonies and rituals, especially in Trinidad.

Like their Jamaican myalist precursors, the adherents of both Revivalist and neo-African religious movements were hostile to and fearful of obeah, which they understood as dangerous and hostile spiritual power. Their means of protecting themselves from obeah were spiritual, including prayer and ritual. For many outsiders, including but not limited to law makers and enforcers, these techniques shows that such religions incorporated, or even were themselves, forms of obeah.

All these religions – Bedwardism, Revival and Spiritual Baptism, and 'neo-African' movements – were subject to harassment and prosecution in the early twentieth century. The Vincentian Shakerism Prohibition Ordinance of 1912, the Trinidadian Shouters' Prohibition Ordinance of 1917, and the Grenadian Public Meetings (Shakerism) Prohibition Ordinance made worship in a style defined by the laws as associated with Shouting, and Shakerism, illegal.[134] In St Vincent the building of 'Shakers Houses' was prohibited, while the holding of 'Shakers Meetings',

---

[131] 'Religious Fanatics', *POSG*, 1 September 1908, 6.
[132] Gibson, *Comfa Religion*, 56; Roback, 'The White-Robed Army'.
[133] Trotman, 'Reflections on the Children of Shango'; Pollak-Eltz, 'The Shango Cult'.
[134] CO 262/26, Ordinance No. 13 of 1912: An Ordinance to render illegal the practices of 'Shakerism' as indulged in the Colony of St Vincent; CO 297/22, Ordinance No. 27 of 1917: An Ordinance to render illegal indulgence in the practice of the body known as the Shouters, Trinidad and Tobago; CO 103/26, Ordinance No. 11 of 1927: The Public Meetings (Shakerism) Prohibition Ordinance, 1927 (Grenada). For further discussion of these laws see Paton, 'Obeah Acts'; Henry, *Reclaiming African Religions in Trinidad*, 32–5.

defined, tautologously, as 'a meeting or gathering... at which the customs and practices of Shakerism are indulged in', were also outlawed.[135] The Trinidad and Tobago statute similarly prohibited meetings of and the building of houses by 'Shouters', and listed a series of bodily and ritual practices that characterized 'shouting', including the use of bells, candles, flowers, and white head cloths, 'violent shaking of the body and limbs', and 'shouting and grunting'.[136] The Grenadian law prohibited, even more broadly, any gathering of two or more persons at which 'any obscene or immoral behaviour or practices are indulged in, or at which behaviour or practices are indulged in which tend to exercise a pernicious or demoralizing effect upon persons attending such meeting'.[137] No equivalent law was passed in Jamaica, but there were repeated proposals for laws against Revival, in particular from the turn of the nineteenth century to the 1930s. A *Gleaner* editorial asked whether 'low class revival meetings should not be brought within reach of the law' because they were 'becoming more and more the feeders of obeahism and are causing a great deal of demoralization among the ignorant mass of the people'.[138] A few years later a petition was submitted against Revival.[139]

The ordinances against 'Shouters' and 'Shakerism' were passed after press and police campaigns in each colony, which also frequently led to prosecutions under the laws against breach of the peace and disorderly conduct.[140] Press coverage was both hostile towards and fascinated with the forms of worship associated with the Spiritual Baptist faith. Even some lengthy and partially sympathetic descriptions referred to practices of spirit possession, speaking in tongues, and night-time worship as 'barbarism', 'blasphemy', 'fetishism', and 'devilish'.[141]

Members of other religious communities also faced hostile policing, even where no law was explicitly made against them. In Jamaica, for instance, the 1911 Night Noises Prevention Law, which prohibited loud noises between 11 p.m. and 6 a.m., was largely directed against Revivalist meetings.[142] In several colonies Acts regulating the practice of medicine

---

[135] CO 262/26, Shakerism Ordinance.
[136] CO 297/22, Shouters' Prohibition Ordinance.
[137] CO 103/26, Shakerism Ordinance.
[138] 'Obeahism Extraordinary', *Gleaner*, 5 May 1899.
[139] 'A Disgraceful State of Things', *Gleaner*, 27 March 1905.
[140] In Trinidad, for reasons that are unclear, this press campaign diminished after 1912, giving way to a series of articles expressing hostility to wakes for the dead.
[141] 'Cleaver Lane and its "Shouter" Band', *POSG*, 17 January 1911; 'A Shouter's Meeting Down South', *Mirror* (Trinidad), 29 April 1906, enclosed in CO 321/269.
[142] CO 139/111, Law 31 of 1911: A Law to compel persons to desist in the night time from disturbing others.

produced the crime of practising medicine without a licence, which was also an offence in England.[143] In the Caribbean it was frequently used to bring charges against ritual specialists who used spiritual power to heal. In Trinidad night-time wakes for the dead were frequently prosecuted in the teens and twenties, usually under the law against breach of the peace.[144] The same law was used to harass open-air meetings for worship, especially in urban communities. The Shouters' Prohibition Ordinance did not apply to outdoor worship and preaching, but the law against breach of the peace was sometimes very broadly interpreted. Frederick Monroe, 'a well-known itinerant preacher', was arrested and fined for breach of the peace along with three women who were supporting him, after they organized an open-air meeting in Port of Spain that attracted a crowd of around 200 listeners.[145] A Pentecostal preacher named Jane Moseley was prosecuted in 1926 for obstruction, after a crowd of about 100 people gathered around her while she led them in song and prayer, preventing the passage of trams along Woodford Street. Moseley was released with a warning, but those whose religious practice involved healing were vulnerable to more serious charges, including obeah.[146]

Unlike the practices of the Spiritual Baptist faith, Shango worship was not specifically outlawed, but there are indications that some of those prosecuted for obeah were engaged in Orisha Worship. An early example took place in 1902, when Francis Caradose, an African, was charged with obeah. His house was marked by a bamboo flagstaff, underneath which 'three old cutlasses planted in a triangular position were found'. Caradose had another arrangement of three cutlasses under a kerosene oil pan, and sang 'a jargon song in his own tongue' to an image found in a neighbour's garden.[147] Nearly forty years later Albertha Isidore was charged under the obeah laws. The evidence against her included the presence in her house of a bowl containing stones, feathers, and seeds, another with oil and a wick, a crucifix, a statue, an old Bible, an axe, wooden hatchets, and swords.[148] Neither of these defendants mentioned Shango in their defence, but the presence of cutlasses, axes, and swords

---

[143] This was a crime in Jamaica from at least 1899, and in the Leeward Islands from at least 1903.
[144] For instance, 'A Motley Crowd', POSG, 26 November 1917.
[145] 'Open Air Service Interrupted', POSG, 9 July 1920.
[146] 'Pentecostal Preacher before the Court', POSG, 26 November 1926.
[147] 'The Alleged Obeah Man', POSG, 10 April 1902; 'The Obeah Case', POSG, 17 April 1902.
[148] 'Court Cases', POSG, 10 January 1940. For another case in which the defendant may well have been associated with Shango worship see 'Alleged Obeahism in Siparia', POSG, 16 January 1910.

arranged in ritual ways strongly suggests that they were participants in Orisha Worship. Swords and cutlasses are symbolically associated with Ogun and St Michael.[149] Caradose was acquitted of the charge against him, something that, given the interest that the case aroused, probably substantially increased his reputation and power.

Not only were Revival and Orisha increasingly prominent in this period, they were also increasingly politicized. In Jamaica this political religion was promoted most forcefully by Alexander Bedward, who preached to his thousands of followers that the 'black wall has become bigger than the white wall and we must knock the white wall down'.[150] As Elkins suggests, and as the subsequent history of religion in the Caribbean bears out, popular religion was repeatedly the site of the most intense expression of hostility to colonialism and racial oppression, rejecting white dominance in a language that was often densely allusive and metaphorical and thus difficult for colonial authorities to understand and engage with; difficult even for them to co-opt, as could more easily be done with more secular and reform-oriented politics.[151] The wave of legislation in the late nineteenth and early twentieth centuries must be seen as a response to this intensification of political, liberation-oriented, religion.

The renewal of the obeah laws also took place in the context of the expansion of British imperial power, and in particular the colonial encounter with indigenous religion and healing practices in new colonies, especially in Africa. As the empire expanded, information circulated rapidly between different imperial regions, through official networks of colonial administration, through the movement of officials, settlers, and colonized people, and through newspapers, pamphlets, and books. People in the Caribbean thinking about obeah were aware of the legal responses being developed to what would later become known as African 'traditional religion' and 'traditional healers', as well as towards 'witchcraft'. In London, colonial officials began to evaluate the appropriateness of anti-obeah laws by comparing them to laws in African colonies about witchcraft or religion.[152] References to writers on African society, such as Alfred Ellis and Mary Kingsley, began to appear in discussions of obeah.[153] Colonial African terms such as 'medicine man' and 'juju'

---

[149] Houk, *Spirits, Blood and Drums*; Simpson, 'The Shango Cult'.
[150] Post, *Arise Ye Starvelings*, 7.    [151] Elkins, *Street Preachers*.
[152] For example, a comment by 'WDR', 27 July 1901, on CO 137/620, Hemming to Chamberlain No. 406, 5 July 1901, evaluates Jamaican obeah law by reference to an 1893 law in Lagos prohibiting possession of amulets.
[153] 'What is Obeah?', 14 October 1904; 'Obeah and Myal', 18 October 1904; 'A Disgraceful State of Things', 27 March 1905, all in the *Gleaner*; 'Tracing the Origin of

began appearing in analyses, such as the claim by the commissioner of the Virgin Islands, Robert Earl:

> Obeah-Voodoo or Ju-Ju is best understood if it is regarded as the whole body of primitive belief and customs of fetichistic African tribes which has undergone a certain amount of change by their fusion, by being placed in a different environment ie the West Indies, and by contact with a civilization having higher and different beliefs... The obeah men officiate for a primitive people in the three-fold capacity of priests, magicians, and medicine men.[154]

For Earl, obeah revealed the Caribbean's continued primitive state and ongoing connection to Africa. Caribbean people's exposure to the allegedly 'higher' civilization of the British Empire had, it seemed, made little impact.

As Earl's comments suggest, Caribbean law and policy regarding obeah was produced in dialogue with the development of related laws regulating witchcraft and spiritual healing in African colonies.[155] As early as the 1850s British colonial administrators and magistrates in southern Africa were negotiating witchcraft accusations, debating whether or not to punish those who were said to be witches or those who accused others of witchcraft. The witchcraft-related laws passed in the Cape of Good Hope, Natal, Zululand, and Southern Rhodesia in the 1880s and 1890s, which provided a model for later African witchcraft legislation, worked differently to Caribbean obeah law.[156] They prohibited accusing others of witchcraft, not practising witchcraft; in contrast, accusing someone of obeah was not an offence in the Caribbean, although if it didn't lead to prosecution, it might lead to a suit for slander. Nevertheless, the two bodies of law shared the use of flogging as a punishment, and were understood in the Colonial Office as related to one another.[157] Early African laws related to witchcraft also included prohibitions on the work of ritual specialists, such as the 1883 Natal Penal Code that provided both for fining people making allegations of witchcraft and imprisonment for 'habitual *isanuse*' (diviners). This provision is more similar to

---

Obeahism', *Correo del Atlantico* (Limón, Costa Rica), 5 November 1911 (thanks to Lara Putnam for this source).

[154] Robert S. Earl to Colonial Secretary, 9 May 1905, enclosed in CO 152/287, Knollys to Lyttleton No. 218, 19 May 1905. For a similar use of the language of 'fetishism' and 'juju' see 'Obeah Fetish', *Gleaner*, 9 November 1907.

[155] For discussion of the emergence of 'witchcraft' as a significant trope in relation to Africa, replacing 'fetishism', see Pels, 'The Magic of Africa'.

[156] Niehaus, 'Witchcraft in the new South Africa', 201n210; Jeater, *Law, Language, and Science*, 133; Flint, *Healing Traditions*, 104–9.

[157] See the Colonial Office minutes to CO 137/676, Joseph Collinson to Crewe, 14 May 1909, which lists several African witchcraft laws in response to a query about Caribbean obeah law.

Caribbean obeah law than were the provisions of African witchcraft law, but it did not last in this form. By 1891 the Natal legislature had changed its policy, licensing a specific category of African healers, so long as they worked only with herbs, while maintaining the prohibition on 'supernatural' healers.[158] Such a policy, the equivalent of the licensing of balm healers, was never attempted in the Caribbean, where law makers did not consider practices they perceived as African to have any traditional authenticity.

News of religiously inspired anti-colonial movements and rebellions of the late nineteenth and early twentieth centuries also travelled from Africa to the Caribbean, influencing the official response to 'obeah'. The dangers of obeah appeared particularly prominent at a moment when apparently similar practices led to revolutionary challenges to colonial power. Although obeah had not been directly linked to rebellion in the Caribbean since the early nineteenth century, the possibility that it might be mobilized in such a way remained an underlying concern of authorities. In the aftermath of the Morant Bay Rebellion, which grew out of Revival religion, an alleged obeah man, Arthur Wellington, was executed by firing squad on a hillside.[159] The authorities were concerned about the political consequences of obeah. Awareness of these possibilities combined with knowledge of concurrent events as colonial power expanded in Africa, where resistance to colonial expansion was frequently religious inspired. In the Cape Colony, Xhosa anti-colonial campaigns in the 1850s were inspired by religious prophecy.[160] Later, in Southern Rhodesia in 1896–7 and Malawi in 1915, British colonists also met resistance from those they interpreted as inspired by witchcraft.[161] Despite the differences between the two bodies of law, the outcome was similar. In Africa, as in the Caribbean, legislation was used against local religious movements, and helped to construct a sense of African difference. In southern Ghana, for instance, oracle shrine movements were made illegal in a series of specific ordinances between the 1890s and 1920s.[162] Such laws have significant parallels with the Shouters and Shakers Prohibition Ordinances of Trinidad, St Vincent and Grenada.

Obeah laws were remade in the late nineteenth century in response to debates about Caribbean modernity and its relationship to race. Such debates intersected with a developing religious politics in the region, in which the everyday religious practice of the majority was more and

[158] Flint, *Healing Traditions*, 109, 120.
[159] Heuman, 'The Killing Time'; Holt, *The Problem of Freedom*, 302.
[160] Ross, 'Ambiguities of Resistance'; Peires, *The Dead Will Arise*.
[161] Ranger, *Revolt in Southern Rhodesia*; McCracken, *A History of Malawi*, 127–46.
[162] Gray, 'Independent Spirits'; Gray, 'Witches, Oracles, and Colonial Law'.

more clearly separate from the religion of the powerful. The increasingly obvious attractions of various forms of African and African Christian religions, and their stimulus to political opposition, revealed the failure, by the late nineteenth century, of the post-emancipation project of cultural hegemony. This failure stimulated an anxious effort to suppress religious heterodoxy in the form of obeah alongside other movements. The next two chapters investigate the practical workings of these revived laws.

# 5    Obeah in the courts, 1890–1939

'Arrest of an Alleged Obeah Woman'; 'The Black Art. Jackson Pleads Guilty Quite Promptly'; 'Alleged Larceny and Obeahism'.[1] These and similar headlines provided one means by which people in the late nineteenth- and early twentieth-century Caribbean learned about obeah. Knowledge of obeah circulated in many other ways as well – written, oral, and experiential – but the printed medium of the newspaper played a particular role in the spread of information and understanding. Newspaper reports of obeah trials had a repetitive quality produced by the formulaic structure of the trial itself, moving through charge, evidence, verdict, and sentence, often packaged within an explicit message to readers provided by the magistrate judging the case, the journalist reporting on it, and sometimes both. The court rites of obeah trials, to adapt Mindie Lazarus-Black's phrase, led to the fashioning of a particular set of stories about obeah, constructed in relation to the needs of modern legal cultures to mark clear boundaries between the guilty and the not guilty, and to adjudicate the severity of offences through precisely calibrated punishments.[2] The definition of obeah in law from the second half of the nineteenth century onwards, and thus the requirements for a successful prosecution, led to trials that focused on three things: objects, ritual and money. Through direct spectatorship in court and newspaper reporting of trials, these elements over time acquired a larger status as the defining characteristics of obeah beyond the courtroom. They existed in tension with other aspects of Caribbean ritual practice that might in some circumstances be construed as obeah, but which rarely featured in court.

This chapter investigates obeah as a prosecuted crime from 1890 to 1939 in order to tease out the ingredients that made up official understandings of obeah in this period. It also examines the patterns that emerge from reports of obeah prosecutions to answer some empirical

[1] *Gleaner*, 23 March 1901; *Gleaner*, 11 September 1908, 3; *POSG*, 5 July 1907, 4.
[2] Lazarus-Black, *Everyday Harm*.

questions about them. How frequently were the obeah laws invoked? Who was likely to be prosecuted? How did people end up being charged with obeah? When people were prosecuted, were they generally convicted or acquitted, and if convicted, what punishments did they experience? How, if at all, were these patterns different in different places? To what extent did they change over time?

The chapter traces the stages of policing and prosecution of obeah, from the emergence of an individual as a suspect to their punishment or release. We can think of these proceedings as a set of journeys travelled by those known to be spiritually powerful or who were accused of practising obeah, journeys that might have a range of different outcomes, and might be repeated on several occasions over the course of a person's life. People arrested on suspicion of obeah might be prosecuted or released without prosecution; the charge they faced could change from obeah to one of several other crimes; they might, with or without the help of a lawyer, offer a range of arguments in their defence, or plead guilty and offer no defence at all. They might be convicted or found not guilty, if found guilty might appeal, and could experience a range of sentences. What emerges through this analysis is that, despite the official rhetoric that surrounded the obeah law, which emphasized that it was intended to suppress belief in obeah and thus to produce a more 'civilized' population, in everyday use the laws regulating obeah had no such impact. Prosecutions might be used to bolster police reputations, to attack religious leaders, to pursue conflicts between individuals and groups within local communities, or in response to relationships between ritual specialist and client that had for some reason gone awry. That is, prosecutions were part of a world in which ritual healing practices were ordinary.

People were prosecuted for obeah in every British colony in the Caribbean. Rather than trying to track cases across the entire region, this chapter focuses on Trinidad and Jamaica, while occasionally supplementing evidence about them with material from other colonies.[3] Along with the next chapter, it is based on a large body of material about obeah prosecutions, collected through a systematic search of the dominant newspaper in Jamaica and Trinidad in the period 1890–1939. I begin in 1890 for two reasons. The first is analytic: my initial research on the development of the law and of politics strongly suggested an upsurge in concern about obeah after this date, with laws passed in many colonies

---

[3] While I did not set out to exclude Tobago from the study, in practice the sources I was using did not report on Tobagonian trials. Although I sometimes refer to Trinidad as a 'colony', it should be noted that after 1888 it was part of the colony of Trinidad and Tobago.

in the 1890s and 1900s. There is also a pragmatic reason: newspapers from before 1890 are less systematically available, and, where digital editions have been produced, the optical character recognition of newspaper text printed prior to 1890 is poor, making searches unreliable. The initial systematic research was on Jamaica, again for a mix of analytic and pragmatic reasons: it was the first place that criminalized obeah; concern about obeah was particularly intense there; and the law against obeah was particularly harsh, and perceived as such. Pragmatically, the existence of a digitized edition of the main newspaper, the *Gleaner*, made it possible to locate cases relatively quickly. With the help of research assistants I was able to collect newspaper reports on obeah cases from 1890 to 1989.[4] We searched the digital edition of the Jamaica *Daily Gleaner* and *Sunday Gleaner*, using the keywords 'obeah', 'obeahman', 'obeahwoman' and 'obeahism', and also looked for cases of practising medicine without a licence that were connected to obeah. I also investigated obeah cases from Trinidad, chosen because it was another large jurisdiction within the Caribbean, but one with a history that in many ways contrasts with that of Jamaica. Trinidad was a late addition to Britain's Caribbean empire, with a very culturally mixed elite and a large East Indian population. For Trinidad, court cases were collected from the microfilmed *Port of Spain Gazette*.[5] As this process was much more time consuming than searching the *Gleaner*, and it was not possible to search until 1989, I limited the period searched to 1890 to 1939 as the likely peak period for prosecutions, because the search of the *Gleaner* had revealed a significant decline in prosecutions after 1939. Investigating two colonies in this way avoids the problems of assuming that a single territory stands for the entire Caribbean, while providing a larger and more systematic body of evidence than can be obtained by selecting examples from across the region. Trinidad and Jamaica were both large colonies within the British Caribbean context, with contrasting histories. These differing histories meant that – to emphasize only the most obvious difference between them – by the turn of the twentieth century there was a significant Indian-origin population in Trinidad but only a small one in Jamaica, a result of the importance of indentured labour in post-emancipation Trinidad. The

---

[4] See chapter 8 for analysis of cases from 1940 to 1989.
[5] The digital edition of the *Gleaner* is available through www.newspaperarchive.com. The *Port of Spain Gazette* was examined at the British Library newspaper library and newsroom. These searches were conducted with the assistance of Suzie Thomas, Helen McKee, and Jennifer Kain for the *Jamaica Gleaner*, and Maarit Forde for the *Port of Spain Gazette*. Forde is also using the material she collected in her own research. I am grateful for the work of all these colleagues, and for the support of the British Academy and Leverhulme Trust which funded it. For reflection on the methodological issues raised by this kind of research see Upchurch, 'Full-Text Databases'.

two colonies also exemplify the two main types of obeah law that existed across the region: Jamaica had specific 'Obeah Acts', revised on multiple occasions in the 1890s and early 1900s, while in Trinidad obeah was illegal under the 'Summary Conviction Ordinance', a composite statute that defined and specified punishments for many minor offences.

In addition to collecting arrests and prosecutions for practising obeah, we collected reports about related offences. In Jamaica, but not Trinidad, a significant group of people was charged with consulting an obeah practitioner, and some were charged under vagrancy laws with being persons 'pretending to deal in obeah'. A few individuals in each colony were prosecuted for possession of 'materials to be used in the practice of obeah' or 'instruments of obeah'.[6] We also included cases where obeah was explicitly considered as a potential charge, but where the defendant was ultimately charged with another crime: larceny or practising medicine without a licence.

Both the *Gleaner* and the *Port of Spain Gazette* filled considerable space with reports of the proceedings of magistrates' courts. The papers did not, however, claim to be comprehensive; undoubtedly there were trials for obeah that they never reported. Sometimes cases trail off frustratingly, with reports that a verdict or sentence will be delivered the next day, but no follow-up story. In addition, we will certainly have missed some cases due to flaws in the optical-character-recognition digitizing process and through oversights when scanning the microfilm editions. Thus although I present figures for the prevalence of different trial outcomes and punishments, and the different characteristics of defendants by gender and ethnicity, these should be taken as broad rather than precise indicators. Nevertheless, these chapters are certainly based on the largest compilation of obeah cases any researcher has so far collected. This material allows us to raise and begin to answer some questions that would otherwise be impossible to consider.

The mass of evidence acquired from the newspapers demonstrates that obeah was a contested category. There are recognizable patterns in the actions, objects, and words that were presented as evidence that someone was practising obeah, and these fed into the reproduction of the stereotype of the obeah man. But these patterns do not exhaust what can be gleaned from the evidence. A tremendous range of practices and of contexts came before the courts. The evidence also hints

---

[6] There was some disagreement over whether this was actually a crime. Newspapers regularly reported people being charged with 'possession of instruments of obeah' in Jamaica, but in 1919 the Jamaican appeal court ruled that this was not in itself a crime, although it could be used in evidence that an individual was practising obeah. 'Conviction Quashed', *Gleaner*, 6 April 1933.

at the existence of other activities, popularly known as obeah, that were never or very rarely prosecuted because they did not fit obeah's legal definition. This large body of evidence also allows for comparison and for the evaluation of similarity and difference over time and across space. It reveals important similarities between Trinidad and Jamaica, but also some significant differences. It shows Jamaica to have been a colony with a harsher judicial system than Trinidad, at least with regard to obeah. Obeah was prosecuted more regularly there, those prosecuted for it were found guilty more frequently, and those found guilty were punished more severely. Obeah acquired a particularly powerful symbolic and political role in Jamaica as *the* activity that in the early twentieth century represented the population's backwardness, a cultural weight that was spread more diffusely among a range of cultural objects and practices in Trinidad.

Jamaica and Trinidad, like other British colonies, shared with the metropolis a common-law tradition characterized by a nested hierarchy of courts, an adversarial system of prosecution, and a judicial process that took place in public. Cases were brought by a prosecuting lawyer or police officer acting on behalf of 'the Crown', a legal fiction that implied the representation of collective interest in the prosecution of criminals. Those prosecuted, known as defendants, had the right to be represented by lawyers, if they could pay for them. In both colonies obeah cases were tried at the lowest level of the criminal justice system, in courts known as police courts, petty sessions courts, or resident magistrates' courts. These courts were presided over by magistrates most of whom had no legal training and were part of the local elite. In the capital cities of Kingston and Port of Spain the magistrate's court was known as the police court, met every day, and was overseen by paid magistrates; in the rural areas the resident magistrates' courts (in Jamaica) and petty sessions courts (in Trinidad) met every few weeks in a local town and were overseen by an unpaid magistrate. The magistrate decided on verdicts and sentences without the aid of a jury. Except when their decisions were appealed, records of the business of these courts were not formally archived. As a result, in most cases the reports of their proceedings that appeared in newspapers provide the only evidence available about the proceedings of these courts. In total, we recorded 813 reports of arrests and prosecutions for obeah-related crimes in Jamaica and 121 for Trinidad (see Table 5.1).[7]

---

[7] This counts each occasion when an individual is charged, rather than each incident, so if two people were prosecuted for the same act we counted each individual's prosecution separately.

Table 5.1 *Arrests and prosecutions for obeah and related offences, reported in the* Daily Gleaner *and* Port of Spain Gazette, *1890–1939*

|  | Jamaica | Trinidad |
|---|---|---|
| Practising obeah | 625 | 91 |
| Practising obeah and additional charge | 29 | 3 |
| Consulting an obeah man/woman | 50 | 0 |
| Vagrancy (obeah related) | 38 | 0 |
| Larceny (obeah related) | 24 | 9 |
| Possession of obeah materials | 21 | 1 |
| Obtaining money by false pretences (obeah related) | 9 | 12 |
| Practising medicine without a licence (obeah related) | 17 | 0 |
| Aiding and abetting the practice of obeah | 0 | 5 |
| **Total** | **813** | **121** |

The choice to charge someone with obeah was one of several possibilities open to police who made arrests. The elements that made up the crime could also, if put together in other ways, contribute towards prosecutions for other offences, some of them more serious than obeah. Most significant was larceny, which regularly led to multiple years' imprisonment, compared to obeah's maximum penalty of a year's imprisonment and a flogging.[8] Larceny charges were usually brought in relatively unusual situations that did not involve entrapment and where the parties did not know each other in advance. The clients involved in cases that led to larceny charges had generally been coerced or tricked into passing over money, rather than doing so in the context of a ritual. Other charges that frequently overlapped with prosecutions for obeah involved less serious charges, including practising medicine without a licence, obtaining money by false pretences, pretending to tell fortunes, and, in Jamaica but not Trinidad, vagrancy. Practising medicine without a licence overlapped with obeah but could only be punished with a fine, not a prison sentence or a flogging. Some of those prosecuted for it were not doing anything that could be interpreted as obeah, but many were offering ritual and spiritual healing services that shared a good deal with some of the activities that were prosecuted as obeah.

The most striking finding is the much larger number of cases reported for Jamaica than for Trinidad. One would expect to find more Jamaican than Trinidadian cases, since the Jamaican population was more than

---

[8] Only men could be flogged, so for women the maximum sentence was a year's imprisonment.

twice the size of that of Trinidad and Tobago, and the *Port of Spain Gazette* rarely reported the proceedings of Tobagonian courts.[9] But even taking this into account, as well as the possibility that some of the difference is due to the *Gleaner*'s greater resources or its greater interest in reporting obeah cases, it is clear that obeah was more vigorously pursued in Jamaica than in Trinidad. In addition to the larger number of prosecutions in Jamaica, this chapter will show that those prosecuted were more likely to be found guilty, and that those found guilty received harsher sentences. Jamaican authorities were also more concerned to promulgate new obeah laws, and paid more attention to obeah as a problem.

One reason for the greater intensity of prosecutions in Jamaica was the existence in Trinidad for the second half of this period of the Shouters' Prohibition Ordinance, which, as discussed in Chapter 4, made it illegal after 1917 to participate in the services of the Spiritual Baptist faith. No such law ever existed in Jamaica. We found twenty-nine prosecutions brought under the Shouters' Prohibition Ordinance between 1917 and 1939. Spiritual Baptists sometimes appeared in court on their own or in groups of one or two, but frequently in groups of 16, 20, 26, or even 130 defendants.[10] Altogether at least 500 people were prosecuted under the Ordinance, many more than under the obeah and related laws.[11] In court, hundreds of co-religionists appeared to support their brethren and sistren: 200 attended a hearing in Chaguanas in 1918.[12] As the next chapter demonstrates, in Jamaica people involved in Revival religion, which played a similar cultural role in Jamaica to that of the Spiritual Baptist faith in Trinidad, were regularly prosecuted for obeah. In contrast I found almost no evidence of people affiliated with Spiritual Baptist communities being prosecuted for obeah in Trinidad.[13] The absence of

---

[9] The 1911 censuses counted the Jamaican population as 831,383 and the population of Trinidad and Tobago as 333,552. Harewood, *The Population of Trinidad and Tobago*, 6; Roberts, *The Population of Jamaica*, 43.

[10] Prosecutions under the Shouters' Prohibition Ordinance are discussed in more depth in the next chapter. For a case with 130 defendants see '"Shouting" at St James', *POSG*, 5 July 1927, 2. Stephen Glazier raises the question of whether the Shouters' Prohibition Ordinance was enforced, noting that some contemporary Spiritual Baptists claim that 'not a single church was closed nor was a single Baptist leader imprisoned'. This may well be true, but significant fines were certainly imposed on Spiritual Baptist leaders, forcing the community to expend considerable practical and financial effort on evading the law and paying fines. Glazier, 'Funerals and Mourning'.

[11] This count includes three cases that were reported in the *Trinidad Guardian* but not the *Port of Spain Gazette*. Thanks to John Cowley for providing details of the *Trinidad Guardian* reports.

[12] 'Shouters in Court', *POSG*, 9 January 1918.

[13] One possible case involves Archibald Forbes, prosecuted for obeah in 1904 ('Amusing Obeah Case', *POSG*, 30 December 1904). A man of the same name was prosecuted twice, in 1918 and 1919, under the Shouters' Prohibition Ordinance. 'Shouters'

an equivalent law in Jamaica making Revival illegal – despite the efforts of some individuals to pass one – meant that the circumstances in which obeah laws, along with some other laws such as the Night Noises Law and laws against breach of the peace, were used in Jamaica were different from their application in Trinidad.

The availability of the Shouters' Prohibition Ordinance does not fully account for the difference between Jamaica and Trinidad, however. Jamaica's much longer history of official preoccupation with obeah also played a significant role. In addition, as I will show, the significant East Indian population of Trinidad seem to have been less likely to experience prosecutions for obeah than people of African descent, whereas in Jamaica Indians were more likely, in relation to their proportion of the population, to be prosecuted for obeah than African Jamaicans.[14] The fact that obeah prosecutions were, in the ethnically divided society of Trinidad, more likely to be used against African Trinidadians may be another reason for the greater intensity of Jamaican obeah prosecutions.

In both Jamaica and Trinidad the number of cases brought fluctuated considerably over time (see Figure 5.1). Fluctuations could result from policy decisions within the higher ranks of the police force, sometimes prompted by press and political agitation for a campaign against obeah. In Jamaica there was a clear peak in 1898 and 1899, a result of determined efforts to enforce the newly passed 1898 Obeah Act. In the wake of its passage, the Clarendon police went on a 'vigorous crusade' against obeah practitioners, resulting in thirteen convictions in that parish in the first year of the new law's existence.[15] Similarly, in the year following the passage of the 1904 Leeward Islands Obeah Act, significant numbers were convicted of obeah in some of the territories it covered, most notably Nevis, where thirteen were convicted within a year.[16] Anti-obeah campaigns could also take place without a change of the law. In 1916, the year of the largest peak in obeah prosecutions, two policemen in Manchester, Jamaica, were assigned specifically to prosecute obeah practitioners, leading to reported arrests of one group of seven people and one of five.[17]

---

Meeting Interrupted by Police', *POSG*, 22 January 1918, 'Keeping Shouters' Meeting at Clifton Hill', *POSG*, 26 September 1919. This may well be a different Archibald Forbes.

[14] This does not, of course, mean that a higher percentage of obeah defendants in Jamaica were of East Indian origin than in Trinidad, only a higher percentage in relation to share of overall population.

[15] 'A Baker's Dozen and a Word of Praise for the Clarendon Police', *Gleaner*, 28 July 1899 (also in Scrap Book 1894–1901 kept by John Henry McCrea, Deputy Inspector General of Police, JA 7/97/3 (henceforth McCrea Scrap Book), f. 133 (follows f. 65)).

[16] CO 152/287, Knollys to Lyttelton No. 208, 12 May 1905.

[17] 'Arrests Made', *Gleaner*, 10 March 1916, 'Mandeville Obeah Charges', *Gleaner*, 17 March 1916.

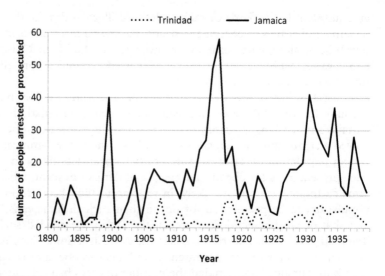

Figure 5.1 Arrests or prosecutions for obeah and related offences in Jamaica and Trinidad, 1890–1939.
*Source*: Jamaica *Gleaner* (newspaperarchive.com); *Port of Spain Gazette* (microfilm).

Jamaican prosecutions then fell back for most of the 1920s before rising to sustained higher levels during the 1930s. Convictions and gendered patterns of arrest followed the same pattern as overall prosecutions, as did the pattern for the various specific crimes. In Trinidad, with fewer cases altogether, the pattern is even more jagged. There too, there were sometimes police campaigns against obeah. In 1933 the *Port of Spain Gazette* reported that a Tobago policeman 'has been digging out the seers of the Island'.[18] In some years we found no obeah cases at all. The peak year for cases was 1907, a year which saw a single case in which five people were charged with obeah.

Who was prosecuted for obeah? As Table 5.2 shows, in both colonies, but especially in Jamaica, defendants in obeah cases were predominantly male, as had also been true during the period of slavery. The charges of practising medicine without a licence and of consulting an obeah practitioner (only found in Jamaica) were somewhat more evenly distributed by gender, although still dominated by men, while larceny charges were

[18] 'Magistrates Court', *POSG*, 30 September 1933.

Table 5.2 *Gender of defendants in obeah and related cases (percentages are of those of known gender)*

|  | Jamaica | | | Trinidad | |
| --- | --- | --- | --- | --- | --- |
|  | Men | Women | Unknown | Men | Women |
| Practising obeah | 552 (90%) | 61 | 12 | 68 (75%) | 23 |
| Practising obeah and additional charge | 20 (69%) | 9 | 0 | 3 (100%) | 0 |
| Consulting an obeah man/woman | 30 (60%) | 20 | 0 | 0 | 0 |
| Vagrancy (obeah related) | 31 (82%) | 7 | 0 | 0 | 0 |
| Larceny (obeah related) | 22 (92%) | 2 | 0 | 9 (100%) | 0 |
| Possession of obeah materials | 19 (90%) | 2 | 0 | 1 (100%) | 0 |
| Obtaining money by false pretences (obeah related) | 7 (78%) | 2 | 0 | 11 (91%) | 1 |
| Practising medicine without a licence (obeah related) | 13 (76%) | 4 | 0 | 0 | 0 |
| Aiding and abetting the practice of obeah | 0 | 0 | 0 | 1 (20%) | 4 |
| All cases | 694 (87%) | 107 | 12 | 93 (77%) | 28 |
| **Total** | **813** | | | **121** | |

with only two exceptions brought against men.[19] These patterns reflect patterns both of prosecution and of practices of spiritual healing.

Women's spiritual healing practices were less likely than men's to be construed as obeah and thus to be prosecuted, because they tended to take place in collective settings. When women *were* prosecuted for obeah, they were much more likely than men to be arrested for actions undertaken within a religious community. Ellen Barnes, for instance, was found guilty of obeah after she was entrapped by a man who claimed to be ill but was in fact a policeman in disguise. Her premises in the parish of Hanover, Jamaica, were marked by a flag on a 48-foot pole; she carried a Bible, candle, and whip. Barnes led the assembled members of her church in worship that involved drumming, singing, prayer, and

[19] One of the obeah-related larceny charges brought against a woman was very different from those brought against men. It involved a woman stealing a dress from another woman in order to take it to an obeah man to use in hostile magic against the woman from whom it was stolen. 'Stole Garments to Give to Obeahman', *Gleaner*, 23 June 1930. The larceny charges against men involved a form of con trick involving the promise of supernatural aid. The second woman charged with obeah-related larceny was working with a man, who was also prosecuted. 'Man Returning from Cuba Relieved of his Money', *Gleaner*, 7 February 1927.

the reading of chapters from the Bible before attempting to heal the policeman, whom she said had three spirits on him. Her activities were recognizably related to Revival religion and her healing, which involved further reading of Bible verses and the provision of medicinal liquids, was a part of the Revival tradition.[20]

Defendants came from predominantly poor and working-class communities. They reported that they made their living through a range of almost entirely working-class occupations such as labourer, bricklayer, poultry-rearer, gardener, higgler, washerwoman, or cultivator. The prosecution of an occasional middle-class person for obeah was surprising enough to attract crowds, extensive comment from journalists, and sometimes special treatment from the magistrate. The *Gleaner* described the prosecution of David Bates, a schoolmaster and inspector for the poor, as 'sensational', noting the 'very great interest throughout the parish on account of the position once occupied by the accused', while the prosecution of Victoria Doyle, former schoolmistress in Guapo, southern Trinidad, attracted a large crowd of spectators to the courtroom.[21] Defendants lived in both urban and rural settings; many had lived overseas or had been born outside Jamaica or Trinidad.

Representations of obeah continued to tie it tightly to Africa throughout this period, although defendants in obeah cases were by this time very rarely African born. I found only five cases in the 1890–1939 evidence that described obeah defendants as African: two in Jamaica and three in Trinidad.[22] Nor was prosecution for obeah limited to people of African descent, although they were the majority in both colonies. People of Indian birth or descent also appeared in court for obeah-related crimes, although I found no reports of people identified as white being prosecuted for obeah.[23]

Prosecutions for obeah played a distinctive but different role in constructing race in the two colonies. In Trinidad, East Indians were significantly underrepresented among those prosecuted for obeah, in relation to their share of the population. Sixteen of the 121 obeah defendants (13 per cent) were described as East Indian or 'coolie', in a colony

---

[20] '"Obeah" woman sent to prison for 6 months', *Gleaner*, 8 November 1932.
[21] 'A Sensational Obeah Case', *Gleaner*, 21 September 1893; 'Alleged Obeah at Guapo', *POSG*, 21 April 1929.
[22] 'Practiced Obeah', *Gleaner*, 20 October 1902; 'The Alleged Obeah Man', *POSG*, 10 April 1902; 'Obeah Charge', *Gleaner*, 14 January 1911; Police Court Brevities', *POSG*, 1 February 1935; 'Lopinot Obeah Case', *POSG*, 26 February 1936.
[23] Both the *Gleaner* and the *Port of Spain Gazette* seem to have always noted when a defendant was of Indian origin, using terms such as 'coolie' or 'East Indian'. The more frequent defendants of African descent were not always described in terms of race in the reports, although sometimes descriptions of their skin colour were included.

in which people of Indian origin made up just over a third of the population.[24] It seems that, in a colony where division between people of African and Indian descent was a crucial element of colonial control, prosecution for obeah was part of what marked out African Trinidadians as a distinct group. Also markedly disproportionate to their share of the population, but in the other direction, was the prosecution of Indians for obeah in Jamaica. There, where blackness was much more of an assumed norm and people of Indian origin never exceeded 2 per cent of the population, people identified as 'East Indian' or 'coolie' made up 4 per cent of those prosecuted for obeah (thirty-five individuals). This was a small proportion of the total, but at least twice what would be expected if the prosecutions took place without regard to ethnicity.[25] In Jamaica, then, Indians had come to be understood as particularly likely to practise spiritual work, while at the same time their small numbers meant that Indian spiritual traditions were assimilated to 'obeah'. If Jamaicans sought out people of Indian origin as spiritual workers, believing them to have access to particularly strong spiritual power, this was interpreted by all concerned as the Indians practising obeah. A *Gleaner* article published in 1890 hinted at this, reporting that 'our people say "the Coolies are the best obeahmen"'.[26] In contrast, in Trinidad, although East Indians were sometimes understood to be obeah men, their spiritual practice was also understood as taking place within Hindu or Muslim ritual contexts, and thus as something other than obeah – Kali Mai Puja, for instance.[27] People of Indian origin certainly undertook rituals that involved the use of spiritual power to heal, but these were relatively infrequently labelled 'obeah' and were less likely to lead to arrest, although not guaranteed to be allowed to take place freely.[28] In the end, though, all this may simplify the complex understanding of race and ethnicity at work in both Trinidad and Jamaica. In Trinidad a man who called himself Baboo Khandas Sadoo was charged with practising obeah in 1919. Described as a man 'of the bold negro type' and as being 'of African descent', he had converted to Hinduism and spoke 'Hindustani', and had an altar

[24] Harewood, *The Population of Trinidad and Tobago*, 91.
[25] Roberts, *The Population of Jamaica*, 43, 131. For another discussion of Indians arrested for obeah in Jamaica see Moore and Johnson, *'They Do as they Please'*, 387.
[26] 'The Land we Live in', *Gleaner*, 15 November 1890.
[27] For an analysis of Kali worship in contemporary Trinidad, with some discussion of the period analysed here, see McNeal, *Trance and Modernity*.
[28] For one case in which an Indian's use of spiritual power was interpreted as obeah see '"Obeah" Case Dismissed', *POSG*, 11 September 1936. In this case Soolal Singh, described as a 'village spiritualist', was prosecuted for obeah after offering 'orations to Allah' in exchange for $5 from a woman who believed her jewels had been stolen. It is notable, however, that this prosecution did not stick and the case was dismissed.

Table 5.3 *Numbers of defendants in obeah and related cases (number of cases is stated first, followed by number of defendants in parentheses)*

|   | Jamaica | Trinidad |
|---|---|---|
| 1 | 539 (539) | 88 (88) |
| 2 | 85 (170) | 9 (18) |
| 3 | 18 (54) | 3 (9) |
| 4 | 4 (16) | 0 |
| 5 | 5 (20) | 0 |
| 6 | 0 | 1 (6) |
| 7 | 2 (14) | 0 |
| **Total** | **653 (813)** | **101 (121)** |

with 'figures of Hindoo gods and devils'.[29] His case suggests the complex movement that could take place across apparently stable categories.

In both colonies, about two-thirds of those arrested for obeah-related offences were prosecuted as individuals, with most of the rest taken to court in pairs (see Table 5.3). A few in each colony were brought to trial in larger groups of up to seven defendants. In some of these group cases one individual was prosecuted for obeah and several others for consulting an obeah man.[30] Women were significantly more likely than men to be prosecuted in groups of two or more people, suggesting again that they tended to be prosecuted for obeah for activities undertaken in the context of collective religious practice.[31]

People tried for obeah were very likely to be convicted. In Jamaica 81 per cent of those charged with obeah-related offences, where the outcome is known, were convicted. In Trinidad convictions were slightly less likely, but at 78 per cent still represented a very high proportion of prosecutions.[32] As Table 5.4 shows, at least in Jamaica, those charged

---

[29] 'Alleged Assumption of Supernatural Powers', *POSG*, 7 February 1919, 9–10.
[30] For example, 'St Elizabeth', *Gleaner*, 9 July 1891; 'Obeah Charge', *Gleaner*, 14 January 1911.
[31] In Jamaica, 63 of 107 women (59 per cent) were involved in cases with more than one defendant, compared to 274 of 813 (34 per cent) of all defendants. In Trinidad, 12 of 28 women (43 per cent) were involved in cases with more than one defendant, compared to 33 of 121 (27 per cent) of defendants as a whole.
[32] This high conviction rate is confirmed by a report on all obeah prosecutions in Jamaica for the period 1887 to 1892, in which even higher proportions of people were convicted. Of eighty-seven people charged with practising obeah or consulting an obeah practitioner, seventy-seven were found guilty (89 per cent). CO 137/550, Table showing... cases of obeah and myalism adjudicated... from 1 August 1887 to 31 July 1892.

Table 5.4 *Outcomes of obeah cases (percentages are of known outcomes)*

|  | Jamaica | | | Trinidad | | |
| --- | --- | --- | --- | --- | --- | --- |
|  | Guilty | Acquitted | Unknown | Guilty | Acquitted | Unknown |
| Practising obeah[a] | 391 (84%) | 73 | 160 | 59 (79%) | 15 | 17 |
| Practising obeah and additional charge | 14 (78%) | 4 | 11 | 1 (33%) | 2 | 0 |
| Consulting an obeah man/woman | 25 (58%) | 18 | 7 | 0 | 0 | 0 |
| Vagrancy (obeah related) | 17 (81%) | 4 | 17 | 0 | 0 | 0 |
| Larceny (obeah related) | 12 (63%) | 7 | 5 | 5 (63%) | 3 | 1 |
| Possession of obeah materials | 7 (50%) | 7 | 7 | 1 (100%) | 0 | 0 |
| Obtaining money by false pretences | 4 (50%) | 4 | 1 | 8 (89%) | 1 | 3 |
| Practising medicine without a licence (obeah related) | 14 (100%) | 0 | 3 | 0 | 0 | 0 |
| Aiding and abetting the practice of obeah | 0 | 0 | 0 | 3 (75%) | 1 | 1 |
| Subtotal | 484 (81%) | 117 | 211 | 77 (78%) | 22 | 22 |
| Total | **812** | | | **121** | | |

[a] One Jamaican case in which the defendant died before trial is excluded. Therefore the total number of Jamaican cases in this table is 812, rather than the 813 in Table 5.1.

with practising obeah itself were more likely to be convicted than were people charged with most other obeah-related offences. The main exceptions were the cases of practising medicine without a licence, for which there were fourteen convictions and no reported acquittals. This outcome probably results from the fact that these cases often represented a kind of plea bargain, in which someone initially charged with obeah agreed to plead guilty to unlicensed medical practice in order to get a lower punishment.[33] These rates of conviction echo high conviction rates for prosecutions heard in lower courts across the common-law world.[34] They significantly exceed the conviction rates for obeah charges brought during slavery, when, as shown in Chapter 3, between 40 and 56 per cent of defendants were convicted. Thus, the transition from a regime where obeah was a very serious crime to one where it was a minor offence meant expanded scope for prosecutions and a greater likelihood of conviction for those prosecuted.

People convicted of obeah might receive a fine or a prison sentence; the prison sentence could be accompanied by flogging if the defendant was male.[35] The maximum allowable sentence for practising obeah in Jamaica was until 1898 twelve months' imprisonment and up to seventy-five lashes; the 1898 Obeah Act maintained the maximum prison sentence but reduced the maximum number of lashes to eighteen. Maximum punishments in Trinidad were lower: six months' imprisonment and corporal punishment (no maximum number of lashes was specified in the legislation, but the most I found in practice was twelve).[36] Other crimes were subject to different punishments: obeah-related vagrancy and possession of obeah materials could be punished with fines or imprisonment, while those convicted of practising medicine without a licence could not receive a prison sentence, only a fine. People convicted for larceny could not be flogged, but could receive long prison sentences, of up to eight years.

Overall, Jamaican magistrates, as well as being more likely to convict, tended to impose more severe punishments. This is not surprising since the maximum allowable punishments under the obeah laws were harsher there. Nevertheless, as Table 5.5 shows, Jamaican magistrates reached for the heavier end of the spectrum of permitted punishments more

---

[33] This practice will be explored in more depth in the next chapter.
[34] For England, Scotland, and Wales see Mitchell, *British Historical Statistics*, 779–82, table 772.
[35] The 1903 Jamaican Obeah Act also provided for the possibility of 'police supervision' following a prison sentence, but this was rarely used.
[36] The Obeah Law 1898, Jamaica (CO 139/108); An Ordinance for rendering certain Offences punishable on Summary Conviction, Trinidad (CO 297/8).

Table 5.5 *Punishments of those found guilty in obeah and related cases (percentages are of known outcomes)*

| | Jamaica | | | | | Trinidad | | |
|---|---|---|---|---|---|---|---|---|
| | Fine | Imprisonment | Imprisonment and flogging | None | Unknown | Fine | Imprisonment | Imprisonment and flogging |
| Practising obeah | 36 (10%) | 248 (67%) | 83 (22%) | 4 (1%) | 20 | 23 (39%) | 31 (53%) | 5 (8%) |
| Practising obeah and additional charge | 2 (15%) | 10 (77%) | 1 (8%) | 0 | 1 | 0 | 0 | 1 (100%) |
| Consulting an obeah man/woman | 14 (58%) | 8 (33%) | 2 (8%) | 0 | 1 | 0 | 0 | 0 |
| Vagrancy (obeah related) | 3 (18%) | 14 (82%) | 0 | 0 | 0 | 0 | 0 | 0 |
| Larceny (obeah related) | 0 | 12 (100%) | 0 | 0 | 0 | 0 | 5 (100%) | 0 |
| Possession of obeah materials | 0 | 6 (100%) | 0 | 0 | 1 | 0 | 1 (100%) | 0 |
| Obtaining money by false pretences | 0 | 4 (100%) | 0 | 0 | 0 | 0 | 8 (100%) | 0 |
| Practising medicine without a licence (obeah related) | 14 (100%) | 0 | 0 | 0 | 0 | 0 | 0 | 0 |
| Aiding and abetting the practice of obeah | 0 | 0 | 0 | 0 | 0 | 1 (33%) | 2 (67%) | 0 |
| Subtotal | 69 (15%) | 302 (66%) | 86 (19%) | 4 (1%) | 23 | 24 (31%) | 47 (61%) | 6 (8%) |
| Total | 484 | | | | | 77 | | |

frequently than did those in Trinidad. When the law gave them the choice they were more likely to send people to prison, more likely to add a flogging to a prison sentence, and less likely to use fines.[37] Prison sentences in Jamaica were also considerably longer than in Trinidad, reflecting the maximum allowable prison sentence of twelve and six months, respectively: the median term of imprisonment for obeah was six months in Jamaica and four months in Trinidad, while the most frequent prison sentence in Jamaica was twelve months, compared to six months in Trinidad (the maximum allowable sentence in each case).[38] As well as ordering longer prison sentences, Jamaican magistrates also allotted more lashes. In Trinidad, the six sentences of flogging were for twelve lashes on four occasions and six on one (on one occasion the number of lashes was not reported); in Jamaica the median number of lashes was also twelve, but the most commonly awarded number of lashes was eighteen.[39] Sentences of eighteen lashes or more were passed in Jamaica on thirty-five occasions, and in five cases the maximum sentence allowed by the 1898 Obeah Law of eighteen lashes was exceeded.[40]

People who were acquitted usually disappeared from written sources, although some later reappeared as defendants, and occasionally as witnesses. Those convicted were taken to serve their prison sentences or to pay their fines. Some of them contested their convictions through appeals, which were decided in courts overseen by professional judges, either in Kingston or Port of Spain. The judges did not hear witnesses, but discussed the evidence that had been presented in the light of arguments from defence lawyers that the magistrates' decisions had been faulty. Table 5.7 shows appeals, representing 14 per cent of both Jamaican and Trinidadian cases that resulted in conviction. Appeal cases are probably overrepresented, because cases in the appeal court were more likely

---

[37] Brian Moore and Michele Johnson state that punishments in obeah cases in the period 1865–1920 usually involved flogging. Moore and Johnson, *Neither Led nor Driven*, 30. This is not confirmed by my data from the *Gleaner*, which covers a slightly later period. It is also not confirmed if one excludes the post-1920 cases (23 per cent of those found guilty between 1890 and 1920 were flogged), nor is it true of the cases from 1887–1892 reported to the Colonial Office in 1892, of which four out of seventy of those found guilty of practising obeah were flogged. My evidence suggests that flogging was a frequent punishment for obeah, but not the dominant one. Table showing.... cases of obeah and myalism adjudicated... from 1 August 1887 to 31 July 1892, enclosed in CO 137/550, Blake to Ripon No. 329, 28 September 1892.
[38] This excludes punishments for larceny, where sentences were considerably longer.
[39] There was also one case in Trinidad and three in Jamaica where the number of lashes was not reported.
[40] 'Country Notes', 6 March 1899; 'Little London: Obeah', 14 March 1901; 'The Supreme Court: Appeal in Obeah Case Upheld', 17 March 1903; 'An Obeah Case', 1 February 1916; 'Annotto Bay News', 4 October 1923, all in the *Gleaner*.

Table 5.6 *Extent of prison sentences in obeah-related cases, in months (percentages are of known outcomes)*

| | Jamaica | | | | | | Trinidad | | |
|---|---|---|---|---|---|---|---|---|---|
| | ≤3 | 4–6 | 7–9 | 10–12 | >12 | unknown | ≤3 | 4–6 | >12[a] |
| Practising obeah | 63 | 103 | 26 | 135 | 0 | 4 | 17 | 19 | 0 |
| Practising obeah and additional charge | 2 | 4 | 1 | 4 | 0 | 0 | 0 | 1 | 0 |
| Consulting an obeah man/woman | 6 | 3 | 0 | 1 | 0 | 0 | 0 | 0 | 0 |
| Vagrancy (obeah related) | 11 | 1 | 0 | 1 | 1 | 0 | 0 | 0 | 0 |
| Larceny (obeah related) | 4 | 0 | 1 | 2 | 5 | 0 | 1 | 3 | 1 |
| Possession of obeah materials | 2 | 2 | 1 | 1 | 0 | 0 | 1 | 0 | 0 |
| Obtaining money by false pretences | 0 | 1 | 2 | 1 | 0 | 0 | 1 | 6 | 1 |
| Aiding and abetting the practice of obeah | 0 | 0 | 0 | 0 | 0 | 0 | 1 | 1 | 0 |
| Subtotal | 88 | 114 | 31 | 145 | 6 | 4 | 21 | 30 | 2 |
| **Total** | **388** | | | | | | **53** | | |

[a] There were no sentences of more than six months and less than three years' imprisonment.

Table 5.7 *Appeals against obeah and related convictions*

| | Jamaica | | | | | Trinidad | | | |
|---|---|---|---|---|---|---|---|---|---|
| | Number of appeals | Conviction upheld | Sentence reduced | Conviction overturned | Unknown outcome | Number of appeals | Conviction upheld | Unknown outcome |
| Practising obeah | 55 | 28 | 5 | 17[a] | 5 | 8 | 6 | 2 |
| Practising obeah and additional charge | 6 | 5 | 1 | 0 | 0 | 0 | 0 | 0 |
| Consulting an obeah man/woman | 4 | 1 | 0 | 3 | 0 | 0 | 0 | 0 |
| Vagrancy (obeah related) | 0 | 0 | 0 | 0 | 0 | 0 | 0 | 0 |
| Larceny (obeah related) | 0 | 0 | 0 | 0 | 0 | 2 | 0 | 2 |
| Possession of obeah materials | 1 | 0 | 0 | 1 | 0 | 0 | 0 | 0 |
| Obtaining money by false pretences | 0 | 0 | 0 | 0 | 0 | 1 | 1 | 0 |
| Practising medicine without a licence | 0 | 0 | 0 | 0 | 0 | 0 | 0 | 0 |
| Aiding and abetting the practice of obeah | 0 | 0 | 0 | 0 | 0 | 0 | 0 | 0 |
| **Total** | **66** | **34** | **6** | **21** | **5** | **11** | **7** | **4** |

[a] Includes one case where the initial appeal was unsuccessful, but the defendant was later granted a 'free pardon' by the governor. 'Woman Convicted under Obeah Law is Granted Pardon', *Gleaner*, 10 March 1924.

to have been reported in the newspapers than those that did not result in appeal. This is confirmed by the fact that in several of the appeals we found no report of the earlier conviction. Nevertheless, even if an overestimate, this still suggests a considerable effort made to appeal against convictions for obeah-related crimes. Despite their regularity, appeals were unlikely to succeed. Less than a third of Jamaican appeals were successful, while in Trinidad we did not find a single successful appeal.[41]

How did these prosecutions for obeah and related crimes work? How did people come to be prosecuted, and what did prosecution mean to defendants, their families, and to people around them? The crime of obeah existed as one element in a larger culture in which concern about spiritual danger was all around. In this context a reputation as an obeah man or obeah woman was a double-edged sword. On one hand, some people prosecuted for obeah presented themselves in court with a sense of pride in ritual practice or spiritual power. In one of his several trials in Montserrat for obeah, Charles Dolly (pictured in Figure 5.2) explained that a board with a piece of glass attached was a tool for divination ('for the purpose of showing him what had happened'), and offered to 'give a demonstration of his skill in Court' before prophesying that an accident would befall 'some members of the Commissioner's family'. He also said 'that the police knew nothing of obeah' but were 'aware of his skill'.[42] On the other hand, for many the allegation of obeah use was a serious slur worth fighting, not least because it suggested that their achievements or status were not authentically gained. When Amelia Baker of Trinidad responded to a policeman's caution by telling him that he had 'got his stripes by the aid of obeah', this was a serious insult; he responded by arresting her and charging her with using 'violent language'.[43]

The negative popular perception of obeah as something dangerous and malicious is visible in the considerable number of slander cases, especially in the Jamaican courts, in which allegedly defamatory words included accusations that an individual had used obeah.[44] These suits were brought despite the fact that in bringing them plaintiffs risked drawing attention to the very accusation that they rejected.[45] Ellen Knight won

---

[41] We were unable to trace the outcome in four of the eleven appeals.
[42] 'Obeah in the Island of Montserrat', *POSG*, 19 December 1908, reprinting report from the *Montserrat Herald*.
[43] 'The Dust Plague', *POSG*, 21 May 1898, 3.
[44] Because practising obeah was a crime, the accusation that an individual had used it was actionable.
[45] We collected forty-nine reports of suits for slander involving accusations of obeah from the *Gleaner* and *Port of Spain Gazette* between 1890 and 1939. Two took place in Trinidad, one in Panama, and the rest in Jamaica.

Figure 5.2 Charles Dolly, front row, far right, pictured in 1905 in the Antigua gaol as one of a group of convicts serving prison sentences for obeah.
Source: The National Archives, CO 152/287

damages from another woman she accused of saying that she 'was holding the communion cup in the one hand and obeah in the other' and also that Knight had worked obeah and killed her accuser's mother.[46] Two years later another slander suit turned on the allegation that a man consulted an obeah man 'to work obeah' against two rival businessmen, and 'that he had a croaking lizard in his store licking his goods to give him luck'.[47] Slander cases reveal both that people accused each other of obeah use, meaning it in wholeheartedly negative terms, and that those so accused felt themselves to be seriously wronged. The slur that someone used obeah threatened their efforts to become a respectable person, distanced from poor and working-class behaviour and cultural practices. Popular understandings of obeah were complex: it inspired fear and anxiety when people suspected that it had been used against them, and it was

[46] *Gleaner*, 6 May 1909.
[47] 'Peculiar Case', *Gleaner*, 18 November 1911. For a further example see 'Cases at the Linstead Court', *Gleaner*, 25 June 1914.

something that most did not want to be associated with. At the same time, it was a form of power that many hoped to be able to access for themselves.

Slander cases invariably focused on accusations that obeah had been used to harm, and, in particular, as in two of the three cases quoted above, to kill. Suing for slander was no doubt an unusual reaction to accusations that one had hurt someone with obeah. Another response, also occasionally made visible through newspaper accounts of court proceedings, was to more directly attack the person making the accusation. Charles Moore, for instance, was prosecuted for beating a woman who claimed that he practised obeah.[48] In another case two men appeared in court for wounding each other in a fight which followed an attempt by one of them to 'advise' the other 'to stop the practising of obeah and ganga [sic] smoking'.[49] People also sometimes physically attacked those they thought had used obeah against them. In Trinidad, James Scipio attacked another man with his cutlass, declaring as he did so that 'it is you who work obeah on me and prevent me from getting work'.[50] These cases allow a glimpse into what we might call a common or reputational knowledge about obeah practice. They emphasize that although the laws against obeah were created by elites who hoped to use them to demonstrate the colonies' modernity and to control popular religion, they were also sustained from below. Prosecutions for obeah existed within a broader framework in which obeah was widely considered dangerous, even while some of the practices prosecuted as obeah were part of everyday life.

In some senses then, the obeah laws simply reinforced popular hostility to dangerous obeah practice. Yet not all actions popularly considered to involve elements of obeah were vulnerable to prosecution. Obeah was defined in Jamaican law as the act of 'any person who, to effect any fraudulent or unlawful purpose, or for gain, or for the purpose of frightening any person, uses, or pretends to use any occult means, or pretends to possess any supernatural power or knowledge'. In Trinidadian law it was 'every pretended assumption of supernatural power or knowledge whatever, for fraudulent or illicit purposes, or for gain, or for the injury of any person'.[51] In both societies, as well as in other colonies, the crime of obeah had two elements: the pretence to 'supernatural power or knowledge'; and the fact that this was done for gain, fraud, or to hurt someone.

---

[48] 'The Magistrate Took No Notes', *Gleaner*, 14 January 1916.
[49] 'Interesting Items from Port Maria', *Gleaner*, 1 February 1926.
[50] 'The Evil of Superstition', *POSG*, 7 June 1919, 7.
[51] The Obeah Law 1898, Jamaica (CO 139/108); An Ordinance for rendering certain Offences punishable on Summary Conviction, Trinidad (CO 297/8).

In practice, obeah cases almost always focused on the 'gain' rather than on the other purposes listed in the laws, and thus required the prosecution to demonstrate that money or, very occasionally, goods, had been exchanged for ritual services. Spiritual work that did not involve these elements was not vulnerable to prosecution as obeah. People who undertook ritual activity on their own behalf or on behalf of a friend or neighbour without any obvious payment or intended harm were not in law practising obeah, although what they did might well be popularly understood as obeah. In Port of Spain, a woman serving as a witness in a court case was arrested for 'strewing coarse salt on the staircase' of the court, which everyone involved interpreted as an attempt to use supernatural means to influence the trial's outcome. Rather than facing prosecution for obeah, she was charged with 'indecent behaviour'.[52] Popular and commercial culture was full of depictions of women using obeah to 'tie' their lovers, often by placing ritual objects including menstrual fluid or vaginal secretions in their food.[53] Prosecutions for obeah did sometimes revolve around relationships, especially men's desire to use spiritual power to force or persuade women who had left them to return. But they included very few prosecutions in which women were alleged to have 'tied' men. One of the few such cases that we found was a 1902 Trinidadian desertion suit, in which Mrs Humphrey sued her husband for leaving her three years previously to live with another woman. Mr Humphrey's defence was that his wife had practised obeah on him by placing a collection of crushed bone, grave dirt, and his nails and skin under his pillow. Her anger when he confronted her over this was what led him to leave, he claimed. It does not seem to have occurred to Mr Humphrey that he might try to prosecute his wife for obeah, and indeed a case brought on the basis of such evidence might well have failed. Mrs Humphrey's activity was understood by everyone in the court as a form of obeah practice, yet was not legally defined as such.[54] Another took place in Jamaica in 1913 when Cecelia Daley and Frank Campbell were charged with vagrancy for actions that, the *Gleaner* reported, 'amount to obeah' – but, it seems, were not quite legally considered to be so. The two had provided a woman with ritual material designed to increase her husband's love for her.[55] The rareness of such cases may be because 'tying' took place much less frequently than the fears expressed in calypsos and stories suggest, but probably also results from the fact that it

---

[52] 'Superstition', *POSG*, 30 November 1894, 3.
[53] Rohlehr, *A Scuffling of Islands*, 238. Perhaps the most well-known such depiction is the Mighty Sparrow's calypso 'Obeah Wedding' (also known as 'Melda').
[54] 'Allegations of Obeah', *POSG*, 7 February 1902, 4.
[55] 'Failing Love', *Gleaner*, 6 October 1913, 14.

Figure 5.3 'Obeah' in Jamaica, *The Graphic*, 2 July 1898, p. 22. This illustration to an article about Jamaica in the context of the Spanish–Cuban–American war shows the ubiquity of obeah as a symbol of the Caribbean more generally. The obeah bottle was part of standard representation of obeah, but is rarely found in obeah prosecutions.
Courtesy of the National Library of Scotland

could be done privately by women without the involvement of a paid ritual specialist. Similarly, obeah prosecutions very rarely heard evidence about the placing of protective 'obeah bottles' in trees and around houses, despite the frequent depiction of this as an obeah activity in works of fiction, folklore, and travel writing (see Figure 5.3).[56] Prosecutions for obeah, then, intersected only partially with the activities that were popularly deemed to constitute obeah. Yet because the legal definition of obeah made the paid encounter between ritual specialist and client a defining characteristic of the crime, such encounters became an important model for obeah practice.

[56] For instance Bell, *Obeah*; Lanaghan, *Antigua and the Antiguans*, II, 54. 'Results of the Christmas Story Competition', *Gleaner*, 24 December 1896; 'The Obeahman', *POSG*, 17 January 1897, 3–4.

In order to show how the legal definition of obeah affected broader understandings, much of the rest of this chapter traces the experience of being prosecuted for obeah, from arrest to conviction. It examines two cases at length, one Trinidadian and one Jamaican, while drawing on other material to show alternative outcomes or trajectories. The first case I attend to is the prosecution in 1910 of Mary Clement and her husband Arthur, of Woodbrook in Port of Spain. The second involved Theophilus Neil of the rural community of Princess Hill, near Linstead in central Jamaica, in 1924. These prosecutions were not typical, but they are particularly telling and were reported in detail. The two cases also exemplify the two main modes by which obeah prosecutions came about: through civilian reports to the police, on the one hand, and through entrapment by police or their agents, on the other.

The story of how someone might end up in court for obeah could be narrated with many starting points, but the evidence available to the historian dependent on newspaper reports usually begins at or shortly before the individual's arrest. Let us start, then, with the earliest information we have about Mary and Arthur Clement and Theophilus Neil. In the Trinidadians' case, a woman named Annie Stewart, who described herself as a Wesleyan, testified that in May 1910 she and her husband had visited the Clements, seeking relief from Mr Stewart's serious illness. A friend had advised them of the Clements' healing abilities. Arthur Clement diagnosed Mr Stewart as having 'devil spirits' on him that were causing his ill health, and treated him by sacrificing a fowl, placing its blood on a plate between his legs, reciting prayers, and burning a 'filthy scented liquid' mixed with rum. He then instructed Mr Stewart on how to take a daily herbal bath for the next six days. Mr Stewart's health did not improve, and not long afterwards he died. On 22 June, a month after the Stewarts had visited the Clements, Corporal Joseph Alexander went to search the healers' house under warrant for 'articles used in the practice of obeah'. Alexander, also known as Cola or Kola, became notorious in early twentieth-century Trinidad for his police work, including several prominent arrests for obeah.[57] He did not explain in court why he sought the warrant, but Annie Stewart's evidence suggests that he did so because she went to the police in the aftermath of her husband's death. Stewart stated in court that she had never believed in the Clements' power, but had visited them with her husband in order to 'please' him.[58]

---

[57] Forde, 'Religious Persecution from Below'.
[58] 'The Brabant Street Obeah Case', *POSG*, 13 July 1910, 5; Alexander, *Recollections of a Trinidad Detective*.

The prosecution of the Clements was thus initiated by a civilian, in this case because of Annie Stewart's disappointment at the failure of their healing and her distress at her husband's death.

Cases like this, initiated by a member of the public reporting someone to the police in the hope of instigating a prosecution for obeah, accounted for more than half of Jamaican cases, and around a third of Trinidadian.[59] In Annie Stewart's case it is relatively clear why she went to the police. Even so, she might have responded in many other ways to her husband's death; why she chose this course of action over others is less easy to judge. In this and in many similar cases it is hard to get much insight into the motivations of those who reported people to the police for practising obeah, because the discourse of newspaper reporting and of the courtroom relied on two fictions: first, that any citizen would report any breach of the law to the police; and second, that the illegal act of 'practising obeah' was clearly distinguishable from other similar, but legal, acts. As a result, in many cases the motivations of the person who went to the police with information about an alleged obeah practitioner were actively excluded from reports and testimony. For instance, according to the *Gleaner* a man named Thomas told a policeman that he had been approached by Thomas Mortimer Hood. Hood told him that he 'had seen a ghost on his wife' and could remove it through spiritual means. Thomas later accompanied two policemen to Hood's house in order to trap him into contravening the obeah law.[60] We do not know why Thomas initially went along with Hood's suggestions and then later reported him. Nor did the magistrate who heard Hood's case raise the question. Thomas could have simply ignored Hood, or refused his offers of help. Why did he, instead, go to the trouble of reporting the situation? Such questions are in many cases unanswerable. They remind us of the limitations of the knowledge that we can achieve through written records about the encounters that led to obeah prosecutions.

As the cases of the Clements and of Thomas Hood show, people who offered ritual or spiritual services risked arrest, especially when, like Thomas Hood, they actively sought out people to treat. Yet the risk must have been relatively low. Incidents in which people went to the police must have been strongly outnumbered by those in which the practitioner

---

[59] For further discussion of the initiation of arrests see Paton, 'The Trials of Inspector Thomas', 186–9, parts of which are incorporated in this chapter.
[60] 'Obeah Charges', *Gleaner*, 20 October 1913. For a similar case see 'Arrested on Obeah Charge', *Gleaner*, 6 April 1912.

succeeded in recruiting a client, or else these approaches would not have continued.

In some cases, often those in which a defendant employed a solicitor to argue his or her case in court, testimony or contextual information reveals something of the reason why the person who eventually became a witness went to the police. In many of these incidents, testimony suggests a breakdown in the client's confidence in the spiritual worker. This might be, as in the case of Annie Stewart and her husband, because the spiritual work failed.[61] Or it could be because the client concluded that the work was excessively costly, as in a case when a man named Moody consulted Charles Johnson in the hope of getting a job. He and his friend later reported Johnson to the police because (according to Johnson's lawyer) 'they thought the amount charged was too much and they doubted the man's powers'.[62] In other cases the ritual specialist failed to return to complete the work promised, despite accepting money, and as a result the client eventually reported him. Letitia Gilbert, for instance, initially accepted William Francis's offer to remove the duppy that he said was causing her long-term sickness. Francis began a ritual, sprinkling white rum in her room, and then left, promising to return the next day. He did not come back. Gilbert took no further action until, after more than two months, she encountered Francis by chance, at which point she reported him to nearby police, who arrested him.[63] In this case it seems that Gilbert initially trusted Francis's powers, but felt cheated by his failure to return.

The involvement of the police in cases like these seems to have been a last resort, a back-up technique when informal efforts to resolve conflict had failed. Letitia Gilbert would not have reported William Francis if he had returned the next day, as he had promised. In a similar case, Eliza Walker consulted Isabella Francis after two biomedical doctors were unable to help her sick daughter. Francis gave her 'two bottles of some liquid and a little bag for the child to wear to keep off the evil spirit which was on the child'. After several weeks during which her daughter's health did not improve, Walker returned to Francis, asking for the return of the bangles that she said she had given in payment. Only when Francis refused to return the bangles did Walker go to the police.[64] In these cases police enforcement of the obeah laws resembled not so much an effort to

---

[61] For similar cases see 'Failing Love', 6 October 1913, 'Cases in the Rural Tribunal', 10 August 1918, and 'Trial of Zachariah Thomas', 10 July 1920, all in the *Gleaner*.
[62] 'Full Court Continues to hear Criminal Appeals', *Gleaner*, 22 September 1932.
[63] 'Obeah Charge', *Gleaner*, 14 April 1909.
[64] 'Cases Tried in the Courts of Two Parishes', *Gleaner*, 7 April 1922. See 'Obeah Charge', *Gleaner*, 13 January 1914 for a case that arose after a spiritual healer who sold ritual

eradicate obeah as a kind of regulatory procedure through which unsatisfied clients could deal with unscrupulous or incompetent practitioners. Despite official rhetoric about the usefulness of prosecution in ridding Jamaica or Trinidad of obeah and belief in obeah, in practice obeah cases often worked in response to the demand of clients for whom obeah was most definitely real.

On other occasions the police were, apparently willingly, drawn into disputes in working-class communities. Those who persuaded the police to prosecute someone for obeah could damage their rivals or enemies. Thus, for instance, Eliza Barnett was prosecuted, her defence lawyer claimed, because she refused to lend money to a neighbour, Boaz Bryan. Angry at being turned down, Bryan worked with the local policeman, Constable Lewis, to trap Barnett into committing ritual acts to remove hostile spiritual power. The trap led to Barnett receiving a six-month sentence for obeah.[65] In a similar case, Emanuel Faulkner and John Barnes were charged with possessing 'implements of obeah'. Under cross-examination two key witnesses who had provided information to the police leading to the raid on Faulkner and Barnes's yard revealed that they were former tenants of Faulkner with whom he had frequently 'quarrelled', and that they had left owing him rent.[66] In such cases, the person who went to the police had known the person reported for some time, and could have reported him or her earlier, but chose to do so at this particular moment because of the developing conflict between them.

In contrast to these cases initiated by civilians, the majority of cases in Trinidad, and a large minority of those in Jamaica, resulted from a policeman's decision to attempt to arrest a ritual specialist. The other case that I will trace in detail provides a good example of this situation, which often involved extended effort to entrap the suspect. Theophilus Neil's arrest in 1924 followed a decision by Detective Euriel Augustus Watson of the Linstead police in Jamaica to pursue him.[67] Detective Watson

---

medicine by post refused to accept an unsatisfied client taking back the horse he had given in payment.

[65] 'Obeah Charge', *Gleaner*, 23 May 1907; 'Obeah Charge', *Gleaner*, 27 May 1907. Barnett denied that she had performed the ritual, and argued that Bryan and Lewis were attempting to frame her. We cannot know whether or not the ritual described by Lewis in court really occurred, but Barnett's claim that Bryan initiated contact with the police because of his resentment at her refusal to lend him money was the only explanation offered at the trial for his behaviour.

[66] 'Interesting Case at Halfway Tree', *Gleaner*, 13 May 1916.

[67] Evidence on this case comes from the following articles published in the *Gleaner* in 1924: 'Theophilus Neil Charged with Practicing Obeah', 5 November; 'The Practising of Obeah is Charged', 14 November; 'A Charge of Practising the Black Art', 15 November; 'Obeah Trial', 17 November; 'Practising the Black Art', 21 November; 'Appeal in the Case of Rex vs Theo Neil', 6 December.

learned of Neil's reputation as an obeah man while investigating the murder of Leah Malcolm, for which Neil's cousin Christopher Fletcher was eventually convicted. Neil's brother George, also a spiritual healer, became an accessory to the murder because he helped Fletcher dispose of the body, although he emphasized that his work was not about killing or harm: 'It is not me who kill the woman. I don't work that sort of obeah. The sort of obeah that I work is to drive away spirits and to cure sickness.'[68] In the course of a lengthy investigation, Watson must have come to see Theophilus Neil as a possible target for prosecution as well, although there were no claims that he had anything to do with Malcom's death. Watson persuaded David Rennals to visit Theophilus Neil at his home in Princess Hill with the deliberate intention of acquiring evidence that he had broken the obeah law. Rennals was not a policeman, but acted on the promise that he would receive a reward if Neil was convicted. He went to Neil's place along with a friend, James Morgan, and claimed that he needed to get treatment for a sick man for whom he was responsible. Neil, although initially reluctant, eventually agreed to advise him. Asking first for 10 guineas, Neil accepted 25 shillings from Rennals, which Rennals paid in notes that Watson had marked for later identification. Neil then worked to 'dismiss' a ghost which he said was 'squeezing the sick man in his stomach'. After working with a pack of cards and three dice which he placed on a mirror, Neil gave Rennals three bottles of liquid and explained how he should use them to treat the sick man, who should also be anointed with a few drops of the blood of a fowl, mixed with the liquid provided. Rennals returned to the police station and gave the bottles of medicinal liquid and other material to Watson, who then went with a warrant for Neil's arrest under both the Obeah Law and the Medical Law.

Police-led arrests sometimes took the form of raids on the premises of suspected obeah practitioners, or opportunistic arrests of people with a reputation while they were going about their business. More commonly, as in Neil's case, they were achieved through subterfuges, sometimes elaborate, designed to entrap ritual specialists into committing illegal acts. The people employed to act as decoys in these cases were more frequently women, and they often appeared in multiple cases and collaborated closely with the police.

The arrest of Theophilus Neil shares many features with other entrapment cases, including the use of pairs of policemen or police spies so as

---

[68] 'Further Evidence Given at Murder Examination at Spanish Town', *Gleaner*, 30 June 1924. For Watson's involvement in this investigation see 'Examination into Murder Charge was Continued at Spanish Town', *Gleaner*, 28 June 1924.

to have corroborating witnesses, deployment of marked money, and the production of convincing narratives by plain-clothes police or civilians acting on behalf of the police. Entrapment narratives often involved ill health, but also revolved around employment, the success of businesses, court cases, and other matters. Either the police or their agents participated in the ritual activity, then revealed their identity and arrested the practitioner.

What led the police to pursue particular individuals at particular moments? As explained above, Neil came to Watson's attention because of his brother George's conviction as accessory to murder in a prominent trial. In other cases the police had apparently wanted to prosecute particular individuals for a long time, but had not been able to do so because of the suspects' knowledge of police techniques and ability to protect themselves against them. When Jasper Roberts was prosecuted for practising obeah, a newspaper reported that the police had been watching him for 'some three years', but 'all attempts to get at him had proved futile'. They were finally able to entrap him when two men who had sought his help in a court case in which they were defendants described his practice to the police after their conviction. Two constables then posed as the relatives of the convicted men and went to ask why they had not succeeded in getting off. (Roberts said it was because they had not consulted him early enough.) The constables then asked for spiritual help with their own (invented) problems, in order to be able to testify to his 'pretending to supernatural power'. Even then, Roberts was extremely cautious. He made the two constables take an oath before he would discuss anything of substance with them, then refused to take payment for his work because his 'concubine' said that 'the detective had been seen down the road that morning'. When they returned to try to pay the following week, Roberts refused to have anything to do with them. He was nevertheless arrested, convicted, and sentenced to a year's imprisonment and ten lashes.[69]

Roberts's caution was commonplace among successful ritual specialists, who knew how the police operated and took precautions to defend themselves against arrest. Like Roberts's 'concubine', their friends and kin warned them against potential police surveillance. While police were hiding in the hope of arresting a man in Diego Martin on the outskirts of Port of Spain, a 'little girl' called out a warning: 'Don't work tonight

---

[69] 'The King of St Thomas Obeahmen', undated newspaper clipping from unnamed source, National Library of Jamaica Clippings File – Obeah and Voodoo. From contextual information it seems likely that this case took place in July 1893. For another case, featuring the arrest of a ritual specialist who had been 'baffling the best efforts of the police for over six months', see 'Arrest is Made', *Gleaner*, 21 March 1916.

because the police hiding in the cocoa.'[70] Ritual specialists took note of other signs that a trap was being set. Joseph Reid, confronted with a putative client claiming to be in need of spiritual treatment for poor health, recognized that the man was a police constable and chased him away with a cowskin whip.[71] Suspect Joseph Donald refused to continue a ritual when his client produced the money provided to her by the police, saying that 'he could not work because the money had marks on them'.[72] Theophilus Neil had been suspicious of David Rennals when he arrived asking for help, initially deflecting him by asking whether there were not people who could help him closer to where he lived, and why he had not sought help from a biomedical doctor, before eventually agreeing to treat him. Ritual specialists operated with an awareness of the illegality of their practice and considerable knowledge of police tactics. It is therefore likely that on many occasions they were able to prevent police from collecting sufficient evidence to enable them to prosecute. Indeed, the police regularly complained of their difficulty in arresting obeah suspects. A policeman giving evidence at the trial of Joseph Paddy of Smith Village in 1915 testified that 'we used to hear a lot about him but we couldn't catch him', while a press report about an arrest the previous year noted that 'the police in their many attempts at bringing [George Black] to book were always beaten'.[73]

The police involved in obeah arrests were often stimulated by personal ambition, since successfully prosecuting obeah practitioners was a means to professional advancement. They were also at times motivated by personal grudges or hostilities against those they prosecuted. Such grudges, although usually concealed in the sources, occasionally emerge, as for example in another case brought by Joseph Alexander (Kola) a few years before he arrested the Clements. In 1907 he arrested Leopoldine Moise at her house a few blocks from Port of Spain's central Woodford Square. Moise's defence lawyer argued that the arrest, through entrapment, was a 'filthy conspiracy' brought as a result of Kola's 'individual grudge' against his client, which arose because Moise had provided ritual services to Kola's former partner Natalie Contreville. Kola believed that Moise had supported Natalie in her court case against him for breaking

---

[70] 'A Family of Obeahists', *POSG*, 2 August 1922, 9.
[71] 'Old Man is Found Guilty of Practising Obeah – Fined £15', *Gleaner*, 30 July 1931.
[72] 'Case of Alleged Obeah', *Gleaner*, 23 July 1929. For similar cases, in which alleged obeah men refused to work because of their awareness of police traps, see 'Cases heard in Resident Magistrate's Court', *Gleaner*, 5 August 1915; 'Charge of Practicing Obeah', *Gleaner*, 6 April 1916.
[73] 'An Obeahman Goes to Prison', *Gleaner*, 30 November 1915; 'Obeah Charge', *Gleaner*, 12 November 1914.

into her house, and had harmed his new partner through spiritual work. Contreville testified that on leaving the courthouse after her successful case against him, Kola said to her that 'the Guadalupe woman' – meaning Moise – 'made you bring this case'. Moreover, Moise claimed that, when he entered her house to arrest her, Alexander stated, in Trinidadian Creole: 'I am Cola Alexander. You have made Natalie win her case over me before the Magistrate, and to-day you have fallen into my hands.'[74] The statement suggests something of Kola's pride in his reputation, as well as his personal motivations. Despite the compromised motivations of a major witness, Moise was found guilty and her later appeal was unsuccessful: according to the appeal court judges it was 'obvious' that Moise had been practising obeah.[75] This case gives a sense of how far the reality of obeah prosecutions might differ from the idealized legal process in which prosecution for obeah served to break down popular belief in its power. Kola seems to have been as convinced as anyone of Moise's ability to use spiritual power to help Natalie; indeed, it was the fact that she had done so that motivated him to bring the prosecution.

Entrapment, though ubiquitous, could be controversial. Charles Frederick Lumb, an English-born judge who practised in Trinidad and Jamaica between 1887 and 1909, opposed its use in obeah cases, declaring it 'loathsome and unEnglish'.[76] A Colonial Office official agreed, describing the use of 'agents provocateurs' as 'discreditable', while the *Port of Spain Gazette* questioned the ethics of cases in which 'the principal witness for the police [might be] a bare-faced and hardened perjurer'.[77] Nevertheless, the practice of entrapment continued throughout the period, in both Trinidad and Jamaica. The Colonial Office refused to endorse Lumb's critique, approving the use of entrapment while noting that it should be used 'as little as possible'.[78] The Chief Justice of

---

[74] 'The Nelson Street Obeah Case', *POSG*, 16 January 1908.
[75] 'Prosecution Alleged by Defence to be a "Filthy Conspiracy"', *POSG*, 23 January 1908; 'Court of Appeal', *POSG*, 18 March 1908.
[76] Lumb's comments were made in the course of his judgment in an appeal. Rex v Chambers, 29 May 1901, enclosed in CO 137/620, Hemming to Chamberlain No. 406, 5 July 1901. On Lumb's career see 'Obituary: Sir Charles Frederick Lumb', *The Times*, 24 February 1911.
[77] Minute by 'RVV' in CO 137/620, Hemming to Chamberlain No. 406, 5 July 1901; 'The Police Informer', *POSG*, 16 September 1922. For a similar argument in a letter from a Kingstonian to the Colonial Office see CO 137/676, J. Cowell Carver to Secretary of State for the Colonies, 27 January 1909.
[78] CO 137/625, Secretary of State to Lucas, 15 October 1901. The Colonial Office advice was in part based on the comments of the chief justice of Jamaica, Sir Fielding Clarke, who argued that 'convictions can rarely be obtained except by means of decoys', because those who had witnessed their crimes were afraid to report them, in part because they were themselves guilty of the crime of consulting an obeah practitioner. CO 137/625,

Trinidad also approved of entrapment.[79] The Colonial Office's directive that entrapment should be used sparingly hardly restrained police practice, since in any individual case it could be argued that it had been necessary to gain a conviction. It became a standard part of police procedure, featuring, for instance, in material such as the *Trinidad Constabulary Manual*, which noted: 'It is almost always necessary to employ "Police Spies" in order to detect & prosecute to conviction persons charged with the practices of Obeah.'[80]

In entrapment cases there was usually a moment when the subterfuge was revealed: at a certain point within a ritual the policeman stopped posing as a client seeking spiritual help, declared his real identity, and physically took hold of the ritual specialist, announcing his or her arrest. This was a dramatic point of crisis and transition, when the police revealed themselves and thus asserted – or attempted to assert – the superior power of the state over that of the ritual specialist and his or her spiritual power. In cases where the police had been posing as the client of the obeah practitioner, there were usually additional police officers hiding outside the house in which the ritual was being undertaken, who rushed into the room and grabbed the accused when a previously agreed signal – a cough or some specific words – was given. Theophilus Neil's arrest departed from this pattern in taking place at a later date, when the people arrested were surprised by police with warrants.

The process of arrest was usually presented in court as smooth and straightforward, despite evidence that it was frequently violent or at least confrontational, often attracting considerable attention. Joseph Paddy's arrest in Smith's Village created a 'furore'.[81] Those arrested and their families and neighbours sometimes tried to fight off arrest, or to dispose of objects that they feared would be used as evidence against them. Mary Clement ran to the back of her yard when the police arrived, apparently trying to hide. When Theophilus Neil was arrested his family, according to Detective Watson, tried to 'make away with things', and he threw away a thread bag, later produced in court, which contained a phial of liquid, a set of human teeth, some coins, a mirror, a smaller bag, and a stone. Others protested their innocence, giving explanations about why what they

---

Sir Fielding Clarke (Chief Justice of Jamaica) to C. P. Lucas, 24 September 1901. For a similar argument see minute by 'WDE' in CO 137/620, Hemming to Chamberlain No. 406, 5 July 1901.

[79] 'Supernatural Power Case', *POSG*, 29 September 1915, 5.

[80] Notes on Trinidad Constabulary Manual, p. 67, Melville and Frances Herskovits Papers, MG 261, Box 17, Folder 106, Schomburg Center for Research in Black Culture, New York.

[81] 'The Case from Smith's Village', *Gleaner*, 26 November 1915.

were doing did not constitute obeah. Victoria Doyle told the arresting officer that 'she didn't work obeah but only makes prayers', having previously told her putative client that 'I do things to make a case drop but I don't work obeah'.[82] Arthur Stewart in Jamaica protested on his arrest, 'Me not working obeah. Me only burning candles.'[83] These efforts to discriminate between practising obeah and other kinds of spiritual work would later be echoed in court.

After making an obeah arrest, the police usually searched the suspects, their homes, and their possessions, often seizing large quantities of material. When Matthew Russell Gordon was arrested in Spanish Town three men were hired to carry his possessions from his home to the police station, where they 'filled the entrance room'. Anything that might remotely be connected to obeah was taken. In Gordon's case, this included 'human skulls, jaw bones, charms, bundles of bush, vials of evil-looking and evil-smelling liquids' – all items from the 'traditional' repertoire of obeah practice – but also a ledger, a bank book, cash, and foreign bank notes.[84] Joseph 'Kola' Alexander stated that he searched the Clements' premises and found a series of rather ordinary objects which he nonetheless described as evidence of obeah: 'a vessel with oil into it and a wick burning... two demijohns containing a liquid that to him tasted like sea water [and] a saucepan with something that smelt like rum'. Detective Watson searched Theophilus Neil's house in Neil's presence, and found a selection of objects, all of which might have multiple uses, but which Watson and the court interpreted as evidence of obeah practice: mirrors, phials, nails, bottles containing liquids, human hair, letters addressed to Neil, books, and two lamps. All were seized and later presented in court as evidence against him. These searches and seizures were driven by the law, which in Jamaica explicitly stated that someone found in possession of 'instruments of obeah' could be assumed to be an obeah practitioner, unless evidence to the contrary could be presented. Instruments of obeah were very broadly defined, as 'any thing used, or intended to be used by a person, and pretended by such person to be possessed of any occult or supernatural power'.[85] In Trinidad the law was not explicit on this point, but nevertheless the display of objects in court was an important part of the practice of obeah prosecutions. Objects seized by police could eventually find their way into works of anthropology and folklore.[86]

---

[82] 'Alleged Obeah at Guapo', *POSG*, 21 April 1929.
[83] 'Pay £10 to Kill', *Gleaner*, 14 July 1932.
[84] 'Alleged Obeahman', *Gleaner*, 4 November 1920.    [85] Obeah Law 1898, clause 3.
[86] Paton, 'The Trials of Inspector Thomas', 178–81.

Some of those arrested for obeah were no doubt released without being charged, and certainly without being brought to trial. Many press reports of arrests where no follow-up trial was reported may well have ended in this way. But in many cases the suspected obeah practitioner was formally charged and taken for trial at the magistrates' court, police court, or petty sessions court. Theophilus Neil was arrested on Sunday 2 November, held in the Linstead lock-up for a few days, and brought to the Linstead resident magistrates' court the following Wednesday for a brief hearing which simply stated the bare facts of the prosecution's case. He was then remanded in custody back to the lock-up before his full trial, which took place over two days the next week. The Clements' full trial also began ten days after their initial arrest. Others might await trial for considerably longer. Leopoldine Moise, for instance, was arrested on 1 November 1907 and brought before the Port of Spain city police court the next day, but her full trial did not take place until the following January.

There were minor differences between the two colonies in the charges brought, due to the wording of the respective laws prohibiting obeah. The charge against Theophilus Neil was framed straightforwardly, as was usually the case in Jamaica, as 'practicing obeah'. Arthur and Mary Clement were both charged with 'obtaining money by false pretenses with intent to defraud by the practice of obeah', a charge that was more specific in directly naming obeah than were many Trinidadian charges, where the phrase used was frequently 'obtaining money by the false assumption of supernatural power or knowledge'. This wording paraphrased text in the Summary Conviction Ordinance of 1868. In both cases the precise charge that was appropriate was discussed in court. The police hedged their bets in prosecuting Neil, charging him, in addition to practising obeah, with practising medicine without a licence. The Clements were initially charged with receiving money 'under the pretence that they could restore [Mr Stewart] to health' – effectively, a charge against the medical licensing law – but this was altered in court at the suggestion of the police to the charge already quoted. These shifts and multiple charges were common in obeah cases, because the offence overlapped with a range of other prohibitions and illegalities. The decision about which specific charge to bring lay initially with the police, and took into account the relative seriousness with which the law treated different offences and the charge that was most likely to result in conviction. The offence of breaching the medical law might be used if there was no explicitly 'supernatural' element to the ritual healing that had taken place. In addition, the Jamaican legal definition of vagrancy – like vagrancy legislation in many other parts of the Caribbean – included 'pretending to use any subtle craft or device by palmistry or any such superstitious means to deceive or impose on any person'.[87] A conviction for 'using superstitious means to deceive or impose' might be obtained in circumstances where the more stringent requirements for a conviction under the Obeah Act had not been met. This produced a number of prosecutions under the vagrancy law that were understood by all concerned as obeah cases. For instance, the prosecution of Benjamin James ('Benjy Two-Face') for vagrancy was reported under the headline 'An Obeah Case'.[88] Indeed, magistrates sometimes commented that a defendant was lucky to have been charged with vagrancy rather than obeah, because of the lesser punishment, or noted that if there had been further evidence they would have changed the charge to one of obeah.[89]

As this discussion shows, police decisions about what charge to bring might not be final. An initial charge of obeah could be reduced to one of practising medicine without a licence, or vagrancy. A defendant's perceived class standing could soften a prosecution. Jane Philips, whose husband was a schoolmaster, was caught at 5 a.m. scattering what some said to be 'a mixture of salt and grave-yard dirt and crushed bones' – although others said it was merely salt – outside the entrance to a neighbour's house. She was brought to court to be prosecuted for obeah, but at the beginning of the trial the prosecuting lawyer asked for permission to reduce the charge, because Philips was 'a respectable woman and a woman of some sense who, in his opinion, must certainly have lost her head when she committed so foolish, such an utterly nonsensical act'. The magistrate agreed, and Philips was bound over to keep the peace for three months.[90] While the obeah prosecution was unlikely to have succeeded in this case anyway, because there was no exchange of money or client–specialist relationship, it is notable that the argument made and accepted in court related to Philips's status rather than what she had done. On other occasions, cases that began as more minor charges were changed to obeah during the course of a trial. Robert Stone, for instance, was initially prosecuted for vagrancy because he had told a woman that an 'iniquity' was buried in her yard, and offered to kill the man who wanted to hurt her. The magistrate in the case, Mr S. C. Burke, ordered that Stone be prosecuted for practising obeah instead, because he 'would very much like to give him a licking'. As it turned out, Burke did not get his way: at Stone's retrial that afternoon, presumably under a

---

[87] Jamaican Vagrancy Act, 1902, cited in Bryan, *Jamaican People*, 29.
[88] *Gleaner*, 19 September 1916, 13.
[89] 'Old Offender Tries his Hand at Black Art', *Gleaner*, 3 November 1930; 'Court News from Port Maria', *Gleaner*, 17 December 1915.
[90] 'A Respectable Woman Caught Practicing Obeah', *POSG*, 30 January 1902, 6.

different magistrate, he received a punishment of two months' imprisonment, which might well have been the outcome of the vagrancy trial.[91] Both examples show that the charge was not a straightforward consequence of the event that allegedly precipitated it, nor was it simply decided on by the police. Rather, it resulted from interactions among police, magistrates, and prosecution lawyers.

Once the initial charge was fixed, the defendant or defendants entered their plea. Most, including Theophilus Neil, Arthur Clement, and Mary Clement, pleaded not guilty. Indeed, those charged with obeah had a reputation for contesting prosecutions. In one case where a guilty plea was entered, the journalist reported surprise, 'as obeahman normally fight their cases to the bitter end'.[92] The trials of the small group of defendants who did plead guilty were quick because little evidence was presented; the main question was the extent of punishment to be imposed. People pleaded guilty in the hope of obtaining a lighter sentence, as one defendant revealed when appealing against a sentence of twelve months' imprisonment and twelve lashes, on the grounds that he had only pleaded guilty because a policeman told him that he would receive no punishment if he did not contest the charge.[93] Those who pleaded guilty in Jamaica do appear to have been less likely than those who did not to be sentenced to flogging, and were less likely to receive the longest possible prison sentences of twelve months. Nevertheless, the median term of imprisonment was the same as for all cases, at six months.[94]

In the majority of cases, in which defendants pleaded not guilty, the plea was followed by the case for the prosecution. These cases were presented either by a senior policeman – in the case of the Clements, Inspector May of the Port of Spain police – or by an official known as the clerk of the court – in Theophilus Neil's case, Mr C. A. McIntosh. Both Neil and the Clements' prosecutions followed standard procedure in that the first and most important prosecution witness was the arresting policeman. Detectives Euriel Watson and Joseph Alexander, respectively, described how they had arrested the defendants, then searched their premises. In Neil's case the other prosecution witnesses were David Rennals and James Morgan, the two men who had entrapped him, along with another policeman who had been present at the time of his arrest. In

---

[91] 'Trickster Punished', *Gleaner*, 2 June 1915.
[92] 'Obe in Clarendon', *Gleaner*, 1 November 1898.
[93] 'Issues Argued before the Appeal Court', *Gleaner*, 15 December 1936. The appeal court ordered a retrial, but I have not been able to locate a report of it.
[94] As I only found six guilty pleas in Trinidad, I have not attempted to draw any conclusions about sentencing there.

the Clements' case the prosecution relied on Joseph Alexander's evidence followed by that of Annie Stewart, the husband of the Clements' patient. Most cases relied on a similar array of witnesses, although sometimes larger numbers of police or clients and informants testified for the prosecution. Occasionally the prosecution also called on technical experts such as the island chemist or his deputy to provide information about the chemical constitution of powders or liquids discovered on the premises of accused obeah practitioners.[95] The witnesses crafted narratives about the events that led up to arrest, with the police in particular keenly aware of the need to demonstrate that key elements of the law against obeah had been transgressed. When the defendant had employed a lawyer, he would then cross-examine the prosecution witnesses; in other cases they were cross-examined by the defendant him- or herself, or did not face cross-examination.[96]

Those orchestrating the prosecution of obeah cases aimed to demonstrate three crucial points: the presence of material objects that could be interpreted as contributing to the practice of obeah ('instruments of obeah' in Jamaican legal terminology); the defendant's practice of ritual activity that could be interpreted as 'pretending to' or 'assuming supernatural power'; and the transfer of money from client to ritual specialist in a way that could be interpreted as a process of exchange for ritual services. If all three of these elements were clearly present, the prosecution was very likely to be successful. As a result, the marking of notes and coins by police officers loomed large in obeah prosecutions. In Neil's case, for instance, Detective Watson described in detail how he 'initialed the back of the three notes "E. A. W." and ran my pen with ink through each initial, so as to make them indistinct' and 'placed a stroke on each of the silver coins by way of a mark'.[97] The fact that a defendant was in possession of coins and notes previously marked by police was usually interpreted as clear evidence that he or she had been paid for ritual activity – had, in the words of the law, undertaken it 'for gain'. Cases that did not involve entrapment, such as the prosecution of the Clements, did not include the marking of money as part of their evidence, but testimony about payment was still important. Annie Stewart explained in detail how Arthur Clement had initially asked her and her husband for $15

---

[95] For example, 'Human Skulls Part Paraphernalia of a Kingston Obeahman', *Gleaner*, 10 May 1932.

[96] To practise law in the Caribbean in this period one had to have been called to the bar in England. These lawyers were either locally born men who had trained in England or English expatriates. On Caribbean legal education see Lazarus-Black, 'After Empire'.

[97] 'The Practising of Obeah is Charged', *Gleaner*, 14 November 1924.

to remove the spirits that he said were causing Mr Stewart's illness, but eventually accepted $5.[98]

In both the Neil and Clement cases the material that had been seized from the defendants' houses was presented in court as evidence of their obeah practice. In Jamaican trials this material was now legally designated 'instruments of obeah'. Even when the objects themselves were not produced, lists of objects frequently formed part of the verbal testimony of prosecution witnesses. In the Neil and Clement cases the assemblages of items exhibited were composed of many kinds of everyday materials that could have all kinds of legitimate uses: oil lamps, saucepans, mirrors, bottles, demijohns, nails, books, letters, and (perhaps the only item that has little other than ritual use) human hair. This was typical of the physical evidence presented in obeah trials. In the prosecution of Alexander Williams, for instance, objects brought before the court included a 'marble crucifix, candles in their stands, [and] a pack of cards', while at Susan Facey's trial 'a basket of curious implements' including 'slate and lead pencils, buttons, looking-glass, fowl egg, calabash cup, silver spoons, marbles, several bottles with liquid and a bundle of letters from correspondents' were shown to the court.[99]

The law assumed that the status of any given item as an 'instrument of obeah' was clear, but in the daily practice of the courtroom this was not the case. In the Leeward Islands in the aftermath of the passage of the 1904 Obeah Act, modelled closely on the Jamaica 1898 Obeah Act and including the same provision about 'instruments of obeah', magistrates laboured to produce lists of objects that might be taken as such 'instruments'.[100] Yet in the end, both there and in Jamaica, this was an impossible task, because spiritual work could use such a wide range of things. The objects presented in court were often mundane, and the law gave no guidance on how to determine whether something was an 'instrument of obeah'. The need to interpret the evidence led those involved in obeah arrests to develop courtroom personae as specialists, with authority in recognizing obeah. One policeman testified that he had 'seen obeah worked' and therefore knew 'what the implements of obeah are', going on to explain that 'an obeah man, in practising, uses looking glass, cards, rice, rum, teeth of dogs, camphor, white fowls, grave dirt etc.'. In fact, the objects under discussion in the case in which this testimony was given included only two of the items from this stereotypical list of

---

[98] 'The Brabant Street Obeah Case', *POSG*, 13 July 1910.
[99] 'Before Metropolitan Courts', *Gleaner*, 1 September 1916; 'In the Rural Courts of Justice', *Gleaner*, 3 August 1916.
[100] Dr Robert S. Earl (Commissioner of the Virgin Islands) to Colonial Secretary, 9 May 1905, enclosed in CO 152/287, Knollys to Lyttleton No. 218, 19 May 1905.

conventional materials used in obeah – a pack of cards and two lumps of grave dirt. Many more objects that the policeman did not list as typical of obeah were also presented to the court, including a rubber ball, a bottle containing a whitish powder, an electric battery, patent medicine, and a doll. Nevertheless, the policeman's claim to knowledge served to authorize his interpretation of these other things as also used in obeah practice.[101] Similarly, a policeman serving as a witness in the trial of two men arrested in Admiral Town, Kingston, testified that because he had 'experience of obeah cases' he could confirm that a large body of material produced in court, including bones, shells, an imitation egg, camphor, candles, a compass, two mirrors, thread, chalk, pimento, garlic, and some dirt, were indeed 'implements of obeah'.[102] In the end, court cases turned on things being deemed instruments of obeah because people with authority – usually policemen – declared them to be so, and because magistrates recognized them as such.

Those constructing prosecution cases thus worked with a triad of narrative strategies, involving money, rituals, and objects, to produce a compelling case that would convince a magistrate of a defendant's guilt. If they could only present two of these elements the case was more vulnerable, although it frequently still led to conviction. The repeated telling of these stories of obeah practice in courtrooms, reproduced in newspapers, drew on but also reinforced the dominance of a wider archetype of obeah as a one-to-one encounter between client and practitioner, in which money is transferred, and objects are manipulated in ritual ways, with ritual words.

This archetype was also produced by defence strategies, which of necessity worked with the construction of obeah as it appeared in legislation and in the narratives created by prosecution lawyers and witnesses. The defence case was presented after the prosecution witnesses had been examined and cross-examined. In many cases – more than half in Trinidad, a slightly smaller proportion in Jamaica – defendants in obeah cases were represented by lawyers, who shaped the presentation of the defence case.[103] Since there was no entitlement to a lawyer in either colony at the time, this suggests that defendants were engaged with and knowledgeable about the functioning of the legal system, and also that many of them had considerable resources – either their own or those of friends and family who were prepared to pool funds to employ a defence

---

[101] 'Cases in the Courts', *Gleaner*, 27 March 1916.
[102] 'Interesting Case at Halfway Tree', *Gleaner*, 13 May 1916.
[103] 46 out of 79 cases in Trinidad. In Jamaica I found 178 cases where defendants were represented.

lawyer. It also suggests that they trusted that a lawyer would be able to help them. Many defence lawyers appeared multiple times in obeah cases. Gaston Johnston, who defended Mary and Arthur Clement, appeared regularly as a defence lawyer in obeah cases for at least twenty-five years in Trinidad.[104] In Jamaica the prominent lawyers Norman Manley and J. A. G. Smith regularly represented people accused of obeah, alongside other regular lawyers including H. A. Lake, Aston Simpson, and H. A. L. Simpson, all of whom represented obeah defendants in trials from the early twentieth century to at least the 1930s.[105]

The goal of the defence in an obeah case, as in all criminal trials in the common-law system, was to convince the magistrate that there was sufficient doubt of the defendant's guilt to render a conviction unsafe. Some defendants and their representatives claimed that the entire charge was fabricated: that they neither possessed the objects presented as evidence against them nor carried out the actions of which they were accused. In these cases defendants sometimes argued that they were being prosecuted for ulterior motives, such as a grudge held against them by the person who had reported the case to the police, or by members of the police force. Samuel Bailey, arrested in Linstead, Jamaica, argued that the man for whom he allegedly performed a ritual to remove ghosts 'hated him, because he would not work in his field'.[106] Albert Thompson of St Thomas, Jamaica appealed unsuccessfully against his conviction for obeah on the grounds that the policeman who brought the charges against him had fabricated them out of 'enmity'.[107]

---

[104] The earliest obeah case in which I have found Gaston Johnston defending was in 1902 ('Allegations of Obeah', *POSG*, 7 February 1902), the latest in 1920 ('Lothians Road Obeah Case', *POSG*, 7 October 1920), although he also appeared as a criminal defence lawyer for other offences until at least 1927 ('Aftermath of a Village Wake', *POSG*, 2 July 1927). Also prominent in Trinidadian obeah cases were two members of the coloured Scipio-Pollard family: Emmanuel, active in the 1890s, and his son Clare Noel, active in the 1920s. See for instance 'An Obeahman in Court', *POSG*, 9 December 1893 and 'Princes Town Obeah Case', *POSG*, 7 October 1920. On Emmanuel see Brereton, *Race Relations in Colonial Trinidad*, 200.

[105] For obeah cases in which Manley acted for the defence see, for example, 'The Home Circuit Court', 7 October 1926; 'Yesterday's Supreme Court', 18 January 1927; 'Bog Walk Obeah Case in Spanish Town Court', 20 April 1931; 'Issues before Appeal Court', 17 March 1942; 'Obeah Charge Against "Professor Brown"', 4 August 1944; 'Charged with Having Prohibited Book – Acquitted', 26 July 1949; 'Faith Healing Submissions Fail in Obeah Appeal', 26 July 1949 all in the *Gleaner*. For examples of J. A. G. Smith's involvement as a defence lawyer in obeah trials see for instance 'Cases Brought before Court', 5 April 1915; 'The High Court', 14 March 1917; 'Session of the Appellate Court', 8 July 1920; 'Appellate Division of the Supreme Court', 27 November 1928 all in the *Gleaner*. In many of these examples Manley or Smith took the cases at the appeal stage.

[106] 'Linstead Court', *Gleaner*, 24 February 1923, 16.

[107] 'Obeah Appeals', *Gleaner*, 6 April 1933, 5.

More commonly, defendants admitted to at least part of the prosecution's account of the facts of the case, but provided alternative explanations for what had been happening, unpicking the triad of ritual objects, ritual activity, and the transfer of money. A successful defence effectively inverted the prosecution. Aside from points that might lead to the failure of any prosecution, such as technical irregularities in search warrants or indictments, cases where the defence could show the absence of one of the three crucial elements were more likely to result in acquittals, although they were never guaranteed.[108] Arguments made by defence lawyers thus revolved around claims that no payment had been made, that the ritual material used to 'prove' obeah in fact had a mundane explanation, or that the rituals reported did not really involve 'pretence to supernatural power'. A person might give or sell to another a substance or object for healing or protective purposes, but if the transfer of the material was not accompanied by ritual activity the court might rule that this could not be construed as obeah. For instance, evidence was presented at James Grandier's trial that he gave Grace Coney a bottle of 'liniment' in exchange for a silver chain, and also cut cards in order to heal her niece. The defence successfully argued that this did not constitute pretence of supernatural powers: the necklace was simply payment for medicine to be used in an 'ordinary way'.[109] In a similar case, John Henry's lawyer argued that 'accused gave medicine, there was nothing supernatural about it', and Henry was acquitted, even though part of the evidence was that Henry had mixed medicine with fragments of bone.[110]

Many other defendants claimed that the things that the prosecution interpreted as instruments of obeah were in fact ordinary objects, with everyday uses. The vagueness of the definition of 'instruments of obeah' gave defence lawyers scope to argue that objects presented in court had not in fact been 'used' and/or 'pretended to be possessed of occult power'. Popo Samuel argued in his defence that the materials that the prosecution claimed demonstrated his practice of obeah were in fact the 'playthings of the children' of his household.[111] David Simon said that a bottle of liquid which the prosecution argued was for ritual purposes was in fact olive oil to soothe his sore toe, and that a pack of playing cards was simply

---

[108] For acquittals on technicalities see 'The Parishes: Sav La Mar', *Gleaner*, 28 June 1893; 'Charged with Working Obeah', *Gleaner*, 20 December 1911; 'Magistrate Refuses to Convict', *POSG*, 22 October 1931.
[109] 'Charge of Obeah Dismissed', *Gleaner*, 14 October 1899.
[110] 'Charge of Obeah', *Gleaner*, 31 July 1903. See also 'Capture of an Alleged Obeahman', *Gleaner*, 8 July 1903.
[111] 'A Family of Obeahists', *POSG*, 2 August 1922, 9.

for games.[112] If objects were found in someone's house or on their person but there was no evidence that he or she had used them as part of a ritual, there was a reasonable chance that the defendant would avoid conviction. Francis Caradose was arrested because a policeman suspected him of having removed body parts from a grave. On searching Caradose's house the police found no evidence of the graveyard robbery, but discovered pieces of bone, animal skulls, a parcel of hair, some reels of thread, and 'several small bottles filled with most foul smelling compounds and liquids', as well as some letters and a copy of the Bible. Caradose was charged with obeah, but despite press speculation that human bones had been found on his premises, the crown solicitor at his trial did not present evidence, stating that he could not prove that Caradose had contravened the obeah Ordinance in any way. Simply having this material in his house was not sufficient in this case to lead to a full trial, let alone to a conviction, because there was no evidence that Caradose had made ritual use of it.[113]

Another strategy, also used in appeals, was to question the reliability of prosecution witnesses. Raphael Landeau appealed against his conviction for practising obeah in Port of Spain on all these grounds, arguing that the material brought before the court to prove that he was practising obeah was simply a domestic 'chapelle', commonly found in Catholic homes, that the dollar he had been given was not payment for ritual services but rather a contribution to have a mass said in church, and that the witnesses against him were police spies and thus were motivated to lie.[114]

Theophilus Neil's defence made an argument based in part on class, emphasizing his settled economic position and his respectability. Neil's father testified that his son owned 40 acres of land from which he sold the produce, rented out a shop, and had two houses. A man with this level of economic security would not, the implication was, be involved in obeah. The defence acknowledged Neil's guilt in the charge of practising medicine without a licence, but challenged the obeah charge by focusing on the element of ritual, the weakest part of the prosecution's case. Neil's lawyer did not deny that his client had accepted money, nor that the items described as 'instruments of obeah' had been found in his

[112] 'Six Months for Obeahman', *Gleaner*, 14 December 1933. For similar cases see 'Before Country Tribunals', *Gleaner*, 8 September 1917, 18; 'RM Court at Spanish Town', *Gleaner*, 11 November 1920, 6.
[113] 'Desecration of a Grave', 10 April 1902; 'The St James Obeah Case', 13 April 1902; 'The Obeah Case', April 13 1902, all in *POSG*. For an acquittal in a similar case see 'Obeah Charges at Morant Bay', *Gleaner*, 5 April 1916. Caradose's case was also briefly discussed in Chapter 4 of this book.
[114] 'Appeal Court before the Chief Justice and Mr Acting Justice Deane', *POSG*, 22 September 1915; 'Supernatural Power Case', *POSG*, 29 September 1915.

home. But he argued, with the support of the testimony of Neil and his father, that no ritual involving 'supernatural power' had taken place. Both father and son contested David Rennals's claim that Theophilus had said that the sick man's stomach pain resulted from ghosts squeezing his stomach, instead claiming that Theophilus had said that 'it must be what *you people* call ghosts' (emphasis added). The medicine provided, they claimed, was not 'occult' but rather 'normal', the sort of thing that a biomedical doctor might supply. Many other obeah defendants also made use of Neil's argument that they were not practising obeah but providing everyday health advice. Representing Hensley Lindo in his appeal against a conviction for practising obeah in 1927, Norman Manley argued that the evidence that Lindo had instructed a man to 'wash his face in the morning with some peppermint water' did not constitute obeah, but rather was 'wholesome' advice.[115] Theophilus Bailey, who was accused of trying to heal a baby suffering from malaria by means of a ritual healing bath of cock's blood mixed with water, argued similarly. He admitted that he had given advice to the child's parents, but denied that he had used a ritual bath, claiming that he merely recommended that they give the boy cod-liver oil, 'as that was a good remedy'.[116]

The defence of the Clements similarly unpicked the triad of ritual, money, and objects. Gaston Johnston argued that what they were doing was not obeah but simply ordinary, legitimate religion. The crucifix 'and other articles' in their home were 'mere symbols used in their faith as Roman Catholics'.[117] Arthur Clement also explained that his wife was a mesmerist, who had cured him of his own long-standing illness when a biomedical doctor had not been able to help him. She had 'slept for a large number of persons in the community in all stations of life and has cured them when doctors failed'. He denied that either he or she practised obeah, and said that no fowl had been sacrificed, nor had he diagnosed a need to remove spirits. Arthur also gave an alternative account of his wife's treatment of Mr Stewart. Mary (or 'Ma Joe') Clement had 'hypnotized herself' by staring at a candle that Stewart held. She fell asleep, and while she was sleeping Mr Stewart 'told her to try and see what she could do for him as he was suffering very long'. In her trance state, Mary listed some remedies that Mr Stewart should use, which he wrote down. Arthur acknowledged that money had changed hands, but said it was a mere 4 shillings paid on two separate occasions, rather than the $5 that Annie Stewart had claimed.

---

[115] 'Yesterday's Supreme Court', *Gleaner*, 18 January 1927.
[116] 'Bathed Baby in Fowl Blood to Cure Malaria', *Gleaner*, 18 November 1929.
[117] 'The Brabant Street Obeah Case', *POSG*, 13 July 1910.

The Clements' description of themselves as Catholics and mesmerists was found in other cases: Beatrice Hanson of Kingston based her defence on the argument that she was a 'clairvoyant medium' rather than an obeah practitioner; she had studied spiritualism while living in the United States, with a pupil of Sir Arthur Conan Doyle. Moreover, the images of Jesus, Joseph, and the Virgin Mary found in her house and used as evidence against her 'could be found in any devout Roman Catholic home'.[118] Similarly, Norman Greaves of Siparia in southern Trinidad argued at his obeah trial that he was simply a preacher; the occult books found in his house and used as evidence against him were to 'advance him in the study of his ministry.'[119] Thomas Carter was acquitted on a charge of obeah despite evidence presented that he had dipped his finger in a glass containing liquid and sprinkled it about the room, saying: 'By this Holy Water I command that your wife come back to you'. Even though he had also spoken in an 'unknown tongue', something frequently taken as a sign of obeah in other cases, the magistrate decided that there was no evidence of 'pretence of supernatural power'.[120] The similarity between what he had done and ordinary Christian ritual, which was both legal and respectable, seems to have saved him from conviction.

As all these cases show, most of the defences against obeah prosecutions, not surprisingly, accepted the terms of the law, but sought to show that those accused of obeah had not broken it. This was no doubt the best way to work within the courts for any individual client. Very occasionally defence lawyers took a more dramatic step, challenging the validity of the law itself. Defending Maria Ramcharan in Trinidad, Gaston Johnston criticized the obeah law as 'very drastic', creating an 'almost indefensible' crime.[121]

We have already established that relatively few defences were successful. Even a defence that appears to have been effective in dismantling the triad of money, ritual, and objects embedded in obeah law did not inevitably lead to acquittal. There is often little to distinguish cases that resulted in conviction from those that did not, and it is hard to resist the conclusion that to a considerable extent the outcomes of trials were arbitrary, resulting from factors beyond the extent to which the evidence presented met the legal requirements for securing a conviction. Several convictions took place in cases that appear similar to those that led to acquittals on the grounds that there was no evidence of supernatural

---

[118] 'Claims to be Spiritualist', *Gleaner*, 11 January 1933. For a similar claim see 'Obeah Case Heard in San Fernando', *POSG*, 3 August 1895, 3.
[119] 'Siparia Magistrate's Court', *POSG*, 31 May 1931.
[120] 'Obeah Charge Fails in Court at Old Capital', *Gleaner*, 19 April 1927.
[121] 'Assumption of Supernatural Powers', *POSG*, 19 February, 10.

power being 'assumed'. Isabella Francis received a twelve-month prison sentence for practising obeah in a case where the main evidence against her was that she had provided 'two bottles of some liquid and a little bag' for a sick child to wear 'to keep off the evil spirit'.[122] Presumably it was the provision of the bag for the child to wear, and the interpretation that her illness was caused by an evil spirit that distinguished this case from others like those of John Henry and James Grandier, discussed above, but there is little difference between them. Joseph Reid was also convicted in a case very similar to that of Francis Caradose, in which police searched his house and found items they interpreted as 'instruments of obeah', but did not put forward witnesses to show that these 'instruments' were used for ritual purposes.[123]

The line between conviction and acquittal was fine, sometimes non-existent, in part because, despite the ideology of the rule of law, decisions did not always follow clear-cut rules. Even so, the possibility of acquittal meant that police had to be careful: it was in their professional interest to follow a set of procedures designed to maximize the likelihood of conviction. Entrapment was more likely to lead to conviction than was a raid on someone's house and confiscation of their possessions. It was also more likely to be successful than cases where civilians reported the ritual specialist after a ritual had taken place, because civilians often did not know the rules by which an obeah conviction might be obtained. Hezekiah Hudson, for instance, was arrested after he offered to anoint Adina McCoy with a liquid 'to prevent the spirit from following her'; this would cure her of her long-term ill health. Although the evidence showed that Hudson had been paid, his defence lawyer was able to use the fact that he had been arrested before he anointed McCoy to successfully argue that no obeah had actually taken place.[124] Within entrapment cases, the police needed to be well trained to make sure they did not reveal themselves too early, before the suspect had conducted a ritual, or before money had changed hands.

If they convicted the defendant, magistrates followed this by announcing the sentence. Theophilus Neil received a twelve-month prison sentence. Arthur Clement was imprisoned for three months, while Mary was sent to prison for only one month. The different sentences of these three individuals follow the pattern in which Jamaicans received more

---

[122] 'Cases Tried in the Courts of Two Parishes', *Gleaner*, 7 March 1922.
[123] 'Old Man is Found Guilty of Practicing Obeah', *Gleaner*, 30 July 1931. For a similar case, in which a man was convicted of obeah on the basis of having human bones in his possession, despite there being no evidence about ritual activity, see 'Some Cases in Rural Courts', *Gleaner*, 15 May 1916.
[124] 'Charged at Retreat Mountain', *Gleaner*, 16 December 1915.

severe punishments than Trinidadians, and men than women. Magistrates described their sentencing decisions as calibrated to the circumstances of specific offences, with acts that they considered especially egregious, and people who had previous convictions, getting the more serious punishments.[125] Some got severe punishments in order to make a strong example: when sentencing Francis Harmit, whose trial attracted a great deal of attention, the magistrate explained that 'when a man like the accused', that is, a well-off and well-dressed Kingstonian, 'resorted to such a thing as obeah he ought to be heavily punished'.[126] At the same time, magistrates distributed punishments depending on the personal characteristics of the convict. This type of calibration was encoded into the law, which had since the end of slavery made the flogging of women illegal. In addition to gender, magistrates took age into account in deciding on sentences, occasionally noting that they had not allocated a flogging, or had given a relatively short prison sentence, because the defendant was old.[127]

Obeah cases, like court cases more generally, had an audience beyond the individual being prosecuted. Magistrates often elaborated on their decisions with comments officially directed to the accused, but also aimed at the wider audience in court, and, via the press, at a newspaper-reading public.[128] These comments often reflected on the Caribbean's relationship to 'civilization', something that was always at stake in discussion of obeah. Magistrates did not argue straightforwardly that the Caribbean was uncivilized, but rather that it was *almost* civilized, on the brink of achieving civilization. In this context the existence or prevalence of obeah was preventing the region from attaining full civilization. A Jamaican magistrate commented that obeah was 'an offence peculiar to this country' and that he knew of 'no other civilised country in the world where this thing exists', thus including Jamaica within the category of civilized countries while also marking obeah as a challenge to

---

[125] Nine of the twenty-seven men (33 per cent) in Jamaica who received punishments of twelve months' imprisonment and eighteen lashes had previous convictions noted in court, compared to 65 of all the 461 known punishments (14 per cent).

[126] 'The Allman Town Obeah Case', *Gleaner*, 24 October 1907.

[127] For examples see 'Another Obeah Conviction in Clarendon', 29 August 1899; 'Practiced Obeah', 20 October 1902; 'Practiced Obeah', 19 June 1906; 'Charges Heard', 20 October 1913; 'Cases Tried by Mr H. Robinson in Police Court', 22 August 1922, all in the *Gleaner*; 'Lopinot "Obeahists" Convicted', *POSG*, 1 March 1936. Previous convictions could trump age, though. Jacob Hatfield, with nine previous convictions, received the maximum punishment of twelve months and eighteen lashes, despite being a 'grey-haired old man'. 'Obeah Cases', *Gleaner*, 16 June 1915.

[128] On judicial comments more generally see Paton, *No Bond But the Law*, 157–8; Hay, 'Property, Authority, and the Criminal Law', 27–9.

that status.[129] Magistrates often emphasized that people who aspired to 'respectability' or 'civilization' should reject 'superstitious practices' such as obeah. One contrasted the 'poor ignorant people... practically living in the bush' of the country where he'd previously lived (which he did not name) with Jamaicans who had 'the opportunity of being taught in schools', stating that he could 'hardly believe they [Jamaicans] were so foolish as to allow themselves to be duped that way'.[130] Another attacked the 'mere ignorance' of the woman who came before him charged with obeah, while a third complained that the practice of obeah was 'a very silly thing and he saw no reason why these people should believe in it to such an extent'.[131] In two separate Trinidadian cases where religious practice led to prosecution, defendants were sternly told: 'You are not in the wilds of Africa.'[132]

Magistrates also emphasized the significance of obeah convictions as a sign that state power was stronger than the power of obeah. They enjoyed pointing out that a successful prosecution for obeah revealed that the defendant was not, despite what he or she claimed, able to determine the outcome of court cases. One magistrate gloated to a convicted obeah defendant that 'whilst people like you pretend to have supernatural power... they have no power whatever to prevent the witnesses speaking the truth and proving a crime against you, and that must show to the public that they are imposters and frauds'.[133] The claim that convictions for obeah would reveal the fraudulence of its practitioners was also frequently made in commentaries on the law.[134]

Yet this was a risky game for state authorities, because it made every obeah case a potential comment on the reality or otherwise of obeah's power. Given that not all prosecutions could lead to convictions, there would inevitably be cases that could be taken to prove the power of ritual specialists as individuals, and of obeah as a spiritual force. Robert Elleston, for example, was said to have boasted of his powerful spiritual work, which he said was proved by the fact that he had not been convicted at a previous trial. He was prosecuted for obeah again for this boast, and once

---

[129] 'An Obeahman', *Gleaner*, 31 August 1915.
[130] 'Obeah Charge', *Gleaner*, 14 January 1911.
[131] 'July Courts in the Rural Districts', *Gleaner*, 17 July 1915; 'A Family of Obeahists', *POSG*, 2 August 1922.
[132] One was a case for breach of the peace following a wake: 'Peace Disturbers', *POSG*, 31 January 1914, 9. The other was a Shouters' Prohibition Ordinance case: '"Shango" Dancers Beware!', *POSG*, 10 July 1919, 5.
[133] 'The Hardware Gap Obeah Case', *Gleaner*, 14 August 1899.
[134] See for example the comments of Charles Frederick Lumb reported in 'The Obeah Law: Dr Lumb Recommends the Stocks', *Gleaner*, 4 December 1901, enclosed in CO 137/625, Eustace Greg to Joseph Chamberlain, 13 December 1901.

more acquitted, no doubt adding to his confidence and reputation.[135] When a policeman involved in a Trinidadian obeah trial was injured in an accident, forcing postponement of the trial, it led to considerable speculation, and the widespread view that the defendant had 'worked obeah to bring about the accident'.[136] Even cases of conviction where a lighter sentence than expected was given could be interpreted as a sign of the spiritual worker's power. Some 'respectable' people disapproved of James Edwards's sentence of thirty days' imprisonment for practising obeah because his 'supporters believe that the light sentence is due to his skill'.[137] Magistrates in cases where the defendant was acquitted sometimes commented that it would have been better if the prosecution had not been brought. After the prosecution case against William Gale collapsed when a key witness refused to give evidence, the magistrate lamented the fact that the defendant was likely to 'tell the people that he had defeated the police and the judge', and as a result would acquire a 'bigger clientele'.[138] News of the acquittal of Matthew Russell Gordon would convince 'the illiterate people' that he 'were really an obeahman', lamented the magistrate who oversaw his case.[139]

These words by magistrates emphasize the public nature of obeah trials. Many provoked considerable public interest. A crowd outside the courthouse was ecstatic in response to the acquittal of James Brown, also known as Tata, displaying 'excitement ... beyond description'.[140] Crowds did not always support the accused practitioner. Samuel Rooms's conviction was greeted with approval by the crowd outside the court, who followed him as he was taken from the court to the prison, 'making a tremendous mocking noise'.[141] Whether supportive or hostile towards the defendant, crowds provided a public commentary on the judicial procedure, emphasizing that it did not belong only to the state but was also a public event.

The end of the trial was not the end of the story. For the defendant, most obviously, it was followed either by time in prison (including sometimes a flogging), the need to pay a fine, or a return to ordinary life with a reputation as someone who had defeated an obeah charge in court. Police involved in obeah trials were sometimes rewarded financially for

[135] 'Obeah Charge at Linstead', *Gleaner*, 30 November 1905.
[136] 'Accident to Detectives', *POSG*, 29 August 1894, 3; 'The Obeah Case', *POSG*, 30 August 1894, 3.
[137] 'Complaints from Annotto Bay', *Gleaner*, 28 November 1894.
[138] 'No Practice of Obeahism', *Gleaner*, 26 October 1905.
[139] 'Business before Criminal Courts', *Gleaner*, 11 November 1920. Perhaps as a result of this warning, Gordon was immediately rearrested and convicted later the same day of vagrancy.
[140] *Gleaner*, 16 May 1908.   [141] 'Rural Court', *Gleaner*, 9 October 1918.

successful prosecutions; for many their involvement was part of the path of building a professional career as a specialist police officer. Magistrates and lawyers also developed expertise in obeah through their repeated participation in obeah trials.

Obeah prosecutions were sometimes used to legitimize attacks on those whose religious practice posed a political or cultural threat. But this was not the primary way in which the law functioned in practice. Its use came partly from below, from the neighbours and enemies of those prosecuted, and for whom obeah was a frightening use of power. From the point of view of the everyday state, especially the police officers who made the arrests, obeah prosecutions provided a way of climbing a career ladder, demonstrating one's competence, and, sometimes, extorting resources and damaging enemies and rivals. And from the point of view of the people who drove policy, obeah prosecutions served to demonstrate the civilizing drive within the Caribbean, the effort by the social elite to reform the population and bring them 'up' to a better standard by clearly marking out unacceptable practices. The conjunction of all these interests cohered to make obeah prosecution a regular part of the landscape of the law in the early twentieth-century Caribbean.

# 6  Obeah prosecutions from the inside

The previous chapter examined reports of obeah trials largely from the point of view of state activity. It investigated the process of prosecution and showed how legal practices and agents of the state contributed to the dominance of a concept of obeah as bounded by specialist–client interactions involving financial exchange. Within the parameters established by law, however, the trials also reveal much more. We have seen that trials worked within a legal framework that produced an emphasis on rituals, money, and objects, but we have not yet considered the nature of the rituals, the process of transfer of money, or the kinds of material objects that were used in trials. Nor have we investigated the meanings of the practices that led to trial from the point of view of those engaged in them. In this chapter, then, I look more closely at the evidence gathered from obeah trials. The prosecutions do not allow us to define what obeah is or was. But they do enable us to build a rich picture of the range of activities undertaken for the purposes of spiritual and ritual healing in the early twentieth-century Caribbean, and to investigate how these related to one another and to the law. The evidence presented in obeah prosecutions demonstrates the fluidity and multiplicity of healing and spiritual work. It reveals the influence of concepts of the power of the dead that resonate strongly with what we know about African understandings of the ancestors, conjoined with magical techniques that drew on long-standing European traditions, all naturalized within the Caribbean. Meanwhile, these traditions jostled with and interacted with recently invented curative practices such as homeopathy, electrical healing, and mesmerism. The most significant concept informing Caribbean spiritual work was that the spirits of the dead, known as duppies, jumbies, and ghosts, influenced the world of the living. This idea can be discerned in many of the techniques for diagnosis and healing displayed in the records of arrests and prosecutions for obeah. But much else is to be found in these trials as well. This chapter also examines the social position of individuals prosecuted for obeah, the role of place in ritual practice, the reasons that people consulted obeah practitioners or those perceived as obeah practitioners, the interpretations made by spiritual workers, and the range of ritual techniques they employed.

The prosecutions also suggest some pan-Caribbean practices, enabling us to distinguish them from the locally specific. Certain techniques found regularly in Jamaica never appear in the Trinidadian material, and vice versa, but much of what appears in the trial records was present in some form across the Caribbean. Similarly, the material reveals the evolution of ritual practice over time. Some techniques found regularly in nineteenth-century cases are almost never present in the twentieth-century sources, while new methods and interpretations are found in the twentieth century that had not previously existed. The most notable innovation is the use of published books, especially those produced by the DeLaurence company in Chicago.

In this chapter I seek to use, as historians frequently do, evidence that was created in the process of legal attacks on people to write about those people's beliefs, practices, and relationships. This is a necessarily difficult task. The prosecutions mediated through newspaper reports that provide the evidence used in this chapter were conducted in a context in which there was already a strong stereotype of the obeah practitioner. Decisions about whom to prosecute, the likely success or failure of those prosecutions, and the discourse through which they were reported all drew on that stereotype, while also reaffirming and developing it. Thus to use the evidence of reports of prosecutions to learn about the meanings those prosecuted ascribed to their practices risks several naïve assumptions: that there was a reality 'behind' the prosecutions that existed separately from them, and that this reality can be disentangled from the evidence produced by the prosecutions. We need to avoid using the court cases in the same way as did the colonial state, as a means of homogenizing the range of healing practice that existed in the Caribbean and of condensing a wide range of everyday activity into a singular object, 'obeah'. And yet not to use the richly detailed evidence produced by the prosecutions to extend our knowledge of everyday practices of healing would also be a loss. It would wilfully close to us a layer of evidence about the conflicts, struggles, and meanings of everyday life in the Caribbean, and would reinforce a focus on the discourse of the elite. The evidence from the newspapers, while partial, does give us information about the ritual practice of those prosecuted for obeah and the people who turned to them for help, including the problems they sought help with, their understanding of harm and how it was caused, and the materials, words, and actions they employed. To find evidence about obeah that is comparable in depth and detail to that collected from the newspapers, we have to turn to anthropological studies of Caribbean ritual healing work.[1] These, although they have some important advantages over material collected through newspaper reports of prosecutions, did not begin until the mid-twentieth century, and never produced the volume of evidence gathered here. In order to avoid the assumption that prosecution evidence gives us direct access to the meaning and experience of Caribbean ritual practice, while still learning as much as we can from it, in this chapter I analyse the evidence of prosecutions in the light of the stereotype of the obeah practitioner, paying particular attention to the points at which practices recorded in the prosecution evidence seem to depart from that stereotype.

The stereotype of the obeah practitioner established during slavery persisted with little change into the late nineteenth and twentieth centuries. A good example appears in 'The Obeah Man', the winner of the *Gleaner*'s Christmas short-story competition for 1896. The story is narrated by a police inspector who seeks out an obeah man who is sheltering a murderer. The obeah man lives in a remote 'mud hovel' on a mountainside, with soot-blackened interior walls hung with reptiles and bats. He is a 'most hideous old African', with 'shaggy white eyebrows' and 'shrivelled lips.'[2] This fictional obeah man differs little from slavery-era obeah men such as Amalkir in William Burdett's *Life and Exploits of Mansong* or the 'wrinkled and deformed' Bashra of William Earle's *Obi*, who lives in a 'sequestered hut', both of whom drew on Benjamin Moseley's description of obeah practitioners as 'ugly, loathsome creatures' who were inhabitants of 'woods, and unfrequented place'.[3] The 1896 story's obeah man is also a descendant of the mid-nineteenth-century character Fanty in Mary Wilkins's *The Slave Son*, who also lives in a remote location and is physically grotesque.[4] Fictional obeah practitioners of the stereotyped kind found in this story and in its precursors were almost always solitary individuals of African descent who lived in isolated rural cabins or caves. They were elderly men, frequently physically repulsive. Their practice is drawn from generic African traditions, and has no hint of Christian theology or ritual. Such obeah men continue to appear in twentieth-century Caribbean fiction, most notably Claude McKay's

---

[1] For example, Mischel, 'Faith Healing and Medical Practice'; Moore, 'Religion of Jamaican Negroes'; Hogg, 'Magic and "Science"'; Hogg, 'Jamaican Religions'; Mischel, 'A Shango Religious Group'; Simpson, 'Jamaican Revivalist Cults'; Seaga, 'Revival Cults in Jamaica'.

[2] Godfrey Brian, 'The Obeahman', in 'Results of the Christmas Story Competition', *Gleaner*, 24 December 1896.

[3] Burdett, *Life and exploits of Mansong*; Earle, *Obi* (2005), 104; Moseley, *A Treatise on Sugar*, 171.

[4] Wilkins, *The Slave Son*.

*Banana Bottom* (1933).⁵ A few individual fictional characters, such as Hamel in the eponymous novel and Feruare in Earle's *Obi*, were more complex, but the composite stereotype of the obeah man was of someone amoral or evil, willing to cause harm when asked to do so, and making use of mysterious and spooky techniques of power, with an element of Gothic and an association with violence.⁶ In the *Gleaner*'s prize-winning story the police inspector at one point fears for his life as the obeah man approaches him with a knife, although it turns out he only wants a few drops of blood to put in a magical charm.

The stereotype of the isolated obeah man implied a Caribbean that was apart from the rest of the world, separate from the sense of modern life that was so much part of the consciousness of the late nineteenth and early twentieth centuries. Yet the Caribbean has since the early seventeenth century been intensely connected to other parts of the world through forced migrations and trade, the site of 'landmark experiments in modernity', as Sidney Mintz explains.⁷ At the turn of the twentieth century the connectedness of the region to places elsewhere was reinforced by the intense intra-regional mobility of the circum-Caribbean population. Drawn by US investment in banana and sugar plantations in Central America, Jamaica, Cuba, and the Dominican Republic, the discovery of oil in Trinidad and Venezuela, and the construction of the Panama Railroad and later the Panama Canal, tens of thousands of Caribbean people in the late nineteenth and early twentieth centuries moved around the region, often moving several times, producing extended networks of knowledge, sociability, and kinship.⁸ As Lara Putnam points out, Caribbean ritual and spiritual practice was reconstructed within this mobile matrix; obeah, she says, was a 'ritual complex created by, for, and about people on the move'.⁹ Many of the ritual specialists prosecuted in the early twentieth century had lived in two or more colonies prior to their arrest. Their clienteles, some of which were quite extensive, often included people from overseas.

Circuits of mobility in ritual practice followed those of Caribbean labour migration, in which there were two major migratory networks. Trinidad was an important node within a southern Caribbean circuit involving Guyana, Grenada, Barbados, and Venezuela, while Jamaica was part of a partially overlapping northern Caribbean circuit that involved

---

⁵ McKay, *Banana Bottom*.   ⁶ Williams, *Hamel*; Earle, *Obi*.
⁷ Mintz, 'Enduring Substances', 295.
⁸ Putnam, *The Company they Kept*; Newton, *The Silver Men*; Giovannetti, 'The Elusive Organization of "Identity"'; Mcleod, 'Undesirable Aliens'; Ayala, *American Sugar Kingdom*.
⁹ Putnam, 'Rites of Power', 245.

movement to and from Cuba, Haiti, Central America, and to some extent British Guiana.[10] Many defendants in obeah trials had moved from smaller islands in the Eastern Caribbean to larger, more industrialized colonies, such as Trinidad. Samuel Benkins, who described himself as a bush doctor and said he could divine the source of illness through a 'gift from the Gods', was prosecuted for obeah in 1913 in Barbados. He had previously lived 'in Tobago, Trinidad, Demerara, Grenada, and other places'. In court he produced a long list of people he had effectively treated.[11] Those moving around the southern migratory circuit had relatively little contact with Jamaicans, who mostly followed the northern routes. In Jamaica, obeah defendants frequently reported previous residence in Costa Rica, Panama, Haiti, or Cuba. Dewry Williams, an 'elderly black man' prosecuted for obeah in 1930 after an encounter at Kingston race course, had previously lived in Cuba.[12] According to the testimony of a policeman, George Washington Pitt had offered his ritual services with the claim that he had 'learned his trade in Panama'.[13] William Fraser and Citira Reid had originally met their client Margaret Davis when all three were living in Costa Rica.[14] Others had spent time in the United States.[15] Knowledge and connections were made and sustained through movement, often over long distances.

Transnational connections were sustained through the circulation of letters. Theophilus Dascent of Nevis was said to have received letters from people 'far and near', including one from Tortola.[16] David Compass was arrested in Jamaica in 1915 with letters from Haiti and Canada on his person.[17] Herbert Brathwaite, who was said to be keeping an 'obeahism house' in Port of Spain, corresponded with people in England.[18] Many more ritual workers used the postal system to communicate with clients within the colonies in which they lived.[19] Dr Williams, who lived in Siparia, Trinidad, was originally from Grenada; letters from many clients

---

[10] Putnam, *Radical Moves*, 23–32.
[11] 'The Holetown Obeah Case', *POSG*, 15 May 1913, 5.
[12] 'Represented Himself as Man of Vision', *Gleaner*, 12 June 1930. For other examples of defendants who had lived elsewhere in the Caribbean see 'Richmond Court', *Gleaner* 31 July 1931; 'Obeah Case tried in Sav-La-Mar Court', *Gleaner*, 17 May 1932.
[13] 'Mechanic Fined £12 10/ on Charge of Practising Obeah', *Gleaner*, 9 January 1934.
[14] 'Ex-Soldier Fined for Practising Obeah', *Gleaner*, 19 February 1940.
[15] 'Obeah Charge', *Gleaner*, 25 November 1909; 'Claims to be Spiritualist', *Gleaner*, 11 January 1933.
[16] Udal, 'Obeah', 277–78.
[17] 'Versatile Law Breaker Finds Himself in the Police Meshes', *Gleaner*, 14 May 1915.
[18] 'Hypnotist on Arson Charge', *POSG*, 8 May 1927.
[19] For example, 'Sent to Prison', *Gleaner*, 2 October 1911; 'Alleged Obeahman', *Gleaner*, 4 November 1920; 'Leprous Obeah Man Convicted', *POSG*, 21 February 1917.

thanking him or soliciting further help were read out in court at his 1910 trial for obeah.[20]

Yet while mobility is crucial in understanding the social world in which obeah practice took place in this period, rootedness was also important. Ritual practice was often deeply connected to particular physical locations. Specific places – sometimes small islands and isolated villages, but also symbolically important urban sites – could gain ambivalent reputations, among elites and popular classes alike, as centres of spiritual power. For instance, the St Kitts acting inspector of police commented in 1906 that obeah still 'flourished' in Nevis, which he described as 'always a hot bed of superstition'.[21] Melville Herskovits's field notes from his 1939 research in Toco, a village on the north coast of Trinidad, relatively close to Tobago, record his informant Margaret's comment that knowledge of obeah (Herskovits used the spelling 'obia') in Tobago was especially strong.[22] The connection between spiritual authority and place goes beyond this discursive or imaginative level, however. First of all, enduring social relations and face-to-face interaction with people were essential for successful ritual practice. These called for a sedentary lifestyle instead of frequent relocations. Given the illegality of their practice, ritual specialists attracted clients by word-of-mouth augmentation of their reputation and authority, and often expected references from people who sought to consult them for the first time. Large clienteles such as that of Dr Williams and other successful ritual workers could not have been sustained by highly itinerant practitioners. In other words, being settled in a particular address for long enough was a prerequisite for popular practice, and the accumulation of social networks stretching across colonial borders added to the credibility and authority of Williams and his colleagues.[23]

Against the evidence of the significance of mobility and long-distance connections to the formation and organization of obeah practices, the stereotype of the isolated practitioner continued to influence the lawyers, magistrates, police, and witnesses who participated in obeah trials, and thus the evidence through which we try to discern the meaning of obeah for ordinary Caribbean folk. This stereotype's influence on everyday trials can, paradoxically, be seen most clearly in cases that diverged from it. One magistrate explicitly contrasted his expectation that obeah defendants

---

[20] '"Dr" Williams Sentenced to Six Months Hard', *POSG*, 27 February 1910.
[21] CO 152/290, enclosure in Sweet-Escott to Elgin No. 307, 9 August 1906.
[22] Trinidad Notes Book I Toco, Melville and Frances Herskovits Papers MG 261, Schomburg Center for Research in Black Culture, New York.
[23] This paragraph and parts of the previous two include revised material from a conference paper originally written with Maarit Forde. I thank her for permission to include it here.

would be 'the admitted obeahmen, the old Africans' with the reality that the defendant in the case he was trying was a migrant from Panama, or, as the magistrate put it, one of 'you fellows who come here and want money'.[24] Similarly, at the 1944 Jamaican trial of Thaddeus 'Professor' Brown, the magistrate contrasted Brown's practice of reading a glass of salted water in order to diagnose a problem with what he understood to be typical obeah cases, characterized by 'sprinkling of blood on a white rooster, scattering of rice and speaking in an unknown tongue'.[25] As we will see, the magistrate was not wrong to note the prominence of sacrificial roosters, rice, and the 'unknown tongue' in obeah cases. But in highlighting these characteristics of trials, he overlooked a range of other practices that were also typical of the rituals and materials in obeah trials, but did not conform to the long-standing stereotype of what obeah practitioners did.

A second stereotype of the obeah man, that of the obeah practitioner as swindler or fraud, existed alongside the idea of the old, isolated African. A few individuals prosecuted for obeah or obeah-related offences do seem to have conformed to this image and were actively defrauding vulnerable people out of their money. Many of these seem to have preyed on the fears, insecurities, and desires generated by the intense mobility of the early twentieth-century Caribbean. Particularly targeted were people who were either about to travel abroad or who had recently arrived in a new place. A series of cases took place over several years in which people were approached within a few blocks of each other in downtown Kingston: on King Street, Duke Street, Orange Street, Barry Street or Tower Street.[26] Several similar cases took place in Port of Spain as well.[27] These cases differed from most in that they did not involve entrapment, or a long-standing relationship gone wrong. Instead, witnesses reported that they were approached on the street by people who claimed to recognize them from overseas, or to be able to help them with information about their intended destination. The people or person who approached them then took them somewhere private, where they conducted a ritual that involved the transfer of significant amounts of money for 'luck' in their travels, often with the promise that the money would be returned.

---

[24] 'Obeah Charge', *Gleaner*, 21 May 1915.
[25] 'Obeah Charge against "Professor" Brown', *Gleaner*, 4 August 1944; 'Brown Sentenced to 12 Months with 18 Lashes in Obeah Case', *Gleaner*, 10 August 1944.
[26] For examples see the cases cited in notes 28–30 and 'Charged with Obeah Claims', 12 April 1906; 'City Sharpers at New Game', 3 May 1906; 'Tell it to the Judge', 15 October 1929; 'Around the Courts', 13 May 1930, all in the *Gleaner*.
[27] 'A Medicine Man in the Toils', 23 March 1897; 'Exploits of an East Indian Necromancer', 21 July 1907; 'Alleged Assumption of Supernatural Power', 19 July 1912; 'A Trickster Trapped', 7 February 1914, all in the *POSG*.

Others told stories of 'Spanish Jars' filled with gold and protected by spirits on people's land, often claiming to have learned how to locate and unearth these while overseas.[28] These individuals were often tried for larceny rather than obeah, but their trials usually referred to obeah.

William Samuels, for instance, described in court how in 1919, during the Cuban sugar boom known as the 'Dance of the Millions', he had come from western Jamaica to Kingston with the aim of travelling on to Cuba for work. In Kingston he met a man who said that he knew someone who could give him information about Cuba. The man then took him and two others to a private house where he introduced each of them in turn to Charles Johnson, who, a later trial revealed, also went by the alias Colon, suggesting his connection to other migratory circuits. Johnson persuaded Samuels to hand over £5, which he placed in an envelope over a glass, then appeared to burn the envelope and its contents. He placed ash on the sole of Samuels's foot (his 'foot bottom'), and told him that he would get the money back, and more, in nine days. Samuels became suspicious and demanded his money back; when Johnson would not return it, he went to the police.[29] I was unable to find a report of the outcome of this case, but two years later Johnson was in court again for a very similar incident. Again, it involved a man from western Jamaica who came to Kingston on his way to Cuba and met Johnson, who claimed to be able to give him information about Cuba. Johnson again conducted a ritual that involved placing money in an envelope and set it on fire, and told his victim that he would receive it back later. This time Johnson received a sentence of three years for larceny, and it was revealed that he had nineteen previous convictions.[30] Ten years later a similar trick involving the apparent burning of money inside an envelope was still taking place in downtown Kingston and still targeted people involved in migration: Gilbert Morais and Justin McGrath were imprisoned for seven years for larceny, having convinced a man who had just returned from Cuba to hand over £70 which he believed they then burnt in an envelope, promising that he would find £20,000 in his trunk a few days later.[31] In Port of Spain a similar case involved Jordan, a migrant from Tobago who had come to the city to look for work, and met a man at Marine Square (now Independence Square), near the docks. The man took him to see a friend, Budsey Williams, who he said could 'work' for him to ensure that he found and kept a job, but then disappeared

---

[28] See, for instance, 'Daring Spanish Jar Swindle', *Gleaner*, 13 January 1908.
[29] 'Preliminary Enquiries Held by Actg Supernumary RM', *Gleaner*, 27 August 1919.
[30] 'The Home Circuit Court', *Gleaner*, 14 January 1921.
[31] 'Two City Sharpers Get 7 Years Each', *Gleaner*, 2 October 1931.

once Jordan handed over money.³² Such cases suggest the vulnerability of both potential and returning migrants, isolated in a city that they did not know well, and anxious about what the future might bring.

Yet if some individuals clearly did take advantage of others' hopes and fears to trick them out of money, they were a small proportion of the overall group of people prosecuted for obeah and related offences. Even fewer individuals prosecuted for obeah fully conformed to the stereotype of the sinister, isolated old African obeah man. Even those who in some respects seemed to fit the traditional picture diverged from it in other ways. Walter William Christian, for instance, did indeed appear to be an amoral individual prepared to do harm as well as to heal; he was alleged to have said, 'I can pull, and I can put' – that is, he claimed both to be able to cause harm through spiritual means and to remove harm caused by others' spiritual work. But, far from living in a remote isolated community, he had worked for the United Fruit Company in Costa Rica, where he had lost a leg in an industrial accident.³³ Goopoul Marhargh also seemed to conform to the stereotype of the sinister obeah man, in that he offered to kill the enemies of his client, who were 'keeping him down'. But he also diverged from it: he was not an African or of African descent, but was described as a 'coolie'.³⁴ In another case the *Port of Spain Gazette* reported that the defendant, Daniel Young, lived in a 'small cottage hid away in the heart of a lonely area, with nothing around but dense foliage' – apparently a stereotypical obeah practitioner par excellence. Yet at his trial it was revealed that Young received letters from clients all over Trinidad, used books acquired by mail order from Chicago, and helped at least one client get a better job in the department of education.³⁵ He was thoroughly integrated into the modern, transnational life of the Caribbean. The *Gazette*'s easy recourse to a language that located Young as hidden, mysterious, and isolated, despite these other elements, reveals the power of the discourse about obeah.

If those prosecuted for obeah rarely conformed fully to the image of the isolated, evil, or amoral obeah man, how did the practice of Caribbean ritual specialists work? What were their goals and aims? Why did people seek them out? The information in obeah trials allows for at least partial answers to these questions, although we must recognize that events and interactions that led to prosecutions represent only some of the ritual

---

[32] 'An Attempt at Obeah', *POSG*, 12 September 1917.
[33] 'Rural Court', *Gleaner*, 25 August 1915, 15.
[34] 'Obeah Man Caught', *Gleaner*, 27 October 1927.
[35] 'Obeah Raid at San Juan', *POSG*, 22 May 1931. For the end of the case see 'Obeah Man Sent to Jail', *POSG*, 17 June 1931. Putnam, 'Rites of Power', discusses some similar cases, as does Forde, 'The Moral Economy of Spiritual Work'.

healing encounters that took place in the Caribbean. The next section of this chapter unpacks what the newspaper evidence tells us about some of the commonalities that underlay ritual practice, while the last part emphasizes the diversity of contexts in which people worked.

People turned to ritual specialists to deal with the full spectrum of human problems. Saying more than this is complicated by the fact that so many of the cases were entrapment stings, in which the individuals seeking help invented problems in order to provoke the suspect into committing the crime of obeah. This was especially the case in Trinidad, where more than half of obeah prosecutions collected were produced by entrapment. As a result, the cases serve as an echo chamber, amplifying the patterns that people embodying the everyday state – low-level police officers and their informants – expected would be plausible reasons for a person to seek ritual help. Some apparently frequent reasons for turning to obeah practitioners appear to be almost entirely artefacts of entrapment. For instance, at first sight it appears that the most common reason people sought out ritual specialists in Trinidad was to resolve problems to do with employment: to get, or to keep, a job. Looking more closely, however, sixteen of the twenty-one cases of this kind were accomplished through entrapment, so what we are really seeing is that those who set up entrapments thought that approaching a suspected obeah practitioner with a story about employment problems would be plausible.[36] If we exclude entrapment cases, including those involving professional informers rather than police officers, we find that prominent reasons for consulting a ritual specialist included court cases (both civil suits and criminal prosecutions); improving the prospects of a business such as a shop or higglering business, especially when it was doing badly; and problems in relationships (especially men's and sometimes women's desire to keep a partner who was thought to be straying). Some of the myriad circumstances in which people sought ritual help included a person who could not successfully raise livestock, a man who needed to get his driving licence, and a butcher who was being prevented from making sales by a spiritual obstruction.[37] Overall, the most common reason for consulting an obeah practitioner in both Trinidad and Jamaica, by a considerable margin, was for concerns to do with physical and mental health. The wide range of problems for which people sought ritual help implies something that was also frequently stated outright: that one's

---

[36] In Jamaica, too, entrapment stories focused disproportionately on employment, although to a lesser extent. Twelve of thirty-three cases involving employment resulted from entrapment.

[37] 'Sent to Prison', 2 October 1911; 'Obeah Charge Fails', 2 May 1938; 'Case of Obeah Tried at Frankfield', 27 August 1915, all in the *Gleaner*.

overt problems in employment, business, relationships, or health were mere symptoms of an underlying spiritual affliction.

In most of the cases where individuals sought help with their health, the newspaper reports provide little information about the nature of those problems. Reporters generally revealed only that the person was sick, ill, or in pain. Those that do give more information, however, cluster in a few important areas: abdominal pain or disturbances; poor vision or blindness; sores, pains, swellings, or worm infestations in the feet or legs; and mental health problems. In most of the last group of cases it was family members, who described their relatives as insane or mad, rather than the patients themselves, who sought out the ritual specialist. These four clusters may have been the health problems that biomedicine was particularly poor at dealing with – although they may also simply be an inventory of some of the most commonly causes of ill health in the region. Certainly, the cases reveal overlap between the use of ritual specialists and of biomedicine. Many clients stated that they had previously consulted a biomedical practitioner who had not been able to help them – a phenomenon also noted in studies of contemporary Caribbean health culture.[38] A Guadeloupean woman convicted of obeah in Dominica was said to specialize in 'the cure, by occult means, of sick persons who had failed to obtain relief from duly qualified medical practitioners'.[39] Hubert Satchell, in Jamaica, was arrested for attempting to heal a man who had attended the Kingston public hospital eleven times over several months, without improvement in his condition.[40] Ephraim Napier also attended the hospital when he began to go blind, but, on realizing that its staff could not heal him, sought help from John Wright. Wright told him that his eye problems were caused by an evil spirit, perhaps a more convincing explanation in a context in which biomedicine was unable to provide much help.[41]

The move from biomedical healer to ritual specialist was sometimes stimulated by the sick person concluding that biomedicine had failed because their problem had a spiritual cause. This seems to have been why Iris Cross, who was hospitalized in Port of Spain when she became sick after childbirth, eventually discharged herself. After three days in hospital, and with 'no sign of improvement', her 'reputed husband' took her home and sought treatment from another healer, because Cross believed

---

[38] For similar findings in studies of contemporary Jamaica see Payne-Jackson and Alleyne, *Jamaican Folk Medicine*, 81; Fumagalli and Patrick, 'Two Healing Narratives'.
[39] Douglas Young to Sir Ernest Bickham Sweet-Escott, 20 June 1906, enclosed in CO 152/290, Sweet-Escott to Earl of Elgin No. 275, 23 July 1906.
[40] 'Hubert Satchell Fined £10', *Gleaner*, 14 October 1933.
[41] 'Human Skulls Part Paraphernalia of a Kingston Obeahman', *Gleaner*, 10 May 1932.

that her problems were caused by spirits that her aunt had put on her.[42] Like Cross, some people arrived at a ritual specialist having already concluded that they were bothered by a duppy, ghost, or hostile spirit. In one case a woman who had been having 'fits' saw a dispenser, who advised her that 'three duppies were on her' and she therefore needed to be treated by ritual specialists who were skilled in removing duppies.[43] More often people simply reported their difficulties to the ritual specialist, although the very fact that they approached (or accepted the approaches of) a ritual healer suggests that they at least suspected that a spiritual cause underlay their problems. On some occasions it seems that spiritual workers immediately knew that the problem was caused by ghosts or spirits without needing to investigate. In others, ritual workers used diagnostic techniques, which varied by place.

Descriptions of diagnostic and curative techniques reveal an overlapping ritual complex found in both Jamaica and Trinidad, as well as elements that were specific to each location. In Jamaica, but not in Trinidad, ritual specialists frequently used a procedure they termed 'eyesight'. Healers would ask for a coin 'for his (or her) eyesight' or to 'clear his/her eyesight'.[44] This technique anticipates a method analysed by Edward Seaga in 1969, based on his work with Revivalists. Seaga described a popular Jamaican means of determining the nature of a person's problem, involving 'reading a glass of water into which a silver coin has been placed. The glass is set near a candle, or in the sun, so that the light reflects in the water. The operator then concentrates on the coin visually until it separates into two images, at which time the impression or message is received [from the spirits].'[45] Seaga did not use the term 'eyesight', but his description closely echoes those found in the many Jamaican trial reports that used that term. Several reports described ritual specialists who placed coins presented for 'eyesight' in glasses of rum or water. Joseph Telfer, for instance, put a ring of his own, along with a 2-shilling coin from his client, in a glass of rum; the newspaper report noted that the coin 'was called Eyesight'.[46] George Williams also asked

---

[42] 'Obeah Charge Fails', *POSG*, 5 May 1922. In this case it was contested whether the healer suggested the presence of spirits or whether this was Cross's interpretation and he in fact offered more conventional biomedical treatment for fever. What is important is that Cross and her husband sought out an alternative to biomedicine after they believed that it had failed them.
[43] 'Obeah Case in Clarendon', *Gleaner*, 7 July 1905, 11.
[44] For instance, 'Practiced Obeah', *Gleaner*, 20 October 1902; 'Obeah Charge', *Gleaner*, 9 September 1903.
[45] Seaga, 'Revival Cults in Jamaica', 11–12.
[46] 'Obeah Charge', *Gleaner*, 7 November 1908.

his client to place 2 shillings in a glass 'as an "eyesight"'.[47] A report of the 1929 trial of James Campbell provides one of the most detailed of these descriptions. A witness, Jeremiah Johnson, testified that Campbell 'filled a glass with water and ordered him to put the 9/ in it'. Campbell then lit a candle, then – just as Seaga would describe forty years later – 'passed the glass around the candle three times' while he 'talked in an unknown tongue'. Having done this, Campbell interpreted Johnson's situation to him, telling him that 'a man has spent £15 on you five is left and when it is paid you are going to steal and it mean handcuff'.[48] Contrary to Seaga's evidence, however, in the early twentieth century 'eyesight' was used not just as a diagnostic or 'reading' technique but also frequently took place after the healer had provided an initial interpretation of the problem. It functioned as a means to cure as well as to diagnose. Eyesight was a routine part of ritual practice in Jamaica, to the extent that it was well known to the magistracy: one magistrate enquired of a witness 'did he not clear his eyesight'.[49] The courts were particularly interested in eyesight because it involved the transfer of money and could thus be interpreted as a means by which the practitioner worked 'for gain'. However, eyesight was clearly more than a means of payment.[50] In many cases a relatively low-value coin was given for eyesight, and a larger additional payment was also made. Thomas Stewart, for instance, requested 4 shillings for eyesight. However, for the full 'job' of removing the damage that had been done by rivals to a couple's market-trading business, he asked for £6, including an initial payment of 40 shillings.[51]

Eyesight was a common technique in Jamaica, but I found no evidence of its use in Trinidad. Although there was a great deal of communication across different parts of the Caribbean, Jamaica and Trinidad were involved in different migratory circuits. Relatively little exchange of knowledge about ritual practice and techniques seems to have taken place between them.

A diagnostic technique shared by ritual specialists in both Jamaica and Trinidad involved packs of cards, presumably imported. Spiritual workers often opened a session by shuffling or cutting cards and either selecting one themselves or asking the client to do so, then interpreting the chosen card or cards. In Jamaica this method might be used in combination with

---

[47] 'Charges Heard', *Gleaner*, 8 October 1913. For another example see 'Court at May Pen', *Gleaner*, 16 June 1917.
[48] 'James Campbell: Obeah Man, Sent to Prison', *Gleaner*, 5 September 1929.
[49] 'The Black Art', *Gleaner*, 18 February 1909.
[50] On the symbolic role of money in obeah practice, focusing on Trinidad, see Forde, 'The Moral Economy of Spiritual Work'.
[51] 'Charged at Richmond for Practising Obeah', *Gleaner*, 8 August 1931.

'eyesight', or as an alternative to it.[52] Daniel Smyth cut a pack of cards, from which he drew a black card, which led him to explain that 'he could do no good as the child had gone bad and the black card shewed that death had passed over her already' because a 'ghost had mingled with the child'.[53] Picture cards had particular interpretative value. Catherine Thomas, in Trinidad, had a client pick out two cards from several piles. The queen of clubs, she said, signified his wife, while the queen of spades denoted 'a bundle of troubled spirits, bad devils and young spirits'.[54] In a Jamaican case a defendant was said to have pulled out four queens from a pack of cards, interpreting them as indicating that four women were interrupting his client's ability to sell at market.[55] William Hall interpreted the jack of clubs to mean that a 'black man ... had obeahed the boy's leg'.[56]

As well as ordinary playing-cards, some practitioners in both colonies used packs of specially printed tarot-style cards. The earliest example of these appears in a 1909 Jamaican case, where William Bruce drew a card with a picture of a man with a walking-stick and told his client: 'After I have finished my work you shall walk like that man – in the street.'[57] Edith Cook made use of cards with pictures of insects, snakes, cats, and dogs, as well as people in various poses, to tell Miriam Hinds which of her acquaintances were in fact her enemies.[58] Nathaniel Stephens used a pack of cards with pictures of people which he interpreted. In the case that led to his prosecution he showed his client a card with a picture of a 'girl' on it, interpreting it as 'a sign of madness meaning to say his wife was mad'. Another card, which showed the devil with two people, was 'the two duppies upon your wife', while a third card with a picture of a girl with her clothes torn off revealed 'what your wife going to do'.[59] These interpretative strategies appear to share much with European traditions of card reading, both of regular packs and tarot. There is little evidence about wider Caribbean interpretations of the uses of cards, but in Europe, and especially in Britain, tarot was widely thought to be of Egyptian origin, perhaps revealing a convergence between contemporary fascination with Egypt and Africa in the Caribbean and in Europe.[60]

---

[52] 'Matters before Tribunals in the Parishes of the Island', *Gleaner*, 5 February 1919.
[53] 'Supreme Court: Hearing of Appeals', *Gleaner*, 18 March 1902.
[54] 'Commander of Spirits Caught', *POSG*, 23 August 1921.
[55] 'Charged at Richmond for Practising Obeah', *Gleaner*, 8 August 1931.
[56] 'St Catherine Obeahman to Serve 6 Month Prison Term', *Gleaner*, 28 April 1933.
[57] 'Obeah Charge', *Gleaner*, 25 November 1909.
[58] 'Matters before Tribunals in the Parishes of the Island', *Gleaner*, 5 February 1919.
[59] 'Obeah Case Tried in Sav-la-Mar court', *Gleaner*, 17 May 1932.
[60] Farley, 'Out of Africa'.

As these examples suggest, the diagnosis that widely varying problems were caused by hostile spirits or ghosts was ubiquitous. The significance of the spirits of the dead in the lives of the living indicates continuity with the period of slavery. Such a diagnosis was usually revealed when evidence of any length was reported. The spirits were often described as almost tangible, physical beings. Although they could only be seen by the ritual specialist, they used physical means to do harm. Joseph Miller, for instance, examined a young woman with a baby before revealing that she was being harmed by two spirits, also a woman and baby. The adult spirit was 'blowing' food served to the woman, making it indigestible, while the baby spirit was sitting on her chest.[61] Theophilus Neil, whom we met in the previous chapter, allegedly explained a client's abdominal pains by stating that an 'evil spirit [was] upon the sick man pressing him in his stomach'.[62] Isaac Niles diagnosed a client's problems as stemming from another family who had paid to put a spirit on him.[63] It seems likely that diagnoses of hostile spirit intervention underlay many or even all of the other cases as well. That it did not always appear in newspaper reports may derive as much from the fact that it was not an essential part of the means by which obeah was proved as it does from its conceptual absence.

The purpose of the ritual treatment offered by those accused of obeah was usually to catch, remove, or drive out the ghost, duppy, or spirit that was causing the problem. Healing techniques were directed to this end. Some healers literally aimed to catch the harmful ghost. Samuel Edwards caught a ghost with white calico and string, then tied it to an ackee tree.[64] George Williams likewise tied a duppy with a strip of white calico, having caught it underneath a bed.[65] Archibald Forbes buried nails under a tree at a cemetery and held a cutlass in his hand to kill a 'bothersome spirit', and later chased away another spirit from a house by throwing dirt and stones on it.[66] More often, healers used more indirect means of driving away the malevolent spirits, integrating elements found during the slavery era with new methods. The skills with which they did so were often very similar to those found by anthropologists who studied Caribbean healing techniques in the second half of the twentieth century.[67]

[61] 'A Bush Doctor', *Gleaner*, 5 April 1916.
[62] 'The Practising of Obeah is Charged', *Gleaner*, 14 November 1924.
[63] 'Leprous Obeah Man Convicted', *Gleaner*, 21 February 1917.
[64] 'Cases Tried in the Courts of Two Parishes', *Gleaner*, 16 February 1922. This is reminiscent of the case of Polydore, discussed in Chapter 3, who had a man's shadow tied in a tree.
[65] 'Charges Heard', *Gleaner*, 8 October 1913.
[66] 'Amusing Obeah Case', *POSG*, 30 December 1904.
[67] Wedenoja, 'The Origins of Revival'; Moore, 'Religion of Jamaican Negroes'; Hogg, 'Magic and "Science"'. These anthropological works were based on fieldwork which

Some specialists worked in graveyards to attempt to control the spirits of the dead. David Bates and Henrietta Harris, for instance, both conducted rituals at graves, in both cases pouring rum onto a grave, then flogging or switching it.[68] Others used bones or skulls, sometimes animal and sometimes human, to maintain a connection with the dead. Charles Dolly, a prominent ritual specialist who worked in Montserrat and whom we met briefly in the previous chapter, had a human skull which was 'dressed' with horse hair and a tin band wrapped around it.[69] The skull symbolized and instantiated the dead with whose spirits Dolly worked. Scrapings from bones were sometimes used as particularly ritually powerful substances. Dirt from graves was also powerful, used in combination with other materials and sprinkled in significant places to do ritual work.[70] Teeth were also often included in lists of objects taken from obeah defendants' houses.[71] In both Trinidad and Jamaica the human body was an important source of ritually powerful objects.

Rum was another central component of the ritual complex, and was also intimately connected to the relationship with the dead just discussed. Almost every case that gives details of ritual material refers to rum. The spirit was used in all sorts of ways: it was mixed with powders, with rice and grave dirt, with cock's blood, or with scrapings from bone.[72] The resulting mixtures were sometimes drunk, and at other times used to anoint a sufferer's body in a ritual bath. Rum was rubbed into cuts, set on fire, or placed in a glass in the centre of a circle around which ritual activity took place.[73] Most frequently it was used as a libation – sprinkled on the ground inside or outside the house for the ancestors, the spirits of the dead. Rum featured in complex combinations of ritual substances. Alfonso McDermott, for instance, made a mixture of rum, corn, rice, and bone, then shook it together in a vial. After a further ritual

---

allowed for more sense of the connection of ritual healing to religious communities than is usually visible in the newspaper reports.

[68] 'A Sensational Obeah Case', *Gleaner*, 21 September 1893; 'Arrests Made', *Gleaner*, 23 June 1915. For another similar case see 'Cases Brought before the Country Courts', *Gleaner*, 30 June 1916.

[69] Udal, 'Obeah', 271.

[70] For instance, 'Charge of Practising Obeah', *Gleaner*, 6 April 1916.

[71] 'Cases Heard in Country Courts', *Gleaner*, 17 August 1923; 'The Criminal Courts of the Metropolis', *Gleaner*, 20 February 1926.

[72] 'Charge of Practising Obeah', 6 April 1916 (rum mixed with rice and grave dirt); 'Daring Spanish Jar Swindle', 13 January 1908 (rum mixed with cock's blood and Florida water); 'Clever Capture of Men on an Obeah Charge', 20 December 1926 (scrapings of bone with rum poured over it), all in the *Gleaner*.

[73] 'Obeah Trial at Montego Bay', *Gleaner*, 1 October 1907; 'Cases in the Rural Tribunals', *Gleaner*, 7 December 1914; 'A Night Raid', *Gleaner*, 25 January 1909; 'The Brabant Street Obeah Case', *POSG*, 13 July 1910.

involving spinning a pimento grain within a pipe shank, he threw some of the mixture outside.[74] The words that ritual specialists spoke while scattering rum, rice, blood, or a combination of these substances reveal that the purpose was often to provide sustenance for spirits with whom they worked. Stewart Carter took a drink of rum, then sprinkled the rest of it on the ground saying, 'Take this and do the work.'[75] William Bruce similarly sprinkled rum on the ground, saying, 'Come and take yours.'[76] John Daly threw rice outside his house, saying 'Feed, good ones, and do my work,' then a few minutes later threw more rice outside, along with rum, saying 'Come forth at once, you are required.'[77] Carter, Bruce, and Daly directly addressed the spirits of the dead that they hoped would work for them. Rum was one of the most long-standing elements of Caribbean ritual practice; it had been mentioned in the 1760 Jamaican law that outlawed obeah. It drew on even longer traditions of sprinkling an alcoholic drink on the ground as a libation for spirits – a widespread practice in the African cultures from which some of the ancestors of the twentieth century had originated.[78]

The other central element of the ritual complex found in obeah trials was the sacrifice of fowls, usually white. Like rum, fowls were mentioned in many cases. In one example, a group of ritual specialists had reportedly requested two fowls, one old and one young. One healer dug a hole while another severed the head of the young fowl with a cutlass, allowing the blood to trickle into the hole, then placing the head on top. The old fowl was then washed in a basin containing rum and placed under the floor of the house. Between them the two fowls were said to be guarding the yard, preventing anything dangerous from entering.[79] In other cases, fowls were cooked and eaten after sacrifice.[80]

Along with sacrifices and libations, healing rituals frequently involved anointing, rubbing, or bathing the body of the person to be healed. Ritual specialists frequently prescribed healing baths, involving herbs and other materials boiled in water. The substances used in the bath might be gathered from growing plants, as in the case of Joanna Grant, who instructed her assistant to 'go outside quickly and pick plenty bush, and boil a bath', which she then used to bathe Rhoda Steel, who was sick

---

[74] 'The Black Art', *Gleaner*, 19 February 1909.
[75] 'Obeah Cases in St Andrews', *Gleaner*, 17 October 1899.
[76] 'Obeah Charge', *Gleaner*, 25 November 1909.
[77] 'Obeah Charge', *Gleaner*, 12 May 1915.
[78] On the history of the libation see Smith, *Caribbean Rum*, 100. On libations in contemporary Kumina practice in Jamaica see Stewart, *Three Eyes*, 151–2.
[79] 'Obeah "Aces" Sent to Prison by Mr Rennie', *Gleaner*, 27 August 1929.
[80] 'Alleged that Baby was Bathed in Fowl Blood', *Gleaner*, 26 October 1929.

because, Grant diagnosed, 'Spirit is troubling her'.[81] Ritual baths sometimes also used the blood of sacrificed fowls, mixed with other material.[82] At least as commonly, however, material for ritual baths was purchased from shops. Henry Padmore, for instance, told Nathaniel Burke to 'go to the apothecary and get 20 cents in musk, a phial of essence, 5 cents red lavender, and half-bottle of strong rum'. On Burke's return Padmore mixed these items together in order to give him a bath.[83] As one practitioner explained, such bathing or rubbing the body would 'keep away ghosts'.[84]

Ritual specialists did not just employ objects, but also had access to esoteric knowledge, both spoken and written. Many court reports described how spiritual workers spoke in an 'unknown tongue'.[85] In Jamaica, evidence against those accused of obeah sometimes included the fact that they had made esoteric marks, often in chalk – signs that are common within the Revival and Spiritual Baptist traditions.[86] Jacob Hatfield, for instance, drew a chalk circle on the floor, with a cross inside it, on which he placed lighted candles and the money received from his client.[87] George Williams 'traced quaint figures' in chalk on a piece of board.[88] In Trinidad, however, making chalk marks was more likely to be included in evidence in cases brought under the Shouters' Prohibition Ordinance.[89]

Christian ritual, language, and iconography featured prominently in the activities that led to obeah prosecution, often integrated within other kinds of ritual practice. Most significant were the Psalms, which were frequently recited during ritual activity. Sheppard Moncrieffe, for instance, diagnosed that two duppies were causing an old man's illness. In his efforts to heal he asked the man's daughter to read a Psalm, then himself said the Lord's Prayer, spoke in an unknown tongue, and asked for a fowl and some rum for ritual use.[90] The Bible was also used, both to read from and as a ritual object. Rossabella Rennals passed a Bible over

---

[81] 'Obeah Charge in Portland', *Gleaner*, 27 January 1914.
[82] 'Bathed Baby in Fowl Blood to Cure Malaria', *Gleaner*, 18 November 1929.
[83] *POSG*, 30 November 1909.
[84] 'City Court's Criminal Work', *Gleaner*, 20 November 1905.
[85] For instance, 'San Juan "Obeahman" Jailed', *POSG*, 12 April 1935; 'Obeah Charge', *Gleaner*, 18 May 1915.
[86] For brief descriptions of such chalk marks see Moore, 'Religion of Jamaican Negroes', 129; Wedenoja, 'The Origins of Revival', 94.
[87] 'Obeah Cases', *Gleaner*, 16 June 1915.
[88] 'Charges Heard', *Gleaner*, 8 October 1913. For a similar case see 'The Hardware Gap Obeah Case', *Gleaner*, 14 August 1899.
[89] 'Keeping a Shouter's Meeting', *POSG*, 15 July 1920; 'Alleged Shouters Meeting', *POSG*, 12 December 1925.
[90] 'Cases in the Rural Tribunal', *Gleaner*, 10 August 1918.

a pan of liquid, while George Forbes waved a Bible over his client's head while speaking in an unknown tongue.[91] Other practitioners put coins inside a Bible, or used it in divination rituals.[92] Elizabeth McPherson, for instance, used a Bible and some eggs to reveal the location of some stolen coffee.[93]

Alongside rituals designed to remove ghosts, others focused on protection. Many practitioners provided 'guards' for their clients: assemblages of ritual substances, often tied in cloth, which were to be worn around the neck, kept in a pocket, or placed under a pillow.[94] Joseph Harvey, for instance, gave a client 'what he called a guard' to be worn around the waist, 'made of a piece of new calico, in which was stitched a small bag containing a pebble, and threepence'.[95]

Many of the materials and actions discussed so far feature prominently in other accounts of obeah practice.[96] The cases also reveal a ritual repertoire not always so visible in other sources. For instance, the cases reveal a significant role for eggs and eggshells in ritual practice. They were used in the preparation of ritual guards, as when Nathaniel Hall made a paste out of egg, vinegar, and powder, put it on a piece of flannel, and told his client to tie it to her stomach to protect her.[97] Eggs could also be used to influence: Walter Christian oversaw the burial of an egg, with rum and powder poured on top of it, outside his client's door, telling him not to remove it until after the court case whose outcome it was intended to affect had taken place.[98] The cases also demonstrate the importance of thread, often black, which was sometimes tied in knots while the names of people were called.[99] Beyond these regularly used materials, a huge range of other objects and substances played an occasional role in spiritual work. Prominent natural materials included garlic, lime juice, calabashes, asafoetida, lavender, pimento, and cedar wood or

---

[91] 'Spanish Town: Obeahism and Revivalism', *Gleaner*, 28 June 1899; 'Cases in the Mandeville Court', *Gleaner*, 7 April 1916.
[92] 'Evidence does not Establish Obeah Charge', *Gleaner*, 15 April 1932; '"Obeah" Woman Sent to Prison for 6 Months', *Gleaner*, 8 November 1932.
[93] 'Obeahwoman Punished', *Gleaner*, 17 June 1916.
[94] 'Witchcraft Again', *POSG*, 21 February 1917; 'Obeah Charge', *Gleaner*, 12 November 1914; 'Jamaican Obeahman in British Honduras to Be Deported Home', *Gleaner*, 31 August 1931.
[95] 'Obeah Charge', *Gleaner*, 9 February 1916.
[96] For instance, Wedenoja, 'The Origins of Revival'; Hogg, 'Magic and "Science"'; Moore, 'Religion of Jamaican Negroes'.
[97] 'Charged under the Obeah Law', *Gleaner*, 14 March 1908.
[98] 'Rural Court', *Gleaner*, 25 August 1915.
[99] 'County Courts', *Gleaner*, 23 April 1924. For other cases involving thread see for instance 'Obeahman Imprisoned', *POSG*, 15 October 1927; 'Curious Obeah Case', *Gleaner*, 13 July 1899.

sawdust.[100] Ritual specialists also frequently made use of manufactured and purchased objects, especially mirrors, candles, marbles, and beads; and abrasive or pungent materials such as camphor, washing blue, brimstone, or carbolic balls.[101] A wide range of healing oils were also used. In a couple of cases these were manufactured oils labelled for specific occult purposes: Arthur Stone, arrested in Jamaica in 1922, had 'oil of turn back' and 'oil of love', while a later Jamaican defendant possessed oils including 'oil of the rising man', 'oil of death', and 'oil of kill him'.[102] More common were oils with names denoting their ingredients rather than their function: variants on 'oil of rignam' were very common; also found were oils of cloves, of amber, of cinnamon, and of peppermint, along with products frequently sold as health-giving substances such as castor oil, camphorated oil, Epsom salts, and cod-liver oil.[103]

The patterns in practices that led to prosecution for obeah drew on a repertoire of ritual practice that at its heart was about mediating between the living and the dead. The healing and cleansing rituals that led to obeah prosecutions were by no means all the same, but they drew on a shared pool of knowledge, although with geographical differences. The scattering of rum and rice, sacrifice of fowls and occasionally other animals, and use of human bones were all offerings to spirits, while other practices such as bathing and anointing with oils sought to alter a suffering person's relationship to the world of the spirits. Taken together, and even despite the hostile framework that generated the evidence, these

[100] See for example 'Obeah Charge in Portland', *Gleaner*, 27 January 1914 (garlic); 'Grace Garrison is Arraigned on Obeah Charge', *Gleaner*, 28 September 1926 (lime juice); 'Obeah Charge in Portland', *Gleaner*, 27 January 1914 (calabash); 'Alleged "Obeah Maker" Dismissed', *POSG*, 12 August 1930 (lavender); 'Cases on Appeal before the Supreme Court', *Gleaner*, 11 May 1909 (asafoetida); 'Interesting Case at Halfway Tree', *Gleaner*, 13 May 1916 (pimento); 'Desecration of a Grave', *POSG*, 10 April 1902 (cedar wood); 'Alleged Obeah Men', *Gleaner*, 12 June 1922 (sawdust). In many cases, combinations of these and other objects were presented as evidence in court.
[101] See for example 'Exorcising a Jumby', *POSG*, 3 February 1899 (mirrors, marbles, washing blue); 'Interesting Case at Halfway Tree', *Gleaner*, 13 May 1916 (candles, chalk, camphor); 'Obeah Charges at Morant Bay', *Gleaner*, 5 April 1916 (brimstone); 'The Allman Town Obeah Case', *Gleaner*, 14 October 1907 (carbolic).
[102] 'Cases tried by Mr H. Robinson in Police Court', *Gleaner*, 22 August 1922; 'Blind Man is Convicted on Charge under Obeah Law', *Gleaner*, 18 March 1938.
[103] For instance, Thornton, '"Obeah" in Jamaica', 264 (variants on oil of rignum); 'Obeah Charges at Morant Bay', April 5 1916; 'Before Country Tribunals', 21 April 1917; 'The Case against Professor Henderson', 10 March 1908 (oil of cloves, oil of amber); 'Spanish Town Court', 11 August 1917 (oil of origanum, oil of cinnamon, oil of sanna, camphor, and assafoetida); 'Man Charged with having Ganja and Obeah Implements', 18 November 1935 (oil of peppermint); 'Obeah Charge in Portland', 27 January 1914 (castor oil); 'Obeah Worker', 5 April 1916 (camphorated oil); 'Alleged Revivalist and Healer before Court on 2 Charges', 2 March 1934 (Epsom salts); 'Bathed Baby in Fowl Blood to Cure Malaria', 18 November 1929 (cod-liver oil), all in the *Gleaner*.

similarities suggest deep underlying unities in what many of those prosecuted for obeah were doing, in their interpretations of problems, and their methods for addressing them.

The ritual practices revealed through these newspaper reports suggest strong resonances with African ways of interpreting and responding to harm and trouble. People prosecuted for obeah in the early twentieth-century Caribbean drew on a set of ideas and practices that had long histories and shared a great deal with other forms of New World African religious practice. That shared approach included openness to innovation and to incorporation of new elements and practices within an existing cosmological framework. The evidence thus speaks to some important questions in Caribbeanist historiography and anthropology, which has been preoccupied with the extent to which the Anglophone Caribbean societies did or did not maintain cultural practices derived from Africa, and whether they can be connected to specific African societies. At some important levels it does make sense to identify some of the ritual practices that were prosecuted as obeah as 'African', even while avoiding the pitfalls of tracing African 'continuities' identified by scholars such as Stephan Palmié.[104] Even so, in the early twentieth century, Anglo-Creole Caribbean ritual practice was primarily connected to Africa through parallels identified by observers, rather than through the direct consciousness of the practitioners. There is little evidence of connection to any specific region within the continent. Identification of certain phenomena as 'African', such as the actions of spirits in the lives of the living and the need to feed those spirits with rum and fowls, is the interpretation of the observer rather than of the practitioners. For early twentieth-century ritual specialists such ways of thinking and acting were part of a common-sense cosmology and embodied habitus which we can identify as incorporating African-derived elements, rather than an explicit orientation towards Africa. Spiritual workers today tend to be more consciously oriented towards Africa than were those practising in the early twentieth century. As the next section of this chapter will show, alongside important shared cosmological elements of obeah practice, there was also much diversity in the context in which ritual specialists practised their arts, within individual societies as well as between them.

The activities of those who appeared before the courts contravened the obeah laws in many ways. Some were religious healers who undertook healing work within a religious community or a balm yard. For instance Samuel Reid, also known as Doctor Reid, was involved with a Revival community in Clarendon. As part of his religious work Reid 'kept a

[104] Palmié, *The Cooking of History*.

regular dispensary and hospital with a matron and other assistants'. He was first prosecuted for obeah in 1899. The evidence against him was that he had treated Sarah Fraser who, according to the *Gleaner*'s reporter, had 'got light-headed and half crazy from attending revival meetings'. Reid, in contrast to the *Gleaner* journalist, diagnosed that Fraser had three duppies inside her. She stayed at his hospital for three days, receiving treatment that involved taking 'medicine'. In addition:

He... threw her on the ground and walked several times up and down on her body, to expel the ghosts. He also squeezed and kneaded her stomach with his hands for the same purposes. He then flogged her with a supple jack and afterwards his assistants or 'soldiers'... formed a ring round Reid and all danced and shouted, and sang revival songs, Reid also sprinkled Mrs Fraser with... medicine, which he said would cut the duppies eyes 'fine as linen'.[105]

Reid's practice was thus a collective one, including many of the core elements established in the earlier part of the chapter as central to the practice of spiritual healing in the Caribbean – most fundamentally, techniques to rid his patient of the duppies that were causing her harm. Reid served at least some of his time in prison, but re-established his practice on his release. He was soon in court again, this time not for obeah but for practising medicine without a licence.[106] He was, according to the *Gleaner*, selling for '1s per bottle' a cure-all 'draught' described as 'a decoction of boiled weeds', the recipe for which he had received by revelation and which was said to be popular with 'great numbers of the peasantry of North-west Clarendon and the adjoining districts of Manchester'. Reid promptly paid his fine of £6 plus costs, but was convicted again for breach of the medical law in 1902.[107] The communal setting of Reid's practice distinguishes it from the stereotype of the isolated obeah practitioner, but was itself typical of a particular subset of religious healers whose work made them vulnerable to charges both of obeah and of practising medicine without a licence. This double illegality, however, also gave them some scope to use one law against another, in a form of plea bargaining.

We can see this plea bargaining in practice in two cases brought against the famous healer Rose Anne (Mammy) Forbes and her husband George, who together ran a popular balm yard (referred to in one newspaper article as a 'Balming sanitorium') at Blake's Pen, Clarendon, to which

---

[105] 'Obeahism Extraordinary', f. 45, 'Charged with Obeah, must be Flogged', f. 48. Both in McCrea Scrap Book.
[106] 'A Heaven-taught "Doctor"', 16 August 1900, press cutting from unnamed newspaper in McCrea Scrap Book, f. 112 (misnumbered: page is between 49 and 50)
[107] 'Bush "Doctoring" in Clarendon', *Gleaner*, 30 October 1902.

'people from far and near parishes suffering from various complaints travelled by the hundreds'.[108] The folklorist Martha Beckwith described Forbes, pictured in Figure 6.1, as 'the most renowned' of the balm healers in Jamaica.[109] Her balm yard operated under her daughter, Mother Rita, until well into the 1970s, and continues a more limited practice today.[110] Mammy Forbes pleaded guilty to a charge of practising medicine without a licence in 1910 and was warned by the magistrate to 'destroy all her implements when she got home... for if the police found anything, such as bottles and feathers and took them to Court, a charge of obeah could be brought against her'.[111] While I have found no evidence that Mammy Forbes ever faced an obeah prosecution, her husband George was charged with obeah in 1916. At that trial, after hearing evidence about a ritual that involved words spoken in an unknown tongue, the words 'praise father, praise son, and praise holy ghost', a Bible, a basin of water, and the prescription of 'balm' liquid, the presiding magistrate ordered the charge reduced to one of practising medicine without a licence. The prosecuting policeman advocated imposing a fine that would be high enough to put the healers out of business. The £10 fine that Forbes actually received was clearly not enough to do this, although it may well have had serious economic effects.[112] In several other cases in the 1910s, prosecutions for obeah were effectively plea-bargained into charges of breach of the medical law. George Morgan, a St Lucian-born healer who worked in Jamaica and was also known as Clement Clarke, had a regular healing practice, indicated by a piece of paper found in his possession, stating: 'Dr C. C. Clarke attends Mondays, Tuesdays and Saturdays.' He was initially charged with obeah, but this charge was withdrawn when he agreed to plead guilty to a charge of practising medicine without a licence.[113] Sometimes it is hard to tell what, if anything, distinguishes such cases from those where obeah charges led to convictions, although the strong element of Christian worship must be part of what enabled George Forbes to avoid conviction for obeah.[114]

[108] 'Under Arrest at Mandeville', *Gleaner*, 7 March 1916.
[109] Beckwith, *Jamaica Folk-Lore*, 9.
[110] For a description of the balm yard under Mother Rita see Barrett, 'The Portrait of a Jamaican Healer'. I was able to visit Blake's Pen in 2011. The balm yard is now run by Mother Rita's granddaughter. Thank you to Robert Hill for facilitating my visit.
[111] 'Charge of Practicing Medicine against a Woman', *Gleaner*, 5 August 1910.
[112] 'Cases in the Mandeville Court', *Gleaner*, 7 April 1916.
[113] 'Before Court', *Gleaner*, 20 April 1916.
[114] Martha Beckwith placed her discussion of the Forbes's balm yard in her chapter 'The Revivalists'. Beckwith, *Black Roadways*, 171–3; Beckwith, *Jamaica Folk-Lore*, 9. Other cases of prosecution for collective healing rituals include that of Albert Josephs for practising obeah after he led two days of rituals in an effort to heal a paralysed man. Josephs wore a red gown and red cloth on his head in court, and said that 'he was a

Figure 6.1 'Mammy Forbes, the Healer', photograph of Rose Anne ('Mammy') Forbes, from Martha Beckwith, *Black Roadways: A Study of Jamaican Folk Life*.
Courtesy of the National Library of Scotland

Further diversity of practice among Caribbean ritual healers is revealed in the widespread use of written and especially imported printed materials. A few of those arrested, including Popo Samuel, had books of handwritten notes and prayers. The police seized from Samuel 'a copy book containing a number of prayers in which were the words "hallelujah... against my enemy, etc"'.[115] Printed books appeared more frequently than handwritten ones. Most often reported was the use of Bibles and prayer books, the contents of which were intimately familiar to most Caribbean people.[116] Ritual techniques often involved reading or reciting Psalms, both as something done by practitioners in the presence of clients and as a technique that ritual specialists instructed clients to undertake on their own at a later date.[117]

Alongside Bibles, ritual specialists made use of occult and esoteric published works. As many studies have noted, spiritual practice in the Caribbean became intimately linked in the twentieth century to the publications of the DeLaurence publishing company in Chicago.[118] The newspaper evidence confirms this, and suggests the rapid circulation of DeLaurence books in the Caribbean after William DeLaurence published his first book in 1902. Evidence in the 1910 obeah trial of Dr Williams, of Siparia, Trinidad, included the fact that the defendant had a copy of a book described as 'the Seventh Book of Moses'.[119] Versions of this book, more commonly named the *Sixth and Seventh Book of Moses*, appeared repeatedly in obeah trials.[120] The text, derived from medieval

---

preacher and was on a Gospel spreading expedition when he was arrested'. 'Full Court Opens before Three Judges', *Gleaner*, 27 January 1931. A similar case is reported in 'Spanish Town: Obeahism and Revivalism', *Gleaner*, 28 June 1899. The seven accused in this case ran what was referred to as a 'Balm House' or 'Balm Yard' and conducted a collective healing ceremony that included singing, drumming, and praying. Six of the seven received sentences of twelve months' imprisonment, and all the men found guilty were also flogged. Another case took place in Smith's Village, a centre for Revival: 'Duppy Catchers to Follow the "Messiah" from City Suburb', *Gleaner*, 25 April 1914.

[115] 'A Family of Obeahists', *POSG*, 2 August 1922, 9.
[116] For instance, 'An Alleged Obeahist', *POSG*, 15 October 1927.
[117] We found more reports of the reading of Psalms in Jamaica than in Trinidad. See for example 'Man and Woman Arrested on Obeah Charge in St Ann', *Gleaner*, 24 May 1930, in which the patient was instructed to read a Psalm during a ritual bath; 'Arrested on Charge of Practising Obeah', *Gleaner*, 18 December 1933, in which the accused obeah practitioner read Psalm 109 as part of a ritual. For a Trinidadian case involving a Psalm see the case of Anita Smith and Charles Carter, discussed below, pp. 238–9.
[118] Simpson, *Black Religions in the New World*, 116; Brodber, 'Brief Notes on DeLaurence'; Davies, *Grimoires*, 227–31; Elkins, 'William Lauron DeLaurence'; Herskovits and Herskovits, *Trinidad Village*, 225; Payne-Jackson and Alleyne, *Jamaican Folk Medicine*.
[119] 'Alleged Obeahism in Siparia', *POSG*, 16 January 1910.
[120] Examples of trials reporting the defendant's possession of the *Sixth and Seventh Book of Moses* include 'Expensive Obeah', *POSG*, 5 April 1918; 'Six Months for Man who Practised the Black Art', *Gleaner*, 30 January 1934; 'Blind Man is Convicted on Charge

European *grimoires*, was brought by German migrants to the United States in the nineteenth century, translated into English, and published in various American editions, including most significantly by DeLaurence, Scott and Company in 1910. Dr Williams may have owned this, or perhaps another edition, possibly that published (also in Chicago) by Feliks Markiewicz.[121] In Jamaica, the earliest evidence of the circulation of DeLaurence publications that I have found is in the 1915 trial of Joseph Paddy of Smith's Village. Paddy had 'several books', including *The Devil's Legacy* and *Mysteries of Magic* as well as DeLaurence's *Sixth and Seventh Book of Moses*.[122] *The Devil's Legacy*, which originated in America and was available at least from 1880, juxtaposes details of European witchcraft trials with quotes from Macbeth and instructions on how to 'tincture silver into gold'.[123] A. E. Waite, the author/compiler of *Mysteries of Magic*, was a sceptical member of the Order of the Golden Dawn, a British occult organization founded in 1888. *Mysteries of Magic* was his 1886 translation and digest of work by the influential French occult writer Éliphas Lévi.[124]

Among the many titles of esoteric books that appeared in obeah trials, the *Sixth and Seventh Book of Moses* and its variants were by far the most prominent. Also produced as evidence in several trials were two further DeLaurence publications, *Egyptian Secrets* and the *Great Book of Magical Art*.[125] The former was *Egyptian Secrets of Albertus Magnus*,

---

under Obeah Law', *Gleaner*, 18 March 1938. Other defendants reportedly owned books including the *First, Sixth and Seventh Books of Moses* ('Alleged Obeah Man', *Gleaner*, 12 June 1922), the *Sixth Seventh and Eighth Chapters of Moses* ('Alleged Obeah', *Gleaner*, 7 March 1928), the *Seventh and Sixth Books of Moses* (Man Alleged to Have Obeah Tools Arrested', *Gleaner*, 14 January 1929), and the *Sixth Book of Moses* ('Obeah Raid at San Juan', *POSG*, 22 May 1931).

[121] Davies, *Grimoires*; Long, *Spiritual Merchants*, 121–2.
[122] 'An Obeahman goes to Prison', *Gleaner*, 30 November 1915. Kevin J. Hayes's claim that from the 1880s copies of the *Sixth and Seventh Book of Moses* 'could be found among the Obeah men of the West Indies' is based on slim evidence: an article from the *Philadelphia Press* that describes the West Indian obeah man as having a unnamed 'cabalistic book... full of strange characters, crude figures, and roughly traced diagrams and devices'. While this may imply an earlier edition of *The Sixth and Seventh Books of Moses*, it could also refer to books written by hand in Jamaica. Hayes, *Folklore and Book Culture*, 18, 120n122. Hayes's claim also appears in ten Kortenaar, *Postcolonial Literature*, 153.
[123] *The Devil's legacy*.   [124] Davies, *Grimoires*, 175–7, 181–3.
[125] Cases in which ritual specialists possessed versions of *Egyptian Secrets* include 'Blind Man is Convicted on Charge under Obeah Law', *Gleaner*, 18 March 1938 and 'Siparia: Alleged Practice of Obeah', *POSG*, 18 September 1931. Versions of the *Great Book of Magical Art* appeared in evidence in 'Obeah Man Trapped', *POSG*, 24 March 1931; 'Siparia Magistrates Court', *POSG*, 31 May 1931; 'Obeah Prosecution Fails', *POSG*, 13 August 1931; 'Six Months for Man who Practised the Black Art', *Gleaner*, 30 January 1934.

another German-origin collection of folk medicine and spells, published in translation in the United States in the late nineteenth century and republished by DeLaurence.[126] The latter, appearing under a range of slightly different titles, were versions of DeLaurence's *Great Book of Magical Art, Hindu Magic, and East Indian Occultism and Talismanic Magic*, published under DeLaurence's name and consisting largely of a reworked version of Francis Barrett's *The Magus, or Celestial Intelligencer* (1801), itself compiled from earlier occult works.[127] By 1931 the Jamaica *Gleaner* was calling for action against the 'numerous more or less ignorant persons [who] import from certain firms in the United States books dealing with such subjects as magical art (Hindu magic particularly), East Indian occultism, talismanic magic and other subjects very much akin to what is locally called the ritual of obeah'.[128] In 1940 the Jamaican Undesirable Publications Act made it illegal to import publications of the DeLaurence company, along with Communist literature and other literature deemed subversive.[129]

These books suggest the flexibility of Caribbean spiritual work and ritual practice. Although drawing on African interpretations of harm with spiritual causes, healers were clearly deeply attracted to what was presented to them as 'East Indian' or 'Hindoo' mysticism. DeLaurence, although an American of European ancestry, presented himself and his products as connected to India, using images of himself wearing a turban on his books and in catalogues and newspaper advertisements (for an example, see Figure 6.2).[130] He thus appealed to the orientalist fascination with 'Eastern' spiritual traditions common in late nineteenth-century Europe and America, expressed, for instance, in the appeal of theosophy.[131] Yet he seems quickly to have found that this form of marketing was also particularly appealing to African, African American, and Caribbean customers – including those who were themselves of Indian birth or descent.[132] People arrested in possession of the *Great Book of Magical Arts* included Gockool Maraj, who said he was a 'Hindi priest', and Beharry, who was described as 'a middle aged East Indian man'.[133]

---

[126] Long, *Spiritual Merchants*, 121.    [127] Ibid., 122; Davies, *Grimoires*, 216–17, 135.
[128] 'Books on Magic Coming from US through Post', *Gleaner*, 2 May 1931.
[129] Palmer, *Freedom's Children*, 232–6. For a 1961 list of banned items and proposed additions see FCO 141/5473: Banning of Undesirable Publications.
[130] Davies, *Grimoires*, 228 fig. 22.
[131] Dixon, *Divine Feminine*, 159–62; McGarry, *Ghosts of Futures Past*; Oppenheim, *The Other World*.
[132] On the African and African American markets for DeLaurence's publications see Davies, *Grimoires*; Long, *Spiritual Merchants*.
[133] 'Obeah Man Trapped', *POSG*, 24 March 1931; 'Obeah Prosecution Fails', *POSG*, 13 August 1931.

The attraction of DeLaurence's works for those brought up as Hindus was perhaps as much in the unfamiliarity of what was presented within them as it was the books' Indianness, for although they claimed connection with Hindu traditions, in practice their actual content was largely derived from older European works.

The use of printed books was one of several methods by which Caribbean ritual workers integrated forms of knowledge from Europe and the United States into their practice. Additionally, many ritual specialists employed modern healing techniques that had not been integrated into biomedicine, such as magnetism, mesmerism, electrical healing, and hypnotism. Others drew on European methods of communication with the world of the dead, naming themselves faith healers and spiritualists. In some of these cases the police charged people with practising medicine without a licence rather than obeah. Professor E. J. Hall, who had worked in Jamaica and Trinidad before setting up a healing practice in Georgetown, Guyana, told the *Demerara Chronicle* that he 'cured without drugs or surgery' and specialised in 'electro-therapeutics, radio-therapy, phototherapy, thermotherapy, hydrotherapy, diaduction, vibratology'.[134] In Jamaica, Professor Robert Bird Henderson used magnetism and massage in his healing practice. Both were charged with practising medicine without a licence.[135] Perhaps most prominent among this group was Alfred Mends of Kingston, who practised homeopathy and produced a certificate in court showing that he was licensed by the 'Thompsonian College' in the United States.[136] He was prosecuted on multiple occasions for practising medicine without a licence, and campaigned for changes to the medical laws that would enable homeopathic doctors to practise legally.[137] He would later become the editor of the nationalist journal *Plain Talk*, and a supporter of Marcus Garvey.[138]

---

[134] '"Professor" Hall in Demerara', *POSG*, 12 March 1903, 3; 'The Charge against Professor Hall', *POSG*, 14 March 1903, 3.

[135] 'Case against Prof Henderson', *Gleaner*, 3 March 1908; 'The Charge against Professor Henderson', *Gleaner*, 10 March 1908.

[136] According to W. F. Elkins, Mends had 'obtained the degrees of Doctor of Medicines and Master of Electro-Therapeutics from the Thompsonian Medical College, Allen Town [sic], Pennsylvania' through a correspondence course based on the system of botanical medicine developed by Samuel Thomson. Elkins, *Street Preachers*, 52–3. According to John Haller, the Thomsonian Medical College of Allentown was organized in 1904, but 'there is no evidence that classes were ever held'. Haller, *Kindly Medicine*, 86. On Thomsonianism more generally see Haller, *The People's Doctors*.

[137] 'Charge under the Medical Law', *Gleaner*, 29 January 1909; 'Charge under the Medical Law', *Gleaner*, 27 June 1912. For a similar case see the prosecution for practising medicine without a licence of Edmund Dicks, a 'duly qualified homeopath or electro-homeopath': 'Business of the Courts of the Metropolis', *Gleaner*, 18 May 1918.

[138] Hill, ed., *The Marcus Garvey and Universal Negro Improvement Association Papers*, 106.

THE GREATEST ADEPT

———

EASTERN ORDER OF SACRED MYSTERIES

Artist's Conception of de Laurence Wearing a Turban

The Orient

Egypt

## When You Buy Get The Best
### de LAURENCE'S BOOKS IN DEMAND ALL OVER THE WORLD

There are more of de Laurence's Volumes and Self-educational Books on Spiritism, Hypnotism, and Occultism sold in New York, Chicago, Boston, San Francisco, Havana, Cuba; Mexico; London, England; Bocas Del Toro, Republic of Panama; Colon in the Canal Zone, Republic of Panama; Trinidad, Jamaica; Black River and Kingston, British West Indies; Durban, Cape Town, Johannesburg and Natal, Transvaal, South Africa; Port Limon and Cuba Creek, Costa Rica, Central America; Belize, British Honduras, Central America; Christ Church, New Zealand; Georgetown, British Guiana; Honolulu, H. I.; Buenos Ayres, Argentine Republic; Curacao, Dutch West Indies; Bombay, Calcutta, Delhi and Benares, India; Melbourne and Sydney, Australia; Port Said, Egypt; Glasgow, Scotland; Dublin and Castlebar, Ireland; Berlin, Germany, and Madrid, Spain, than all other authors, teachers and writers on these subjects combined.

The Publishers.

ATTRACTING ATTENTION BY FAKE ADVERTISING

de Laurence Says: It is more commendable to set a just price on a book, or an article you know to be good, than to be so deceitful as to sell at any price a thing you know to be worthless; or to pretend to give away something for nothing, with the sole object of attracting attention by fake advertising.

Figure 6.2 Advertisement from the DeLaurence company catalogue. Similar advertisements were published in Caribbean newspapers such as the Jamaican *Gleaner*.
Source: personal collection of Owen Davies

Others who did similar work used (relatively) new healing techniques including electrical healing in order to achieve goals such as removing afflictions caused by the spirits of the dead, thus becoming vulnerable to prosecution under the obeah laws. Professor Dawkins de Brown of Jamaica circulated printed advertisements for his electrical and herbal healing treatments, and also issued shares in his United Blue Ribbon Medical Electricity and Herbal Company. He was fined four times for practising medicine without a licence before receiving a twelve-month prison sentence in 1919 for practising obeah. The difference between the prosecutions for the two charges was that in 1919 a witness claimed that de Brown had 'claimed to have power over evil spirits', even while his main activity involved 'electrical and herbal treatments'.[139] Another 'Medical Electrical Specialist', Simeon Luther Blagrove, was charged with both obeah and practising medicine without a licence, having received £10 from a man who wanted him to remove duppies. His practice included the use of an electrical machine that 'pass[ed] healing power through the body'.[140]

Even less apparently African than the mesmerists and hypnotists – and nevertheless still sometimes prosecuted – were people who combined work as ritual healers with performances designed to entertain. Travers Wright was arrested in Jamaica after he had advertised that he would 'hold an entertainment to give an exhibition of his magic skill'. On arrest he said he was 'a magician in the modern sense of the word and not an obeahman'.[141] Professor Joseph Maria Williams was prosecuted in Trinidad for practising medicine without a licence because he sold liquid medicine for an eye complaint; in his defence he argued that he was a conjuror who performed sleight-of-hand tricks, and had even performed before the governor of Jamaica and his wife.[142] Hubert Carrington likewise denied practising obeah, explaining that he used massage and electricity in his healing work and 'used to give big performances on the stage and he never pretended to be able to work obeah'.[143]

Other ritual specialists combined new European healing technologies with established African–Caribbean practices. As we saw in the last chapter, Arthur and Mary Clement described their work as mesmerism, but

---

[139] 'The Case of Professor Dawkins', 6 September 1919; 'Cases Heard by Resident Magistrates', 8 September 1919; 'Court Work of Montego Bay', 15 September 1919, all in the *Gleaner*.
[140] *Kingston Daily Chronicle*, 18 October 1915, quoted in Elkins, *Street Preachers*, 95–7, at 96.
[141] 'Alleged Black Art Worker Held at Frankfield', *Gleaner*, 9 December 1930.
[142] 'More about "Professor" Joseph of Sagwa Fame', *POSG*, 24 June 1896.
[143] 'Expensive Obeah', *POSG*, 5 April 1918.

faced obeah charges for activities that included bush baths and the sacrifice of fowls. Beatrice Hanson described her work as spiritualism and said she had trained with Arthur Conan Doyle. Her ritual work included asking for 'eye sight' and speaking in an unknown tongue.[144] Such cases led to complex discussions in court that repeatedly circled around the need to distinguish between obeah and legitimate healing practices, while bemoaning the impossibility of doing so. The prosecution of Anita Smith and Charles Carter in Port of Spain is a particularly clear example. Smith and Carter were prosecuted after their entrapment by Detective Lambert, one of the several Trinidadian policemen who specialized in obeah cases.[145] Lambert organized a sting involving a man and a woman who posed as a couple claiming that the man had been having trouble in his job as an overseer on a sugar estate. According to the testimony of Margaret Thomas, who posed as the wife of the supposed overseer, Anita Smith went into a trance and told them that their problems were caused by 'the bad spirit upon you'; they should 'take a bath on the Third Stage of Science'. Thomas also reported that Smith stated that 'it is not I speaking but the dead spirit in my body. I am now at the 12th stage of science and when I wake from here I will not know what I have said.'

In her trial, Anita Smith's defence was that Carter had induced her to act as a medium, hypnotizing her using techniques derived from Franz Mesmer. She did not know what took place while she was in a trance. Her defence lawyer read from the *Encylopaedia Britannica*'s entry on hypnotism to prove that Smith's practice was not supernatural but rather was 'genuine science'. In contrast, the prosecution argued that 'the form of obeah in this case was that of mesmerism'. The trial was complicated by the fact that Charles Carter was a former police officer, that Margaret Thomas admitted to being Detective Lambert's lover and said she would do anything to help him, and that witnesses called Lambert's integrity into question in other ways, claiming for instance that he and others in the police regularly used mesmerism and hypnotism to work out whom to arrest in obeah and other cases. Rather than pitting rationality against superstition, as advocates of obeah law claimed it would, in this trial everyone involved was entangled in similar work in which multiple forms of magical and esoteric practices intertwined.

---

[144] 'Claims to be Spiritualist', *Gleaner*, 11 January 1933. Similar cases include 'Alleged Obeah', *POSG*, 19 July 1907; 'Man before Court on Obeah Charge', *Gleaner*, 2 February 1940.

[145] All information on this trial comes from 'Ex-Constable Alleged Obeahist', 18 August 1922, 7; 'Medium Victim of Hypnotist', 23 August 1922, 6; 'Obeah Case Continued', 26 August 1922, 8, all in *POSG*. Unfortunately we were unable to locate a report of the outcome of the trial.

This case also reveals how the use of techniques such as mesmerism and hypnotism challenged the legal and discursive conception of obeah as an African phenomenon in the Caribbean. Few of the material objects removed from Smith and Carter's house were overtly connected to Africa. Nor, to the extent that there was any ritual described, did the ritual practice that they undertook seem particularly 'African'. There was no animal sacrifice, no sprinkling of rice or libations of rum. There were candles involved but, the prosecution admitted, they were 'ordinary ones with no obeahist marks upon them', while a book and a letter taken had 'nothing on them [that] showed they were obeahistic'. This left a leather-and-braid charm that was taken from Anita Smith. Cut open in court, the charm turned out to contain 'some quicksilver and the bark of some tree' as well as a handwritten copy of the twenty-third Psalm.[146] The magistrate was very interested in this charm, wondering if it was African or not. As he noted, 'Obeah is supposed to go on in Africa and if this thing came from Africa it was possible that it had something to do with obeah.' It turned out that the charm was indeed from Africa: a witness, Leopold Clarke, testified that he was a seaman and had acquired it in Durban, South Africa, from a 'sweetheart' there who gave it to him, telling him to 'wear this and remember me'. He had brought the charm to Trinidad where he became Anita Smith's 'sweetheart', moved into her house, and passed it on to her. Asked whether the 'charm' was supposed to protect him, and whether he knew that 'Africa is a great place for obeah', Clarke reasonably replied that he didn't: 'Africa is a big place,' he said. The prosecution focused on the 'charm' in order to distinguish between obeah as something that is 'supposed to go on in Africa' and hypnotism as a European science. For the defendants, the charm may not have been particularly important, or it may have been one among several ritual objects. As a South African item, it had little to do with the ancestral West or West–Central African cultures that were said to underlie obeah. Yet from the court's point of view this was irrelevant; anything African was as good as anything else in proving both obeah and obeah's link to Africa. Although the legislation that prohibited obeah did not specify that it had to be African, the practical working out of the law in the courtroom meant that 'magical' practices that seemed to be connected to Africa were more easily prosecutable than those that appeared European.

The early twentieth-century Caribbean was the site of an intensely pluralistic healing arena, in which European biomedicine shaded into 'alternative' European-derived practices, which themselves overlapped

---

[146] The twenty-third Psalm begins 'The Lord is my Shepherd'.

with 'traditional' techniques derived from older European folk medicine, African means of healing, and skills imported by Indian migrants. Private healing sessions and collective religious rituals existed side by side with public performances that played with the uncertainty of illusions. Many individuals must have experienced or made use of multiple healing techniques and magical performances. Some descriptive terms, such as 'mesmerism', have clearly identifiable European origins, but it is in general neither possible nor analytically useful to attempt to clearly separate practices of European origin from those that are 'traditionally' African Caribbean or African, especially if the purpose of so doing is to suggest that the latter are more authentic than the former. Healers experimented with multiple traditions and techniques, as did those seeking treatment. Among the stories that emerged from obeah trials of people who sought relief from ritual specialists, we find many who had previously consulted biomedical and other kinds of practitioners. The laws about obeah, and most of the contemporary commentary on them, assumed that it was an African import or survival within the Caribbean region, and that its prosecution would enable the suppression of fraudulent African techniques of healing. In practice, it was difficult to distinguish obeah as African from other kinds of healing powers and practices that also, in a variety of senses, involved ritual, money, and objects. Meanwhile, the state and the medical profession were also involved in a battle to maintain boundaries between biomedicine and other forms of healing practice that were of low status, indeed that in Europe were often stigmatised. In the Caribbean, though, because of underlying anxiety about African culture, a claim that what one was doing was in fact mesmerism, electrical healing, homeopathy, or some kind of other unorthodox but not African-derived practice was a method by which people sought to distinguish what they did from the site of most intense stigma: obeah itself.

# 7 Protest, development, and the politics of obeah

The 1930s were a watershed decade for the Caribbean and wider British Empire, transforming the dynamics of colonial rule. The global depression triggered by the Wall Street Crash of 1929 had a massive impact on the region. A world-wide slump in the price of sugar led to lay-offs and wage cuts in the sugar industry both in the Anglo-Creole Caribbean and in other parts of the region, where large numbers of people from the British colonies had moved in search of work. Housing and health were very poor; poverty was extreme. These factors, intertwined with political and ideological discontent, led to an explosive series of riots, strikes, and popular protests across the Caribbean which permanently changed its political culture and shocked its rulers. In the wake of these labour rebellions, the British government reached for an established tool of empire: a royal commission of inquiry to investigate 'social and economic conditions' in the region. The report of what became known as the Moyne Commission, published in 1945, contained nearly 500 pages of descriptions and recommendations, revealing the desperate poverty and lack of development of Britain's oldest colonies. Among their accounts of poverty, overcrowded housing, poor health, and insufficient work, the commissioners included a telling piece of historical–anthropological analysis. The 'coloured West Indian peoples' had a different history to those of 'native inhabitants of other parts of the Colonial Empire', the commissioners wrote. They had 'lost their original cultures, and constructive efforts to provide a satisfactory alternative [were] long overdue'.[1]

For centuries Caribbean people had been deemed primitive and inferior because of their connection to Africa. Caribbean religious and healing practices, symbolized above all by obeah, had been the most significant exemplars of the Caribbean's lack of civilization, and, as we saw in Chapter 4, the prime exhibit for arguments against the region's people having the political rights accorded the white empire. The structure of these arguments shifted significantly in the mid-twentieth century. As

---

[1] *West India Royal Commission Report* (henceforth Moyne Commission Report), 358, 429.

Africa moved from being an exotic location on a map, dominated by blank space, to a continent containing many British colonies, the implications of the association between Africa and the Caribbean shifted too. Colonial government in Africa gave rise to the ideology and policy of indirect rule, accompanied by anthropological ideas about Africa as a continent of small-scale tribes. In the light of these theories Britain's Caribbean colonies started to look less African and more like a diluted and degenerated Africa. After the Second World War Caribbean social science and social policy had a great deal to say about family life in the region, and rather less about religion and religious healing. The focus of attention shifted from religion to the family as the main site of Caribbean difference.

This change had complex implications for the government of obeah, and more generally of religion and healing practices in the Caribbean. As the new view of the Caribbean's link to Africa became more pronounced, there was less effort to transform the region's religious culture, and less to say about religion. The Moyne Commission's inquiry – indeed, its very remit to investigate 'social and economic conditions' – derived from an approach that saw protest as a reflex response to poverty and poor conditions. Religion, along with other forms of consciousness, was largely excluded from this analysis. It was certainly not considered an important part of the reason for rebellion.

The lack of attention to religion in the Moyne Commission's analysis was particularly noteworthy because the period leading up to the rebellions was one of religious ferment. These years saw an explosion of religious movements across the Caribbean, especially in its rapidly growing cities. The religious movements that expanded in the interwar period did not produce the most visible participants in the labour protests, but nevertheless were crucial in creating a space for the development of autonomous ideologies that fed into the rebellious moment of the 1930s. Revivalist and other African-oriented religions themselves attracted attention and suppression in these years. The criminal category of obeah was one among many statutes mobilized for the harassment of popular religions. This chapter explores the relationship of obeah as a legal category to the religious ferment of the first half of the twentieth century, and situates this in the light of broader debates and concerns about obeah in the 1920s and 1930s. As we will see, concern about obeah was a widespread element of public discourse in this period, and worked on multiple levels. Obeah, understood as a malevolent practice and power, was a preoccupation of ordinary people across the region, including adherents of religions that were themselves vulnerable to prosecution for it. Obeah was also a marker of difference in relation to the concerns of doctors and public-health campaigners. It was rejected explicitly by the adherents of the various Revivalist, neo-African, and political religions of the region as well as by emerging respectable nationalist leaders. At the same time, it was, as a sign of the primitive state of the population's belief, a concern alongside popular religions for respectable political leaders and for medical professionals who aimed to reform health care and public health.

The labour protests began in Belize in 1934 and spread to almost every Anglophone Caribbean colony. Protests took place on a large scale, including hunger marches of the unemployed and underemployed, strikes of oil workers, sugar workers and dock workers, and open riots in towns and cities. By 1937 the protests had become region-wide, with strikes and riots that year in Trinidad, Barbados, Jamaica, St Lucia, Antigua, and British Guiana. The authorities responded in most places with violence, turning out the military and the police in force, and in many cases shooting at protesters. Barbados saw the largest numbers of casualties, with fourteen people killed during the rebellion of July 1937. In Jamaica in 1938 the colonial government came close to losing control of the island for a few days, re-establishing its authority by granting significant concessions in the form of higher wages and a land settlement scheme.[2]

The immediate response of Caribbean elites to these events was to blame outside agitators and rabble rousers for mobilizing people to strike or demonstrate. The *Daily Gleaner* invoked 'mob rule' and 'lawlessness' as the cause of the events, while a Jamaican magistrate criticized the 'hooliganism and ruffianism' involved.[3] Yet by the summer of 1938 the events had come to look systemic rather than colony-specific, and the British government sent the Moyne Commission to investigate the region as a whole. The Commission's report amplified the conclusions of its predecessors in blaming the rebellion on poverty, underemployment, and deprivation across the region.[4]

Caribbean people were indeed poor and had experienced a real contraction in opportunities over the previous few years – not just in the rise in unemployment but also in the reduced chance for migration overseas that accompanied the tighter border restrictions of the late 1920s

---

[2] The fullest account of the events across the region is Bolland, *The Politics of Labour*, 212–378, at 288 for the deaths in Barbados. See also Post, *Arise Ye Starvelings*; Bakan, *Ideology and Class Conflict*, 94–133; Palmer, *Freedom's Children*; Thomas (ed.), *The Trinidad Labour Riots*.
[3] *Gleaner*, 6 June 1938, 1; *Gleaner*, 2 June 1938, 3, quoted in Post, *Arise Ye Starvelings*, 287.
[4] For instance, Orde Browne, *Labour Conditions*.

and 1930s. Across the circum-Caribbean, states that had in earlier years provided work for large numbers of migrants now instituted nativist policies that forced many to return to their places of birth, exacerbating problems of unemployment, underemployment, and low wages in the British colonies.[5] But poverty and social deprivation do not inevitably produce protest, nor do they explain the form that protest takes. Scholars have argued that a combination of factors led to changing consciousness in the 1930s. Particularly significant were the attraction of Garveyism, the radicalizing experience of the First World War, the development of new labour organizations and trade unions, and the expanding demands of movements for political reform such as the Trinidad Labour Party, Jamaica Reform Club, and, in Barbados, the Democratic League.[6] Historical studies have also identified the explosion of radical and autonomous religious movements in the 1930s, particularly in Jamaica, as a significant development.[7]

Some earlier historians interpreted religious consciousness, even in its radically anti-colonial Ethiopianist form, as a distraction from appropriate secular class-based ideologies.[8] Ken Post dismissed Pocomania as a 'retreat' into 'fantasies', even while seeing it as playing a 'most important part in refocusing the consciousness of the rural and urban poor'.[9] Similarly, Abigail Bakan framed religious activity as an 'idiom' that inhibited the development of full political consciousness in Jamaica.[10] More recent investigations have been more willing to pursue non-teleological investigations of the relation between religion and social protest.[11] In Trinidad, in particular, there was a clear connection between religious movements and the social protests of the 1930s, in the person of Uriah 'Buzz' Butler, a leader of oil workers in the south of the colony who was also a Baptist preacher.[12] In Jamaica the links were not as closely embodied in those who became political leaders, but nevertheless popular religion was significant in forming the consciousness of the 'sufferers' who were at the heart of the 1938 protests. Robert A. Hill locates the key impetus here in Rastafari, arguing that the movement's 'millenarian ideology functioned as an active catalyst on the developing popular consciousness that led to

---

[5] Putnam, *Radical Moves*, 100–10.
[6] Bolland, *The Politics of Labour*, 167–209; Ewing, 'Caribbean Labour Politics'; Johnson, 'The Black Experience', 326–33.
[7] Putnam, *Radical Moves*, 214–22; Bakan, *Ideology and Class Conflict*, 95–8.
[8] Ethiopianism focused on the connection of black people to Africa, and especially Ethiopia, drawing inspiration in particular from Psalms 68:31: 'Ethiopia shall soon stretch our her hands unto God'. Price, '"Cleave to the Black"'.
[9] Post, *Arise Ye Starvelings*, 246.   [10] Bakan, *Ideology and Class Conflict*, 98–9.
[11] Hill, *Dread History*; Putnam, *Radical Moves*.
[12] Brereton, *A History of Modern Trinidad*, 172, 180; Jacobs, *Butler versus the King*.

the labor uprising of 1938'.[13] This assessment is accurate, but should be expanded to recognize the role of other religious movements too. Their adherents' vulnerability to state harassment, arrest, and prosecution contributed to the oppositional consciousness of Caribbean urban sufferers and poor rural folk in the 1930s, and thus was an important element of the labour rebellions.

Autonomous religious communities were hardly mentioned in official inquiries. Nevertheless, across the region, and in particular in its rapidly growing urban and industrial centres, participation in religious movements contributed to feelings of solidarity, community, and cohesion, while also framing popular senses of injustice and anger. As Lara Putnam has shown, encounters around the Caribbean migrant communities of the Americas intensified religious feeling in these communities and fed into the construction of new religious movements in sending islands, especially at the moment of return migration of the 1930s.[14]

In Jamaica the late 1920s and early 1930s saw an upsurge in popular religious activity, especially in Kingston. Most well known today is the fact that this was the period of the emergence of Rastafari, which synthesized Revival religion, religious Ethiopianism, Garveyism, and esotericism.[15] More explicitly political than any other Caribbean religious movement, and possessing an urgency in its millennial tones, the message of early Rastafari was potentially revolutionary. Leonard Howell preached in Kingston and St Thomas against loyalty to the British Empire, and for a transformation in the condition of the black poor.[16]

At the time, though, Jamaican middle-class people were relatively unaware of the Rastafari movement, and far more concerned about what they called 'Pocomania', a term that began to appear in print from the mid-1920s.[17] This suggests that, although most scholars and adherents locate the origins of Pocomania (also often spelled Pukkumina to be closer to Jamaican speech) in the 1861 Revival, the movement was

---

[13] Hill, *Dread History*, 33.  [14] Putnam, *Radical Moves*, 51–76.
[15] Chevannes, *Rastafari*, 78–118; Hill, *Dread History*, 27–30; Post, *Arise Ye Starvelings*, 163–7.
[16] Edmonds, *Rastafari*, 37; Hill, *Dread History*.
[17] This is confirmed by a Google n-gram viewer search, books.google.com/ngrams/graph?content=pocomania&year_start=1800&year_end=2000&corpus=0&smoothing=3 (conducted 19 April 2012) and by a search of the online *Jamaica Gleaner*, whose first hit for the term 'Pocomania' is a 1926 article, 'Interesting Notes from Hampstead', *Gleaner*, 4 September 1926, 17. Elkins finds 'Pokomania' in 1909 and 'Pokomaniac' in 1912. Elkins, *Street Preachers*, 30–2. I have also found 'Pocomia' and 'Pocomaneans' in 1911 and 'pockoo mania' in 1915 (*Gleaner*, 8 May 1915). These variant spellings suggest that the term existed in the early twentieth century but was not yet widely used.

expanding and becoming more public in the inter-war period, even while drawing on longer traditions.[18] Indeed, Dianne Stewart convincingly argues, on the basis of her own field research and an interview with Edward Seaga, that the term 'Pocomania' and its cognates were not used self-ascriptively, but rather 'were always externally derived and derisively employed to humiliate and belittle Revivalists'.[19] Thus the relatively sudden preoccupation with 'Pocomania' in the newspapers of the late 1920s and 1930s suggests an upsurge of Jamaican Revival religion as a whole in this period.[20]

With the emergence of Pocomania into public discourse in the early 1930s, there were renewed and increasingly vociferous calls for the use of the law to suppress both it and Revival. The *Gleaner* was filled with letters and articles opposing balm yards, Revival, and Pocomania. Some were hostile to the point of describing them as 'demoniac'.[21] Others took a more exoticizing tone, such as the pseudonymous Jack O'Kingston's article 'Kingston after Dark', which described the author's intrepid progress through the city: 'North past delapidated zinc fences from behind which came sounds – a queer admixture of prayers, murder yells, singing, wailing, loud laughter, curses and children playing ring games.'[22] The Legislative Council considered 'A Law for the Suppression of Balm or Obeah Yards' in 1931, although the bill did not become law.[23] For reasons that are unclear and probably contingent, proposals to legislate against Pocomania were also unsuccessful, and no equivalent to the Shouters and Shakerism Prohibition Ordinances of St Vincent, Trinidad and Tobago, and Grenada was ever passed in Jamaica.[24]

Even without specific laws against them, worshippers in independent religious movements faced considerable legal attacks. In Jamaica Alexander Bedward's Native Baptist Free Church, established in the late nineteenth century, attracted thousands of adherents in the early 1920s. In 1921 nearly 700 of Bedward's followers were arrested as they made a pilgrimage from August Town to Kingston, wearing white, carrying crosses and wooden swords, and singing 'Onward Christian Soldiers'. More than 200 received prison sentences for vagrancy in a series of collective trials. All were pardoned a couple of days later except Bedward himself,

---

[18] Besson, *Martha Brae's Two Histories*, 243–7.   [19] Stewart, *Three Eyes*, 271n253.
[20] See also Hill, *Dread History*, 24.
[21] 'Wild Scenes at Night in Portland', *Gleaner*, 12 July 1931; 'The Pocomania Evil', *Gleaner*, 16 November 1932.
[22] 'Kingston after Dark', *Gleaner*, 15 June 1935. See also 'With the Pocomaniacs – At the Balmyard', *Gleaner*, 1 August 1936.
[23] 'Suppression of "Balm Yards"', *Gleaner*, 18 November 1931.
[24] Hill, *Dread History*, 23–4.

who remained incarcerated on grounds of mental illness.[25] No leader emerged to replace him, but many of his followers moved into other religious communities. Even though the sentences were later rescinded, the use of vagrancy law effectively demonstrated to the Bedwardites the power of the state and its ability to harass them. Similarly, early leaders of Rastafari experienced extensive state harassment. Leonard Howell was sentenced to two years' imprisonment for sedition in 1934.[26] On his release, the government prohibited his Ethiopian Salvation Society from holding meetings, on the grounds that 'the racial feeling evoked by these meetings rendered them definitely prejudicial to the public safety'.[27] The comments of a St Thomas land-owner provide additional insight. Byron F. Caws, of Trinity Ville, the St Thomas village where Howell preached that 'George the Fifth is no more our King', forwarded a copy of the Rastafari text *The Promised Key* to the Moyne Commission.[28] Describing it as a 'farrago of nonsensical lies', Caws explained that he had acquired it 'through the Clerk of the Courts for St Thomas'. It had, he said, been taken from a 'Rasta' at Port Morant. While Caws did not name the individual from whom the book was taken, or explain the legal context of the confiscation, this suggests an additional level of police harassment of the community at the time. Caws explained that 'the Ras Tafari cult took hold of a section of the people and some of them ceased working for a time'.[29] Employers and members of the elite repeatedly complained about Rastafarians' and Revivalists' prioritization of religious worship and community above employment.

This was only the tip of the iceberg of arrests and prosecutions of religious leaders. A range of other legislative powers, from laws against vagrancy, 'night noises', and disorderly conduct to laws against practising medicine without a licence and, of course, laws against obeah, meant that people who worshipped in ways that included catching the spirit, trances, and drumming, and people whose religious practice included spiritual healing, were subject to prosecution and other forms of state harassment. In 1938, shortly before the labour disturbances, the mayor of Kingston, Oswald Anderson, announced his intention to make a 'clean sweep' of the thirty-five 'balm yards and healing fountains' across Kingston and

---

[25] Satchell, 'Colonial Injustice'; Austin-Broos, *Jamaica Genesis*, 86; Elkins, *Street Preachers*, 16–17.
[26] Stewart, *Three Eyes*, 121–2; Hill, *Dread History*, 34.
[27] CO 137/840/6, Richards to MacDonald, 9 April 1940.
[28] CO 950/944, 'Memorandum of the Small Cultivators of Jamaica as observed on Island Head Estate, Trinity Ville, St. Thomas, by B F Caws from 1912–1938', 10 October 1939.
[29] Ibid.

St Andrew. These were, he claimed, 'dens of disease, hotbeds of obeah and witchcraft', which caused 'untold misery' by diverting people from consulting 'medical men'. The following year a 'census' of balm yards and Pocomania assembly places in and around Kingston was conducted, allegedly proving the need for direct repressive measures.[30] In Montserrat, Joseph Fenton of a group that called itself the Farnborough Missionaries was fined for holding disorderly services, offering as a defence that 'the noise they made was caused by the descent of the Holy Spirit'.[31] In Port Limón, Costa Rica, members of the New Jerusalem Revelation Baptist Church were attacked as Pocomania people and obeah practitioners, and deported to Jamaica.[32] Nathaniel Jordan, the leader of the White-Robed Army in Guyana, was arrested for sedition.[33]

In Jamaica, laws against obeah were regularly used to arrest Revivalists and other church leaders. These laws provided state authorities with the means to harass religious groups whenever they wanted to, for anyone who conducted healing rituals and accepted money without being a qualified doctor was potentially vulnerable to prosecution. For example, in one obeah case the defendant stated that he had 'formed a church on his own and was a leader of a sect which believed in cure by faith and prayer'.[34] In another, a banner across the gate of the premises of the defendant, Adina McLeod, read: 'Divine Healing Society, Jesus the Light of the World'. McLeod stated in court that she was a 'divine healer' whose work was 'faith healing'.[35]

As well as Revivalists, several significant figures in the spread of Ethiopianism and millennial religion in early twentieth-century Jamaica experienced prosecution for obeah. Grace Jenkins Garrison and Charles F. Goodridge began a Jamaican branch of the Afro-Athlican Constructive Gaathly in 1925.[36] The AACG was founded by Robert Athlyi Rogers, the author of the *Holy Piby*, a Garveyite-influenced work part of which Leonard Howell incorporated into *The Promised Key*.[37] In 1926 Garrison was arrested for obeah at her yard near Half Way Tree in St Andrew after she was entrapped into providing instructions on how to conduct a ritual bath and cleansing to a man who turned out to be a policeman. Her church and the healing operation of which it was part was clearly

---

[30] 'Pocomania and Balm Yards Form Grave Menace', *Gleaner*, 19 September 1939.
[31] 'Item of News', *POSG*, 9 May 1908, 4.
[32] 'Religious Cult: Not Devil Worship', *Gleaner*, 19 January 1937.
[33] Roback, 'The White-Robed Army', 239.
[34] 'Yesterday's Sitting of Appellant Court in Metropolis', *Gleaner*, 15 May 1928.
[35] 'Obeah Pretence Case in Half-Way Tree Court', *Gleaner*, 17 November 1938; '£7 10s or 2 Months for Obeah Pretence', *Gleaner*, 21 November 1938.
[36] Lee, *The First Rasta*, 42.
[37] Hodges, *Soon Come*, 93–6; Lee, *The First Rasta*, 38–42; Hill, *Dread History*, 18.

successful: about 200 people were waiting in the yard when the policemen visited, holding numbers written on slips of paper to indicate their place in the queue.[38] Ten years later Charles Goodridge, Garrison's cofounder of the Jamaican AACG, was fined for practising obeah. In court he described himself as a 'Divine Healer' and a 'Divine Scientist'.[39] But probably the most sustained series of attacks on religious leaders were those suffered by Annie and David Harvey. The Harveys were Ethiopianists who had spent time in Port Limón, Panama, Cuba, and New York, where they knew Leonard Howell. In the mid-1920s they went to Ethiopia, where they spent about five years. Returning to Jamaica, and probably bringing with them the image of Emperor Haile Selassie that became a sacred image for Rastafari, they founded a group called the Israelites or the Black Israelite Church.[40] The Harveys were prosecuted several times in the early 1930s: she for obeah in 1932 (she was acquitted), she and others for disorderly conduct arising out of a religious service on Palm Sunday, 1933, then both of them together for combined charges of obeah and breach of the medical law in 1933 and again in 1934 (they were both convicted on both counts).[41] In 1932 Annie was accompanied to court by '11 members of the band, the women dressed in red, green and yellow, with the word "Israelites" across the front of their red and white hats'. During her 1934 trial a journalist described her as 'resplendent in a scarlet robe with a cloth breastplate of white and wearing a helmet which gave her an appearance of military authority'.[42] Harvey's military styling parallels Marcus Garvey's adoption of military uniform as a sign of black pride and a counter to the reservation of symbols of authority for whites. The repeated prosecutions of the Israelite leaders over this two-year period suggests a concerted police campaign against them, one that was resisted assertively by the Harveys and their supporters.

The frequent use of obeah law to prosecute religious leaders is ironic, because such leaders were often keen to demonstrate that their form of worship was *not* obeah. This was sometimes because they wanted to

---

[38] 'Held as Being 'Black Art' Worker', 28 July 1926; 'Motor Drivers Figure Largely in Court List', 9 September 1926; 'Grace Garrison is Arraigned on Obeah Charge', 28 September 1926, all in the *Gleaner*.
[39] '"Spiritual Healer" Convicted on Charge of Practicing Obeah', *Gleaner*, 27 April 1936.
[40] Hill, *Dread History*, 27; Lee, *The First Rasta*, 56–7.
[41] 'Head of Alleged Band of Faith Healers Discharged by Court', 3 October 1932; 'Charged with Breach of Medical Law and Practising Obeah', 20 October 1933; 'Alleged Revivalist and Healer before Court on 2 Charges', 7 February 1934; 'Man and Wife are Convicted on Charge of Working on Obeah', 31 March 1934, all in the *Gleaner*.
[42] 'Head of Alleged Band of Faith Healers Discharged by Court', *Gleaner*, 3 October 1932; 'Alleged Revivalist and Healer before Court on 2 Charges', *Gleaner*, 7 February 1934.

prove their own respectability, as was the case with the New Jerusalem Revelation Baptist Church, founded by Jamaicans in Costa Rica who were subsequently deported to Jamaica. In an interview with the *Gleaner*, members of the church repeatedly emphasized that what they did was neither obeah nor Pocomania: 'We are not Pocomanians, we do not work any black magic, as some people have been saying,' one of their members said. Another read from a Bible then declared, with heavy irony, 'This is the obeah that we are supposed to be working.'[43] The desire to distance oneself from obeah was not just about status and respectability. It also resulted from many people's genuine fear and hostility to the evil work that the term connoted. Indeed, Revival in Jamaica was rooted in opposition to obeah, defined as evil magic, in the myal movement of the early years after slavery.[44] Much of the healing work undertaken within religious communities was designed to counter obeah. Grace Garrison protested on her arrest, 'I am not working obeah I can pull obeah.'[45] Rastafarian texts were intensely hostile to obeah, despite or perhaps because some early leaders were reputed to be able to access supernatural power.[46] *The Royal Parchment Scroll of Black Supremacy* (1926), one of the earliest texts of Rastafari, included a section attacking 'Obeah dogs', associating obeah with 'witch, Old Hige, ghost, lizard': 'You will not plant your Obeah Self, with no Man or Woman, so that they cannot get RID of you until the Obeah ROTTEN.'[47] Leonard Howell incorporated these passages with minor alterations into his *The Promised Key*.[48]

There was, then, widespread and contested religious activity in the Caribbean of the 1920s and 1930s. All this was significant for the upsurge of protest in the 1930s. It is difficult to prove definitively that the rebellions were connected to the religious upsurge, since most of the events that made up the strikes, riots, and urban disturbances did not have clear leaders. Those who stepped in to lead the protests were mostly men such as Norman Manley and Alexander Bustamante, products of the light-skinned middle class who sought to represent the protesters while urging them to resist escalation. Moreover, it is likely that many of the Shepherds and Mothers of the Revival and Spiritual Baptist traditions did not encourage their members to join in with protests, seeing it as a diversion from their religious focus. And yet, at the same time, the sustenance of

---

[43] 'Religious Cult: Not Devil Worship', *Gleaner*, 19 January 1937.
[44] Austin-Broos, *Jamaica Genesis*, 51–9.
[45] 'Grace Garrison is Arraigned on Obeah Charge', *Gleaner*, 28 September 1926.
[46] The anthropologist George Eaton Simpson recalled that Joseph Hibbert was 'regarded as a "scientist"'. Simpson, 'Personal Reflections', 223.
[47] Pettersburg, *Royal Parchment Scroll*, chapters 6 and 7, last accessed 19 September 2013.
[48] Maragh (Leonard Howell), *The Promised Key*, last accessed 19 September 2013.

a different value system and the ideological autonomy transmitted by involvement in independent religion certainly had a big impact. There is clear evidence that in the poorer areas of West Kingston, in Trinidad among the supporters of Uriah Butler, and in Georgetown, Guyana, many of those who got involved in protest did so through religious organizing. In Guyana the followers of the Reverend Claude Smith's Church Army of America protested against homelessness, destitution, and hunger.[49] Una Marson reported on a crowd of 500 people who marched from West Kingston to the *Jamaica Standard* offices on 23 May 1938, a day of intense confrontation between the people and the police. The marchers sang 'Onward Christian Soldiers' and played drums; their leader wore 'a crown of cardboard, trimmed with green crepe paper and draped with rows of yellow beads, [and] carried a wooden sword in his hand'.[50] The green and yellow of the parade suggests an Ethiopianist orientation of the marchers, while 'Onward Christian Soldiers' was a political hymn in Jamaica, widely used in the labour movement; it would later be adopted by the Jamaica Labour Party. The songs and slogans of striking workers frequently drew on religious rhetoric and symbolism.[51] The connections between Revival and politics are perhaps revealed most clearly in the flock of the Trench Pen Revival or Pocomania leader Shepherd Levi Jackson, who became a supporter of the Bustamante Industrial Trade Union. Zora Neale Hurston visited Jackson, to whom she referred as 'Brother Levi', during her 1936 research trip to Jamaica, and described him and his mother Mother Saul (or Sol) as the 'greatest leaders of the [Pocomania] cult in Jamaica'.[52] When Shepherd Levi was killed in a railway accident in 1939, both Bustamante and his ally St William Grant participated in his funeral. The event was attended by 25,000 people, some of whom were beaten by police trying to keep them out of the May Pen cemetery near the Kingston waterfront. Grant allied himself with Levi's church, wearing its 'scarlet robes and turban' and taking part in the burial rites, while Bustamante's connection with the mourners was emphasized when he 'appealed for order' in a speech from an impromptu earthen podium.[53]

---

[49] Cudjoe, *Caribbean Visionary*, 125–7.
[50] Una Marson in *Jamaica Standard*, 24 May 1938, quoted in Post, *Arise Ye Starvelings*, 280.
[51] Hodges, *Soon Come*, 92; Sewell, 'Music in the Jamaican Labour Movement'.
[52] Hurston, *Tell my Horse*, 3. On Hurston's Caribbean research see Nwankwo, 'Inside and Outsider'.
[53] 'Roaring Mob of Twenty-Five Thousand at "Shepherd" Levi's Burial', *Gleaner*, 20 April 1939. Both Bustamante and William Grant also attended Levi's massive Nine Night in Trench Pen. 'Shepherd Levi Jackson's Ninth Night', *Gleaner*, 28 April 1939. On Grant,

Religious leaders also contended with competition from newly prominent biomedical practitioners and public health campaigners. The health of the people had been largely neglected for most of Caribbean history, but in the early twentieth century it became a matter of increasing interest. The British imperial government began to implement anti-hookworm measures in the first decade of the twentieth century, while the Rockefeller Foundation's international campaign against hookworm was established in many of the British West Indian colonies in the 1910s. Other diseases, including tuberculosis, yellow fever, and malaria also came to be seen as both significant and preventable.[54]

Public health interventions required changes in behaviour, and thus brought public health campaigners into potential conflict with the population as a whole. Public health workers and their supporters frequently blamed popular 'superstition' for the poor health of the people, who allegedly refused to act on health-promoting advice in areas such as ventilation and nutrition. The Jamaican Anti-Tuberculosis League argued that a 'great cause of the spread of TB is the belief in ghosts and the obeahman'. People kept homes tightly shut and ill ventilated in order to keep out duppies, making the transmission of TB more likely. When TB was contracted 'such people, despite the most thorough instruction in the principles of Hygiene, will prefer to restore to the obeahman for aid in case of illness than to go to the physician or surgeon'.'[55] Mental health problems were also attributed to obeah and more generally to popular religion. The Jamaican Lunatic Asylum's annual reports always listed 'religious excitement' as a cause of insanity. Newspaper commentary blamed lunacy on both obeah and the fear of it.[56]

Public health professionals and other commenters frequently decried the popular preference for the obeah man above the doctor. Caribbean people's common understanding of ill health as resulting from spiritual affliction caused particular concern. A 1906 article in the *Gleaner* complained that 'in the country districts... almost every misfortune is attributed to non-human agencies'. As a result children are 'smoked and

---

who had been a Garveyite prior to his involvement in the labour movement and BITU, see White, 'St William Wellington Grant'.

[54] Pemberton, 'A Different Intervention'; Palmer, *Launching Global Health*, 57.
[55] 'Anti-Tuberculosis League', *Gleaner*, 1 July 1931. See also 'Dr Escoffery Speaks about Tuberculosis', *Gleaner*, 8 June 1936; 'Tuberculosis Still a Major Problem Here', *Gleaner*, 16 September 1937. For a very similar argument made in 1892 see Jones, *Public Health in Jamaica*, 93, citing CO 140/205, Report of the Island Medical Department, 1892, 9.
[56] All the Jamaican *Annual Reports of the Superintending Medical Officer* between 1908 and 1934 that I have been able to consult (nineteen years in total) listed 'religious excitement' as a cause of insanity. For newspaper commentary see 'The Causes of Insanity', *Gleaner*, 3 July 1899; 'A Disgraceful State of Things', *Gleaner*, 27 March 1905.

doctored, not through cruelty, but through kindness, for the object of their treatment is to free them from their affliction'. Education was necessary to get people to see the doctor rather than the obeah man, the article concluded.[57] Similarly, a sneering account in the *Port of Spain Gazette* described the process by which sick people might move from one practitioner to another. The imagined patient visits the doctor, but is told by a friend, 'Doctah medicine aint gwine do you no good – you want a "bart," me dare [a bath, my dear] – why you aint try Pa Sammy?' The article ends by emphasizing the competition that this represents and the problems for biomedical doctors in this situation: 'Pa Sammy has gained another five dollars and the qualified Medical Man, who has sacrificed his youth to his profession, is kept out of his honest practice, through crass superstition and unbending faith in the "obeah" doctor.'[58] Such complaints were regularly repeated through the 1910s, 20s and 30s.[59] This article also suggests the breadth of the practices described as obeah by the promoters of biomedicine. Like Grace Garrison, 'Pa Sammy', who offers treatment via a 'bart' would more likely have been popularly understood as a balm healer who aimed to cast out obeah than an obeah man.

Biomedical doctors intensely disliked the competition from other healers, both the literal competition for work and the epistemological challenge to their authority. Charles Joseph Stuart, a white Jamaican biomedical doctor and public health inspector interviewed for an oral history project in 1992, remembered his confrontation with Mr Mannie (Emmanuel Williams), whom he described as 'the greatest obeah man you can find... as you call the name Mannie everybody tremble you know'. Mannie managed a very substantial healing practice; Stuart described seeing 'bout twenty or thirty people pouring out medicine bottles after bottles [of] medicine', which he described as 'oil a gu back, come back, come back... tun him roun'.[60] This almost industrial scale of production of medicines suggests that Mannie was not straightforwardly an 'obeahman', as Joseph Stuart described him. Mannie was successful

---

[57] 'Obeah and the Child', *Gleaner*, 5 July 1906.
[58] 'A Bush Doctor's Bath', *POSG*, 19 January 1911.
[59] See for example 'Elections for Members of the Parish Boards', 11 June 1924; 'On Health Week', 2 June 1932; 'Problems that Face Jamaica', 5 October 1934, all in the *Gleaner*.
[60] Mr Charles Joseph Stuart, transcript of interview by Hazel Ramsay-McClune, 28 October 1992, African Caribbean Institute of Jamaica Memory Bank, Tape 1369–3. Stuart does not give his age in the interview, and would have had to have been in his eighties or older to have been practising medicine in the 1930s; it is possible that his memory of this encounter is from a later period. Nevertheless, it is of interest in shedding light on this area of competition between healers.

enough to own two houses, and for his wife to have 'gold rings on her wedding finger almost to the tip'. Stuart took particular pleasure in recounting a story about how he exerted his authority over Mannie by persuading him to accept biomedical treatment. The encounter involved a hookworm-eradication campaign in which Stuart managed to persuade Mannie to be treated. In Stuart's account a stand-off followed, in which through an exchange of written notes Mannie demanded that Stuart come to his home if he wanted to treat him, while Stuart refused, insisting that the 'great obeah man' attend his surgery. Stuart claimed eventually to have won the contest by threatening to have Mannie arrested for obeah. When Mr Mannie finally arrived his presence produced consternation among observers: 'All of a sudden I saw the lady the owner of the house running to me dacta, dacta... dacta a begging you sar Mr Mannie is coming careful... I don't want them to send back you dead body to Kingston, docta please sar careful.'

Stuart demonstrated his control of the situation and also differentiated himself from the householder's fear by making Mannie wait until the hundred patients already present had been treated, and then insisting that he climb the steps to the treatment room. When Mannie returned the following week for the second dose of the course of treatment, the interest from others 'wasn't as great because they said that I had beaten Mannie'.[61] No doubt Mannie's account would have been rather different; one can imagine many equivalent encounters in which the dynamics between the two healers would have been reversed. The incident also implicitly reveals the medical pluralism and flexibility of healers such as Mannie, who was prepared to take biomedical treatment for hookworm, while continuing with his practice.

The hookworm-eradication campaign was the most substantial public health initiative in this period, and it directly addressed the competition between different forms of healing. Across the Caribbean, people involved in the campaign attempted to get their message across through methods that included didactic short stories, public meetings, and informational leaflets. In Jamaica these materials, published from the early 1920s on, included pamphlets and educational dialogues between invented characters who reflect on obeah, among other matters. The central characters in these stories included Aunt Eliza, an older woman who promoted 'bush tea' and all forms of superstition, and her young nephew Thomas Ezekiel Brown and niece Retinella Francis, who showed Aunt Eliza the errors of her ways. *Jamaica Public Health* envisaged a change as

---

[61] Ibid. Stuart also told another story in similar vein, in which Mannie accepted his treatment for fever, and recovered.

Jamaica's Aunt Elizas gave way to the new generation: 'The passing of Aunt Eliza with her quaint superstitions and fatalistic attitude to sickness symbolises, we hope, the death of obeah and ignorance and the birth of a new intelligence which will help Government in its efforts to make our naturally healthy and beautiful island still happier and safe.'[62] Similar publications were produced in both Trinidad and British Guiana. In British Guiana the anti-hookworm initiative published a story, 'Superstition vs Parasites', in which the use of obeah in the form of material sprinkled on the ground was revealed to be ineffective in getting rid of hookworm, in contrast to the adoption of biomedical treatment. In Trinidad an equivalent story targeted Indian popular medical practice.[63]

From 1923 in Jamaica, public health efforts were concentrated in an annual Health Week, part of 'Empire Health Week', which involved intensive propaganda about public health matters.[64] Participants in spreading the public health message frequently complained that popular belief in obeah or 'bush medicine' was a central problem in getting their messages accepted. A Health Week talk in Port Antonio included the point that the people 'considered too much of the obeahman and believed too much in bush medicine', while a similar talk aimed at children claimed that obeah was responsible for 'all the evil in Jamaica'.[65] Similar talks on the damaging nature of belief in obeah can be found in reports of Health Week into the 1960s.[66]

The contest between biomedicine, spiritual healing, and public health intervention went beyond propaganda. As the hookworm campaign began under the auspices of the Rockefeller Foundation, one of the major difficulties was the need to convince people of the value of taking hookworm medication. For many of the professionals working in this area, Jamaicans' belief in obeah and their affiliation with Revival religion were linked phenomena that made their work more difficult. A generally positive report on the pilot programme in the parish of St Catherine, Jamaica,

---

[62] 'The Education in Matters of Health Here', *Gleaner*, 5 February 1936, reproducing an article from *Jamaica Public Health*, January 1936. For an analysis of these public health pamphlets see Jones, *Public Health in Jamaica*, 126–36.
[63] Palmer, *Launching Global Health*, 170.
[64] On the history of Health Week see 'First of Series of Health Week Meetings Held in Ward Theatre Last Night', *Gleaner*, 6 October 1936. For Health Week in other parts of the empire see Naono, 'Burmese Health Officers', 125–8. Health Week also took place in Trinidad, where its proponents seems to have paid less attention to obeah. See, for instance, 'Health Week, 1932', 25 September 1932; '1935 Health Week Opens', 10 November 1935; 'His Excellency Opens Health Week Exhibition', 8 November 1936, all in *POSG*.
[65] 'The Celebration of Health Week in the Country Parts', *Gleaner*, 10 October 1932; 'Wait-a-Bit Weather and Health Meeting', *Gleaner*, 18 October 1937.
[66] For example, 'PTA's Health Week Programme Ends', *Gleaner*, 21 December 1964.

noted the difficulty of persuading the large community of Revivalists in the parish to undertake treatment. According to the report, Revivalists were reluctant to take hookworm medication because they believed it would counteract or make ineffective the religious healing that took place within their community. They were also more likely to visit the 'Obeah man who is regarded as a high dignitary in the community' than to seek help from biomedical doctors. This article reveals the intertwining of hookworm intervention with disapproval of broader cultural practices. It describes Revival worship as 'frenzy', as 'religious superstition', and 'especially dangerous to children'. Nevertheless, in this instance the hookworm campaigners dealt with their concerns pragmatically, recognizing the significance of Revival in the community and trying to find ways to cooperate with Revivalists rather than antagonizing them. They circumvented Revivalists' suspicion of hookworm treatment by convincing them that it would 'strengthen their bodies and render them more receptive to the lasting results of the [religious] "healing"'.[67] Thus some of those carrying out public health campaigns came to believe that their interventions were more effective if they sought common ground with those they aimed to influence. The hookworm campaign in St Catherine seems to have been successful, treating nearly 1,000 people out of a district population of 1,500 over a relatively short period. This campaign also reveals, if inadvertently, the medically pluralist worldview of rural Jamaicans. Neither Revivalists nor ritual healers such as Mannie Williams simply rejected biomedical interventions. Both were willing to engage with the public health campaign against hookworm, without giving up their own practices of healing and worship. As Steven Palmer has argued in his study of the international campaign against hookworm, public health campaigns often involved overt denunciation of popular health beliefs, but practical cooperation with local people, who frequently welcomed interventions if they were genuinely effective.[68]

Thus far this chapter has demonstrated the significance of radical religious movements and the extent of their suppression through law, as well as the challenge that spiritual healers faced from campaigns around public health and from biomedical doctors. Popular religion and spiritual healing were also subject to criticism from the emerging leaders of Caribbean nationalism and radicalism, both within the region and abroad. Leaders of organizations such as the League of Coloured Peoples, based in London, the Jamaica Progressive League, based in New York, and within

---

[67] 'The Hookworm Campaign in St Catherine', *Gleaner*, 21 May 1924.
[68] Palmer, *Launching Global Health*. For a similar argument see Riley, *Poverty and Life Expectancy*.

the region Jamaica Welfare, the Trinidad Labour Party, and the Negro Workers Association (in Trinidad) differed in their political orientations but shared their origins in the respectable brown and black middle and lower middle classes, precisely those people who had since slavery proved their respectability by emphasizing their distance from the culture of the poor, and their mastery of British culture. These were the descendants, politically and culturally, of John Jacob Thomas. For these individuals popular religion presented a problem. This was partly because it did not fit within norms of respectability, but also, for some, because they were, as secular socialists, opposed to all religion.[69] As the events of the 1930s unfolded, some of this group rose to positions of leadership. The considerable numbers of people involved in popular religion suggested a potentially large group that might be mobilized in support of reform, but the fact that Revival, Pocomania, Spiritual Baptism, and Rastafari had their own structures of leadership and authority made it difficult for middle-class secular nationalist leaders to engage with them, even if they might attract their electoral support. In addition, the enormous gulf in political language and symbolism that separated most early Caribbean nationalist leaders from popular religion made interaction very difficult, even if it was desired.

Some nationalist and radical leaders acknowledged the existence of popular religion, but discussed it primarily as a sign of the degradation of the people under colonial rule. Such interpretations shared with elite views a disapproval of popular religion and spiritual healing, but where elite defenders of the status quo argued that this showed that Caribbean people were inherently debased and thus could not qualify for self-government or the expansion of representative structures, secular nationalists argued that they showed the problems of colonialism. Harold Moody, the leader of the League of Coloured Peoples, participated in a debate on the letters page of *The Times* of London. Responding to a letter that described obeah as a problem, he argued against legislation as a solution. For Moody, obeah demonstrated colonial neglect of the Caribbean colonies. The fact that more than 30 per cent of the Jamaican population remained illiterate was the source of the problem, and it led to ill health and was a sign of the weakness of colonial education. The cure for obeah was therefore better educational services and, in general, more investment by the colonial government.[70] From a different political perspective, the Jamaican labour leader Hugh Buchanan wrote that the

[69] Putnam, *Radical Moves*, 78–9.
[70] Dr Harold A. Moody, 'Witchcraft in the West Indies', *The Times*, July 1936, clipping in Bell Papers 5 (files) /A12 (Obeah and Fetichism).

problems caused by obeah would not be solved by education because no education system 'that will liquidate the backwardness upon which obeah thrives' would be 'sponsored by British Imperialism'. Instead, he concluded, 'the path to the liquidation of obeah, as indeed of all other superstitions, is the path to Trade Unionism and peasant action'.[71]

Other reformers made similar arguments with regard to public health. Oswald Anderson, a black biomedical doctor who as mayor of Kingston would in 1938 lead the campaign against balm yards discussed above, attacked Health Week propaganda as a distraction from more serious problems: the island's poverty and maldistribution of land and power. Speaking at a Kingston Health Week event in 1936 he decried its focus on providing nutritional information to the poor. It was no good telling people to look after themselves, drink fresh milk, and eat fresh meat when they could not afford good food, he argued. People were moving to the city, where less fresh food was available and diets were worse, because of the 'tyranny of the plantations'. For reformers such as Anderson, complaints about popular ignorance and superstition – whether this was prejudice against fresh meat, refusal to sleep with the windows open due to fear of duppies, or consultation of the obeah man rather than the biomedical doctor – were all part of an ideological formation that blamed the poor for their own ill health while refusing to tackle the fundamental injustices of the island.[72] Clearly a contradictory figure, Anderson's willingness to attack balm yards while also critiquing the domination of the plantocracy was characteristic of secular nationalism in this period.

Other nationalists were more straightforwardly dismissive of popular religion. A 1938 article in the reforming nationalist newspaper *Plain Talk* disparaged the large number of churches in the poor Kingston area of Jones Pen: 'Mid-day jumpings! Cock-killings! Candle burnings! Ghost calling! Stupid low down antiquated immorality which does as much harm to a locality as to an individual person, not to mention the effect they have on little children who ought to be in school during the time of these nefarious practices.'[73] Another article in *Plain Talk*, 'The Truth about Obeah', was similarly hostile.[74]

Garveyites shared the secular reformers' hostility to popular religion, although their relationship to religion was different to that of the secular

---

[71] Hugh C. Buchanan, 'Obeah: What Solution?', *Public Opinion*, 30 October 1937.
[72] 'Acting Governor Officially Opens Health Week Exhibition in Edmondson Hall', *Gleaner*, 6 October 1936.
[73] Post, *Arise Ye Starvelings*, 146, quoting 'Detestable Cult Molests Citizens', *Plain Talk*, 23 April 1938.
[74] 'The Truth about Obeah', *Plain Talk*, 21 August 1937.

left. While not itself explicitly a religious movement, Garveyite culture was infused with religion. As Lara Putnam has argued, 'the UNIA's rhetoric, ritual, and mission made it a community of faith as much as a political movement'.[75] Meetings began with prayers, and Garvey enjoined his followers to participate in the respectable Christian churches. The perception of Garvey as a prophet or as himself divine played an important role in the development of Rastafari.[76] Robert A. Hill has documented popular perceptions of him as a spiritually powerful figure – even a 'scientist' – and suggests that at some level Garvey encouraged this perception.[77]

Marcus Garvey's explicit pronouncements, however, were resolutely and unequivocally hostile to African-oriented religion, to spirit possessions and manifestations, and to anything perceived as obeah.[78] Like many African American and African-diaspora leaders, Garvey's programme of racial uplift included the idea that 'the race' needed to be culturally transformed. At an early Universal Negro Improvement Association (UNIA) meeting in Jamaica in 1915, he presented a plan for a Tuskegee-inspired institute for industrial and agricultural training in Jamaica, necessary because 'the bulk of our people are in darkness and are really unfit for good society'. 'The country parts of Jamaica', Garvey explained, were dominated by 'villainy and vice of the worst kind, immorality, obeah and all kinds of dirty things', which this training institute would act to redress.[79] The Garveyite International Convention of the Negro Peoples of the World held in 1934 in Kingston took a similar view, passing resolutions 'recognizing the doctrine of Jesus Christ known as Christianity' and condemning 'religious fanaticism and commercialization'. Another resolution, moved by a Jamaican delegate and seconded by one from Honduras, went further, urging 'Negro Organizations' and others to:

seek the sympathy and co-operation of government and police departments... to assist in putting down and discouraging the existence... of all immoral, viscious [sic], criminal and unreasonable forms of cult worship and the practice of religious frenzy calculated to injure the morals, culture, mind and general health of simple minded and ignorant Negroes who may be influenced to join such cult and frenzied organizations.[80]

[75] Putnam, *Radical Moves*, 72. See also Chevannes, *Rastafari*, 93–4.
[76] Chevannes, *Rastafari*, 100–6.
[77] Hill, 'Marcus Garvey and the Discourse of Obeah'. See also Hodges, *Soon Come*, 98.
[78] Lewis, 'Marcus Garvey and the Early Rastafarians', 154.
[79] 'Universal Negro Improvement Association: Address Delivered by the President at the Annual Meeting', *Gleaner*, 26 August 1915.
[80] 'Resolutions of the Seventh International Convention of the Negro Peoples of the World Held under the Auspices of the Universal Negro Improvement Association August 1st

The UNIA thus adopted a position explicitly in support of the prosecution of obeah and of adherents of Revival, Pocomania, the Spiritual Baptist Faith and other forms of religious worship designated 'cults'. In the same period Garvey, echoing public health commentary on religion and mental illness, reported frequently encountering 'Jamaica Negroes who had . . . become crazy over local pocomania religions'.[81]

Garvey shared with Moody and Anderson the view that the expansion of religions such as Pocomania was a symptom of the problem of empire, turning on its head the dominant view of such religions as a sign of the inherent inferiority of black people. Introducing a piece of sensationalist reportage on Pocomania, Garvey's Jamaican newspaper *The Black Man* suggested that the report revealed that Jamaica was home to 'a large number of ignorant Negroes who have been neglected educationally and culturally by the Imperial and Local Governments. This neglect', *The Black Man* continued, 'includes their economic, social, and general educational conditions, thereby leaving them entirely to themselves to reflect the lowest of their animal natures and dispositions.' The attraction of religions such as Pocomania revealed the paucity of education.[82] While no less hostile to popular healing religions than the official perspective, this view used the evidence of popular degradation to argue for change in the ordering of imperial power.

When the Moyne Commission convened in London in 1938 it was thus preparing to visit a region where popular religion and its healing practices were items of considerable public interest and debate, in multiple locations and arenas. The Commission began its work by inviting people to submit 'memoranda' about the issues that they felt were important. Hundreds of individuals and organizations across the Caribbean and beyond responded. The contributors included a range of Caribbean society – colonial officials, representatives of the churches, social workers, land-owners and planters, trade unionists, Garveyites and other political leaders. They wrote and testified on myriad topics, from the very specific and personal to the abstract and general. The Commission heard proposals for a federation of the West Indies, analyses of the Caribbean family, discussions of the problems of trade union law, protests against local racism, diatribes about the laziness of the black and Indian populations,

---

to 31st 1934 at Kingston, Jamaica, BWI', in Garvey, *The Black Man*, 1, 6 (November 1934), 25.

[81] 'Sanity or Madness or Is it Blasphemy', in Garvey, *The Black Man*, 1, 8 (July 1935), 12. For discussion of Garvey's hostility to Revival see Hill, 'Leonard P. Howell and Millenarian Visions', 30–2.

[82] 'West Indian Negro Mystic Cult Called "Pocomania"', in Garvey, *The Black Man*, 1, 12 (March 1936), 16–17. This article was reprinted from the *Gleaner*.

descriptions of local conditions in housing, education, and health care, and testimony on the economic difficulties of the sugar and banana industries, among other matters.[83] From the written memoranda received, the commissioners selected those they thought significant to give evidence in person, first in London and then on a series of visits to the Caribbean colonies.

Obeah was first brought to the commissioners' attention while they were still in London. Peggy Cox, a woman from a white Barbadian planter family, submitted a written memorandum that attributed much of the Caribbean's problems to obeah. She argued that the Caribbean's problems resulted from its history of racial diversity, including the fact that 'the negroes, whether chieftains or slaves in their native Africa, brought with them the belief in black magic, obeah and voodoo'. This claim attracted considerable interest from the commissioners, who questioned Cox on the contemporary implications of such beliefs. She asserted that belief in 'black magic, obeah and voodoo' had a negative impact on 'economic conditions, social conditions, and the health of the native', citing her experience of a recently deceased female servant whose children believed that another woman, who hated her, had caused her death through supernatural means. More generally, according to Cox, obeah caused problems in the region because people spent money on it rather than on more wholesome things, and because of the negative effects on the health of people who believed they had been spiritually attacked.[84]

Their interest raised by Cox's comments, the commissioners heard some further evidence on the topic when they went to the Caribbean. The most significant and prominent attention to independent religion and to obeah came from the mainstream churches, with which they were direct competitors. In Jamaica, leaders of the Church of England, the Catholic Church, Methodists, Presbyterians, Moravians, the Salvation Army, and the Jamaica Baptist Union submitted a joint memorandum that took up the question of obeah at length. They emphasized that poverty was not the island's only problem: 'Side by side with the attempt to solve Jamaica's economic problems must go an equally intensive effort to combat the moral and social evils of our Island and to raise the whole stand[ard] of living among the peasantry, ideologically as well as economically.' Of their twenty-six-page document, seven pages were devoted to obeah and a further three to what they termed 'peculiar cults', along

---

[83] The oral testimony and written evidence is held in nearly 1,000 items in the National Archives' CO 950 series. For analysis of this testimony see La Guerre, 'The Moyne Commission and the West Indian intelligentsia'; La Guerre, 'The Moyne Commission and the Jamaican Left'.

[84] CO 950/8, Memorandum of evidence and transcript of oral interview, Miss Peggy Cox.

with sections dealing with overpopulation, illegitimacy and the home, housing, education, the uses of leisure, and prison conditions.[85]

Jamaica's 'peculiar cults', the clergy said, were most prominently represented by 'Pocomania, Ras Tafarianism, and Balmism'. Such religions were growing in prominence and drew large numbers of worshippers, who often travelled considerable distances to participate in their gatherings. They were subversive, both of the established political order and of mainstream religious leaders: 'These people preach against the Government and discourage the education of children,' stated the memorandum. Moreover, and perhaps this was their most substantial objection, 'they endeavour to destroy the people's faith in their religious leaders, who are called faithless shepherds'. The memorandum proposed that such 'peculiar cults' should be effectively banned through the establishment of a legal requirement that any preacher carry a licence from a recognized religious body.

Even more threatening than these 'cults', said the Christian leaders, was obeah, 'a dreadful evil and curse in Jamaica, which is increasing in influence'. Echoing the public health campaigns of the previous two decades, the memorandum stated that obeah was damaging because it was used in preference to the work of biomedical doctors, because it encouraged conflict, and because people spent large sums on a practice that could not help them. Obeah and the 'peculiar cults' were intimately connected, the former having increased in prominence recently as a result of the expansion of the latter. In particular, the clergy emphasized the close connection between obeah and 'balmism', while distinguishing between them on the grounds that obeah practitioners charged more and made use of 'things other than medicine'. Their evidence emphasized the strong popularity of the balm yards, and included an account of how one truck driver was able to make more money driving people to a balm yard in Hanover than he made from driving bananas to the ports for export. They ended by calling for a government enquiry specifically into 'the practice of Obeah and Balmism'. In their appearance before the Commission, the Christian leaders elaborated on their concerns, with the commissioners returning repeatedly to obeah in their questions. The encounter was prominently reported in the press, with two double-page spreads reporting their evidence.[86]

---

[85] CO 950/98, 'A Memorandum presented by the leaders of certain Christian bodies in Jamaica to the chairman and members of the West Indian Royal Commission', quotation at 2.

[86] 'Heads of 9 Denominations tell Commissioners about Conditions in Island', *Gleaner*, 11 November 1938.

While the leading clergy gave the most prominent evidence about obeah and independent religions, similar points were made by other Christian leaders, in Jamaica and elsewhere. Reverend R. W. McLarty of Kingston discussed obeah alongside complaints about gambling, illegitimacy, and other social issues. He argued for increased police attention to obeah, suggesting that the police should enquire 'into the occupation of individuals who manifestly have a number of callers for some business purpose'. Like the Jamaican Christian leaders, he linked obeah to 'its concomitants the Balmyard and Pocomania'.[87] In British Honduras a delegation of the clergy said that obeah and balm yards were treated with 'far too much levity, and the existence of the obeahman accepted with far too much equanimity'. Far from dying away of its own accord, they noted, these phenomena were growing; action was needed.[88]

Yet by no means all who submitted evidence to the Commission agreed with this point. The Jamaican Christian leaders were countered by another churchman, the black Baptist minister J. P. Dillon. Dillon did not raise the issue of obeah, Pocomania, or balm yards himself, but, when he appeared a few weeks after the Christian leaders had been questioned, the commissioners raised the topic with him. Rachel Crowdy, one of two female commissioners, asked him if he thought that 'superstition in this country affects the health of the people? I am thinking obviously of obeah again.' Dillon answered that he did not think so, and indeed that he was 'sorry that the question has come up'. Referring indirectly to the evidence of the clergy, he went on to say:

It has been represented to this Commission that the people of this country are superstitious and that they are an obeah-loving people. I am sorry that has gone out. The superstition exists in nearly every country I know, in one form or another... I believe that by the teaching of the schools and the work of the Christian Churches in Jamaica we have done wonderfully in that direct, in one hundred years. It takes more than a short time to eradicate superstition from any people... Children are taught science, and some of the things that the obeah man used to use – the mixing of chemicals – is done in our secondary schools and colleges, and the folly of the whole thing is recognised.[89]

Dillon's view thus echoed the line taken by Harold Moody and Oswald Anderson in the debates over public health: that obeah and popular belief was a distraction, which drew attention from the region's more serious problems of poverty.

---

[87] CO 950/272, Memorandum to the West India Royal Commission from Rev R. W. McLarty of Kingston, Jamaica, 19 November 1938, 11.
[88] 'The Clergy and the Commission', *Gleaner*, 6 December 1938, 24. I was unable to locate this testimony in the CO 950 files.
[89] CO 950/109, Transcript of testimony of Rev J. P. Dillon.

Similarly, representatives of the Elementary Teachers' Association of Barbados resisted the Commission's efforts to get them to testify on the subject of 'superstition'. Asked if their members 'give the children any teaching with regard to ghosts jumbies and things of that sort?', the Teachers' Association said no, because the question did not arise. The Teachers' Association argued that there was no more 'superstition' in Barbados than anywhere else in the world, although another of their party did admit that 'there are some of us that deal with the problem when it comes up. If we hear someone talking of obeah, we try to explode the theory altogether.'[90]

While I have documented here considerable testimony dealing with questions of religion and ritual healing, such discussions in fact formed a small proportion of the Moyne Commission's enquiries. The commissioners heard detailed evidence about obeah only in Jamaica. Nationalists, reformers, and trade unionists largely steered clear of these issues except when directly confronted with them during questioning. They focused instead on issues related to race, material deprivation, and political change. I only found evidence of two reformers or political leaders raising questions about independent religion or ritual healing, neither of whom was able to give oral testimony to the Commission. One was Uriah Butler of Trinidad, who was in prison for sedition when the Moyne Commission visited the island, and so could not testify in person. He submitted a petition listing six demands, including home rule for a 'United West Indian Free State'. The sixth demand was 'Freedom of "Workers" Religious Worship'. Although Butler did not elaborate, this probably referred primarily to the Shouters' Prohibition Ordinance.[91] The other was Alfred Mends, a long-standing figure in Jamaican nationalism, editor since 1935 of the newspaper *Plain Talk*, and one-time defendant for the offence of practising medicine without a licence. Mends spoke up obliquely in his submission for a broader view of medical practice. He did not mention obeah directly, but indirectly referred to it in his call for 'medical freedom', which he argued for by analogy with the religious freedom that (allegedly) existed in Jamaica. He pointed out that 'herbalists etc, are allowed practice in England' and asked, 'Why not allow the same in Jamaica without molestation?'[92] Although Mends' own healing practice, as revealed by his prosecutions, suggests that he worked hard

---

[90] CO 950/920, Barbados, Transcripts of Oral Evidence, Elementary Teachers Association, 27 January 1939.
[91] CO 950/959, Circulars to the Commission, 'Extract from a Petition from Uriah Butler, dated the 14th March, 1939'.
[92] CO 950/250, Memorandum of Evidence, Mr A. A. Mendes (*sic*), 12 November 1938.

to distinguish his work from obeah, the generous space of that 'herbalists etc' might have enabled a wide range of spiritual healers to practise. The Commission did not invite Mends to elaborate on his views in oral testimony.

Although testimony like that of Peggy Cox and the Jamaican Christian leaders roused the commissioners' interest, overall they paid little attention to cultural concerns, focusing instead on more generic economic questions. Their lack of interest in the Caribbean as a specific place, or indeed as a series of specific places, rather than a generic poor place, was reflected in the relative inattention to cultural specificity in the commissioners' report, when it was finally published in 1945.[93]

The minor place of religion flowed in part from the Commission's underlying understanding of Caribbean culture, which focused on absence and lack. 'The negroes', wrote the commissioners, 'were taken from lands where they lived no doubt in a primitive state, but at any rate under certain social traditions and subject to customs and usages which modern anthropology increasingly shows to have definite social, economic and cultural value.' In the West Indies, however, these traditions, customs, and usages disappeared: 'Their transfer to the West Indies... did not involve the transfer of any important traces of their traditions and customs, but rather their almost complete destruction.'[94] This analysis was crucial to the Commission's approach to Caribbean culture. While the commissioners acknowledge that a 'primitive state' had 'certain... value', the Caribbean was deemed to be a region devoid of any culture at all, and thus particularly in need of education.

The claim that people in the Caribbean had entirely lost their original cultures represented a significant shift from earlier arguments such as Froude's that Caribbean people were essentially African. Related to this was the argument that 'modern anthropology' had demonstrated the 'definite value' of primitive cultures. The commissioners were invoking the growing prominence of British structural-functionalist social anthropology, which focused in particular on African societies. Structural-functionalist analyses argued that African societies were – or had recently been – closed, small-scale, and tribal; societies in which equilibrium was preserved. These societies might be primitive, but they worked. A year before the Moyne Commission began its investigations, E. E. Evans-Pritchard had published *Witchcraft, Oracles, and Magic among the*

---

[93] The report was finalised in 1939, but remained unpublished until 1945, as a result of the British government's fear that it would 'feed the German propaganda machine' by revealing the dire situation of its colonies during wartime. Whitham, *Bitter Rehearsal*, 10–11.

[94] Moyne Commission Report, 29.

*Azande*, arguing for the coherence and rationality of Zande, and by extension other African, thought on its own terms. Evans-Pritchard argued that Zande understandings of witchcraft and magic derived from different premises to those of modern European society, but that once those premises were understood, Zande behaviour could be shown to be rational and logical. It should not, therefore, be dismissed as superstition.[95] Although the Moyne Commission did not refer by name or title to any specific anthropologist or anthropological study, 'modern anthropology' for educated British people in the late 1930s referred to the group of scholars who dominated the major centres of anthropology in Britain at the time: Bronislaw Malinowski at the London School of Economics (he left in 1938) and A. R. Radcliffe-Brown and E. E. Evans-Pritchard at Oxford University.[96]

The reference to 'modern anthropology' and the claim for the value of the primitive were also oblique references to the political theory of indirect rule. This policy, initiated in India under a different nomenclature, was elaborated by Lord Lugard, the governor of Northern Nigeria in the 1910s, and then generalized across much of Africa. Lugard argued that colonial rule should not intervene in the everyday life of colonial subjects; government should be carried out through indigenous political, judicial, and social institutions.[97] The natural leaders of the people should be respected, so long as they submitted to British tutelage. Indirect rule led to institutional features such as native courts and laws governing specific ethnic groups. In the Caribbean indirect rule was largely absent, although elements of it can be seen in the existence of different laws for marriage for Hindus and Muslims in Trinidad and Tobago and British Guiana, and to some extent in the relationship between the colonial state and the Maroons in Jamaica and indigenous groups in British Guiana.[98] Caribbean people could not be ruled indirectly through indigenous leaders and institutions, because there were no indigenous leaders or institutions – or, at least, none recognized by the British Empire.

In a major change from earlier dominant forms of colonial discourse, which had deemed Caribbean people primitive and inferior because of their alleged Africanness, the commissioners recognized the 'value' of cultural life in African societies, along with other societies deemed

---

[95] For assessments of the impact of *Witchcraft, Oracles and Magic* see Falk Moore, *Anthropology and Africa*, 31–2.
[96] Mills, *Difficult Folk?*, 29–67; Kuklick, *The Savage Within*.
[97] On indirect rule in India see Ramusack, 'The British Construction of Indirect Rule'. For a recent analysis and history of indirect rule in Africa see Beidelman, *The Culture of Colonialism*.
[98] Moore, *Cultural Power*, 173–5.

primitive. Yet, with considerable irony, the Caribbean was excluded from this recognition: for the Moyne Commission, Caribbean people were defined not by their African culture but by their lack of culture. The problem of civilization identified by the Commission was not so much that Caribbean people – specifically, Caribbean people of African descent – were outside the modern world, but rather that they exhibited all the negative but none of the positive aspects of modernity. Isolated and individualist, lacking family life, proper religion, and morality, focused on consumerism but without adequate income to purchase consumer goods: these were people whose situation could be explained to a considerable extent by their cultural deficiencies.

From this analysis flowed the relatively low priority that the Moyne Commission accorded obeah and other aspects of religion and spiritual healing. These apparently undeniably African elements of Caribbean culture did not fit well with the Commission's overarching analysis. The Commission did not mention obeah or spiritual healing at all in its extensive discussion of public health and the Caribbean's medical services. Nevertheless, they could not be completely ignored. No doubt as a result of the intervention of the Jamaican Christian leaders, obeah and the 'peculiar cults' did feature briefly in the Moyne Commission's final report. The commissioners described obeah as 'a variety of witchcraft... akin to the much more powerful Voodoo cult prevalent elsewhere in the Caribbean area' and suggested that it had 'serious... psychological effects... leading now and then to unrest, madness, violence and even murder'. Drawing on the Jamaican clergy's evidence, they argued that obeah's 'greatest danger is the preaching of hatred and fear', and also drew attention to the high costs of consulting obeah practitioners. These points were relegated to the final page of the section on 'Social Services, Existing Position and needs.'[99]

Despite basing their understanding of the nature of obeah and of Caribbean religion on the Jamaican clergy's evidence, the commissioners did not agree with their analysis of the measures necessary for suppression. They opposed 'legislative suppression of the peculiar cults' and also argued that the continuing prevalence of obeah, despite its illegality, demonstrated the weakness of existing legal measures in getting rid of it. (They did not, apparently, realize that in Trinidad and Tobago, St Vincent, and Grenada there were already laws that rendered followers of certain religions – 'Shouters' and 'Shakers' – liable to prosecution.) Rather, they proposed 'better education and the healthy occupation of leisure hours' as a solution that would lead to the 'disappearance' of

[99] Moyne Commission Report, 240.

both 'peculiar cults' and obeah. The Commission thus sided with the long-standing liberal view in which obeah – and Caribbean culture more generally – was a problem, but one that should be resolved through methods other than the law.

In the Moyne Commission's analysis, obeah and the 'peculiar cults' with which it was associated were exceptions to the general rule of the decultured Caribbean, rather than signs of a larger problem. This analysis influenced the next generation of Caribbeanist social science and social policy, which focused attention most centrally on problems of 'the' Caribbean family, downplayed the significance of religion, and argued that Caribbean people lacked a coherent culture. Crucial to the development of this paradigm was the work of Thomas Simey, a Liverpool University professor of sociology who in 1941 was appointed social welfare adviser to the new comptroller of development and welfare in the West Indies, Frank Stockdale.[100] Simey's analysis of the Caribbean, published as *Welfare and Planning in the West Indies*, was even more influential than the Moyne Commission in framing Caribbean social policy and its application in the post-war period.[101] It became required reading for Jamaican trainee social welfare workers and, according to Raymond Smith, 'the received wisdom of social planners'.[102] Simey's analysis differed in some important respects from that of the Moyne Commission. Where the commissioners dealt only obliquely with political questions, Simey placed them at the heart of his analysis. The opening sentence of *Welfare and Planning* declared that the 'most important problem' for the British Empire was to manage the transition from Crown Colony government to 'a form of government suitable for those who have advanced up to or within a measurable distance of social and political self-reliance'.[103]

Despite this significant difference, Simey's analysis of Caribbean social life echoed and expanded upon the Moyne Commission's interpretation of the relationship of Caribbean people to the modern world. Simey agreed with the commissioners that people in the Caribbean lacked a coherent culture. Neither properly African nor properly Western, 'the West Indian,' he argued, 'was forcibly divorced from his African culture and has not been able to establish himself securely as an inheritor of the "western" way of life'.[104] 'African tradition', Simey believed, could

---

[100] Both Stockdale and Simey's positions were direct responses to the Moyne Commission. Chamberlain, *Family Love*, 31–3.
[101] Simey, *Welfare and Planning*.
[102] Smith, 'Caribbean Families', 51. For an important analysis of Simey's work see Smith, *The Matrifocal Family*, 81–4.
[103] Simey, *Welfare and Planning*, v.      [104] Ibid., 18.

not form 'the basis of the construction of social or economic institutions to meet contemporary needs.' The one exception that Simey allowed to his argument about the lack of continuity with African life was in the area of religion. However, Simey dismissively categorized this continuity as 'superstitious beliefs' and focused on the problems that such beliefs allegedly produced:

> The religious life of the peoples of the West Indies is shot through in every direction with superstitious beliefs which obviously stem from African religions. Nowhere in the British West Indies has African religion been elevated to the position of second religion in the land, as has occurred with Vodun in Haiti, but everywhere there are sects and practices which are a constant source of trouble to Governments and Churches alike. 'Obeah' and 'pocomania' abound in Jamaica, the 'shouters' and the Shango cult have many adherents in Trinidad, as have the 'shakers' in St. Vincent. All these sects pander to superstition. Day by day 'healers' extract money from the credulous who come from the middle classes as well as the masses. The 'services' in bush churches and chapels not only undermine the work of the regular Christian denominations, but by exciting deep emotion and maintaining it at a high pitch for hours on end, perhaps all through the night or even for longer periods, the energies of the devotees are sapped, and the economic life of the people is as deeply undermined as the spiritual.[105]

Thus, for Simey, religion was the exception that proved the rule of the overall lack of African cultural influence in Jamaica. From being a symbol of the Africanness and therefore the backwardness of the region, religion had become the odd man out.

In its application to the Caribbean, this argument was boosted by the publication in the same year as the Moyne Commission undertook its investigations of E. Franklin Frazier's *The Negro Family in the United States*. Frazier made a case for African Americans in the United States that paralleled the claims of the Moyne Commission Report, while

---

[105] Ibid., 37–8. Intriguingly, Simey's private letters suggest a somewhat more sympathetic, if condescending and primitivist, approach to African-oriented Caribbean religion. In one, he describes his visit in St Vincent to a 'Shaker' church and his discussion with the leader. He concluded that 'any intelligent government would study' the Shakers and other 'spontaneous upbursts of religion and social organization amongst the people', and criticized the illegality of the Shakers and the influence of mainstream Christian denominations, especially the Catholic Church. Later in the same letter he jokingly declared that 'All I can say is that *my* religion so far as the West Indies is concerned will be Voodoo in the future' because it is 'the most efficient way of releasing the inhibitions of modern life.' Thomas Simey, circular letter to EIB, Stanley Dumbell, Bertran Nelson, Nancy Parkinson and Miss Spensley, 8 November 1942, Liverpool University Archives, Papers of Professor Lord Simey of Toxteth and Dr Margaret Simey (1836–2003) (henceforth Simey Papers), D396/4/1/2.

arguing that the American situation stood in contrast to the West Indian. 'Probably never before in history', Frazier claimed, 'has a people been so nearly completely stripped of its social heritage as the Negroes who were brought to America.'[106] Although Moyne and his commissioners do not appear to have been aware of Frazier's work, the social scientists who followed them were, and took it as confirmation of their interpretation. Thomas Simey in particular was strongly influenced by Frazier's work, describing *The Negro Family* as 'not only an indispensable guide to the social problems of the West Indies, but also ... a major contribution to the general science of sociology'.[107] In this it appears that he was guided by Caribbean intellectuals, particularly the Jamaicans E. A. Maynier, Philip Sherlock, and Tom Girvan, all of whom wrote to him emphasizing the significance of Frazier's work.[108] Simey concluded that there were no 'opportunities for utilizing African tradition as the basis of the construction of social or economic institutions to meet contemporary needs', but argued that religion provided the exception to this conclusion.[109]

Simey's use of Frazier's work located British studies of the Caribbean within the emerging debate between Frazier on the one hand and Melville Herskovits and his followers on the other. In 1941 Herskovits responded to Frazier's *The Negro Family* with *The Myth of the Negro Past*.[110] Focused largely on the United States, Herskovits nevertheless drew on studies of the wider African diaspora. He and his students were drawn to more 'obviously' African locations, including Suriname, Haiti, and Cuba, where there were also indigenous anthropological traditions associated with Fernando Ortiz and Jean Price-Mars.[111] But they had also from the 1930s begun attending to the British colonies. Katherine Dunham and Zora Neale Hurston, both students of Herskovits, spent brief periods studying Jamaica in the mid-1930s, while Dunham also spent time in Trinidad. Hurston published *Tell my Horse*, a hybrid, part scholarly, part popular work that included a section on the Jamaican Maroons.[112] Dunham did not publish on Jamaica or Trinidad, but sent detailed

---

[106] Frazier, *The Negro Family*, 15.   [107] Simey, *Welfare and Planning*, 49.
[108] See letters to Simey from E. A. Maynier, 29 May 1943, 1 May 1945, and 23 July 1945; from Philip Sherlock, 1 July 1945; and from D. T. M. Girvan, 21 June 1945, all in Simey Papers D396/8/1. I would like to thank Lara Putnam for generously telling me about these letters and sharing her notes from them. For her analysis, which has influenced mine, see Putnam, 'T. S. Simey's Anonymous Interlocutors'.
[109] Simey, *Welfare and Planning*, 37.   [110] Herskovits, *Myth*.
[111] For an important discussion of Herskovits's relationship to other intellectuals within and beyond the United States, see Kevin A. Yelvington, 'The Invention of Africa'.
[112] Hurston, *Tell my Horse*.

observations of her experiences there to Herskovits.[113] Melville and Frances Herskovits spent the summer of 1939 in Toco, Trinidad, shortly after the Moyne Commission completed its visit, publishing *Trinidad Village* in 1947 as a result.[114] George Simpson, having worked in Haiti in the 1930s, conducted research in Jamaica in 1953 and in Trinidad in 1960, eventually publishing 'Jamaican Revivalist Cults' in 1956 and articles on Trinidad in 1962 and 1964.[115] Joseph Moore undertook fieldwork in Jamaica in the early 1950s for a doctorate, 'Religion of Jamaican Negroes'.[116] Simey, however, while aware of the work of the Herskovitses and some of Melville's students, was more convinced by E. Franklin Frazier's arguments. British colonial policy in the last years before decolonization thus paid little attention to the new literature on religion emerging from American anthropology.

At least as important as the parallels that Simey drew with Frazier's analysis of US African Americans was the influence of an emerging problem in colonial governmentality: that of the 'detribalized African', which was the concomitant of the theory of the tribe. Drawing on old suspicions of urbanization and industrialization as processes that undermined hierarchy and traditional forms of authority, the concept of the detribalized African crystallized in Northern Rhodesia (Zambia) in response to a series of strikes in the copper-mining belt in 1935, at the same time as the labour conflicts in the West Indies. The government of Northern Rhodesia responded with the time-honoured method of establishing a commission of inquiry. The commission concluded that 'detribalisation' among the mining population who shared space with 'unemployed or unemployable natives who are not under any effective control is one of the most important predisposing causes of the temper which led to the strikes'. The answer was the 'establishment of native authority' within the mines and an effort to ensure that miners frequently returned to their home villages where 'tribal authority should, as far as possible, be preserved'.[117] These arguments were underscored by the analysis of anthropologists Godfrey and Monica Wilson, who argued that colonial economic

---

[113] Katherine Dunham to Melville Herskovits, 25 August 1935 and 15 November 1935, Herskovits Papers, Northwestern University Archives, Evanston, Ill., Series 35/6, Box 7, Folder 12.
[114] Herskovits and Herskovits, *Trinidad Village*.
[115] Simpson, 'Folk Medicine'; Simpson, 'Jamaican Revivalist Cults'; Simpson, 'The Shango Cult'.
[116] Moore, 'Religion of Jamaican Negroes'.
[117] Cooper, *Decolonization and African Society*, 58–9, quoting *Report of Commission Appointed to Enquire into the Disturbance in the Copperbelt, Northern Rhodesia* (Lusaka, 1935), 38–40, 59.

development had produced a 'disequilibrium' in a previously balanced society, and that this would probably produce 'maladjustments' until radical readjustment took place to bring the society back into equilibrium.[118]

The analysis of African problems, especially problems of industrial Africa, as symptoms of detribalization and of a broader maladjustment in African society became standard within colonial government. Urban Africans and African workers in industry were understood as a negative by-product of colonial development. They were most likely to be influenced by Communism, most likely to agitate for nationalism, and were also likely to be morally and socially degenerate. In effect, the detribalized African was the flip side to the 'definite social, economic and cultural value' of 'traditional' African 'customs and usages' that the Moyne Commission praised.[119]

The Moyne Commission's analysis of the West Indies, and the social scientific and development work that flowed from the Moyne Commission Report, positioned the region within this framework. Indeed, Caribbean people were in a sense the epitome of the detribalized African, having been removed from their 'tribal' origins generations before. Like detribalized Africans, but even more so because there was no hope of re-establishing 'tribal' authority, Caribbeans were understood as divorced from valuable traditions of authority – especially the authority of the family – and as buffeted by modernity. They were characterized by all the negative elements of modern life that the social theories of the period emphasized, but were not seen as fully able to participate in valued elements of modernity, such as democracy or rational thinking.

The Moyne Commission set the scene for the new policy embodied in the Colonial Development and Welfare Act of 1940. As the work of Simey and his colleagues shows, the Commission's intellectual trajectory was largely accepted by post-war social science and social policy. In terms of its implications for religion, healing, and in particular the interpretation of obeah, this was an ironic shift in policy. At precisely the moment that African culture began to be to be taken seriously and recognized as a culture, the Caribbean came to be excluded from the category of 'African'. Instead, within British policy and social science, it was interpreted as insufficiently African. Where religion and healing had symbolized the region's connection to Africa, they now became exceptions to an overall rule that posited minimal cultural links between the African continent

---

[118] Wilson, *Economics of Detribalization*, 15. Although published only under Godfrey Wilson's name, the text states that these ideas were developed jointly with his wife Monica. For discussion of the anthropology of detribalization in the copper-belt context see Ferguson, *Expectations of Modernity*, 86–93.
[119] Füredi, *Colonial Wars*, 123–8.

and its diasporic cultures. The effect was to exclude Caribbean cultural forms that had ideological or historical connections with Africa from the re-evaluation of African cultures; they remained easy to dismiss or diminish well into the nationalist period. As the colonies moved towards independence in the 1960s, the nationalists who had been part of this effort to avoid considering popular religions that involved spiritual healing became the new political elite. Their agenda included both a desire to reconnect with Africa and a concern to maintain the region's respectability. This created new approaches to obeah and new debates, to which we turn in the next, final, chapter.

# 8    The post-colonial politics of obeah

In 1964, two years after Jamaica became an independent nation, a woman named Cindy Brooks received a parcel from the United States containing material from the DeLaurence company. The parcel, labelled 'novelty oil, incense kits, candles', drew attention at the post office, and Brooks was arrested and charged with practising obeah and with possession of 'instruments of obeah'. Taken before the resident magistrate's court at Richmond, she was found guilty and sentenced to a fine of £25 for each of the two charges. Brooks's was the last conviction for obeah that I have found reported in the *Gleaner*.[1] As Jamaica established itself as an independent state, no changes were made to the obeah law, but its enforcement came to an end.

This chapter examines the politics of obeah after the Second World War, as Britain's Caribbean colonies attained, first, full internal self-government and then, in most cases, independence. The political systems established by colonial rule remained in place, as did economic relationships. The dates of formal independence, 1962 for Jamaica and Trinidad and Tobago, 1966 for Barbados and Guyana, and other territories in the 1970s and 1980s, were only a single step along a gradual chain. Arguably more significant turning-points were the beginning of mass political participation in the 1930s, and the challenges to the existing social, political, and cultural status quo that accompanied the emergence of the Black Power movement in the late 1960s. The rise of Black Power led to a responsive transformation in the style and to some extent the substance of the mainstream Caribbean nationalist tradition. This can be seen most clearly in the politics of Michael Manley, but also in the later politics of Eric Williams and Forbes Burnham.

The victories, limitations, and contradictions of the cautious but genuine social democratic nationalism of constitutional decolonization in the

---

[1] 'Woman fined £25 for Practicing Obeah', *Gleaner*, 26 March 1964. I found three subsequent reports of arrests, one in 1965, two in 1970, and one in 1977, but no trials following these arrests were reported. My search of the *Gleaner* ended in 1989.

Caribbean have been the subject of sustained critique by recent scholars.[2] Caribbean nationalism emerged from the brown middle class who had been educated in British models of respectability. It was transformed by the 1930s rebellions and subsequent elections, which forced putative leaders to appeal to a mass base. Nevertheless, the leadership of the post-war nationalist movement remained largely drawn from the professional middle classes, black, brown, and Indian, whose cultural orientation was distinctly separate from that of those they sought to represent. A few significant exceptions were individuals such as Uriah Butler and Eric Gairy: populist leaders who emerged from working-class and peasant backgrounds and gained authority through leadership in the labour movement. They more easily spoke the language of the masses, including an ability to make emotional and spiritual connections with popular religion. Even leaders such as Butler and Gairy, if they achieved power, tended to become differentiated from their base as they achieved a very different life from that of their supporters. The era of mass politics, inaugurated by the first full adult suffrage elections in Jamaica in 1944 and Trinidad in 1946, was characterized by the struggles of the emerging leadership to find a way of recuperating Caribbean culture while retaining middle-class power and authority.

The cultural difference between leaders and followers was amplified by the religious affiliations and hostilities of left and labourist politics, which in different ways influenced both the mainstream Caribbean nationalist tradition and the Marxist critics to the left of that mainstream. Mainstream nationalism was often allied to the 'respectable' churches which defined themselves against African-Christian religious communities. Meanwhile, the Marxist left drew on a Continental European tradition that developed out of conflicts in which the church was an arm of the state and actively rejected progressive social change.[3] Their default common sense understood religion – all religion, not just state-sponsored religion – as a diversion from struggle in this world. Popular religion, in the view of many, represented backwardness and superstition, and was likely to inhibit radical consciousness, stimulating as it did a reliance on external saviours.[4] In the Caribbean this theoretical position rubbed shoulders with an empirical awareness of the centrality of religion to all the major popular radical movements, from marronage to slave rebellions to Bedwardism and Rastafari, producing contradictory politics that was

---

[2] Among the most important studies are Thomas, *Modern Blackness*; Lewis, *The Growth of the Modern West Indies*; Scott, *Conscripts of Modernity*; Bolland, *The Politics of Labour*; Macpherson, *From Colony to Nation*; Crichlow, *Negotiating Caribbean Freedom*.
[3] Kaiser, "'Clericalism'".     [4] Putnam, *Radical Moves*, 78–80.

cognizant of the significance of popular religion, and often sought to use it, while at the same time hoping to overcome it.

Obeah remained symbolically significant within these developments. On the one hand, as a form of Caribbean cultural practice that had been made illegal by colonial rule, it could be read as a sign of cultural resistance. But, as a form of practice that started from the assumption that spirits and ancestors could act in the human world, and could be prevailed upon by human beings to act in certain ways, it was, for nationalists, easily understood as one of the most negative forms of religion. Because obeah was seen as individualistic and usually focused on improving the personal circumstances of individuals, sometimes at the expense of other individuals, it was difficult to mould into a more positive view of religion as part of Caribbean culture. In a world in which the modernity and civilization of the Caribbean region continued to be questioned, nationalist leaders struggled to emphasize what they thought of as the positive elements of folk culture while often disavowing the less positive, including obeah. The treatment of obeah – both as actual practice and as signifier – by the new elites thus worked as a kind of litmus test for wider issues about the relationship between the middle class and the population as a whole in these new nations-in-formation. It was a particularly complex litmus test, however, because of the multifaceted nature of popular views of obeah, which continued to include use of its arts, fear of its power, and knowing awareness of its stigmatized status.

This chapter, then, investigates the place of obeah as the subject of political debate, cultural representation, and continuing illegality within the emerging independent nation-states of the Caribbean. It has three main sections. First, it shows that there was a decline in prosecutions for obeah in Jamaica, beginning in the 1940s. Practically no prosecutions for obeah took place after independence. This decline in prosecution was not accompanied by formal decriminalization, and obeah's continued illegality had real effects on popular practice, despite the lack of enforcement of the law. This section of the chapter asks why prosecutions for obeah ended without decriminalization taking place. The second section examines two places where obeah became the site of intense political debate during the 1970s: Guyana and Grenada. In both, authoritarian populist leaders were under pressure from the rise of a radical, cultural nationalist and Marxist left. In both, these leaders made symbolic use of obeah to help consolidate their power. In Guyana, Forbes Burnham announced in 1973 that he would decriminalize obeah, provoking discussion and analysis across, and indeed even beyond, the Caribbean. The debate revealed the ethnic terms in which a proposal for decriminalization of obeah was understood in the ethnicized politics of 1970s Guyana, as well as the multiple points of view, from conservative religious bodies to the Marxist left, that could lead to a denunciation of the proposal. In Grenada, at around the same time, Eric Gairy, also an authoritarian populist leader, came to be associated with the use of obeah, and the opposition to his government, in the form of the New Jewel Movement, denounced him for its use, in the process also denouncing popular 'superstition'. These events reveal not only the ability of authoritarian politicians to co-opt the power of Caribbean religion – the pre-eminent example of which took place under the Duvalier regime in Haiti – but also the difficulty even of left-wing movements that wanted to rehabilitate pride in the Caribbean's African past in moving beyond the stigmatization of obeah and all that it represented.

If obeah was no longer a regularly prosecuted crime, it certainly did not disappear from Caribbean discourse. The chapter's third section investigates the place of obeah within post-war Caribbean cultural production, focusing in particular on theatre and performance. As Caribbean artists sought to produce an authentically Caribbean culture, many of them used obeah as a key theme within their work. This took place in many art forms, from novels to poetry to music, but the chapter focuses on theatre as a publicly shared art form that has been less discussed by scholars than have some of these areas.[5] Theatre is also of particular interest because of the participatory role of its audience, and the parallels between the theatrical stage and the court of law as a kind of stage, which featured prominently in many dramatic works. The chapter examines popular forms of theatre, especially the comic variety shows that were a staple of the Caribbean stage, alongside the more explicitly cultural nationalist theatre of playwrights Barry Reckord, Errol Hill, and Dennis Scott. Theatrical portrayals of obeah were frequently comic and, despite the fact that they often worked within an explicitly cultural nationalist paradigm, often reiterated and reinvigorated, from a nationalist point of view, long-standing stereotypes of the obeah man as fraud and charlatan. However, in theatre, far more than in formal politics, there were also serious and sensitive portrayals of Caribbean religion as an aesthetic and spiritual realm of life worthy of serious representations. Such stagings included aspects of Caribbean religion that were deeply integrated with

---

[5] On music see Bilby, 'An (Un)natural Mystic', 65. On obeah in Caribbean fiction and poetry see Fernández Olmos and Paravisini-Gelbert, *Sacred Possessions*; ten Kortenaar, *Postcolonial Literature*, 152–6; Paul, '"Bad Name Worse Dan Obeah"'; Johnson, 'Shamans, Shepherds, Scientists'; Collins, '"We Shall All Heal"'.

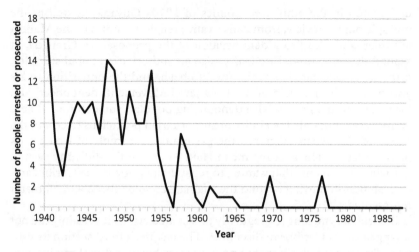

Figure 8.1 Arrests or prosecutions for obeah and related offences in Jamaica, 1940–1989.
Source: Jamaica *Gleaner* (newspaperarchive.com).

practices generally deemed to be obeah. However, those that did this in a sympathetic way, such as Dennis Scott's *An Echo in the Bone* (1974), avoided all mention of obeah itself in representing Caribbean religion. Obeah, it seems, could not be rehabilitated in the terms that other aspects of Caribbean culture could.

Obeah continued to be a criminal act throughout the Anglophone Caribbean until 1980, but stasis in its criminal status does not mean that there was no change in the enforcement of the law.[6] The postwar period saw a dramatic decline of obeah prosecutions in Jamaica.[7] Figure 8.1 shows the distribution of prosecutions between 1940 and 1989. Although there are fluctuations, it demonstrates a clear downward trend over time; in no year after 1940 did the total number of arrests and prosecutions exceed the mean average for prosecutions between 1890 and 1939. Between 1940 and 1962, when Jamaica became independent, I located 164 cases, an average of 7 per year. Between 1963 and 1989 (after which I stopped collecting evidence), prosecutions almost completely ended. There was, that is, a gradual decline in the use of the obeah law from the Second World War until independence, and

---

[6] Handler and Bilby, *Enacting Power*, 74.
[7] From 1940 on, I only systematically collected reports of prosecutions from Jamaica, where prosecution numbers were always considerably higher than in Trinidad. The methods of collection were the same as those described in Chapter 5.

Table 8.1 *Outcomes of Jamaican obeah and related cases, 1940–1989 (percentages are of known outcomes)*

|  | Guilty | Acquitted | Unknown |
|---|---|---|---|
| Practising obeah | 89 (86%) | 15 (14%) | 47 |
| Practising obeah and additional charge | 8 (100%) | 0 | 6 |
| Vagrancy (obeah related) | 5 (83%) | 1 (17%) | 0 |
| Possession of obeah materials | 0 | 0 | 2 |
| **Total** | **102 (86%)** | **16 (14%)** | **55** |

a sharp curtailment of its use after independence. We cannot be certain that the decline in obeah prosecutions evident in the Jamaican sources also took place in other territories, but the Jamaican evidence is suggestive.

During this period of declining prosecutions, the consequences of prosecution continued to be serious. Conviction became even more likely than it had been before 1940, probably suggesting that prosecutions were now undertaken more selectively, in cases where prosecutors were confident of securing convictions (compare Table 8.1 with Table 5.4). Although the proportion of those convicted who were fined rather than imprisoned and/or flogged increased significantly, they remained a minority; the majority of those convicted continued to be sent to prison, and two-fifths of those imprisoned were also flogged (see Table 8.2). The dominance of men among those prosecuted declined a little, from 85 per cent in the earlier period to 78 per cent in the later.

This decline in prosecutions took place without any change in the criminal law governing obeah, and was accompanied by very little public debate about the law's validity. The almost total termination of prosecutions for obeah after 1962 is particularly striking. Without, as far as I have been able to discover, any official discussion, enforcement of the obeah law ceased, apparently seeming inappropriate in an independent state. Like many changes in the implementation of criminal law, especially with regard to largely victimless 'moral' crimes, shifts in prosecutions for obeah responded to subtle changes in the perspective of those responsible for enforcing the law and to shifts in the wider public mood. These changes are evident in the debates about the Caribbean's social problems in the wake of the Moyne Commission. In the view of post-war social science and social policy, as discussed in the previous chapter, the region's problems derived primarily from family forms, not religion. These might be seen as intertwined, as for instance in Basil Matthews's book

Table 8.2 *Punishments of those found guilty in Jamaican obeah and related cases, 1940–1989 (percentages are of known outcomes)*

|  | Fine | Imprisonment | Imprisonment and flogging | None | Unknown |
|---|---|---|---|---|---|
| Practising obeah | 28 (36%) | 28 (36%) | 20 (26%) | 2 (3%) | 11 |
| Practising obeah and additional charge | 6 (75%) | 1 (13%) | 1 (13%) | 0 | 0 |
| Vagrancy (obeah related) | 1 (20%) | 3 (60%) | 1 (20%) | 0 | 0 |
| Total | 34 (38%) | 32 (36%) | 22 (24%) | 2 (2%) | 11 |
| **Total** | 102 | | | | |

*The Crisis of the West Indian Family*, which argued that obeah was a problem associated with family breakdown.[8] Nevertheless, even in Matthews's argument it was the family that was seen as the primary cause, with obeah as a consequence. Popular religion continued to be considered problematic and a sign of the region's backwardness, but in the long-standing conflict among policy makers, those who favoured education and 'uplift' had quietly but finally come to dominate over those who argued for suppression through criminal law. Obeah was coming to be seen as something exotic and quaint, rather than dangerous. To the extent that religion caused anxiety, obeah was being displaced in elite and middle-class concern with the growing – in both size and militancy – Rastafarian communities of Kingston and rural Jamaica. In the 1950s these were the subject of intense anxiety, as the source of militant protest and rejection of the reforming direction of nationalist policy, which peaked in 1960 when Claudius Henry's group began armed protest.[9] Rastafarians experienced continued police harassment, but the obeah laws, which before the Second World War had been used to target a very wide range of people whose practice extended a long way beyond what most Jamaicans considered 'obeah', were rarely used for the suppression of Rastas. Rastafarians were instead targeted through laws about dress, drugs, noise, and vagrancy, and perhaps most importantly through the police's near-unchecked ability to intervene in everyday life, especially life lived in urban public spaces, as part of the control of 'public order'.[10]

The decline in prosecutions did not mean that the law had become irrelevant. Threats of prosecution for obeah continued after actual

---

[8] Matthews, *Crisis of the West Indian Family*, 24–5.
[9] Lacey, *Violence and Politics*, 82–5; Thomas, *Modern Blackness*, 70–2; Chevannes, 'The Repairer of the Breach'.
[10] King, *Reggae, Rastafari*, 78–82.

prosecutions became rare. In 1954 the *Gleaner* published a vivid complaint about police abuse of the obeah law. Jamaican police, the pseudonymous author 'Ceiba' complained, used the law to harass and extort money from Revival communities, illegally bullying their way into religious premises with threats and without warrants:

> At times, the purpose is to conduct a genuine search for evidence of what the law loosely terms 'obeah' but at other times the agent of the Law is merely intent upon extortion.
>
> This is accompanied by seizing a few paper notes or coins of value and claiming they were 'marked' by the Police previously and used in a trap in which the victim supposedly accepted them in payment for obeah.
>
> Identification of any mark on the paper is used as evidence. The officers then pocket these funds and disappear with threats of returning. Needless to say, nothing more is heard of the money nor of the officers, and since the plainclothes type usually refuse to present credentials on demand there is no way of investigating the matter.[11]

Such corrupt police practices, according to Ceiba, also enabled people from outside the police force to steal from Revivalists.

Ceiba's article made public a set of practices that must long have accompanied the policing of obeah. It is significant that police abuses were still complained of by the mid-1950s, at a time when actual prosecutions were at a level of less than a third compared to their high point in the 1930s. Indeed, popular memory of the use of the obeah law suggests that threats of prosecution continued until very recently. Dianne Stewart's informants in the 1990s, who were active in Kumina and Revival Zion, told her that the Night Noises Prevention Law of 1911 and Obeah Law of 1898 were both enforced until Seaga 'cut the ribbon', suggesting that this continued until the 1980s.[12] Meanwhile informants of Anthony Harriott in research conducted in 1989 'complained of recent police harassment and repeated searching of their homes for "instruments of obya"'.[13] These complaints suggest the significant consequences of the law remaining officially in force even while prosecutions declined. Obeah law continued to be used to target adherents of the religions associated with poor Jamaicans.

The maintenance of obeah's illegality may have been a deliberate choice by political leaders. Given the almost total end of prosecutions after independence, it is noteworthy that there was almost no public debate about the repeal of obeah laws. All Caribbean colonies maintained obeah

---

[11] Ceiba, '"Della": An Unfaithful Picture of a Shepherd's Life', *Gleaner*, 29 June 1954.
[12] Stewart, *Three Eyes*, 282n107. Stewart's informants presumably referred to Seaga's period as Jamaican prime minister, which began in 1980.
[13] Harriott, 'Captured Shadows', 117.

law intact as they became independent nations. Although a few have since decriminalized obeah, most Caribbean nations maintain legislative provisions against it, including Jamaica, where the 1898 Obeah Act remains technically in force.[14] In the case of Jamaica, the maintenance of the law against obeah was not simply an oversight or a case of allowing a law to remain in force even while it had fallen into disuse. Rather, the governments of independent Jamaica actively maintained the law even while not enforcing it. This was made clear in 1972, when Michael Manley's democratic socialist government amended the list of items prescribed under the Undesirable Publications Act of 1940. The Act had banned the importation into Jamaica of the publications of the DeLaurence company, along with a much longer list of left-wing and trade unionist publications. The list had been extended in 1968 to include Rastafarian publications, especially those of Claudius Henry's group.[15] With almost no publicity, Manley removed seventy-four publications from the list of banned items, all of them political (socialist or sympathetic to Black Power). Of the thirteen items that remained banned, eight were publications of the DeLaurence company.[16] Even at the high point of cultural nationalism represented by his government, a period when Jamaica was establishing new heroes, including Nanny, whose reputation included her use of obeah, and when Manley himself used some of the symbols of Revival religion to demonstrate his connection with the Jamaican people, the illegality of obeah continued to do significant work. It separated acceptable folklore, which was to be celebrated, from the unacceptable elements of the past in the present, which would continue to be illegal.

Black Power played a significant role in these developments. Manley's unbanning of Black Power literature is a sign of the movement's broader challenge to the political process. This challenge was made prominent in Jamaica through the political action of some sections of Rastafarianism, and by the riots after Walter Rodney was prevented from returning to Jamaica in 1968. In Trinidad the Black Power rebellion of 1970 seriously challenged Eric Williams's government. In other parts of the region, too, Black Power was seriously destabilizing for the newly consolidating nationalist middle class, providing a genuine challenge that was very

---

[14] Handler and Bilby, *Enacting Power*, 74, 57, 60, 91. In 2013 the Obeah Act was revised to remove the possibility of punishment by flogging, but the crime remained unchanged. The Obeah (Amendment) Act 2013, www.japarliament.gov.jm/attachments/341_The%20Obeah%20%28Amendment%29%20Act,%202013.pdf (accessed 1 February 2014).

[15] Davies, *Grimoires*, 229–30; Gray, *Radicalism and Social Change*, 149–150.

[16] 'Academic Freedom: Manley's Heritage', *Gleaner*, 18 February 1973. See also Elkins, 'William Lauron DeLaurence', 215.

attractive to young middle-class people as well as to the mass of the population.[17] Much of the politics of obeah that followed, the subject of the next section of the chapter, can be seen as a response to the pressure of Black Power activism.

The issues at stake were perhaps revealed most clearly in Guyana, where a proposal to decriminalize obeah initiated a debate across the Caribbean. In 1973 Forbes Burnham, whose People's National Congress (PNC) had recently won a third consecutive term in government, announced that he would repeal the laws that made the practice of obeah a criminal offence. Burnham argued that rather than being interpreted as a crime, obeah should be treated as part of Guyana's rich culture; its outlawing, he said, was an instance of 'cultural imperialism'.[18]

In the event, Burnham never repealed the anti-obeah provisions of the Guyanese criminal code, which remain in place today.[19] Nevertheless, Burnham's announcement was an important and controversial symbolic move, with ramifications across the Caribbean. Although no action was taken to decriminalize obeah, many Guyanese understood Burnham's statement of intent to mean that obeah was no longer a crime, and claims that Burnham did in fact legalize obeah are commonplace in Guyanese reflections on the period.[20] The continuation of such statements also suggests that prosecutions came to a complete halt with Burnham's announcement, if they had not already done so. In a sense, then, the change in policy meant a form of back-door decriminalization.

Debate about decriminalization took place in the Guyanese and wider Caribbean public sphere over several months. Burnham's proposal brought to the fore conflicts about the nature of new Caribbean nations' relationship to Africa and to modernity, and provides insight into the continuing illegality of obeah not just in Guyana but throughout the region. The controversy over obeah reveals the dilemmas of a nationalism that needed to ground itself in claims about the legitimacy of Caribbean culture, but also to present that culture as respectably modern and rational. Obeah became, in this period, an instrument of populist politics; for some a complex signifier of state support for African culture, for others a symbol of corrupt power whose promotion by those in control of the state

---

[17] On Caribbean Black Power see Quinn, ed., *Black Power in the Caribbean*; Swan, *Black Power in Bermuda*.
[18] Burnham, quoted in 'Obeah Law will be Repealed: PM', *Guyana Graphic*, 2 November 1973. For another discussion of the controversy over decriminalization see Quinn, 'Governing National Cultures', 231–3.
[19] Handler and Bilby, *Enacting Power*, 65.
[20] This claim is based on conversations and interviews during a research trip to Georgetown in 2006.

emphasized the illegitimacy of that control. It also became enmeshed in multiple discourses about ethnic and national authenticity and purity. Within Guyana's complex and tense ethnic politics, Burnham's promotion of obeah at a symbolic level signified his government's favouring of African rather than Indian concerns.

Burnham's proposal to decriminalize obeah was part of his declared 'Cultural Revolution' that aimed to emphasize the existence of and raise pride in 'authentic', 'indigenous' Guyanese culture. This policy took shape under pressure from radical activists and intellectuals who, across the region, were denouncing the limits of the changes brought by independence, and demanding genuine transformation. The Rodney Riots in Jamaica in 1968 and the Black-Power-inspired 'February Revolution' in Trinidad in 1970 had demonstrated the significance of Black Power within the region.[21] Within Guyana, Burnham was pulled towards cultural nationalism by the prominence of the African Society for Cultural Relations with Independent Africa (ASCRIA), which would in 1974 co-found the Working People's Alliance with Walter Rodney, but which in 1973 still gave critical support to his government.[22] Burnham's public position on Black Power was to argue that it was unnecessary in Guyana, where 'the black man has achieved political and social gain'.[23] Burnham also used cultural nationalism to mark out a distinct territory for the PNC in opposition to the People's Progressive Party (PPP), led by Cheddi Jagan, which he attacked as Communist and oriented to the Soviet Union rather than authentically Caribbean.[24] The cultural policies of the Burnham government included the elevation of Cuffy, the leader of a major slave rebellion in Berbice in 1763, to the status of National Hero; the declaration of Hindu and Muslim religious holidays as national holidays; the official recognition of the Jordanite religion; and the hosting of the first Caribbean Festival of Arts (Carifesta) in 1972.[25] Carifesta had a particularly profound regional significance, attracting representation from across the Caribbean to showcase an independent Caribbean culture, including African-derived religions. Burnham's cultural nationalism accompanied a declared policy of 'cooperative socialism', which included nationalization of the major foreign-owned industries, and a high-profile role in the Non-Aligned Movement.

---

[21] Meeks, *Radical Caribbean*, 8–36, 65–77; Palmer, *Eric Williams*, 290–303; Lewis, 'Jamaican Black Power'; Samaroo, 'The February Revolution'.
[22] Quinn, '"Sitting on a Volcano"'; Latin America Bureau, *Guyana: Fraudulent Revolution*, 49–50.
[23] Quoted in Manley, *Guyana Emergent*, 96.   [24] Burnham, *The Case of Pedro Beria*.
[25] Roback, 'The White-Robed Army'; Quinn, 'Governing National Cultures'.

Announcing the new policy on obeah, Burnham attacked what he described as a widespread Guyanese 'tendency to look down on our way of life, our expressions of joy or sorrow, our ancient forms of worship and our mysteries'.[26] Burnham's use of the first-person plural emphasized the unity of the nation, a unity also stressed in the new official national slogan, 'One People, One Nation, One Destiny'. At the same time, Burnham also praised Guyana's 'diversity of ethnic origin', and linked obeah to two other religious forms, Kali Mai Puja (linked to Hindu Indo-Guyanese culture) and Comfa (linked to Afro-Guyanese culture and more closely associated with obeah). In so doing, he implied that each of these diverse 'forms of worship' was attached to a singular ethnic group.[27] Although his speech placed obeah, Kali Mai, and Comfa on the same plane, only obeah was illegal. As a result, the debate that followed focused almost exclusively on obeah.

Burnham's proposal did not reject an understanding of obeah as primarily negative. His speech proposing decriminalization noted that obeah practitioners would still be liable to prosecution should they use deception 'for capitalist gain', thus mobilizing the trope of the obeah man as a fraud or a charlatan.[28] Despite its assertive anti-colonial rhetoric, then, in content Burnham's proposal did not go further than long-standing suggestions that specific laws against obeah were unnecessary because those who committed it could be prosecuted by other means. ASCRIA recognized this, attacking Burnham's emphasis on prosecution of those who practised obeah for capitalist gain as 'double talk', and criticizing the ruling PNC for coming late to the promotion of African culture.[29]

Nevertheless, Burnham's attempt to use the legalization of obeah as a means of securing his own popularity was at least partially successful. The PNC's newspaper *New Nation* unsurprisingly editorialized in favour of the move, suggesting that those Guyanese who saw obeah as 'superstition' were 'slavish pupils of the colonial master'. The government-owned *Daily Chronicle* supported the proposal to place obeah in the 'rightful category of the culturally acceptable'. The *New Nation* also ran supportive letters to the editor arguing, for instance, that obeah was 'a science more powerful than most medicine' and 'the black man's religion'.[30] Journalists and commentators in other newspapers also supported the

---

[26] 'Obeah Law will be Repealed: PM', *Guyana Graphic*, 2 November 1973. [27] Ibid.
[28] 'Burnham to Legalize Obeah', *Daily Gleaner*, 2 November 1973.
[29] 'Confusion, says ASCRIA', *Guyana Graphic*, 11 November 1973.
[30] 'Editorial: Our Culture', *New Nation*, 3 November 1973; 'Odingo in Letter to Editor Says Obeah Mystic Cult for Good and Bad', *New Nation*, 10 November 1973. *Daily Chronicle* editorial reported in 'Archbishop Suggests Study into Obeah', *Trinidad Guardian*, 7 November 1973.

move, some suggesting that decriminalization was 'clearing the way for a revival of our legend and mysteries brought from ancient Africa'.[31] Afro-Guyanese informants of the anthropologist Brackette Williams, who did fieldwork in Guyana in the late 1970s, praised Burnham for his efforts to 'treat Obeah fairly', even while being 'disenchanted with [his] political and economic policies'. For these Guyanese obeah was a positive symbol of African culture in Guyana.[32]

In the context of a society that had become increasingly bitterly divided on ethnic lines since the British state deposed the first elected government in 1953, these comments about obeah's link to Africa were not simply assertions of anti-colonialism. The fragile anti-colonial alliance between Indo- and Afro-Guyanese was shattered in the wake of that coup. By the 1970s Guyanese politics was divided between Burnham's PNC, which drew its support primarily from the mainly urban African-descended population, and Cheddi Jagan's PPP, with a base among the Indo-Guyanese who made up just over 50 per cent of Guyana's total population, mainly sugar workers and rice farmers.[33]

It is thus not surprising that Burnham's announcement that he would decriminalize obeah was widely interpreted as specifically promoting Afro-Guyanese culture and therefore a move that privileged Burnham's Afro-Guyanese constituency. For some this was positive, while for others it was a problem, but all parties in the debate accepted the symbolic link between obeah and Afro-Guyanese. In fact, there is considerable evidence that, in Guyana as in Jamaica and Trinidad, the practices labelled obeah were very widespread and were not confined to a single ethnic group. To the extent that they were used at all by this time, anti-obeah laws might be used against spiritual practitioners of a range of ethnic and religious affiliations. A number of famous obeah practitioners were Indo-Guyanese, including Buckridee, a man of Indian origin, who was the key defendant in an infamous early twentieth-century murder case that was linked to obeah.[34] According to one commentator, Indo-Guyanese obeah men outnumbered those of other ethnic backgrounds, while clients of the obeah men 'came from all races and classes'.[35] Nevertheless, the debate about obeah law worked to deny these cross-cutting allegiances, emphasizing instead the ethnic specificity of distinctive spiritual practices.

Burnham's announcement was met with considerable hostility as well as with some support. Some of the opposition derived from, as Burnham

---

[31] Carl Blackman, 'Mumbo Jumbo', *Daily Chronicle*, 4 November 1973.
[32] Williams, *Stains on my Name*, 209.   [33] Lewis, *The Growth of the Modern West Indies*.
[34] Campbell, *Obeah: Yes or No?*, 5.
[35] Wordsworth MacAndrew, 'O-b-e-a-h', *Sunday Chronicle*, 11 November 1973, quoted in Quinn, 'Governing National Cultures', 232n105.

put it, a perspective linked to that of 'our former colonial masters'.[36] Many opponents of the proposal replicated long-standing hostile representations of obeah as witchcraft, devil-worship, evil, and even murderous and cannibalistic. Opponents of decriminalization repeatedly associated obeah with child-murder. Friar Andrew Morrison, a senior Guyanese Catholic, said that obeah could include ritual murder of children, although he did not oppose legalization, because murder was already illegal. The Barbados *Advocate-News*, one of several newspapers outside Guyana that picked up the story, reminded its readers of the 'Salt Pond murder case' in which 'a child was sacrificed in an obeah ritual'.[37] A commentator in the Guyana *Sunday Chronicle* said that 'we cannot forget the horrible ritual murders which have occurred from time to time in the past and which allegedly have been connected with the practice of obeah'.[38] Reuters, in picking up the story, glossed obeah as 'a form of witchcraft', replicating precisely the problem that Burnham attacked.[39] The *Advocate-News* argued that 'we would hate to believe that we are so desperate for a cultural identity that we would encourage people to literally turn to the devil in our frantic search'.[40]

While some African-oriented independent religious organizations such as the African Apostolic Brotherhood supported the decriminalization proposal, those connected to international religious hierarchies mainly opposed it, apparently seeing obeah as a threat to their cultural authority.[41] The Guyana Council of Churches expressed 'concern' and 'uneasiness' at the proposal, while the Caribbean Conference of Churches, meeting in Jamaica and thus less concerned about offending the Guyanese government, resolved that 'legislation designed to foster unchristian principles [is] unacceptable to this Conference'.[42] Some

---

[36] 'Obeah Law will be Repealed: PM', *Guyana Graphic*, 2 November 1973.
[37] 'Obeah and our Cultural Past', *Advocate-News*, 3 November 1973.
[38] Mohammed Hamaludin, 'Archbishop Wants Obeah Commission', *Sunday Chronicle*, 4 November 1973. Archie Codrington in the *Guyana Graphic* referred to a famous 1950s murder case of a girl named Lillawattee and the 'infamous Cotton Tree Maraj who dispensed raw arsenic as love philtres', in order to argue that 'cultural heritage' was not necessarily positive. Archie Codrington, 'Let's Think Hard on Obeah', *Guyana Graphic*, 11 November 1973.
[39] 'Burnham to Legalize Obeah', *Gleaner*, 2 November 1973.
[40] 'Obeah and our Cultural Past', *Advocate-News*, 3 November 1973.
[41] 'Obeah – Why all this Hue and Cry', letter to the editor from A. G. Green, *New Nation*, 10 November 1973.
[42] 'GCC Wants to Interview PM on Obeah', 3; 'CCC Resolution on Anti-Christian Legislation', 5, both *Sunday Graphic*, 2 December 1973. The Anglican bishop of Barbados described obeah as 'witchcraft' and as 'unchristian', and said that 'from a Christian point of view [decriminalization] cannot be supported' while a Catholic leader in Dominica argued that obeah 'detracts from the faith due God and ... creates fear in the minds of people'. 'Church Blasts Move to Legalise Obeah', *Guyana Graphic*, 3 November 1973.

Islamic authorities also attacked the move, the Islamic Brotherhood of Guyana calling obeah 'unholy and uncivilised'.[43] Much of the opposition to Burnham's move thus fairly straightforwardly reproduced colonial discussions of obeah.

Others presented their opposition in more complex terms, connected to the question of whether obeah was authentically African and authentically a religion. The Anglican archbishop of the West Indies, Dr Alan Knight, called for the establishment of an academic commission to research obeah before decriminalization took place, to include experts on African religion. Only if obeah could be shown to be a 'proper' religion should it be legalized, he suggested.[44] A Briton who had spent considerable time in Ghana, Knight pre-empted the conclusions of his proposed investigation, arguing that African religion as practised in Africa was legitimate because it was based on learning and controlled by 'tribal law'. Obeah, on the other hand, was a corrupt and degenerate form, mere 'hocus-pocus' rather than proper 'fetish religion'.[45] Another commentator wrote that obeah did not represent genuine African culture, but rather was the province of 'get-rich-quick rascals'.[46] Similarly, a Barbadian commentator argued that obeah was not a 'religion in any true sense of the word' but rather 'consists of mere vestiges of a number of African beliefs'. Instead of legalizing obeah, this writer suggested, Burnham should introduce Haitian Vodou to Guyana.[47] These suggestions inverted earlier attacks on obeah that presented it as problematic and dangerous precisely because of its association with Africa and Haiti, instead taking on the perspective established in the late 1930s, which positioned African 'traditional religion' as more acceptable because more authentic than its Caribbean equivalents. Where obeah's association with both Africa and Haiti had in the past been used to condemn it, it was by this time its *lack* of cultural purity, its creole or hybrid status, that made it suspect.

While Burnham and his allies represented the debate about decriminalization as a straightforward contest between an anti-colonial faction and the dupes of colonialism, the reality was more complex. Many who opposed the move, including the opposition PPP, were stalwarts of the

---

[43] 'Criticism Mounts against Bid to Legalise Obeah', *Guyana Graphic*, 4 November 1973; although a representative of the Guyana Muslim Centre supported legalization on grounds of freedom of religion: 'Mr Ali Welcomes Law to Allow Practice of "Obeah Religion"', *Sunday Graphic*, 16 December 1973.
[44] Mohammed Hamaludin, 'Archbishop Wants Obeah Commission', *Sunday Chronicle*, 4 November 1973.
[45] 'Present-Day Obeah in Guyana All Hocus-Pocus', *Guyana Graphic*, 6 December 1973.
[46] Archie Codrington, 'Let's Think Hard on Obeah', *Guyana Graphic*, 11 November 1973.
[47] 'Papaloi Burnham Creates a Religion', *Advocate-News*, 5 November 1973.

anti-colonial struggle. The PPP was primarily concerned at the time with economic issues and, especially, with contesting Burnham's increasingly authoritarian rule. It expressed little interest in cultural issues outside education policy and promotion of the arts.[48] The PPP described Burnham's regime as 'semi-fascist', and was boycotting parliament in protest at electoral fraud in the 1973 election.[49] It argued that the move to decriminalize obeah was a distraction from the failure of the post-colonial state under Burnham. Burnham's focus on obeah, the PPP argued, was an attempt to use a peripheral issue for political advantage. The party's public statement said: 'The people cannot be fed on superstitions. Obeah cannot solve their day-to-day problems of unemployment, poor housing and hunger brought on by rising prices and shortages.'[50] It was already becoming apparent that the PNC government's promotion of 'cooperative socialism', and nationalization of important foreign-owned companies such as the Demerara Bauxite Company, was not enabling the 'small man [to] become a real man', as the PNC's gendered slogan put it. Rather, it was channelling resources to a small political elite, while increasing ethnic division by restricting access to public-service employment to African Guyanese.[51] Burnham's announcement, according to the PPP, focused attention on 'our former colonial masters' in order to distract from the limits of his own government's success and its lack of electoral legitimacy. A commentator in the *Guyana Graphic* echoed this view, suggesting that the obeah issue had pushed stories about high food prices and shortages of essential goods out of the newspapers.[52] Such a view was in many ways accurate, and Burnham's policy was surely instrumental. Yet by counterposing cultural and economic decolonization the PPP showed its formation within a Caribbean secular nationalism that would always struggle to connect with popular belief.

The PPP's use of the term 'superstitions' to display its hostility to Burnham's policy is telling. In another statement the party attacked the move on the grounds that obeah was inappropriate for the modernity that newly independent Guyana should be trying to achieve: 'In a century when science had made so many advances, when man had already

[48] This claim is based on materials at the Cheddi Jagan Research Centre, Georgetown, Guyana, including two folders of 'Articles by Cheddi Jagan 1973'.
[49] For the PPP's description of the PNC regime as 'semi-fascist', see Jagan's speech to the eighteenth congress of the PPP, Leonora, 3–5 August 1974, published in *Thunder: Quarterly Theoretical and Discussion Journal of the People's Progressive Party*, Guyana, 6, 3 (1974): 2–52, quotation at 11.
[50] 'Criticism Mounts against Bid to Legalise Obeah', *Guyana Graphic*, 4 November 1973.
[51] Latin America Bureau, *Guyana: Fraudulent Revolution*.
[52] C. Hamilton, 'Sunday Opinion: Follow the Leader', *Guyana Graphic*, 18 November 1973.

walked on the moon, to go back to an era of superstition and denial of science and logic is nothing short of tragic.'[53] This stance was shaped by Cheddi Jagan's Soviet-influenced modernist secularism which counterposed religion – any religion – to progress. However, by focusing on obeah rather than, for instance, on Anglicanism, as the mark of the irrational, it preserved the hierarchy among different forms of religion characteristic of the colonial era.[54] Other commentators also emphasized the contrast between obeah and modernity. Archie Codrington argued that while Christianity had given Europeans the strength for imperial conquest, 'traditional' African religion had failed to protect its adherents. 'We are embarking on the exciting adventure of making Guyana into a modern nation,' Codrington stated, 'and with so may honourable and worthwhile tasks awaiting our energies we should have no time for dark, morbid and ill understood things and cultures like obeah, fraught with so many possibilities for evil.' This view also drew on traditional hostility to obeah as evil – Codrington also suggested that legalizing obeah might mean setting up altars to 'a Deity with a grinning skull for a face'.[55]

Burnham's nationalism, in contrast to that of the PPP, allowed obeah to be conceptualized as part of the modern nation. Yet the extent to which Burnham could bestow legitimacy on obeah was constrained by the limits to his own legitimacy. Burnham had first come to power in 1964 after strikes and 'race riots' supported by the CIA brought down Cheddi Jagan's government. The 1968 and 1973 elections were both characterized by significant electoral fraud.[56] As the 1970s went on, Burnham's government became increasingly repressive. With the possible exception of Eric Gairy of Grenada, to whom we will turn in a moment, Burnham became the most authoritarian post-colonial political leader in the Anglophone Caribbean.

In such a context it may be that, far from bestowing the legitimacy associated with state power on obeah, Burnham's announcement drew attention to the illegitimacy of his own rule. The PPP declared that the people 'cannot be fooled by circuses and political obeah men', a remark that maintained the opposition between the cultural and economic nationalism of PPP policy, and at the same time implicitly positioned Burnham

---

[53] PPP statement, quoted in Mohammed Hamaludin, 'Archbishop Wants Obeah Commission', *Sunday Chronicle*, 4 November 1973.
[54] It is also revealing that the PPP invoked the Cold War moon landings as their symbol of scientific progress, rather than praising science for a more obviously useful result.
[55] Archie Codrington, 'Obeah – Tainted with Sorcery and Murder', *Guyana Graphic*, 25 November 1973, 4.
[56] For discussions of Guyanese politics in this period see Manley, *Guyana Emergent*, 5–16.

as an obeah man. The cryptic reference to 'political obeah men' drew on widespread rumours in Guyana that linked Burnham to obeah. Brackette Williams's informants, for instance, believed that Burnham 'had his own private obeahman', and people who had been politically active in the 1970s remembered similar rumours when interviewed in 2006.[57] The PPP's rhetoric drew on an image of obeah as fraudulent, rather than as powerfully evil; the obeah man was responsible for tricking people into belief in something that wasn't true. More explicit was a columnist in the Jamaican *Daily Gleaner*, who sardonically described Burnham as 'Head Witch Doctor' and 'Guyana's No 1 Obeahman' and suggested that the next Guyanese election would be known as the 'Obeah election'.[58] Guyana's foremost poet, Martin Carter, had referred to obeah in similar terms in a 1971 lecture, where he argued that 'in the Caribbean, the political leader and the obeahman have much in common ... Both seek short cuts; the former through history; the latter through reality.'[59] Carter, who had recently resigned as minister of information and culture in Burnham's government, did not explicitly name Burnham, yet his critique of politics seems directed against Burnham among other Caribbean political leaders. By the late 1970s, as Burnham's government increasingly turned to the use of political violence to preserve its rule, Carter would attack the regime as based on 'degradation', 'corruption', and 'authoritarian bullying'.[60] For now, when the regime maintained some popularity based in part on a still relatively buoyant economic situation, the comparison to an 'obeahman as charlatan' – another phrase from Carter's lecture – was sufficient.

In Guyana in the 1970s, then, obeah became a site for debate on the power of the post-colonial state and the nature of the post-colonial nation. In the context of a state with important power to distribute resources, which it used to bolster its ethnically based support, obeah's symbolic link to African culture was both politically powerful and politically sensitive. The re-evaluation of Caribbean culture that had taken place as part of the nationalist movement had created space for a view of obeah as morally neutral rather than dangerous or fraudulent. Yet this space was unstable and contested, in part because of the power of notions of

---

[57] Williams, *Stains on my Name*, 209. Interviews with Rupert Roopnarine and David Granger, Georgetown, Guyana, September 2006.
[58] Thomas Wright, 'Obeah and Burnham', *Gleaner*, 9 November 1973, 10.
[59] Martin Carter, *Man and Making – Victim and Vehicle: The 1971 Edgar Mittelholzer Memorial Lectures* (Georgetown: National History and Arts Council and Ministry of Information and Culture, *c.* 1971). Thanks to Gemma Robinson for alerting me to this source.
[60] 'Open Letter to the People of Guyana' (1971), in Carter, *University of Hunger*, 217.

ethnic and cultural purity to which obeah did not conform. Moreover, the association of the move to decriminalize obeah with the personalized government of Forbes Burnham brought to the fore the negative and frightening connotations of obeah.

Burnham was not alone in seeking to use obeah to make political capital. Rumours that politicians used obeah were widespread in the independent Caribbean. Eric Williams, for instance, was said to use it to maintain his power.[61] However, the politician most widely associated with obeah was Eric Gairy. Like Forbes Burnham, he was an authoritarian and populist ruler who in the 1970s was struggling to fight off challenges from the left, including those influenced by Black Power. Gairy came to prominence as a labour leader in 1950. Recently returned from Aruba where he had been an active trade unionist, he rapidly acquired a following among sugar workers. He led several successful strikes, culminating in a general strike in 1951 which won a 50 per cent wage increase for agricultural workers.[62] Later that year he was elected the colony's first prime minister, his Grenada United Labour Party gaining 63 per cent of the vote in the first elections under universal adult suffrage.[63] Unlike other Grenadian politicians at the time, he was from the black working class. Part of his political success rested on his ability to make connections with the majority of the population, especially the peasantry, in particular through using a familiar set of religious metaphors.[64] He was close to the Spiritual Baptist community, whose religious practices had been made illegal in 1927.[65] He deliberately made use of religious symbolism in his politics, inviting Spiritual Baptist and Orisha ('Shango') leaders to act as chaplains at his rallies while also sponsoring masses at rural Catholic churches.[66] The brown middle class scorned him as uncultured and uncultivated.

Gairy's politics were populist and his style charismatic. He inspired loyalty among his followers, but once in power did little to change their everyday lives. He made no significant changes to improve health and education systems, for instance, and used his position to enrich himself. His policies worked primarily to preserve his own power. Over time he became more authoritarian, especially when he began to be challenged

---

[61] Beck, 'The Implied Obeah Man', 30.
[62] Singham, *The Hero and the Crowd*, 153–67; Benoit, 'Ressentiment and the Gairy Social Revolution'.
[63] Singham, *The Hero and the Crowd*, 171. Despite his electoral victory, the constitution gave Gairy little real power at this point. See ibid., 117–20, 172–3.
[64] Noguera, 'Charismatic Leadership', 13–14.
[65] CO 103/26, Public Meetings (Shakerism) Prohibition Ordinance, Ordinance No. 11 of 1927.
[66] Franklyn, *Bridging the Two Grenadas*, 44.

from the left by Black Power-influenced radicals who would eventually form the New Jewel Movement.[67]

It is in this context that Gairy's reputed connections to obeah must be situated. Rumours linking him to obeah developed early in his career. When he lost the 1957 election to the Grenada National Party, which represented the light-skinned middle class, he suggested that his defeat was related to his opponents' use of obeah.[68] In later years rumours made him the user, rather than the victim, of obeah. This was an image he encouraged, because it emphasized his power. His reputation was such that foreign journalists asked him about his connections to obeah. In one interview, part of a feature published in the Jamaica *Gleaner* but apparently written for a British or North American audience, he refused to either confirm or deny a connection to obeah, claiming instead to be 'psychic', 'telepathic', and 'clairvoyant' and stating that it was God's will that he rule Grenada.[69] The use of obeah was said to be implicated in the 1973 general election. Gairy was rumoured to have visited an obeah woman in Guyana in advance of the election; with her help he was declared the victor, with 90 per cent of the vote. The opposition argued, convincingly, that the outcome was due to electoral fraud. The story had a sting, however: Gairy allegedly refused to pay the woman in full, and as a result she sent a backu through the mail to torment him. Gairy eventually managed to get rid of the backu from his own residence, but it remained in Grenada, causing trouble for everyone.[70]

Stories about Gairy's use of obeah for his electoral benefit led to his links to obeah becoming a prominent part of the opposition's discursive repertoire. At an anti-Gairy rally in January 1974, the culmination of several weeks of strikes and demonstrations against the government, the crowd at one point chanted:

> Gairy hiding, hiding, hiding
> Gairy hiding from the crowd
> g o = go Gairy bound to go (Repeat three times)
> He go to Guyana

[67] Schoenhals and Melanson, *Revolution and Intervention*; Singham, *The Hero and the Crowd*.
[68] 'Political Obeah', *Gleaner*, 15 October 1957.
[69] Bob Neiland, 'Grenada's Eric Gairy: One of the Mystics of this World', *Gleaner*, 14 July 1974.
[70] Beck, 'The Implied Obeah Man'. According to Beck: 'A backu takes the form of a little man and if "set" on someone does all sorts of harmful and irritating things' (30). Once Gairy got rid of the backu 'the wretched little backu continues his mischief on the island, particularly venting his spleen on his new hosts. In fact, the latest report is that he is busy burning houses' (31).

> He go and wuk obeah
> He wuk obeah
> In Guyana (Repeat)[71]

The crowd's chant tapped into the common belief that Gairy's electoral victory had been aided by obeah. By bringing this into public discourse the crowd exposed it, and thus hoped to undermine his power. The opposition also made use of religious language: Mrs Sybil La Granade gave a speech stating that, since 'the Voice of the people is the voice of God', and there were 30,000 people demonstrating against Gairy, God was asking him to go. The crowd, she added, would treat Gairy 'as God did Lucifer – throw him out of the heavenly land'.[72]

The crowd's reference to Gairy's use of obeah seems to work within the terms of the discursive universe within which obeah was genuinely powerful. Gairy is mocked or denounced for going to Guyana to 'wuk obeah', but not for believing in its power. The anti-Gairy stories about the obeah woman sending a backu functioned similarly within the terms of obeah discourse. At the same time, some opposition leaders spoke of Gairy's alleged use of obeah in more distant and distancing terms, emphasizing a difference between their own sophisticated rejection of obeah and the mass of the population who were said to be in thrall to Gairy's use of it. In the 1974 article quoted above, New Jewel Movement leader Chester Humphrey spoke of Gairy's 'mystical hold' over the people, especially the peasantry, who, he said, were 'superstitious':

> Whatever he might say, we have reliable evidence that he [Gairy] does indulge in obeah – he has been seen taking a herb bath with some country people. This sitting in a hut with steaming herbs and [sic] is said to bring good fortune. I have also heard of him going to a taraka, an obeah ceremony in which a goat is sacrificed for the good fortune of the person who called the ceremony. The people at these events work themselves into a state of frenzy with African-style dancing and chants.[73]

Humphrey's words suggested a capacious understanding of obeah to mean collective African-oriented religion, not just one-to-one

---

[71] *Duffus Commission* (last accessed 4 October 2012). The crowd may well have been referencing the Barbadian group Drayton's Two song, 'G.O. Go', which was released in 1973 and included the lyrics 'G.O. Go/ Gal, a weh you go?/ Me ben down Speightstown/ Me ben a wuk obeah/ Me wuk obeah'. Bilby, 'An (Un)natural Mystic', 52. For a recording see http://www.youtube.com/watch?v=biZZVanNNsU (accessed 1 February 2014).

[72] *Duffus Commission*, 208 (digital page 212). This demonstration was soon after attacked by Gairy supporters and police. It turned into a riot during which one person, Maurice Bishop's father, was killed by police. See www.thegrenadarevolutiononline.com/bloodymonday.html.

[73] Bob Neiland, 'Grenada's Eric Gairy: One of the Mystics of this World', *Gleaner*, 14 July 1974.

consultations aimed at using spiritual power to influence the world. His view that African-style ceremonies were in themselves problematic or negative is telling, speaking to the middle-class and respectable milieu from which he came, and to which the New Jewel Movement oriented itself. Maurice Bishop to some extent shared this point of view. In a speech to a union-organized event in Trinidad entitled 'Fascism: A Caribbean Reality', Bishop argued that fascism has six 'faces', one of which was 'A Pseudo-Philosophical or (Occult) Face where belief in divine Providence, obeah, magic, superstition, and intuition takes the place of reason, planning and participation by the people'. In Grenada, he argued, Gairy's self-proclaimed 'mysticism', and his promotion of national prayers calling on God to 'save us from those who intend to destroy us by speech, by writing, by fire and all other ways and means... confuse and confound our enemies in their wickedness and remove them from our paths of progress' were part of this sixth face of fascism; indeed, 'neo-fascism is fairly well entrenched in Grenada'.[74]

After the New Jewel Movement overthrew Gairy in 1979, it gave considerable publicity to the fact that 'obeah' material was found in his residence. The journalist Alister Hughes ran an article in his *Grenada Newsletter* headlined 'Gairy's Witchcraft Room', which described his visit to the prime minister's official residence, where he was shown a room with an altar on which were 'crucifixes, statutes of saints, rosaries, together with balls of indigo, pieces of salt-petre and small bags of a white powder', along with several ceremonial gowns, a bishop's staff, wooden sword, candles, and incense.[75] In an unpublished book Hughes claimed that Bishop had shown him this material personally.[76] A syndicated article by the Caribbean News Agency (CANA) expanded the list to include 'a skeleton' and 'liquid that could be blood', neither of which Hughes reported the presence of.[77] Most damning in Hughes's account was the fact that Gairy possessed, as well as several Bibles, a number of books 'suggesting witchcraft' and, most telling of all, a list of thirty names headed 'May God Grant Me Eric Mathew Gairy to Overcome These Enemies'.[78]

Gairy's relationship to obeah also figured in musical celebrations of his downfall. 'Natty Dread in the PRA' referred to the persecution of

---

[74] Bishop, 'Fascism – A Caribbean Reality' (accessed 4 October 2012).
[75] 'Gairy's Witchcraft Room', *Grenada Newsletter*, 31 March 1979, 8–10 (last accessed 1 February 2014).
[76] Hughes, Untitled and undated book manuscript (last accessed 1 February 2014).
[77] 'Bishop's Cousin Kills Himself', *Gleaner*, 2 April 1979, 12.
[78] 'Gairy's Witchcraft Room' and 'Gairy's List of Enemies', both in *Grenada Newsletter*, 31 March 1979, 8–12, consulted online at http://ufdc.ufl.edu/AA00000053/00195/8 (last accessed 1 February 2014).

Rastafarians which had been a prominent part of Gairy's regime in the 1970s. It attacked Gairy as an 'obeah dictator':

> The dreadlocks have been kept down
> By the obeah dictator
> And now they are being given a chance
> To show they are fellow West Indians
> Natty never been so gay.[79]

The following year the Grenadian-born, Trinidadian-based calypsonian Mighty Sparrow released 'Wanted: Dead or Alive', which celebrated not only Gairy's downfall in 1979 but also that of Somoza of Nicaragua, Idi Amin of Uganda, and the Shah of Iran. He too couldn't resist a reference to Gairy's reputation for obeah:

> Grenadian Mongoose was bad and so brave
> They send the old Bishop straight to his grave
> After that, well Gairy skip town
> With his diary and him obeah gown
> No more people to enslave[80]

The New Jewel Movement's exposure of Gairy's 'use of obeah' was complicated. The 'evidence' presented did not in itself suggest anything more than a set of religious practices that appeared to draw on Spiritual Baptism or other African Christian religions that made use of complex altars and tables. Moreover, as I have argued throughout this book, the stigmatization of obeah was an intrinsic part of a way of seeing the world in which obeah's negative reputation resulted from a wider hostility to Africa and to anything in the Caribbean perceived as partially or wholly African. This analysis remains useful in the context of 1970s Grenada. Maurice Bishop and other members of the New Jewel Movement were largely drawn from the middle class, a group which had traditionally opposed Gairy, as was Alister Hughes. When they came together to 'expose' Gairy as an obeah user or even an obeah man, their actions followed in the footsteps of attacks on African Caribbean cultural practices through which the Caribbean middle class had marked out its distinction from the poor ever since slavery. When Bishop personally invited Alister and Cynthia Hughes to see, and publicize, Eric Gairy's 'obeah room', they were emphasizing Gairy's low class and race status as much as his authoritarian use of power, even if this was not the deliberate message. In an interview with Hughes, Bishop reportedly characterized the

---

[79] 'Natty Dread in the PRA' (last accessed 1 February 2014).
[80] Mighty Sparrow, 'Wanted Dead or Alive' (last accessed 1 February 2014).

'situation of Grenada' as dominated by 'backwardness, illiteracy, superstition, rumour-mongering, certainly functional illiteracy'.[81]

Nevertheless, Gairy can clearly not be understood in any straightforward way as a victim of colonial-style racism. Both he and Burnham were, indisputably, political leaders who used authoritarian methods to maintain their power, and enriched themselves in doing so. Gairy deliberately fostered a climate of fear and intimidation, using a personally loyal corps of unaccountable thugs, the 'Mongoose Gang', to attack opposition. The lack of any deep legitimacy of his regime explains the relative ease with which the New Jewel Movement was initially able to take power in 1979.

It makes more sense to see Gairy's association with obeah as part of the wider politics of race and class in the Caribbean in this period. A worldview that encompassed the possibility of spiritual action in this world – obeah – was not at all out of place among the peasant community in which he grew up. It became out of place for a statesman, who from the standpoint of the middle class should be secular and rationalist, or at least whose religion should be of the respectable, unemotional Christian kind. Gairy's refusal to become this kind of leader was intrinsically related to his own egomania, but was also part of his populism and continued ability to maintain a sense of personal connection with the people, even while his regime faltered and lost legitimacy.

The New Jewel's criticism of Gairy's use of obeah was not often spelt out. Obeah's negative connotation made it unnecessary to do so. However, I would suggest that it functioned as a dual critique. On one level, Gairy was being criticized for encouraging superstition, not being appropriately rationalist, and therefore as failing to project the appropriate 'modern', Western way of being that middle-class Caribbean people, including radicals, wanted to see represent their nations. At the same time, he was also being criticized for his actual use of obeah to attack his enemies and control people. This is why the list of 'enemies', some of whose names were ticked off, was seen as so sinister. These two critiques sat side by side but were not really compatible.

Meanwhile, attacks in popular culture on Gairy's use of obeah encompassed both these critiques. When Sparrow mocked Gairy for his 'obeah gown' he was both ridiculing Gairy's belief in obeah and, at the same time, emphasizing his threatening use of hostile magic to sustain his power. Different audiences would be likely to interpret the critique in different ways. In large part because of Gairy's deliberate fostering of his own mystical image, criticisms of his corruption, personalistic power, and violent authoritarianism became entangled in hostility to the everyday

[81] Maingot, *The United States*, 126.

understandings of the nature of spiritual power shared by many Caribbean people, in ways that made cultural decolonization more challenging.[82]

Political discussion of the relationship of obeah to Gairy and Burnham's regimes took place against a backdrop of other debates about obeah, as people across the Caribbean region sought to redefine what it meant for independent nations. Although prosecutions declined, obeah remained an important symbol of Africa. As the Caribbean struggled to reassess its relationship with Africa in the move towards and in the wake of independence, obeah figured prominently in the debate. Cultural workers were particularly drawn to it, alongside other manifestations of African Caribbean culture. The role of obeah in some of these cultural forms, particularly the novel, have already been extensively discussed or are the subject of important ongoing work.[83] I focus here on performance, partly because it has been very little analysed, and partly because of its significant position as a form of cultural production that spanned the class divide in the Caribbean, reaching multiple audiences through both popular and 'serious' theatre. Evidence for this section is drawn mainly from published and manuscript play scripts, supplemented by press reports and reviews of performances from Jamaica and Trinidad.

Postwar Caribbean theatre included two related but distinct traditions, both of which incorporated significant representations of obeah. On one hand, popular comic performance drew on traditions of slapstick, verbal comedy, and variety performance, and made use of – while also mocking – the 'man-of-words' West Indian tradition of high-blown rhetorical skill.[84] In Jamaica this kind of performance originated in the Christmas Morning Concerts that were performed from the 1890s in downtown Kingston to a largely working-class audience.[85] Performers in this tradition helped make the Garveyite pageants of the 1930s successful. In the post-war period they were some of the most commercially successful performers, regularly selling out downtown Kingston's Ward Theatre while also taking their shows around the country, playing in hotels, nightclubs, and sometimes schools. Ernest Cupidon was one of the earliest such performers, sometimes playing alongside his partner 'Abe'. Their comedy developed into a form that from the 1960s became

---

[82] Although violent attacks on spiritual workers did not take place in Grenada, there are clear parallels with the use of Vodou imagery and *vodouisants* by the Duvaliers, and the attacks on Vodou practitioners during the *dechoukaj* that followed Jean-Claude Duvalier's overthrow in 1986. Ramsey, *The Spirits and the Law*, 11–13.
[83] See the work cited in note 5 above.
[84] Abrahams, *The Man-of-Words in the West Indies*.
[85] Banham, Hill, and Woodyard, *Cambridge Guide*, 200, 206.

known as Roots Theatre, a popular genre presenting original comic plays to a mass audience, presented in *patwa* and using sexual innuendo to comic effect, while often also including commentary on contemporary social and political issues. This mass-oriented tradition developed alongside the work of playwrights, especially from the 1930s, who wanted to develop a contemporary serious Caribbean art theatre. Such artists connected their work with developments in international theatre, for instance challenging theatrical realism and formal chronological structures, while seeking to develop an 'authentic' Caribbean idiom. Both genres can be seen as embodying cultural nationalism; the latter explicitly, with manifestos and considered thought, the former in a more down-to-earth way, simply by appealing to the masses and addressing them in their own language. Between these two stood a range of other performance material: in Jamaica, the Little Theatre Movement's Jamaica National Pantomime, which became an institution from the mid-1940s onwards, transforming the pantomime genre through the use of Caribbean folk traditions such as anansi; and across the region a repertoire of middle-brow plays, mostly performed by amateur or school groups, which, while depicting Caribbean life, stuck fairly closely to traditional realist depictions and were not formally experimental.[86]

All these performance genres frequently represented obeah, often in the form of the stock character of 'the obeah man'. This ubiquity suggests the extent to which obeah was a concern of Caribbean people, and also how the representation of obeah allowed something that was understood as specifically Caribbean to be portrayed on stage – a kind of insider knowledge. However, as I will show, some of the plays that have most successfully staged Caribbean religious culture from within, such as Dennis Scott's *Echo in the Bone*, avoided directly representing obeah, or naming it as such, even while staging events that involve the actions of the dead in the lives of the living, a theme that is at the heart of obeah.

Caribbean popular comedy is rarely discussed in scholarly literature, because of the 'low' status of the genre, and because the fact that play scripts were not preserved and sometimes never existed means that we have few sources. These ephemeral performances, which at most toured for a few months and were rarely re-staged, left little in the way of archival traces. Nevertheless, the huge popularity of this genre is indicated by the long runs of the shows, evidenced by newspaper advertisements.

One particular interesting form of popular Jamaican theatre was the 'mock trial', notices of which appear sporadically in the press from

---

[86] Canfield, 'Theatralizing the Anglophone Caribbean'; Omotoso, *The Theatrical into Theatre*.

the early twentieth century.[87] The genre drew on both European and Caribbean traditions of carnivalesque inversion; mock trials are reported, for instance, as part of festivals during slavery.[88] It also developed out of Jamaicans' famous love of attending and commenting on real trials, something that had been much commented on, often disapprovingly, by elites ever since the early post-emancipation period. The mock trial developed the pleasure of spectatorship at an actual trial into public entertainment. Mock trials followed the familiar conventions of the courtroom, with actors and well-known public figures playing a defendant, judge, witnesses (including policemen), and clerks of the court. They were played for laughs, with the comedy directed at the pomposity and hypocrisy of the legal system as well as at the defendant's bathetic attempts to justify his behaviour or deny his guilt. Jamaica's leading comedian of the 1930s, Ernest Cupidon, performed regularly in these trials, frequently taking up the role of the defendant.[89]

Many theatrical mock trials were for the crime of obeah, confirming Jamaican audiences' familiarity with the conventions of obeah prosecutions. Although we lack scripts, newspaper reports often reveal the names of the actors and the characters they played, sometimes describe the plot, and frequently assert the comic success of the productions. The trials featured exotically or comically named defendants. Quako, Uncle Fixam (also known as Big Buller Big Price), Mr Boodu, Obeahman Taffea, Kajan Tenderfoot, John Augustus Catawampoo, and Judas Iscariot Braggadap all appeared as obeah men on Jamaican stages between 1930 and 1950. Ernest Cupidon was involved in at least three mock obeah trials: as defendant Quako in 1930, as Uncle Fixam the obeah man in 1932, and as the judge in the trial of Kajan Tenderfoot in 1936.[90] 'Uncle Fixam' was performed in multiple versions. The success of the initial mock trial in which the defendant, played by Cupidon, was convicted, led to the staging of an 'appeal', which played at Edelweiss Park

---

[87] The *Gleaner* provides substantial evidence of 'mock trials' as both amateur and professional theatrical events. For examples of mock trials not relating to obeah see *Gleaner*, 26 May 1891; *Gleaner*, 27 January 1921; 'Mock Trial Tonight', *Gleaner*, 30 September 1931, 16.

[88] Frey and Wood, *Come Shouting to Zion*, 55. Frey and Wood's evidence for mock trials comes from the United States.

[89] On Cupidon see Baxter, *Jamaica*, 269–70.

[90] 'Mock Trial to be held at Y.M. tonight', 30 May 1930 (Quako); 'Comedian is Convicted on Obeah Charge', 2 August 1932 (Fixam); 'Function at St Mark's School, Brown's Town', 21 September 1932 (Boodu); 'Four Paths Concert', 12 December 1933 (Taffea); 'Mock Trial To-Night', 22 July 1936 (Tenderfoot); 'The Metcalfe Club', 31 December 1936 (Catawampoo); 'Settlers' Asson. to Hold Mock Trial', 16 January 1950 (Bragaddap), all in the *Gleaner*.

with Marcus Garvey himself in the role of the presiding judge.[91] In later productions in Falmouth and Spanish Town Uncle Fixam was acquitted, and other participants, including the attorney general, either ran from the courtroom or were seized and beaten.[92] The plot, as described in reports in the *Gleaner*, is nearly indistinguishable from the many accounts of actual obeah trials published in that newspaper, except for the profuse use of inverted commas to indicate that this was a performance, not a real trial. The comedy revolved around a double mocking: of both the legal system and of Jamaican popular religion.

At the explicit level, these mock trials reiterated Jamaican middle-class contempt for popular religion, and indeed for the popular classes. *Uncle Fixam's Obeah Trial* centred on a dispute within a popular church, the 'Wash Foot' denomination of the 'Half a Foot' district of St Andrews, led by the Reverend Sky Pilot.[93] The name of the preacher made a sly, knowing reference to Alexander Bedward's claims that he would be able to fly to heaven, while 'Half a Foot' signified the area's poverty. The audience was thus invited to laugh at and feel superior not simply to the obeah man but also to the Bedwardites and by extension other Revivalist groups and poor Jamaicans. The performances were certainly popular with middle-class Jamaicans, with some newspaper reports specifically naming the respectable people in attendance, while one reported an audience 'including many of the best class'.[94] Yet the audiences were large, and could not have been made up simply of the great and the good. A working-class and plebeian audience also took pleasure in the downfall of the obeah man and enjoyed the mockery of his pretensions. Perhaps the comic pleasure came as much from the ridiculing of the officials as of the defendant, whose position, while ridiculous, also enabled an anansi-style flummoxing of the state system. At the same time, the distancing laughter provoked by the mock trials depended on an awareness that they depicted the audience's own desires and practices. The plays depict the use of obeah as both pervasive and unrespectable. The laughter in response could distance people from the reality of their desire for security through spiritual work. In addition, these comedies engaged popular fear of obeah: by making the obeah man the butt of laughter, they reduced anxiety about it.

---

[91] 'Comedian is Convicted on Obeah Charge', *Gleaner*, 2 August 1932; 'Double Attraction at Edelweiss Tonight', *Gleaner*, 6 September 1932. Hamilton, 'Marcus Garvey and Cultural Development', 98.
[92] '"Uncle Fixam's Obeah Trial" in the Country', *Gleaner*, 17 October 1932.
[93] 'Comedian is Convicted on Obeah Charge', *Gleaner*, 2 August 1932.
[94] 'Cupidon in Great Form at Mock Trial', *Gleaner*, 5 June 1930; '"Uncle Fixam's Obeah Trial" in the Country', *Gleaner*, 17 October 1932.

Evolving in part out of the mock trials of the 1930s were the comedy double acts of the mid-twentieth century. Among the most successful were Bim and Bam (Ed Lewis and Aston Wynter), African Jamaican performers who initially performed in blackface and who produced and performed in a stream of successful shows from the early 1940s to the 1970s. The plots of these productions, which travelled across Jamaica, also frequently revolved around court cases, interspersing comic routines with singing and dance acts by the performers who played the witnesses in the trials.[95] Bim and Bam's shows mixed entertainment with satire, social commentary, and references to current events. For instance, their 1949 show *Rygin's Ghost* (sic) drew on the recent death in a shoot-out of Ivanhoe 'Rhygin' Martin (later to inspire the film *The Harder They Come*), while their 1950 show *Finger in the Ink* poked fun at politicians and electoral officials, in the wake of the recent general election won by the Jamaica Labour Party.[96]

By the early 1950s Bim and Bam had discovered that satire focused on African Jamaican working-class religion and folk belief in ghosts and duppies was reliably popular. Their shows throughout the 1950s incorporated these themes, although little evidence remains about them aside from brief descriptions in newspaper advertisements. They produced *Wappy King Ghost* in 1952 and *The Headless Corpse* in 1953, while the very successful *Healing in De Balmyard* ran from late 1953 to 1955.[97] After a couple of plays that dealt with other themes they returned to Revival religion and spiritual healing in 1956 with *Duppy Biznezz*, followed later that year with *Obeahman Ben*. The advertisement for *Duppy Biznezz* proclaimed:

The mysterious stone throwing and money disappearing did not bother Mrs Tiny Martin much ... But when her 3 yrs old son vanished from the bed that was too much for her. Then it was that the ever popular Mother Banner was called in to solve the mystery. You will howl ... scream, rock, with laughter at the awe-inspiring cymballing of the mother as she drives her Flocks to the Rhythm of the Pocomania Drums.[98]

The central focus of comedy was thus a Revival/Pukkumina 'Mother' and her community, along with the threat of supernatural stone-throwing.

---

[95] Banham, Hill, and Woodyard, *Cambridge Guide* 204; Baxter, *Jamaica*, 265.
[96] Advertisement for *Rygin's Ghost*, *Gleaner*, 11 April 1949; '"Finger in the Ink" at Ward Tonight', *Gleaner*, 19 April 1950. See also Neely, 'Calling all Singers'.
[97] Advertisements for *Wappy King Ghost*, 18 August 1952; for *The Headless Corpse*, 28 March 1953; for *Healing in de/the Balmyard*, 9 December 1953, 13 July 1954, 15 October 1954, 3 October 1955, all in the *Gleaner*.
[98] Advertisement for *Duppy Biznizz*, *Gleaner*, 22 July 1956; for *Obeahman Ben*, *Gleaner*, 27 December 1956.

Mother Banner's movement to the 'Pocomania drums' was played for laughs, relying on the audience's sense that it knew what a real 'Pocomania' dance involved. These comedies relied on the audience's knowledge to emphasize its distance from the events depicted.

In 1961 Bim and Bam embarked on the production of what was perhaps their most successful play, *The Case of John Ras I*, followed by the sequel *The Execution of John Ras I*. The play mocked the newly prominent Rastafarian community while linking it to obeah in a way that Rastas themselves would never have done.[99] Centring on a trial, the story blended questions of gender, sexuality, and religion. The central character and defendant, John Ras I, was a stereotypical Rastafarian with 'curly locks and colourful robe', who was also an obeah man and on trial for ill-treating his wife. The show involved an entrapment scene, as well as a scene in *The Execution* where Ras I sets duppies on the hangman who is supposed to execute him. These were staples of the traditional mock obeah trial shows, but centred now on a Rastafarian, with scant regard for the Rastas' actual disdain for obeah.[100]

Popular comedies that moved beyond the mock trial genre also featured obeah. Perhaps the most significant was *Obeah Wedding*, a 'roots play' produced by Ed Lewis ('Bim'), and written by Ralph Holness, the founder of the genre. It opened in July 1979 at the Ward Theatre, played regularly around Jamaica until 1984, and was revived in 1988–9 with a video of the show a Jamaican bestseller in 1990.[101] The play, which included flashy dancehall-style numbers, was about a middle-class woman who goes to an obeah man when she finds herself pregnant by her former lover. The obeah man is an obvious fraud, exaggeratedly working for the money he can procure from the vulnerable, but also foolish, woman. This was the stock presentation of obeah on Caribbean stages.

Similar depictions of obeah appeared in popular theatre elsewhere in the Caribbean. In Trinidad, comic plays that attracted a broad audience were an important part of the cultural scene, and also frequently revolved around obeah. In the 1930s and 1940s Arthur Roberts, the headmaster

---

[99] Banham, Hill, and Woodyard, *Cambridge Guide*, 204. A Rastafarian character had previously appeared in *Finger in the Ink* in 1950. Farley, *Before the Legend*, 125, quoting *Gleaner*, 13 February 1950.
[100] Advertisement for *The Case of John Ras I*, 30 October 1961 ('curly locks'); *The Trial of John Ras I*, 3 January 1962; *The Execution of John Ras I*, 26 July 1962, all in the *Gleaner*.
[101] 'End of Bim's last season: "Obeah Wedding" takes over from "Gun Court"', *Sunday Gleaner Magazine*, 22 July 1979. *Obeah Wedding* was regularly advertised in the *Gleaner*, with a 'final chance' to see it on 19 September 1984. Advertisements for a new touring production appear from 10 November 1988 until 7 June 1989. A video of the stage show was advertised as for sale from 20 December 1989. An advertisement published on 2 November 1990 lists *Obeah Wedding* as a Jamaican bestseller.

of Nelson Street Roman Catholic Boys School, staged a series of 'topical farces' that he wrote himself and staged at the Empire cinema in Port of Spain. One of his most successful plays was called, simply, *Obeah*, and he was sometimes referred to as 'Obeah' Roberts as a result.[102] The leading Trinidadian writer and producer of popular dialect comedy was Freddie Kissoon, whose most well-known play, *Zingay*, centred on the comic potential of obeah. *Zingay* was the first live drama performed on Trinidadian television, in 1966.[103] The action takes place in the village home of a couple, Doris and Paul, and centres on conflict between them. Seeing a mark on her son Sonny's toe, Doris believes that he has been attacked by a soucouyant and must be treated by a healer, who is sometimes referred to as an obeah man. Paul is sceptical, and wants to take Sonny to a doctor instead. Doris persuades Paul to allow the obeah man, Man Man, to come to their home, where he performs a ritual before producing a mixture that he tells Sonny to drink. Rather than drink the concoction, Sonny confesses that he hurt his toe while attempting to steal the neighbour's mangoes, and then deliberately made the injury appear like the mark of a soucouyant in order to avoid being discovered. At this point Doris turns on Man Man, who is reduced to a pathetic character and driven away.[104] As with *Obeah Wedding* and many of Bim and Bam's productions, the obeah man is pompous and exaggeratedly flamboyant. The audience is invited to enjoy his fall.

Guyanese comic theatre also referred to obeah. At the height of the controversy over Burnham's announcement of the legalization of obeah, a leading comedian, Habeeb Khan, included a prominent sketch about obeah in his annual review, trailed by press advertisements in the preceding week which promised the appearance of 'Dr Obadiah (UDO), Unofficial Doctor of Obeah, from Swindleland'. Khan's comedy played on the imagined incongruity of obeah as a legal, state-licensed profession, a comic image also picked up on by others, including a columnist who envisioned future advertisements for individuals such as 'Obediah Brown D.O. (doctor of obeah), hundreds of satisfied clients'.[105] Khan presented the obeah man as by definition a fraud, a charlatan – from

---

[102] Stone, *Theatre*, 22. Advertisements for *Obeah* ran in the *Port of Spain Gazette* from 26 April to 24 May 1936.
[103] Banham, Hill, and Woodyard, *Cambridge Guide*, 237.
[104] Kissoon, *Zingay*.
[105] Archie Codrington, 'Let's Think Hard on Obeah', *Guyana Graphic*, 11 November 1973; 'Rescuing Obeah', *Trinidad Guardian*, 3 November 1973. Similarly, a letter writer suggested a new criminal offence that might be a source of revenue for the state: the practice of obeah by those unqualified to do so. 'Obeah and Revenue', *Guyana Graphic*, 7 November 1973.

'Swindleland', a name that also evoked, in negative and stereotypical terms, an imaginary African country.

In many ways these comedies confirm Dianne Stewart's comments about the deep anti-Africanism – even 'Afrophobia' – within Jamaican (and, more broadly, African diasporic) culture.[106] The blackface of Bim and Bam suggests its complicity with a long tradition of racist comedy as well as more complex processes of masking and imitation that were part of the black-on-black minstrel tradition.[107] Certainly, audiences enjoyed laughing at elements of Caribbean culture, and by doing so emphasized their own distance from those elements. In laughter members of an audience could make community with one another, demonstrating both their awareness of and their distinction from the figure of the obeah man–charlatan, the self-righteous Rastafarian, or the over-involved Revival Mother. The very broad appeal of comedies like this – Bim and Bam were one of the few acts that could sell out the Ward Theatre – makes this a partial interpretation, however. This was knowing laughter, for a working-class Caribbean audience familiar with the subtleties of working-class Caribbean life. With dialogue largely in patois, and references to the specifics of popular religion, part of the pleasure of the Bim and Bam shows, of *Obeah Wedding*, and of *Zingay* must have been their integration with everyday working-class life, in all its complexity. The fact that working-class Jamaicans, Trinidadians, and Guyanese found jokes about obeah so funny that performers came back to them time and time again reveals that complexity. In the same way that many reports to police about suspected obeah practitioners emerged from within working-class communities and as a result of conflicts between members of those communities, yet those arrested had large and often loyal clienteles, these popular performances reveal the common-sense view that people with reputations for practising obeah were frequently self-aggrandizing or fraudulent. Such a view could without contradiction sit alongside concern about the intervention of the dead in the lives of the living, and the use of spiritual healing at moments of particular concern or crisis.

Alongside the popular comedies that aspired to mass appeal developed a Caribbean performance tradition that aspired to be taken seriously as art. 'Serious' dramatists flourished in the immediate pre-war and post-war period. Significant plays produced in the 1930s included Una Marson's *Pocomania*, whose theme was middle-class alienation and desire for connection with 'authentic' African culture.[108] After the

---

[106] Stewart, *Three Eyes*, 43–4, 179–80.   [107] Chude-Sokei, *The Last 'Darky'*.
[108] Marson, *Pocomania (a Play)*; Ford-Smith, 'Unruly Virtues'; Rosenberg, *Nationalism*, 165–80.

Second World War serious Caribbean dramatists worked to develop a genuinely Caribbean theatre, and at times debates raged about the value of using indigenous creative forms such as carnival as a basis for more formal, European-style theatre.[109] In contrast to the comedies already discussed, these plays tended to have multiple stagings, and were often produced in Britain or the USA as well as in the Caribbean; indeed, one might say the playwrights had half an eye on international audiences while writing them, even while attempting to create a national and nationalist theatre.

One of the earliest such plays was Barry Reckord's *Della*, first performed in 1953 at the Ward Theatre. It was produced in London as *Adella* in 1954, performed at the Ward again in 1958, before being produced as *Flesh to a Tiger* as one of the early plays at the Royal Court Theatre in London the same year.[110] In London it attracted significant attention, largely because of the presence of Cleo Laine in the title role, but reviews were mostly hostile.[111] Although written while Reckord was a student at Cambridge University, and clearly influenced by the contemporary social realism of the 'Angry Young Man' movement, it was advertised in Jamaica as a 'real Jamaican Theatre Night', with 'Jamaicans acting Jamaican parts ... speaking Jamaican dialect ... in a play by a Jamaican author'.[112] Set uncompromisingly in present-day Trench Town, *Della* was unusual in that it broke with the comic frame within which obeah was usually portrayed on stage. The action takes place over two days and centres on the relationships between the eponymous character, a poor, black Trench Town mother, and two powerful men. One is Shepherd Aaron, who maintains his power over his largely female flock through the brutal use of obeah to induce fear. The other is the white biomedical Doctor, known by both Shepherd Aaron and Della as White Wolf. Although Doctor initially appears more gentle and less dominating than Aaron, he also refuses to give Della what she wants, which is his love and a way out of Trench Town through a job as his servant. Instead, while desiring her and happy to have sex with her ('Your body like dark supple water draws my thirst') he refuses to kiss her on the lips, stating crudely that 'too many mouths have drooled over them'. Doctor and Shepherd compete for Della's allegiance in healing her sick baby, Tata. Their contest is also a struggle between Revivalist religion and white medicine for the wider loyalty of the Jamaican urban poor. There is no easy resolution

---

[109] Omotoso, *The Theatrical into Theatre*, 49–52.
[110] Brewster, ed., *For the Reckord*, 18.
[111] Royal Court, *Flesh to a Tiger*, Press Cuttings File, English Stage Co. Archive THM 1273/7/2/13, National Art Library, London.
[112] Advertisement for *Della*, *Gleaner*, 15 June 1954.

to this conflict, for Della is also full of rage at her poverty and exclusion by White Wolf and the uptown system he represents. The melodramatic story ends with Della killing first her child, Tata, and then the predatory Revivalist Shepherd Aaron.

*Della* presents a more complex picture of obeah than most theatrical portrayals. It did not suggest that obeah was only the specialist property of the 'obeah man'. Rather, it understands obeah as one aspect of the work of the shepherd, his balm yard, and his followers. The play endorses the standard understanding of obeah as fraudulent, but in contrast to many fictions and dramas about obeah where the exposure of the obeah man's charlatanism reconciles everything, enabling people to be liberated from its grasp, *Della* has no such happy ending. Della liberates herself from Shepherd Aaron's power, but because of Jamaica's extreme and intertwined inequalities of race, class, and gender, she is unable to ally herself with white society. Her efforts to do so fail and she ends up bitterly angry with White Wolf. The play is also written from a perspective that is resolutely hostile to Jamaican popular religion. Its 1958 production at the Ward Theatre advertised it as 'a woman's fight against obeah and a Trench Town shepherd'.[113]

Shepherd Aaron is a malign force in the play, but his power operates on a small scale. As his struggle to control Della reveals, power is slipping away from him as Jamaica moves to a more secular modernity. The play positions itself as sympathetic to Della's plight and critical of her exploitation from all sides; the audience is invited to pity her inability to escape her position. But it rejects any possibility of solutions to her situation coming from within the cultural repertoire of the Jamaican poor. In this understanding of Jamaican popular religious culture as something that must be overcome, *Della* echoed secular nationalist arguments made in more direct political commentaries.

*Della* was relatively straightforward in its form and structure. The story unfolds chronologically and is told through extensive dialogue. More formally experimental was Errol Hill's *Man Better Man*, also probably the most successful serious play in which obeah played a major part.[114] With this, which would become his best-known play, Hill extended his lifelong project of producing a Caribbean theatre that drew on the region's folk culture 'not as curiosities but as the fibre from which a national drama is fashioned'.[115] He had already written plays that focused on steel-band music and on the Chinese illegal gambling game whe-whe

---

[113] Advertisement for *Della*, *Gleaner*, 6 March 1958.
[114] Hill, ed., *Plays for Today*, 139–233.
[115] Hill, 'The Emergence of a National Drama', 34.

(Wey-wey).[116] *Man Better Man* centred on stick-fighting (kalinda), the martial art out of which Trinidad's calypso and carnival had developed. The play was initially written in prose and performed in Jamaica in 1957, while Hill was teaching at what was then the University College of the West Indies, Mona. Seeking a form that would be more authentically Caribbean, Hill in 1960 reworked the play into what would become the final version. He left the plot and structure largely unchanged, but expanded the role of the calypsonian, rewrote the dialogue in calypso verse, and added music and songs.[117] *Man Better Man's* first production in Trinidad was in 1965, and it was performed in London and Glasgow as part of the 1965 Commonwealth Arts Festival, where mainstream reviewers praised the 'blazing, electrifying feast of rhythm and colour' but did not recognize the calypso influence on the dialogue or comment on the stick-fighting theme.[118]

*Man Better Man* portrayed the seriousness of Trinidadian village life and the stick-fight as a cultural activity with deep meaning – a form of Geertzian 'deep play'. Nevertheless, it approached the religious significance of stick-fighting and the broader religious culture within which the art was embedded as a sign of village folk's foolishness and their vulnerability to manipulation. Stick-fighting, like many other martial arts of the African diaspora and elsewhere, developed within a religious framework in which the fighters sought protection and strength from ancestral spirits. As Maureen Warner-Lewis explains, 'victory in the gayelle (stickfight ring) is not achieved by physical skill alone but by magic, too – it is a contest of spirit forces'.[119] Alongside the fight, the songs of the chantwell – the predecessor of the calypsonian – carried religious force and protective power. Such protection would be mediated through a religious specialist, possibly an Orisha/Shango priest, who might be termed an obeah man.[120] In *Man Better Man* the stick-fight and calypso are authentic, serious, and worthy parts of folk culture, but their religious context is presented as illegitimate rather than intrinsic. Indeed, in the first scene the defeated fighter, Pogo, angrily denounces the champion, Tiny Satan, as a cheat and a coward because he 'fight with a mounted stick/ He had a charm, else I woulda lick/ In his flank. . . . Obeah save him from my poui.'[121] The rest of the play's action develops out of Tiny's desire to prove that he can win with any stick and does not use spiritual protection. This, then,

---

[116] Stone, *Theatre*, 24–6.    [117] Hill, ed., *Plays for Today*, 15.
[118] 'Musical Feast of Rhythm and Colour', *The Times* 1 October 1965, 15; Gerard Fay, 'Man Better Man at the Scala', *The Guardian*, 2 October 1965, 6. On the Commonwealth Arts Festival see Craggs, 'The Commonwealth Institute'.
[119] Warner-Lewis, *Guinea's Other Suns*, 177.    [120] Rohlehr, *Calypso and Society*, 52.
[121] Hill, ed., *Plays for Today*, 153.

is a secularized version of the stick-fight. In its effort to secularize 'folk culture' in order to produce a respectable, acceptable version of it *Man Better Man* exemplifies Caribbean cultural nationalism more broadly.

The illegitimacy of the spiritual protection provided to the stick-fighter is made clear by the character of Diable Papa, described in the stage directions and by multiple characters as 'obeahman'. Diable Papa is in many ways a stock obeah man, whose characterization draws on long-developed stereotypes that date back to the obeah men of the eighteenth-century stage and were reproduced in the mid-twentieth-century obeah comedies. He lives isolated in the woods, is a fraud, motivated by greed rather than genuine religious belief, and exerts power over the rest of the village through deluding them. While the ritualized conflict of the stick-fight is central to the play's action, the most important conflict of the play is not the fight between Tiny Satan and his new challenger, the inexperienced Tim Briscoe, but the fight for the villagers' allegiance between Diable Papa and Portagee Joe, the sceptical keeper of the village rum-shop. This conflict between the black obeah man and the (near) white sceptic parallels that between Shepherd Aaron and Doctor in Della, although Joe is a far more sympathetic character than Doctor. Joe, according to an opening passage in the script that describes several of the characters, is 'popular with the villagers' and 'considered one of them', but is nevertheless an outsider, having come to Trinidad from Madeira.[122] As a 'Portagee' he is not precisely white, but nevertheless in Trinidad's racial hierarchy stands above the black and Indian Trinidadians who make up the rest of the village community. Joe, the village atheist and racial outsider, provides the moral heart of the play. At the beginning, only he sees through Diable Papa's claims to magical power. In Act 3 it is he who leads the villagers to understand that Diable Papa has deceived them, that he is the 'faker behind the fraud'.[123] In emphasizing Joe's ability to understand what the villagers cannot, and lead them to higher consciousness, *Man Better Man*, even while aiming to produce an indigenous Caribbean aesthetic, reinforces the existing racial order.

Where *Della* flowed from Barry Reckord's secular socialist politics, *Man Better Man* represents Hill's cultural nationalist viewpoint in which progress for the nation is gained through valuing and promoting a secularized version of the region's arts and culture. Portagee Joe's line in the final scene precisely represents this perspective: 'Superstition is a rope round the neck/ Of the village, choking your intellect'.[124] Spoken by the sympathetic, generous, and wise Joe, this line can be taken to represent Hill's authorial perspective: the village constitutes a microcosm of the

[122] Ibid., 146.   [123] Ibid., 212.   [124] Ibid., 228.

Caribbean nation, which also needs to remove its neck from the rope of superstition in order to move forward into independence. By the end of the play Crackerjack, speaking for the whole village, praises Briscoe for his 'lion courage' in 'rescu[ing] the game [of stick-fighting]/ From obeah, greed and politics, and you give it back to the poui sticks.'[125] Importantly, obeah is here linked to the negative side of 'politics' – the kind that would be labelled 'politricks' by Rastafarians – in a denunciatory discourse that was becoming increasingly common in the independence era.

Nevertheless, even within the play, 'superstition' is not totally vanquished. There is plenty of room for audiences to dispute Joe's point of view, and to read the villagers' beliefs as more than just foolishness. Diable Papa's ritual is shown with much greater seriousness than is Shepherd Aaron's in *Della*: Papa's assistant Minee becomes possessed, apparently genuinely, and speaks in tongues. Both Minee and Diable Papa invoke Yoruba orishas, including Damballa, Shango, and Ogun. These rituals are thus more than cues for mockery and laughter, and are not simply generic depictions of obeah. In invoking the orishas, they show the locatedness of the obeah practice within Trinidad, and they draw on Hill's knowledge of Trinidadian forms of spiritual healing. Moreover, even Diable Papa's openly fraudulent spiritual work might be understood as at least partially effective. Tim Briscoe's failure to defeat Tiny Satan in the stick-fight could be not because the obeah did not work but because he lied to Diable Papa about his opponent, pretending that he wanted protection in a contest with a novice stick-fighter rather than the champion. Moreoever, Briscoe's initial request to Diable Papa was not for victory in the fight per se but for ritual help to win the love of Lily, the 'belle of the village', and he does in the end gain this, albeit in defeat rather than in victory.[126] Thus audiences might conclude that some genuine spiritual power had intervened, perhaps in the art of the more sympathetic figure Minee, rather than the villainous Diable Papa. Finally, the village community's interpretation of illness and healing beliefs could also be understood sympathetically. When Briscoe lies seriously ill, having been wounded in the stick-fight and cursed by Diable Papa, characters suggest burning candles, using an aloes plaster, snake-oil, turning a broom upside down, scattering salt on the floor, putting a cross on the door, and calling for 'Cassirip, the old sorcerer'. Lily declares that she has 'explore[d] every piece of science in the book' to heal Briscoe.[127] Joe attacks this approach and runs to fetch a 'real' doctor, but in the end Briscoe gets up and walks away to vanquish Diable Papa before Joe returns. Thus although the play pits Joe's biomedicine against the community's 'science', Briscoe is in fact

[125] Ibid., 232.   [126] Ibid., 151, 163.   [127] Ibid., 208.

successfully healed without biomedical intervention. The script suggests that Briscoe's consumption of 96 per cent proof imported Barbadian rum has done the trick, but audiences might well read the spiritual ministrations of Briscoe's sister Inez and newly won lover Lily as effective healing agents. Hill's script therefore leaves open the possibility of a relatively sympathetic understanding of the religious context of the Caribbean folk culture the play depicts, even while its overt message traces a direct line back to hostile and mocking colonial depictions of obeah as nothing more than foolish superstition.

'Serious' Caribbean writers who represented obeah framed their stories around predatory obeah men, who were generally much more threatening, because more powerful, than the comic obeah men. Representations of obeah, or at least its practitioners, on stage appeared to lead inevitably to the predator, the comic fraud, or both. Yet other Caribbean playwrights did struggle to present the intervention of the dead in the life of the living, and the world of religious ritual that was bound up with obeah, in dramatic form without either mocking it or presenting it as malign. To do so, however, they turned away from the direct representation of obeah itself.

The most significant example of this form of dramatic representation of obeah is Dennis Scott's *An Echo in the Bone*, first produced by the Drama Society at the University of the West Indies, Mona, in 1974.[128] *Echo* stands out from the other plays discussed here in its use of tragedy rather than comedy or melodrama, its formal complexity, and the challenges that it presents for an audience. As it opens the central character, Rachel, is preparing for the Nine Night memorial for Crew, her husband. Crew is missing and presumed to be dead, having just killed the local white landowner, Mr Charles. Early in the play the theme of the dead reappearing through and intervening in the lives of the living is introduced, as Crew and Rachel's son Sonson is possessed by his father's spirit at the Nine Night. The action then moves to a series of scenes that take place in earlier times, moving back and forth between the near past and the distant past: a slave ship; the village shop two days ago; the office of a slave auctioneer in 1820; a confrontation between a Maroon and white man in 1833; in Rachel's home four years earlier as she rebuffs Mr Charles's advances; at a Great House on the eve of the end of slavery in 1834; on the estate the previous Monday as Crew confronts Mr Charles who has diverted the river that previously watered his land, and is turned away and insulted;

---

[128] Scott, *Echo*. For critical analysis of the play see Thieme, 'Repossessing the Slave Past'; Juneja, 'Recalling the Dead'; Balme, *Decolonizing the Stage*; Batra, *Feminist Visions and Queer Futures*, 29–46.

and finally, in the immediate aftermath of Crew's killing Mr Charles. These fragmented scenes reveal the larger history that leads up to Crew's actions. History is shown to work on both a local, short-term scale – the appropriation of resources by Mr Charles, and the assumption of sexual power by Charles over Rachel and his angry response to her eventual ability to reject him – and on a deeper-time, Atlantic-world scale – the continuing reverberations of slavery and the complex relationships it established. The play deals with big, serious themes: the quiet desperation of the poor peasant; the familial conflict generated by the crowded lives of poor people; the continuing power relationship between white landowner and black women and men, despite the end of slavery.

*An Echo in the Bone* is deeply engaged with African Caribbean religious culture, which it presents as normal and unremarkable; it is the common sense of the world that the characters inhabit. By setting the play within a Nine Night ritual and staging Sonson's possession, Scott emphasizes early on the presence of the dead in the lives of the living. The subsequent performance of scenes that take place chronologically earlier within this frame makes them more than 'flashbacks'; rather, these people from the past are truly with us in the present. This is also emphasized by the fact that in order to act the parts of the play set in other times characters change roles while continuing to inhabit their initial characters. The script continues to index their lines with the original character's name. The implication is that theatre itself is a form of, or a metaphor for, possession.[129] The play thus presents a key cosmological principle of African Caribbean religion – the idea that the spirits of the dead can and do act in the living human world – as a serious way of understanding the human condition. This is a principle on which obeah, in the sense of spiritual action involving the intervention of the dead, depends. Nevertheless, Scott does not make any specific reference to obeah in the play, even though the possession that takes place within it would be conceptually linked to obeah for many in its audience. In his effort to move the representation of African Caribbean religion into the realm of the serious and away from the comic or melodramatic, Scott chose to avoid the representation of obeah activity as such. Indeed, it seems that obeah could not be represented within a framework that presented African Caribbean religion seriously. It was so closely discursively linked to manipulation, domination, and fraud that it could not be rehabilitated or even addressed in the context of a play like this. The same is true of other serious theatrical efforts to represent Caribbean folk culture or

---

[129] This is a theme discussed in more depth in Balme, *Decolonizing the Stage*, 91–4, and, specifically in relation to *An Echo in the Bone*, at 100–1.

religious culture from this period, such as Sylvia Wynter's *Maskarade*, which focuses on Jonkanoo, or Rawle Gibbons's *Shepherd*, which depicts the Spiritual Baptist mourning ritual.[130]

This chapter has turned to theatre as a site for the playing out of post-colonial debates about obeah, and more broadly, the value of African Caribbean religion. Such theatre, even when strongly culturally nationalist, was not, as some critics have suggested, straightforwardly anti-imperialist.[131] Rather, it negotiated with and attempted to mediate layers of inherited scorn and pride with regard to obeah, the central site for the representation of the Caribbean's link to Africa. Such debates took place in other areas of post-colonial life too, and could be extremely complex, as the use of obeah symbolism in the service of the authoritarian regimes of Forbes Burnham and Eric Gairy show most dramatically. Despite the rapid decline of prosecution for obeah in the independence period, it remained a crucial symbol throughout the region, a means by which relationships of power were contested and maintained.

[130] Gibbons, 'Shepherd'; Wynter, *Maskarade*.   [131] Savory, 'Strategies for Survival'.

# Conclusion

Today, obeah remains a source of possible harm for many in the Caribbean, as well as a site of embarrassment and anxiety for some. In contrast to more clearly defined religions such as Vodou, regla de ocho/santería, Revival, Spiritual Baptism, or Orisha Worship, obeah lacks the affiliated public intellectuals who will act as its advocates and defenders. This should come as no surprise. The story of the cultural politics of obeah across more than two centuries that this book has told shows that obeah has from its earliest appearance been as much an artefact of colonial law and the colonial imagination as it has been a coherent, self-defined religious or healing formation. The term obeah has been used to criminalize and to stigmatize the real healing practices associated with many Caribbean religions, and has been a means by which a multitude of specific religious identities have been hidden under a single, hostile, term. The specifics of anti-obeah law have shifted, and in the recent past in some parts of the region it has been entirely decriminalized. Despite this, throughout the whole period discussed in this book, the weight of the negative construction of ordinary aspects of Caribbean religion, through their designation as obeah, has borne down on people going about their everyday religious lives.

Scholarly knowledge of obeah has been deeply entangled with its prohibition and with popular hostility to it. Attacks on obeah practitioners became means by which individuals who made up the everyday state, particularly policemen, could differentiate themselves from the mass of the population, and achieve professional advancement. In doing so, these everyday state agents also contributed substantially to state knowledge of obeah, which, in the longer term, informed scholarly knowledge too, not least in the form of the evidence from obeah trials on which this book draws. This book, then, tells not the history of obeah itself, but of the swirling layers of representation that surround it.

The history of obeah is entangled in complex ways with the history of autonomous Caribbean religions such as myal, Revival, the Spiritual Baptist religion, and Orisha Worship. These organic religions conducted healing rituals as integral parts of their practice. Their healing techniques were routinely described as obeah, not just by state authorities but also by ordinary people who were not affiliated with them. Such description served to differentiate those doing the naming from the religions in question, which have largely been associated with the poor. Adherents of these religions were adamant that what they did was not obeah. Indeed, they understood much of their healing practice as designed to combat obeah. Obeah thus became an ever-receding object of suspicion and danger, a process which has made attitudes towards it difficult to change. Yet the many and various practices and belief that have been invoked by the encompassing term 'obeah' are all part of the range of beliefs found in any society, not something that marks out the Caribbean as particular or unusual.

The prohibition of and hostility to obeah has not just been about religion. It has also been, as Kei Miller argues, about policing the Caribbean's symbolic connection to Africa: its blackness.[1] During slavery and for some time after, the primary dynamic of this policing was colonial and racial. It was between colonized and colonizer, black and white. Representations of obeah became a central means by which the Caribbean was condemned as savage and backward. The all-too-real terror and harm of slavery became symbolically inverted through stories about the supernatural terror and harm inflicted by obeah practitioners. From the late nineteenth century on, this dynamic shifted. Obeah became less well known internationally, and during the years of the US occupation of Haiti was displaced by 'Voodoo' as a signifier for African Caribbean backwardness. Hostility to obeah became centred within the Caribbean region, and its primary dynamic shifted to one in which religion, class, and race were deeply intertwined. Claims to respectability came to be tied to the rejection of obeah. Such rejection was often particularly important to people whose assertions of respectability were most precarious. Even some of those who overtly and politically embraced Africa often rejected obeah, Africa's symbolic manifestation in the Caribbean, as a sign of the poor, the black, the uncivilized, and the non-modern. The ongoing hostility to and rejection of obeah reflects, perhaps most of all, the distance between classes in the Anglo-Creole Caribbean.

Hostility to obeah is not, though, simply the preserve of the elite or the middle class. Rather, it taps into broader fears about competition and lack of solidarity that may not be more acute in the Caribbean than

---

[1] Kei Miller, 'The Banning of the Drums', or 'How to be a Good Nigger in Jamaica', *Under the Saltire Flag* 13 July 2014, http://underthesaltireflag.com/2014/07/13/the-banning-of-the-drums-or-how-to-be-a-good-nigger-in-jamaica.

in other societies, but are certainly an everyday presence there. The slippage between the (at least) double meanings of obeah – as dangerous power that might be mobilized against one, and as a catch-all term for religious-oriented cultural forms associated with the poor and with Africa – is at the heart of this phenomenon. Pervasive concern about what my neighbour might do to me has been harnessed over centuries so that rejection of obeah in both senses works effectively to maintain class and race relationships in the contemporary Caribbean.

# Bibliography

ARCHIVAL SOURCES

GUYANA

Cheddi Jagan Research Centre, Georgetown
  Articles by Cheddi Jagan, 1973 (two files)

JAMAICA

African Caribbean Institute of Jamaica, Kingston
  Mr Charles Joseph Stuart, transcript of interview with Hazel Ramsay-McClune, 28 October 1992, Memory Bank, Tape 1369-3
Institute of Jamaica, Kingston
  'Of Things Sacred', unpublished catalogue
  'Of Things Sacred' files
Jamaica Archives, Spanish Town
  Hanover Slave Court, Hanover Courts Office, Lucea, 1A/2/1/1
  Scrap Book 1894–1901 kept by John Henry McCrea, Deputy Inspector General of Police, 7/97/3
  St Ann Vestry Orders, Local Government 2/9/1
  St Thomas in the Vale, Vestry Minutes, Local Government 2/1, 1
National Library of Jamaica, Kingston
  Frank Cundall, 'The British West Indies To-day', unpublished manuscript, MS934
  Clippings File – Obeah and Voodoo

UNITED KINGDOM

British Library, London, Manuscripts Division
  Add Ms 12431 Miscellaneous Papers and original Letters relating to the affairs of Jamaica
  Add Ms 12432: Report of the Committee of the Assembly of Jamaica on the Slave Trade (printed), 1792, with letters to Mr Long on the subject
  Add Ms 36499: 1801–June 1804. Reverend Richard Denison Cumberland: Correspondence with his brother George
  Add Ms 38416: Liverpool Papers Vol. 127: Papers relating to the slave trade, 1787–1823

Add Ms 51819: The Holland House Papers. Jamaica: General Papers
Cambridge University Library
   Sir Henry Hesketh Bell Collection, Royal Commonwealth Society Library GBR/0115/RCMS 36
Liverpool University Library, Special Collections and Archives
   Papers of Professor Lord Simey of Toxteth and Dr Margaret Simey (1836–2003) D396
National Library of Scotland, Edinburgh
   Nisbet Papers, Ms 5466
National Archives, London
   Board of Trade (BT) 6/10, 6/12
   Colonial Office (CO): multiple files
   Foreign and Commonwealth Office (FCO) 141/5473: Banning of Undesirable Publications
   Treasury (T) 1/3482 Berbice, Winkel Department (Slavery)
School of Oriental and African Studies, Library, Archives, and Special Collections
   Council of World Missions Archives, British Guiana–Berbice, Incoming Correspondence, 1813–50
National Art Library, London
   Press Cuttings File, English Stage Co. Archive THM 1273/7/2/13

UNITED STATES OF AMERICA

Northwestern University Archives, Evanston, Illinois
   Melville J. Herskovits Papers, Series 35/6
Schomburg Center for Research in Black Culture, New York
   Melville and Frances Herskovits Papers, MG 261

## NEWSPAPERS AND PERIODICALS

*Advocate-News* (Barbados), 1973
*Annual Reports of the Superintending Medical Officer*, Jamaica
*Antigua Standard*, 1904
*Daily Chronicle* (Guyana), 1973
*Daily Gleaner* and *Sunday Gleaner* (Jamaica), newspaperarchive.com, 1890–1989
*Falmouth Post* (Jamaica), 1850–64
*Grenada Newsletter*, Digital Library of the Caribbean, available at http://ufdc.ufl.edu/AA00000053/00195/allvolumes
*Guyana Graphic*, 1973
*New Nation* (Guyana), 1973
*Plain Talk* (Jamaica), 1938
*Port of Spain Gazette* (Trinidad and Tobago), 1890–1940
*Royal Gazette* (Jamaica), 1791–2
*Sunday Chronicle* (Guyana), 1973
*The Times* (London), 1911, 1965
*Trinidad Guardian*, 1973
*Thunder: Quarterly Theoretical and Discussion Journal of the People's Progressive Party*, 1974

## PUBLIC DOCUMENTS

Calendar of State Papers Colonial, America and West Indies, Volume 38: 1731 (1938), no. 25

*Parliamentary Papers* 1789 (70), A Statement of the Laws at Large, Respecting Negroes in the West India Islands

*Parliamentary Papers* 1789, Report of the Lords of the Committee of Council appointed to the Consideration of all Matters relating to Trade and Foreign Plantations: submitting to his Majesty's consideration the evidence and information they have collected in consequence of his Majesty's Order in Council, dated the 11th of February 1788, concerning the present State of the Trade to Africa, and particularly the Trade in Slaves; and concerning the Effects and Consequences of this Trade, as well in Africa and the West Indies, as to the general Commerce of this Kingdom

*Parliamentary Papers* 1814–15 (478) vii, Papers relating to the West Indies

*Parliamentary Papers* 1823 (348) xviii, Trial of a Slave in Berbice, for the Crime of Obeah and Murder: Return to an Address to His Majesty, by the Honourable House of Commons, dated 29th of July 1822; for Copy of any Information which may have been received concerning the Trial of a Slave, for the Crime of Obeah, in the Colony of Berbice

*Parliamentary Papers* 1825 (66) xxv, Papers relating to the manumission, government and population of slaves in the West Indies, 1822–1824

*Parliamentary Papers* 1825 (476) xxv, Further papers relating to slaves in the West Indies. (Berbice)

*Parliamentary Papers* 1826–7 (36) xxiv, Third report of the commissioner of inquiry into the administration of civil and criminal justice in the West Indies. Antigua, Montserrat, Nevis, St. Christopher, and the Virgin Islands

*Parliamentary Papers* 1830–1 (262) xv, Copy of any Reports which may have been received from the Protectors of Slaves ... Part II: Berbice

*Parliamentary Papers* 1836 (166-I) xlviii, Papers ... in explanation of the measures adopted by His Majesty's government, for giving effect to the act for the abolition of slavery throughout the British colonies

*Parliamentary Papers* 1839 (107-I) xxv, Papers Relative to the West Indies. Part I. Circular Instructions, Jamaica and British Guiana

*West India Royal Commission Report, presented by the Secretary of State for the Colonies to Parliament by Command of His Majesty.* London: HMSO, 1945

## MISCELLANEOUS ONLINE SOURCES

Album of Anti-Slavery News Cuttings, 1824–6, Merseyside Maritime Museum D/CR/13, in *Slavery, Abolition and Social Justice* (online collection) (Marlborough: Adam Matthews Digital, 2007), available at www.slavery.amdigital.co.uk/Contents/DocumentDetails.aspx?documentid=45443&prevPos=45443&vpath=Default&pi=2

Bishop, Maurice, 'Fascism – A Caribbean Reality', text of speech given on 17 October 1975 in Trinidad at the Oilfield Workers Trade Union

Leadership Seminar, The Grenada Revolution Online, available at www.thegrenadarevolutiononline.com/bishspkfascism.html

Brown, Vincent. 'Slave Revolt in Jamaica, 1760–61: A Cartographic Narrative', available at http://revolt.axismaps.com/project.html

Burney Collection newspapers, seventeenth–eighteenth centuries, online, available at http://find.galegroup.com/bncn/infomark.do?page=BasicSearch&userGroupName=new_itw&prodId=BBCN&type=static&version=1.0&source=gale

Cox, Jeffrey N. 'Theatrical Forms, Ideological Conflicts, and the Staging of Obi'. Romantic Circles Praxis Series, available at www.rc.umd.edu/praxis/obi/cox/cox.html

Fawcett, John. 'Obi, or, Three-Finger'd Jack! a serio-pantomime, in two acts'. Romantic Circles Praxis Series, available at www.rc.umd.edu/praxis/obi/

Gardelin Slave code, 5 September 1733, English translation available at www.eurescl.eu/images/files_wp3/danishregulations/17330905.pdf

Hughes, Alister, Untitled and undated book manuscript, available at http://grenadabroadcast.net/pastshows/Alister%27s%20book

Maragh, G. G. (Leonard Howell), *The Promised Key* (c. 1935), available at www.sacred-texts.com/afr/tpk/

Mighty Sparrow, 'Wanted Dead or Alive', lyrics available at http://musicandmessage.pbworks.com/w/page/615124/Wanted%20Dead%20or%20Alive%20-%20Lyrics%20and%20Project%20Outline

Murray, William Henry Wood. 'Obi; or, Three-Finger'd Jack. A Melo-drama in Two Acts'. Romantic Circles Praxis Series, available at www.rc.umd.edu/praxis/obi/

'Natty Dread in the PRA', recording available on youtube at www.youtube.com/watch?v = orWApKB0qYw; lyrics available at www.thegrenadarevolutiononline.com/page14a.html

Paton, Diana. 'Histories of Three-Fingered Jack: A Bibliography', available at www.brycchancarey.com/slavery/tfj/

Pettersburg, Fitz Ballantine *The Royal Parchment Scroll of Black Supremacy* (1926), available at www.sacred-texts.com/afr/rps/

*Report of the Duffus Commission of Inquiry into the Breakdown of Law and Order, and Police Brutality in Grenada* (Grenada: The Commission, 1975). Digital Library of the Caribbean, available at http://ufdc.ufl.edu/AA00010419/00001

Rzepka, Charles. 'Obi Now'. Romantic Circles Praxis Series, available at www.rc.umd.edu/praxis/obi/

## UNPUBLISHED DISSERTATIONS AND CONFERENCE PAPERS

Anderson, Claudette Andrea. 'Gnostic Obia from Chukwu Abiama to Jah Rastafari: A Theology of the JamAfrica Obia Catholic Church'. Unpublished Ph.D. dissertation, Emory University, 2010.

Bollettino, Maria Alessandra. 'Slavery, War, and Britain's Atlantic Empire: Black Soldiers, Sailors, and Rebels in the Seven Years' War'. Unpublished Ph.D. dissertation, University of Texas at Austin, 2009.

Browne, Randy. 'Slavery and the Politics of Marriage in Berbice, 1819–1834'. Paper presented at the Annual Conference of the Association of Caribbean Historians, Martinique, 11–16 May 2014.

Forde, Maarit. 'Religious Persecution from Below: Colonial Police and Ritual Specialists in Trinidad, 1900–1930'. Paper presented at the Annual Conference of the Caribbean Studies Association, Barbados, 24–28 May 2010.

Hill, Robert A. 'Marcus Garvey and the Discourse of Obeah'. Paper presented at the conference 'Obeah and Other Powers', Newcastle University, July 2008.

Hogg, Donald W. 'Jamaican Religions: A Study in Variations'. Unpublished Ph.D. Dissertation, Yale University, 1964.

Mischel, Frances Osterman. 'A Shango Religious Group and the Problem of Prestige in Trinidadian Society'. Unpublished Ph.D. Dissertation, Ohio State University, 1958.

Moore, Joseph. 'Religion of Jamaican Negroes: A Study of Afro-American Acculturation'. Unpublished Ph.D. Dissertation, Northwestern University, 1953.

Paul, Maritza Adriana. '"Bad Name Worse Dan Obeah": The Representation of Women and Obeah in Caribean Oral and Written Literatures'. Unpublished Ph.D. dissertation, University of Colorado, 2000.

Putnam, Lara. 'T. S. Simey's Anonymous Interlocutors: Local Intelligentsia and the Transnational Pathologization of the Black Family'. Paper presented at the Annual Conference of the Society for Caribbean Studies 38th Annual Conference, Glasgow, 2–4 July 2014.

Quinn, Katherine. 'Governing National Cultures in the Caribbean: Culture and the State in Castro's Cuba and Burnham's Guyana c.1959–c.1989'. Unpublished Ph.D. Dissertation, University College London, 2005.

Robertson, James. 'The Experience and Imagination of a Slave Revolt: An Uprising in St Mary's Parish, Jamaica, in 1765'. Unpublished paper in author's possession, n.d.

BOOKS AND ARTICLES

Abrahams, Roger D. *The Man-of-Words in the West Indies: Performance and the Emergence of Creole Culture*. Baltimore: Johns Hopkins University Press, 1983.

Adair, James M. *Unanswerable Arguments against the Abolition of the Slave Trade, with a defence of the Proprietors of the British Sugar Colonies, against certain malignant charges contained in letters published by a Sailor, and by Luffman, Newton &c. Remarks on the dispositions and characters of the African slaves; and means suggested for the distribution of their labour; the regulation of their habitations, foods, cloathing, and religious instruction; the accommodation of the sick, and cure of their diseases; which may be most conducive to render them Faithful, Obedient, and Happy.* London: J. P. Bateman, n.d. [1790].

Alexander, Joseph. *Recollections of a Trinidad Detective*. n.p. [Port of Spain]: n.p. [Trinidad], n.d. [1920].

Alleyne, Mervyn. *Roots of Jamaican Culture*. London: Pluto Press, 1988.

Allsopp, Richard, ed. *Dictionary of Caribbean English Usage*. Oxford: Oxford University Press, 1996.

Anstey, Roger. *The Atlantic Slave Trade and British Abolition 1760–1810*. London: Macmillan, 1975.

Aravamudan, Srinivas. 'Introduction'. In *Obi or, The History of Three-Fingered Jack by William Earle*, edited by Aravamudan, Srinivas. 7–51. Peterborough, Ontario: Broadview Editions, 2005.

Atwood, Thomas. *The History of the Island of Dominica, containing a description of its situation, extent, climate, mountains, rivers, natural productions, &c, &c.* London: J. Johnson, 1791.

Austen, Ralph A. 'The Moral Economy of Witchcraft: An Essay in Comparative History'. In *Modernity and its Malcontents: Ritual and Power in Postcolonial Africa*, edited by Comaroff, Jean and John Comaroff. 89–110. Chicago: University of Chicago Press, 1993.

Austin-Broos, Diane J. *Jamaica Genesis: Religion and the Politics of Moral Order.* Chicago: University of Chicago Press, 1997.

Ayala, César J. *American Sugar Kingdom: The Plantation Economy of the Spanish Caribbean, 1898–1934.* Chapel Hill: University of North Carolina Press, 1999.

Bakan, Abigail B. *Ideology and Class Conflict in Jamaica: The Politics of Rebellion.* Montreal and Kingston: McGill-Queen's University Press, 1990.

Balme, Christopher B. *Decolonizing the Stage: Theatrical Syncretism and Post-Colonial Drama.* Oxford: Clarendon Press, 1999.

Banbury, Thomas R. *Jamaica Superstitions; or the Obeah Book: A Complete Treatise of the Absurdities Believed in by the People of the Island.* Kingston: DeSouza, 1894.

Banham, Martin, Errol Hill, and George Woodyard. *The Cambridge Guide to African and Caribbean Theatre.* Cambridge: Cambridge University Press, 1994.

Barclay, Alexander. *A practical view of the present state of slavery in the West Indies: or, an examination of Mr. Stephen's 'Slavery of the British West India colonies': containing more particularly an account of the actual condition of the negroes in Jamaica: with observations on the decrease of the slaves since the abolition of the slave trade, and on the probable effects of legislative emancipation: also, strictures on the Edinburgh Review, and on the pamphlets of Mr. Cooper and Mr. Bicknell.* London: Smith, Elder & Co, 1826.

Barrett, Leonard. 'The Portrait of a Jamaican Healer: African Medical Lore in the Caribbean'. *Caribbean Quarterly* 19, no. 3 (1973): 6–19.

Batra, Kanika. *Feminist Visions and Queer Futures in Postcolonial Drama.* London: Routledge, 2011.

Baum, Robert M., *Shrines of the Slave Trade: Diola Religion and Society in Precolonial Senegambia.* Oxford: Oxford University Press, 1999.

Baxter, Ivy. *Jamaica: The Arts of an Island.* Metuchen, NJ: Scarecrow Press, 1970.

Beattie, John. *Crime and the Courts in England 1660–1800.* Oxford: Clarendon Press, 1986.

Beck, Jane. 'The Implied Obeah Man'. *Western Folklore* 35, no. 1 (1976): 23–33.

Beckles, Hilary M. *A History of Barbados: From Amerindian Settlement to Caribbean Single Market.* Cambridge: Cambridge University Press, 2006.

Beckwith, Martha. *Black Roadways: A Study of Jamaican Folk Life.* Chapel Hill: University of North Carolina Press, 1929.

*Jamaica Folk-Lore.* New York: American Folk-Lore Society, 1928.

Beidelman, T. O. *The Culture of Colonialism: The Cultural Subjection of Ukaguru*. Bloomington: Indiana University Press, 2012.

Bell, Hesketh J. *Obeah: Witchcraft in the West Indies*. London: Sampson Low, Marston, Searle & Riving, 1889.

Benn, Denis. *The Caribbean: An Intellectual History 1774–2003*. Kingston: Ian Randle, 2004.

Benoit, Oliver. 'Ressentiment and the Gairy Social Revolution'. *Small Axe* 22 (2007): 95–122.

Besson, Jean. *Martha Brae's Two Histories: European Expansion and Caribbean Culture-Building in Jamaica*. Chapel Hill: University of North Carolina Press, 2002.

Bewell, Alan, ed. *Medicine and the West Indian Slave Trade*. Vol. VII of *Slavery, Abolition, and Emancipation: Writings in the British Romantic Period*, edited by Lee, Deborah and Peter Kitson. London: Pickering & Chatto, 1999.

Bilby, Kenneth. 'An (Un)natural Mystic in the Air: Images of Obeah in Caribbean Song'. In *Obeah and Other Powers: The Politics of Caribbean Religion and Healing*, edited by Paton, Diana and Maarit Forde. 45–79. Durham: Duke University Press, 2012.

*True-Born Maroons*. Gainesville: University Press of Florida, 2005.

Bilby, Kenneth M., and Jerome S. Handler. 'Obeah: Healing and Protection in West Indian Slave Life'. *Journal of Caribbean History* 38 (2004): 153–83.

Blackburn, Robin. *The Overthrow of Colonial Slavery, 1776–1848*. London: Verso, 1988.

Blay, Yaba Amgborale. 'Obeah'. In *Encyclopedia of the African Diaspora: Origins, Experiences, and Culture*, edited by Davies, Carole Boyce. 725–6. Santa Barbara: ABC Clio, 2008.

Blouet, Olwyn. 'Bryan Edwards, FRS, 1743–1800'. *Notes and Records of the Royal Society* 54, no. 2 (2000): 215–22.

Bohls, Elizabeth. 'The Gentleman Planter and the Metropole: Long's History of Jamaica'. In *The Country and the City Revisited: England and the Politics of Culture, 1560–1840*, edited by Landry, Donna, Gerald MacLean, and Joseph Ward. 180–96. Cambridge: Cambridge University Press, 1999.

*Romantic Literature and Postcolonial Studies*. Edinburgh: Edinburgh University Press, 2013.

Bolland, O. Nigel. *The Politics of Labour in the British Caribbean: The Social Origins of Authoritarianism and Democracy in the Labour Movement*. Kingston: Ian Randle, 2001.

Bosman, Willem. *A New and Accurate Description of the Coast of Guinea: Divided into the Gold, the Slave, and the Ivory Coasts*. London: Frank Cass, 1967. [1704].

Bostridge, Ian. *Witchcraft and its Transformations, c. 1650-c. 1750*. Oxford: Oxford University Press, 1997.

'Witchcraft Repealed'. In *Witchcraft in Early Modern Europe: Studies in Culture and Belief*, edited by Barry, Jonathan, Marianne Hester, and Gareth Roberts. 309–34. Cambridge: Cambridge University Press, 1996.

Botkin, Frances R. 'Questioning the "Necessary Order of Things": Maria Edgeworth's "The Grateful Negro", Plantation Slavery, and the Abolition of the

Slave Trade'. In *Discourses of Slavery and Abolition: Britain and its Colonies, 1760–1838,* edited by Carey, Brycchan, Markman Ellis, and Sara Salih. 194–208. Basingstoke: Palgrave Macmillan, 2004.

'Revising the Colonial Caribbean: "Three-Fingered Jack" and the Jamaican Pantomime'. *Callaloo* 35, no. 2 (2012): 494–508.

Boulukos, George. *The Grateful Slave: The Emergence of Race in Eighteenth-Century British and American Culture.* Cambridge: Cambridge University Press, 2008.

'Maria Edgeworth's "Grateful Negro" and the Sentimental Argument for Slavery'. *Eighteenth-Century Life* 23, no. 1 (1999): 12–29.

Brathwaite, Edward Kamau. *The Development of Creole Society in Jamaica, 1770–1820.* Oxford: Clarendon Press, 1971.

'The African Presence in Caribbean Literature'. *Daedalus* 103, no. 2 (1974): 73–109.

Brereton, Bridget. 'Haiti and the Haitian Revolution in the Political Discourse of Nineteenth-Century Trinidad'. In *Reinterpreting the Haitian Revolution and its Cultural Aftershocks,* edited by Munro, Martin and Elizabeth Walcott-Hackshaw. 123–49. Mona, Jamaica: University of the West Indies Press, 2006.

*A History of Modern Trinidad, 1783–1962.* London: Heinemann, 1982.

'John Jacob Thomas: An Estimate'. *Journal of Caribbean History* 8–9 (1977): 22–42.

*Race Relations in Colonial Trinidad, 1870–1900.* Cambridge: Cambridge University Press, 1979.

Brereton, Bridget, Rhonda Cobham, Mary Rimmer, and Lisa Winer. 'Introduction'. In E. L. Joseph, *Warner Arundell: The Adventures of a Creole.* xi–lii. Kingston: University of the West Indies Press, 2001.

Brewster, Yvonne, ed. *For the Reckord: A Collection of Three Plays by Barry Reckord.* London: Oberon Books, 2010.

Bristol, Joan Cameron. *Christians, Blasphemers, and Witches: Afro-Mexican Ritual Practice in the Seventeenth Century.* Albuquerque: University of New Mexico Press, 2007.

Brodber, Erna. 'Brief Notes on DeLaurence in Jamaica'. *ACIJ Research Review* 4 (1999): 91–9.

Brown, David H. *Santería Enthroned: Art, Ritual, and Innovation in an Afro-Cuban Religion.* Chicago: University of Chicago Press, 2003.

Brown, Vincent. *The Reaper's Garden: Death and Power in the World of Atlantic Slavery.* Cambridge, Mass.: Harvard University Press, 2008.

'Spiritual Terror and Sacred Authority in Jamaican Slave Society'. *Slavery and Abolition* 24, no. 1 (2003): 24–53.

Browne, Randy. 'The "Bad Business" of Obeah: Power, Authority, and the Politics of Slave Culture in the British Caribbean'. *William and Mary Quarterly* 68, no. 3 (2011): 451–80.

Bryan, Patrick. *The Jamaican People 1880–1902: Race, Class and Social Control.* London: Macmillan Caribbean, 1991.

Burdett, William. *Life and exploits of Mansong, commonly called Three-finger'd Jack, the terror of Jamaica: with a particular account of the Obi; being the only true one of that celebrated and fascinating mischief so prevalent in the West Indies*. 3rd edn. London: A. Neil, 1800.

Burnard, Trevor. *Mastery, Tyranny, and Desire: Thomas Thistlewood and his Slaves in the Anglo-Jamaican World*. Chapel Hill: University of North Carolina Press, 2004.

Burnham, L. F. S. *The Case of Pedro Beria: Statement by the Hon L. F. S. Burnham, Q.C., Prime Minister, at a Special Broadcast Press Conference held on Saturday, November 30, 1968*. Georgetown: Government Printery, 1968. [pamphlet]

Burton, Richard D. E. *Afro-Creole: Power, Opposition, and Play in the Caribbean*. Ithaca: Cornell University Press, 1997.

Bush, Barbara. 'Defiance or Submission? The Role of the Slave Woman in Slave Resistance in the British Caribbean'. In *'We Specialize in the Wholly Impossible': A Reader in Black Women's History*, edited by Hine, Darlene Clark, Wilma King, and Linda Reed. Brooklyn. 147–69. New York: Carlson Publishing, 1995.

*Slave Women in Caribbean Society 1650–1838*. London: James Currey, 1990.

Byrd, Alexander X. *Captives and Voyagers: Black Migrants across the Eighteenth-Century British Atlantic World*. Baton Rouge: Louisiana State University Press, 2008.

Campbell, John. *Obeah: Yes or No? A Study of Obeah and Spiritualism in Guyana*. Georgetown, Guyana: Labour Advocate Job Printing Department, n.d. [1976].

Candlin, Kit. *The Last Caribbean Frontier, 1795–1815*. Basingstoke: Palgrave, 2012.

Canfield, Rob. 'Theatralizing the Anglophone Caribbean, 1492 to the 1980s'. In *A History of Literature in the Caribbean*, vol. II: *English- and Dutch-Speaking Regions*, edited by Arnold, A. James. 285–326. Amsterdam: John Benjamins Publishing Company, 2001.

Caretta, Vincent. *Equiano, the African: Biography of a Self-Made Man*. New York: Penguin, 2005.

Carey, Brycchan. *British Abolitionism and the Rhetoric of Sensibility: Writing, Sentiment, and Slavery, 1760–1807*. Basingstoke: Palgrave Macmillan, 2005.

Carmichael, Gertrude. *The History of the West Indian Islands of Trinidad and Tobago, 1498–1900*. London: Alvin Redman, 1961.

Caron, Aimery, and Arnold R. Highfield. *The French Intervention in the St John Slave Revolt of 1733–34*. St Thomas: Bureau of Libraries, Museums, and Archaeological Services, Dept. of Conservation and Cultural Affairs, 1981.

Carter, Martin. *University of Hunger: Collected Poems and Selected Prose*. edited by Robinson, Gemma. Tarset: Bloodaxe, 2006.

Chamberlain, Mary. *Family Love in the Diaspora: Migration and the Anglo-Caribbean Experience*. New Brunswick: Transaction, 2006.

Chambers, Douglas B. 'Ethnicity in the Diaspora: The Slave-Trade and the Creation of African "Nations" in the Americas'. *Slavery and Abolition* 22, no. 3 (2001): 25–39.

'My Own Nation: Ibo in the Diaspora'. *Slavery and Abolition* 18, no. 1 (1997): 72–97.

'Tracing Igbo into the African Diaspora'. In *Identity in the Shadow of Slavery*, edited by Lovejoy, Paul E. 55–63. London: Continuum, 2000.

Chevannes, A. Barrington. 'The Repairer of the Breach: Reverend Claudius Henry and Jamaican Society'. In *Ethnicity in the Americas*, edited by Henry, Frances. 263–90. The Hague: Mouton, 1976.

——. *Rastafari: Roots and Ideology*. Syracuse: Syracuse University Press, 1995.

Chireau, Yvonne P. *Black Magic: Religion and the African American Conjuring Tradition*. Berkeley: University of California Press, 2003.

Chude-Sokei, Louis. *The Last 'Darky': Bert Williams, Black-on-Black Minstrelsy, and the African Diaspora*. Durham: Duke University Press, 2006.

Clark, Stuart. *Thinking with Demons: The Idea of Witchcraft in Early Modern Europe*. Oxford: Clarendon Press, 1997.

Clarkson, Thomas. *The History of the Rise, Progress, and Accomplishment of the Abolition of the African Slave-Trade by the British Parliament*, 2 vols. London: Longman, Hurst, Rees, & Orme, 1808.

Clery, E. J. *The Rise of Supernatural Fiction, 1762–1800*. Cambridge: Cambridge University Press, 1995.

Collins, Loretta. '"We Shall All Heal": Ma Kilman, the Obeah Woman as Mother-Healer in Derek Walcott's "Omeros"'. *Literature and Medicine* 14, no. 1 (1995): 146–62.

Cooper, Frederick. *Decolonization and African Society: The Labor Question in French and British Africa*. Cambridge: Cambridge University Press, 1996.

Cooter, Roger. 'The History of Mesmerism in Britain: Poverty and Promise'. In *Franz Anton Mesmer und Die Geschichte Des Mesmerismus*, edited by Schott, Heinz. 152–62. Stuttgart: Franz Steiner Verlag Wiesbaden GMBH, 1985.

Cousins, Phyllis. *Queen of the Mountain*. London: Ginn & Company, 1967.

Cox, Edward. 'The British Caribbean in the Age of Revolution'. In *Empire and Nation: The American Revolution in the Atlantic World*, edited by Gould, Eliga H. and Peter S. Onuf. 275–94. Baltimore: Johns Hopkins University Press, 2005.

Craggs, Ruth. 'The Commonwealth Institute and the Commonwealth Arts Festival: Architecture, Performance and Multiculturalism in Late-Imperial London'. *The London Journal* 36, no. 3 (2011): 247–68.

Craton, Michael. *Testing the Chains: Resistance to Slavery in the British West Indies*. Ithaca: Cornell University Press, 1982.

Craton, Michael, James Walvin, and David Wright, eds. *Slavery, Abolition and Emancipation: Black Slaves and the British Empire*. London: Longman, 1976.

Crichlow, Michaeline A. *Negotiating Caribbean Freedom: Peasants and the State in Development*. Lanham, Md.: Lexington, 2005.

Cudjoe, Selwyn R. *Caribbean Visionary: A. R. F. Webber and the Making of the Guyanese Nation*. Jackson: University Press of Mississippi, 2009.

Davies, Owen. *Grimoires: A History of Magic Books*. Oxford: Oxford University Press, 2009.

——. *Murder, Magic, Madness: The Victorian Trials of Dove and the Wizard*. Harlow: Pearson Education, 2005.

——. *Popular Magic: Cunning-Folk in English History*. London: Continuum, 2007.

——. *Witchcraft, Magic and Culture, 1736–1951*. Manchester: Manchester University Press, 1999.

Davis, David Brion. *The Problem of Slavery in the Age of Revolution, 1770–1823.* Ithaca: Cornell University Press, 1975.

Davis, N. Darnell. 'Mr Froude's Negrophobia: or Don Quixote as Cook's Tourist'. *Timehri: Journal of the Royal Agricultural and Commercial Society of British Guiana* 2, new series (1888): 85–129.

Davis, Natalie Zemon. 'Judges, Masters, Diviners: Slaves' Experience of Criminal Justice in Colonial Suriname'. *Law and History Review* 29, no. 4 (2011): 925–84.

Day, Lynda. *Gender and Power in Sierra Leone: Women Chiefs of the Last Two Centuries.* New York: Palgrave Macmillan, 2012.

Dayan, Colin. *The Law is a White Dog: How Legal Rituals Make and Unmake Persons.* Princeton: Princeton University Press, 2011.

De Barros, Juanita. '"Race" and Culture in the Writings of J. J. Thomas'. *Journal of Caribbean History* 27, no. 1 (1993): 36–53.

'"Setting Things Right": Medicine and Magic in British Guiana, 1803–38'. *Slavery and Abolition* 25, no. 1 (2004): 28–50.

de Mello e Souza, Laura. *The Devil and the Land of the Holy Cross: Witchcraft, Slavery, and Popular Religion in Colonial Brazil,* translated by Whitty, Diane Grosklaus. Austin: University of Texas Press, 2003.

de Verteuil, Anthony. *A History of Diego Martin 1784–1884.* Port of Spain, Trinidad: Paria, 1987.

Debbasch, Yvan. 'Le crime d'empoisonnement aux îles pendant la période esclavagiste'. *Revue d'histoire d'outre-mer* 51, no. 2 (1963): 137–88.

Delbourgo, James. *A Most Amazing Scene of Wonders: Electricity and Enlightenment in Early America.* Cambridge, Mass.: Harvard University Press, 2006.

*The Devil's legacy to earth mortals: being the key note to black arts!! witchcraft, devination, omens, forewarnings, apparitions, sorcery, dm̃onology, dreams, predictions, visions, and compacts with the devil!!: with the most authentic history of Salem witchcraft!* Palmyra, Penn.: Diamond, 1880.

Dillon, Elizabeth Maddock. 'Obi, Assemblage, Enchantment'. *J19: The Journal of Nineteenth Century Americanists* 1, no. 1 (2013): 172–8.

Dirks, Nicholas B. *Castes of Mind: Colonialism and the Making of Modern India.* Princeton: Princeton University Press, 2001.

Dixon, Joy. *Divine Feminine: Theosophy and Feminism in England.* Baltimore: Johns Hopkins University Press, 2001.

Drescher, Seymour. *Capitalism and Antislavery: British Mobilization in Comparative Perspective.* London: Macmillan, 1986.

*Econocide: British Slavery in the Era of Abolition.* Pittsburgh: University of Pittsburgh Press, 1977.

*The Mighty Experiment: Free Labor versus Slavery in British Emancipation.* Oxford: Oxford University Press, 2002.

Duffy, Michael. 'World-Wide War and British Expansion, 1793–1815'. In *The Oxford History of the British Empire,* vol. II: *The Eighteenth Century,* edited by Marshall, P. J. 184–207. Oxford: Oxford University Press, 1998.

Earle, William. *Obi or, The History of Three-Fingered Jack,* edited by Aravamudan, Srinivas. Peterborough, Ontario: Broadview, 2005 [1800].

*Obi: or, The history of three-fingered Jack: in a series of letters from a resident in Jamaica to his friend in England.* London: Earle & Hemet, 1800.

Ebroin, Ary. *Quimbois, magie noire et sorcellerie aux Antilles.* Paris: Jacques Grancher, 1977.
Edgeworth, Maria. *Belinda. The Novels and Selected Works of Maria Edgeworth Volume 2*, edited by Kilfeather, Siobhan. London: Pickering & Chatto, 2003 [1801].
  *The Grateful Negro.* In *The Novels and Selected Works of Maria Edgeworth*, vol. XII: *Popular Tales, Early Lessons, Whim for Whim*, edited by Eger, Elizabeth, Clíona ÓGallchoir, and Marilyn Butler. 49–63. London: Pickering & Chatto, 2003 [1804].
Edmonds, Ennis Barrington. *Rastafari: From Outcasts to Culture Bearers.* Oxford: Oxford University Press, 2003.
Edmonds, Ennis Barrington, and Michaelle A. Gonzalez. *Caribbean Religious History: An Introduction.* New York: New York University Press, 2010.
Edwards, Bryan. *The History, Civil and Commercial, of the British Colonies in the West Indies.* 2 vols. Vol. II, London: John Stockdale, 1793.
Elkins, W. F. *Street Preachers, Faith Healers and Herb Doctors in Jamaica 1890–1925.* New York: Revisionist Press, 1977.
  'William Lauron DeLaurence and Jamaican Folk Religion'. *Folklore* 97, no. 2 (1986): 215–18.
Ellis, Markman. *The Politics of Sensibility: Race, Gender and Commerce in the Sentimental Novel.* Cambridge: Cambridge University Press, 1996.
Epstein, James. 'The Radical Underworld Goes Colonial: P. F. McCallum's Travels in Trinidad'. In *Unrespectable Radicals? Popular Politics in the Age of Reform*, edited by Davis, Michael T. and Paul A. Pickering. 147–66. Aldershot: Ashgate, 2008.
  *Scandal of Colonial Rule: Power and Subversion in the British Atlantic during the Age of Revolution.* Cambridge: Cambridge University Press, 2012.
Ewing, Adam. 'Caribbean Labour Politics in the Age of Garvey, 1918–1938'. *Race and Class* 55, no. 1 (2013): 23–45.
Falk Moore, Sally. *Anthropology and Africa: Changing Perspectives on a Changing Scene.* Charlottesville: University Press of Virginia, 1994.
Falola, Toyin, and Matt D. Childs, eds. *The Yoruba Diaspora in the Atlantic World.* Bloomington: Indiana University Press, 2004.
Fara, Patricia. 'An Attractive Therapy: Animal Magnetism in Eighteenth-Century England'. *History of Science* 33, no. 2 (1995): 127–77.
Farley, Christopher. *Before the Legend: The Rise of Bob Marley.* New York: HarperCollins, 2006.
Farley, Helen. 'Out of Africa: Tarot's Fascination with Egypt'. *Literature and Aesthetics* 21, no. 1 (2011): 175–95.
A Fellow of the Royal Geographic Society. *Jamaica and its Governor during the last six years.* London: Edward Stanford, 1871.
Ferguson, James. *Expectations of Modernity: Myths and Meanings of Urban Life on the Zambian Copperbelt.* Berkeley: University of California Press, 1999.
Fernández Olmos, Margarite, and Lizabeth Paravisini-Gebert. *Creole Religions of the Caribbean: An Introduction from Vodou and Santeria to Obeah and Espiritismo.* New York: New York University Press, 2003.
Fernández Olmos, Margarite, and Lizabeth Paravisini-Gelbert, eds. *Sacred Possessions: Vodou, Santería, Obeah, and the Caribbean.* New Brunswick: Rutgers University Press, 1997.

Fett, Sharla M. *Working Cures: Healing, Health, and Power on Southern Slave Plantations*. Chapel Hill: University of North Carolina Press, 2002.
Flint, Karen. *Healing Traditions: African Medicine, Cultural Exchange and Competition in South Africa, 1820–1948*. Athens: Ohio University Press, 2008.
Fluehr-Lobban, Carolyn. 'Anténor Firmin: Haitian Pioneer of Anthropology'. *American Anthropologist* 102, no. 3 (2000): 449–66.
Ford-Smith, Honor. 'Unruly Virtues of the Spectacular: Performing Engendered Nationalisms in the UNIA in Jamaica'. *Interventions* 6, no. 1 (2004): 18–44.
Forde, Maarit. 'The Moral Economy of Spiritual Work: Money and Rituals in Trinidad and Tobago'. In *Obeah and Other Powers: The Politics of Caribbean Religion and Healing*, edited by Paton, Diana and Maarit Forde. 198–219. Durham: Duke University Press, 2012.
Foucault, Michel. 'Governmentality'. In *The Foucault Effect*, edited by Burchell, Graham, Colin Gordon, and Peter Miller. 87–104. Chicago: University of Chicago Press, 1991.
Franklyn, Omowale David. *Bridging the Two Grenadas: Gairy's and Bishop's*. St. George's, Grenada: Talented House, 1999.
Frazier, Edward Franklin. *The Negro Family in the United States*. Chicago: Chicago University Press, 1966 [1939].
Frey, Sylvia R., and Betty Wood. *Come Shouting to Zion: African American Protestantism in the American South and British Caribbean to 1830*. Chapel Hill: University of North Carolina Press, 1998.
Froude, James Anthony. *The English in the West Indies or The Bow of Ulysses*. London: Longman, Green, & Co, 1888.
Fullarton, Colonel William. *Substance of the Evidence Delivered Before The Lords of His Majesty's Most Honourable Privy Council, in the Case of Governor Picton, under the Statute 23d of King Henry VIII which relates only to treason and murder, submitted, with all due deference and respect, to the consideration of the Imperial Parliament, as the Supreme Legislative Authority of these Kingdoms*. Edinburgh: Murray & Cochrane, 1807.
Fumagalli, Maria Cristina, and Peter L. Patrick. 'Two Healing Narratives: Suffering, Reintegration, and the Struggle of Language'. *Small Axe* 10, no. 2 (2006): 61–79, 287–8.
Füredi, Frank. *Colonial Wars and the Politics of Third World Nationalism*. London: I. B. Tauris, 1994.
Games, Alison. *Witchcraft in Early North America*. Lanham, Md.: Rowman & Littlefield, 2010.
Garraway, Doris. *The Libertine Colony: Creolization in the Early French Caribbean*. Durham: Duke University Press, 2005.
Garvey, Marcus. *The Black Man: A Monthly Magazine of Negro Thought and Opinion*, edited by Hill, Robert A. Millwood. New York: Kraus-Thomson Organization Limited, 1975.
Gaspar, David Barry. *Bondmen and Rebels: A Study of Master–Slave Relations in Antigua: With Implications for Colonial British America*. Baltimore: Johns Hopkins University Press, 1985.
——'"To Bring their Offending Slaves to Justice": Compensation and Slave Resistance in Antigua, 1669–1773'. *Caribbean Quarterly* 30, no. 3/4 (1984): 45–59.

Gatrell, V. A. C. *The Hanging Tree: Execution and the English People, 1770–1868*. New York: Oxford University Press, 1994.

Gerzina, Gretchen. *Black London: Life before Emancipation*. New Brunswick: Rutgers University Press, 1997.

Gibbons, Rawle. *Shepherd*. In *Love Trilogy: I Lawah, Shepherd, Ogun Ayan*. 91–160. Tunapuna, Trinidad: Canboulay Productions, 2012.

Gibson, Kean. *Comfa Religion and Creole Language in a Caribbean Community*. Albany: State University of New York Press, 2001.

Gikandi, Simon. *Slavery and the Culture of Taste*. Princeton: Princeton University Press, 2011.

Gill, Gordon E. A. 'Doing the Minje Mama: A Study in the Evolution of an African/Afro-Creole Ritual in the British Slave Colony of Berbice'. *Wadabagei* 12, no. 3 (2009): 7–29.

Giovannetti, Jorge L. 'The Elusive Organization of "Identity": Race, Religion, and Empire among Caribbean Migrants in Cuba'. *Small Axe* 10, no. 1 (2006): 1–27.

Glazier, Stephen D. 'Funerals and Mourning in the Spiritual Baptist and Shango Traditions'. *Caribbean Quarterly* 39, no. 3/4 (1993): 1–11.

*Marching the Pilgrims Home: Leadership and Decision-Making in an Afro-Caribbean Faith*. Westport, Conn.: Greenwood Press, 1983.

Gloster, Archibald. *A Letter to the Right Honourable the Earl of Buckinghamshire, late secretary of the Colonial Department, respecting Affairs in Trinidad in 1803, and in answer to William Fullarton, Esq*. London: D. N. Shury, 1807.

Gomez, Michael A. *Exchanging our Country Marks: The Transformation of African Identity in the Colonial and Antebellum South*. Chapel Hill: University of North Carolina Press, 1998.

Gottlieb, Karla. *'The Mother of us All': A History of Queen Nanny Leader of the Windward Maroons*. Trenton, N.J.: Africa World Press, 2000.

Goveia, Elsa V. *Slave Society in the British Leeward Islands at the End of the Eighteenth Century*. New Haven: Yale University Press, 1965.

Graham, Eric J. *Burns and the Sugar Plantocracy of Ayrshire*. Ayr: Ayrshire Archaeological and Natural History Society, 2009.

Gray, Natasha. 'Independent Spirits: The Politics of Policing Anti-Witchcraft Movements in Colonial Ghana, 1908–1927'. *Journal of Religion in Africa* 35, no. 2 (2005): 139–58.

'Witches, Oracles, and Colonial Law: Evolving Anti-Witchcraft Practices in Ghana, 1927–1932'. *International Journal of African Historical Studies* 34, no. 2 (2001): 339–63.

Gray, Obika. *Radicalism and Social Change in Jamaica, 1960–1972*. Knoxville: University of Tennessee Press, 1991.

Hall, Catherine. *Civilising Subjects: Metropole and Colony in the English Imagination, 1830–1867*. Cambridge: Polity Press, 2002.

Hall, Douglas. *In Miserable Slavery: Thomas Thistlewood in Jamaica, 1750–86*. London: Macmillan, 1989.

Hall, Gwendolyn Midlo. *Africans in Colonial Louisiana: The Development of Afro-Creole Culture in the Eighteenth Century*. Baton Rouge: Louisiana State University Press, 1992.

*Slavery and African Ethnicities in the Americas: Restoring the Links.* Chapel Hill: University of North Carolina Press, 2005.
Hall, Neville A. T. *Slave Society in the Danish West Indies: St Thomas, St John & St Croix,* edited by Higman, B. W. Mona, Jamaica: University of the West Indies Press, 1992.
Haller, John S. *Kindly Medicine: Physio-Medicalism in America, 1836–1911.* Kent, Ohio: Kent State University Press, 1997.
*The People's Doctors: Samuel Thomson and the American Botanical Movement, 1790–1860.* Carbondale: Southern Illinois University Press, 2000.
Hamilton, Beverly. 'Marcus Garvey and Cultural Development in Jamaica: A Preliminary Survey'. In *Garvey: His Work and Impact,* edited by Lewis, Rupert and Patrick Bryan. 87–111. Trenton, N.J.: Africa World Press, 1991.
Handler, Jerome S., and Kenneth M. Bilby. *Enacting Power: The Criminalization of Obeah in the Anglophone Caribbean, 1760–2011.* Mona, Jamaica: University of the West Indies Press, 2012.
'On the Early Use and Origin of the Term "Obeah" in Barbados and the Anglophone Caribbean'. *Slavery and Abolition* 22, no. 2 (2001): 87–100.
Harewood, Jack. *The Population of Trinidad and Tobago.* New York: Committee for International Co-ordination of National Research in Demography, 1975.
Harriott, Anthony. 'Captured Shadows, Tongue-Tied Witnesses, "Compellants" and the Courts: Obya and Social Control'. In *Jamaica in Slavery and Freedom: History, Heritage and Culture,* edited by Monteith, Kathleen E. A. and Glen Richards. 115–43. Mona, Jamaica: University of the West Indies Press, 2002.
Hart, Richard. *Slaves who Abolished Slavery: Blacks in Rebellion.* Mona, Jamaica: University of the West Indies Press, 2002 [1985].
Harvey, Alison. 'West Indian Obeah and English "Obee": Race, Femininity, and Questions of Colonial Consolidation in Maria Edgeworth's *Belinda*'. In *New Essays on Maria Edgeworth,* edited by Nash, Julie. 1–29. Aldershot: Ashgate, 2006.
Havard, Robert. *Wellington's Welsh General: A Life of Sir Thomas Picton.* London: Aurum Press, 1996.
Hay, Douglas. 'Property, Authority, and the Criminal Law'. In *Albion's Fatal Tree: Crime and Society in Eighteenth-Century England,* edited by Hay, Douglas, Peter Linebaugh, John G. Rule, E. P. Thompson, and Cal Winslow. 17–63. New York: Pantheon Books, 1975.
Hayes, Kevin J. *Folklore and Book Culture.* Knoxville: University of Tennessee Press, 1997.
Henry, Frances. *Reclaiming African Religions in Trinidad: The Socio-Political Legitimation of the Orisha and Spiritual Baptist Faiths.* Mona, Jamaica: University of the West Indies Press, 2003.
Herskovits, Melville J. *The Myth of the Negro Past.* Gloucester, Mass.: P. Smith, 1970 [1941].
Herskovits, Melville J., and Frances S. Herskovits. *Trinidad Village.* New York: Octagon Books, 1964 [1947].
Heuman, Gad. *Between Black and White: Race, Politics, and the Free Coloreds in Jamaica, 1792–1865.* Westport, Conn.: Greenwood Press, 1981.

'*The Killing Time*': *The Morant Bay Rebellion in Jamaica*. London: Macmillan Caribbean, 1994.

Higman, B. W. *Slave Populations of the British Caribbean 1807–1834*. Mona, Jamaica: University of the West Indies Press, 1995 [1984].

———. *Writing West Indian Histories*. London: Macmillan, 1999.

Hill, Donald R. *Caribbean Folklore: A Handbook*. Westport, Conn.: Greenwood Press, 2007.

Hill, Errol. 'The Emergence of a National Drama in the West Indies'. *Caribbean Quarterly* 18, no. 4 (1972): 9–40.

Hill, Errol, ed. *Plays for Today: Longman Caribbean Writers*. Harlow: Pearson Education, 1985.

Hill, Richard. *Light and Shadows of Jamaican History, being Three Lectures delivered in aid of the Mission schools in the colony*. Kingston: Ford & Gall, 1859.

Hill, Robert A. *Dread History: Leonard P. Howell and Millenarian Visions in the Early Rastafarian Religion*. Chicago: Research Associates School Times Publications, 2001.

———. 'Leonard P. Howell and Millenarian Visions in Early Rastafari'. *Jamaica Journal* 16, no. 1 (1983): 24–39.

Hill, Robert A., ed. *The Marcus Garvey and Universal Negro Improvement Association Papers Volume I: 1826–August 1919*. Berkeley: University of California Press, 1983.

Hodges, Hugh. *Soon Come: Jamaican Spirituality, Jamaican Poetics*. Charlottesville: University of Virginia Press, 2008.

Hogg, Donald W. 'Magic and "Science" in Jamaica'. *Caribbean Studies* 1, no. 2 (1961): 1–5.

Holt, Thomas C. *The Problem of Freedom: Race, Labor, and Politics in Jamaica and Britain, 1832–1938*. Baltimore: Johns Hopkins University Press, 1992.

Hörmann, Raphael. 'Thinking the Unthinkable: Representations of the Haitian Revolution in British Discourse, 1791–1805'. In *Human Bondage in the Cultural Contact Zone: Transdisciplinary Perspectives on Slavery and its Discourses*, edited by Hörmann, Raphael and Gesa Mackenthun. 137–70. Münster: Waxmann, 2010.

Houk, James T. *Spirits, Blood and Drums: The Orisha Religion in Trinidad*. Philadelphia: Temple University Press, 1995.

Hurston, Zora Neale. *Tell my Horse: Voodoo and Life in Haiti and Jamaica*. New York: Perennial Library, 1990 [1938].

Jacobs, W. Richard, ed. *Butler versus the King: Riots and Sedition in 1937*. Port of Spain, Trinidad: Key Caribbean Publications, 1976.

Jaudon, Toni Wall. 'Obeah's Sensations: Rethinking Religion at the Transnational Turn'. *American Literature* 84, no. 4 (2012): 715–41.

Jeater, Diana. *Law, Language, and Science: The Invention of the 'Native Mind' in Southern Rhodesia, 1890–1930*. Portsmouth, NH: Heinemann, 2007.

Jennings, Judith. *The Business of Abolishing the British Slave Trade, 1783–1807*. London: Frank Cass, 1997.

Johnson, Howard. 'The Black Experience in the British Caribbean in the Twentieth Century'. In *Black Experience and the British Empire*, edited by Morgan,

Philip D. and Sean Hawkins. 317–46. Oxford: Oxford University Press, 2004.
Johnson, Joyce. 'Shamans, Shepherds, Scientists, and Others in Jamaican Fiction'. *New West Indian Guide/Nieuwe West-Indische Gids* 67, no. 3/4 (1993): 221–38.
Johnston, Harry. *The Negro in the New World*. London: Methuen, 1910.
Jones, Margaret. *Public Health in Jamaica, 1850–1940: Neglect, Philanthropy and Development*. Kingston: University of the West Indies Press, 2013.
Joseph, E. L. *History of Trinidad*. London: Frank Cass, 1970 [1838].
Juneja, Renu. 'Recalling the Dead in Dennis Scott's "An Echo in the Bone"'. *Ariel: A Review of International English Literature* 23, no. 1 (1992): 98–114.
Kaiser, Wolfram. '"Clericalism – That is our Enemy!": European Anticlericalism and the Culture Wars'. In *Culture Wars: Secular–Catholic Conflict in Nineteenth-Century Europe*, edited by Clark, Christopher and Wolfram Kaiser. 47–76. Cambridge: Cambridge University Press, 2003.
Kennedy, W. R. *Sport, Travel, and Adventure in Newfoundland and the West Indies*. Edinburgh and London: William Blackwood & Sons, 1885.
Khalili, Laleh. *Time in the Shadows: Confinement in Counterinsurgencies*. Stanford: Stanford University Press, 2013.
King, Stephen A. *Reggae, Rastafari and the Rhetoric of Social Control*. Jackson: University Press of Mississippi, 2002.
Kingsley, Charles. *At Last: A Christmas in the West Indies*. London: Macmillan, 1871.
Kissoon, Freddie. *Zingay: A Play in One-Act*. Diego Martin, Trinidad: F. Kissoon, 1961.
Konadu, Kwasi. *The Akan Diaspora in the Americas*. Oxford: Oxford University Press, 2010.
*Indigenous Medicine and Knowledge in African Society*. New York: Routledge, 2007.
Kopytoff, Barbara K. 'The Early Political Development of Jamaican Maroon Societies'. *William and Mary Quarterly*, 3rd series, 25 (April 1978): 287–307.
*The Koromantyn Slaves; or, West-Indian Sketches*. London: J. Hatchard & Son, 1823.
Kostal, R. W. *A Jurisprudence of Power: Victorian Empire and the Rule of Law*. Oxford: Oxford University Press, 2005.
Kuklick, Henrika. *The Savage Within: The Social History of British Anthropology, 1885–1945*. Cambridge: Cambridge University Press, 1991.
La Guerre, John. 'The Moyne Commission and the Jamaican Left'. *Social and Economic Studies* 31, no. 3 (1982): 59–94.
'The Moyne Commission and the West Indian Intelligentsia, 1938–39'. *Journal of Commonwealth Political Studies* 9, no. 2 (1971): 134–57.
Lacey, Terry. *Violence and Politics in Jamaica, 1960–1970: Internal Security in a Developing Country*. Manchester: Manchester University Press, 1977.
Laitinen, Maarit. *Marching to Zion: Creolisation in Spiritual Baptist Rituals and Cosmology*. Helsinki: Helsinki University Press, 2002.

Lanaghan, Mrs. *Antigua and the Antiguans: A Full Account of the colony and its Inhabitants from the time of the Caribs to the Present Day, interspersed with anecdotes and legends, also, an impartial view of slavery and the free labour systems; the statistics of the island, and biographical notices of the principal families.* London: Saunders & Otley, 1844.

Landers, John. *Death and the Metropolis: Studies in the Demographic History of London, 1670–1830.* Cambridge: Cambridge University Press, 1993.

Lang, John. 'Extract of the Diary of Brother John Lang at Carmel, in Jamaica, giving an account of the progress of the Mission at Carmel, Peru, &c during the year 1816'. In *Periodical Accounts Relating to the Missions of the Church of the United Brethren, established among the Heathen.* 363–73. London: W. McDowell, 1814.

Latin America Bureau. *Guyana: Fraudulent Revolution.* London: Latin America Bureau, 1984.

Lazarus-Black, Mindie. 'After Empire: Training Lawyers as a Postcolonial Enterprise'. *Small Axe* 25 (2008): 38–56.

——— *Everyday Harm: Domestic Violence, Court Rites, and Cultures of Reconciliation.* Urbana: University of Illinois Press, 2007.

Lee, Debbie. *Slavery and the Romantic Imagination.* Philadelphia: University of Pennsylvania Press, 2002.

Lee, Hélène. *The First Rasta: Leonard Howell and the Rise of Rastafarianism*, translated by Davis, Lily. Chicago: Chicago Review Press, 2003.

Letí, Geneviève. 'L'empoisonnement aux antilles françaises à l'époque de l'esclavage (1724–1848)'. In *L'esclave et les plantations: de l'établissement de la servitude à son abolition: un hommage à Pierre Pluchon*, edited by Hroděj, Philippe. 209–27. Rennes: Presses Universitairesde Rennes, 2008.

Levack, Brian P. 'The Decline and End of Witchcraft Prosecutions'. In *Witchcraft and Magic in Europe: The Eighteenth and Nineteenth Centuries*, edited by Gijswijt-Hofstra, Marijke, Brian P. Levack, and Roy Porter. 3–89. London: Athlone Press, 1999.

——— *The Witch-Hunt in Early Modern Europe.* Harlow: Longman, 1995 [1987].

Lewis, Gordon K. *The Growth of the Modern West Indies.* Kingston: Ian Randle, 2004 [1968].

——— *Main Currents in Caribbean Thought: The Historical Evolution of Caribbean Society in its Ideological Aspects, 1492–1900.* Baltimore: Johns Hopkins University Press, 1983.

Lewis, Matthew. *Journal of a West Indian Proprietor, kept during a residence in the island of Jamaica.* Oxford World's Classics. Edited by Terry, Judith. Oxford: Oxford University Press, 1999 [1834].

Lewis, Rupert. 'Jamaican Black Power in the 1960s'. In *Black Power in the Caribbean*, edited by Quinn, Kate. 53–75. Gainesville: University Press of Florida, 2014.

——— 'Marcus Garvey and the Early Rastafarians: Continuity and Discontinuity'. In *Chanting Down Babylon: The Rastafari Reader*, edited by Murrell, Nathaniel Samuel, William David Spencer and Adrian Anthony McFarlane. 145–58. Philadelphia: Temple University Press.

Long, Carolyn Morrow. *Spiritual Merchants: Religion, Magic, and Commerce.* Knoxville: University of Tennessee Press, 2001.

Long, Edward. *The History of Jamaica, or General Survey of the Antient and Modern State of that Island: With reflections on its situations, settlements, inhabitants, climate, products, commerce, laws, and government*. London: Frank Cass, 1970 [1774].

Lum, Kenneth Anthony. *Praising his Name in the Dance: Spirit Possession in the Spiritual Baptist Faith and Orisha Work in Trinidad, West Indies*. Amsterdam: Harwood Academic Publishers, 2000.

MacGaffey, Wyatt. 'The Cultural Tradition of the African Forests'. In *Insight and Artistry in African Divination*, edited by Pemberton, John, III. 13–24. Washington: Smithsonian Institution Press, 2000.

——— *Kongo Political Culture: The Conceptual Challenge of the Particular*. Bloomington: Indiana University Press, 2000.

——— *Religion and Society in Central Africa*. Chicago: University of Chicago Press, 1986.

Macpherson, Anne S. *From Colony to Nation: Women Activists and the Gendering of Politics in Belize, 1912–1982*. Lincon: University of Nebraska Press, 2007.

Madden, R. R. *A Twelvemonth's Residence in the West Indies, during the Transition from Slavery to Apprenticeship ...* Philadelphia: Carey, Lea & Blanchard, 1835.

Maingot, Anthony P. *The United States and the Caribbean*. London: Macmillan, 1994.

Mair, Lucille Mathurin. *A Historical Study of Women in Jamaica, 1655–1844*, edited by Shepherd, Verene A. and Hilary M. Beckles. Mona, Jamaica: University of the West Indies Press, 2006.

Manley, Robert H. *Guyana Emergent: The Post-Independence Struggle for Nondependent Development*. Boston: G. K. Hall, 1979.

*Marly, or a Planter's Life in Jamaica*. Glasgow: Richard Griffin & Co., 1828.

Marsden, Peter. *An Account of the Island of Jamaica with Reflections on the Treatment, Occupation, and Provisions of the Slaves. To which is added a Description of the Animal and Vegetable Productions of the Island. By a gentleman lately resident on a plantation*. Newcastle: S. Hodgson, 1788.

Marshall, P. J. 'The British State Overseas, 1750–1850'. In *Colonial Empires Compared: Britain and the Netherlands, 1750–1850*, edited by Moore, Bob and Henk Van Nierop. 171–84. Aldershot: Ashgate, 2003.

Marson, Una. Pocomania (a Play). In *Anglophone Karibik-USA: Peripherie und Zenbrum in der 'neuen Welt'*, edited by Hoenisch, Michael and Remco von Cappelleveen. 117–47. Hamburg: Argument, 1991.

Matory, J. Lorand. *Black Atlantic Religion: Tradition, Transnationalism, and Matriarchy in the Afro-Brazilian Candomblé*. Princeton: Princeton University Press, 2005.

——— 'The "Cult of Nations" and the Ritualization of their Purity'. *South Atlantic Quarterly* 100, no. 1 (2001): 171–214.

Matthews, Basil. *Crisis of the West Indian Family: A Sample Study*. Port of Spain: Extra Mural Department, University College of the West Indies, 1953.

Maya Restrepo, Luz Adriana. '"Brujería" y reconstrucción étnica de los esclavos del Nuevo Reino de Granada, Siglo XVII'. In *Geografía humana de Colombia: los Afrocolombianos: Tomo VI*, edited by Arocha Rodriguez, Jaime, Martha

Luz Machado Caicedo, and William Villa. Santa Fe de Bogota: Instituto-Colombiana de Cultura Hispanica, 1998. Available at www.banrepcultural.org/blaavirtual/geografia/afro/brujeria.

McCallum, Pierre F. *Travels in Trinidad during the months of February, March, and April, 1803, in a series of letters, addressed to a Member of the Imperial Parliament of Great Britain*. Liverpool: W. Jones, 1805.

McCann, Andrew. *Cultural Politics in the 1790s: Literature, Radicalism and the Public Sphere*. New York and London: St Martin's Press and Macmillan Press, 1999.

McCaskie, T. C. *State and Society in Pre-Colonial Asante*. Cambridge: Cambridge University Press, 1995.

McClellan, James E., III. *Colonialism and Science: Saint Domingue in the Old Regime*. Baltimore: Johns Hopkins University Press, 1992.

McCracken, John. *A History of Malawi, 1859–1966*. Woodbridge: James Currey, 2012.

McGarry, Molly. *Ghosts of Futures Past: Spiritualism and the Cultural Politics of Nineteenth-Century America*. Berkeley: University of California Press, 2008.

McKay, Claude. *Banana Bottom*. London: Pluto, 1966 [1933].

McLaren, Angus. *The Trials of Masculinity: Policing Sexual Boundaries, 1870–1930*. Chicago: University of Chicago Press, 1997.

Mcleod, Marc C. 'Undesirable Aliens: Race, Ethnicity, and Nationalism in the Comparison of Haitian and British West Indian Immigrant Workers in Cuba, 1912–1939'. *Journal of Social History* 31 (1998): 599–623.

McNaughton, Patrick R. *The Mande Blacksmiths: Knowledge, Power, and Art in West Africa*. Bloomington: Indiana University Press, 1988.

McNeal, Keith E. *Trance and Modernity in the Southern Caribbean: African and Hindu Religions in Trinidad and Tobago*. Gainesville: University Press of Florida, 2011.

Meeks, Brian. *Radical Caribbean: From Black Power to Abu Bakr*. Mona, Jamaica: University of the West Indies Press, 1996.

Metcalf, George. *Royal Government and Political Conflict in Jamaica 1729–1783*. London: Longmans, 1965.

Millette, James. *The Genesis of Crown Colony Government: Trinidad, 1783–1810*. Curepe, Trinidad: Moko Enterprises, 1970.

Mills, David. *Difcult Folk? A Political History of Social Anthropology*. New York: Bergahn Books, 2008.

Mintz, Sidney. 'Enduring Substances, Trying Theories: The Caribbean as Oikumene'. *Journal of the Royal Anthopological Institute* 2, no. 2 (1996): 289–311.

Mintz, Sidney W., and Richard Price. *The Birth of African-American Culture: An Anthropological Perspective*. Boston: Beacon Press, 1992 [1976].

Mischel, Frances Osterman. 'Faith Healing and Medical Practice in the Southern Caribbean'. *Southwestern Journal of Anthropology* 15, no. 4 (1959): 407–17.

Mitchell, B. R. *British Historical Statistics*. Cambridge: Cambridge University Press, 1988.

Moore, Brian L. *Cultural Power, Resistance and Pluralism: Colonial Guyana 1838–1900*. Montreal: McGill-Queen's University Press, 1995.

Moore, Brian L., and Michele A. Johnson. *Neither Led nor Driven: Contesting British Cultural Imperialism in Jamaica, 1865–1920*. Kingston: University of the West Indies Press, 2004.

'They Do as they Please': *The Jamaican Struggle for Cultural Freedom after Morant Bay*. Mona, Jamaica: Unviersity of the West Indies Press, 2011.

Morgan, Kenneth. *Materials on the History of Jamaica in the Edward Long Papers held at the British Library: An Introduction to the Microfilm Collection*. Wakefield: Microform Academic Publishers, 2006. Available at www.microform.co.uk/guides/R50027.pdf.

Morgan, Philip D. 'Africa and the Atlantic, c. 1450–c. 1820'. In *Atlantic History: A Critical Appraisal*, edited by Greene, Jack P. and Philip D. Morgan. 223–48. Oxford: Oxford University Press, 2009.

*Slave Counterpoint: Black Culture in the Eighteenth-Century Chesapeake and Lowcountry*. Chapel Hill: University of North Carolina Press, 1998.

Moseley, Benjamin. *A Treatise on Sugar*. London: G. G. and J. Robinson, 1799.

Mullin, Michael. *Africa in America: Slave Acculturation and Resistance in the American South and the British Caribbean, 1736–1831*. Urbana and Chicago: University of Illinois Press, 1992.

Munasinghe, Viranjini. 'Culture Creators and Culture Bearers: The Interface between Race and Ethnicity in Trinidad'. *Transforming Anthropology* 6, no. 1–2 (1997): 72–86.

Murphy, Joseph M. 'Black Religion and "Black Magic": Prejudice and Projection in Images of African-Derived Religions'. *Religion* 20 (1990): 322–37.

Murray, Deryck. 'Three Worships, an Old Warlock and Many Lawless Forces: The Court Trial of an African Doctor Who Practised "Obeah to Cure", in Early Nineteenth Century Jamaica'. *Journal of Southern African Studies* 33, no. 4 (2007): 811–28.

Naipaul, V. S. *The Loss of El Dorado: A History*. London: Andre Deutsch, 1969.

Naono, Atsuko. 'Burmese Health Officers in the Transformation of Public Health in Colonial Burma in the 1920s and 1930s'. In *Public Health in the British Empire: Intermediaries, Subordinates, and the Practice of Public Health, 1850–1960*, edited by Johnson, Ryan and Amna Khalid. 118–34. New York: Routledge, 2012.

Neely, Daniel T. 'Calling all Singers, Musicians and Speechmakers: Mento Aesthetics and Jamaica's Early Recording Industry'. *Caribbean Quarterly* 53, no. 4 (2007): 1–15, 110.

Newton, Velma. *The Silver Men: West Indian Labour Migration to Panama*. Mona, Jamaica: Institute of Social and Economic Research, University of the West Indies, 1984.

Niehaus, Isak. 'Witchcraft in the New South Africa: From Colonial Superstition to Postcolonial Reality?' In *Magical Interpretations, Material Realities: Modernity, Witchcraft and the Occult in Postcolonial Africa*, edited by Moore, Henrietta L. and Todd Sanders. 187–205. London: Routledge, 2001.

Noguera, Pedro A. 'Charismatic Leadership and Popular Support: A Comparison of the Leadership Styles of Eric Gairy and Maurice Bishop'. *Social and Economic Studies* 44, no. 1 (1995): 1–30.

Nordius, Janina. 'Racism and Radicalism in Jamaican Gothic: Cynric R. Williams's Hamel, the Obeah Man'. *ELH* 73, no. 3 (2006): 673–93.

Nwankwo, Ifeoma C. K. 'Inside and Outsider, Black and American: Rethinking Zora Neal Hurston's Caribbean Ethnography'. *Radical History Review* 87 (2003): 49–77.

O'Rourke, James. 'The Revision of Obi; or Three-Finger'd Jack and the Jacobin Repudiation of Sentimentality'. *Nineteenth Century Contexts* 28, no. 4 (2006): 285–303.

*Obi or, Three Fingered Jack. A Popular Melo-drama in two acts (as performed at Drury Lane Theatre)*. London: Penny Pictorial Plays, n.d.

Oldfield, J. R. *Popular Politics and British Anti-Slavery: The Mobilisation of Public Opinion against the Slave Trade 1787–1807*. London: Frank Cass, 1998 [1995].

Omosini, Olufemi. 'C. S. Salmon: Pre-Lugardian Advocate of Indirect Rule in British West Africa'. *Odu* 20 (1980): 49–66.

Omotoso, Kole. *The Theatrical into Theatre: A Study of the Drama and Theatre of the English-Speaking Caribbean*. London: New Beacon, 1982.

Oppenheim, Janet. *The Other World: Spiritualism and Psychical Research in England, 1850–1914*. Cambridge: Cambridge University Press, 1985.

Orde Browne, G. St J. *Labour Conditions in the West Indies*. London: HMSO, 1939.

Ortiz, Fernando. *Brujas e inquisidores (Defensa póstuma de un inquisidor cubano)*. Havana: Fundación Fernando Ortiz, 2003.

Palmer, Colin A. *Eric Williams and the Making of the Modern Caribbean*. Chapel Hill: University of North Carolina Press, 2006.

*Freedom's Children: The 1938 Labor Rebellion and the Birth of Modern Jamaica*. Chapel Hill: University of North Carolina Press, 2014.

Palmer, Steven. *Launching Global Health: The Caribbean Odyssey of the Rockefeller Foundation*. Ann Arbor: University of Michigan Press, 2010.

Palmié, Stephan. *The Cooking of History: How Not to Study Afro-Cuban Religion*. Chicago: University of Chicago Press, 2013.

'Other Powers: Tylor's Principle, Father Williams's Temptations, and the Power of Banality'. In *Obeah and Other Powers: The Politics of Caribbean Religion and Healing*, edited by Paton, Diana and Maarit Forde. 316–40. Durham: Duke University Press, 2012.

*Wizards and Scientists: Explorations in Afro-Cuban Modernity and Tradition*. Durham: Duke University Press, 2002.

Parish, Susan Scott. *American Curiosity: Cultures of Natural History in the Colonial British Atlantic World*. Chapel Hill: University of North Carolina Press, 2006.

'Diasporic African Sources of Enlightenment Knowledge'. In *Science and Empire in the Atlantic World*, edited by Delbourgo, James and Nicholas Dew. 281–310. New York: Routledge, 2008.

Parker, Robert. *On Greek Religion*. Ithaca: Cornell University Press, 2011.

Paton, Diana. 'The Afterlives of Three-Fingered Jack'. In *Slavery and the Cultures of Abolition: Essays Marking the Bicentennial of the British Abolition Act of 1807*, edited by Carey, Brycchan and Peter Kitson. 42–63. Woodbridge: Boydell & Brewer, 2007.

'An "Injurious" Population: Caribbean–Australian Penal Transportation and Imperial Racial Politics'. *Cultural and Social History* 5, no. 4 (2008): 449–64.

*No Bond But the Law: Punishment, Race, and Gender in Jamaican State Formation, 1780–1870*. Durham: Duke University Press, 2004.

'Obeah Acts: Producing and Policing the Boundaries of Religion in the Caribbean'. *Small Axe* 13, no. 1 (2009): 1–18.

'Punishment, Crime, and the Bodies of Slaves in Eighteenth-Century Jamaica'. *Journal of Social History* 34, no. 4 (2001): 923–54.

'The Trials of Inspector Thomas: Policing and Ethnography in Jamaica'. In *Obeah and Other Powers: The Politics of Caribbean Religion and Healing*, edited by Paton, Diana and Maarit Forde. 172–98. Durham: Duke University Press, 2012.

'Witchcraft, Poison, Law and Atlantic Slavery'. *William and Mary Quarterly* 69, no. 2 (2012): 235–64.

Patterson, Orlando. *The Sociology of Slavery: An Analysis of the Origins, Development and Structure of Negro Slave Society in Jamaica*. London: Macgibbon & Kee, 1967.

Paugh, Katherine. 'The Politics of Childbearing in the British Caribbean and the Atlantic World during the Age of Abolition, 1776–1838'. *Past and Present* 221 (2013): 119–60.

Payne-Jackson, Arvilla, and Mervyn C. Alleyne. *Jamaican Folk Medicine: A Source of Healing*. Mona, Jamaica: University of the West Indies Press, 2004.

Peel, J. D. Y. *Religious Encounter and the Making of the Yoruba*. Bloomington: Indiana University Press, 2003.

Peires, J. B. *The Dead Will Arise: Nongqawuse and the Great Xhosa Cattle-Killing Movement of 1856–7*. Johannesburg: Ravan Press, 1989.

Pels, Peter. 'The Magic of Africa: Reflections on a Western Commonplace'. *African Studies Review* 41, no. 2 (1998): 193–209.

Pemberton, Rita. 'A Different Intervention: The International Health Commission/Board, Health, Sanitation in the British Caribbean, 1914–1930'. *Caribbean Quarterly* 49, no. 4 (2003): 87–103.

Pennington, Brian K. *Was Hinduism Invented? Britons, Indians, and the Colonial Construction of Religion*. Oxford: Oxford University Press, 2005.

Perkins, Maureen. *The Reform of Time: Magic and Modernity*. London: Pluto, 2001.

Pettinger, Alasdair. 'From Vaudoux to Voodoo'. *Forum for Modern Language Studies* 40, no. 4 (2004): 415–25.

Phillippo, James M. *Jamaica: Its Past and Present State*. London: John Snow, 1843.

Pietz, William. 'The Problem of the Fetish II: The Origin of the Fetish'. *Res* 13 (1987): 23–45.

'The Problem of the Fetish, IIIa: Bosman's Guinea and the Enlightenment Theory of Fetishim'. *Res* 16 (1988): 105–23.

Pitman, Frank Wesley. 'Slavery on British West India Plantations in the Eighteenth Century'. *Journal of Negro History* 11, no. 4 (1926): 584–668.

Pluchon, Pierre. *Vaudou, sorciers, empoisonneurs de Saint-Domingue à Haïti*. Paris: Karthala, 1987.

*Poems Chiefly on the Superstition of Obeah*. London: Gale & Fenner, 1816.

Pollak-Eltz, Angelina. 'The Shango Cult and Other African Rituals in Trinidad, Grenada, and Carriacou and their Possible Influence on the Spiritual Baptist Faith'. *Caribbean Quarterly* 39, no. 3/4 (1993): 12–26.
Porter, Dale H. *The Abolition of the Slave Trade in England, 1784–1807*. Hamden, Conn.: Archon Books, 1970.
Porter, Roy. 'Witchcraft and Magic in Enlightenment, Romantic, and Liberal Thought'. In *Witchcraft and Magic in Europe: The Eighteenth and Nineteenth Centuries*, edited by Gijswijt-Hofstra, Marijke, Brian P. Levack, and Roy Porter. 191–282. London: Athlone Press, 1999.
Post, Ken. *Arise Ye Starvelings: The Jamaican Labour Rebellion of 1938 and its Aftermath*. The Hague: Martinus Nijhoff, 1978.
Price, Charles Reavis. '"Cleave to the Black": Expressions of Ethiopianism in Jamaica'. *New West Indian Guide* 77, no. 1/2 (2003): 31–64.
Price, Richard. 'Kwasimukamba's Gambit'. *Bijdragen tot de Taal-, Land en Volkenkunde* 135, no. 1 (1979): 151–69.
Purkiss, Diane. *The Witch in History: Early Modern and Twentieth-Century Representations*. London: Routledge, 1996.
Putnam, Lara. *The Company they Kept: Migrants and the Politics of Gender in Caribbean Costa Rica, 1870–1960*. Chapel Hill: University of North Carolina Press, 2002.
— *Radical Moves: Caribbean Migrants and the Politics of Race in the Jazz Age*. Chapel Hill: University of North Carolina Press, 2013.
— 'Rites of Power and Rumors of Race: The Circulation of Supernatural Knowledge in the Greater Caribbean, 1890–1940'. In *Obeah and Other Powers: The Politics of Caribbean Religion and Healing*, edited by Paton, Diana and Maarit Forde. 243–67. Durham: Duke University Press, 2012.
Quinn, Kate. '"Sitting on a Volcano": Black Power in Burnham's Guyana'. In *Black Power in the Caribbean*, edited by Quinn, Kate. 136–58. Gainesville: University Press of Florida, 2014.
Quinn, Kate, ed. *Black Power in the Caribbean*. Gainesville: University Press of Florida, 2014.
Ragatz, Lowell Joseph. *The Fall of the Planter Class in the British Caribbean, 1763–1833: A Study in Social and Economic History*. New York: The Century Co., 1928.
Ramsey, Kate. *The Spirits and the Law: Vodou and Power in Haiti*. Chicago: University of Chicago Press, 2011.
— 'Vodouyizan Protest an Amendment to the Constitution of Haiti'. *Journal of Haitian Studies* 19, no. 1 (2013): 272–81.
Ramusack, Barbara N. 'The British Construction of Indirect Rule'. In *The New Cambridge History of India*, vol. III.6: *The Indian Princes and their States*, edited by Ramusack, Barbara N. 48–87. Cambridge: Cambridge University Press, 2004; also available at *Cambridge Histories Online*, http://dx.doi.org/10.1017/CHOL9780521267274.
Ranger, Terence. 'The Invention of Tradition in Colonial Africa'. In *The Invention of Tradition*, edited by Hobsbawm, E. J. and T. O. Ranger. 211–62. Cambridge: Cambridge University Press, 1983.

*Revolt in Southern Rhodesia, 1896–97: A Study in African Resistance.* London: Heinemann, 1967.

Regourd, François. 'Mesmerism in Saint Domingue: Occult Knowledge and Vodou on the Eve of the Haitian Revolution'. In *Science and Empire in the Atlantic World*, edited by Delbourgo, James and Nicholas Dew. 311–32. New York: Routledge, 2008.

Richardson, Alan. 'Romantic Voodoo: Obeah and British Culture, 1797–1807'. In *Sacred Possessions: Vodou, Santería, Obeah, and the Caribbean*, edited by Fernández Olmos, Margarite and Lizabeth Paravisini-Gelbert. 171–94. New Brunswick: Rutgers University Press, 1997.

Riley, James C. *Poverty and Life Expectancy: The Jamaican Paradox.* Cambridge: Cambridge University Press, 2005.

Roback, Judith. 'The White-Robed Army: An Afro-Guyanese Religious Movement'. *Anthropologica* 16, no. 2 (1974): 233–68.

Roberts, George W. *The Population of Jamaica.* Cambridge: Cambridge University Press, 1957.

Rohlehr, Gordon. *Calypso and Society in Pre-Independence Trinidad.* Port of Spain: G. Rohlehr, 1990.

*A Scuffling of Islands: Essays on Calypso.* San Juan, Trinidad: Lexicon Trinidad, 2004.

Roper, Lyndal. *Oedipus and the Devil: Witchcraft, Sexuality, and Religion in Early Modern Europe.* London: Routledge, 1994.

Rosenberg, Leah Reade. *Nationalism and the Formation of Caribbean Literature.* New York: Palgrave Macmillan, 2007.

Ross, Robert. 'Ambiguities of Resistance and Collaboration on the Eastern Cape Frontier: The Kat River Settlement 1829–1856'. In *Rethinking Resistance: Revolt and Violence in African History*, edited by Abbink, Jon, Mirjam de Bruijn, and Klaas van Walraven. 117–40. Leiden: Brill, 2003.

Roughley, Thomas. *The Jamaica Planter's Guide; Or, A System for Planting and Managing a Sugar Estate...* London: Longman, Hurst, Rees, Orme, & Brown, 1823.

Salmon, C. S. *The Caribbean Confederation: A Plan for the Union of the Fifteen British West Indian Colonies, preceded by an Account of the Past and Present Condition of the Europeans and the African Races Inhabiting them, with a True Explanation of the Haytian Mystery.* London: Frank Cass, 1971 [1888].

Samaroo, Brinsley. 'The February Revolution (1970) as a Catalyst for Change in Trinidad and Tobago'. In *Black Power in the Caribbean*, edited by Quinn, Kate. 97–116. Gainesville: University Press of Florida, 2014.

Sanderson, John. *An Appeal to the Imperial Parliament upon the Claims of the Ceded Colony of Trinidad, to be Governed by a Legislature and Judicature, Founded on Principles Sanctioned by Colonial Precedents and Long Usage.* London: J. M. Richardson, 1812.

Sandiford, Keith. *Theorizing a Colonial Caribbean-Atlantic Imaginary: Sugar and Obeah.* New York: Routledge, 2011.

Sansi, Roger. 'Sorcery and Fetishism in the Modern Atlantic'. In *Sorcery in the Black Atlantic*, edited by Paré, Luis Nicolau and Roger Sansi. 19–39. Chicago: University of Chicago Press, 2011.

Satchell, Veront M. 'Colonial Injustice: The Crown v the Bedwardites, 27 April 1921'. In *The African-Caribbean Worldview and the Making of Caribbean Society*, edited by Levy, Horace. 46–67. Mona, Jamaica: University of the West Indies Press, 2009.

Savage, John. 'Between Colonial Fact and French Law: Slave Poisoners and the Provostial Court in Restoration-Era Martinique'. *French Historical Studies* 29, no. 4 (2006): 565–94.

Savory, Elaine. 'Strategies for Survival: Anti-Imperialist Theatrical Forms in the Anglophone Caribbean'. In *Imperialism and Theatre: Essays on World Theatre, Drama and Performance*, edited by Gainor, J. Ellen. 237–50. London and New York: Routledge, 1995.

Schiebinger, Londa. 'Scientific Exchange in the Eighteenth-Century Atlantic World'. In *Soundings in Atlantic History: Latent Structures and Intellectual Currents, 1500–1830*, edited by Bailyn, Bernard and Patricia L. Denault. 294–328. Cambridge, Mass.: Harvard University Press, 2009.

Schoenhals, Kai P., and Richard A. Melanson. *Revolution and Intervention in Grenada: The New Jewel Movement, the United States, and the Caribbean*. Boulder: Westview Press, 1985.

Schuler, Monica. *'Alas, Alas, Kongo': A Social History of Indentured African Immigration into Jamaica, 1841–1865*. Baltimore: Johns Hopkins University Press, 1980.

Schwarz, Philip J. *Twice Condemned: Slaves and the Criminal Laws of Virginia, 1705–1865*. Baton Rouge: Louisiana State University Press, 1988.

Scott, David. *Conscripts of Modernity: The Tragedy of Colonial Enlightenment*. Durham: Duke University Press, 2004.

Scott, Dennis. *An Echo in the Bone*. In *Plays for Today*, edited by Hill, Errol. 73–137. Harlow: Pearson Education, 1985.

Seaga, Edward. 'Revival Cults in Jamaica: Notes towards a Sociology of Religion'. *Jamaica Journal* 3, no. 2 (1969): 3–13.

Sensbach, Jon F. *Rebecca's Revival: Creating Black Christianity in the Atlantic World*. Cambridge, Mass.: Harvard University Press, 2005.

Sernett, Milton C., ed. *African American Religious History: A Documentary Witness*. Durham: Duke University Press, 1999.

Sewell, Lileth. 'Music in the Jamaican Labour Movement'. *Jamaica Journal* 43 (1979): 43–55.

Sharpe, Jenny. *Ghosts of Slavery: A Literary Archaeology of Black Women's Lives*. Minneapolis: University of Minnesota Press, 2003.

Shaw, Rosalind. *Memories of the Slave Trade: Ritual and the Historical Imagination in Sierra Leone*. Chicago: University of Chicago Press, 2002.

Sheller, Mimi. *Consuming the Caribbean: From Arawaks to Zombies*. London: Routledge, 2003.

Simey, T. S. *Welfare and Planning in the West Indies*. London: Oxford University Press, 1946.

Simpson, George Eaton. *Black Religions in the New World*. New York: Columbia University Press, 1978.

'Folk Medicine in Trinidad'. *Journal of American Folklore* 75 (1962): 326–40.

'Jamaican Revivalist Cults'. *Social and Economic Studies* 5 (1956): 321–442.

'Personal Reflections on Rastafari in West Kingston in the Early 1950s'. In *Chanting Down Babylon: The Rastafari Reader*, edited by Murrell, Nathaniel Samuel, William David Spencer and Adrian Anthony McFarlane. 217–28. Philadelphia: Temple University Press, 1998.

'The Shango Cult in Nigeria and in Trinidad'. *American Anthropologist* 64, no. 6 (1964): 1204–19.

Singham, A. W. *The Hero and the Crowd in a Colonial Polity*. New Haven: Yale University Press, 1968.

Smith, Faith. *Creole Recitations: John Jacob Thomas and Colonial Formation in the Late Nineteenth-Century Caribbean*. Charlottesville: University of Virginia Press, 2002.

Smith, Frederick H. *Caribbean Rum: A Social and Economic History*. Gainesville: University Press of Florida, 2005.

Smith, Raymond T. 'Caribbean Families: Questions for Research and Implications for Policy'. In *Caribbean Families in Britain and the Trans-Atlantic World*, edited by Goulbourne, Harry and Mary Chamberlain. 48–62. London: Macmillan, 2001.

*The Matrifocal Family: Power, Pluralism, and Politics*. New York: Routledge, 1996.

Snelgrave, William. *A New Account of some parts of Guinea, and the Slave Trade*. London: J. J. & P. Knapton, 1734.

St John, Spenser. *Hayti, or The Black Republic*. London: Smith, Elder, 1884; 2nd edn. 1889.

Stedman, John Gabriel. *Narrative of a Five Years Expedition against the Revolted Negroes of Surinam, Transcribed for the First Time from the Original 1790 Manuscript*, edited by Price, Richard and Sally Price. New York: iUniverse, 2010.

Stewart, Dianne M. *Three Eyes for the Journey: African Dimensions of the Jamaican Religious Experience*. Oxford: Oxford University Press, 2005.

Stewart, John. *A View of the Past and Present State of the Island of Jamaica; with Remarks on the Moral and Physical Condition of the Slaves, and on the Abolition of Slavery in the Colonies*. Edinburgh: Oliver & Boyd, 1823.

Stone, Judy S. J. *Theatre*. London: Macmillan Caribbean, 1994.

Swaminathan, Srividhya. *Debating the Slave Trade: Rhetoric of British National Identity, 1759–1815*. Farnham: Ashgate, 2009.

Swan, Quito. *Black Power in Bermuda: The Struggle for Decolonization*. Basingstoke: Palgrave Macmillan, 2010.

Sweet, James H. *Domingo Álvares, African Healing, and the Intellectual History of the Atlantic World*. Chapel Hill: University of North Carolina Press, 2011.

*Recreating Africa: Culture, Kinship, and Religion in the African-Portuguese World, 1441–1770*. Chapel Hill: University of North Carolina Press, 2003.

ten Kortenaar, Neil. *Postcolonial Literature and the Impact of Literacy: Reading and Writing in African and Caribbean Fiction*. Cambridge: Cambridge University Press, 2011.

Thicknesse, Philip. *Memoirs and Anecdotes of Philip Thicknesse Late Lieutenant Governor, Land Guard Fort, and Unfortunately Father to George Touchet, Baron Audley*. Dublin: William Jones, 1788.

Thieme, John. 'Repossessing the Slave Past: Caribbean Historiography and Dennis Scott's *An Echo in the Bone*'. In *Theatre and Slavery: Ghosts at the Crossroads*, edited by Walling, Michael. 42–52. Enfield: Border Crossings, 2007.

Thomas, Deborah. *Modern Blackness: Nationalism, Globalization, and the Politics of Culture in Jamaica*. Durham: Duke University Press, 2004.

Thomas, J. J. *Froudacity: West Indian Fables by James Anthony Froude*. London: New Beacon, 1969 [1889].

*The Theory and Practice of Creole Grammar*. London: New Beacon, 1969 [1869]

Thomas, Roy, ed. *The Trinidad Labour Riots of 1937: Perspectives 50 Years Later*. St Augustine, Trinidad: Extra-Mural Studies Unit, University of the West Indies, 1987.

Thompson, Alvin O. *A Documentary History of Slavery in Berbice 1796–1834*. Georgetown, Guyana: Free Press, 2002.

*Unprofitable Servants: Crown Slaves in Berbice, Guyana, 1803–1831*. Mona, Jamaica: University of the West Indies Press, 2002.

Thornton, John. *Africa and Africans in the Making of the Atlantic World, 1400–1800*. Cambridge: Cambridge University Press, 1998.

*The Kongolese Saint Anthony: Dona Beatriz Kimpa Vita and the Antonian Movement, 1684–1706*. Cambridge: Cambridge University Press, 1998.

Thornton, S. Leslie. '"Obeah" in Jamaica'. *Journal of the Society of Comparative Legislation* 5 (1903): 262–70.

Trotman, David V. 'Reflections on the Children of Shango: An Essay on the History of Orisa Worship in Trinidad'. *Slavery and Abolition* 28, no. 2 (2007): 211–34.

Trouillot, Michel-Rolph. 'The Caribbean Region: An Open Frontier in Anthropological Theory'. *Annual Review of Anthropology* 21 (1993): 19–42.

*Global Transformations: Anthropology and the Modern World*. New York: Palgrave Macmillan, 2003.

Turner, Mary. *Slaves and Missionaries: The Disintegration of Jamaican Slave Society, 1787–1834*. Urbana: University of Illinois Press, 1982.

Udal, J. S. 'Obeah in the West Indies'. *Folk-Lore: A Quarterly Review of Myth, Tradition, Institution, & Custom* 26 (1915): 255–95.

Umeh, John Anenechukwu. *After God is Dibia: Igbo Cosmology, Divination and Sacred Science in Nigeria*. London: Karnak House, 1997.

Upchurch, Charles. 'Full-Text Databases and Historical Research: Cautionary Results from a Ten-Year Study'. *Journal of Social History* 45, no. 1 (2012): 89–105.

van Wetering, Ineke. 'Polyvocality and Constructions of Syncretism in Winti'. In *Reinventing Religions: Syncretism and Transformation in Africa and the Americas*, edited by Greenfield, Sidney M. and André Droogers. 183–200. Oxford: Rowman & Littlefield, 2001.

Vansina, Jan. *Paths in the Rainforest: Toward a History of Political Tradition in Equatorial Africa*. London: James Currey, 1990.

Vincent, David. *Literacy and Popular Culture: England 1750–1914*. Cambridge: Cambridge University Press, 1989.

Viotti da Costa, Emilia. *Crowns of Glory, Tears of Blood: The Demerara Slave Rebellion of 1823*. New York: Oxford University Press, 1994.

Ward, Candace. '"What Time has Proved": History, Rebellion and Revolution in *Hamel, the Obeah Man*'. *Ariel: A Review of International English Literature* 38, no. 1 (2007): 49-73.
Ward, Candace, and Tim Watson. 'Introduction'. In Cynric Williams, *Hamel, the Obeah Man*. 9-46. Peterborough, Ontario: Broadview, 2010.
Warner-Lewis, Maureen. *Guinea's Other Suns: The African Dynamic in Trinidad Culture*. Dover, Mass.: The Majority Press, 1991.
Waters, Hazel. *Racism on the Victorian Stage: Representation of Slavery and the Black Character*. Cambridge: Cambridge University Press, 2007.
Watson, Tim. *Caribbean Culture and British Fiction in the Atlantic World, 1780–1870*. Cambridge: Cambridge University Press, 2008.
Weaver, Karol K. *Medical Revolutionaries: The Enslaved Healers of Eighteenth-Century Saint Domingue*. Urbana: University of Illinois Press, 2006.
Wedenoja, William. 'Mothering and the Practice of Balm in Jamaica'. In *Women as Healers: Cross-Cultural Perspectives*, edited by McClain, Carol Shepherd. 76-97. New Brunswick: Rutgers University Press, 1989.
'The Origins of Revival, a Creole Religion in Jamaica'. In *Culture and Christianity*, edited by Saunders, George. 91-116. New York: Greenwood Press, 1988.
Weise, Kesia. *Guzzum Power: Obeah in Jamaica*. Kingston: African Caribbean Institute of Jamaica/Jamaica Memory Bank, 2010.
Westergaard, Waldemar. *The Danish West Indies under Company Rule (1671–1754) with a Supplementary Chapter 1755–1917*. New York: Macmillan, 1917.
White, Noel. 'St William Wellington Grant: A Fighter for Black Dignity'. *Jamaica Journal* 43 (1979): 56-63.
Whitham, Charlie. *Bitter Rehearsal: British and American Planning for a Post-War West Indies*. Westport, Conn.: Praeger, 2002.
Whyte, Iain. *Scotland and the Abolition of Black Slavery, 1756–1838*. Edinburgh: Edinburgh University Press, 2006.
Wilberforce, William. *An Appeal to the Religion, Justice, and Humanity of the Inhabitants of the British Empire*. London: Hatchard, 1823.
Wilkins, Mary Fanny. *The Slave Son*. In *Adolphus, a Tale and The Slave Son*, edited by Winer, Lisa. 93-324. Kingston: University of the West Indies Press, 2003 [1854].
Williams, Brackette F. *Stains on my Name, War in my Veins: Guyana and the Politics of Cultural Struggle*. Durham: Duke University Press, 1991.
Williams, Cynric R. *Hamel: The Obeah Man*, edited by Ward, Candace and Tim Watson. Peterborough, Ontario: Broadview, 2010 [1827].
*A Tour through the Island of Jamaica, from the Western to the Eastern End, in the Year 1823*. London: T. Hurst, E. Chance & Co., 1827.
Williamson, Karina, ed. *Contrary Voices: Representations of West Indian Slavery, 1657–1834*. Mona, Jamaica: University of the West Indies Press, 2008.
Wilson, Godfrey. *An Essay on the Economics of Detribalization in Northern Rhodesia*. Livingstone, Northern Rhodesia: Rhodes–Livingstone Institute, 1941.
Winterbottom, Thomas M. *An account of the native Africans in the neighbourhood of Sierra Leone, to which is added an account of the present state of medicine among*

*them*. London: J. Hatchard & J. Mawman, 1803; facsimile repr. London: Cass, 1969.
Wise, K. S. *Historical Sketches of Trinidad and Tobago*. Vol. II. Port of Spain: Trinidad Historical Society, 1936.
Wisecup, Kelly. 'Knowing Obeah'. *Atlantic Studies* 10, no. 3 (2013): 406–25.
Wynter, Sylvia. Maskarade: A 'Jonkonnu' Musical Play. In *Mixed Company: Three Early Jamaican Plays*, edited by Brewster, Yvonne. 17–132. London: Oberon Books, 2012.
Yelvington, Kevin A. 'The Invention of Africa in Latin America and the Caribbean: Political Discourse and Anthropolical Praxis, 1920–1940'. In *Afro-Atlantic Dialogues: Anthropology in the Diaspora*, edited by Yelvington, Kevin A. 35–82. Santa Fe: School of American Research Press, 2006.
Young, Jason R. *Rituals of Resistance: African Atlantic Religion in Kongo and the Lowcountry South in the Era of Slavery*. Baton Rouge: Louisiana State University Press, 2007.

# Index

Abercromby, Sir Ralph, 79
abolition, 10, 49, 87, 116–18
*Account of the Island of Jamaica* (Marsden), 69
*Account of the Native Africans in the Neighbourhood of Sierra Leone* (Winterbottom), 71
Act to remedy the evils arising from irregular assemblies of slaves (Jamaica, 1760), 17–18, 31, 39–42, 43, 88–9, 90, 91, 98
Adair, James, 60, 62, 63, 64
*Advocate-News* (newspaper), 287
Africa
　anti-colonialism, 156
　detribalization, 271–2
　government of British colonies, 136–7, 154–6, 266, 271–2
　influence on Caribbean culture, 9, 134, 135–6, 137, 138, 148–55, 156, 224, 227–8, 241, 265, 266–9, 272–3, 283–4, 286, 288, 296, 315
　labour protests, 271–2
　magic and spiritual power, 265–6
　religions, 17–18, 22–5, 288
*Africa and Africans* (Thornton), 23
African Americans, 269–70
African Apostolic Brotherhood, 287
African Caribbean Institute of Jamaica, 4–5
African Society for Cultural Relations with Independent Africa (ASCRIA), 284, 285
African spiritual power, 17–18, 22–5
　and Christian missionaries, 94
　and politics, 156
　and slave rebellions, 91–2, 99
　in popular religion, 177–82
　post-emancipation period, 121
　terminology, 85–90, 93
Afro-Athlican Constructive Gaathly (AACG), 248–9

Aitken, Richard, 146
Akan, 9
　etymology of obeah, 28, 30
　*obayifo*, 24
　obeah practitioners, 30, 31–2, 36–7, 39
Alexander, Joseph 'Kola', 182–3, 188–9, 191, 194
Alleyne, Mervyn C., 7, 57
Álvares, Domingo, 14
amelioration, 90, 93–4
*American Curiosity* (Parish), 20
Anderson, Oswald, 247–8, 258
Anderson, William, 110–14
Andrews, William, 145
Anguilla, 5
animal magnetism, comparison with obeah, 63
anthropology, 45–6, 265, 268–70
anti-Africanism, 305
anti-colonialism, 154, 156, 244, 260, 286, 288–92
Antigua
　anti-obeah legislation, 90, 122, 123, 127
　political role of obeah practitioners, 39
　post-emancipation period, 122, 123, 127
　responses to parliamentary inquiry on slave trade, 60, 61–2, 63, 64–5
　slave rebellions, 35–8
*Antigua Standard* (newspaper), 144
anti-obeah legislation, 9–11, 17–18, 89–97, 116–18, 120, 153–4, 267–8
　and white practitioners, 92–3
　Antigua, 90, 122, 123, 127
　Barbados, 90, 91–2, 125, 142, 143
　Belize, 92
　Berbice, 92, 96
　British Guiana (Guyana), 120, 123, 127–8, 143, 286
　British Honduras, 90
　Dominica, 64, 90, 91, 93
　Grenada, 143

347

## Index

anti-obeah legislation (*cont.*)
  Jamaica, 6–7, 17–18, 31, 39–42, 43, 88–9, 90, 91, 92, 96–7, 120, 122, 123, 124, 126, 127–8, 132, 142, 144, 145–7, 152–3, 281–2
  Leeward Islands, 132, 143–4, 165
  Nevis, 92, 93
  post-emancipation period, 121, 142–8
  St Lucia, 143
  St Vincent, 92, 123–4, 125–6
  Trinidad and Tobago, 77–8, 81–2, 143
anti-Revival legislation, 151–4, 164–5
anti-witchcraft legislation, 155–6
Aravamudan, Srinivas, 57
art theatre, 299, 305–13
assemblages, 98–9, 112–13, 140, 153, 161, 191, 196–7, 223–4, 226–7
*At Last* (Kingsley), 120–1
Atwood, Thomas, 69
Austin-Broos, Diane, 149

Bailey, Samuel, 198
Bailey, Theophilus, 201
Bakan, Abigail, 244
Baker, Amelia, 177
balm yards, 150, 229–30, 246, 247–9, 258, 262, 263
*Banana Bottom* (McKay), 210–11
Banbury, Thomas R., 28, 132
Barbados
  anti-obeah legislation, 90, 91–2, 125, 142, 143
  decriminalization of obeah, 5
  education, 264
  obeah trials, 212
  post-emancipation period, 125, 127, 142, 143
  responses to parliamentary inquiry on slave trade, 60, 61, 62, 63, 64–5
  slave rebellions, 94
  social protests, 243
Barclay, Alexander, 117
Barkly, Henry, 127
Barnes, Ellen, 167–8
Barnes, John, 185
Barnett, Eliza, 185
Barrett, Francis, 234
Bates, David, 168, 223
baths, in rituals, 224–5
Beckwith, Martha, 230
Bedward, Alexander, 150, 154, 246–7
Bedwardism, 150, 154, 246–7, 301
Begorrat, St Hilaire de, 79, 83
*Belinda* (Edgeworth), 72
Belize (British Honduras), 90, 92

Bell, Hesketh J., 28, 131, 139–42
Benkins, Samuel, 212
Berbice, 77–8, *see also* Guyana (British Guiana)
  anti-obeah legislation, 92, 96
  obeah trials, 83–8, 108–9, 115
  punishments, 97
Berbice Dutch, 85–6
Bible, use in ritual, 225–6, 232
Bilby, Kenneth M., 1, 29, 31–2, 45, 71, 122, 277
Bim and Bam, 302–3
biomedicine, 218–19, 252–6, 262
Bishop, Maurice, 295, 296–7
*Bizoton, affaire de* (1863), 128–9
Black Israelite Church, 249
*Black Magic* (Chireau), 22
*Black Man* (newspaper), 260
Black Power movement, 274, 282–3, 284, 293
Black, George, 188
Blagrove, Simeon Luther, 237
Board of Trade, 45–69, 89, 96
Bohls, Elizabeth, 60
Bolland, O. Nigel, 243
Bollettino, Maria Alessandra, 39
Bomfim, Seu Martiano de, 6
books, use in rituals, 209, 232–5, 282
Bosman, Willem, 24
Brathwaite, Herbert, 212
Brathwaite, John, 60, 61, 62, 63, 64, 76
Brathwaite, Kamau, 77
Brazil, 5–6, 20, 23, 83
Brereton, Bridget, 82, 198
Bridgens, Richard, 105–6
British Guiana (Guyana). *See* Guyana (British Guiana)
British Honduras. *See* Belize (British Honduras)
British Humanitarian League, 146
'British West Indies Today' (Cundall), 3–4
British–Maroon war, 32–5, 39
Brooks, Cindy, 274
Brown, David, 6
Brown, James 'Tata', 206
Brown, Thaddeus 'Professor', 214
Brown, Vincent, 9, 39, 41, 58, 77, 95, 100, 110
Browne, Randy, 113
Bruce, William, 221, 224
Brutus (Captain Brutus), 101
Bryan, Boaz, 185
Bryant, Jacob, 28, 53
Buchanan, Hugh, 257–8
Buckridee, 286

# Index

Burdett, William, 72–4, 210
Burke, Nathaniel, 225
Burke, S. C., 193–4
Burnham, Forbes, 274, 276–7, 283–92
Bush, Barbara, 46
Bustamente, Sir Alexander, 251
Bustamante Industrial Trade Union, 251
Butler, Uriah 'Buzz', 244, 264, 275

Caesar, Doctor, 96
Calderón, Luisa, 79
*calundú*, 20
calypso, 180–1, 296, 307–8
Campbell, Colonel (*c*. 1730), 34
Campbell, Frank, 180
Campbell, James, 220
Candlin, Kit, 79, 81
Candomblé, 5–6, 20
cannibalism, 128–30, 131, 132–4, 137
capital punishment, 99, 100, 116, 123
Caradose, Francis, 153, 154, 200, 203
cards, use in rituals, 220–1
*Caribbean Confederation* (Salmon), 136–8
Caribbean Conference of Churches, 287
Carifesta (Caribbean Festival of Arts), 284
Carrington, Hubert, 237
Carter, Charles, 238–9
Carter, Martin, 291
Carter, Stewart, 224
Carter, Thomas, 202
Carver, J. Cowell, 146
*Case of John Ras I* (Bim and Bam) (play), 303
Castello, John, 124, 125
*Castes of Mind* (Dirks), 8
Catholicism, 25, 140, 141, 200, 201–2, 287, 292, 303–4
Caws, Byron F., 247
censorship, 234, 282
chalk marks, in rituals, 225
Chalmers, George, 49
Chambers, Douglas B., 29
child sacrifice, 129–30, 131, 287
Childs, Matt D., 9
Chireau, Yvonne P., 22
Chisholme, James, 28, 38–9, 51–60, 61, 66, 70, 110, 114
Christian, Walter William, 216, 226
Christianity
and obeah, 201–2, 225–6, 232
influence on Caribbean culture, 134, 135, 136, 148
opposition to obeah, 261–3, 287, 288
Church Army of America, 251
*Civilising Subjects* (Hall), 148

Clark, Stuart, 26
Clarke, Clement, 230
Clarke, Sir Fielding, 190
Clarkson, Thomas, 50
clearing rituals, 112–13
Clement, Mary and Arthur, 182–3, 190, 191, 192, 194–6, 197, 198, 201–2, 203–4, 237–8
clergy, memorandum to Moyne Commission, 261–3
Codrington, Archie, 287, 290
Colebrooke, William, 125–7, 145
Colonial Development and Welfare Act (Great Britain, 1940), 272
Colonial Office
  African colonies, 136–7, 154–6, 266
  entrapment policy, 189
  indirect rule, 136–7, 266
  post-emancipation colonial policy, 120, 122–3, 144–5, 154–6
  post-emancipation period, 147–57
  public health campaigns, 252–6
  slavery period, 13, 20, 31, 32, 77–8, 117
comedy, 298–305
Comfa, 285
Committee on Trade and Plantations (Board of Trade), 45–69, 89, 96
Compass, David, 212
Confou man, 85–6, 93
conjure, 21–2
Consolidated Slave Act (Barbados, 1826), 92
Consolidated Slave Law (Jamaica, 1801), 115
Cook, Edith, 221
Cooter, Roger, 63
corporal punishment, 6–7, 91, 97, 122, 124, 125, 142–7, 172, 174, 203–4, 279
  in England, 146
Court, 30, 37, 39
Cousins, Phyllis, 32
Cox, Peggy, 261
*Creole Religions of the Caribbean* (Fernández Olmos and Paravisini-Gebert), 1
creole slave society
  and sexual relationships, 109–15
  enslaved men, 113–14
creolization, 9
*Crisis of the West Indian Family* (Matthews), 279–80
Cross, Iris, 218–19
Cuba, 5–6, 23, 270
Cudjoe, 32, 88

culture, 1, 177–82, 241, 268–73
  African influences, 9, 134, 135–6, 137, 138, 148–55, 156, 224, 227–8, 241, 265, 266–9, 272–3, 283–4, 286, 288, 296, 315
  (East) Indian influences, 169, 285
  and national identity, 283–92, 299, 309–10
  and politics, 3, 147, 162, 265–6, 283–92
  and religion, 3, 147–57, 169–70, 259–60, 268–9, 275–8, 314–16
  Carifesta, 284
  effects of detribalization, 271–2
  European influences, 18–19
  fiction and poetry, 69, 71–5, 83, 115–16, 210–11, 277
  music, 180–1, 277, 294, 295–6, 307–8
  theatre, 277–8, 298–313
Cundall, Frank, 3–4
Cupidon, Ernest, 298–9, 300–1

Daley, Cecelia, 180
Daly, John, 224
Danish West Indies, 20–1
Dascent, Theophilus, 212
Davis, David Brion, 47
Davis, N. Darnell, 134–6, 137, 138, 145
de Brown, Dawkins, 237
Debbasch, Yvan, 20
decolonization, 274–7, 292–8
decriminalization of obeah, 5, 6, 10, 276–7, 285–6, 287, 296
DeLaurence publications, 209, 232–5, 282
*Della* (Reckord) (play), 306–7
Demerara, 94
Denmark, 20–1
Depression (Great Depression), 241
*Description de la Côte Occidentale d'Afrique* (Fernandes), 24
determinism, 9–10
detribalization, 271–2
*Devil's Legacy* (Anon.), 233
*dibia*, 29
Dicks, Edmund, 235
Dillon, J. P., 263
Dirks, Nicholas B., 8
divination rituals, 105–6, 108–9, 177
  Minje Mama dance, 84–5, 86
Dolly, Charles, 14, 177, 178, 223
Dominica
  amelioration, 90
  anti-obeah legislation, 64, 90, 91, 93
  slave trade, 31
  slavery period, 116
Donald, Joseph, 188

double acts (comedy), 302–3
Doyle, Victoria, 168, 191
drama, 277–8
Drescher, Seymour, 48, 120
DuBois, W. E. B., 28
Dundas, Henry, Viscount Melville, 49
Dunham, Katherine, 270–1
duppies (jumbies), 22, 141, 184, 208, 219, 222–4, 225, 227–8, 237, 252
*Duppy Biznezz* (Bim and Bam) (play), 302–3
Duvalier, Jean-Claude, 5, 277, 298

Earl, Robert S., 154–5
Earle, William, 72, 74–5, 210
East Indians, 165, 168–70, 216, 234–5, 284, 285
Ebroin, Ary, 22
*Echo in the Bone* (Scott) (play), 277–8, 299, 311–13
economy, 241, 243, 289
  industrialization, 271–2
  transnational networks, 211–13, 214–16, 243–4
Edgeworth, Maria, 71–2
Edo, 29
education, 11, 257–8, 259, 260, 264, 267–8, 279–80
  public information campaigns, 254–5
Edwards, Bryan, 45, 69–71, 74, 75, 89
Edwards, James, 206
Edwards, Samuel, 222
Efik, 30
eggs and eggshells, use in ritual, 113, 226
Egyptian etymology, obeah, 28, 53
*Egyptian Secrets of Albertus Magnus* (DeLaurence), 233–4
elections, 275, 289, 290, 291, 292, 302
electric shock, 58
electrical healing, 237
Elementary Teachers' Association of Barbados, 264
Elkins, W. F., 149, 154
Elleston, Robert, 205–6
Eltis, David, 9
employment problems, 217
*English in the West Indies* (Froude), 119, 121, 129–33, 137
  criticism of, 133–42
English law, influence on colonial law, 126
Enlightenment, 18–19
entertainers, 237
entrapment cases, 167–8, 183, 185–7, 203, 217, 238–9, 248–9
Epstein, James, 79, 82
Equiano, Olaudah, 50

# Index

esoteric knowledge, 225–6
Ethiopianism, 244, 249, 251
etymology, 27–31
  Akan theory, 28
  Egyptian theory, 28, 53
  Igbo theory, 29
European witchcraft, 18–19, 25–7, 40–2
  comparison with obeah, 91, 99, 141–2
Evans-Pritchard, E. E., 265–6
*Exchanging our Country Marks* (Gomez), 9, 22
*Execution of John Ras I* (Bim and Bam) (play), 303
'eyesight', 219–20

Facey, Susan, 196
*Falmouth Post* (newspaper), 124, 125, 149
Falola, Toyin, 9
family life, 124–5, 268–70, 279–80
Fara, Patricia, 63
Faulkner, Emanuel, 185
Fawcett, John, 72, 77
February Revolution (Trinidad, 1970), 284
*feitiço*, 20
Fenton, Joseph, 248
Fernandes, Valentim, 24
Fernández Olmos, Margarite, 1
fetish, definition, 20
Fett, Sharla M., 22
fiction, 69, 71–5, 83, 115–16, 210–11, 277
fines, 172
Firmin, Anténor, 6
flogging, 6–7, 91, 97, 122, 124, 125, 142–7, 172, 174, 203–4, 279
  in England, 146
folk beliefs, 140, *see also* witchcraft
Fon, 30
Forbes, Archibald, 165, 222
Forbes, George, 14, 226, 229–30
Forbes, Rose Anne (Mammy), 14, 229–30
Forde, Maarit, 160
Foucault, Michel, 147
fowls, sacrifice, 214, 224
France, colonial policy, 20, 22
Francis, Isabella, 203
Francis, William, 184
Fraser, William, 212
fraud, 214–16, 304–5
Frazier, E. Franklin, 269–70, 271
Frey, Sylvia, 46
*Froudacity* (Thomas), 119–20, 133–4, 137, 138
Froude, James Anthony, 119, 121, 129–33
  criticism of, 133–42

Fry, John, 108
Fullarton, William, 80, 81, 116
Fuller, Stephen, 28, 38–9, 51–60, 61, 66, 70

Gairy, Eric, 275, 277, 292–8
Gale, William, 206
Games, Alison, 20
Gardelin Slave Code (1733), 20–1
Garraway, Doris, 27
Garrison, Grace Jenkins, 248–9, 250
Garvey, Marcus, 249, 259–60, 301
Garveyism, 248, 258–60
Geffrard, Fabre, 128–9
genres, 298–9
George, 99
ghosts, 141
Gikandi, Simon, 43
Gilbert, Letitia, 184
Girvan, Tom, 270
Glazier, Stephen D., 6, 164
*Gleaner* (newspaper), 10, 132, 138, 145, 146, 150, 152, 161, 164, 169, 210–11, 234, 243, 246, 252–3, 291
*Global Transformations* (Trouillot), 1
Gomez, Michael A., 9, 22
Goodridge, Charles F., 248–9
Gordon, Matthew Russell, 191, 206
Gottlieb, Karla, 32
governmentality, 271–2
Grandier, James, 199, 203
Grant, Joanna, 224
Grant, St William, 251
*Great Book of Magical Art, Hindu Magic, and East Indian Occultism and Talismanic Magic* (DeLaurence), 234–5
Great Britain
  judicial flogging in England, 146
  Moyne Commission, 14, 241, 243, 247, 260–8, 269–70, 272
  Parliamentary Report into the Slave Trade (1789), 12
Great Depression, 241
Greaves, Norman, 202
Grenada
  anti-obeah legislation, 143
  labour protests, 292
  obeah trials, 14, 102, 104, 118
  politics, 276, 277, 292–8
  post-emancipation period, 143
  responses to parliamentary inquiry on slave trade, 60, 61, 63, 81
  Revival, 151–2, 292
  slave trade, 31
Grenville, William Wyndham, Baron, 49

Guadeloupe, 22
Guerra, Fernando, 6
Guyana (British Guiana), 251, *see also* Berbice
  anti-obeah legislation, 120, 123, 127–8, 143, 286
  decriminalization of obeah, 276–7
  East Indian community, 284, 285
  ethnic divisions, 286
  independence, 283–92
  obeah trials, 235, 286
  politics, 276–7, 283–92
  popular culture, 304–5
  post-emancipation period, 120, 123, 124, 127–8
  Revival, 151, 248
Guyana Council of Churches, 287
Guyana Muslim Centre, 288
'Guzzum Power: Obeah in Jamaica' (exhibition, 2011), 4–5, 7

Haiti, 121, 128–9, 270
  British perceptions of, 128–9, 132–3, 134–5, 137
  constitution, 5, 22
  US occupation of, 315
  Vodou, 5, 6, 22, 23, 121, 128–9, 134–5, 137, 261, 269, 298, 315
Hall, Catherine, 148
Hall, E. J., 235
Hall, Gwendolyn Midlo, 22
Hall, Nathaniel, 226
Hall, Neville, 20
Hall, William, 221
Hamaludin, Mohammed, 287
Handler, Jerome S., 1, 29, 31–2, 45, 71, 122
Hanson, Beatrice, 202, 238
harmful practices, 25, 104–8, 109–15, 177–9, 293
Harmit, Francis, 204
*Harpers*, 132
Harriott, Anthony, 281
Harris, Henrietta, 223
Hart, Richard, 103
Harvey, Annie and David, 249
Hatfield, Jacob, 204, 225
Havard, Robert, 79
Hawkesbury, Robert Banks Jenkinson, Lord, 49, 51, 66
Hayes, Kevin J., 233
*Hayti, or the Black Republic* (St John), 128–9, 130, 132–3
health and healing, 92, 96, 118, 149, 150, 167–8, 182–3, 184, 192, 200–1, 203, 216–18, 222–3, 228–32, 235–40, 264–5
  diagnostic techniques, 219–22
  legislation, 152–3, 155–6
  mental health, 252–3
  role of biomedicine, 218–19, 252–6, 258, 262
Health Week, 255, 258
Henderson, Robert Bird, 235
Henry, Claudius, 280, 282
Henry, Frances, 6
Henry, John, 199, 203
Herskovits, Frances, 271
Herskovits, Melville, 9, 29, 213, 270–1
Hibbert, Joseph, 250
Higman, B. W., 134
Hill, Donald, 30
Hill, Errol, 277, 307–11
Hill, Robert A., 244–5, 259
Hinds, Miriam, 221
Hinduism, 169–70, 234–6, 285
*History of Jamaica* (Long), 52, 74
*History of the Island of Dominica* (Atwood), 69
*History of Trinidad* (Joseph), 82
*History, Civil and Commercial of the British West Indies* (Edwards), 45, 69–71, 74
Hodges, Hugh, 47
Hogg, Donald, 6
Holness, Ralph, 303
*Holy Piby* (Rogers), 248
homeopathy, 235
Hood, Thomas Mortimer, 183
hookworm, eradication measures, 252, 253–4, 255–6
Houk, James T., 150
House, Thomas, 109–10, 113
Howell, Leonard, 245, 247, 248, 250
Hughes, Alister, 295, 296–7
Humphrey, Chester, 294–5
Humphreys, Mrs, 180
Hurston, Zora Neale, 251, 270–1
Hutchinson, William, 60, 62, 64
hypnotism, 238–9

Ibibio, 30
identity, 5, 283–92, 299, 309–10, 314–16
Igbo, 29, 110
independence, 268, 274–7, 282, 292–8, 313
India, 130–1, 266, 284
indirect rule, 136–7, 266
industrialization, 271–2
Inquisition, 14, 20
Institute of Jamaica (IoJ), 4–5

Index

International Labour Organization, 5
Isidore, Albertha, 153–4
Islam, 288
Israelites (Black Israelite Church), 249

Jack (Three-Fingered Jack), 69, 72–5, 89
Jack, of St George, Jamaica, 102–3
Jackson, Shepherd Levi, 251
Jackson, Thomas Witter, 126
Jagan, Cheddi, 284, 286, 290
Jamaica
   anti-obeah legislation, 39–42, 43, 88–9, 90, 91, 92, 96–7, 120, 122, 123, 124, 126, 127–8, 132, 142, 144, 145–7, 152–3, 281–2
   censorship of occult literature, 234, 282
   East Indian community, 165, 168–70, 216
   independence, 274, 282
   legal status of obeah, 6–7, 17–18, 31, 59, 274, 276, 278–82
   Maroon communities, 32–5, 39, 270
   Morant Bay Rebellion (1865), 120, 129, 156
   myalism, 112–13, 126, 145, 148–9
   obeah trials, 13–14, 95–6, 97, 98–102, 109–15, 159–82, 183–8, 189–91, 192–6, 197–203, 212, 214–16, 219–22, 225, 235, 237, 274, 276, 278–82
   popular culture, 299–303
   population, 164, 165
   post-emancipation period, 120, 122, 123, 124, 126, 127–8, 131, 138, 145–7
   public health campaigns, 255–6
   punishments, 6–7, 58
   Rastafari, 245, 247, 250, 280, 282, 303
   religion and politics, 148–9, 244–5, 280
   responses to parliamentary inquiry on slave trade, 51–60, 61, 62–3, 64–6, 67–8, 70, 75, 89
   Revival, 150, 152–3, 164, 244, 245–6, 250, 251, 255–6, 258, 302–3
   Rodney Riots, 284
   slave rebellions, 17, 27, 30, 31, 38–9, 41–2, 94
   social protests, 243, 244–5, 251
   spiritual healing practices, 13, 150
   transnational networks, 211–12
Jamaica Constabulary Force, 5
Jamaica Standard Occupational Classification 2003 (Statistical Agency of Jamaica), 5
Jamaican Anti-Tuberculosis League, 252
Jaudon, Toni Wall, 46, 58
Johanna, of Clarendon, Jamaica, 110–14
Johnson, Charles, 184, 215
Johnson, Jeremiah, 220
Johnson, Michele, 147, 174
Johnston, Gaston, 198, 201–2
Johnston, Harry, 29
Jordan, Nathaniel, 248
Joseph, E. L., 82
Josephs, Albert, 232
jumbies (duppies), 22, 141, 184, 208, 219, 222–4, 225, 227–8, 237, 252
justice system, 162

Kain, Jennifer, 160
Kali Mai Puja, 169, 285
Kerr, George, of Jamaica, 97
Kingsley, Charles, 120–1
Kingston, 38, 98–9, 146–7, 150, 162, 174–7, 196–7, 202, 204, 212, 214–16, 218–19, 235, 244–5, 246, 247–8, 252, 258, 262, 280, 298–9
Kissoon, Freddie, 304
Knight, Alan, 288
Knight, Ellen, 177–8
'Kola'. *See* Alexander, Joseph 'Kola'
Konadu, Kwasi, 9, 20, 28, 30, 37
*Kongo Political Culture* (MacGaffey), 23
Kopytoff, Barbara, 32–4
*Koromantyn Slaves* (Anon.), 74, 115–16
Kwasi, Graman. *See* Quacy, Graman

La Fortune, 80
La Granade, Sybil, 294
Labat, Jean-Baptiste, 27
labour protests, 243, 271–2, 292
Lake, H. A., 198
Landeau, Raphael, 200
larceny trials, 163, 166–7, 168, 172, 214–16
*Last Caribbean Frontier* (Candlin), 81
Lazarus-Black, Mindie, 158
League of Coloured Peoples, 257
Lee, Debbie, 51
Leeward Islands, 132, 143–4, 165
   obeah trials, 196–7
Leeward Maroons (Jamaica), 32–4
left-wing movements, 275–7, 290, 293
Letí, Geneviève, 20
Levack, Brian, 26
Lévi, Éliphas, 233
Lewis, Gordon K., 52
Lewis, Matthew, 97
liberalism, 10–11

*Life and Exploits of Mansong* (Burdett), 72–4, 210
Lindo, Hensley, 201
Liverpool, Robert Banks Jenkinson, Earl of. *See* Hawkesbury, Robert Banks Jenkinson, Lord
London Missionary Society, 87
Long, Edward, 28, 38–9, 51–60, 61, 66, 70, 74, 89
loupsgarou, 141
Lugard, Frederick, Lord, 266
Lumb, Charles Frederick, 10, 189
lwa, 23

MacGaffey, Wyatt, 22, 23, 25
Madden, R. R., 28
magicians (entertainers), 237
magistrates' courts, 162, *see also* obeah trials
*Magus, or Celestial Intelligencer* (Barrett), 234
*Main Currents* (Lewis), 52
Makandal's conspiracy (1760?), 27
Mamadoe, 115
*Man Better Man* (Hill) (play), 307–11
Manley, Michael, 274
Manley, Norman, 198, 201, 282
Marble, Andrew, 105–6, 107–8, 109–10
*Marching the Pilgrims Home* (Glazier), 6
Marhargh, Goopoul, 216
*Marly, or a Planter's Life in Jamaica* (Anon.), 96–7
Maroon communities (Jamaica), 32–5, 39, 270
  Leeward Maroons, 32–4
  Windward Maroons, 32, 34
Marsden, Peter, 69
Marson, Una, 251, 305
Martinique, 22, 83
Marxism, 275–7, 290
Matory, J. Lorand, 5, 6, 9
Matthews, Basil, 279–80
Maynier, E. A., 270
McDermott, Alfonso, 223–4
McGrath, Justin, 215
McKay, Claude, 210–11
McKee, Helen, 160
McLaren, Angus, 146
McLarty, R. W., 263
McLeod, Adina, 248
McNeal, Keith E., 169
media
  and decriminalization of obeah, 10, 285–6, 287
  campaigns against Revival, 152
  campaigns against ritual healing, 252, 258
  reports on labour protests, 243
  reports on obeah trials, 158, 161, 164, 204–7
*Medical Revolutionaries* (Weaver), 20
medicine, regulation of, 152–3, 163, 172, 192, 200, 228–32, 235–40, 264–5
'Melda' (Mighty Sparrow) (song), 180
Melville, Henry Dundas, viscount. *See* Dundas, Henry, Viscount Melville
*Memories of the Slave Trade* (Shaw), 24
Mends, Alfred, 235, 264–5
mental health, 252–3
mesmerism, 63, 201–2, 237–9
methodology, 11–12
  criminal justice history methods, 12–14, 15
  critical theory, 15–16
  cultural history methods, 12, 13, 15
  data collection and sources, 97–8, 159–61
  limitations, 161
  research questions, 8–9, 11–12
  structural-functionalist approach, 265
  translation, 85–6, 88
middle classes
  and popular culture, 301
  as obeah practitioners, 168, 193, 200
  opposition to anti-obeah legislation, 145
  political leaders, 256–60, 275–6, 296–7
  support for anti-obeah legislation, 11, 124–5, 132, 143–4, 146
Mighty Sparrow, 180, 296
migration, 211–13, 214–16, 243–4
millennialism, 244–5
Miller, Joseph, 222
Millette, James, 79
Minje Mama dance, 84–5, 86
*minkisi (nkisi)*, 22–3
Mintz, Sidney, 9, 211
missionaries, 94, 134, 148
  support for anti-obeah legislation, 144
mock trials, 299–302
modernity, and obeah, 2, 133–42, 145, 147, 156–7, 283–4, 289–90
Modest, Wayne, 4
Moise, Leopoldine, 188–9, 192
Moncrieffe, Sheppard, 225
Monroe, Frederick, 153
Montalembert, Baron de, 79, 81
Montserrat, 51, 177, 248
Moody, Harold, 257
Moore, Brian, 147, 174
Moore, Charles, 179

# Index

Moore, Joseph, 6, 271
Morais, Gilbert, 215
Morant Bay Rebellion (1865), 120, 129, 156
Morgan, George (Clement Clarke), 230
Morgan, Kenneth, 52
Morgan, Philip D., 20, 22
Morris, S. C., 145
Morrison, Andrew, 287
Moseley, Benjamin, 69, 72, 74, 106, 210
Moseley, Jane, 153
Moyne Commission, 14, 241, 243, 247, 260–8, 269–70, 272
Mullin, Michael, 103
Munasinghe, Viranjini, 132
Murray, Deryck, 105, 108
Murray, William Henry Wood, 72
music, 180–1, 277, 294, 295–6, 307–8
Muslims. *See* Islam
myalism, 126, 145, 148–9
  clearing rituals, 112–13
*Mysteries of Magic* (Waite), 233
*Myth of the Negro Past* (Herskovits), 270

Naipaul, V. S., 80
Nanny, 32, 34, 282
Napier, Ephraim, 218
narrative, 15–16
Natal, 155–6
national identity, 5, 283–92, 299, 309–10
nationalism, 139, 256–60, 274–7, 283–92
'Natty Dread in the PRA' (song), 295–6
*Negro Family in the United States* (Franklin), 269–70
Neil, Theophilus, 182, 185–7, 188, 190, 191, 192, 194–6, 197, 200–1, 203–4, 222
*Neither Led nor Driven* (Moore and Johnson), 174
neo-African religious movements, 151
Netherlands, colonial policy, 31–2
Nevis, 92, 93, 165
  obeah trials, 213
*New Account of Some Parts of Guinea and the Slave Trade* (Snelgrave), 55, 66
*New and Accurate Description of the Coast of Guinea* (Bosman), 24
New Jerusalem Revelation Baptist Church, 248
New Jewel Movement, 277, 293, 294–5, 296–7
*New System of Ancient Mythology* (Bryant), 28, 53
*ngangas*, 24
Nigeria, 266

Night Noises Prevention Law (Jamaica, 1911), 152–3, 281
Niles, Isaac, 222
Nine Night ritual, 311–13
Nketia, J. H., 29
Northern Rhodesia (Zambia), 271–2

oaths, 34–5, 36–7, 88–9, 101–2
*obayifo*, 24, 28
obeah
  and cultural identity, 1, 314–16
  comparison with European witchcraft, 141–2
  comparison with Vodou, 121, 128–9, 132–3, 134–5, 137, 261, 269
  decriminalization of, 5, 6
  definition, 1, 7–8, 11–12, 18–19, 30–2, 83–8, 90, 93, 103, 121, 133–4, 136, 137, 158, 161–2, 179–80, 181, 237–40, 249–50, 253, 267, 277–8
*Obeah: Witchcraft in the West Indies* (Bell), 131, 139–42
Obeah Act (Jamaica, 1898), 142–3, 281
  amendments to, 7
Obeah and Myalism Amendment Act (Jamaica, 1893), 145
obeah practitioners
  and place, 213
  and slave rebellions, 91–2, 99, 101–3
  as political leaders, 32–40, 156
  class, 168, 193, 200, 204
  clienteles, 213, 305
  correspondence, 212–13
  ethnicity, 30, 31–2, 36–7, 39, 92–3, 110, 168–70, 216, 234–5, 286
  gender, 100–1, 143, 166–8, 170, 180–1
  stereotypes, 209–10, 213–14, 216, 277, 299, 305, 311
  transnational networks, 211–13
obeah trials, 2, 158–207
  and public opinion, 158, 204–7
  appeals, 174–7
  Barbados, 212
  Berbice, 83–8, 108–9, 115
  British Guiana (Guyana), 235, 286
  charges, 163–5, 168, 192–4, 228–32, 235
  conviction rates, 100, 101, 170–2, 202–3, 279
  defence strategies, 197–203
  entrapment cases, 183
  gender of defendants, 100–1, 166–8, 170
  Grenada, 14, 102, 104, 118
  group cases, 170

obeah trials (*cont.*)
　'instruments of obeah', 161, 191, 195, 196–7, 199, 223–4, 226–7, 239
　Jamaica, 13–14, 95–6, 97, 98–102, 109–15, 159–82, 183–8, 189–91, 192–6, 197–203, 212, 214–16, 219–22, 225, 235, 237, 274, 276, 278–82
　larceny and fraud, 163, 166–7, 168, 214–16
　Leeward Islands, 196–7
　legal definition of obeah, 2, 18–19, 30–2, 40–2, 158, 161–2, 179–80, 181, 197, 202, 238–9
　mock trials, 299–302
　newspaper reports of, 158, 161, 164
　number of prosecutions, 162–6, 278–80
　of religious leaders, 246–50
　pleas, 194, 229–32
　prosecution strategies, 194–7
　sentencing, 172–4, 194, 203–4
　slander cases, 177–9
　slavery period, 13–14, 83–8, 97–115
　social class of defendants, 168, 193, 204
　spiritual healing practices, 167
　transfer of money, 195–6, 199, 220
　Trinidad and Tobago, 13–14, 159–82, 188–91, 192, 197–203, 215–16, 217, 218–19, 220–1, 225, 237, 238–9
　witnesses, 109, 182–3, 194–7, 200, 206
*Obeah Wedding* (Holness) (play), 303
'Obeah Wedding' (Mighty Sparrow) (song), 180
Obi (Three-Fingered Jack), 69, 72–5, 89
'Of Things Sacred' (exhibition, 2006), 4
oils, use in ritual, 226–7
*okomfos*, 24
Oliver, Henry, 102–3
Oliver, Sidney, 146
Op Hoop van Beter (Berbice), 83–8
Orde, Sir John, 93
orishas, 6, 23, 151, 292
Orisha Worship, 6, 23, 151, 292
Ortiz, Fernando, 6, 270
othering, 141
*Oxford English Dictionary*, 29

Paddy, Joseph, 188, 190, 233
Padmore, Henry, 14, 225
paganism, 137
Palmié, Stephan, 5, 6, 228
Paravisini-Gebert, Lizabeth, 1
Parish, Susan Scott, 20
Parliamentary Report into the Slave Trade (1789), 12, 260–8

Parry, David, 62
patriarchy, and slavery, 113–14
Patterson, Orlando, 28, 45–6, 76–7
Paugh, Katherine, 52
Payne-Jackson, Arvilla, 57
Pelete, Louis, 81
Pennington, Brian K., 9
People's National Congress (Guyana), 283, 285, 286
People's Progressive Party (Guyana), 284, 286, 288–91, 292
Perkins, Maureen, 122
petty sessions courts (Trinidad and Tobago), 162, *see also* obeah trials
Phillippo, James M., 148
picqueting, 79
Picton, Thomas, 79–83, 116
Pierre of Grenada, 14, 118
Pietz, William, 20
Pitman, Frank, 46
Pitt, George Washington, 212
Pitt, William, the Younger, 48, 49
place, 213, 219–22
*Plain Talk* (newspaper), 258
planters
　authority of, 93–4, 95–7
　compensation for loss of slaves, 105
　use of obeah, 108–9, 139–42
Pluchon, Pierre, 20
*Pocomania* (Marson) (play), 305
Pocomania (Revival Zion), 112–13, 150, 244, 245–6, 251, 267–8, 281, 301
　and biomedicine, 255–6
　opposition to obeah, 249–50
poetry, 277
poisonings, 23–4, 101
police
　anti-obeah campaigns, 165–6, 188–9, 281
　arrests and search procedures, 190
　entrapment cases, 167–8, 185–7, 203, 217, 238–9, 248–9
　harassment of Revivalists, 249, 281
　investigation procedures, 182–3, 184–5
　rewards and career development, 206–7
police courts, 162, *see also* obeah trials
political rights, 133–8, 142
politics, 241–73
　and culture, 147, 162, 265–6
　and religion, 3, 147–57, 241–3, 244–52, 256–60, 262, 264, 275–6, 280, 289–90, 291–2, 294–5, 298, 313
　and social class, 292
　anti-colonialism, 154, 156, 244, 260, 286, 288–92

Black Power movement, 274, 282–3, 284
elections, 275, 289, 290, 291, 292, 302
independence, 268, 274–7, 282, 313
indirect rule, 136–7, 266
leaders, 32–40, 156, 256–60, 275–7, 283–98
left-wing, 275–7, 290, 293
nationalism, 5, 139, 256–60, 274–7, 283–92
radicalism, 274, 282–3, 284, 293
self-government, 268
slave trade debate, 43–75
*Politics of Labour* (Bolland), 243
Polydore of Jamaica, 14, 106–8, 109
Popo woman, 44–5, 58–60, 74, 96
popular culture, 180–1, 297–313
popular religion, 147–57, 177–82, 241–3, 244–52, 256–60, 262, 264
Port of Spain, 79–80, 81, 119, 150–1, 153, 162, 174–7, 182–3, 187–9, 192, 195–6, 200, 212, 215–16, 218–19, 238–9, 303–4
*Port of Spain Gazette* (newspaper), 150–1, 161, 164, 189, 216, 253
Porter, Roy, 26
Porteus, Beilby, bishop of London, 49
Portuguese Inquisition, 14
Post, Ken, 244
postcolonial society, 268, 274–7, 282, 292–8, 313
poverty, 241
power relationships, 148
prayer books, use in ritual, 232
Price, Richard, 9
Price-Mars, Jean, 6, 270
primitivism, 2, 119, 133–42, 145, 147, 154–5, 156–7, 265, 283–4, 289–90
*Problem of Slavery in the Age of Revolution* (Davis), 47
*Promised Key* (Howell), 247, 248, 250
protective rituals, 23–4, 38–9, 140, 151, 181, 226
Psalms, use in ritual, 225
public health, 252–6, 258, 262
public information campaigns, 254–5
Pukumina (Revival Zion), 112–13, 150, 244, 245–6, 251, 267–8, 281, 301
and biomedicine, 255–6
opposition to obeah, 249–50
punishments, 9–11, 91, 116–17, 126, 143–5, 172–4, 194, 203–4
death penalty, 99, 100, 116, 123
electric shock, 58
fines, 172
flogging, 6–7, 91, 97, 122, 124, 125, 142–7, 174, 203–4, 279
for vagrancy, 122, 125, 143, 172, 192–3
gender and age differences, 143, 203–4
picqueting, 79
Picton's slave code, 81–2
solitary confinement, 143
transportation, 91, 100
Putnam, Lara, 211, 245, 259, 270

Quacy, Graman, 30, 31–2
Quamina, 36–7
Quao, 32
Quaon, 98
Quashe, Jinney, 95
Quashie, 88
Quawcoo, 30, 36–7, 39
quilundo, 20
quimbois, 22
*Quimbois, magie noire et sorcellerie aux Antilles* (Ebroin), 22

race, 9–10, 133–42, 145, 147, 156–7, 283–4, 289–90
racist comedy, 305
radicalism, 256–60, 274, 282–3, 284, 293
Ramcharan, Maria, 202
Ramsey, Kate, 5, 22, 128–9
Ramusack, Barbara N., 266
Ranger, Terence, 8
Rastafari, 244–5, 247, 250, 280, 282, 295–6, 303
*Reaper's Garden* (Brown), 9
rebellions, 27, 91–2, 243, 284
labour protests, 243
Reckord, Barry, 277, 306–7
*Reclaiming African Religions in Trinidad* (Henry), 6
*Recreating Africa* (Sweet), 9
Reeves, Sir Conrad, 132–3
Reid, Citira, 212
Reid, Joseph, 188, 203
Reid, Samuel, 228–9
religion, 266–8, 314–16, *see also* ritual practices
African traditional religions, 17–18, 288
and politics, 3, 147–57, 241–3, 244–52, 256–60, 262, 264, 275–6, 280, 289–90, 291–2, 294–5, 298, 313
and public health, 255–6
harassment of Revivalists, 151–4, 164–5, 246–50, 267–8, 280, 281, 295–6
Hinduism, 169–70, 285
leaders, 244–5
missionaries, 94, 134, 144, 148
Revival, 149–54, 256–60, 268–9, 302–3

Rennals, David, 200–1
Rennals, Rossabella, 225–6
resident magistrates' courts (Jamaica), 162
Revival, 6, 149–54, 244–5, 268–9, 301, 302–3
   harassment of, 151–4, 164–5, 246–50, 267–8, 280, 281, 295–6
   leaders, 150
Revival Zion (Pocomania/Pukumina), 112–13, 150, 244, 245–6, 251, 267–8, 281, 301
   and biomedicine, 255–6
   opposition to obeah, 249–50
Rex v. Chambers (29 May 1901), 10
Rheder, Mr, 58
Richardson, Alan, 69
Richardson, David, 9
riots, 284
ritual practices, 206–7, 213–40
   and biomedicine, 255–6
   and place, 209, 213, 219–22
   and transnational networks, 211–13
   assemblages, 98–9, 112–13, 140, 153, 161, 191, 196–7, 223–4, 226–7
   baths, 224–5
   books, 209, 232–5, 282
   cards, 220–1
   Christian rituals, 201–2, 225–6, 232, 249–50
   clearing rituals, 112–13
   control of spirits, 222–3
   diagnostic techniques, 219–22
   divination rituals, 84–5, 86, 105–6, 108–9, 177
   esoteric knowledge, 225–6
   European influences, 221, 235, 237–40
   'eyesight', 219–20
   for causing harm, 25, 104–8, 109–15, 177–9, 293
   for protection, 23–4, 38–9, 140, 151, 181, 226
   healing, 92, 96, 105–8, 118, 149, 150, 155–6, 167–8, 182–3, 184, 192, 200–1, 203, 216–18, 222–3, 228–32, 235–40, 253, 264–5
   Hinduism, 169–70, 234–6
   innovations in, 209
   Nine Night ritual, 311–13
   oaths, 34–5, 36–7, 88–9, 101–2
   pan-Caribbean rituals, 209, 224
   Revival, 152, 249–50
   rum, 223–4
   sacrifice, 129–30, 131, 214, 224, 287
   tarot, 221
   'tying', 180–1

*Rituals of Resistance* (Young), 22
Roberts, Arthur, 303–4
Roberts, Jasper, 187
Robertson, James, 98
'Rock alias Venture', 30
Rockefeller Foundation, 252
Rodney Riots (1968), 284
Rodney, Walter, 284
Rodrigues, Raymundo Nina, 6
Rogers, Rogert Athlyi, 248
Rooms, Samuel, 206
root work, 21–2
Roots Theatre, 298–9
Roper, Lyndal, 26
Roughley, Thomas, 109
*Royal Parchment Scroll of Black Supremacy* (1926), 250
rum, use in ritual, 223–4

sacrifice, 214, 224
Sadoo, Baboo Khandas, 169–70
Saint-Domingue, 27, 63
Salmon, C. S., 136–8
Samuel, Popo, 199, 232
Samuels, William, 215
Sanderson, John, 82, 89
santería, 5–6
Sarra, 34–5
Satchell, Hubert, 218–19
Savage, John, 83
Schiebenger, Londa, 46
Schwarz, Philip J., 20
Scipio, James, 179
Scipio-Pollard family, 198
*Scotland and the Abolition of Black Slavery* (Whyte), 60
Scott, David, 15
Scott, Dennis, 277–8, 299, 311–13
Seaga, Edward, 219, 220, 246, 281
secularism, 256–60, 290
self-government, 268
sexuality, 124–5
Shakers, 151–2, 270
Shango. *See* Orisha Worship
Shaw, Rosalind, 24
Sheller, Mimi, 130
Sherlock, Philip, 270
Shouters (Spiritual Baptists), 6, 150–1, 152, 153, 164–5, 225, 292
Shouters' Prohibition Ordinance (1917), 6, 153, 164–5, 225
Sierra Leone, 24
Simey, Thomas, 268–9, 270, 271
Simon, David, 199–200
Simpson, Aston, 198

Simpson, George Eaton, 149, 150, 151, 250, 271
Simpson, H. A. L., 198
*Sixth and Seventh Book of Moses* (DeLaurence), 232–3
slander cases, 177–9
slave codes, 81–2, 88–9, 93
*Slave Counterpoint* (Morgan), 20
*Slave Son* (Wilkins), 83, 210
slave trade debate, 43–75
Slave Voyages database, 31
*Slavery and African Ethnicities* (Hall), 22
*Slavery and the Romantic Imagination* (Lee), 51
slaves
 discipline and punishment of, 6–7, 93–4, 95–7, 116–17
 manumisson, 114
 rebellions, 27, 32–40
 spiritual beliefs, 22–5
 use of obeah, 110–14, 116
Smith, Anita, 238–9
Smith, J. A. G., 198
Smith, Raymond, 268
Smith, Reverend Claude, 251
Smyth, Daniel, 221
Snelgrave, William, 55, 66
social class, 140
social policy, 242, 268–70, 272–3, 279–80
social science, 45–6, 268–70, 271–2, 279–80
Society for the Abolition of the Slave Trade, 48–9, 68
Society of West India Planters and Merchants, 49
*Sociology of Slavery* (Patterson), 45–6
soul, 22
southern Africa, 155–6
Spain, 14, 20, 79
spelling, standardization of, 89
spirit world, 22–5
Spiritual Baptists (Shouters), 6, 150–1, 152, 153, 164–5, 225, 292
spiritualism, 202, 238
Spooner, Charles, 60, 61, 63, 64, 81
St John, Spenser, 128–9, 130, 132–3
St Kitts, 60, 61, 63, 64–5, 81
St Lucia, 5, 143
St Vincent, 92, 123–4, 125–6
 Revival, 151–2
Statistical Institute of Jamaica (STATIN), 5, 7
Stedman, John Gabriel, 31
Steel, Rhoda, 224
Stephens, Nathaniel, 221

stereotypes, 209–10, 213–14, 277, 299, 305, 311
Stewart, Annie, 182–3, 195
Stewart, Arthur, 191
Stewart, Dianne, 94, 246, 281, 305
Stewart, John, 115
Stewart, Thomas, 220
stick-fighting, 307–11
Stone, Arthur, 227
Stone, Robert, 193–4
strikes and labour protests, 243, 271–2, 292
structural-functionalist anthropology, 45–6, 265
Stuart, Charles Joseph, 253–4
sugar industry, 241, 292
*Sunday Chronicle* (Guyana), 287
superstition, 1, 9–10, 34, 46–7, 58–9, 61–3, 66–8, 69, 87, 116–17, 119, 125, 126–7, 132, 133–42, 147, 148, 192–3, 204–5, 238, 252–3, 254–6, 258, 268–9, 272–3, 275–6, 277, 285, 289–90, 294–5, 296–7, 309–11
Suriname, 31–2, 270
Sweet, James H., 9, 14, 83

Tacky's Rebellion (1760), 17, 27, 30, 31, 38–9, 41–2
tarot cards, 221
'Tata'. *See* Brown, James 'Tata'
Telfer, Joseph, 219
*Tell my Horse* (Hurston), 270
theatre, 277–8, 298–313
 art theatre, 299, 305–13
 comedy, 298–305
*Theory and Practice of Creole Grammar* (Thomas), 133, 134
Thicknesse, Philip, 34
*Thinking with Demons* (Clark), 26
Thisbe, 80
Thistlewood, Thomas, 95–6, 112
Thomas, Catherine, 221
Thomas, John Jacob, 119–20, 133–4, 137, 138, 145, 257
Thomas, Suzie, 160
Thompson, Albert, 198
Thompson, Alvin O., 92
Thornton, John, 23, 25
Thornton, S. Leslie, 143
thread, use in ritual, 226
Three-Fingered Jack, 69, 72–5, 89
Toco (Trinidad), 213
torture, 58, 79
*Trance and Modernity* (McNeal), 169
Transatlantic Slave Trade Database, 9

translation, 85–6, 88
transnational networks, 211–13, 243–4
transportation, 91, 100
*Treatise on Sugar* (Moseley), 69, 72
Trench Pen Revival, 251
Trinidad and Tobago, 13
  anti-obeah legislation, 77–8, 81–2, 143
  breach of the peace legislation, 152–3
  creole slave society, 77–83
  decriminalization of obeah, 5, 6
  East Indian community, 165, 168–70
  February Revolution, 284
  obeah trials, 13–14, 159–82, 188–91, 192, 197–203, 215–16, 217, 218–19, 220–1, 225, 237, 238–9
  Orisha Worship, 23, 151
  popular culture, 303–4, 307–11
  population, 79, 164, 165
  post-emancipation period, 131
  slave trade, 31
  social protests, 244
  Spiritual Baptists, 6, 150–1, 152, 153, 164–5, 225
  transnational networks, 211
*Trinidad Constabulary Manual*, 190
*Trinidad Village* (Herskovits and Herskovits), 271
Trouillot, Michel-Rolph, 1, 6, 7–8
tuberculosis, 252
Tunnicliff, James, 126
Twi (Akan). *See* Akan
*Twice Condemned* (Schwarz), 20
'tying', 180–1

Umeh, John Anenechukwu, 29
*Unanswerable Arguments against the Abolition of the Slave Trade* (Adair), 60
Undesirable Publications Act (Jamaica, 1940), 234, 282
United States, 21–2
Upchurch, Charles, 161
urbanization, 271–2

Vagrancy Act (Great Britain, 1824), 122
Vagrancy Acts, 122–3, 125, 143
vagrancy trials, 192–3
vampires, 141
Vansina, Jan, 25
*Vaudou, sorciers, empoisonneurs* (Pluchon), 20
vindicationists, 139
Vodou, 27, 298, 315
  cannibalism allegations, 128–30, 131, 132–4, 137

  comparison with obeah, 121, 128–9, 132–3, 134–5, 137, 261, 269
  decriminalization of, 5, 6, 22

Waite, A. E., 233
Wall Street Crash (1929), 241
'Wanted Dead or Alive' (Mighty Sparrow) (song), 296
*Was Hinduism Invented?* (Pennington), 9
Watson, Euriel Augustus, 185–7, 190, 191, 194
Watson, Tim, 32
Weaver, Karol K., 20
*Welfare and Planning in the West Indies* (Simey), 268–9
Wellington, Arthur, 156
werewolves (loupsgarou), 141
White, Noel, 252
White-Robed Army, 248
Whyte, Iain, 60
Wilberforce, William, 10, 49, 87, 116–17
Wilkins, Mary Fanny, 83, 210
Willem, trial of, 83–8, 93
Williams, Alexander, 196
Williams, Brackette, 286, 291
Williams, Budsey, 215–16
Williams, Cynric R., 94
Williams, Dewry, 212
Williams, Dr, 212–13, 232, 233
Williams, Emmanuel (Mr Mannie), 253–4
Williams, Eric, 274, 292
Williams, George, 219–20, 222, 225
Williams, Joseph J., 28
Williams, Joseph Maria, 237
Williamson, Karina, 57
Wilson, Godfrey and Monica, 271–2
Windward Maroons, 32, 34
Winterbottom, Thomas, 71
winti, 31–2
witchcraft, 18–27, 40–2
  comparison with obeah, 91, 99, 141–2
  in Africa, 22–5, 155–6, 265–6
Witchcraft Act (Great Britain, 1736), 40–1
*Witchcraft in Early North America* (Games), 20
*Witchcraft, Oracles, and Magic among the Azande* (Evans-Pritchard), 265–6
women
  as obeah practitioners, 34, 100–1, 143, 166–8, 170, 180–1, 193
  as religious leaders, 150
  punishments, 143, 203–4
  sexual coercion of, 109–15, 125